Special Education

for All Teachers

Sixth Edition

Ronald P. Colarusso, Colleen M. O'Rourke,
and Melissa A. Leontovich
Georgia State University

Kendall Hunt
publishing company

Book Team
Chairman and Chief Executive Officer   Mark C. Falb
President and Chief Operating Officer   Chad M. Chandlee
Vice President, Higher Education   David L. Tart
Director of National Book Program   Paul B. Carty
Development Editor   Angela Willenbring
Assistant Vice President, Production Services   Christine E. O'Brien
Senior Production Editor   Carrie Maro
Permissions Editor   Caroline Kieler
Cover Designer   Heather Richman

Cover image © Shutterstock, Inc.

Brief Contents

Contents

3   The Response to Intervention, Referral, and Placement Process   59
Gwendolyn T. Benson and John O'Connor

4   Collaboration with Families and Professionals   93

Ronald P. Colarusso, Editor

The editors of *Special Education for All Teachers* appreciate the contributions of the following individuals: Peggy A. Gallagher, Debra Schober-Peterson, Cheryl A. Rhodes, Lauren Stern Wynne, and JoAnna White

8 Students with Behavior Differences Affecting Achievement   207
L. Juane Heflin and Ginny L. Van Rie

9 Managing Behavior for Effective Learning   245
L. Juane Heflin and Kristine Jolivette

Preface

This textbook is for all professionals who are interested in the education of students with special needs. These students include not only those with disabilities, but also those who are culturally and linguistically diverse, and those who are at risk of academic failure for any reason. The intent of this book is to provide information and increase knowledge about these students in the hope that greater understanding will lead to the acceptance of them and their diverse needs in our schools and our society. This book is to serve as a text for students enrolled in preservice courses addressing at-risk learners. It also is intended to provide instructional and management strategies for general education classroom teachers who interact with these students on a daily basis. In addition, it can serve as a supplemental text or resource for those professionals currently serving students with special needs. The goals of *Special Education for All Teachers* are:

- To present the philosophy of inclusion, and the application and implementation of laws related to the education of students with special needs;
- To discuss the identifying characteristics of students with special needs; and
- To provide practical information relative to:
  - the response to intervention, referral, and placement process
  - collaboration with families and professionals
  - instructional accommodations, modifications, and adaptations needed to provide special education in the general classroom
  - instructional methods and strategies for students with learning difficulties
  - the management of behavior

Every student has the right to a free appropriate education and this education should occur in the least restrictive environment appropriate for each student's individual educational needs. For this to become a reality, educators must accept the responsibility for the education of all students regardless of their abilities, disabilities, or differences. Perhaps the greatest challenge to the classroom teacher is to meet the educational needs of the diverse student population in our schools today. Students with differing abilities contribute to the diversity in the classroom and there is no doubt that many of them will have special needs that must be addressed. We believe that good teachers have the desire and ability to accept the challenge of meeting the needs of diverse students in the general education classroom if they are provided with the appropriate knowledge and resources.

The classroom teacher must have the ability and willingness to make appropriate referrals and to integrate students with special needs into the general education program; however, they cannot succeed alone. The successful education and integration of all students requires cooperation and collaboration among classroom teachers, special educators, parents, students, administrators, and other professionals. For this reason, this textbook focuses on relevant and practical issues in educating students with special needs and students who are at risk for learning problems in the general education classroom.

In this sixth edition we have made extensive revisions to expand some content and consolidate other areas while continuing to incorporate the latest research. There are now 13 chapters in this textbook.

Chapters 1 and 2: Introduce the concept of inclusion and the laws that impact the education of all students.

Chapter 3: Reviews the processes of response to intervention, referral, evaluation, and placement.

Chapter 4: Presents techniques to develop effective relationships and enhance collaboration with parents, administrators, and other professionals.

Chapter 5: Explores the issues of cultural and linguistic diversity in our schools today.

Chapter 6: Provides information about the characteristics and needs of students with specific learning disabilities and mild intellectual disabilities.

Chapter 7: Addresses the strategies and methods general educators can use for academic instruction of students who have, or are at risk for, learning problems.

Chapter 8: Provides information about students with behavior differences that affect their achievement and the general education classroom environment.

Chapter 9: Offers strategies for managing behavior in the classroom.

Chapter 10: Reviews the characteristics, prevalence, and educational issues related to students with Autism Spectrum Disorders.

Chapter 11: Describes the characteristics and needs of students with sensory, communication, physical, and health impairments.

Chapter 12: Focuses on the issues relevant to educating students with moderate and severe intellectual disabilities.

Chapter 13: Presents information pertinent to educating students who are gifted and talented.

Other key features of this textbook include: web resources, key terms defined in the glossary, classroom application activities, internet resources, case studies to illustrate the application of information and strategies, comprehensive reference lists, and a bank of test questions for instructors.

It is our hope that the content of this textbook will assist all teachers and school professionals in ensuring success for all students.

Ronald P. Colarusso
Colleen M. O'Rourke
Melissa A. Leontovich
2013

Acknowledgments

We wish to thank the contributors to all six editions of this text for sharing their collective knowledge and expertise in this book. This text is a collective effort of select experts and we are pleased to have several new authors in this sixth edition. This book was written in response to a recognized need to provide teachers with information about how they might serve students with special needs more effectively in the general education classroom. We appreciate the authors' commitment to this goal and their willingness to revise and expand their chapters.

To the instructors and students at Georgia State University, we are grateful for your feedback and suggestions. You prompted the initial writing of this book and taught us some valuable lessons in writing an introductory textbook.

We are especially grateful to the external reviewers whose comments and suggestions guided us as we developed the sixth edition of this textbook.

R.P.C.
C.M.O'R.
M.A.L.

About the Editors

Ronald P. Colarusso

Ronald Colarusso is currently Professor Emeritus of Special Education and Dean Emeritus of Georgia State University's College of Education. He served as Dean of Georgia State University's College of Education from 2001 through 2007. Previously, Dr. Colarusso was Chair and Professor of the Department of Educational Psychology and Special Education at the University. He held a joint appointment in the Department of Special Education and Early Childhood Education. His public school teaching experience and background are in the areas of early childhood special education, intellectual disabilities, learning disabilities, assessment, and parent involvement.

His teaching philosophy takes a collaborative, student-centered approach to projects in order to get students involved in real research and real activity. As Dean he instated Professional Education programs that are field based in high needs urban schools and give the University faculty the opportunity to work with schools in the community.

Dr. Colarusso's interests focus on the preparation of Special Educators and General Educators in high needs urban schools. He holds several committee assignments and memberships with various academic, community, and professional associations that focus on special education and urban education issues. Dr. Colarusso earned his B.S. at Bloomsburg State College and his M.Ed. and Ed.D. at Temple University.

Colleen M. O'Rourke

Colleen O'Rourke is an Associate Professor in the Department of Educational Psychology and Special Education at Georgia State University in the College of Education. She served as the program coordinator for the Communication Disorders Program in the College for 17 years. She has been active in the American Speech-Language-Hearing Association for many years, serving as the Vice President for Academic Affairs in Audiology, a member of the Board of Ethics and as Convention co-chair. She also was a member of the Board of the Council on Academic Accreditation in Audiology and Speech-Language Pathology and the Board of the Council of Academic Programs in Communication Sciences and Disorders.

Dr. O'Rourke was instrumental in the design and development of the College's undergraduate course that addresses the educational needs of students with disabilities. She received the College's Outstanding Teaching Award for that work. The course is now required for all students who plan to earn certification and work in a school setting (general educators, special educators, counselors, speech-language pathologists, etc.).

Her approach to teaching and supervision is to assist students in the application of theory to practice, promoting hands-on learning and evidence-based practice. Dr. O'Rourke earned her B.S. at the University of Cincinnati and her M.A. and Ph.D. at Wayne State University.

Melissa A. Leontovich

Melissa Leontovich is a Clinical Assistant Professor in the Department of Educational Psychology and Special Education at Georgia State University. She coordinates the Introduction to Special Education course that all GSU College of Education majors are required to pass. This textbook is also used in her Characteristics and Instructional Strategies for Students with Disabilities course. She is active in the development of both traditional and online classes.

Dr. Leontovich taught students with moderate and severe intellectual disabilities for six years in the Cobb County, Georgia public school system. She served as a behavior invention specialist and intellectual disabilities specialist in Cobb before joining Georgia State University. While at Georgia State, Dr. Leontovich also spent ten years working with the Georgia State Department of Education implementing their Best Practices for Inclusion of Students with Disabilities in the General Education Classroom project.

Dr. Leontovich earned her B.S. at the University of Mississippi and her M.Ed. and Ph.D. at Georgia State University. She continues to focus on preparing teachers to work with students with disabilities in the least restrictive environment, supervising student teachers and perfecting effective instructional practices for students with moderate and severe intellectual disabilities.

CHAPTER ONE

Teaching Every Student: A Mandate for Today

Colleen M. O'Rourke and Melissa A. Leontovich

CHAPTER OBJECTIVES

- to examine special education in schools today;
- to provide an overview of the characteristics and special needs of students with disabilities;
- to discuss the diversity in today's public schools and its relevance in the identification of students who need special education services;
- to explore the controversy of labeling and the impact it can have on students and teachers;
- to examine the history of special education and how society's attitudes have changed toward individuals with disabilities;
- to present the educational options and service delivery models used in today's schools to meet the special needs of students; and
- to provide an overview of the impact of No Child Left Behind and IDEA on today's classrooms and schools.

KEY TERMS

education • special education • accommodations • modifications • related services • cognitive disabilities • behavior disorders • emotional disturbances • communications disorders • sensory disabilities • physical disabilities • normalization • free, appropriate, public education (FAPE) • least restrictive environment (LRE) • mainstreamed • inclusion • Response to Intervention (RTI) • No Child Left Behind (NCLB)

Today's classrooms are a reflection of our society and its diversity, and we have come to expect full participation in our educational system for all students. Classrooms in schools today are more diverse than ever. Students come to school with unique personalities, abilities, attitudes, and values, not to mention the diversity found in gender, race, religion, culture, language, ethnic background, and socioeconomic status. Three events have drastically changed the educational system in the United States and created great diversity in our schools. In 1954 the U.S. Supreme Court ruled that the policy of separate but equal schools was unconstitutional (*Brown v. Topeka, Kansas, Board of Education,* 1954). This ruling began the integration of classrooms in the United States. In 1974 President Gerald Ford signed into law the Education of All Handicapped Children Act, which is known today as the Individuals with Disabilities Education Improvement Act (IDEA). IDEA, first enacted in 1975, mandates that children and youth aged 3 to 21 with disabilities be provided a free and appropriate public school education. This law marked the beginning of a mandated public education for children with disabilities. In addition, America's racial and ethnic profile is rapidly changing. Based on 2010 U.S. Census data, 27.6% of the U.S. population is from a racial group other than white and 16.3% is of Hispanic or Latino origin (U.S. Census Bureau, 2010). It is projected that by 2020, 35% of the U.S. population will be racial or ethnic minorities (U.S. Census Bureau, 2007).

The sentiments behind the laws that have been passed reflect American values and beliefs that all individuals should have an equal opportunity for an appropriate education. Some students in our schools today need specialized instruction, or special education, if they are to have that equal opportunity for learning. In this chapter, we examine special education and the rationale for its existence, as well as its history and current status. In addition, we explore the issues of diversity and labeling as they relate to the provision of special education services.

Today's teachers will find students with many types of disabilities in their classrooms. These students may be from different races and ethnic backgrounds. Students with disabilities come from every cultural, socioeconomic, and linguistic group, and many do not fit into neat categories. As you will see in this chapter, the education of students with disabilities is the responsibility of everyone affiliated with the school: classroom teachers, special educators, administrators, and parents. Today's educators must understand how children learn and develop and must be able to provide learning opportunities to support these diverse students.

Defining Special Education

Education is the process of learning and developing as a result of schooling and other experiences. Through education we promote literacy, personal autonomy, and economic self-sufficiency. For a variety of reasons (cognitive, behavioral, communicative, or physical), students with disabilities or special needs may need special education to ensure that they have the opportunity to participate fully in the educational process. Special education is defined in IDEA as "specially designed instruction, at no cost to parents, to meet the unique needs of a child with a disability, including instruction conducted in the classroom, in the home, in hospitals and institutions, and in other settings; and instruction in physical education" (IDEA, 2004). As Kaplan (1996) stated, "Special education is not a place, but a group of services tailored to the special needs of an individual student" (p. 36).

The National Center for Educational Statistics (2008) defines special education as:

Direct instructional activities or special learning experiences designed primarily for students having exceptionalities in one or more aspects of the cognitive process or as being underachievers in relation to general level or model of their overall abilities. Such services usually are directed at students with the following conditions: (1) physically handicapped; (2) emotionally handicapped; (3) culturally different, including compensatory education; (4) mentally retarded; and (5) learning disabled. Programs for the mentally gifted and talented are also included in some special education programs.

Today there are 13 categories of disabilities in special education. According to IDEA, the students in need of special education services have one or more of these 13 conditions which include: specific learning disability, speech or language impairment, mental retardation (intellectual disability[1]), emotional disturbance, multiple disabilities, hearing impairment (including deafness), orthopedic impairment, other health impairments, visual impairment (including blindness), autism, deaf–blindness, traumatic brain injury, and developmental delay.

The general education classroom is just one of many places special education services can be provided.

As you can see from these categories, there is a wide range of disabilities and needs among students, and since the 1970s, schools have been required to provide specialized education services to all students with disabilities. Special education services can be provided in many different places or environments: the general education classroom, a special classroom, or even at home. The decisions regarding when, where, what, and how special education services occur are made according to what is appropriate for the individual student. For example, students with emotional or behavioral disabilities may need more structured, smaller classes, whereas students with physical disabilities may need special equipment. Other students may need special teaching strategies or a revised curriculum.

Some students with mild disabilities may only require **accommodations** to be successful in school. Accommodations are any changes made to the instruction or materials that do not change the curriculum expectations. Students with disabilities receiving accommodations would be held to the same curriculum standards as general education students. Some students with more significant disabilities may require **modifications** to achieve their educational goals. Modifications are significant changes made to instruction or materials that result in the student no longer meeting the standards of the general education curriculum. Adapting the curriculum might allow students with significant disabilities to access the general education curriculum and classroom.

Students who have been evaluated and identified as having a disability and are determined eligible for special education services may also need additional services. These are known as **related services** and may be required to assist a student in benefiting from special education. Related services fall into such categories as transportation, both to and from school as well as within the school, or developmental, corrective, and other supportive services. Other examples of related services are special services such as speech-language therapy, audiology services, interpreting services, psychological services, physical and occupational therapy, and counseling services.

---

[1] The term "mental retardation" is used in the federal law; however, the professional community is now using the preferred term *intellectual disability*. The national professional organization, formerly the American Association on Mental Retardation, has changed its name to the American Association on Intellectual and Developmental Disabilities. The term "intellectual disability" is used throughout this textbook.

Students with disabilities have the same needs as their peers, as well as different needs specific to their disabilities. As we look more closely at these students throughout this book, you will discover that they have some similarities, but you will also find that they are a heterogeneous group. Students who have physical disabilities may require special desks and communication devices but may not need any modification of the general education academic curriculum. In contrast, students with learning disabilities may not require any physical adaptations of the classroom but may need accommodations to the curriculum or instructional strategies. Students usually are targeted to receive special education because they exhibit cognitive, behavioral, communication, sensory, or physical differences from their peers. These differences are examined briefly in this chapter. Chapters 6, 8, 10, 11, and 12 explore the causes of these differences and more fully describe the characteristics and educational needs of students with specific disabilities.

Cognitive Differences

Cognitive disabilities affect the student's ability to acquire and/or express knowledge and may be demonstrated by difficulties with attention, perception, memory, and the generalization of knowledge and skills. Cognitive differences may be exhibited in students with intellectual disabilities, learning disabilities, or traumatic brain injuries. These students typically develop academic skills at a slower rate than other students do, taking longer to perform academic tasks and requiring more practice and repetition. For example, if the typical student can complete a worksheet of math problems in 20 minutes, the student with a cognitive disability may need twice that time to complete it. These students may not reach a developmental level that allows for abstract thinking and will need concrete objects and experiences to understand and remember concepts and skills.

To ensure that students with cognitive differences participate as fully as possible in general education classrooms, some modifications or adaptations of curriculum, materials, and/or instructional methods will be needed. Without this special education, these students generally experience steadily decreasing performance in all subjects. Many academic skills must be learned in a specific sequence. If students do not master one step in a sequence, or a prerequisite skill, they will not be able to acquire the ones which follow. A student who cannot recognize and remember the letters of the alphabet will not be able to read. These skill deficits are compounded as new skills continue to be taught and new tasks become more difficult. Students get behind academically and never catch up.

Behavioral Differences

Although behavioral differences among people are expected, some students, those with behavior disorders or emotional disturbances, will act in a way that is chronically and significantly different from their peers. We are all unique individuals who act and react according to our personalities, our cultural backgrounds, and our life experiences. As long as our behavior is acceptable according to social standards, it is considered normal. Yet everyone has exhibited unacceptable or inappropriate behavior at some time. Teachers know that their students will not act in an acceptable manner at all times. Effective teachers use a variety of strategies to prevent misbehavior and encourage appropriate behavior in the classroom. However, some students may exhibit significant behavior problems. Their inappropriate behaviors are so severe as to interfere with their own learning and the learning of other students in the classroom. For example, a student who constantly bullies other students or steals and destroys classmates' belongings will be a serious problem for the teacher. Other students with disabilities also may demonstrate mannerisms or behaviors that are considered unacceptable. For example, students who are blind may rock back and forth; students who have intellectual disabilities may display affection inappropriately; students who have experienced traumatic brain injury may act impulsively. All of these students need intervention programs, or special education, to learn new and acceptable behaviors. Students with serious behavior disorders who are not provided with assistance will be unable to function in the classroom and will be a constant disruption to both their teachers and their classmates.

Communication Differences

Communication disorders are any disruption in an individual's ability to understand or express thoughts, feelings, and ideas. Most individuals take the ability to communicate for granted. Although communication styles, voices, and dialects may vary, we express our thoughts and listen to others with ease on a daily basis. We use oral and written communication to exchange ideas, to learn, and to build relationships. These skills are the basis of interpersonal interactions as well as the foundation of academic instruction in the classroom.

Speech and language impairments, or communication disorders, can have a significant impact on a student's academic performance and social interaction. Individuals with speech or language impairments may have difficulty producing speech sounds accurately and fluently. They may be unable to express their thoughts in a way others understand, or they may fail to understand the communication of others. They may have trouble learning to read and write. In some students, a communication disorder may accompany another disability; for example, students with learning disabilities, intellectual disabilities, or hearing impairments often have language processing problems. These problems affect their ability to perform required school tasks such as reading and writing. Other students may exhibit communication disorders with no additional disability; they will have the same cognitive, behavioral, and physical abilities as their peers. Students with communication disorders need special services provided by speech-language pathologists to improve and facilitate their communication abilities. This special education assists students in their academic learning and in developing positive social interactions.

Sensory and Physical Differences

Sensory disabilities occur whenever any sensory system (vision, hearing, taste, touch, etc.) is impaired. **Physical disabilities** result from diseases or disorders that affect normal physical development or functioning. The most common sensory disabilities are vision and hearing impairments. Such sensory impairments may impose certain restrictions on students. For example, a visual impairment may prohibit the use of a standard print textbook. Large-print textbooks, exams written in Braille, raised maps, and other materials may be needed for students with impaired vision. Students with a hearing loss may need amplification devices, sign language interpreters, note takers, and other assistance to succeed in the classroom. Without these forms of special education, students with sensory disabilities would not be able to reach their full academic potential.

All students have varying levels of physical abilities, strength, and stamina. Some are better coordinated than others. Although certain students may tire quickly, others never seem to run out of energy. Students with physical disabilities (orthopedic impairments or health problems) may have special needs with regard to their ability to function fully in the general education classroom setting. Students who use braces or wheelchairs require changes in the school's physical environment to allow access to classes and activities. Other accommodations that students with physical disabilities might require include augmentative communication devices, lap boards, oral examinations, adapted physical education activities, and accessible restrooms.

When Ms. McDonnell reported to preplanning for her new job of teaching middle-school language arts, she found that she would have a "co-teacher" for the students with disabilities who were placed in her classroom. She wondered how she should approach her co-teacher. Should she suggest ideas about how to divide up the work that needed to be done, or should she assume that she was the "regular" teacher and let her co-teacher know what she expected? If you were Ms. McDonnell, what approach would you take?

Defining Disability

When is a difference, a disorder, or a condition considered a disability? Currently schools define disabilities according to the guidelines and regulations established by their state. These state regulations are based on the federal law that defines disabilities and provides states with funding for students who qualify for special education services. As shown in **Table 1.1,** the federal law, Public Law 108-446, the Individuals with Disabilities Education Improvement Act of 2004 (IDEA, 2004), defines students with disabilities as those with specific learning disabilities, speech or language impairments, mental retardation (intellectual disabilities), emotional disturbance (behavior disorders), multiple disabilities, hearing impairments (including deafness), orthopedic impairments, other health impairments, visual impairments (including blindness), autism, deaf–blindness, or traumatic brain injury who need special education or related services as a result of the disability.

Other students who do not meet the eligibility criteria specified in IDEA still may qualify for special education services under Section 504 of the Rehabilitation Act of 1973. For example, attention deficit/hyperactivity disorder (ADHD) is not listed as a specific category of disability under IDEA. This could mean that these students would not be eligible for special education services and the federal government would not provide funds to serve them. However, the impact of ADHD on the ability of students to learn is widely recognized, and these students may be eligible for services under Section 504. Students who are gifted and talented also may receive special services in schools, but they are not protected by the same laws that mandate services to students with disabilities. The federal laws that mandate special education services are discussed in more detail in Chapter 2.

Prevalence of Disabilities

Prevalence refers to the number or percentage of the population that have been identified as having a particular disability or exceptionality. The percentage of special education students who are identified as having disabilities has changed considerably over the last 40 to 50 years. In 1976 3.7 million children received special education services. Currently in the United States, over 6.5 million children receive special education services according to the U.S. Department of Education (2011).

TABLE 1.1
Disability Categories Specified in Public Law 108-446 (IDEA, 2004)

• Specific learning disabilities	• Orthopedic impairments
• Speech or language impairments	• Other health impairments
• Mental retardation	• Visual impairments (including blindness)
• Emotional disturbance	• Autism
• Multiple disabilities	• Deaf–blindness
• Hearing impairments (including deafness)	• Traumatic brain injury

TABLE 1.2

Number of Students Age 6 through 21 Served Under IDEA, Part B, and Percentage of Students as a Percentage of Population Age 6 through 21, by Disability Category, for Fall 2010

Disability Category	Number of Students	Percentage of Population
All disabilities	5,818,074	8.46
Specific learning disabilities	2,412,801	3.51
Speech or language impairments	1,089,976	1.59
Intellectual disability	444,894	0.65
Emotional disturbance	387,368	0.56
Multiple disabilities	123,417	0.18
Hearing impairments	69,685	0.10
Orthopedic impairments	55,704	0.08
Other health impairments	703,912	1.02
Visual impairments	25,632	0.04
Autism	369,774	0.54
Deaf–blindness	1,281	0.00
Traumatic brain injury	4,594	0.04
Developmental delay	109,036	0.16

U.S. Department of Education (2011). Office of Special Education Programs, Data Analysis System (DANS), OMB #1820-0043: "Children with Disabilities Receiving Special Education Under Part B of the Individuals with Disabilities Education Act," 2010. Data updated as of July 15, 2011. From: https://www.ideadata.org/

Table 1.2 shows that over 8% of children and youth age 6 through 21 in the total public school enrollment were served under IDEA in 2010. The number and percentage of children and youth age 6 to 21 receiving special education services in each disability category also is shown in Table 1.2. Among students served under IDEA in 2007, about 1% were American Indian/Alaska Native, 2% were Asian/Pacific Islander, 18% were Hispanic, 21% were black, and 58% were white.

As can be seen in Table 1.2, the highest percentage of students receiving special services in schools in 2010 had specific learning disabilities (3.51%). A specific learning disability is a disorder of one or more of the basic psychological processes involved in understanding or in using spoken or written language that may manifest itself in an imperfect ability to listen, think, speak, read, write, spell, or do mathematical calculations. This includes conditions such as perceptual disabilities, brain injury, minimal brain dysfunction, and dyslexia.

In addition to specific learning disabilities, there are other categories of disabilities that are considered high prevalence, or high incidence, due to the large numbers of students requiring services. These include speech or language impairments, mental retardation (intellectual disabilities), emotional disturbances, and autism. The remaining categories specified under IDEA often are described as low incidence, due to the limited number of students exhibiting those types of disabilities. Based on the prevalence figures, general education teachers certainly will find students with learning disabilities, speech or language impairments, intellectual disabilities, behavior disorders, and autism in their classrooms. Due to their lower incidence, students with physical or sensory disabilities, or traumatic brain injury will be encountered in the general education classrooms less frequently. In addition, some of these students (i.e., those with physical disabilities health impairments, or sensory impairments) may function quite well in the general education classroom and can perform in academic areas at a level equal to their peers without disabilities.

The number of students who receive special education services is not equally distributed across the ages of 6 through 21 years. As seen in **Figure 1.1,** equal percentages of students

Figure 1.1   Percentage of Students Served by IDEA, by Age Group, for Fall 2010

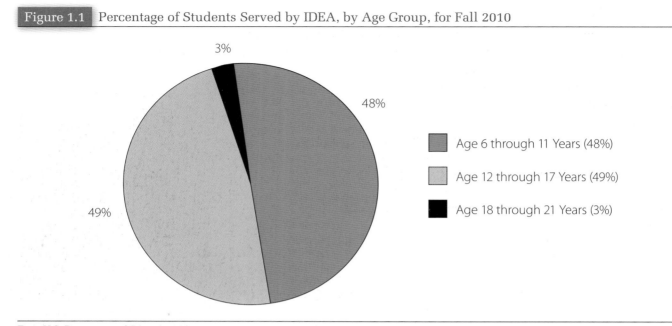

From U.S. Department of Education (2011). Data Accountability Center: https://www.ideadata.org.

age 6 through 11 years and 12 through 17 years receive services, whereas a significantly smaller percentage of students age 18 through 21 years receive them. There are also gender differences in the number of students receiving special education services: approximately 70% of students are male and 30% are female.

The Issue of Diversity

A major focus of this book is diversity: the diversity of students with disabilities and other students with special needs bring to the learning environment. These students may exhibit differences from (and similarities to) their peers in the classroom in their cognitive and learning abilities, behavior, communication styles, or physical and sensory capabilities. However, those with disabilities also bring their own unique competencies, attitudes, and learning styles to the classroom. For students with disabilities, the issue of diversity can become a complex one. In addition to the differences associated with their disabilities, these students may exhibit differences due to their ethnic, racial, cultural, or linguistic backgrounds.

Diversity is an issue that has been prominent in special education from its very beginning and remains in the forefront today. As a group, individuals with disabilities were considered different (or diverse) and were segregated from the mainstream of education in the past. They were placed in institutions, special schools, and self-contained classes. These segregated options still may be appropriate educational placements for some individuals, if these options are selected on an individual basis. However, when an entire group is segregated as a means of avoidance due to prejudice, then it is discrimination against a diverse group. The issue of diversity in relation to race, ethnicity, culture, and language also has played a role in special education. The number of minority students in special education is disproportionate to the general school population (Artiles, Rueda, Salazar, & Higareda, 2005; Artiles & Trent, 1994; Aud, Fox, & KewalRamani, 2010; National Research Council, 2002). If students belong to a minority group, they may be at risk for inappropriate placement in special education.

Cultural Diversity

Over time, educators have come to understand that students need a multicultural education to succeed in a nation and a world rich in cultural diversity. Today's classrooms reflect the variation in gender, race, religion, sexual orientation, language, socioeconomic status, family structure, motivation, talents, and abilities found in the community at large. Based on U.S. Census data, it is predicted that by the year 2020, the U.S. population will be more than 35% racial and ethnic minorities and by 2050 what is now the majority will be the minority (U.S. Census Bureau, 2007). To be effective in the classroom, teachers will need to be prepared to consider the cultural values, lifestyle, and language of each student in their classes.

Multicultural education is based on the premise that all students benefit from exposure to different people, beliefs, and ideas.

Culture can be defined as "a complex frame of reference that consists of patterns or traditions, beliefs, values, norms, and meanings that are shared in varying degrees by interacting members of a community" (Ting-Toomey, 1999, p.10). Culture pervades every aspect of our lives. It influences the way we view life, the way we think, and the way we behave. The values and beliefs we acquire from our cultural group guide us in social interactions, which affect family and interpersonal relationships and the expectations we have of others.

Cultural pluralism is the belief that cultural differences and the contributions of various groups can strengthen and enrich society. Multicultural education is based on the premise that all students benefit from exposure to different people, beliefs, and ideas. It promotes the strength and value of cultural diversity as well as human rights and respect for those who are different from oneself.

Cultural differences may be mistaken for abnormality when one's own cultural group is viewed as setting the standard for all others. The dominant cultural group in a community or a nation generally considers itself the standard and views other groups as deviations. Cultural groups may vary markedly in their use of eye contact, physical proximity and contact, nonverbal communication, or verbal interaction with persons in positions of authority. If a teacher is speaking to a student who avoids eye contact with her, does she assume the student is ignoring her or doesn't care what she is saying, or is showing disrespect? In some cultures, direct eye contact with adults in positions of authority is considered disrespectful. Teachers and students must realize that what they consider inappropriate or unacceptable behavior based on their own cultural beliefs and actions may be normal and standard in another cultural group.

Some cultures highly value group success and therefore encourage cooperative behavior over competitive behavior whereas other cultures value and foster individual success and achievement. One culture might encourage spontaneity and creativity in children, and another may teach the importance of restraint in all behaviors. This disparity in values can result in differences in behavior that are viewed and judged as appropriate or inappropriate based on the viewer's cultural perspective.

Appreciation of one's own cultural heritage and acceptance of others is the key to success in multicultural classrooms and communities. Appreciation and acceptance of differences do not develop spontaneously. Some people fear and avoid what is different and unknown to them. Teachers must provide students with experiences that foster an acceptance and appreciation of diversity. The school curriculum and instructional materials must reflect the contributions of diverse individuals and groups to our world. With knowledge and understanding, differences due to culture or disability become less frightening and easier to accept. See Chapter 5 for additional information on issues of cultural and linguistic diversity.

Diversity and Disability

The percentage of students in special education from minority groups is disproportionately high given their percentage in the school-age population at large (Aud, Fox, &KewalRamani, 2010; Gollnick & Chinn, 2006; National Research Council, 2002). **Table 1.3** shows the percentage of students receiving special education services by disability and race/ethnicity for fall 2007 (U.S. Department of Education, 2008). The distributions are similar to those of previous years, and you can see that the racial/ethnic distribution differs from that of the school-age population (age 6 through 21) at large. Asian/Pacific Islander students made up 4.2% of the general school-age population, yet they constituted only 2.3% of students receiving special education services. Students who are black were 15.1% of the general school population, but they represented 20.5% of students receiving services. The largest discrepancies found with black students were in the categories of intellectual disability (31.9% receiving services compared to 15.1% of the general school-age population) and emotional disturbance (28.9% compared to 15.1% of the general population). The white school-age population, which comprised 60.9% of the general population, accounted for 57.7% of special education services. The greatest discrepancy for white students was found in the category of intellectual disability (49.5% compared to 60.9% of the general school-age population). The American Indian/Alaska Native and Hispanic populations at large most closely matched their total percentages receiving special education services (1.0% vs. 1.5% and 18.9% vs. 18.0%). In addition to overall racial/ethnic discrepancies, African American and Hispanic males also are overrepresented in special education (Nichols et al., 2008). You will see in Chapter 13 that discrepancies are found in gifted and talented programs as well, with students from minority cultures, particularly African American, Hispanic, and Native American students, being underrepresented in those programs.

According to Harry and Klingner (2007), "Those categories with the highest incidence of disproportionate minority-group placement are also those categories whose criteria are based on clinical judgment: educable mental retardation, emotional/behavior disorders, and learning disability. The categories whose criteria are based on biologically verifiable conditions—such as deafness or visual impairment—do not show disproportionality by ethnicity" (p. 17).

Students' cultural values or customs, their linguistic abilities, or their experiential backgrounds may set them apart from their peers. This diversity presents a unique challenge for educators in the areas of assessment, instruction, and socialization. If differences in culture or language are not considered when selecting assessment tools, instructional strategies, and social activities, the result may be academic failure, social isolation, and inappropriate referral to special education for students who are culturally or linguistically different.

As cultural and linguistic diversity increase in the population at large, it also increases in the population of individuals with disabilities. It is difficult for any family to accept and adjust to having a child with special needs. The family's attitude toward disabilities and their resultant behavior can be a major factor in the identification of the disorder and the implementation of an intervention program. Families from diverse cultural backgrounds may have beliefs about disabilities that differ significantly from the beliefs of the majority culture. Language differences between the family and school personnel may inhibit the communication of test results and recommendations as well as the expression of parental questions and

TABLE 1.3

Percentage of Students Served by Disability and Race-Ethnicity, Fall 2007, Ages 6 through 21

Disability	American Indian/ Alaska Native	Asian/Pacific Islander	Black (non-Hispanic)	Hispanic	White (non-Hispanic)
Specific learning disability	1.7	1.7	20.7	22.2	53.7
Speech/language impairment	1.4	3.3	15.4	18.3	61.6
Intellectual disability	1.3	2.2	31.9	15.1	49.5
Emotional disturbance	1.6	1.1	28.9	11.6	56.8
Multiple disabilities	1.2	2.8	20.9	13.6	61.5
Hearing impairment	1.2	5.3	16.2	23.4	53.9
Orthopedic impairment	1.0	3.7	14.3	21.9	59.1
Other health impairments	1.3	1.5	17.8	10.5	68.9
Visual impairment	1.3	4.1	17.1	18.6	58.9
Autism	0.7	5.5	14.2	12.4	67.2
Deaf–blindness	1.9	4.2	12.9	19.3	61.7
Traumatic brain injury	1.6	2.4	16.3	13.4	66.3
Development delay	3.6	2.8	22.9	10.4	60.3
All disabilities	1.5	2.3	20.5	18.0	57.7
General population (ages 6–21)	1.0	4.2	15.1	18.9	60.9

From U.S. Department of Education (2008). Data Accountability Center: https://www.ideadata.org.

concerns. Students from diverse cultural and linguistic groups are at greater risk for being mislabeled and receiving inappropriate or inadequate services.

Other Sources of Diversity

The differences associated with cultural background and with disability are not the only sources of classroom diversity. The social and domestic issues of family structure, sexual orientation, poverty, malnutrition, inadequate health care, drug abuse, homelessness, and child abuse or neglect also contribute to the diverse needs of students in today's schools. All of these conditions can affect school attendance, motivation, and academic performance, placing many students at risk for school failure.

Educators are expected to provide effective instruction to all students in spite of the diversity of their needs, learning styles, and other characteristics. If the goal of meeting the educational needs of today's students is to be met, instructional practices must change to accommodate diversity, no matter what the source of that diversity. However, special education cannot be used to serve the needs of students from diverse backgrounds by labeling them disordered when, in fact, they are simply different. The instructional strategies presented throughout this book are strategies not only for students with disabilities. They are strategies that teachers can implement in their classrooms to meet the unique learning styles and needs of all students.

The Controversy of Labeling

When it is determined that a student needs and is eligible for special education services, a label is placed on that individual: intellectual disability, physical handicap, behavior disorder, etc. Unfortunately, most of the labels used to identify and categorize students for special education services have negative connotations. Labels can change the way a student is viewed by teachers, peers, and even family. Suddenly, the biases, myths, and misperceptions associated with certain labels become attached to the student. We look for and expect certain behaviors (or misbehaviors) with certain labels. We become focused on the disability and not the ability of the individual. The actions and reactions of teachers, peers, and parents to these students can have a significant impact on the students' attitudes toward their own behavior and self-concept, as well as their attitudes toward school, their academic goals, and performance.

Educators have argued for many years about whether we must label students in order to provide them with appropriate educational services. Opponents of labeling point to such problems as the potential mislabeling of students, the negative stereotypes associated with labels, the effects of labels on self-esteem, and lowered teacher expectations as reasons not to assign labels (Hardman & Nagle, 2004). Proponents of labeling counter that without labels students would not get the special services they need. The federal government provides special funds to the states for the education of students with disabilities. Labeling students allows schools to receive those additional funds to offer the special programs and services. In addition, categorizing and labeling students provides opportunities for research in both medicine and education. Finally, using labels can assist professionals in communicating about students with disabilities.

As teachers recognize the unique educational needs of all students in their classrooms, not just those with disabilities, the importance of labels becomes minimized. However, since an individualized approach to education is not yet the norm in all schools and classrooms, it is important to examine the impact of disabilities and labeling on teachers and students. How does a teacher react to students who have been labeled "special" or "different"? What do peers think of their classmates who are different?

Teacher Expectations

Teachers' expectations of their students can be influenced by a variety of factors. A student's gender, race, physical appearance, or performance in other classes, even comments from parents or fellow teachers, can impact a teacher's expectations of academic performance and behavior. If teachers are told that a student is gifted, they assume outstanding ability and expect performance at a level above others in the class. If teachers are told a student has an intellectual disability, they assume limited ability and expect performance below others in the class. These teacher attitudes and expectations can have a profound impact on teacher–student interaction which in turn influences the students' own attitudes, expectations, and behaviors (Ferguson, 1998; Rist, 2000; Trouillard, Sarrazin, & Bressoux, 2006; Van Acker, Grant, & Henry, 1996). This may result in positive outcomes when teachers' expectations are high for students; however, it is not difficult to envision the disastrous outcomes when teachers' expectations are low.

Peer Expectations

The attitudes of students toward their peers with disabilities or other differences have been examined by many researchers (Jenkins & O'Connor, 2003; Frederickson & Furnham, 2004; Horne, 1985; Woolfolk, 2004). Such studies have reported conflicting results with some suggesting that students view their peers with disabilities in a positive way and others showing that students view these peers negatively. Students may enter school with misperceptions and stereotypic views of individuals who are different from the norm. This may be due to limited interaction with individuals who are different from them in any way (language, race, culture, sexual orientation, disability, etc.) as well as the result of the influence of negative portrayals of persons with disabilities often seen in the media. It can be difficult for students without disabilities to get beyond labels and their negative connotations. The acceptance or

Mr. Grant has been informed by one of the special education teachers in his school that he will have a new student who is blind in his classroom this year. This student will, of course, be using special equipment, including recording devices. Mr. Grant wonders how he can help this student feel and be a part of the class with the other students. Mr. Grant is also a little concerned about the student using recording devices because he has never worked with a student who has a visual impairment before. If you were Mr. Grant, where would you go for answers to your questions and for additional information?

rejection of students with disabilities may have more to do with their labels than with the students as individuals.

The attitudes and behaviors of school personnel exert a powerful influence on the attitudes of students toward their peers (Garbarino & deLara, 2003; Sapon-Shevin, 2003). Students imitate the attitudes and behaviors they observe on a daily basis. Successful integration and acceptance of students with disabilities or other differences into general education requires the support of the entire educational system. Schools and classrooms that have a positive, inclusive culture will be models for the inclusion and acceptance of all individuals regardless of differences.

The Beginnings of Special Education Services

The attitudes of society toward individuals with disabilities have changed drastically over the centuries. Reviewing the history of these attitudes and the options that have or have not been available to individuals with disabilities provides a perspective for us to view the approaches used today to identify and provide services to these individuals. As our society has evolved, so have our social consciousness and our treatment of those who are perceived as different from the majority of society. Students with special needs, who today receive the full benefit of our educational system, would have been willfully ignored or abused in earlier times. Federal laws not only prevent discrimination in education, housing, and employment based on disabilities but also mandate a free, appropriate education for all students, no matter how severe their disabilities or how limited their abilities.

History of Special Education

Prior to the late 1700s, disabilities and differences were viewed with fear and superstition. Physical disabilities and mental incompetence were thought to be curses from the gods. Emotional problems and seizures were believed to be the result of possession by demons or evil spirits. Adults with disabilities were ignored, abused, or exploited. Large institutions or asylums were built to house individuals who were considered different or deviant. The asylums generally provided overcrowded, unsanitary living conditions and the residents often received little care. These asylums kept persons whom society viewed as undesirable or physically unattractive out of the community at large (Kanner, 1964; Carlson, 1990).

In the United States, the history of special education as described by Cruickshank (1958) begins in the nineteenth century. Physicians, ministers, educators, and social activists were instrumental in establishing the first schools for children who were blind, intellectually disabled, or deaf. However, the provision of the special services was relegated to isolated facilities, segregated from the mainstream of education and the community. Special services or classrooms in local public schools were virtually nonexistent at this time.

Public school programs for students with special needs began early in the 1900s and grew gradually until the middle of the century. As the country's population increased and people congregated in large cities, cities began to establish day-school programs for these special children, particularly those with the most common disorder, mild or moderate intellectual disabilities. These special education schools for the "educable mentally retarded" often were the sole source of special services in the local community.

Later, special education classes were established in the local schools. It was not uncommon to find students who had disabilities other than intellectual disabilities (e.g., learning disabilities, emotional disorders, hearing impairment, etc.) placed in these classes, although the services provided were neither appropriate nor adequate. Sailor and Roger (2005) stated that "in its early days, special education embraced the diagnostic/prescriptive model characteristic of modern medicine, and disability was viewed as pathology. . . . Students referred by teachers and parents were diagnosed in one of the categories of disability and tagged for separate, highly differentiated treatment" (p. 504).

Because students who were deaf or blind were fewer in number than students with other disabilities, public school programs were not commonly available for these children until later in the 1900s. The residential and day-school programs operated by states or private schools typically were the only educational options for these students. Parents of children with severe physical and/or cognitive disabilities were encouraged to place them in residential care facilities, state institutions, or to care for them at home, because the prevailing attitude was that these children could not be educated.

Changing Attitudes

During the 1940s and 1950s, the attitudes of society toward disabilities went through a dramatic change. World Wars I and II left thousands of individuals injured and disabled. Prior to their injuries, these people were respected and accepted members of their families and communities. When they returned home from these wars, their families and communities generally welcomed them back with continued respect and acceptance. Disabilities were viewed in a more favorable light than ever before. This attitude of acceptance began to extend to children and others whose disabilities were not related to war injuries. Head traumas incurred during military service led to research and a better understanding of the brain and its relationship to learning. As medical explanations were discovered for epilepsy, cerebral palsy, and other conditions, the attitudes of society began to change, and some of the myths and misperceptions about individuals with these disorders were dispelled (Cruickshank, 1958).

A powerful force in the evolution of educational services for students with disabilities has been parental concern and its resultant action. During the 1900s, parents began to form local, state, and eventually national and international organizations (Cruickshank, 1958; McCleary, Hardman, & Thomas, 1990). Initially these groups served as a forum for parents to discuss common problems and find sources for services. As they grew, these organizations became effective advocates for individuals with disabilities. Parent and professional groups such as the Association for Retarded Citizens of the United States (ARC) and the Learning Disabilities Association of America (LDA) had significant influence on the actions of local school boards, state legislatures, and even Congress in providing educational services to individuals with disabilities.

Moving into the Mainstream

Programs developed during the 1960s generally followed the model of segregating students with disabilities in separate, or self-contained, classrooms. There was little or no interaction between the students and teachers in these classrooms and the students and teachers in general education classrooms. Some schools during this period still did not offer any special education services. Parents were told to send their children to private schools at their own personal expense or to state-operated schools or institutions.

Countering this common practice of segregated services, some parents and professional organizations were espousing the philosophy of normalization, one of the steps leading to current practices in special education. Normalization (Nirje, 1979) is the belief that individuals with disabilities should be integrated into the mainstream of society. They should live, learn, and work in environments as similar to the norm as possible, having full access to the programs and services available to the community at large. In the schools, this meant that students with disabilities should have appropriate classrooms and access to the cafeteria, gym, etc.

The Office of Special Education Programs (OSEP), originally the Bureau of Education for the Handicapped, was established in 1965 as part of the Elementary and Secondary Education Act. Although education of children with disabilities was not mandated by law, the establishment of such a national bureau was the first sign of special education in national policy (National Information Center for Children and Youth with Disabilities, 1996). By 1972, the Supreme Court ruled in two separate class action lawsuits that children with disabilities have an equal right to publicly funded education like their nondisabled counterparts (National Information Center for Children and Youth with Disabilities, 1996).

With the passage in 1975 of Public Law 94-142, the Education for All Handicapped Children Act, states were required to provide a free, appropriate, public education (FAPE) to all students with disabilities. The law further mandated that the education of these students take place in the least restrictive environment (LRE). The principle of least restrictive environment requires that students with disabilities be educated with their peers who do not have disabilities to the maximum extent appropriate or, in other words, in the mainstream of the general education setting. This led to widespread use of the resource room as the model for educating students with disabilities. In this model, students received their special education in a separate class for the majority of the school day and were mainstreamed, or participated in the same learning and social activities as their peers, for the remainder of the day. Although this model is still used today, the current trend is for the full inclusion of students with disabilities in the general education classroom or schools, with appropriate accommodations and modifications being used. As you will see in Chapter 2, legislation and litigation were used to enhance the rights of individuals with disabilities and to achieve access to programs and services.

The Delivery of Special Education Services in Today's Schools

Classroom teachers play an important role in the identification of students with disabilities. A student does not receive special education services, however, simply because the classroom teacher thinks the student has a disability. Special education services can only be provided following a comprehensive assessment by a team of professionals who have determined the student is eligible for special education. Prior to referral for special education evaluation, students would have participated in the Response to Intervention (RTI) process. RTI is a process initiated by teachers when a student is struggling with academic or behavior issues. The process ensures that students have received appropriate instruction prior to being referred for special education. This approach is designed to provide research-based strategies and high-quality instruction to students. Data are analyzed to determine if students respond to the instruction. Students who continue to exhibit deficits in achievement will referred for a

Throughout the school year, classroom teachers will encounter students who experience difficulty in learning, behaving, or communicating. Not all of these students have disabilities.

special education evaluation. The RTI process is discussed in detail in Chapter 3. Throughout the school year, classroom teachers will encounter students who experience difficulty in learning, behaving, or communicating. Not all of these students have disabilities. A student may have difficulty learning a new math concept, not due to a learning disability, but because the earlier prerequisite skills were not taught. A student may refuse to speak in class, not due to a communication disorder, but out of fear of being teased by peers. Another student may talk back to the teacher or pick fights with classmates, not because of a behavior disorder, but as the result of a temporary conflict at home.

When a teacher encounters a student who is having difficulty in the classroom, the teacher makes whatever adjustments seem appropriate given the individual student's needs. Such strategies as meeting with the student to discuss the problem, providing additional instruction and practice, or speaking with the parents might help to resolve the problem. If the problem persists, additional steps will be taken. Typically the RTI process is the next source for assistance.

Placement Options

As defined earlier, special education is instruction designed to meet the unique learning needs of students with disabilities. The form that the special education takes—adaptations in curriculum or materials, specific instructional methods, or specialized equipment—will vary for each student. The environment in which the special education occurs also will vary. Some students' special needs can be met while the student remains in the general education classroom on a full-time basis. For other students, their needs may be best met by full-time placement in a special education classroom. Still others may benefit from a combination of general education classroom instruction and special education services. For example, some students will remain in the classroom for their academic instruction and receive additional tutoring or instruction in a resource room. The specific special education services and the environment in which they are provided will vary based on the nature of the disability and what is appropriate for the individual student. No two students are the same in abilities and in needs, even though they may share the same disability label. No label can fully describe a student's educational, social, psychological, or physical abilities and disabilities.

Inherent in the requirement of the least restrictive environment is the provision of a variety of educational placement options. States and school districts must offer a variety of educational settings for students with disabilities, including residential programs, separate schools, separate or self-contained classrooms, and resource rooms, as well as the general education classroom. Homebound/hospital programs are additional settings that may be a required placement for some students with disabilities who cannot be in other school settings due to the nature of their disability. Federal law (IDEA) defines all of the possible educational settings as shown in **Figure 1.2**. The appropriate placement for any one student is determined by the multidisciplinary team and is based on the student's needs. The first choice of placement is always to be the least restrictive setting in which the student's educational needs can be met with the option of moving to a more restrictive setting if needed. **Figure 1.3** shows the typical placement options on a scale from least restrictive to most restrictive.

| Figure 1.2 | Definitions of Educational Placement Settings |

General Classroom	Students receive services in programs designed primarily for students without disabilities, for 80% or more of the school day.
Resource Room	Students receive services in programs designed primarily for students without disabilities, for 40% to 79% of the school day.
Separate Class	Students receive services in programs designed primarily for students without disabilities for less than 40% of the school day.
Separate School	Students receive services in publicly or privately operated programs designed primarily for students with disabilities, that are not housed in a facility with programs for students without disabilities. Students receive special education and related services in the separate day school for greater than 50% of the school day.
Residential Program	Students are served in publicly or privately operated programs in which they receive care for 24 hours a day. This includes placement in public nursing home care facilities or public or private residential schools.
Homebound/Hospital Program	Students are served in either a home or hospital setting.

(IDEA, 2004)

| Figure 1.3 | Educational Placement Options from Least Restrictive to Most Restrictive |

Least Restrictive

- General Education Classroom
- Resource Room
- Separate Class
- Separate School
- Residential Program

Most Restrictive

When students with disabilities are placed in the general education classroom, special education teachers consult with the classroom teacher to provide support and assistance to ensure appropriate educational strategies and interventions are implemented. Most students with disabilities are being educated in regular school buildings, and nearly 80% are in general education classrooms for 40% or more of the school day (see **Figure 1.4**). Some students with disabilities may leave the general education classroom during the school day to receive ancillary or support services, which are services other than academic instruction. Examples of support services are physical therapy for students with physical disabilities, mobility training for students with visual impairment, or speech and language therapy for students with communication disorders.

Some students whose instructional needs are significantly different from their peers may spend the majority of the school day in special classes or, in some cases, in special schools. Figure 1.4 shows that 14% of students with disabilities were served in separate classes (they spent less than 40% of the school day in the general education classroom), and only 3% were in separate schools. Although some students are being educated in separate classes, they will participate in instructional and social activities with the other students in the school whenever appropriate. Such inclusion might be instruction in selected academic subjects; instruction in nonacademic subjects such as art, music, or physical education; or participation in school sports, clubs, and extracurricular activities. The extent of participation will differ from student to student, according to each individual's needs and abilities.

Figure 1.4   Educational Placements of Students with Disabilities Ages 6 through 21, for Fall 2010

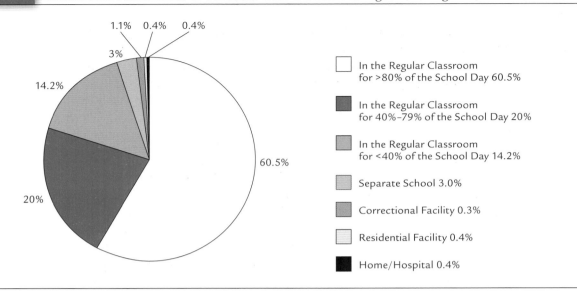

From U.S. Department of Education (2011). Data Accountability Center: https://www.ideadata.org.

TABLE 1.4

Percentage of Students Ages 6 through 21 by Disability in Educational Placements, Fall 2007

Disability	>80% of School Day	Served in the General Education Class 40%–79% of School Day	<40% of School Day
Specific learning disability	59.0%	29.7%	9.2%
Speech-language impairments	86.7	5.7	4.5
Intellectual disability	15.8	27.6	48.9
Emotional disturbance	37.3	19.7	24.1
Multiple disabilities	12.9	16.1	45.2
Hearing impairments	51.9	17.6	16.8
Orthopedic impairments	49.9	17.4	24.5
Other health impairments	59.0	25.4	11.7
Visual impairments	60.1	14.3	12.9
Autism	34.6	18.2	36.9
Deaf–blindness	20.8	13.8	32.4
Traumatic brain injury	43.9	24.7	22.5
Developmental delay	61.6	20.8	16.2

From U.S. Department of Education (2008). Data Accountability Center: https://www.ideadata.org

The educational placements for students with disabilities vary according to the disability category (see **Table 1.4**). Students with speech or language impairments typically spend the least amount of time outside the general education classroom, followed by students with specific learning disabilities. Given that these are high-incidence disabilities and these students will spend the majority of their school day in the general education classroom, teachers need to be particularly knowledgeable about these disability categories and the appropriate educational strategies for these students. Students with multiple disabilities, deaf–blindness, and severe intellectual disabilities will spend the least amount of time in the general education classroom and are more likely to be educated in separate facilities (separate schools, residential facilities, or homebound or hospital environments) than students with other types of disabilities.

The educational placement of students with disabilities has changed over the years with more students being served in less restrictive environments. Students with disabilities are spending more time in general education classrooms and less time in all of the other placement settings today. This reinforces the importance of general education classroom teachers having the knowledge and skills needed to teach students with disabilities.

Inclusive Classrooms

The term inclusion is used to describe the process of educating students with disabilities in the general education setting. Advocates for what is labeled full inclusion believe that the general education classroom is the appropriate educational placement for all students with disabilities, not just those with mild disabilities. They believe that students should not leave the classroom to receive special services, but that the special services needed should be provided in the general education classroom through the collaboration and cooperation of the classroom teacher and special education professionals. Proponents of inclusion argue that pulling students from the classroom to receive special services fragments their education and inhibits communication and collaboration between the classroom teacher and the special educator. There are benefits and drawbacks to inclusion as can be seen in **Figure 1.5.** Both proponents and opponents of inclusion recognize that there are problems with the current delivery of special education services, and their common goal is to improve those services.

The full inclusion movement seeks the elimination of a dual system of education: general education versus special education. Supporters cite the cost of maintaining a dual educational system, the negative result of labeling some students as disabled, and the benefits of individualized instruction for all students (with and without disabilities) as reasons for full inclusion. Full inclusion is a controversial issue among general and special educators and parents. Not all special education professionals and parents believe that full inclusion, or a full-time placement in the general education classroom, will meet the educational needs of all students with disabilities. These educators generally support full inclusion as a placement option when it is appropriate for a student, but they are skeptical that it is the best model of

Figure 1.5   Arguments For and Against Full Inclusion

Proponents of Full Inclusion Argue:

- Labeling is de-emphasized.
- Stigma of leaving class for special instruction is decreased.
- Students remain with their peers full-time.
- Social skills are improved.
- Self-esteem is increased.
- General education students benefit from interaction.
- Interaction and cooperation among all school personnel is enhanced.
- The realities of our society are faced.

Opponents of Full Inclusion Argue:

- Classroom teachers, parents, and students are not prepared.
- Class sizes are too large to allow teachers to meet all students' needs.
- Quality of education to all students will decrease.
- School personnel do not have the necessary collaborative skills.
- Some students need instructional strategies and technology not available in the classroom.

The push for inclusion came with the **No Child Left Behind** rule that 95% of all students had to participate in state assessments for accountability.

service delivery for all students. Researchers have only recently begun to examine the academic progress of students in full inclusion classrooms.

Many classroom teachers are concerned about their ability to meet the diverse needs of the students currently in their classrooms. Many teachers, in both general and special education, fear that students with disabilities will be placed in general education classrooms on a full-time basis without adequate support, ensuring frustration and failure for both students and the teachers. Some parents and professionals are concerned that full inclusion will hurt the students it is proposed to help by eliminating placement options. However, Sailor and Roger (2005) state, "The sum of available evidence overwhelmingly supports integrated instructional approaches over those that are categorically segregated, regardless of the categorical label or severity of the disability" (p. 504). They continue by noting that, "Special education has designed instructional enhancements that can facilitate this outcome, but for these research-based enhancements to benefit all students, special education needs to be integrated with general education" (p. 505).

The real push for inclusion came with the No Child Left Behind (NCLB) rule that 95% of all students had to participate in state assessments for accountability. Schools and districts must now pay attention to the performance of all students, which means students with disabilities are getting attention they did not have before. Because of the assessment requirements of NCLB, educators are promoting and practicing instructional differentiation, adaptations of curricula, and universal design for successful student learning (Schwarz, 2007).

Impact of Federal Legislation

Major changes in the area of special education came into effect as we entered the early 2000s with the passage of the 2001 No Child Left Behind (NCLB) legislation and the 2004 reauthorization of IDEA. As discussed with placement options, the IDEA legislation ensures that all students receive a free appropriate public education, or FAPE, in the least restrictive environment (LRE) and special services to assist in meeting their educational needs. "The reauthorization of IDEA both increased the number of individuals eligible to receive special services and extended the range of services available" (Nichols et al., 2008). These laws are discussed in detail in Chapter 2.

Prior to the passage of IDEA, most school districts provided minimal services to students with disabilities, but with the passage by Congress of the 2001 NCLB legislation, education took a new direction as schools were required to provide effective instruction for all students, including students with disabilities. The power of this new law is in the fact that schools in all states are required to demonstrate the effectiveness of instruction by assessing and measuring the progress of all students, including those with disabilities, in major content areas such as reading and math each academic year.

Since its passage, NCLB has been criticized for many reasons. One of the major criticisms is that it is unfair to include special education students and students with limited English proficiency (LEP) in the testing and accountability of states and to judge them by the same standard used for all other students. In the past, special education students and LEP students were often excluded from high-stakes, large-scale assessment because educators believed it was not in the best interest of those students to take the tests.

Proponents of NCLB counter that the law was designed to ensure that students in subgroups, which traditionally had low percentages of students meeting standards, would receive attention in schools. Recently, educators have become concerned that excluding students from testing may be harmful to students because it allows their needs to remain unknown and unaddressed. Students who are not tested often do not get the services they need to help improve their academic achievement. Many education researchers and policymakers now believe that special education students and LEP students should be included in the assessments to the maximum extent practical so that the needs of those students are not ignored.

The impact of the accountability and testing requirements on special education students and other subgroups listed in NCLB has been significant. Because of the accountability factor, more special education and LEP students have access to the standard or general education curriculum and are in inclusion classes whenever possible. The Council for Exceptional Children (CEC), the major professional organization in special education, supports the assessment of special education students as part of each state's accountability for student achievement under NCLB. CEC stated that the new regulations include a number of provisions that will enable educators to better assess the academic progress of students with disabilities while still maintaining high standards for them.

Special Education Across the Life Span

Although the discussion of special education services in this chapter has focused on students in elementary, middle, and secondary schools, it is important to note that many disabilities will affect individuals throughout their lifetimes, not only during their school years. For example, intellectual disabilities, deafness, or severe physical disabilities can have a significant impact on children's cognitive, physical, communicative, or social/emotional development long before they enter school. These disabilities and others also may affect an individual's ability to obtain employment or live independently in adulthood.

Educators and providers of social services have recognized the importance of providing services as early as a disability can be identified, in infancy if possible, and extending services beyond the typical age for completion of secondary school, 18 years. The federal laws that mandate special education services target infants and toddlers with disabilities and their families for early intervention services. Providing both direct services to the young child and support services to the family can minimize the effect the disability will have on the child's early development and later learning. These laws also target adolescents and young adults through age 21 for transition services. Transition services are designed to assist students with disabilities in making the transition from living at home and attending school to independent living, employment, and community involvement. The laws that require early identification and mandate the provision of transition services are discussed in Chapter 2.

Summary

This chapter examined the role that special education plays and the students it serves in today's educational system. Teachers face a challenging task: to ensure that all students have the opportunity to learn and develop to their potential. When students in general education classrooms exhibit cognitive, behavioral, communicative, sensory, or physical differences from their peers, this task can appear overwhelming. It is only through the cooperation and collaboration of classroom teachers, special education professionals, parents, and school administrators that the goal of full participation in the educational process to the extent that is most appropriate for each student will be met.

Classroom Application Activities

1. Interview a teacher who has an inclusive classroom. Focus your questions on how the teacher makes accommodations and modifications for students in the classroom and on the types of support he receives from the special education teachers for these students.

2. Contact a local school system and make arrangements to observe a self-contained special education classroom. Discuss with classmates why this classroom is self-contained, the disabilities of the students in the classroom, and how the teacher works with these students.

3. Discuss how general education teachers can encourage a multicultural education in their classrooms and in their schools.

4. Check the web sites of schools in your area to determine how their special education students as a group are doing on the state accountability tests. Are these schools making adequate yearly progress (AYP)? If they are not, is it because of the special education subgroup? Discuss the impact of AYP on the education of special education students.

5. Interview a friend or family member who attended elementary or secondary school prior to 1965. Focus your questions on issues involving the education and placement of students with disabilities. Ask about the types of disabilities of students in their schools and the services that were or were not provided to these students. Discuss these topics with classmates.

Internet Resources

Council for Exceptional Children (CEC)
www.cec.sped.org

National Center for Culturally Responsible Educational Systems
www.nccrest.org

National Dissemination Center for Children with Disabilities (NICHCY)
www.nichcy.org

Office of Special Education and Rehabilitative Services
www.ed.gov/about/offices/list/osers/osep/index.html

Special Education Resources on the Internet (SERI)
www.seriweb.com

The National Institute on Disability and Rehabilitation Research
www.abledata.com

IDEA
www.ideadata.org/links.asp

National Association of State Directors of Special Education
www.nasde.org

National Center for Educational Statistics (Institute of Education Sciences), U.S. Department of Education
http://nces.ed.gov/programs/coe/2008

New Horizons for Learning
www.newhorizons.org/spneeds/improvement/jewel.htm

The National Early Childhood Technical Assistance Center
www.nectac.org

References

Artiles, A., & Trent, S. (1994). Overrepresentation of minority students in special education: A continuing debate. *Journal of Special Education, 27,* 410–437.

Artiles, A.J., Rueda, R., Salazar, J.J., & Higareda, I. (2005). Within-group diversity in minority disproportionate representation: English language learners in urban school districts. *Exceptional Children, 71,* 283–300.

Aud, S., Fox, M., & KewalRamani, A. (2010). *Status and Trends in the Education of Racial and Ethnic Groups* (NCES 2010-015). U.S. Department of Education, National Center for Education Statistics. Washington, DC: U.S. Government Printing Office.

Brown v. Topeka, Kansas, Board of Education 347 U.S. 483 (1954).

Carlson, N.R. (1990). *Psychology: The science of behavior.* Boston: Allyn & Bacon.

Cruickshank, W.M. (1958). The development of education for exceptional children. In W.M. Cruickshank & G.O. Johnson (Eds.), *The education of exceptional children and youth* (pp. 3–42). Englewood Cliffs, NJ: Prentice-Hall.

Ferguson, R.F. (1998). Teacher's perceptions and expectations and the Black-White test score gap. In C. Jencks & M. Phillips (Eds.), *The black-white test score gap* (pp. 273–317). Washington, DC: Brookings Institute.

Frederickson, N.L., & Furnham, A.F. (2004). Peer-assessed behavioural characteristics and sociometric rejection: Differences between pupils who have moderate learning difficulties and their mainstream peers. *British Journal of Educational Psychology, 74,* 391–410.

Garbarino, J., & deLara, E. (2003). Words can hurt forever. *Educational Leadership, 60*(6), 18–21.

Gollnick, D.M., & Chinn, P.C. (2006). *Multicultural education in a pluralistic society* (7th ed.). Boston: Pearson.

Hardman, M.L., & Nagle, K. (2004). Policy issues. In A. McCray, H. Reith, & P. Sindelar (Eds.), *Contemporary issues in special education: Access, diversity, and accountability* (pp. 277–292). Boston: Allyn and Bacon.

Harry, B., & Klingner, J. (2007). *Discarding the deficit model.* Alexandria, VA: Educational Leadership, Association for Supervision and Curriculum Development.

Horne, M.D. (1985). *Attitudes toward handicapped students: Professional, peer, and parent reactions.* Hillsdale, NJ: Lawrence Erlbaum Associates.

Individuals with Disabilities Education Improvement Act of 2004 United States 108th Congress (IDEA). (2004). Office of Special Education and Rehabilitative Services. From http://www.ed.gov/about/offices/list/osers/osep/index.html.

Jenkins, J.R., & O'Connor, R.E. (2003). Cooperative learning for students with learning disabilities: Evidence from experiments, observations, and interviews. In H.L. Swanson, K. Harris, & S. Graham (Eds.), *Handbook of learning disabilities* (pp. 417–430). New York: Guilford.

Kanner, L. (1964). *A history of the care and study of the mentally retarded.* Springfield, IL: Charles C. Thomas.

Kaplan, P.S. (1996). *Pathways for exceptional children: Home, school, and culture.* St. Paul, MN: West Publishing.

McCleary, I.D., Hardman, M.L., & Thomas, D. (1990). International special education. In T. Husen & T.N. Postewaite (Eds.), *International encyclopedia of education: Research and studies* (pp. 608–615). New York: Pergamon Press.

National Center for Educational Statistics. (2008). Glossary. Education indicators: An international perspective. From http://nces.ed.gov/pubs/eiip/eiipgls.asp.

National Information Center for Children and Youth with Disabilities. (1996). *The education of children and youth with special needs: What do the laws say?* From https://www.nichcy.org/pubs/outprint/nd15txt.htm.

National Research Council. (2002). *Minority students in special and gifted education.* Committee on Minority Representation in Special Education, Division of Behavioral and Social Sciences and Education. Washington, DC: National Academy Press.

Nichols, S.M.C., Bicard, S.C., Bicard, D.F., & Casey, L.B. (2008). *A field at risk: The teacher shortage in special education.* Bloomington, IN: Phi Delta Kappa International.

Nirje, B. (1979). The normalization principle and its human management implications. In R.B. Kugel & W. Wolfensberger (Eds.), *Changing patterns in residential services for the mentally retarded.* Washington, DC: The President's Committee on Mental Retardation.

Rist, R.C. (2000). HER classic: Student social class and teacher expectations: The self-fulfilling prophecy in ghetto education. *Harvard Educational Review, 70*(3), 257–301.

Sailor, W., & Roger, B. (2005). *Rethinking inclusion: School-wide applications.* Bloomington, IN: Phi Delta Kappa International.

Sapon-Shevin, M. (2003). Inclusion: A matter of social justice. *Educational Leadership, 61*(2), 25–28.

Schwarz, P.A. (2007). *Special education: A service, not a sentence.* Alexandria, VA: Educational Leadership, Association for Supervision and Curriculum Development.

Ting-Toomey, S. (1999). *Communicating across cultures.* New York: Guilford Press.

Trouillard, D., Sarrazin, P., & Bressoux, P. (2006). Relation between teachers' early expectations and students' later perceived competence in physical education classes: Autonomy-supportive climate as a moderator. *Journal of Educational Psychology, 98,* 75–86.

U.S. Census Bureau (2007). From http://factfinder.census.gov.

U.S. Census Bureau (2010). Retrieved April 5, 2012, from http://2010.census.gov/2010census/data/index.php.

U.S. Department of Education (2008). Office of Special Education Programs, Data Accountability Center. From https://www.ideadata.org.

U.S. Department of Education (2011). *Office of Special Education Programs, Data Analysis System (DANS), OMB #1820-0043: Children with Disabilities Receiving Special Education Under Part B of the Individuals with Disabilities Education Act, 2010.* Data updated as of July 15, 2011. From: https://www.ideadata.org.

Van Acker, R., Grant, S.B., & Henry, D. (1996). Teacher and student behavior as a function of risk for aggression. *Education and Treatment of Children, 19,* 316–334.

Woolfolk, A. (2004). *Educational psychology* (9th ed.). Boston: Allyn and Bacon.

CHAPTER TWO

The Legal Foundation for Special Education

Wendy F. Hensel and Colleen M. O'Rourke

CHAPTER OBJECTIVES

- to provide an overview of the legislative history that relates to the special education of students with disabilities;
- to define the key educational provisions required by law for students with disabilities; and
- to review the impact that legislation related to general education has on special education.

KEY TERMS

Brown v. Board of Education • Section 504 of the Rehabilitation Act • The Education for All Handicapped Children Act • The Individuals with Disabilities Education Act (IDEA) • The Americans with Disabilities Act (ADA) • The No Child Left Behind Act (NCLB) • The Family Educational Rights and Privacy Act (FERPA)

According to the U.S. Department of Education (2008–09), over 6 million children currently receive special education services. Historically, our nation's response to students with disabilities has been exclusion from public schools, institutionalization, and segregation from the regular classroom. However, groundbreaking federal legislation in the 1960s and 1970s opened our nation's schools to students with special needs. These laws also served as the catalyst for a major shift toward a more inclusive learning environment for students with disabilities. As seen in Chapter 1, students with disabilities have not always had the same right to education and access to services as their peers.

Federal laws that ensure the rights of today's students with disabilities did not just happen. They were the result of the work and dedication of parents, advocacy groups, and professional organizations that serve individuals with disabilities. In large measure, these groups owe their success in achieving equality in education to minority groups and their struggle to guarantee civil rights for all citizens. As the civil rights movement entered the arena of public education, it resulted in court decisions and legislation that prevented discrimination in education based on race. These decisions and laws were the foundation for parental and professional action to prevent discrimination in education based on disability. Initial right-to-education litigation in the area of special education was based on *Brown v. Board of Education* (1954). In this civil rights case, the U.S. Supreme Court ruled that separate schools for black and white students were unequal and therefore unconstitutional. This case ended racially segregated public education and provided a legal precedent for the elimination of segregated public education based on disability.

Numerous court cases have impacted the education of students with disabilities.

This chapter outlines the primary laws that regulate the field of special education. It addresses some of the important cases that have shaped and determined the rights and services available to individuals with disabilities today. This chapter begins with an in-depth discussion of the Education of All Handicapped Children Act (EAHCA), later renamed the Individuals with Disabilities Education Act (IDEA). It then turns to briefly review the two federal antidiscrimination laws relevant to children with disabilities, Section 504 of the Rehabilitation Act of 1973, and the Americans with Disabilities Act (ADA), as amended by the ADA Amendments Act of 2008. The chapter briefly reviews the No Child Left Behind Act and its intersection with the IDEA and concludes with a summary of the Family Educational Rights and Privacy Act (FERPA). It is critical for classroom teachers to understand the basic provisions of these laws because teachers play a key role in implementing them and delivering the legally required services.

Litigation History

The early history of children with disabilities in public schools is an unhappy one. Many students were excluded from public schools altogether, and those lucky enough to gain entrance were often denied adequate educational services once enrolled. As late as 1969, for example, there was a law in North Carolina making it a crime for parents to insist that a child with disabilities attend public school once a superintendent had rejected the child's placement (Colker, 2009). The exclusion of children with mental retardation, deemed uneducable, and children with physical disabilities unable to access school buildings with stairs, was particularly common and widespread.

Parent activism was a significant factor in the growth and expansion of special education from 1950 to 1974 (Blackhurst & Berdine, 1993). The National Association for Retarded

Children, now known as the American Association on Intellectual and Developmental Disabilities (The ARC), was formed in the 1950s. Its members, many of whom were parents, began to pressure public schools for services. In the 1960s, the Association for Children with Learning Disabilities, now the Learning Disabilities Association of America (LDA), was formed and followed the precedent of the ARC. When schools denied services to students with disabilities or provided inadequate services, parents and professional organizations began to file lawsuits and lobby Congress.

As a result of the success of *Brown v. Board of Education,* however, parents and advocates for children with disabilities began arguing that students with disabilities had a civil right to attend public schools. They argued that schools' refusal to allow the children to attend public schools or to provide adequate services once there violated the Fourteenth Amendment of the U.S. Constitution, which guarantees all citizens the equal protection of the laws and due process under law.

Two important early cases adopted this reasoning and ultimately served as blueprints for the subsequent enactment of federal legislation in this area. The first, *Pennsylvania Association for Retarded Children (PARC) v. Commonwealth of Pennsylvania* (1972), challenged a state law permitting school districts to exclude students with moderate, severe, or profound mental retardation from public education. The district court ruled that the U.S. Constitution required the state to provide these children with a "free program of education and training appropriate to his capacities." Equally important, the court ruled that parents have the right to a hearing when they are dissatisfied with their child's placement, setting the stage for legal enforcement.

In the second case, *Mills v. Board of Education of the District of Columbia* (1972), parents and advocates of students with a wide range of disabilities likewise claimed that the district's failure to admit their children or to provide adequate services once enrolled violated the U.S. Constitution. The district court not only agreed with this argument, but also rejected the school's position that the cost of providing services to these children justified their exclusion from educational services, a commonly held perspective at the time.

These and numerous other cases served as a wake-up call to Congress, who responded by passing the **Education for All Handicapped Children Act** (EAHCA) in 1975. **Table 2.1** outlines several significant cases that have shaped the delivery of special education services. The following section highlights the legislative evolution of EAHCA, which ultimately was renamed the Individuals with Disabilities Act (IDEA) in 1990.

TABLE 2.1	
Rulings in Court Cases Relevant to Special Education	
Case	*Ruling*
Hobson v. Hansen (1967)	• This suit challenged the practice of educational tracking, or ability grouping, based on standardized test scores. The practice was ruled to be unconstitutional as it discriminated against poor and minority students.
Diana v. State Board of Education (1970)	• Parents of Spanish-speaking students filed suit challenging placement of their children in classes for the mentally retarded. They alleged that intelligence tests were culturally biased and resulted in inappropriate labeling of their children. The result was the requirement for nondiscriminatory assessment and testing of students in their primary language.
Larry P. v. Riles (1972)	• Parents of African-American children filed suit challenging inappropriate placements of children in classes for the mentally retarded. The result was a ruling that (a) intelligence tests cannot be the sole basis for placement, and (b) a test must be developed that is not culturally biased.

(continued on next page)

TABLE 2.1

Rulings in Court Cases Relevant to Special Education *(continued)*

Case	Ruling
PARC v. Commonwealth of Pennsylvania (1972)	• The Pennsylvania Association for Retarded Children (PARC) filed suit against the state of Pennsylvania to obtain access to public education for children with mental retardation. Although Pennsylvania provided special classes for some students with disabilities, students with moderate, severe, or profound retardation could be excluded from public education. The case resulted in the provision of educational programs (beyond traditional academic programs) for students with mental retardation. The court also ruled that parents have the right to a hearing when they are dissatisfied with their child's placement. Many of the provisions of Public Law 94-142 were based on this case.
Mills v. District of Columbia Board of Education (1972)	• A group of parents in Washington, DC, filed suit against the public schools for access to education for children with disabilities, including those with behavior problems. The court, which ruled in favor of the parents, expanded the ruling to include all students with disabilities and created a zero reject policy. The court also refused to allow schools to claim fiscal inability as an excuse for not providing appropriate services.
New York State Association for Retarded Children v. Carey (1979)	• This suit challenged the placement of children who were mentally retarded and had hepatitis B (a disease that can be contained) in separate self-contained programs. The court ruled that the students' placement could not be made based solely on the existence of the disease.
Battle v. Commonwealth of Pennsylvania (1980)	• Parents of students with disabilities challenged the state of Pennsylvania to extend education services beyond the 180-day school year. The ruling found that some students with disabilities need an extended school year to prevent significant regression and required the school to provide summer programming.
Rowley v. Hendrick Hudson School District (1982)	• Hendrick Hudson School District in New York provided a student with a hearing impairment a sign language interpreter plus six other things. They then terminated this service the following year because the student was doing so well. The due process hearing officer, federal district court, and federal appellate court supported the parents by requiring the school to provide the interpreter, ruling that it maximized the student's educational achievement. The U.S. Supreme Court reversed the ruling, stating that Congress never intended for schools to "maximize" the educational progress of students with disabilities, but to make available an appropriate educational program. They established a two-part standard for evaluating a "free appropriate public education": (1) the state must provide meaningful access to an education for each disabled child, and (2) sufficient supportive and related services must be provided to permit a child to benefit educationally from special instruction.
Irving Independent School District v. Tatro (1984)	• In this case the family sought for the provision of catheterization services to allow their child to remain in school for the entire school day. The Court ruled that catheterization is a related service needed by some students to maintain access to education and that schools are required to provide related services that students need to remain in school.
Honig v. Doe (1988)	• Parents challenged that children with disabilities should not be expelled from school for inappropriate behavior that is due to the disability. The Court ruled that students cannot be expelled if the inappropriate behavior is related to the disability.
Daniel R. R. v. State Board of Education (1989)	• The Fifth Circuit Court of Appeals held that a segregated class was an appropriate placement for a student with Down syndrome. The Court established two factors for determining compliance with the requirement of least restrictive environment (LRE) for students with severe disabilities: (1) it must be determined whether the student can make satisfactory progress and benefit educationally in the general education classroom with curriculum modifications and using supplementary aids and services, and (2) it must be determined whether the student has been integrated to the maximum extent appropriate.
Timothy W. v. Rochester School District (1989)	• The First Circuit Court of Appeals established that students are entitled to a free and appropriate public education no matter the severity of their disabilities. Education was defined broadly to include functional skill instruction.

(continued on next page)

TABLE 2.1	

Rulings in Court Cases Relevant to Special Education *(continued)*

Case	Ruling
Oberti v. Board of Education of the Borough of Clementon School District (1992)	• The Court ruled that the school must offer placement in a general education classroom with supplementary aids and services to a student with disabilities before considering more segregated placements. The student cannot be denied placement in a general education classroom just because the curriculum and services would need to be modified.
Agostini v. Felton (1997)	• The U.S. Supreme Court reversed a ruling that banned the delivery of publicly funded educational services to students enrolled in private schools. This means that special educators can now provide services to students enrolled in parochial schools.
Cedar Rapids Community School District v. Garret F. (1999)	• The U.S. Supreme Court ruled on the issue of related services, reaffirming that intensive and continuous school health care services (if not performed by a physician) that are necessary for a student to attend school can qualify as related services.
Schaffer v. Weast Superintendent of Montgomery County Schools (2005)	• The U.S. Supreme Court ruled that the burden of proof in an administrative hearing challenging an IEP is placed upon the party seeking relief. This means that if a student, represented by his or her parents, challenges an IEP the burden of proof is their responsibility. However, the rule applies with equal effect for the school system. Some states have laws or regulations that always put the burden of proof on the school district. The court chose not to address these state laws. No such law exists in Maryland where this case was located.

The Education for All Handicapped Children Act (EAHCA) (Public Law 94-142)

EAHCA was a landmark in legislation for special education. It reflected Congress's belief that state and local educational agencies have the responsibility to provide appropriate education to all children. By passage of the law and provision of federal funds, Congress asserted that the national interest is served by the federal government's support of programs to meet the needs of students with disabilities. EAHCA awarded states increased funding to meet the needs of students with disabilities and established specific guidelines for spending the money.

The centerpiece of EAHCA was the requirement that public schools provide a free, appropriate public education (FAPE) and related services to children with disabilities aged 5 to 21, language that mirrored the PARC case discussed previously. No longer could schools refuse to provide services that were needed for the appropriate education of students or provide them at an extra cost to the parents.

Public Law 94-142 addressed numerous issues in the identification and education of students with disabilities. It mandated a comprehensive, nondiscriminatory evaluation prior to special education placement as well as periodic reevaluation. A written, individualized education program (IEP) specifying goals and objectives was required for each student receiving special education services. The special education services had to be provided in the least restrictive environment (LRE). The law also specified procedural safeguards to protect the rights of students and parents. Public Law 94-142 dramatically and permanently changed the delivery of services to students with disabilities. Not only would school systems be required to provide services, they would be held accountable for the appropriateness of those services.

The Education of the Handicapped Act Amendments of 1986 (Public Law 99-457)

When it becomes necessary to update a law or add new provisions to existing laws, Congress can add amendments to a current law. In 1986, Congress amended EAHCA, extending its rights and protections to children with disabilities aged 3 to 5 years and providing funds to assist states in planning, developing, and implementing a comprehensive, statewide system of early intervention for infants and toddlers (birth to age 3 years) with disabilities and their families.

The revised law required an individualized family service plan (IFSP) for children birth to age 3. Like the IEP, the IFSP describes the child's needs and the services to be provided to enhance development. The IFSP also addresses the family's needs and the services to be provided to ensure that the family understands the child's disability and is involved in the intervention program. In fact, if it is determined that services to the family are needed for the appropriate education of the child, those services will be provided even if the child does not need direct services.

The Individuals with Disabilities Education Act (IDEA) (Public Law 101-476)

With the passage of Public Law 101-476 in 1990, Congress again reauthorized EAHCA, renaming it IDEA. IDEA updated the terminology used to describe this population. The term *handicapped*, used previously, no longer was considered acceptable and was replaced with *disabled*. Since the law applies to persons with disabilities from birth through age 21, the label *children* was inappropriate and was changed to *individuals*. To reflect the sentiment that the disability should not define the person, the phrasing of the title of the Act was modified to place the emphasis on the person not the disability. The preferred phrasing became *individuals with disabilities* rather than *disabled individuals*. Thus the law known as the Education for All Handicapped Children Act became the Individuals with Disabilities Education Act (IDEA).

IDEA added two new categories of disability: autism and traumatic brain injury. These students had been receiving services prior to this law, but they were labeled under one of the other existing categories. Parents and professionals advocated for separate categories to ensure accurate identification and appropriate services. The law also defined transition services (services to ensure the progression from school to post-school activities) and required that these services be included on the student's IEP no later than age 16. In addition, IDEA defined assistive technology devices and services and required that students with disabilities have access to this technology if needed.

The Individuals with Disabilities Education Act Amendments of 1997 (IDEA 97) (Public Law 105-17)

After 2 years of discussion and debate in the Senate and House of Representatives, Public Law 105-17 reauthorized and amended IDEA and is often referred to as IDEA 97. IDEA 97 included several major changes and modified some procedures that were included in the previous laws. It required students with disabilities to be included, with accommodations when necessary, in state- and districtwide assessment programs. For example, when states or school districts administer the Iowa Test of Basic Skills to all students in certain elementary grades, students receiving special education services must be included in that assessment. In the past, many of these students were excused from such assessments. For those students who could not participate in regular assessments, IDEA required states to develop alternative assessments. IDEA 97 also added additional specific requirements for an IEP, such as an explanation of the extent to which the student will not participate in the general classroom program.

The law mandated a more significant role for parents in the decision-making process. Parents must be included on any team that makes decisions about their child's educational placement. Mediation was emphasized in resolving conflict between schools and the parents of a student with disabilities. States were required to create a mediation system and to bear the cost of the process. The most controversial and complicated changes were in the area of discipline and alternative placement of students with disabilities.

The Individuals with Disabilities Education Act Amendments of 2004 (IDEA 2004) (Public Law 108-446)

The law amended the language of IDEA to better align it with the requirements of No Child Left Behind, the Elementary and Secondary Education Act (ESEA) of 1965. The amendments made clear that special education students are entitled to highly qualified teachers in core academic subjects just as all other students covered by ESEA, the specifics of which are covered later in this chapter. It is also notable that IDEA 2004 required local education agencies (LEAs) to provide special education services to children with disabilities attending private schools within the LEA. Although these students have no enforceable right to individual services, the LEA must set aside federal dollars to meet the needs of private school students proportionate to their population in the district. Finally, a number of changes were made in an attempt to reduce the time and paperwork burdens placed on special education teachers and administrators.

Implementation of Federal Laws

Before discussing the provisions of IDEA in more detail, it is important to understand that the implementation of federal laws involves both federal and state agencies. Once laws are passed, detailed regulations are written as guidelines for implementation. These regulations describe the procedures that must be followed to comply with the laws. State laws and regulations tend to mirror the federal laws. This results in commonalities across states in their special education programs and procedures. However, differences exist among states in such areas as the language used, the criteria for defining a disability, and the approach to service delivery. Each state must present its plan for the delivery of special education services to the U.S. Office of Special Education Programs for approval. This provides evidence that the state is meeting the intent of the law to provide appropriate educational services to students with disabilities. Prior to submission of the plan, states must provide an opportunity for public review and comment on the plan.

At the local level, school districts and their boards of education are responsible for the delivery of special education services. These local districts must operate their special education programs according to the regulations established at the state and federal levels. Although there may be some degree of local control and autonomy, education is primarily a responsibility of the state. For this reason, teachers should be familiar with the rules and regulations of their local educational agency and state. A copy of your state's special education regulations can be obtained from your state Department of Education or Department of Public Instruction.

Federal funds are provided for the education of students with disabilities. These funds are awarded to each state that has an approved plan for the delivery of special education services. The funds are based on the number of students currently receiving special education services. Although most of this money is passed from the state to the local education agency, additional local funds are needed to fully cover the cost of the special education services. Each state must monitor local education agencies to ensure that their approved plan is being carried out and the monies being spent for special education services. The U.S. Office of Special Education Programs is responsible for monitoring each state.

In spite of the written federal and state regulations for implementation, the laws related to special education are complex. It is difficult to translate the full intent of the laws into regulations that anticipate all possible situations in the education of students with disabilities. Thus, the lawsuits and court decisions discussed earlier in this chapter have played an important role in interpreting the laws. Certainly lawsuits will continue to be filed in the future, and the courts will continue to clarify and provide interpretation of the basic principles underlying the laws.

Major Provisions of IDEA

As noted previously in this chapter, IDEA reflects national support for the public education of all students. The law requires that each state have an approved plan that describes the policies and procedures for the identification and education of all students with disabilities. Until this plan is approved, the state will not receive federal funds to support the education of students with disabilities.

Students with disabilities who exhibit one or more of several specific conditions that result in their need for special education and related services are eligible under IDEA:

- Autism
- Deaf–blind
- Emotional disturbance
- Hearing impairment
- Specific learning disabilities
- Intellectual disability
- Multiple disabilities
- Orthopedic impairment
- Other health impairment
- Speech or language impairment
- Traumatic brain injury
- Visual impairment

IDEA mandates that state and local educational agencies identify, evaluate, and provide services to students who qualify under the definitions of these disability categories. In addition, children ages 3 through 9 may qualify for services if they are experiencing developmental delays (as defined by state law) in physical, cognitive, communication, social or emotional, or adaptive development and need special education and related services. This latter category of eligibility was intended to give states more flexibility in providing early intervention services without the need for a disability label. Definitions and in-depth discussions of each exceptionality are presented in Chapters 6, 8, 10, 11, and 12. It is important to remember that although IDEA has specific criteria for each of the above mentioned categories, ADA and Section 504 define disability in broad terms in relation to one's ability to function in our society (see Table 2.2). The major components of IDEA have implications for the education of students in all settings, especially the general education classroom. A discussion of these provisions and how they must be implemented in educational settings follows.

Free Appropriate Public Education (FAPE)

All students with disabilities have the right to a free and appropriate education at public expense. IDEA ensures that these students will no longer be denied the right to attend school. Prior to the passage of Public Law 94-142, schools could claim that programs were not available or that certain students with disabilities could not be educated. As discussed in Chapter 1, this meant some students were turned away from public schools, and parents were forced to pay for any educational services themselves. Now public schools must provide appropriate education to all students at no cost to parents. The term *appropriate* is not defined in the law, which has proved troublesome for teachers and administrators trying to interpret what level of services the law requires. In *Board of Education v. Rowley* (1982), the Supreme Court provided some guidance on this question. The Court concluded that Congress was primarily concerned with providing access to education for children with disabilities and did not intend to impose a substantive educational standard on schools. As a result, the Court concluded that a school will satisfy the requirements of FAPE by (1) complying with the procedural requirement of IDEA, and (2) "by providing personalized instruction with sufficient support services to permit the child to benefit educationally from that instruction." Notably, the court rejected the idea that schools must maximize the educational outcomes of each child. Instead, evidence that a child is achieving passing marks and advancing from grade to grade will be strong evidence that FAPE has been provided to those with academic difficulties educated in a general education classroom.

The Supreme Court's relatively narrow interpretation of FAPE has been much criticized by disability advocates. Many lower courts have softened the impact of the Rowley language by interpreting it to call for schools to provide a meaningful education benefit to children with disabilities. It is up to teachers, special educators, school officials, and parents to work together to determine what is appropriate for each student under this standard.

Nondiscriminatory Evaluation and Placement

Special education services cannot be provided unless a student meets eligibility criteria based on the results of a comprehensive assessment by a multidisciplinary evaluation team. This assessment must be individualized and nondiscriminatory. The nondiscriminatory provision was added to eliminate errors in the classification and placement of students. It was believed that many students received unreliable and invalid assessments and then were labeled inappropriately and placed in special education classrooms. School personnel must assure that they are using tests that are valid for the purpose for which they are used and that the testing and evaluation materials are fair and unbiased. It is required that states monitor and prevent the inappropriate overidentification of racial or ethnic minority students as having disabilities. This is due to the history of a disproportionate representation of students from minority groups in special education. States must collect data that determines whether there is disproportionate representation by specific impairment, educational placement, or disciplinary actions, including suspensions and expulsions. The intent of this provision is to eliminate discrimination based on cultural background, race, or disability. In addition, IDEA requires that when assessing students suspected of having a disability:

- At least one member of the evaluation team be a specialist (usually a special education teacher) with knowledge in the area of the suspected disability.
- The parent of the student must be a member of the group making evaluation and placement decisions.

- All areas related to the suspected disability be evaluated, including health, vision, hearing, behavior, general intelligence, motor abilities, academic performance, and language abilities.
- Trained personnel select and administer the tests.
- The evaluation be done in the student's native language or other mode of communication (e.g., sign language).
- The results of the assessment reflect the student's aptitude or achievement, not the disability (e.g., sensory, physical, or communication impairment).
- The evaluation determines not only what disability a student might have, but also the most appropriate way to address the disability.
- Eligibility and placement cannot be determined on the basis of the results of a single test, such as a general intelligence test.

In IDEA 2004, Congress made significant changes to the evaluation process for students suspected of having a specific learning disability (SLD). Prior to 2004, many states identified SLD by considering evidence reflecting a severe discrepancy between a student's intellectual ability and actual achievement in oral expression, listening comprehension, written expression, basic reading skill, reading comprehension, mathematical calculation, or mathematical reasoning. Because many educators had criticized this methodology, IDEA 2004 provides that LEAs are not required to use the severe discrepancy model, although they may continue to do so. As an alternative, the law states that LEAs may use a process that determines whether students respond to scientific, research-based intervention as part of the evaluation process. Often referred to as the Response to Intervention (RTI) model, this methodology applies progressive teaching interventions in the classroom to determine whether the source of a student's learning difficulty is an underlying disability.

Individualized Education Program (IEP)

A major component of IDEA is the requirement that every student receiving special education services have an individualized education program (IEP). The IEP is a written statement of the plan designed to meet the student's special needs and to ensure that an appropriate education is provided. It is the product of the comprehensive assessment. The IEP is developed annually by an IEP team. The team members include the student's general education teacher, a special education teacher, a school district representative, an evaluation specialist, the parents or surrogate, the student if appropriate, and other individuals as needed (e.g., psychologist, speech-language pathologist, physical therapist). The IEP must include a statement of the student's present levels of academic achievement and functional performance and a statement of measurable academic and functional annual goals. The IEP must include a description of how the student's progress toward meeting the annual goals will be measured. It must also include a statement of the special education and related services, supplementary aids and services, and program modifications or supports for school personnel that will be provided for the student. Included in the IEP are:

- The student's present level of educational performance.
- The annual goals.
- If necessary, a statement detailing why regular assessments are not appropriate and why a particular alternative assessment is necessary.
- Short-term instructional objectives for students who take alternative assessments.
- A statement of the specific educational services to be provided, including who will provide them and where they will be provided.
- The starting date and expected duration of services.

- A statement of the extent to which the student will be able to participate in general education programming.
- An explanation of the extent to which the student will not participate with nondisabled students in the general class or in extracurricular and nonacademic activities.
- The evaluation plan and criteria to determine whether the objectives are being met.
- Postsecondary goals and transition services beginning no later than age 16.

The IEP documents the student's needs and the school's commitment of resources and services. It can be an evaluation device to determine a student's progress toward stated goals as well as a management tool to assure that special education services are provided. In cases of controversy, the IEP may be important as a legal instrument to provide evidence of whether the requirements of the law have been met.

An IEP must be reviewed by the team annually, or sooner if requested by the parent or teacher. In addition, a student's eligibility for special education services must be reevaluated every 3 years. IDEA 97 modified the procedures required in the reevaluation process. Previously, it was required that tests be administered in this process (e.g., IQ tests, academic achievement tests). Under the reauthorization of IDEA, the IEP team considers all available information in making a decision about the student's continued eligibility for special education services. The team may request the administration of specific tests when needed, but retesting is not required.

Changes to a student's IEP after the annual IEP meeting for a school year may be made without a meeting if the parent and the LEA agree. This can be done by amending the IEP rather than by redrafting the entire IEP. In addition, the parent and the LEA may agree to use alternative means of meeting participation, such as video conferences and conference calls.

Under IDEA 2004, a transition plan is required for all students beginning no later than 16 years of age. The IEP must include appropriate measurable postsecondary goals based upon age-appropriate transition assessments related to training, education, employment, and, where appropriate, independent living skills and the transition services (including courses of study) needed to assist the student in reaching those goals. This plan ensures that students' education is focused on the skills needed for employment and community living after they have left the public school environment.

In the case of a student with a disability who transfers school districts within the same academic year and had an IEP that was in effect, the LEA shall provide the student with a free appropriate public education (FAPE) described in the previously held IEP until a new IEP is developed. If the transfer is to a school district in another state, the same rule applies until the LEA conducts an evaluation if determined to be necessary. To facilitate the transition, the new school must take reasonable steps to promptly obtain the student's records from the previous school in which the student was enrolled; the previous school must promptly respond to the request.

Infants and toddlers who qualify for special education must have an individualized family service plan (IFSP). The significance of this plan is that the family may be offered direct services if they are needed for the child's development. In fact, a family may receive services and assistance even though the child does not receive any direct services. In addition, IDEA 2004 requires that a school transition plan be developed to ensure the appropriate continuation of special education services.

Least Restrictive Environment (LRE)

Educating students with disabilities in the least restrictive environment (LRE) means that they should remain in the school environment with their nondisabled peers to the greatest

Educating students with disabilities in the least restrictive environment means that they should remain in the school environment with their nondisabled peers to the greatest extent possible and appropriate.

extent possible and appropriate. The current law requires that before a student is removed from the general education classroom setting, attempts be made to educate the student in the classroom with supplemental services and aids. Teachers must plan and implement an intervention program for the general education classroom setting. The process of referral and placement is discussed in Chapter 3. However, it must be demonstrated that specific interventions in the general education classroom were unsuccessful before the student is referred for special education. Only when the disability is severe enough that education in the general classroom is not effective are schools allowed to remove students from the general education classroom. This provision is "based on the premise that many creative alternatives exist to help the regular educator serve children with learning or adjustment problems within the context of a regular class setting" (Wood, 1984, p. 11).

A common misperception is that the principle of LRE requires all students with disabilities to be educated solely in general education classrooms. In fact, the law requires that a continuum of placement options be available to students with disabilities. This continuum ranges from the totally integrated, general education classroom setting to a totally segregated, separate school as shown in **Figure 2.1**.

The appropriate placement for any student is determined by the IEP team based on the specific needs of that student. Even though students may have the same disability, the LRE that is appropriate for one may be inappropriate for another. For the majority of students with disabilities, placement in the general education classroom for at least a part of the school day is appropriate.

There is no uniform test applied by courts to determine whether the programming a school provides to a child with disabilities is delivered in the least restrictive environment.

Figure 2.1   Educational Placement Options from Least Restrictive to Most Restrictive

Least Restrictive

Most Restrictive

- General Education Classroom
- Resource Room
- Separate Class
- Separate School
- Residential Program

One set of courts has adopted what is often referred to as a *portability test*, developed in *Roncker v. Walter* (1983) by the Sixth Circuit Court of Appeals. If the school says that superior services are provided in a more restrictive setting, these courts begin by asking whether such services feasibly could be transferred into a less restrictive setting for the child with a disability. If they can, then placement in the more restricted setting is usually inappropriate. In evaluating this question, courts are directed to:

- compare the benefits the child would receive in special education with those they would receive in regular education;
- consider whether the child would be disruptive in the nonsegregated setting; and
- consider the cost of inclusion.

Another set of courts follows a two-part test developed by the Fifth Circuit Court of Appeals in the case of *Daniel R.R. v. State Board of Education* (1989), which gives more leeway to school districts. These courts begin by asking "whether education in the regular classroom, with the use of supplemental aids and services, can be achieved satisfactorily for a given child," and if it cannot, "whether the school has mainstreamed the child to the maximum extent appropriate." To assist in answering these questions, the court identified several relevant factors to consider:

- the steps the school district has taken to accommodate the child in the general education classroom;
- whether the child will receive an educational benefit from general education;
- the child's overall educational experience in general education; and
- the effect the child's presence has on the general education classroom.

Some courts following this approach also consider whether the cost of educating the child with disabilities in the general education classroom is so great that it would significantly impact on the education of other children in the district.

The Supreme Court has never weighed in on which approach is appropriate, and some courts have taken a hybrid approach between these two. Regardless of which approach is adopted, the interpretation of IDEA by the U.S. Office of Special Education Programs in Washington, DC, and recent court rulings have increased dramatically the number of students with disabilities included in the general education classroom.

There is disagreement among both professionals and parents as to the benefits of inclusion for all students, as well as the student with disabilities. Some school systems have eliminated self-contained special classes and have adopted a model of full inclusion. This extreme position eliminates the continuum-of-services option. In this extreme inclusive model, the IEP is no longer the basis for placement, since all students with disabilities are placed in the general education classroom.

Regardless of the final outcome of the debate and controversy surrounding inclusion, more students with disabilities will spend a greater part of their school day in the general education school program. The philosophy of placement has shifted from that of initial placement in a restrictive environment and movement toward the mainstream to that of initial placement in a least restrictive environment and movement toward a segregated environment if needed. As a result, all classroom teachers will interact with students with special needs. The responsibility for the education of all students will be shared by general education teachers and special education teachers. This shared responsibility will require additional skills for all teachers. Chapter 4 discusses the need for collaboration with families and professionals in sharing the responsibilities of educating students with disabilities.

Discipline and Placement in Alternative Educational Settings

Behavior and discipline have been controversial issues under IDEA, especially when determining whether a student with disabilities could be expelled from school for violating school rules (e.g., carrying a weapon) or must "stay put" in the student's current educational placement. These rules were amended significantly in 1997 and 2004.

When students with disabilities violate a code of student conduct, schools are permitted to suspend or transfer them to alternative appropriate educational settings for up to 10 school days, so long as students without disabilities are subject to the same treatment. Within 10 days the IEP team must convene to determine whether the misconduct was caused by, or had a direct and substantial relationship to, the student's disability. If the conduct is a manifestation of the disability, the IEP team must review any existing behavioral intervention plan and modify it as necessary. If prior to the incident the IEP team did not conduct a functional behavioral assessment with a behavior intervention plan, it must do so. At the end of 10 school days, the student must be returned to their original placement if the conduct was a manifestation of the student's disability. If the student's behavior was not a manifestation of a disability, the school may impose the disciplinary consequences applicable to general education students but must continue to ensure that FAPE is provided to the student with a disability.

Suspensions and transfers of more than 10 days are permitted in some cases of serious misconduct whether or not the misconduct is a manifestation of the student's disabilities. Schools may initiate such changes for up to 45 school days for a student with disabilities who carries or possesses a weapon; possesses, uses, or sells illegal drugs; or has inflicted serious bodily injury upon another person while at school, on school grounds, or at a school function. Serious bodily injury is defined as bodily injury that involves a substantial risk of death, extreme physical pain, protracted and obvious disfigurement, or protracted loss or impairment of the function of a bodily member, organ, or mental faculty. In addition, schools with substantial evidence that maintaining the student's current placement is likely to result in injury to the student or to others may request a hearing where a hearing officer may order a change in placement to an appropriate alternative setting for up to 45 school days. In all cases, parents who do not agree with decisions regarding placement may file a due process challenge. While waiting for the hearing, the stay-put placement is the interim alternative educational setting determined by the IEP team.

Notably, these protections may extend to students who have not yet been deemed eligible for special education if the school had knowledge that the student had a disability before the behavior that resulted in the disciplinary action occurred. Knowledge means a parent has expressed concern in writing about the student's behavior, the parent had requested an evaluation of the child, or a teacher or administrator had expressed specific concerns about a pattern of behavior demonstrated by the student to the director of special education or other supervisory personnel. Chapter 9, Managing Behavior for Effective Learning, addresses these issues in greater detail.

One issue that has received increasing focus over the last several years is the use of restraints and seclusion rooms for students with disabilities who act out in the classroom. The use of restraints varies widely, and includes physically holding children on the floor either face down or on their backs, or using mechanical devices or objects, such as bungee cords, to limit the child's range of movement. Students may be isolated in seclusion rooms by themselves without supervision for hours at a time. At times, such techniques have resulted in death or serious injury to children with disabilities. The problem is growing because more children with severe behavioral needs are included in the general education setting without adequate teacher training on how to address their needs.

Currently, the IDEA does not deal directly with the use of restraint or seclusion and leaves the matter to state law. Several recent attempts to pass federal legislation in this regard have failed. Nevertheless, because states' responses to the use of restraints and seclusion, with a few exceptions, have been weak or nonexistent, and reports of abuse of children with disabilities have become increasingly common, it is likely that this issue will remain on the federal agenda in the near future.

Related Services and Supplementary Aids

Each local school system must provide a free appropriate public education for students with disabilities who require special education services and any related services, as specified in each student's IEP. Related services include, but are not limited to, specialized transportation and such developmental, corrective, and other supportive services as are required to help a student with a disability to benefit from special education. These may be assistive technology devices, assistive technology services, audiological services, counseling services (including rehabilitation counseling), early identification and assessment services, educational interpreting services, medical services for diagnostic or evaluation purposes, physical and occupational therapies, psychological services, and recreation services (including therapeutic recreation). Related services also include parent counseling and training, school health services, school nutrition services, and social work services in schools.

Medical services are excluded from coverage, except to the extent that they are provided for the purpose of diagnosis or evaluation. Many students with severe disabilities need health care during the school day in order to attend; however, the cost of such services can be quite expensive. As a result, there has been some controversy over the definition of *medical*. The Supreme Court in *Irving Independent School District v. Tatro* (1984) took a liberal interpretation of this provision, concluding that a skill is medical and therefore excluded only if it is exclusively performed by a physician. If a school nurse can provide the care needed, it is covered under the statute as a related service regardless of the cost. As a result, courts have concluded that things like urinary catheterization, suctioning of tracheotomy tubes, and similar procedures are covered as related services that schools must provide under the IDEA.

Supplementary aids and services include, but are not limited to, assistive technology devices, assistive technology services, educational interpreting services, note takers, preferential seating, provision of assignments in writing, and other such services required to assist a student with a disability to benefit from the general education program. This applies to any education program in which the student may participate, including art, music, physical education, and vocational education.

Rights of Students with Disabilities and Their Parents

IDEA guarantees procedural safeguards for students with disabilities and their parents in all areas relating to identification, evaluation, and placement. At one time, it was common practice to evaluate students and make changes in their educational program without their parents' knowledge or consent. This law makes parents important participants in the planning and execution of the educational program for their child. Parents must be notified and give their consent before the student is assessed or the educational program is changed. IDEA establishes specific procedures that must be followed from evaluation through placement and programming to protect the rights of students and parents. Specific due process requirements under IDEA are:

- Written notice must be provided to parents and written parental permission obtained for the evaluation of a student for special education services. Parent participation in eligibility decisions is required.

- Parents may refuse special education services for their child.

- Written parental permission must be obtained before the school initiates or changes the placement of a student in special education services. Parent participation in all placement decisions is required, except in some disciplinary proceedings.

- Parental notices must provide a description of the proposed actions and be written in the native language of the home.

- All materials and procedures used for evaluation purposes of students with disabilities should be provided and administered in the native language used in the home unless it is not feasible.

- All matters relating to the student must be held confidential.

- Parents have the right to obtain an independent assessment of their child at their expense. The assessment may be at the expense of the school if the school agrees, or if it is required by a hearing officer.

- Parents have the right to inspect and review all educational records of their child. This law expands the privacy rights of all students that were legislated by the Family Rights and Privacy Act of 1974 (Buckley Amendment) to protect the privacy of an individual's records.

- Parents have the right to have records amended if information is inaccurate, misleading, no longer relevant to the child's education, or in violation of any rights of the child.

School systems provide parents with in-depth information about their rights regarding the special education of their child. This is usually presented as a parent's rights statement. These statements include such topics as records, confidentiality of information, independent evaluation, notification of meetings and actions, parental consent, hearings, evaluation procedures, least restrictive environment, private school placement, and alternative educational settings.

In most cases, parents and school officials are able to reach agreement on the appropriate placement and programming for students. Disagreements can arise due to honest differences in opinion as to what is best for the student. When the parents and school do not agree about any part of the special education program, either party may request a due process hearing. When parents have requested a due process hearing, the student is entitled to stay put in his current educational placement, except in some disciplinary cases as discussed earlier, until the administrative or judicial proceedings are concluded.

School districts are required to convene a meeting known as a resolution session prior to a due process hearing to determine whether the complaint regarding a student's educational plan can be resolved amicably. Participants in the resolution session include the parents, a school representative, and members of the IEP team who are knowledgeable about the issues in dispute. The resolution session provides an opportunity for the parents and school district to discuss their concerns and amicably resolve the issues in the complaint. If the dispute is resolved, both the parent and a representative of the school district with decision-making authority should sign a legally binding settlement agreement. However, if the dispute is not resolved through the resolution process, a due process hearing is scheduled. Alternatively, parents and the school district may agree in writing not to participate in the resolution session or to use a mediation process instead.

IDEA emphasizes mediation as the first step in conflict resolution. States now are required to create a mediation system in which parents and schools may participate voluntarily at the state's expense. If mediation is successful, a formal agreement must be written and signed. If mediation is not successful in resolving the dispute, or if the parent or school chooses not to participate, the next step is a due process hearing before an impartial hearing officer. During the due process hearing parents and school officials present evidence to challenge the placement or provision of services.

In *Shaffer v. Weast* (2005), the Supreme Court held that the burden of persuasion during the due process hearing is on the party challenging the IEP. Because most due process hearings are initiated by parents, this means that parents usually will have the obligation to bring forward evidence reflecting that their child's IEP is inadequate to provide FAPE in accordance with IDEA. This is not universally true, however, as some states continue to place the burden of persuasion on the school district as a matter of state law. The Supreme Court has never answered whether such state practices violate the IDEA. In *Arlington Central School District Board of Education v. Murphy* (2006), the Supreme Court held that parents are not entitled to recover expert witness fees even if they are prevailing parties in the due process hearing. As a result of these two decisions, many have argued that school districts have a decisive advantage in IDEA litigation.

It is up to the hearing officer to decide on the appropriateness of the educational program. During the hearing, parents and school officials have the right:

- To have legal counsel.
- To present evidence and call witnesses.
- To a written or taped record of the hearing.
- To a written decision of the disposition of the case.

The decision of the hearing officer must be implemented unless it is appealed to the civil courts at either the state or federal level.

The needs of students with disabilities are best met when schools and parents work together. This partnership between parents and the school is not easily formed and maintained. Some parents may be reluctant to participate, believing they do not have the expertise needed. Others may view schools as adversaries rather than partners. Chapter 14 discusses the importance of parents as team members in the educational process and provides suggestions to facilitate their involvement.

Federal Antidiscrimination Statutes Relating to Disability

Although IDEA is the primary federal law relating to the provision of special education and services, other federal laws also relate to children with disabilities in public schools, including 504 of the Rehabilitation Act, the Americans with Disabilities Act, and its subsequent amendments in 2008. These statutes prohibit discrimination against individuals with disabilities and serve as additional sources of protection for students.

Section 504 of the Rehabilitation Act of 1973 (Public Law 93-112)

This act is considered to be the first federal civil rights law protecting the rights of persons with disabilities. Section 504 states that:

> No otherwise qualified handicapped individual shall, solely by reason of his handicap, be excluded from participation in, be denied the benefits of, or be subjected to discrimination in any program or activity receiving federal financial assistance.

Under Section 504, an individual with a disability is defined as any individual who:

- has a physical or mental impairment which substantially limits one or more of such person's major life activities,
- has a record of such impairment, or
- is regarded as having such an impairment.

In addition, a physical or mental impairment is defined as:

- any physiological disorder or condition, cosmetic, disfigurement, or anatomical loss affecting one or more of the following body systems: neurological; musculoskeletal; special sense organs; respiratory; including speech organs; cardiovascular; reproductive; digestive; genito-urinary; hematic and lymphatic; skin; and endocrine; or
- any mental or psychological disorder, such as mental retardation, organic brain syndrome, emotional or mental illness, and specific learning disabilities. (29 Code of Federal Regulations Part 32.3)

Section 504 applies to any program receiving federal funding, including preschool programs.

The law applies to any private or government agency receiving federal funds. This includes not only state, county, and local governments, but also preschool programs, elementary and secondary schools, and institutions of higher education. These agencies and programs would lose all federal funding if they violated Section 504 by denying individuals with disabilities employment opportunities, benefits, or access to services or activities. As a result of Section 504, major changes have occurred not only in the accessibility of educational, vocational, and social services, but also in architectural accessibility for persons with disabilities. It required that existing structures be modified so as to be accessible to persons with disabilities and that new facilities be designed and constructed to meet standards of accessibility.

Although Section 504 applies to individuals of all ages, school-age individuals benefit from its application to educational programs and school environments. It guarantees a free, appropriate education to all children, including those with handicapping conditions. Section 504 also requires that school districts bear the cost if the lack of appropriate facilities necessitates the transfer of a student to an alternative, appropriate placement. The law specifies that arrangements be made for participation by students with disabilities in nonacademic and extracurricular activities "to the maximum extent appropriate to the needs of the handicapped person in question."

Many of the provisions of Section 504 were later incorporated into IDEA. Section 504 remains an important, comprehensive civil rights statement for students with disabilities. A student may be eligible for protection under Section 504 and IDEA simultaneously. In some cases, however, students with disabilities will not qualify under IDEA, usually because they do not need special education and related services. These same students at times require some reasonable accommodation to succeed in the school environment. A student with severe asthma, for example, may need school policies prohibiting the carrying of an inhaler to be waived during gym class. Likewise, a student with attention deficit/hyperactivity disorder (ADHD) may be performing well in the classroom but need preferential seating in order to maintain their attention during instructional activities.

It is important to note that not all students with impairments will qualify for a 504 plan. Students will only qualify if the impairment significantly limits one or more of major life activities. It is also important to note that if a student qualifies for an IEP under IDEA, they could qualify for a 504 plan; however, they would not need this plan because they are already covered by an IEP which is more comprehensive than a 504 plan. If a student qualifies for a 504 plan, they are allowed accommodations to support their learning. If they need modifications, they should be assessed to determine if they qualify for an IEP. Additionally, it is noteworthy that school systems do not receive additional funding for students who have a 504 plan; however, systems can lose federal funding if they do not follow 504 plans. For this reason some school systems are not quick to suggest 504 plans for students.

Some of the students who qualify for 504 plans include, but are not limited to, those with type 1 diabetes, ADHD, seizure disorders, and sickle cell disorder. Some of the accommodations that are common include:

- ensuring students are in the proper health conditions during standardized and classroom testing;
- having procedures for turning in work when they are being assisted by a nurse;
- excusing students from classes if health conditions warrant;
- providing additional visual or verbal explanations if needed; and
- providing additional assistance for any organizational issues due to absences or their impairment.

Additionally, medical protocol procedures for individual students can be included in their 504 plans. Some students will need only a nursing plan for their impairment. The distinction of whether a student requires a 504 plan or a nursing plan depends on whether the impairment limits one or more of that student's major life activities.

Most school systems have developed 504 Committees to determine whether a student qualifies for accommodations under Section 504. Students who meet the eligibility requirements are entitled to an individualized accommodation plan. This plan should include the support services that are necessary to ensure the student has equal access to education programs and services. Some school systems follow the same procedures as IDEA and complete an IEP for 504 students, although this is not legally required.

The Americans with Disabilities Act (ADA) (Public Law 101-336)

The ADA, signed into law in 1990, prohibits discrimination on the basis of disability. It extends the civil rights protection mandated by Section 504 for persons with disabilities into the private sector. The ADA specifically prohibits discrimination in both public and private employment, accommodations (workplace, hotels, restaurants, stores, etc.), transportation services (buses, trains, airplanes, etc.), and telecommunications.

Employers with 15 or more employees must make reasonable accommodations for persons with disabilities to avoid discrimination in hiring, firing, and promotions.

The ADA requires that public facilities be accessible to those with disabilities.

Public entities, including public schools, must be accessible and may not exclude or discriminate against any individual with disabilities from their services, programs, or activities. Likewise, public accommodations, which include things like private hotels, restaurants, theaters, private schools, banks, and professional offices, must provide equal benefits and access to the extent feasible to people with disabilities. They also must make reasonable modifications to their policies and procedures when necessary to provide such benefits to people with disabilities, unless doing so would fundamentally alter the nature of the services provided.

The ADA overlaps with the Rehabilitation Act but is far broader in its scope because it extends into the private sector. Congress made clear that the two laws would be interpreted consistently with respect to the meaning of disability, and therefore changes to the ADA affect the Rehabilitation Act as well. Both laws define disability to mean an impairment that substantially limits a major life activity, a record of such impairment, or an individual who is regarded as having such impairment.

Although the provisions of the ADA enabled individuals with disabilities to function more independently than ever before, the law was not without its critics. Judges construed the meaning of disability under the act in an extremely narrow way. For example, the Supreme Court determined that the question of whether an individual is substantially limited in a major life activity must take into consideration the ameliorative effects of any medication or devices to correct the impairment. Thus, a student with serious asthma who in most cases could control the asthma with an inhaler would not be considered disabled within the meaning of the act. A student with learning difficulties who nevertheless was able to achieve high grades by spending a substantially longer time studying than typical peers would likewise not be covered under the law. As a result, schools were not required to provide these students with a reasonable accommodation. Unhappy with this turn of events, disability advocates and scholars called for changes in the law to restore the broad protections originally intended by Congress.

The Americans with Disabilities Act Amendments Act of 2008 (ADAAA) (Public Law 110-325)

In 2008, Congress passed the ADAAA, which went into effect at the beginning of 2009. Congress directed courts to interpret the ADA to provide a broad scope of protection to people with disabilities. Although Congress did not change the basic definition of disability, it provided additional guidance on the meaning of each element of the definition. For example, it expanded the list of activities that qualify as major and made it significantly easier to show that an individual is regarded as being disabled. Of major significance, Congress directed that courts evaluate whether a person is *substantially limited* without regard to the effects of medication or corrective devices used by the individual. Because the Rehabilitation Act is to be interpreted consistently with the ADA, these changes also apply to 504 determinations.

The impact of ADAAA has yet to be determined, but there is no question that the law has significantly broadened eligibility under Section 504 and the ADA. The 504 committees will now be required to take a much more liberal perspective in evaluating whether a student is disabled under federal law and thus entitled to a 504 plan. Especially in the area of learning difficulties, it will not be enough to determine whether or not the student is achieving good grades. Instead, 504 Committees must now inquire into the method and manner in which the student learns to determine whether they substantially differ from the average person in the general population. In the future, courts are likely to focus on whether the school has offered reasonable accommodations to the student rather than the question of whether the student has a protected disability.

Comparing Three Current Laws

Of the laws discussed here, three play a major role in the regulation of services provided by schools: IDEA, Section 504, and ADA. **Table 2.2** compares the major provisions of these three laws.

TABLE 2.2

A Comparison of the Provisions of IDEA, Section 504, and ADA, as Amended (P.L. 110-325)

	IDEA	Section 504	ADA
Title of Act	The Individuals with Disabilities Education.	Section 504 of the Rehabilitation Act of 1973.	The Americans with Disabilities Act, 1990.
Description	Ensures the right of all individuals with disabilities to a free appropriate public education.	Antidiscrimination statute, guarantees civil rights to qualified individuals with disabilities.	Same as Section 504.
Purpose	To ensure that all children with disabilities have a free appropriate public education with special education to meet their individual needs.	To eliminate discrimination on the basis of disability in any program or activity receiving federal financial assistance.	To eliminate discrimination on the basis of disability in public or private employment, public entities, and public accommodations.
Funding Provision	Federal money based on number of students receiving special education adjusted for poverty rates in the state. Funds withdrawn for noncompliance.	The loss of federal funds for noncompliance.	Judicial award of damages.
Age	Birth to 21 years.	All ages.	All ages.
Definition of Disability	Individuals with disabilities are defined by category, with criteria specified in the law.	Individuals with a physical or mental impairment that substantially limits one or more major life activities.	Individuals with a physical or mental impairment that substantially limits one or more major life activities.
Due Process	A set of procedures that includes mediation, local hearings, and civil court.	Civil court.	Civil court.
Service Delivery Model	An individualized education plan that specifies the special education services to be provided and the location of these services.	A 504 plan that provides accommodations that meet the educational needs of the student with a disability as adequately as the needs of students without disabilities are met.	

(continued on next page)

TABLE 2.2

A Comparison of the Provisions of IDEA, Section 504, and ADA, as Amended (P.L. 110-325) *(continued)*

	IDEA	Section 504	ADA
Preschool	• Part C provides early intervention for infants birth to 2 years and their families. Part B mandates special education for ages 3–5 and transition from early intervention to preschool.	• Requires that individuals with disabilities have the same opportunities as other individuals. In states where preschool is available to other children, children with disabilities must have the same opportunity.	• Same as Section 504.
Accessibility	• Provides assistance to make schools accessible.	• Requires accommodations so that the individual may receive appropriate education.	• Accessibility codes for public and private entities to accommodate individuals with disabilities as employees and consumers.
Parental Involvement	• Parents have rights to participate fully in all aspects of the process from eligibility to program modification; due process procedures.	• Parents of children with disabilities must be provided with the same opportunity for involvement as parents of typical children.	• Same as Section 504.
Least Restrictive Environment	• Students shall be placed in the least restrictive environment where they can most benefit from their special education. Attempts to educate the student in the general education setting must be demonstrated before a segregated placement is chosen.	• Students shall be placed in the general educational environment unless it is demonstrated that the education of the student in the general educational environment with the use of supplemental aids and services cannot be achieved satisfactorily.	

The No Child Left Behind Act of 2001 (Public Law 107-110)

The No Child Left Behind Act (NCLB) is the latest version of the Elementary and Secondary Education Act of 1965. It redefines the federal role in K–12 education to help improve the academic achievement of all students and to close the achievement gap between disadvantaged and minority students and their peers. Four of the main principles of the education reform plan are:

1. Stronger accountability for results.
2. Expanded flexibility at the local level.
3. Expanded options for parents.
4. An emphasis on teaching methods that have been proven to work.

This general education law will have an effect on the education of all students including those receiving special education services. The following are some of the major provisions that will have a significant impact on the education of all students at-risk for low achievement.

Accountability

NCLB creates assessments in each state that measure what students know and learn in reading and math in grades 3 through 8. Student progress and achievement will be measured for every student every year. The data will be available in annual report cards on school performance and in statewide progress reports. Statewide reports will include performance data for individual groups according to race, gender, and other criteria to demonstrate not only how well students are achieving overall but also the progress in closing the achievement gap between disadvantaged students and other groups of students.

Expanding Options

The parents of children from disadvantaged backgrounds who are attending failing schools are allowed to transfer their child to a better-performing public or charter school immediately after a school is identified as failing. Federal money can be used to provide supplemental educational services such as tutoring, after-school services, and summer school programs for students in failing schools. NCLB also expands federal support for charter schools by giving parents, educators, and interested community leaders greater opportunities to create new charter schools.

Reading

To ensure that every student can read, NCLB increased federal funding for reading and links that funding to scientifically proven methods of reading instruction.

Teacher Quality

NCLB required a highly qualified teacher in every public school classroom by 2005. In addition to specific funds for teacher quality, NCLB allows local schools freedom to spend additional federal funds for hiring new teachers, increasing teacher pay, and improving teacher training and development.

English Proficiency

NCLB consolidates the U.S. Department of Education's bilingual and immigrant education programs in order to focus support on enabling all limited English proficient (LEP) students to learn English as quickly and effectively as possible. All LEP students will be tested for reading and language arts in English after they have attended school in the United States for 3 consecutive years. Parents will be notified that their child demonstrates limited English proficiency and is in need of English language instruction. The new act will focus on helping LEP students learn English through scientifically based teaching methods.

IDEA 2004 Meets NCLB

In 2004, two of the largest pieces of federal education legislation in our nation's history converged with the alignment of IDEA's individualized approach to improving educational outcomes with NCLB's standards-based approach. Collectively, these two pieces of sweeping federal legislation were intended to ensure that all children, including those with disabilities, receive a high-quality education through the implementation of a more results-based

IDEA 2004 and NCLB require that all teachers of core academic subjects be "highly qualified" in all core subjects taught.

system. Under this new system, Title I public schools (schools that enroll a significant percentage of students who are living at or below the federal poverty level) in each state must establish performance goals and indicators for students with disabilities that incorporate NCLB's Adequate Yearly Progress (AYP) measures as a condition for receiving IDEA funding. Each school's performance goals should be aligned with a standards-based curriculum, and schools and districts are legally required to include the achievement outcomes of students with disabilities in their annual report card. Additionally, both laws require that all teachers, including special education teachers who teach core academic subjects, be "highly qualified" in all core subjects taught. Core academic subjects are defined as reading or language arts, science, mathematics, English, foreign languages, economics, civics and government, geography, arts, and history. General education teachers of areas that are not considered core academic subjects, such as vocational education, are not required to be "highly qualified."

The adoption and cross-referencing of the statutory definition of "highly qualified" teachers within these two federal statutes sends a symbolic message that the federal government intends for NCLB and IDEA 2004 to work in tandem toward ensuring that all students receive an equal opportunity to obtain a high-quality education.

Special education teachers are considered "highly qualified" if the following conditions are met:

- Hold a bachelor's degree.
- Possess full state licensure as a special education teacher (teachers will not be deemed highly qualified if they have had state requirements waived on an emergency, provisional, or temporary basis).
- Pass a rigorous state special education licensure examination.

IDEA 2004 provides clarity regarding what type of special education instruction requires individuals to be "highly qualified." Special education teachers who provide direct instruction in core academic subjects in any educational setting are required to meet the "highly qualified" standards for each of the core academic subjects they teach. However, special education teachers who do not teach core academic subjects directly to students are not required to meet the "highly qualified" criteria for academic subjects. For example, special education teachers whose sole responsibility is to provide consultative services (e.g., adapting curricula, selecting appropriate accommodations) to a core content teacher who is "highly qualified" are not required to demonstrate subject matter competency in that area.

To further the goals of NCLB, IDEA 2004 provides alternative routes for veteran special education teachers to be considered "highly qualified" without having to return to school or obtain a degree in every subject area they teach. Under IDEA 2004, veteran teachers must meet the same qualifications as new elementary, middle, and secondary special education teachers in terms of education level (i.e., bachelor's degree). However, states are permitted to create HOUSSE standards (highly objective uniform state standards of evaluation) by which veteran special education teachers can demonstrate competency in the core academic subjects they teach. HOUSSE standards differ from those required of new special education teachers by allowing things such as experience, expertise, and various other evidenced-based practices to be evaluated by the state to determine a teacher's subject matter competency. States are provided with some flexibility regarding the specific evaluation criteria used during the HOUSSE evaluation process.

Recently, the U.S. Department of Education encouraged states to limit the use of HOUSSE procedures when possible, to avoid the practice of allowing teachers assigned to new subject areas to use nonrigorous HOUSSE procedures to quickly demonstrate subject matter competency. The HOUSSE standards are intended to provide states with flexibility in determining the subject matter competency of experienced special education teachers, not to provide an expedited path for teachers of new subject areas to meet NCLB's "highly qualified" standards.

The underlying principle of NCLB and IDEA 2004 is the notion that all students can excel academically if they receive high quality instruction, are held to high expectations, and have clearly defined standards. Despite the laudable goals of NCLB and IDEA 2004 in improving the quality of special education instruction, there is concern among stakeholders in education that the rigid academic subject matter competency requirements for special education teachers may adversely affect teacher recruitment and retention. There is also considerable debate among special education advocates that requiring students with disabilities to participate in a standards-based system may adversely affect the self-esteem of low-performing students and reduce their graduation rates.

As a result of these concerns, there have been increasing calls to reform or repeal NCLB. Congress has made several attempts to eliminate the requirement that schools make adequate yearly progress and instead demonstrate that all students are making continuous improvement and are on track to meet college and career readiness. All of these attempts to date have either been unsuccessful or remain in committee. Frustrated with the slow pace of reform, President Obama granted waivers in 2012 to 11 states that free them from compliance with key provisions of NCLB until 2014. In exchange for more flexibility, these states agreed, among other things, to adopt evaluation systems that support principal and teacher effectiveness, curricula that focus on college and career readiness standards, and accountability standards that differentiate between students based on their performance. A number of additional states are currently under consideration for such waivers.

The ultimate impact of the 2012 waivers and proposed amendments to NCLB remain unclear. Meeting the challenges of NCLB and IDEA will require a united front in which all stakeholders in education are committed to ensuring that these two laws make a substantive, as opposed to symbolic, impact on improving the quality of education for students with disabilities. To this end, all teachers play an integral role in helping to provide every child with the opportunity to reach the highest levels of academic achievement that are within her unique capabilities.

Family Educational Rights and Privacy Act (20 U.S.C. § 1232g)

The Family Educational Rights and Privacy Act, known as FERPA, is another federal statute that plays a significant role in the responsibilities of teachers and school administrators. FERPA gives important privacy rights to all students, including those with disabilities. The statute requires schools that receive funding from the U.S. Department of Education to maintain the confidentiality of student records and to provide access to such records upon request by parents or eligible students. An eligible student is one who is 18 years of age, at which time the rights bestowed by FERPA transfer from the parent to the student exclusively. Teachers need to take this responsibility of maintaining the confidentially of all students' information and records seriously. Schools that fail to comply with FERPA are at risk of losing federal funding.

In most cases FERPA prevents schools from releasing information from a student's records without the permission of the parent or eligible student. The statute does contain exceptions, however, and authorizes the release of records to the following individuals without permission:

- school officials with a legitimate interest;
- other schools to which a student is transferring;
- appropriate parties related to the student's application for or receipt of financial aid;
- specified officials for audit or evaluation purposes;
- certain organizations conducting evaluations or studies on behalf of the school;
- accrediting organizations;
- appropriate officials in health or safety emergencies; and
- state and local authorities in conjunction with a juvenile justice proceeding in accordance with state law.

Not surprisingly, the statute likewise permits release by education officials in response to a subpoena or judicial order.

FERPA also gives parents or eligible students the right to inspect and review students' educational records held by the school. Schools generally are not required to make copies of the record, and may charge a fee if one is requested. If the parent or eligible student believes the record contains an inaccuracy or is misleading, they may petition the school to correct the record. If the school refuses to do so, parents or eligible students are entitled to a formal hearing on the issue. If the school maintains its position following the hearing, the parent or eligible student may place in the record a statement of their views about the material that is in dispute.

Summary

This chapter outlined the legal foundation for special education. The relevant court cases and laws that have determined the rights and services available to individuals with disabilities were reviewed. The discussion of the Individuals with Disabilities Education Act (IDEA) and its requirements offers classroom teachers the basic information needed to understand their role in the provision of services to students with disabilities. The education of students with disabilities is a shared responsibility between general and special educators in partnership with parents. The more knowledgeable each participant in the process is, the more effective the delivery of services will be.

Classroom Application Activities

1. As a teacher or other school professional, if you had a question regarding the federal laws that mandate special education services (or your state's plan for implementation of those laws), what resources are available to you?

2. Why do you think *IDEA* mandated greater parent participation in eligibility and placement decisions for students with disabilities? What impact does this have on schools?

3. Contact your local school system and find out what information and materials are provided to parents of children with disabilities having to do with their legal rights in regard to their child's education.

4. What is transition? Why was it mandated by IDEA? Why do you think IDEA 2004 added a postsecondary plan requirement to the transition plan by age 16?

5. Walk around your college or university campus. How accessible is it for individuals with disabilities? List the modifications or adaptations that you see.

6. Prior to IDEA 97 students with disabilities often were excluded from state- and districtwide assessments. Why might schools want to exclude these students from assessments? Why should these students be included in the assessments?

7. What two court cases having to do with special education have made the most meaningful impact on the education of students with disabilities?

8. What meaningful changes should Congress make with regard to students with disabilities when it is time for the next reauthorization of NCLB?

9. How will the ADAAA of 2008 affect decisions on whether a student is eligible for a 504 Plan?

Internet Resources

ADA Amendments Act of 2008
http://www.access-board.gov/about/laws/ada-amendments.htm

Council for Exceptional Children
www.cec.sped.org

IDEA 2004
http://idea.ed.gov

No Child Left Behind
www.ed.gov/nclb/landing.jhtml?src=ln

U.S. Department of Education, Office for Civil Rights: Frequently Asked Questions About 504 and the Education of Children with Disabilities
http://www.access-board.gov/about/laws/ada-amendments.htm

Office of Special Education and Rehabilitative Services
www.ed.gov/about/offices/list/osers/osep/index.html

Parent Advocacy Coalition for Educational Rights
www.pacer.org

Section 504
www.hhs.gov/ocr/504.html

Special Education Law
www.wrightslaw.com

U.S. Department of Education
www.ed.gov

Case Law Resources

PARC v. Commonwealth of Pennsylvania
http://www.state.me.us/education/speced/cds/training/miscellaneous/partc.pdf

Mills v. D.C. Board of Education
http://outreach.umf.maine.edu/files/2009/10/millsvboardofed.pdf

Rowley v. Hendrick Hudson School District
http://www.wrightslaw.com/law/caselaw/ussupct.rowley.htm

Irving Independent School District v. Tatro
http://scholar.google.com/scholar_case?case=14870986137968601908&hl=en
&as_sdt=2&as_vis=1&oi=scholarr

Honig v. Doe
http://scholar.google.com/scholar_case?case=16042322352248963439&hl=en
&as_sdt=2&as_vis=1&oi=scholarr

Roncker v. Walter
http://scholar.google.com/scholar_case?case=12579313991222842393&q=roncker+v.+walter&hl=en
&as_sdt=2,11&as_vis=1

Timothy W. v. Rochester School District
http://law.justia.com/cases/federal/appellate-courts/F2/875/954/179023/

Oberti v. Board of Education of the Borough of Clementon School District
http://law.justia.com/cases/federal/appellate-courts/F2/995/1204/67463/

Sacramento City Unified School District v. Rachel H.
http://law.justia.com/cases/federal/appellate-courts/F3/14/1398/613232/

Agostini v. Felton
http://scholar.google.com/scholar_case?case=6468982625941805364&q=agostini+v.+felton&hl=en&as_sdt=2,11

Cedar Rapids Community School District v. Garret F.
http://scholar.google.com/scholar_case?case=13901710157337917845&q=cedar+rapids+community+school+district+v.+garrett+f&hl=en&as_sdt=2,11

Schaffer v. Weast Superintendent of Montgomery County Schools
http://scholar.google.com/scholar_case?case=17345534621187318493&q=shaffer+v.+weast&hl=en&as_sdt=2,11

Arlington Central School District Board of Education v. Murphy
http://scholar.google.com/scholar_case?case=3710960681408767889&q=arlington+central+v.+murphy&hl=en&as_sdt=2,11

References

Blackhurst, A.E., & Berdine, W.H. (1993). *An introduction to special education* (3rd ed.). New York: Harper Collins.

Colker, R. (2009). *The law of disability discrimination*. Los Angeles, CA: Mathew Bender & Company.

Haring, N.G., & McCormick, L. (Eds.). (1990). *Exceptional children and youth* (5th ed.). New York: Merrill/Macmillan.

Individuals with Disabilities Education Act Amendments of 2004, Public Law 108–446, 108th Congress.

U.S. Department of Education. (2007). *Part B, Individuals with Disabilities Education Act, Implementation of FAPE Requirements*. Washington, DC: Author.

Wood, J.W. (1984). *Adapting instruction for the mainstream: A sequential approach to teaching*. New York: Merrill/Macmillan.

CHAPTER THREE

The Response to Intervention, Referral, and Placement Process

Gwendolyn T. Benson and John O'Connor

CHAPTER OBJECTIVES

- to examine the Response to Intervention (RTI) process;

- to describe the activities that classroom teachers should implement as part of the RTI framework;

- to present activities that might be completed when students are struggling in school;

- to explain the process of determining if a student has a disability and the responsibilities of the classroom teacher during that process;

- to list and describe the elements of an Individualized Educational Program (IEP);

- to describe the function of other service plans for special education, such as Individual Transition Plans and Individualized Family Services Plans; and

- to specify the rights and roles of parents in the eligibility and staffing process.

KEY TERMS

Response to Intervention (RTI) • curriculum • universal screening • standard intervention protocols • Student Support Team (SST) • Individualized Educational Program (IEP) • ineligible • Individualized Transition Plan (ITP) • Individualized Family Service Plan (IFSP)

In Chapter 2 you read about the laws and regulations that are in place for providing special education services for students with disabilities. In this chapter, you will read about how some of the special education requirements operate in real life. Chapter 3 walks you through the activities that are completed when:

1. a student is having difficulty in school,
2. a student is referred for a special education evaluation,
3. a student is evaluated to determine if the student has a disability,
4. a determination is made whether the student does or does not qualify for special education services, and
5. an Individualized Educational Plan (IEP) is developed to meet the student's unique needs in school.

Much of the material in this chapter focuses on younger students because students typically are referred for assessment and determined eligible for special education services when they are in elementary school. Although the process is the same for students who are identified and placed in later grades, the procedures at grade levels beyond elementary grades focus primarily on IEP review and revision. Examples of students from elementary, middle, and secondary grades are provided throughout the chapter.

As a classroom teacher, you will have students who are having difficulty in class and will have to decide what to do next about meeting the needs of such students. In spite of differences in the ages and specific needs of each student, there are common steps to be followed. This chapter focuses on the role of the classroom teacher in the processes of assisting struggling students, referring a student for a special education evaluation, the determination of eligibility, development of the IEP, and placement.

The Role of the Classroom Teacher

For most students with mild disabilities the initial identification of that disability will be made after the student begins school. It is often the classroom teacher who first notices that the student might have a disability. When a student is struggling in your class or you suspect a disability, the first step is to begin the response to intervention process.

Response to Intervention

Response to Intervention (RTI) is the process to ensure that all students are receiving high quality instruction. Federal law requires that students receive research-based effective instruction tailored to their individual learning needs prior to being referred for special education evaluation. In addition to poor instruction, a student should not be identified as having a disability if the difficulties in school were the result of excessive school absences, or other factors external to the student. In the Individuals with Disabilities Education Act (IDEA, 2004), RTI was codified in federal legislation. IDEA stated:

> When determining whether a child has a specific learning disability . . . a local education agency shall not be required to take into consideration whether a child has a severe discrepancy between achievement and intellectual ability in oral expression, listening comprehension, written expression, basic reading skills, reading comprehension, mathematical calculation, or mathematical reasoning . . . In determining whether a child has a specific learning disability, a local education agency

may use a process that determines if the child responds to scientific, research-based intervention as part of the evaluation procedures.

RTI is a process that applies to all students in schools. It is a framework for addressing the learning needs of any child who is struggling in school and what school personnel can do to address students' learning differences. The RTI process assists educators in systematically analyzing which instructional strategies are effective for increasing student achievement. Often the RTI process is successful in meeting the student's instructional needs and a referral for special education evaluation is not required.

There are different RTI models throughout the country. In most states, the state department of education or similar body has adopted an RTI model or framework that guides the actions of school personnel as they address the various needs of students. All models provide a framework for providing steps or tiers of interventions when students are experiencing difficulty in school including academic and behavioral challenges.

Some frameworks contain three tiers, whereas others use a model with four tiers. Regardless of the number of tiers, most models are similar. Various interventions are provided through the tiers with each set of interventions becoming more intensive. Fewer students participate in each subsequent tier because many students will find success with a less intensive intervention. An example of a three-tiered approach is depicted in **Figure 3.1**.

Tier 1

In this model, all students participate in instructional activities that address the state curriculum or performance standards. State performance standards include descriptions of what students know and should be able to do in the various subject areas, grades, and courses throughout their school career. The performance standards describe what a fourth grade student, for example, will know and be able to do in mathematics, reading, etc. All students should participate in effective instruction that includes differentiation through small group instruction, multiple means of learning material, and demonstrating their learning. According to O'Connor (2009) all students should participate in GREAT instruction, which is:

* Guided by the performance standards
* Rigorous with research-based strategies
* Engaging and exciting
* Assessed continually to guide instruction
* Tailored through flexible group instruction

The entire focus, however, is not on academic success. In every class, schools should provide an environment where students learn and demonstrate appropriate behavior. Classrooms should include effective rituals and routines so that students know how the class operates. They should know the procedures that are used for turning in their homework, requesting a restroom break, answering a question in class, and transitioning to a new learning group. These rituals and routines, when taught and implemented consistently, will create one of the foundational components for positive student behavior. School personnel and teachers should clearly outline the behavioral expectations for students. Many people assume that behavioral expectations include a list of things that are forbidden such as "no sagging pants, talking disrespectfully, or getting out of your seat without permission." Expectations should ultimately include a description of what students should do. Expectations might include: Be Prepared. Be Respectful. Be Kind. Work Diligently. These overall expectations will then need to be clearly defined, demonstrated, and taught to students routinely so that

Figure 3.1   Response to Intervention: A Pyramid of Interventions Approach

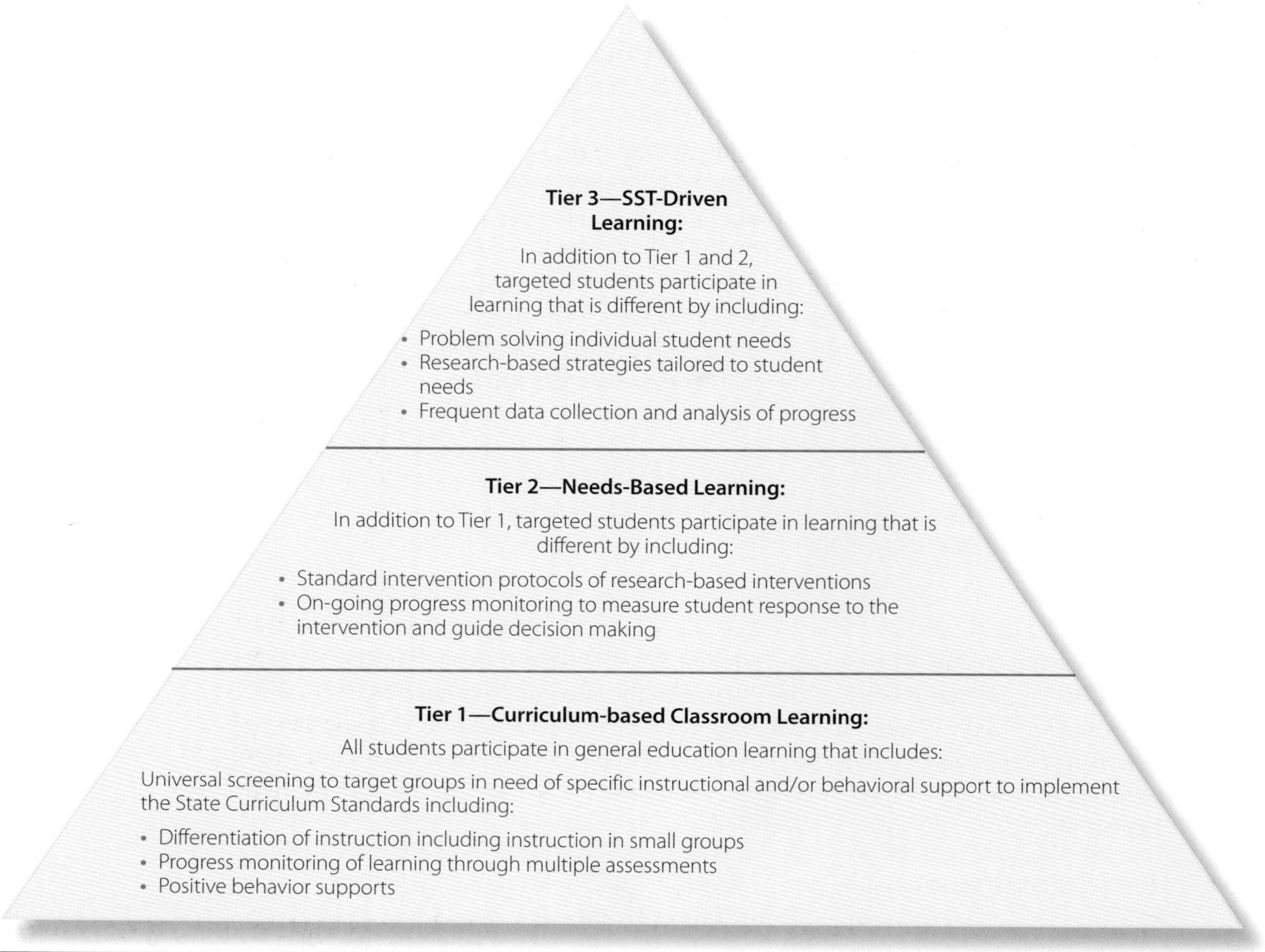

Tier 3—SST-Driven Learning:

In addition to Tier 1 and 2, targeted students participate in learning that is different by including:

- Problem solving individual student needs
- Research-based strategies tailored to student needs
- Frequent data collection and analysis of progress

Tier 2—Needs-Based Learning:

In addition to Tier 1, targeted students participate in learning that is different by including:

- Standard intervention protocols of research-based interventions
- On-going progress monitoring to measure student response to the intervention and guide decision making

Tier 1—Curriculum-based Classroom Learning:

All students participate in general education learning that includes:

Universal screening to target groups in need of specific instructional and/or behavioral support to implement the State Curriculum Standards including:

- Differentiation of instruction including instruction in small groups
- Progress monitoring of learning through multiple assessments
- Positive behavior supports

Adapted from: The Georgia Student Achievement Pyramid of Interventions—Dr. John D. Brage, State Superintendent, October 2011

all adults and students have a clear picture of what preparedness and respect, for example, actually look like in class and in school.

It is not enough to establish and continuously teach students about appropriate behavior, educators must also recognize when students meet those expectations. If a student offers an academic viewpoint that is different from the teacher but does so in a mature and respectful way, then the teacher should verbally recognize that student for being respectful. "Jordan, I am impressed by how you expressed a different opinion so respectfully. I really admire students when they show such respect." Recognizing students when they meet expectations will reinforce the desired behavior.

In addition to providing GREAT instruction and positive behavioral supports, schools should provide **universal screening**. According to the National Center on Response to Intervention (n.d.),

Screening is conducted to identify or predict students who may be at risk for poor learning outcomes. Universal screening tests are typically brief, conducted with all students at a grade level, and followed by additional testing or short-term progress monitoring to corroborate students' risk status.

Quick screenings are typically provided to large groups of students initially at the beginning of the school year (and at multiple times during the year) to determine which students have deficits in core academic areas such as oral reading fluency, reading comprehension, math calculation, and understanding math concepts. By conducting screenings, students can be identified at the beginning of the school year (and at multiple points during that year) so that interventions can be provided.

As a classroom teacher, what should I do to effectively implement Tier 1 interventions?

All classroom teachers should provide GREAT instruction for all students. Their instruction should be driven by the curriculum standards and include instructional activities that are both rigorous and research based. The daily activities should be motivating and engaging for all of the students. In addition, teachers should continually analyze ongoing student information to guide their instruction. Through that constant analysis of ongoing data, teachers should provide differentiated instruction in small groups to meet the needs of all students (O'Connor, 2009). In addition, teachers should ask school leaders what universal screenings will be used to determine if any students are starting the school year or course with deficits that will impact their ability to be successful in school. One of the most important classroom teacher responsibilities in Tier 1 is to effectively analyze and interpret all data gathered to determine which students will require Tier 2 interventions.

Tier 2

Tier 2 includes interventions that address the needs of students who continue to be at-risk following Tier 1 interventions. The universal screenings and other information indicate which students need additional interventions. Tier 2 provides the structure for those interventions. When a student is moved to Tier 2 in the RTI process, there are two general approaches to providing structured interventions: the problem solving approach and the standard intervention protocols approach. School systems across the country will use one or a combination of both approaches.

The Problem Solving Approach

Historically, when students were experiencing difficulty there were two options. First, each teacher individually developed instruction to try to meet the needs of the students in their class, the problem solving approach. This approach is extremely inefficient. Each teacher was working in isolation and not benefitting from the experiences and expertise of other teachers who were trying to solve the same instructional challenges. The second option was for teachers to pursue special education eligibility for the student so that the student could benefit from special education services. Neither of these two options is ideal. The first approach is extremely inefficient. Some of those teachers developed effective instructional approaches while some did not. Even those teachers who implemented effective interventions could have benefited from a school- or districtwide approach. The second approach of pursuing special education eligibility was often premature. Many teachers referred struggling students for special education evaluation because they just did not know how to meet the students' educational challenges.

Standard Intervention Protocols Approach

Standard intervention protocols meet the challenges described previously. Standard intervention protocols are predetermined, research-based interventions that schools make available to meet the specific needs of students as determined by universal screenings. An example of how a school could implement standard intervention protocols is provided in **Figure 3.2**.

Figure 3.2 Example of Implementation of a Standard Intervention Protocol for Reading Fluency

At Vista Lake Elementary School, several fifth grade students have trouble with fluency when reading text orally. Fluency describes a student's ability to read quickly and smoothly. Generally, when students have difficulty with oral reading fluency, there are also difficulties with reading comprehension. If students struggle through text and their oral reading sounds halted and labored then their cognitive energy is spent pulling the words off of the page rather than understanding the text. The students' efforts are on the mechanics of reading rather than developing an ongoing understanding of the material. An effective approach to improve fluency and thereby impact reading comprehension is the use of guided repeated oral reading.

One way to provide guided repeated oral reading is to offer students multiple opportunities to orally read the same text while they are being timed. At Vista Lake Elementary, the teachers in fifth grade provide timed, repeated oral reading practice to students who have trouble with reading fluency. They provide a copy of a text on each student's instructional level. Over the course of a few days, the students orally read and re-read the same text while they are being timed for 1 minute by the teacher. After the minute is complete, the teacher and student review words read correctly and incorrectly. This allows teachers to calculate correct words read per minute. The goal of this activity is to increase the number of words that are read correctly in a minute. The students might challenge themselves to read faster by re-reading the same text twice a day for 3 to 5 days and with more expression each time. Then, a new text is introduced. At the conclusion of each timed drill, the students document their progress by coloring in a bar graph with the correct words read per minute during each timed trial. **Figure 3.3** provides an example of a bar graph developed to record progress on oral reading fluency.

Figure 3.3 Bar Graph to Display Correct Words Read per Minute

Student: Janelle   Date: October 15–19

Selection: Lizards and Reptiles Found in the U.S.

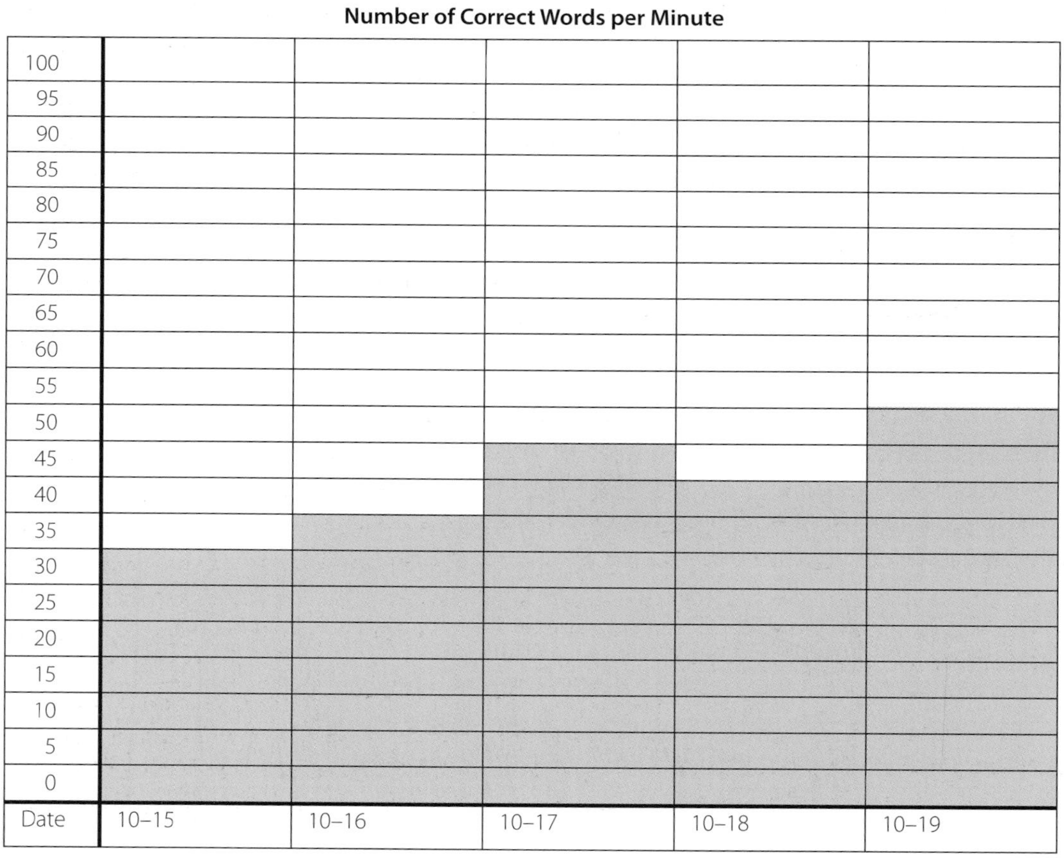

Number of Correct Words per Minute

| Date | 10–15 | 10–16 | 10–17 | 10–18 | 10–19 |

The teachers and administrators at Vista Lake chose this intervention as a standard intervention protocol for several reasons. Across the fifth grade, it was clear that many students were having difficulty with oral reading fluency and thereby having difficulty with reading comprehension. Guided repeated oral reading was also supported in the research as an effective approach to improve fluency with a secondary effect of improving reading comprehension (National Institute of Child Health and Human Development, 2000). Lastly, this intervention could be easily incorporated into the English/Language Arts instructional period by the fifth grade teachers.

The administrators at Vista Lake provided support for this standard intervention protocol by providing all of the materials that were needed for the teachers. They gathered the oral reading fluency passages from all of the grade levels in the school and placed them in one notebook. That way, if a teacher needed a third grade text it was readily available. The texts were specifically designed by the reading textbook company for this purpose so at the end of each line of text, the total number of words in the text was printed. Therefore, the teachers did not have to count the number of words, a task that would have been extremely laborious.

This is one example of a standard intervention protocol. It demonstrates how efficient and effective it can be when a group of educators pull together to develop a standard intervention rather than each teacher attempting to solve instructional challenges in isolation. This intervention also provided an easy way to chart the student's progress. Each teacher can easily review how students are progressing in oral reading fluency and determine if a student is or is not making satisfactory progress. If the student does not make adequate progress, then a different intervention can be implemented.

At the school level, teachers and school administrators meet regularly to review the data on students who are participating in a Tier 2 intervention. At those meetings, the fifth grade teachers report on the progress of their students in Tier 2 and determine the next steps. Some students will have made sufficient progress and may not need to continue participation in this intervention. Other students will be making progress, but they have not reached the desired levels for fifth grade students. They will continue participating in the intervention and the teacher will report their progress at the next school RTI meeting. Some students, unfortunately, will not be demonstrating significant progress. For those students other interventions may be attempted during Tier 2 or the students may be referred to the third tier of the RTI model.

The use of standard intervention protocols does not imply that individual student needs are not considered. Teachers could implement instructional strategies or interventions that are in addition to those provided in the standard protocol. Also, how often, or the duration of the intervention, might be adjusted depending on the needs of the student.

How Are Standard Intervention Protocols Implemented?

There are typically two locations for the implementation of standard intervention protocols: in the general education classroom and during a supplementary instructional time. The supplementary interventions might include after-school tutorial activities. Some schools may provide an extra period during the school day for a particular content area such as mathematics. Other supplementary standard intervention protocols might address social/emotional issues. For example, the school counselor might offer a group session to students who need to address anger management issues.

As a classroom teacher, what should I do to effectively implement Tier 2 interventions?

Classroom teachers are critically important for effective Tier 2 implementation. Tier 2 intervention is distinguished from Tier 1 by the implementation of standard intervention protocols and increased progress monitoring to measure student progress. One of the most important roles of the general education teacher in Tier 2 is data collection of student progress. Collecting data on student learning and behavior is required in addition to work samples or scores obtained on assignments and universal screenings. To meet the requirement of progress monitoring, teachers may need to collect frequency counts of correct and incorrect responses or behaviors exhibited. In Tier 1 it was expected that all students in the class would receive differentiated instruction in small groups and behavior support as needed. In Tier 2, in addition to small group instruction and behavioral supports, students will receive interventions that are tailored to their individual needs.

If supplemental interventions are being used, it will be important to be fully aware of what those interventions are and how they might integrate with the classroom instruction that you are providing. Supplemental interventions include those interventions that are in addition to students' typical class periods. Many schools provide additional support during the school day or tutoring before and after school for specific skills (reading or math) or content areas (chemistry or algebra). Even if you are not providing the supplemental instruction, it is beneficial to communicate with the teacher providing the additional instruction to share information that will support the student in the RTI process. Even with the use of Tier 1 and 2 interventions, some students will need to move to Tier 3 to achieve adequate academic or behavioral progress.

Tier 3

All the procedures from Tier 1 and 2 remain in place for the students that will move into Tier 3. During Tiers 1 and 2, classroom teachers were responsible for the implementation of interventions and were the primary decision makers regarding whether a student should continue in the RTI process. Once in Tier 3, students who continue to struggle with academic and behavioral challenges and their teachers will have a team to support them. Many states require each school to have a **Student Support Team (SST)** in place to provide the support needed for the student to be successful in general education classrooms. Some schools call this team the Prereferral to Special Education Evaluation Team or the RTI Team. By calling this group of professionals the prereferral team, it is implied that the student will in fact be referred for special education evaluation. The purpose of the team is to ensure that everything has been done to prevent the student from needing to be referred for special education evaluation.

The purpose of the SST is to involve a team of professionals in the RTI process to investigate if additional interventions, accommodations, or modifications could provide the support needed for the student to be successful in the general education classroom or if the student will need to have an educational evaluation to determine if the student has a disability. Members of the SST could be the student's teacher, parents or guardians, other teachers, support personnel, and school administrators. It is often helpful to have other teachers on the team who teach at the same grade level or in the same content area in which the student is currently placed (e.g., other third grade teachers or math teachers). In addition to teachers, other support personnel such as a school counselor, a speech-language pathologist, or a special education teacher might be included to provide specific help.

The SST has been found to have several advantages (Craig, Hull, Haggart, & Perez-Sellers, 2000; Strickland & Turnbull, 1990; Stump, 2002).

- Systematic SST intervention tends to reduce the number of inappropriate referrals to special education.
- Teams can reduce the overrepresentation of minority groups in special education.
- These teams gather information that can be used to evaluate a student for possible special education services.

- Teams can provide immediate intervention without waiting for eligibility to be established.

- Teams can promote the inclusion of culturally relevant curricular content.

- The approach takes advantage of the expertise of those teachers who have been working most closely with a student.

- Student support teams can help to refine vague or subjective referrals.

- Teams can promote cooperation between the general and special educator.

- Teams help to promote acceptance and support within the general education program for students with disabilities.

Tier 3 provides an opportunity for a group of adults, and the parent of the student, to brainstorm about the student to determine more closely the needs of the student and why that student may not be responding as desired to the instruction and interventions provided. The adults can analyze the student at a deeper level and determine what interventions are needed.

At times, the team might determine that the student would benefit from continuing the interventions that were provided during Tier 2. The data might suggest that progress has been made, but the rate of progress would increase to an acceptable level by providing the interventions for longer periods and/or for more days during the week. In other scenarios, the team of professionals might determine that the student would benefit from different interventions. See **Figure 3.4** for a description of a student who has been referred to the SST.

As a classroom teacher, what should I do to effectively implement Tier 3 interventions?

Classroom teachers are critically important for effective Tier 3 implementation. Students should be referred for Tier 3 when it is evident that the student needs more intensive interventions than have been provided in the first two tiers. When referring a student to Tier 3, the classroom teacher must have a clear profile of the student including the instruction and interventions that have been provided and how the student responded to those interventions. It is not sufficient to state that the student "is not passing his classes," or "is having trouble in reading." The classroom teacher must provide specific and ongoing information regarding the student's performance.

The information provided must include multiple data points for review by the SST. In our example of reading fluency, the teacher could provide the bar graphs that recorded the student's progress on oral reading fluency. For our second example regarding Trey, the teacher could provide data on Trey's disciplinary referrals and daily data on his behavior. This data does not have to be complex. The teacher could use a self-created rating scale to reflect Trey's behavior in class. The teacher should have clearly defined the specific areas, in observable and quantifiable terms, that are causing the student difficulty. Then, the teacher includes data on the student that shows his progress as a result of the implementation of the interventions. Depicting data in a graph is extremely helpful for the SST.

In addition to providing information to the SST, you will be a fully engaged member of the team. The information you provide will help the team analyze the student and determine appropriate interventions. Your expertise is critical. Many students will be successful with the interventions provided in Tier 3. Other students require a referral for special education evaluation.

If students continue to struggle and do not meet the expectations for success after Tier 1, 2, and 3 interventions, then the SST will request that the student be referred for special education evaluation to determine if the student meets the eligibility requirements of the disability category. In most states, the state department of education has determined the

| Figure 3.4 | Case Study of a Student in the RTI Process |

Trey is a ninth grader who has been recommended for Tier 3 interventions and referred to the student support team (SST). He consistently demonstrates inappropriate behavior such as talking back and becoming argumentative with his teachers. He often makes inappropriate comments in class which generally causes laughter from his peers and frustration for his teacher, Mr. Rhodes.

As part of Tier 1, the school implemented a strong schoolwide discipline plan. All teachers have a list of expectations for student behavior. Those expectations are taught and discussed routinely and students are recognized for meeting those expectations. In addition, strong rituals and routines are implemented so that students have a predictable environment. Even with this type of positive, proactive approach to discipline, Trey's behavior was still inappropriate. He was making learning difficult in the class and was referred to the office for disciplinary reasons nine times during the first 2 months of the school year. His teachers and administrators determined that Trey needed to participate in a supplemental Tier 2 intervention.

During Tier 2, after review of his disciplinary record, it was determined that Trey should participate in a Lunch and Learn group provided by the school counselor, Ms. Harrington. This group met once a week during their lunch period for open discussion. Ms. Harrington facilitated the group discussion with the hopes of helping students grow in social/emotional areas that would help them become more successful in and outside of school. Students discussed various interactions they had during the week and discussed the strength and weakness of those interactions. They brainstormed and practiced a wide variety of social interaction skills.

Even with the implementation of a strong Tier 1 approach to positive discipline and participation in the Tier 2 Lunch and Learn group, Trey's behavior was still consistently inappropriate. He had made some slight improvement but it was decided that Trey should be referred for Tier 3 support and to the SST to determine what other interventions could be implemented. Ms. Harrington, Mr. Rhodes, the Assistant Principal, and Trey's parents participated in numerous SST meetings over several months. During those meetings, they reviewed extensive information about Trey, determined specific interventions, and then analyzed the impact of those interventions. Trey also participated in some of the meetings.

Mr. and Mrs. Silvers, Trey's parents, shared that Trey did not have a pattern of behavioral problems in middle school. On occasion, he would talk too much in class, but he was generally thought to be a respectful young man. The records from his middle school years confirmed this perception. This information was particularly interesting to the SST. Trey's behavior had changed drastically in the last few months once he transitioned to high school. Mr. and Mrs. Silvers questioned their decision to move to the new school district due to Trey's behavioral difficulty in his new school. The SST also tackled some tough questions. None of the SST members had any indication that Trey was using drugs or that he had become involved in any gang activity. In fact, Mr. and Mrs. Silvers stated that he had a very active social life and lots of friends in middle school, but that didn't seem to be the case in his new school. Trey's behavioral and academic records were also reviewed. Trey had always been a better than average student. Most of his report cards indicated a grade of B for most classes with the occasional A. It was rare that he received less than a grade of B. This pattern was evident throughout middle school and during his ninth grade year. In fact, the teachers in his classes stated that he seemed to perform academically well.

Ms. Harrington shared information about Trey's participation in the Lunch and Learn group. She shared that his behavior seemed to be better than it was during academic classes, but that he would sometimes make inappropriate comments to get a reaction from his peers. Ms. Harrington mentioned that Trey did not seem to connect with the other students and did not have strong friendships with the other students. All of the teachers mentioned the same thing regarding Trey's participation in their classes. He didn't seem to have any close friends in his classes. In fact, one of the teachers mentioned that she saw Trey eating alone in the cafeteria the other day. They theorized that the reason he was misbehaving was that Trey was attempting to gain attention and friendships from his peers. In his new school, he has not been successful finding a group of friends. Therefore, as he made the transition to a high school, a school where many of the other students knew each other, he was having difficulty establishing friendships. His need to develop friendships in his new school was quite healthy. Unfortunately, the methods Trey was using for meeting that need were inappropriate.

The SST devised a plan that would enable Trey to develop friendships and a positive peer group in his school. By doing this, his need to become argumentative and make continual inappropriate comments in class would diminish. The SST decided to:

- **Connect Trey with a group of upper class students who were known for being positive leaders in the school.** Ms. Harrington knew these students well and could rely on them to surround Trey with positive friendships. They also regularly attended school sports events as a group. Ms. Harrington would encourage the students to invite Trey to the upcoming football games and sit with them.

- **Encourage Trey to become involved in specific extracurricular activities.** There were a variety of clubs whose meetings were getting started. Mr. and Mrs. Silvers mentioned that Trey enjoyed drawing Japanese Manga cartoons. In the art club, there were a few students who developed online Manga stories. Mr. and Ms. Silvers agreed that this would be great for Trey and they committed to providing his transportation for the art club meetings and activities.

- **Develop a behavioral contract with Trey.** Ms. Harrington would facilitate this effort with all of Trey's teachers. Each teacher would rate Trey's behavior at the conclusion of his daily class on a 1 to 4 rubric. A score of 1 would indicate that Trey was extremely unsuccessful behaviorally in class that day. He was argumentative and verbally inappropriate. A 4 indicated that Trey spoke respectfully and appropriately during the entire class period with ratings of 2 and 3 along the continuum between both extremes. Every morning, Trey would meet briefly with Ms. Harrington for encouragement and to review the behavioral rubrics from the previous day. Ms. Harrington would be in regular contact with Mr. and Mrs. Silvers.

- **Meet monthly in order to discuss Trey's progress.**

The SST approach was successful for Trey and it was decided that he did not need to move to special education evaluation.

---

criteria for eligibility in each of the disability categories. The purpose of the special education evaluation is to review existing information and gather additional information in order to determine if the student meets the eligibility criteria. The purpose of the special education evaluation is to determine if the student has a disability that is impeding his ability to make educational progress.

Students Referred for Special Education Evaluation

After completing the RTI process for Tiers 1, 2, and 3, the SST determines that the student should have a referral for a special education evaluation. What happens next?

The determination of whether a student is eligible for special education is based on the fact that the student has been appropriately evaluated and meets the requirements for one of the federally defined categories of disability (i.e., autism, deaf-blind, serious emotional disturbance, hearing impairment, specific learning disabilities, intellectual disability, multiple disabilities, orthopedic impairments, other health impairments, speech or language impairment, traumatic brain injury, or visual impairment). The impairment must have had

Most students who are eligible for special education services are identified within the first 5 years of school.

a negative impact on the student's educational performance, and special educational services are needed due to the impairment.

A student's eligibility for placement and service in a particular special education program is dictated first by the federal laws, especially the Individuals with Disabilities Education Improvement Act of 2004 (IDEA), which were described in Chapter 2, then by the operational guidelines established by each state's department of education, and finally by the procedural provisions adopted by the individual school system. Eligibility for special education services is established by an evaluation team of school professionals who, through formal and informal assessment procedures, decide whether a student meets the established eligibility criteria. From a teacher's viewpoint, the eligibility for special education services is based on three factors:

1. The student's problem is *significant* enough to require special instruction not available in the general education class.
2. The student's problem is *persistent* to the extent that it interferes with school success from year to year.
3. The student's problem is *inherent to (i.e., based in) the student* rather than just the result of a temporary difficulty, such as a home problem or conflict with a teacher.

Most students who are eligible for special education services are identified within the first 5 years of school. Students whose need for special education services are based on a physical or medical problem frequently are identified before coming to school. This would include students with visual impairment, hearing impairment, orthopedic impairment, or those exhibiting more severe forms of intellectual disability. In general, the more severe a student's disability, the younger the student will be when identified as eligible for special education services. Parents and physicians identify many physical and developmental disabilities and provide the initial referral for special services. Students with more mild or subtle disabilities (e.g., learning disabilities, mild intellectual disability, and even many sensory disabilities) typically are first noticed by an observant elementary-level teacher. Occasionally a student with a disability may not be identified until later if the disability is mild or is the result of some sudden problem, for example, the result of an injury which impacts learning abilities (e.g., a traumatic head injury) that occurred in later school years.

To have a complete understanding of the referral for evaluation, determining eligibility, developing an IEP, and making a placement decision, let's follow one student through the process.

Ms. Winters first noticed that Miguel, age 9, seemed to be in a world of his own. It was clear from his lack of response when she asked him to read that he would require additional support. He also made no attempt to solve the two-digit addition and subtraction problems that she assigned to her lowest math group, and he sat looking out of the window when other students were doing independent seatwork. Ms. Winters began the RTI process immediately. After many months and the completion of Tiers 1, 2, and 3, the SST decided Miguel should be referred for a special education evaluation to determine if he had a disability that was interfering with his ability to make educational progress.

Referral for Special Education Services

The multidisciplinary team, sometimes called the special services team, has the responsibility for determining whether a student referred for possible special education placement actually meets the eligibility requirements for special education as defined by federal and state regulations. They are the ones who collect and analyze the information about a student's referral for possible special education services. The team must include a school psychologist, a special educator, and a representative from general education. The provisions of IDEA specify the rights of students and parents that must be protected during the referral and evaluation process. These rights were presented in Chapter 2.

As noted earlier, most of the students who are placed in special education programs are identified in elementary school. The probability that a student will be referred and receive service in learning disabilities, for example, is primarily due to the likelihood of the general educator making a referral (Colarusso, Keel, & Dangel, 2001). The decision of whether a student needs special education services must include information from a representative of general education, hopefully the classroom teacher, as well as from those specialists trained to evaluate and service students with special needs, that is school psychologists and special education teachers. The general educator is a key member of the team because of the important perspective this professional brings to the decision-making process.

Other professionals involved with the team will depend on the special services needs of the student. Some teams are large, whereas others have only three or four members. Let's discuss the people who may be involved in teams for a student with special needs.

1. **General Education Teacher.** The general education teacher is a valuable member of the team for the student with disabilities who will spend any portion of the day in a general education classroom. The teacher has knowledge of general education curriculum and can share input on programming issues.

2. **Special Education Teacher.** The special education teacher plays a critical role in monitoring and providing services for the student with disabilities. The special educator is mandated by law under Part B of IDEA to be part of the team process to assess and design programs best suited for the student with a disability. Special educators are trained in special education and should be knowledgeable in the areas of assessment, teaching methods, curriculum, and behavior management for students with special needs.

3. **Principal.** The school principal is a valuable ally and important team member. This individual controls the scheduling of classes and rooms and plays a leading role in fostering the climate of the school. The principal can set the stage for collaborative team interactions by allowing time for teams to meet and encouraging team input and group decision making.

4. **Paraprofessional or Aide (Paraeducator).** The paraprofessional or aide may work in the general education classroom or in the special education classroom. This individual can be a critical player in the school life of students with disabilities for it is often the aide who accompanies students to classes and activities in the general education environment. Although aides often are not thought of as formal members of a team, they can be valuable players in ensuring consistency across programming efforts for the student with special needs.

5. **Psychologist.** A psychologist performs a major part of the assessment of a student's cognitive (IQ testing) and behavioral abilities (attentional or adaptive skills). Various procedures such as interviews, standardized IQ and achievement tests, and/or behavioral assessments are used to determine the student's level of functioning and potential.

6. **Audiologist.** An audiologist focuses on a student's hearing. This individual assesses hearing, fits and monitors hearing aids, and provides therapy services related to a diagnosed hearing loss. Audiologists assist the team in making decisions about assistive listening devices and classroom modifications.

7. **Occupational Therapist (OT).** OTs are involved in helping to teach activities of daily living, especially those skills requiring fine motor movements of the arms, fingers, and trunk. An OT's evaluation involves assessing the muscles for strength and tone, as well as monitoring reflexes, posture, and joint motion of the upper extremities and trunk. The OT also assesses self-help skills such as feeding and dressing, and perceptual motor skills, such as drawing, and prevocational skills for the older student. The OT provides therapeutic services to students with fine motor deficits and assists teachers in modifying classroom activities to facilitate fine motor development.

8. **Physical Therapist (PT).** The physical therapist evaluates and provides treatment for the student's motor skills, particularly gross motor skills. The PT is involved in evaluating the student's overall motor function through observing the student's muscle strength and endurance, muscle tone, and posture. The PT is involved with other team members in designing and implementing programs to improve motor skills. They may work with medical personnel to recommend assistive devices such as braces, wheelchairs, or other seating devices.

9. **Speech-Language Pathologist (SLP).** The SLP is concerned with the critical area of communication. A speech-language pathologist evaluates communication by taking a history of communication milestones, assessing language, articulation, voice, and fluency skills, and conducting an examination of the speech mechanism. SLPs provide therapy services if a speech or language problem is diagnosed. SLPs use a variety of techniques in therapy and may assist students in the use of alternative forms of communication such as sign language, communication boards, or computer-assisted devices. They also may be involved in evaluating and treating feeding and swallowing problems. SLPs can be important team members in helping to create classroom environments that foster speech and language development.

10. **Social Worker.** The social worker helps determine family strengths and resources and the family's need for support services to be able to help their child learn and develop. In early intervention programs, a social worker often serves as a service coordinator offering information to parents regarding community resources, coordinating evaluations, and facilitating the development and implementation of the service plan.

11. **Vocational Rehabilitation Counselor.** Vocational rehabilitation counselors are responsible for working with eligible students with disabilities on job training opportunities. Vocational counselors consult with school officials to make and evaluate training arrangements so that persons with disabilities learn effective job skills. They also can facilitate arrangements with other rehabilitation services to obtain job-related equipment such as prosthetic devices.

12. **School Counselor.** The school counselor assists students with personal and/or behavior problems. In high school, the school counselor also advises students in relation to college, career, and job finding skills. School counselors may provide individual or group counseling and consult with parents, teachers, and others regarding student adjustment issues.

13. **Medical Personnel.** Medical personnel, such as the school nurse, a developmental pediatrician, a neurologist, or a psychiatrist, also have important roles on the team for the student with disabilities. The medical community often has been involved with the student and family long before the school. They will be involved in diagnosis, treatment from a medical perspective (medications), and monitoring of ongoing health concerns.

14. **Family Members.** It is important to emphasize a true partnership between all participants, including the child's family members. Family members are a critical part of the team for a student with special needs. Family members know the child in important ways outside of the classroom. Family members who might have input in team decisions include the parents, brothers and sisters, grandparents, cousins, and aunts and uncles, as well as other significant persons who may not be blood relatives but are considered family.

Activities of the Multidisciplinary Team

The multidisciplinary team will conduct several activities in order to determine if the student is eligible for special education services.

Reviewing the Past

Reviewing the student's background documents the extent to which a student's problem has been a persistent problem, offers insight as to the severity of the problem, and provides information as to whether the problem is inherent to the student. Although a student's background and past performance are, at best, imperfect indicators of current and future instructional needs, they should not be overlooked. Potentially valuable information may be available from parents or in a permanent folder (see **Figure 3.5**). By examining a student's past performance the team can answer questions about:

Contact with parents and the information they can provide regarding medical problems, educational history, and the student's perception of school are very important.

© 2013 Lisa S. Under license from Shutterstock, Inc.

- What previous opportunities to learn have been provided?

- What is the pattern of success to previous instruction?

Figure 3.5   Defining Classroom Variables

Reviewing the Past

Opportunities to Learn	Parent information
	Good school attendance
	Attended preschool
Instruction	Previous grades
	Standardized tests
Curriculum	Previous instructional programs
Delivery of Service	Retention
	Previous special programs

- What was the curriculum that was taught previously?
- What types of special provisions have been used to deliver the instructional program?

Conversing with a parent, whether in a formal meeting or in a telephone call, offers an opportunity to assess a student's or even a family's history of access to learning materials and school success. In the case of a young student, a parent's report gives an invaluable picture about developmental milestones and preschool opportunities. A parent can provide information on medical problems that might impact school success. A parent's response to questions about a student's perception of school—such as favorite class activities—can give a different and sometimes important view of a student in school.

Ms. Winters, a member of the team, considers the following questions before meeting with Miguel's parents:

1. What does M. tell you that he likes most (or least) about school this year?

   What do M.'s parents report about the classroom that he likes? Anything? Does it match with what you have observed? How might you use this information to work with M.?

2. What did M. say about school last year? What did he like?

   How does the report of previous years in school match with this year's? Does the report seem accurate? Are there areas of interest that could be included in programming for M.?

3. What does M. enjoy doing in his free time? Does he ever look at magazines or books?

   How does M. spend his time? Is there evidence of M. reading outside of school? Do there appear to be opportunities to interact with reading material?

4. Who are M.'s playmates? What do they do together?

   Does M. interact with any other students from the class outside of school? Does he choose students of the same age or children who are younger? Does he appear to be involved in any organized activities? Does he play games in which he must follow rules and structure?

5. Are there any medical or physical problems of which I should be aware when working with M.?

Is there any information related to M.'s health that might help explain the lack of class involvement? Are there other professionals who have worked with M. who might be helpful?

The team can judge the extent to which he has had access to opportunities to learn by reviewing this information. They note his preschool experiences (he attended both a preschool and kindergarten program), his age (he entered first grade at age 6 years-6 months—at about the same age as other students), his attendance (he has not missed more than 4 days of school in any year), and the extent to which he perhaps has been moved from school to school and, as a result, had his education disrupted (he has been enrolled in the same school system for all of his school experiences).

This information is important because it confirms for the team that Miguel has had appropriate opportunities to learn. Had he not had preschool experiences or been unusually young compared to other students, or been absent from school for extended periods, or moved frequently from one school to another (especially during the school year), some of his academic problems might be attributed to a lack of opportunity or disrupted opportunity to learn rather than to a challenge to learn.

Another source of information about a student's past school performance is the permanent record file. The permanent record is the accumulated information about a student's school performance. It can be used to help evaluate a student's previous access to learning materials and the pattern of previous school progress. The permanent record also can be used to corroborate information received from parents. **Figure 3.6** is a page from Miguel's permanent record file.

In general, the longer a student is enrolled in school, the more potentially valuable information will be accumulated from attendance patterns, grades, standardized achievement measures, and teachers' observations.

Figure 3.6   Permanent Record File—Miguel, page 1

Name   Jones, Miguel R.   *Parents/Guardian*   William and Martha Jones

Address   2342 Newton Street, Summerville, USA

Phone   (770) 555-4321   *Date of Birth*   three-five-nine years ago

Date	School	Placement	Days Present	Days Absent
• 5 years ago	Private preschool	Preschool	na	na
• 4 years ago	Washington Elementary	Kindergarten	178	2
• 3 years age	Washington Elementary	1st grade	176	4
• 2 years ago	Washington Elementary	2nd grade	178	2
• last year	Washington Elementary	2nd grade	179	1
• this year	Washington Elementary	3rd grade		

Placement	Reading Grd./Lev.	Arith. Grd./Lev.	Writing Grd./Lev.	Social Studies	Science Grd.	Conduct	Standard Text Results
• First Grade	C 1.0	C 1.5	C 1.5	B	na	B	Total 1.2
• Second Grade	F 1.2	F 1.5	D 1.2	F	D	D	Not given
• Second Grade	C 1.5	D 2.0	C 1.8	B	C	B	Not given
• Third Grade	D 2.0	F 2.3	F 1.8	C	F	D	Total 1.8

The permanent record also allows the team to review the extent of Miguel's academic progress. They examine the pattern of grades (he did relatively well in first grade but started to earn failing grades in second grade), the pattern of performance on standardized tests (Miguel has been consistently well below average), and any indication of being retained in a grade (Miguel repeated second grade).

The pattern of academic progress in Miguel's permanent record is one of continuing difficulty. The near average grade performance in first grade is the only suggestion of possible average progress. Was this because that teacher saw some achievement progress that has since been lost, or was it because the teacher avoided giving a low grade and was waiting for him to "grow out of it"? The team will need to interpret the achievement information based on what they know about the school's achievement pattern and the program in which Miguel is enrolled. If, for example, his below average academic performance on standardized achievement tests is within the range of what other students in his class have scored, Miguel would not be seen as "at-risk." If, however, other students who experienced the same instruction scored above average on standardized measures, Miguel would be considered "at-risk" and be more likely to need special education services.

Finally, the team will review whether the curriculum or the delivery of services ever have been changed for Miguel. Sometimes a student, such as Miguel, who has been experiencing difficulty in school will have been given some special instruction in addition to the intervention discussed in Tiers 1, 2, and 3. This may be done through a special general education program, such as Title 1 (a federally funded compensatory program for at-risk students), Reading Recovery (an intensive individualized reading program in general education), or special support from a trained paraprofessional. If Miguel has received any of these special services previously and is still having significant problems, we would consider him to be more at-risk for subsequent school failure.

Determining Eligibility

After all evaluations were complete, Ms. Winters and the multidisciplinary team meet to determine if Miguel is eligible for special education services. **Figure 3.7** shows the type of information typically provided by each team member. **Figure 3.8** shows some commonly used assessment instruments for evaluation.

Ms. Faber, the school psychologist, indicated that Miguel had scored slightly above average on the WISC-III (*Wechsler Intelligence Scale for Children—Third Edition*), and he had relatively more difficulty with those subtests that were timed and required a degree of persistence. When Ms. Faber asked if the team members had any comments, Ms. Winters was able to add that she had noticed that Miguel had trouble staying on task and seemed to give up easily once he was frustrated. Ms. Winters went on to briefly summarize Miguel's performance during the RTI process. Ms. Parks, the special education teacher, then described Miguel's low test scores in Word Recognition and Reading Comprehension and his poor performance on Arithmetic Computation. Ms. Winters added that this was consistent with Miguel's performance throughout the RTI process. She went on to note that even though he had trouble with the comprehension questions, he was interested in the story she had been reading to the class each day after lunch and he demonstrated exceptional insight about the feelings of one of the characters. Miguel's parents stated that he liked school and wanted to do well. They had noticed that he had begun to have some behavior issues as his academic performance declined.

After each team member shared all their relevant information, Ms. Faber facilitated a decision about the possibility that Miguel might possibility be eligible for services in learning disabilities. The team decided Miguel met the criteria for learning disabilities for the following reasons:

1. Although his performance on the intelligence test indicated that he should be able to learn the skills and information in third grade, his academic achievement in basic reading skills, reading comprehension, and mathematical calculations showed a severe discrepancy between his achievement and his performance.

2. Data from Tiers 1, 2, and 3 indicated that Miguel has made slight progress but he is still not performing at the accepted level of his same age peers.

3. The achievement problem Miguel displays has been a *persistent* problem for him since first grade.

4. The team concluded that Miguel's learning issues were not based on external factors but rather they were *inherent*. His inability to attend and organize his work task is contributing to his frustration with academic work.

The multidisciplinary team found Miguel eligible for special education services in the area of Specific Learning Disabilities. Ms. Winters played a vital role in the evaluation and eligibility process. It was her systematic and accurate instruction and data collection during RTI that supported the findings of the psychological testing.

Figure 3.7 Sources of Eligibility Information

Source	Information Provided
General Education Teacher	• progress records • intervention results • work samples
Special Educator	• achievement testing • observations • checklists
Psychologist	• intelligence testing • personality testing • adaptive behavior assessment
Other Specialists —Speech-Language Pathologist —Audiologist —Physician —Social Worker	• speech and language assessment • hearing assessment • medical information • information on home environment
Parents	• background information • information on development • interests and activities

Figure 3.8 Assessment Instruments Used for Eligibility Decisions

Intelligence Tests
- Stanford-Binet Intelligence Scale—Revised
- Wechsler Intelligence Scale for Children III
- Wechsler Adult Intelligence Scale—Revised
- Wechsler Preschool and Primary Scale of Intelligence
- Kaufman Assessment Battery for Children

Individual Achievement Tests
- Kaufman Test of Educational Achievement
- Peabody Individual Achievement Test—Revised
- Wide Range Achievement Test—Revised
- Woodcock-Johnson Psychoeducational Battery
- Wechsler Individual Achievement Test

Group Achievement Tests
- California Achievement Tests
- Iowa Tests of Basic Skills
- Metropolitan Achievement Tests
- Stanford Achievement Tests

Ineligibility

If the committee decides that the student does not require special education services or programs, it must provide information indicating why the student is ineligible. If the student is of school age, the committee will also send information to the principal of the child's school. The principal will be able to work with professionals in the school or with the child's current teacher, the reading teacher, the guidance counselor, or another specialist to help the student, and may make a referral under Section 504 of the Rehabilitation Act of 1973 (a federal civil rights law) to another multidisciplinary team within the school. Parents will receive a written notice that explains the committee's decision and the information on which that decision was based. If parents disagree with the decision of the committee, they may request mediation and/or an impartial hearing to resolve the disagreement. (Source: http://www.vesid.nysed.gov/specialed/publications/policy/parentguide#Elig.)

Developing Individualized Educational Programs

Once it has been determined that a student is eligible for special education services, an instructional plan is developed that is appropriate for the eligible student and specifies those persons, both general and special educators, who are responsible for providing each part of it. The Individualized Educational Program (usually referred to as the IEP) is required by law (IDEA) to ensure that the special education services provided to a student are planned and implemented in the prescribed manner. You may want to refer back to Chapter 2 which outlines the specific legal requirements that must be followed when providing special education services to a student. IDEA 2004 includes the following changes related to the IEP:

1. Revises language, regarding members of the IEP Team to include, *not less than one* regular education teacher and *not less than one* special education teacher.
2. Identifies when the IEP Team meeting attendance is not necessary.
3. Authorizes excusals from IEP meetings.
4. Adds new provisions for making changes to the IEP, such as an agreement between the parent and the local educational agency not to convene an IEP meeting for the purposes of making changes, and instead developing a written document to amend or modify the student's current IEP.
5. Encourages consolidations of IEP meetings.
6. Authorizes alternative means of meeting participation, for example, video conferences and conference calls.

Who Plans the IEP?

The process of developing a student's special education program sometimes is referred to as staffing and must include the student's parents or guardian, representation from general education, as well as appropriate special educators. The special educators would have expertise in those areas in which special services are anticipated to be needed. For example, for a third grade student eligible for services in learning disabilities because of a disability in reading, the third grade teacher who referred the student, the teacher of students with learning disabilities, and the parent(s) or guardian would be the minimum group required to develop and approve the IEP. It is conceivable that a school also might want to include a general education administrator (e.g., the principal or assistant principal), school support personnel (e.g., counselor, reading specialist, or social worker), and other special education specialists (e.g., a speech-language pathologist) as team members.

An IEP includes the involvement of parents and students, together with regular and special education personnel, in making decisions that support each student's educational success.

In the case of an older student with multiple disabilities, including orthopedic impairments, the meeting might include most of the individuals listed above plus the student, physical or occupational therapist, a vocational education specialist, and a specialist on transitional services. IDEA emphasizes the importance of including the parent and, when appropriate, the student.

What Does the IEP Include?

IEP requirements emphasize the importance of three core concepts:

- The involvement and progress of each student with a disability in the general curriculum, including addressing the unique needs that arise out of the student's assessment;
- The involvement of parents and students, together with regular and special education personnel, in making individual decisions to support each student's educational success; and
- The preparation of students with disabilities for employment and other post-school activities.

Plan for Developing an IEP

The IEP should evolve naturally from the information and documentation gathered by the multidisciplinary eligibility teams in specifying the elements of the IEP. Ideally, the IEP committee works logically from describing the student's current levels of performance in the context of the classroom (or present instructional setting) to what needs to be provided in an appropriate educational program. Specifically, the IEP committee:

- describes the student's *academic achievement and functional performance*,
- determines the *annual goals* that are appropriate, and helps the student to be involved in and progress in the general education curriculum,
- develops *benchmarks*, aligned to alternate assessments and alternate achievement standards, when appropriate,
- describes the *special education services needed* and who is responsible for providing them, especially as related to helping the student with the general education curriculum,

- describes the extent to which the student will *participate in schoolwide assessment programs,* including appropriate accommodations,
- determines whether the student will take an alternate assessment on a particular state- or districtwide assessment of student achievement and, if so, includes a statement of why the student cannot participate in the regular assessment and why the alternate assessment is appropriate,
- specifies how *progress on the IEP is measured and communicated to parents or guardians,*
- indicates the *extent of time to be spent in general and special education settings,* and explains reasons for any nonparticipation in general education settings,
- describes the *projected dates for initiating services and dates to review annual progress,* and
- addresses requirements for students with disabilities transferring school districts within a state and between states.

Figure 3.9 relates the IEP components to the concerns of the committee.

What Are the Current Levels of Performance?

The current level of performance should include information about the following general areas, as appropriate for a particular student: academic performance relative to the school's curriculum, classroom working behaviors relative to the school's expectations, personal and social behaviors relative to expectations, and a description of particular disabilities that would impact with school performance.

The statement of current level of educational performance would include a brief description of the student's strengths and weaknesses in the school curriculum. For example, "Reads fourth grade material with 75% accuracy in word recognition."

The description of present levels of performance should be tied to the eligibility decision and help to put the eligibility into a school-based context. For example, a team writing a statement of current level of performance for a student eligible for services due to an emotional/behavior disorder would describe the impact of the emotional/behavior disorder on meeting the expectations of the school ("doesn't comply with teacher's directions to begin seatwork" or "has not established friendships with other classmates"). Likewise, for students with visual impairments, learning disabilities, or intellectual disabilities, the team would describe current classroom impact on areas such as seeing words in the text, mastering basic academic skills, and developing appropriate adaptive behaviors respectively for each group.

Figure 3.9 IEP Components

IEP Committee Concern	*IEP Components*
• What are the current levels of performance?	• Current Level of Performance
• What does the student need to be able to do?	• Annual Goals and Relationship to Curriculum
• How will the program be provided to help the student?	• Delineation of Responsibility • Specifying Time in General Education and special education settings • Specifying Dates to Initiate and Review Services • Assessment of Student Progress

The current level of performance might provide information about a student's difficulties as well as describing areas of relative strength. For example, describing other areas of school performance in which emotional/behavior skills might be noted ("follows the rules and competes appropriately with classmates during physical education periods"), or in which vision might be important ("difficulty copying letters even when model is at the desk" or "mastered basic addition facts using manipulatives"), or in which learning skills are needed ("language skills are comparable to classmates"). Other general information may be included in the current level of performance to help provide a context of strengths and weaknesses for individual students.

On the IEPs for most students, the current level of performance should be related to the major objectives of the school's curriculum. For example, if reading is part of a student's general education program, then a statement such as "reads grade level reading material with 80% accuracy in word recognition" and "comprehends grade level factual information at 50%" is important information because it compares the student's performance to the school's expectations for achievement. Information about skills in reading, mathematics, written expression, and language proficiency typically are included for students at the elementary level because these skill areas comprise the core of the academic curriculum. At the secondary level, academic areas also would reflect the school's curriculum, such as "the ability to use content area texts."

Classroom working behaviors would include a description of issues such as whether a student completes work on time, follows directions, brings the needed materials to class, and works cooperatively with others. Personal and social behaviors might include a description of self-help skills, self-concept, interactions with peers, and use of free time. Finally, if appropriate, any impact of disabilities not covered in the other items should be described. These might include a physical or sensory disability that affects classroom performance or stereotypic behavior that interferes with the ability to achieve in the classroom. In the case of preschool students or students with more severe disabilities, a description of the extent to which certain developmental markers have been achieved, such as mobility skills, self-help skills (feeding, toileting), and language skills, are important components of the current level of performance.

As part of IDEA, there are several special factors that must be considered in preparing the information on current level of performance for the IEP. The IEP team must specify whether the student has behavior that interferes with learning or the learning of others. If so, the student's behavior must be assessed and a plan developed to improve the behavior. The IEP team also must indicate whether the student has limited proficiency in English or has some special communication needs. These needs must be described in the present level of performance statement and the student's language needs addressed in the IEP. The team must state whether the student is blind or visually impaired or deaf or hard of hearing and what services will be provided for these sensory disabilities. Finally, any need for assistive technology services or devices must be indicated.

Ms. Winters's role as the general education classroom teacher is to provide special information about the extent to which Miguel's behavior has interfered with his learning or the learning of others and whether there is evidence of any communication problems. She reflects on his off-task and out-of-seat behaviors as well as his relationships with his classmates. She considers whether there have been times when he had difficulty understanding her instructions or could not follow directions she gave to the class. Did he seem able to carry on conversations with her and his classmates?

Two cautions are worth noting here. Use the description of the current level of performance to indicate both what a student does and does not do (i.e., positive and negative behaviors) and avoid relying heavily on standardized test scores to indicate the level of performance. Although test scores may be helpful to summarize and communicate performance information, many times a test score obscures a clear image of what a student is able or unable to do. A 3.5 grade level performance in math does not tell us whether a student has mastered the 4 times multiple tables or the concept of one-half.

What Does the Student Need to Be Able to Do?

The goals on the IEP should be developed from the areas of concern identified in the current level of performance and should be related, but not limited, to the general education curriculum and issues of the student's eligibility. That is to say, the IEP for students eligible for services in emotional/behavior disorders would have goals that relate to the problems such as "exhibited an inability to build or maintain satisfactory personal relationships with peers and teachers" (IDEA, 2004). IDEA 2004 makes several changes to the provisions governing IEPs. One of the most significant changes is the elimination of the requirement that a student's annual goal also contains short-term objectives that are incremental steps toward the goals. Short-term objectives are now a requirement in the IEPs of students with only the most significant cognitive disabilities. Local school districts have the option to continue to require all IEPs to include short-term objectives.

How Will the Program Be Provided?

This part of the IEP specifies the responsibilities for providing the instruction and services for each element of the goals and objectives. The guiding legislation for special education requires students to receive services in the least restrictive environment (LRE), that is to minimize separation from peers of the same age in a neighborhood school. The issue of LRE involves who provides the services (general or special educators) and where the service is to be provided (in a special school, self-contained classroom, resource room, or the general education classroom). Remember, special education is a service, not a place. A student who is eligible for special education services remains the responsibility of all educators in the school, not just the responsibility of special education teachers.

We take the position that the least restrictive environment is not synonymous with only the general education classroom but includes the full continuum of services from special schools to the general education classroom. The key to determining the least restrictive environment for a particular student is that it must be the most effective environment for providing instruction and services. In the great majority of cases, the IEP would indicate times during the day when a student receiving special education services and general education students will be together. This shared responsibility is important because we believe students with disabilities, in order to be part of the general society after their schooling has ended, need to be educated with their age peers to the extent appropriate. The students in general education programs also need the opportunity to be educated with students with disabilities.

The IEP is to be written with the full participation of all those responsible for serving the student, as well as the student's parents or guardian, and even the student, if appropriate. This shared development helps to promote mutual trust and understanding among educators, related service specialists, and parents. The IEP that was developed for Miguel is shown in **Figure 3.10.**

Note that Goals 1, 2, and 3 directly address his low performance level in reading and mathematics and are linked to the general education curriculum. They also are concerns because Miguel is eligible for services in learning disabilities due to achievement in these

Figure 3.10 Miguel's IEP

Annual Goal 1   **Placement**   **Person Responsible**   **Duration**

- Miguel will demonstrate mastery of sight vocabulary on second grade material.

Placement	Person Responsible	Duration
Resource room	Mrs. Parks	1 year

Instructional Objectives	Start Date	Review Dates	Method	Criteria
1.1 Given phonetically regular CVCC and CCVC words from second grade reading book, M. will pronounce the words.	9-25	11-15, 1-15, 3-15, 5-15	Observation	90%
1.2 Given phonetically irregular words in context, M. will pronounce the words.				

Annual Goal 2

- Miguel will demonstrate literal comprehension skills on second grade material.

Placement	Person Responsible	Duration
Resource room	Mrs. Parks	1 year

Instructional Objectives	Start Date	Review Dates	Method	Criteria
2.1 Given a selection from the second grade reader, M. will answer five factual comprehension questions.	9-25	11-15, 1-15, 3-15, 5-15	Work samples	80%
2.2 Given a selection from the second grade reader, M. will paraphrase the major theme and state five supporting details.				

Annual Goal 3

- Miguel will increase fluency in solving addition and subtraction problems requiring regrouping.

Placement	Person Responsible	Duration
Third Grade	Ms. Winters	1 year

Instructional Objectives	Start Date	Review Dates	Method	Criteria
3.1 Given worksheets of mixed two-digit addition and subtraction problems, M. will write the correct answer.	9-25	11-15, 1-15, 3-15, 5-15	Work samples	90%
3.2 Given probes of mixed two-digit addition and subtraction problems, M. will write the correct answer.				> 5 correct/ min.

Annual Goal 4

- Miguel will increase his on-task behavior.

Placement	Person Responsible	Duration
Third Grade	Ms. Winters	1 year

Instructional Objectives	Start Date	Review Dates	Method	Criteria
4.1 M. will complete four of five assignments within the time allotted.	9-25	11-15, 1-15, 3-15, 5-15	Work samples	80%

areas that is significantly below his ability. The IEP committee decides that Miguel will receive his reading instruction from Mrs. Parks in the resource room because she is using the kind of highly structured phonics-based program that would be most beneficial for him. Ms. Winters, with consultation help from Mrs. Parks, will be responsible for the arithmetic goal because his needs in this area seem reasonable within the program Ms. Winters already has established. The fourth goal focuses on increasing on-task behavior. This is supportive content because, although being on-task is not by itself a reason for being eligible for special education, it contributes to Miguel's low achievement in reading and mathematics. Miguel's mother, Mrs. Jones, had reported that Miguel says he enjoys going to school, but that he tells her little about his lessons. She indicates that he seldom looks at books or magazines at home and seems to prefer the company of younger playmates. This information is added to what the team has gathered from the school setting.

Reviewing and Revising IEPs

IDEA includes information about who and by what method the various team members participate in drafting of the IEP. The law encourages the use of alternative ways of meeting, such as conference calls. The law also allows changes to the IEP without the need for the entire IEP team to reconvene for a formal meeting. IDEA legislation also requires school personnel to document the progress of each student with an IEP. General educators are required to participate in the annual review of students' IEPs and to assist in the revisions that are made. The law requires the review to evaluate:

1. The progress or lack of progress to the IEP and, if included, general education goals,
2. Possible revisions of goals, placement, and responsibilities,
3. The results of assessments for the purpose of reevaluation,
4. Information provided by the parents and the student's anticipated needs, and
5. Other relevant information.

Some of the most common problems with IEPs are a lack of coordination with general educators (Lipsky & Gartner, 1996), the failure to include parents in the development of IEPs, and IEP goals and objectives that are not individually designed for a student's instructional needs (Drasglow, Yell, & Robinson, 2001). IDEA 2004 authorizes a new pilot program that will allow up to 15 states to offer parents the option of a multiyear IEP, not to exceed 3 years.

Individualized Transition Plan

The **Individualized Transition Plan (ITP)** was established by IDEA to supplement the services outlined in the IEP and focuses on the demands of the world outside of school. It assures that planning and services are available and coordinated to assist young adults with disabilities in moving from school- to community-based programs, agencies, and services. The ITP is required to be part of the IEP for any student with disabilities beginning with the first IEP that will be in effect when the student turns 16 years of age or earlier if determined by the IEP team. The plan should address issues of vocational preparation (career awareness, job training, placement, and follow-up), independent living skills (consumer skills, community travel, and supportive living), and leisure time options (Cronin & Patton, 1993). The ITP planning should involve the student and parents as well as the community agencies that will provide or coordinate the services.

The planning for a 16-year-old, therefore, would include additional concerns beyond what is included in the IEP of a younger student, such as Miguel. The ITP addresses the problems encountered by students preparing to leave school and has the intention of promoting independent living. That is to say, to ensure that a student leaving school has:

- mastered the skills needed to function independently (e.g., speaking, listening, reading, and writing)
- general knowledge about the world (e.g., consumer information, health, community resources, and responsibilities related to citizenship)

- knowledge of career options and the development of vocational skills
- the ability to apply personal and vocational skills and knowledge to promote self-determination and quality of life (Wiederholt & Dunn, 1995).

The development of a transition plan for Thomas, a 15-year-old who is classified as moderately intellectually disabled, will bridge the gap between the school and community. Thomas's IEP indicates that he is to be served in general education exploratory classes in his middle school where he will rotate through home economics, wood working, and art classes with his age peers. During other times of the day, Thomas is receiving services in the pull-out special education program. This program includes a language arts class in which he learns basic reading and writing skills related to functioning successfully in his neighborhood and community; a functional mathematics program that focuses on mastering money, time, and measurement problems he will face outside of school; a course in citizenship; and a science course on environmental issues. Three additional goals (the ITP portion) have been included to facilitate Thomas's movement from school to the community.

The first of the ITP goals is to develop an awareness of vocational opportunities in the immediate community and involves instruction in identifying the types of jobs in his community, the skills and training needed for each, and the types of activities each job requires. This goal is met through instruction by his special education teacher, Mrs. Phillips, as part of the curriculum for all the students in his class. A second goal is to demonstrate ability to access and use the public transportation system which was selected to enable Thomas to have access to the facilities available throughout his city. For this goal, Mr. Shoemaker, the community education specialist, works with a small group of students to teach them to identify the bus routes, scheduled departure times, and procedures for riding the bus (e.g., having the exact change for the fare and recognizing and signaling when to get off). The final ITP goal is to participate in a community-sponsored leisure activity. This goal is met when Mrs. Phillips contacted Mike Ward, Scoutmaster of a local Explorer Scout group, and enrolled Thomas in an urban scouting program sponsored by a local church. The group not only participates in outdoor leisure activities, but has an active program of community service, such as assisting with food distribution programs and participating in a senior citizens' gardening program. Through the ITP, Thomas should make a smooth transition to the world beyond school.

Individualized Family Service Plan

Whereas the IEP is the formal plan for serving school-aged students, the Individualized Family Service Plan (IFSP) is designed for infants and toddlers (Public Law 99-457). The IFSP has many similarities to the IEP for school-aged students, such as specifying current functioning levels, identifying goals and objectives, indicating services and who will provide them, and indicating the time frame for initiating and reviewing services. There are, however, several important differences. These include a broader approach with the family unit as the focal point for delivering service to the infant or toddler with disabilities and recognizing and building on each family's strengths in developing a service plan, naming a service manager to coordinate services, reviewing the service plan every six months, and indicating the method of providing transition to other services as the child grows older.

Additionally, IDEA 2004 requires changes regarding the IFSP, including the following:

- New child-find criteria with emphasis on at-risk populations;
- New provisions for early childhood transition;

- Additional dispute resolution options; and
- New members to state Interagency Coordinating Councils.

Summary

Over the last several years, the RTI framework has been implemented across the country. Through a multitiered approach, school personnel are routinely identifying students who are struggling or at-risk of struggling and implementing specific, research-based interventions that will increase academic and behavioral performance. The emphasis is on being proactive and working as an entire school to implement universal screenings and interventions that meet the needs of students rather than waiting for students to struggle. Instead of each teacher attempting various interventions in isolation, standard intervention protocols are predetermined and implemented in the classroom and also during supplementary instruction. In addition, problem solving activities are applied as teachers analyze the specific needs of students and match those needs to research-based interventions. If multiple tiers of interventions are not resulting in satisfactory progress and a disability is suspected, then a student will be referred for a special education evaluation to determine if they have a disability. The multidisciplinary team including the student's parents and teachers conducts a thorough analysis of their current efforts and completes a comprehensive evaluation. If eligible for special education services, an Individualized Education Program is developed.

Classroom Application Activities

1. In Chapter 3 you read about Miguel and the development of his Individualized Educational Program (IEP). As a future teacher, whether in general or special education, you will be required to provide input into the development of students' IEPs. Ms. Winters, Mrs. Parks, and Miguel's mother have agreed that he needs special help and modifications for his spelling. They have completed the goal below but not the instructional objective(s). Write two (2) objectives, 5.1 and 5.2, that would be appropriate for Miguel's annual goal in spelling. Remember to apply the guidelines discussed in the chapter for writing IEPs.

Annual Goal 5	Placement	Person Responsible	Duration
• Miguel will increase his spelling of second grade words.	Third Grade	Ms. Winters	1 year

Instructional Objectives	Start Date	Review Dates	Method	Criteria
• 5.1				
• 5.2				

2. You have noticed Miguel's increased achievement in classroom assignments but are saddened to see he continues to perform poorly on standardized tests. Confident in his developing abilities, you consider it plausible that he can still provide you with the correct answers to the lesson review if given another avenue by which to demonstrate his knowledge. Bearing in mind Miguel's learning style and his culture as important factors, your task is to develop two alternative forms of assessment for Miguel: one in math and one in language arts. Choose a lesson objective for each content area, state the original expected outcomes (as prescribed by state standards), describe Miguel's modified assessment plan, and list observable behaviors that will indicate Miguel has successfully met the stated objectives. Explain the scoring rubric if applicable.

3. As the day to reevaluate Ray draws near, your apprehensions about taking part in the deliberations increase. Your role as Ray's history teacher does not seem as vital to the process as one of his other teachers, so you have your doubts about even being present during the meeting. However, you suspect that if the label of "learning disabled" is removed from his file, Ray can potentially become more confident in his own abilities as a student. You want to help him achieve that confidence and decide that you will attend the meeting. In preparation, create an extensive list of those things you have observed about Ray which you believe will be a valuable asset to the deliberation process. Make sure the list includes factors related to his academic performance, behaviors, attitudes, and overall ability. You may also offer your opinion on Ray's demonstrated performance juxtaposed to his true ability. Keep in mind that your honest input will help to determine the outcome of Ray's support within the school.

4. As a first-year teacher at the elementary school, you have been assigned the class with "special students." Unbeknownst to you, this is the class of third graders who have been grouped together because no one else wants to accept the responsibility to teach them. After 2 weeks of frustration, you determine that the only way your students will succeed is if you "remove" their labels. Explain how you will go about meeting the needs of the following students:

- *Chelsea*—Strong in math but weak in language arts. Distracts others during English lessons.

- *Michael*—Stutters a lot when speaking. Hates to read aloud in class.

- *Ennis*—English learner from Puerto Rico. Loves to participate but frequently gives incorrect responses.

- *Leonard*—Chronic tardiness. Unable to concentrate during the day.

What are your expectations? How do you ensure that your students realize success both socially and academically?

Internet Resources

A Web site with IDEA 2004 and updated information about the legislation
http://www.cec.sped.org/law_res/doc/law/index.php

A U.S. Department of Education pdf file with detailed information about IEPs
http://www.ed.gov/policy/speced/guid/idea/tb-iep.pdf

An article about involving parents in the IEP process
http://ericec.org/digests/e611.html

A Web site with information about students with learning disabilities
http://www.ncld.org

A Web site with information about prereferral teams and their role in reducing disproportionate representation in special classes
http://www.emstac.org/registered/topics/disproportionality/index.htm

The Families and Advocates Partnership for Education (FAPE) at PACER Center links families, advocates, and self-advocates
http://www.fape.org

The Policy-Maker Partnership (PMP) at the National Association of State Directors of Special Education increases the capacity of policy makers
http://www.ideapartnership.org

Document providing definition of and process in referral and placement
http://www.aps.edu/aps/policy/Directives/SPEDREFP.FIN.html

Online article addressing issue of overrepresentation of minority students in special education placement
http://www.inmotionmagazine.com/er/charles.html

Document on screening general education students for referral and placement
http://www.sped618.org/PDF/Teacherhandbook/th5.pdf

Example of referral packet used by California school system (Merced County) to place special education students
http://www.mcoe.org/NR/rdonlyres/5B43F939-6AE6-4BCE-ADF5-0BF1F1773DFA/0/Referral_Packet.pdf

Booklet providing parent information on their rights in the referral and placement process in special education (prepared by New Jersey DOE)
http://www.state.nj.us/education/parights/prise.pdf

Web site providing variety of articles on assessment and referral for students with special needs (National Clearinghouse for English Language Acquisition and Language Instructional Programs)
http://www.ncela.gwu.edu/resabout/sped/4_referral.html

Web site discussing when it is most appropriate to make a special education referral
http://www.doe.state.in.us/lmmp/specialeducationreferrals.html

Full-text article on the effect of Reading Recovery on special education referral and placement process
http://www.uky.edu/~kmkram1/CCITLTransfer/fulltext

Document listing referral standards, including legal citations
http://www.asec.net/tses/referral.htm

Web site explaining preschool special education eligibility
http://www.brighttots.com/Preschool_Special_Education.html

Online resource for Americans with disabilities; provides link for local and state resources
http://www.disabilityinfo.gov/digov-public/public/DisplayPage.do?parentFolderId=107

Document describing special education process: child-find, referral, evaluation, and eligibility
http://www.state.nj.us/education/specialed/info/process.pdf

Web site with detailed explanation of special education process with descriptive graphic organizer
http://www.westco.k12.mo.us/special/spedprocess.pdf

Web site explaining seven-step IEP process
http://www.slc.sevier.org/7iep.htm

Handbook with guidelines and regulations for special education assessment process
http://www.tr.wou.edu/eec/assessmentprocess2001.pdf

References

Colarusso R., Keel, M., & Dangel, H. (2001). A comparison of eligibility criteria and their impact on minority representation in LD programs. *Learning Disabilities Research & Practice, 16*(1), 1–7.

Craig, S., Hull, K., Haggart, A.G., & Perez-Selles, M. (2000). Promoting cultural competence through teacher assistance teams. *Teaching Exceptional Children, 32*(3), 6–12.

Cronin M.E., & Patton, J.R. (1993). *Life skills instruction for all students with special needs: A practical guide for integrating real-life content into the curriculum.* Austin, TX: PRO-ED.

Drasglow, E., Yell, M.L., & Robinson, M.R. (2001). Developing legally correct and educationally appropriate IEPs. *Remedial and Special Education, 22,* 359–373.

Georgia Department of Education. (2011). *Response to intervention: Georgia's student achievement pyramid of interventions.* From http://archives.gadoe.org/DMGetDocument.aspx/Response%20to%20Intervention%20Student%20Achievement%20Oct%202011.pdf?p=6CC6799F8C1371F62E73B73604299B7B3848567EA4E6AC015A424285AAFF3923&Type=D.

Individuals with Disabilities Education Improvement Act of 2004, 108th Congress of the United States.

Lipsky, D.K., & Gartner, A. (1996). Inclusive education and school restructuring. In W. Stainback & S. Stainback (Eds.), *Controversial issues confronting special education: Divergent perspectives* (pp. 3–15). Boston: Allyn & Bacon.

National Center on Response to Intervention. (n.d.). *Universal screening.* From http://www.rti4success.org/categorycontents/universal_screening.

National Institute of Child Health and Human Development. (2000). *Report of the National Reading Panel. Teaching children to read: An evidence-based assessment of the scientific research literature on reading and its implications for reading instruction* (NIH Publication No. 00-4769). Washington, DC: U.S. Government Printing Office.

O'Connor, J. (2009). *Turning average instruction into great instruction.* Lanham, MD: Rowman & Littlefield Education.

Strickland, B.B., & Turnbull, A.P. (1990). *Developing and implementing individualized education programs.* Columbus, OH: Merrill.

Stump, C. (2002). Prereferral: The first step in addressing your child's learning disability. SchwabLearning.org. A Parent's Guide to Helping Kids with Learning Difficulties.

U.S. Department of Education. (2011). Office of Special Education and Rehabilitative Services, Office of Special Education Programs, *30th Annual Report to Congress on the Implementation of the Individuals with Disabilities Education Act, 2008.* Washington, DC: U.S. Government Printing Office.

Wiederholt, J.L., & Dunn, C. (1995). Transition from school to independent living. In D.D. Hammill & N.R. Bartel (Eds.), *Teaching students with learning and behavior problems: Managing mild to moderate difficulties in resource and inclusive settings* (pp. 381–417). Austin, TX: PRO-ED.

CHAPTER FOUR

Collaboration with Families and Professionals

Ronald P. Colarusso, Editor

The editors of *Special Education for All Teachers* appreciate the contributions of the following individuals: Peggy A. Gallagher, Debra Schober-Peterson, Cheryl A. Rhodes, Lauren Stern Wynne, and JoAnna White

CHAPTER OBJECTIVES

- to discuss models used to understand families of students with disabilities;
- to discuss family roles in the development of students with disabilities;
- to describe the importance of collaboration with families;
- to provide strategies for building collaboration among professionals and families; and
- to describe effective interpersonal skills that contribute to respectful, encouraging working relationships with individuals and groups.

KEY TERMS

collaboration • family systems approach • nonverbal behavior • empathy

Historically, teaching has been an isolated profession with teachers and their students in their classrooms for most of the day. Educating America's children has become increasingly more complex. Recent educational reforms emphasize that to be effective teachers must be involved in interactions with others outside the walls of their classrooms. Effective teachers serve as members of school teams, consult with parents and other professionals, and provide leadership with respect to their students in schoolwide decision making. Federal law requires that a team approach be used for several aspects of the special education process. Teachers are the best advocate for their students in the classroom, within the school setting and outside of the school. Because student success hinges on a team approach, collaboration is a crucial part of making this teamwork successful. This chapter focuses on collaboration with parents and colleagues and some techniques for positive interaction with each other, with administrators, with support personnel, and with family members.

Families and the Child with Special Needs

When she arrived at school, Chan-sook Park was smiling and Ms. Miller, her teacher, knew why. She said, "Today is your birthday, you are 13 years old!" Chan-sook signed 13 in ASL (American Sign Language). Ms. Miller was glad that Mrs. Park was coming to the class birthday party she enthusiastically planned. The class will love making strawberry rice cakes, the cooking activity Mrs. Park had suggested since this was one of Chan-sook's favorite foods. Ms. Miller thought back to the beginning of the school year when her efforts to communicate with Mrs. Park were ignored. How many notes did she send home in Chan-sook's backpack? Since the family did not have a phone, what choice did she have? Chan-sook's limited communication did not help. Ms. Miller checked with last year's teacher who told her that Mrs. Park attended one IEP meeting but her participation was limited to signing the plan prepared by the team. One day Chan-sook made the sign for baby and with some effort, Ms. Miller found out that Mrs. Park had given birth to her fourth child in early November and that her mother's younger sister had come to stay with the family. Soon after, when Ms. Miller was getting the students from the bus, the bus driver handed her a note from Mrs. Park. Neatly written on floral paper, Mrs. Park said she was very grateful for the assistance Chansook received at school and thanked Ms. Miller for the invitations she received. But, Mrs. Park explained, since she could not attend the meetings, she did not answer the notes that were sent home. After the holidays Ms. Miller was ready to try again. This time, when she sent a message to Mrs. Park, she gave it to the bus driver. The next day, the bus driver handed her another envelope from Mrs. Park; this was the beginning of regular communication culminating nearly 4 months later with Mrs. Park's first visit to Chan-sook's classroom. Somehow Ms. Miller was sure that it would not be the last.

What role did culture play in this situation? With more information and a nonjudgmental attitude, Ms. Miller was able to involve a parent who initially seemed disinterested and unavailable. Collaborating with families from diverse cultures requires an understanding and appreciation of views and behaviors that may be different from your own.

Effective teachers periodically consult with professionals to enhance their skills.

Developing a healthy partnership with families is an important goal for schools. With an active and positive partnership with families, schools can achieve full collaboration. Students are first and foremost members of their families before being members of their school. Families have a lasting and powerful influence on their children.

Today, there is no longer a typical family. The basic family unit has changed substantially over the last several decades with increases in divorce rates, single parent families, married women working outside of the home, and blended families encompassing two adults and children from different unions and extended families (Johnson, Pugach & Hawkins, 2004; Correa et al., 2005). In addition, the increasing number of culturally and linguistically diverse children in our society is reflected in our schools. As a result, school personnel must be prepared to work with a variety of family structures and cultures.

Poverty is another factor that influences families. The National Center for Children in Poverty (2012) reported nearly 15 million children in the United States, and 21% of all children, live in families with incomes below the federal poverty level of $22,050 a year for a family of four. On average families need an income of about twice that level to cover basic expenses. Using this standard, 42% of our children live in low-income families.

Grandparents can be a source of support for the family.

Children with disabilities live in families below the poverty line more frequently than typically developing children. Research suggests that children with disabilities who live in poverty have a greater risk of poor developmental, educational, social, and health outcomes (Parish, 2007).

The family's role in the development of a child with disabilities has gained increasing attention in recent years. The focus has shifted from viewing the development of the child alone to looking at the development of the child as a part of the family and community. As educators, we should be familiar with information and approaches that can be used to better understand and collaborate with the family of a child with disabilities. These include family systems, stressors, needs, adjustment, and empowerment models.

Family Systems

A **family systems approach** views families who have a child with special needs first and foremost like all other families with the same needs, wants, and desires. In this perspective, all families need special help and support at various times. As Fewell and Vadasy (1986) noted, there are differences among families in terms of their family interactions, their capacity to meet the family's basic needs or functions, and the life cycle stage of the family unit (e.g., just married, children finishing high school, etc.). In addition, these differences may be influenced greatly by the family's cultural background. These concepts combined with a broad understanding of the family's dynamics and makeup are the basis for a family systems approach (Turnbull, Brotherson, & Summers, 1985; Turnbull, Summers, & Brotherson, 1984; Turnbull, Turnbull, Erwin & Soodak, 2006). As a system, the family is composed of members. If any outside force affects one member of the family, it will in turn have an effect on the rest of the family system. For example, an economic recession causes a father to lose his job. This in turn creates additional stress in the home that might impact the student's behavior in school. Similarly, a teacher's request that parents spend additional time with a child on homework or self-help skills may put additional stress on an already overworked family system (Pugach & Johnson, 2002).

In family systems theory, a variety of subsystems exist within a family system. They may include a husband-wife system, a parent-child system, a sibling-sibling system, a grandchild-grandparent system, and others. The interaction of these subunits helps to define the family's functioning. All of these subsystems can be a source of support or stress for the family. For instance, if grandparents live in the home and are helpful with childcare, they may be viewed as a source of support. If they live elsewhere and arrive unannounced for extended visits, they may create a source of stress for the family.

Family Stressors

A way to view a family's adjustment to having a child with disabilities is to examine possible family stressors. This suggests that a potentially stressful event such as the birth or diagnosis of a child with special needs may precipitate a family crisis (Hill, 1949; 1958). The resources a family brings to a situation and their response to the situation will vary across families.

Families react to and cope with a child with disabilities in different ways and their strategies for coping may change as the life cycle of the family changes. Some families will be involved at a healthy level whereas others may be over involved at an unhealthy stress level. Others may not be able to cope with the stress and disengage.

Family Needs

The basic tasks that families undertake to meet their needs are called family functions. Turnbull et al. (2006) described eight family functions: economic, daily care, socialization, recreation, self-esteem, affection, spiritual, and education/vocational. Family needs are complex, and all of these functions are important, not only the educational ones. Think about these functions and consider how they influence a family with a child with disabilities.

Economic. A child with a disability can create additional stress on the financial needs of a family. For example, parents may need to pay the costs of additional health care, physical or occupational therapy, adaptive devices, or specialized after-school care.

Daily Care. Parents may be so exhausted from the daily demands of caring and planning for a child with a disability that they neglect their own needs for rest, exercise, or adequate nutrition. Daily living routines are made even more complicated and challenging for parents who must schedule and transport a child to various medical or therapy appointments on the bus or by car.

Socialization and Recreation. Families that have a child with special needs may limit their own opportunities to socialize because of the child's disability or behavior. For instance, a family may feel uncomfortable taking their 6-year-old son with autism to his older sister's school play because he may run off, scream, and interrupt the play. Parents may find it difficult to find time for their personal leisure and needs.

Self-Esteem. Confidence and self-worth are linked to a person's or family's definition of self. The self-identity of the parents is tied strongly to the self-identity of the children regardless of their special needs. Being a parent of a child with special needs can have a negative effect on a parent's self-esteem.

Affection. The needs for love and physical intimacy are expressed through verbal and nonverbal means. Family members may have a hard time reading a child's facial expressions if the child has autism. Or, they may have difficulty understanding a child's speech if she has cerebral palsy, and thus some of the spontaneous give and take of affection may be lost.

Spiritual. Spirituality is displayed in a variety of ways across cultures, often through family values that may be different than ours. Spiritual traditions can be a source of support for families.

Family Adjustment

Another way of viewing families of children with disabilities is to consider how they are adjusting to the unique and complex demands of rearing a child with special needs. An early view equated this process with the specific and predictable stages of grief reported by Kubler-Ross (1969) in her work with dying patients. While the grief cycle theory has been proposed to describe how families adjust to having a child with a disability, research does not support the notion that families go through a set series of emotional reactions such as shock, denial, sadness, anger, and resolution before adapting to their child with a disability (Gallagher, Fialka, Rhodes, & Arceneaux, 2002; Turnbull & Turnbull, 2001). Families of children with special needs may in fact feel grief, shock, or anger at certain points in time and may experience it and express it in a variety of ways. Some families with children with special needs are not adversely affected (Turnbull et al., 2006) and may be as well adjusted as families without a child with a disability (Singer, 2002). Other factors that can affect family adjustment are stress and isolation, especially for families whose children have complex medical needs, high expenses, or challenging behaviors.

Family Empowerment

A family empowerment model regards the family as a true partner in determining needed services, rather than the traditional recipient of services (Dunst, Trivette, & Deal, 1988). Such an approach acknowledges the capability of families to generate their own solutions and reinforces collaborative relationships. These relationships must involve mutual respect among family members and school personnel. A family empowerment model demands that parents and family members have adequate information so that they can participate as equals in the collaboration process.

Families are essential for meeting the basic needs of students. It is important to remember that the family members consist of more than just parents. Brothers and sisters, for instance, are an important part of the family and may need support as they play key roles in the development of their brothers and sisters with disabilities. Specific sibling concerns that may arise include competition, serving in a caregiver role, and a lack of understanding of special education (Gallagher, Powell, & Rhodes, 2006).

Grandparents also may play an important caregiving role in the life of the child with a disability. Many have assumed primary caregiver roles on a temporary or permanent basis and may be involved in as many ways as the parents.

Working with Families

Families can play a crucial role on many of the teams established in schools. Working with families of students with disabilities can be a rewarding and meaningful experience for professionals. After all, parents are the child's first and most important educators. The home setting is a critical factor in the child's success.

Parental involvement in the school enhances a child's chances of school success and significantly improves student achievement (Dettmer, Thurston, & Dyck, 1993; Henderson, 1987; Epstein, 1989; Kroth & Scholl, 1978). Parents also benefit from being involved in their child's education through improved feelings of self-worth and self-satisfaction (Murphy, 1981). Teachers benefit by having more information about their students' backgrounds and home life.

Family Involvement and the Law

IDEA provides guidelines for the team procedures to be used in the special education process. Specifically, the law requires that two teams be formed, the multidisciplinary evaluation team and the IEP (Individualized Education Program) planning team. The multidisciplinary team evaluates students referred for special education services by general education teachers or parents and determines the students' eligibility for services. Parental consent must be obtained before conducting an initial evaluation for placement in a special education program. Although the composition of the multidisciplinary team varies according to the needs of the student, it must include a teacher or other specialist with knowledge in the suspected area of disability. It also should include the student's family and other school professionals with knowledge of the student's academic performance. Once a student is deemed eligible for special education services, IDEA requires that a meeting to develop the IEP be held within 30 calendar days of the determination that the student has a disability and requires special education and related services. The IEP team develops, reviews, and revises the student's IEP. The required participants in IEP meetings include the following:

- Parents (or guardians or surrogate parents) and, when appropriate, the student.
- At least one general education teacher if the student is, or may be, participating in the general education environment.
- At least one special education teacher or, if appropriate, a special education provider.
- A representative of the local school system who is qualified to provide or supervise the provision of specially designed instruction to meet the needs of students with disabilities, has knowledge of the general curriculum, has knowledge of the resources of the local school system.
- An individual who can interpret the instructional implications of evaluation results.
- Other individuals who have knowledge or special expertise regarding the student, including related services personnel, at the discretion of the parent or local school system or state operated program.

The law emphasizes the involvement of parents in the development of the IEP to ensure that they are active participants in decision making regarding their child's educational program (Bateman & Linden, 1998; Correa et al., 2005; Turnbull et al., 2006). Parents must be members of any group that makes decisions on the educational placement of their child. The IEP and placement must be reviewed at least annually, but can be reviewed more often if requested by the parent or teacher. Specific requirements for parental involvement in the IEP process include the following:

- Notifying the parents regarding the purpose, time, location, and participants at the meeting so that they have an opportunity to attend.
- Scheduling the meeting at a mutually agreed upon time and place.
- Ensuring that the parents understand the purpose and tasks of the meeting and that an interpreter is present for parents who are deaf or whose native language is one other than English.
- Providing a copy of the IEP, including the placement meeting minutes, to the parents. Minutes must be taken at every IEP meeting. If parents do not attend the meeting, a copy of the IEP and the minutes must be provided to the parents before the IEP is implemented.

Parents must be afforded every opportunity to participate in the IEP process for their child. If a parent cannot attend the IEP meeting, parents and the local education agency may agree to use alternative means of meeting participation such as video conferencing or a conference call. An IEP meeting can be conducted without the parents being present only if the parents have rejected all attempts by the school system to involve them. The school system must document all efforts to arrange a convenient meeting time and place, including detailed records of telephone calls and responses, visits to the parent's home or place of work, and mailings concerning the IEP meeting (Turnbull et al., 2006).

IDEA also requires that a description of how the student's parents will be regularly informed of the student's progress be included in the IEP. Annual goals on the student's IEP must be addressed in the progress report. These reports must be as frequent as reports received by parents of students without disabilities.

As a result of IDEA, schools have moved toward the development of collaborative teams that include general education teachers, special education teachers, and families. There are many reasons school personnel should strive to interact collaboratively in all aspects of their work with students with disabilities. Probably the most important benefit of a collaborative process is that the student receives the best educational programming possible. Because school personnel, family members, and in many cases the student, provide input into decision making, there is a greater likelihood that plans will be carried out effectively and enthusiastically. In addition, the student's needs are viewed as a whole rather than as separate, possibly unrelated, needs. Families also may feel a stronger connection with their child's school program and be better able to assist in helping their child achieve goals. Collaboration also facilitates effective communication because it fosters an atmosphere of trust and respect among team members. In the collaborative team concept, it is important to emphasize a true partnership with the child's family members. Family members know the child in important ways outside of the classroom. Family members who might have input in team decisions include the parents, brothers and sisters, grandparents, cousins, and aunts and uncles, as well as other significant persons who may not be blood relatives but are considered family.

Johnson, Pugach, and Hawkins (2004) outlined several barriers to family participation. These three barriers were identified by parents and include logistical problems, communication problems, and a lack of understanding of schools.

1. *Logistical Problems.* Situations leading to a lack of transportation or childcare or getting time away from work to attend school conferences have been identified as logistical problems families may face.

2. *Communication Problems.* Teachers often use professional jargon that may intimidate some parents. In turn, teachers may not understand or be put off by the style of communication used by the family. Teachers and administrators may be uncomfortable with parents who are well versed in special education law and advocacy or whose style of communication is authoritative or assertive.

3. *Lack of Understanding of Schools.* Schools have a complex set of written and unwritten operating rules. Families may not understand, for instance, what occurs at an IEP meeting or who will be there or why. If schools are to be family-focused, all families must understand these rules and be a part of what is happening in the schools. This may mean preparing families for who will be at a meeting, their roles, and the process that will occur. It also may mean teaching families how to access the resources of the school and accepting all families as an educational resource for the school.

It is clear that family involvement in schools provides numerous benefits such as improved academic achievement, better school attendance, greater knowledge about how a child learns, better knowledge about the school and opportunities within the school, and better overall behavior at school and at home. Sometimes professionals talk about parents who do not seem to want to be involved in the child's school or who seem angry with the schools. However, in reality most parents, regardless of their background or economic status, do want to be involved but may need assistance in the process. Teachers often misinterpret a lack of involvement as apathy, particularly with respect to families of cultures different from their own (Pugach & Johnson, 2002). Many times the school asks parents to participate in their child's education at a level they are not capable of or require more time than they have.

Pagett (2006) and Summer, Gavin, and Purnell-Hall (2003) provide some useful strategies for involving parents at the school level:

1.   Identify barriers that may prevent family involvement. For example, flexible conference times may make it possible for more families to meet with teachers.
2.   Create a plan for increasing family involvement. Specifically, set a goal to increase parent participation, get input from as many people as possible when developing the plan, post the plan for the school community, and evaluate the plan's success.
3.   Get feedback from families. This might be possible through the school's Web site or by having forms available in the school's office. Schools might seek input on a regular basis.
4.   Involve the entire community. Schools may plan festivals, cook-outs, or other social events that raise the community's knowledge about the school. In addition, schools and community groups or businesses can work together to provide resources for the school.
5.   Encourage parent volunteers. Parents can help out at school events, they can volunteer the classroom, school library, or school office, and they can participate in field trips.
6.   Encourage parents to be involved in the school's parent-teacher association and other school advisory groups that can assist in school-level decisions.
7.   Provide opportunities to extend learning into the home. For example, families might be able to participate in parent-child literacy programs.

How Teachers Can Help

Teachers should be responsive to parental needs including childcare, transportation, or time away from work. Creative ways of getting families and teachers together have to be developed. Meetings can be scheduled in a safe, convenient, and more comfortable location. In addition, meetings could be scheduled on weekends or in the evenings with childcare provided, if needed.

Teachers also can help family members become equal members of a team by giving them information. Teachers can help prepare family members for the IEP process—who will be there and why, what some of the words that are likely to be used may mean, how long the meeting will last, what will occur, etc. so that they can be active participants in the process. In addition to strategies that can improve family involvement schoolwide, teachers can implement specific strategies to encourage family involvement in

Parents can get involved through volunteer work for the school.

their child's education. Parents who have a good sense of self-worth and feel competent as parents will make strong parents for their children.

Some ideas that may be helpful to parents are:

- Support parents' hopes and dreams for their child. Family support groups can be helpful to parents as they allow families the chance to meet others who share their feelings and give them specific strategies to use with their children.

- Suspend judgment of families and their behavior. Learn from each family and respect family differences.

- Don't send work home that requires teaching on the part of a parent. Only ask parents to support the process and supervise homework that you are assured they have the knowledge and ability to supervise.

- Respect and honor the cultural traditions of families. Recognize that parents and professionals may have a different perspective and may not share the same vision of the child and his or her future.

- Help families meet their children's educational and vocational needs by encouraging and facilitating their involvement in the school at a level they can manage. Don't expect all parents to integrate new information about their child in the same manner or within the same time frame as the professional.

- Help siblings by explaining special education to all students in the school, involving siblings as appropriate in IEP or other meetings, and being available to talk to the siblings about concerns as needed.

- Provide links to agencies that offer support services to individuals and families. School personnel can contribute to family adjustment by providing resources, respecting and accepting feelings, and providing opportunities for participation and involvement.

Additionally, as Johnson, Pugach, and Hawkins (2004) noted, teachers have to be honest about their own sincere desire to have families involved. Teachers have not always valued input from families, particularly when meeting the needs of students with disabilities. Teachers need to treat families as equal members of the team for true collaboration to occur. More importantly, families need to begin to see schools as family-centered with positive feelings and outcomes. Families need to be involved as real school decision makers and see that their participation is valued.

Collaboration

Collaboration in the schools is a process in which school personnel and family members work together to provide effective services for students. It is an interactive process that enables people with diverse experiences and expertise to mutually define problems, set goals, and create solutions. In addition, collaboration encourages effective communication and respect for the knowledge of others. In all cases, collaboration results in a team of people making decisions, whether the team consists of two individuals or twenty.

Collaboration defines how individuals interact with each other when working as a team. Team members approach interactions with others by conveying a willingness and desire to work together. Collaboration requires a style of interacting that uses the ideas and contributions of others as a way of affecting one's own thoughts (Coufal, 1993; Friend & Cook, 2007). Individuals who successfully collaborate must consider a variety of viewpoints, take risks, try new ideas, respect others, and use effective communication skills.

Collaborating with Families

A collaborative attitude on the part of a teacher can go along way in creating an effective relationship with parents. Simple strategies can be the most beneficial. Patrikakou, Weissberg, Hancock, Rubenstein, and Zeisz (1997) outlined four essential ingredients to creating effective interactions between teachers and parents. They described these strategies as the four Ps:

1. Be *positive*. Discuss strengths and provide praise and encouragement, not just concerns.
2. Be *personalized*. Write personal notes rather than using form letters to provide feedback to parents.
3. Be *proactive*. Contact parents well in advance of upcoming events and school policies and expectations. Discuss a concern immediately, don't wait and allow the problem to become more severe.
4. Develop a *partnership*. Encourage parents to respond to notes or questions. Show appreciation of feedback.

Teachers can facilitate interactions with family members in a variety of ways. When working with families whose first language is other than English, a translator should be present for face-to-face meetings or telephone contact, and all written materials should be translated. When communicating with any family, provide information in a jargon-free manner and provide specific examples of a student's strengths and weaknesses. In addition, create a safe, positive environment and remember to view the student as an individual (Correa et al., 2005). Provided below are several ideas regarding fostering successful communication with families.

Family Conferences

The most common form of communication is the family-teacher conference. Sometimes the student with special needs also may be included in the conference. In other cases, grandparents, siblings, aunts, uncles, or other family members may attend. Family conferences can be an opportunity to solidify collaborative relationships. Turnbull and Turnbull (2001) see four main reasons for the family conference including:

1. Exchanging information about home and school.
2. Working together to help the student progress.
3. Developing rapport and mutual commitment to the student's development.
4. Cooperating in solving problems and concerns.

Family-teacher conferences should have three phases (Turnbull & Turnbull, 2001):

1. Preconference planning including notification, preparation and planning of the agenda, and arranging the environment;
2. Implementation—conducting the conference; and
3. Postconference follow-up.

Planning includes notification of the meeting and preparing parents for what will happen at the meeting. Notification should be translated into the native language of the family. Parents should know that they can bring someone with them to the meeting if that would be helpful. If parents know what to expect at a meeting, be it an information conference or an IEP meeting, they will be more likely to participate. It also may be helpful to provide parents with a preview of the child's progress on IEP goals or other information before the meeting so that they can be prepared with questions and comments at the meeting.

The teacher should review folders, gather examples of the student's work and progress on IEP goals and objectives, and make an outline of the meeting agenda with the parents if at all possible. Parents should prepare in a similar manner by reviewing the child's progress.

The meeting should be held in a quiet room with adult size chairs at a time convenient for everyone involved that allows for enough time to address all agenda items. Communication skills, discussed later, are the basis for conducting the conference. Be sure that parental concerns are clarified and placed on the agenda, being flexible as new issues are raised. The conference follow-up should summarize and provide written copies of plans for everyone involved. Follow-up communication to family members and other team members are made as needed.

Self-Determination and Self-Advocacy

Self-determination and self-advocacy are familiar concepts in the disability rights field that are important for educators of students with disabilities. Self-determination means that individuals with disabilities have needed tools and resources to make decisions and choices for their own lives, engage in activities that are important to them, and have the same opportunities as other members of their community. Self-determination is a process that assures that individuals with disabilities receive the supports they need to be full participants of their community. Self-advocacy literally means advocating for oneself. Self-advocacy requires decision making and communication skills needed for an individual to determine their rights and responsibilities, and promotes independence.

Student involvement in IEP meetings and IEP planning promotes self-determination and self-advocacy. Students with many types of special needs can participate in the IEP process. (Test et al., 2004). Student involvement varies with student's age, ability, and comfort level but should be implemented as early as possible. Falvey (2005) advises that students should start attending IEP meetings when services begin. IDEA requires that the public agency include the student with a disability, whenever appropriate, as a member of the IEP team and the student must be invited to attend IEP meetings when discussing postschool goals and transition services (U.S. Department of Education, Office of Special Education Programs, 2006). As with any skill, students must learn how to become self-advocates.

Phone Calls, E-mails, and Unplanned Conferences

Frequent communication should be a necessary part of interaction with family members for all students. While calls or e-mails typically are made when there is a problem, it is important to make calls or send e-mails regarding good things as often as possible. Teachers should keep a log of all phone calls and take notes during these exchanges. This is also true of e-mail interactions. If you do not have the information at the time of the interaction, say so and get back to the parents in a reasonable period of time. Give the family member a date by which you will respond but do not promise to do it immediately. For example, you might say: *"I'm glad you took the time to talk to me. I want to be sure I get the correct information, and I'll get back to you by _____."* Give yourself enough time to gather the information and review it before calling back or responding by e-mail.

If the family member is angry during your exchange, talk to the person in a calm voice, listening, and not interrupting, and indicate you will get back with more information by a specific date. Remember that not all families have telephones or home computers, and some may not be comfortable communicating through these media. It is useful only if it is convenient and acceptable to the family.

School, Class, and Course Web Sites

Class and school Web sites are a good way to keep families informed of events that affect the school or your class. Course Web sites also can be established for students in middle school or high school. Class and course Web sites can provide students and their families with information regarding expectations, policies, assignments, test dates, and upcoming events and may help alleviate the need to e-mail information to individual families.

Traveling Notebooks

An excellent way to communicate frequently and in a more informal way with families and professionals is through the use of a traveling notebook. The notebook can go back and forth among all the school personnel with whom the student interacts and be sent home on a daily or weekly basis. Family members and professionals write brief messages to each other to keep everyone informed about the student's current progress and needs.

Observation or Volunteering in the Classroom

Another way to collaborate with families is to encourage family members to spend time observing or participating in their child's classroom. This could be a once-a-year experience or as frequent as a weekly experience. This type of opportunity allows the family to learn more about the student's school day and to see their child's performance on various school tasks. Observations also help parents be more active team members, especially regarding goal setting and program implementation for the student. Parents also might volunteer by sharing a hobby or information about a career, their culture, or travel. In addition, parents can help with a specific project in the classroom or by something as simple as reading to the class.

Educational or Medical Record Notebooks and Portfolios

Strickland and Turnbull (1993) suggested the development and use of a reference book for parents and families. A reference notebook is a good way for parents to gather and maintain information about their child. It might include sections on legal references, names of local or national parent support groups, and names of school or community contacts. Another helpful and innovative tool is a student portfolio. Portfolios are appropriate for students of all ages and abilities. In addition to teacher/parent made portfolios, *Take a Look at Me and Mireme*™ (Spanish version) are printed books that parents can use to create a "snapshot" of their child's current strengths and interests. A portfolio for older children is also available. Rugg (2008) noted that the portfolio process "promotes building supports based on the hopes and dreams of the family for their child" (www. ihdd.uga.edu).

Parental Access

When thinking about parent and professional collaboration for children with disabilities, it is important to remember there are some parents who may not have access to typical collaborative opportunities. These include parents whose native language is not English; or who have limited access to technology, childcare, or transportation; or who have work schedules that do not allow them to be available for conferences or communication with the teacher during the typical school day. An effective strategy may be to hire other parents in similar situations who can be trained to work with their fellow parents or serve as community liaisons or partners with faith-based and community organizations that serve immigrant or migrant communities. Schools might also set up resource centers that are open longer than traditional school hours (evenings and weekends) and provide information and materials in a variety of languages. Providing transportation and childcare may also be helpful in increasing family involvement.

In addition to the ideas presented here, teachers can provide all families with calendars, announcements, or newsletters about what is happening in the classroom. In some schools, Web sites provide good information about school events and the school calendar. Open houses and orientation programs for new parents also may be helpful in facilitating communication with families. Moreover, including families of students with disabilities as volunteers for field trips and other school events will help them feel connected with the general education classroom in which their child participates. Clearly, to foster the best communication possible between families and schools, teachers must encourage frequent communication and be receptive to family input.

Teamwork

As educators we work with many colleagues who care deeply about the well being of the students they serve. It is ineffective for teachers to use a linear cause and effect model of problem solving in educational settings. LaFountain and Garner (1998) encouraged the use of a systemic approach that views cause and effect as "circular, simultaneous, and reciprocal" (p. 7) and requires educators to explore student concerns from a holistic perspective that considers environmental factors both in school and outside of school before drawing conclusions. Student Support Team meetings (SSTs), often known as Response to Intervention (RTI) meetings (as discussed in Chapter 3), are at their best, geared toward a collaborative, systemic approach to problem solving because the important adults in a student's life are invited to contribute their perspective on the student's strengths and weaknesses in the unique environments in which they work with the child. For example, a classroom teacher is able to contribute information about the student's academic work and behavior in a classroom. A reading intervention teacher can offer information about specific reading intervention strategies. Parents or caregivers can contribute information about how the student functions at home and their perspective on their child's development thus far. When everyone works together simultaneously, students are better understood as individuals within the systems to which they belong and more effective and individualized approaches to academic problem solving can be determined and consistently implemented.

Relationship Skills for Teachers

Positive interpersonal skills are necessary to develop alliances with your students, parents, and professional partners. It takes commitment, practice, and constant awareness of your thoughts and emotions for these skills to become natural in daily interpersonal relationships.

Working with Students, Parents, and Teachers
Observing and Attending

One of the most effective skills that a teacher has at their disposal is the skill of observation. Observation can last from as long as a few seconds to an entire school day. The skill of observation involves suspending one's need to take immediate action to fix things (which usually does not work well because the event is so laden with emotion), taking a breath, trying to stay neutral,

During observation, a teacher can learn a great deal from facial expressions, body language, eye contact, and tone of voice.

and concentrating on the other person (Kottler & Kottler, 2007). During observation, attention to **nonverbal behavior** is critical. In most cases a teacher can learn a great deal from attending to facial expressions, body language, eye contact, and tone of voice. Observation without judgment can provide you a window into the student's, parent's, or fellow teacher's world that you would not have if you did not stop and use your senses and intuition. Kottler and Kottler (2007) used the metaphor of the tennis player who, before serving, goes through a ritual to block out emotion and get into a zone. Notes written following observations may reveal patterns of behavior over time.

Listening and Empathizing

Real listening is critical for all good relationships. Passive listening involves observation and attention to nonverbal behavior as well as to what is being said. Listening is only effective if you are " . . . actually listening and can prove that you have understood" (Kottler & Kottler, 2007, p. 52). Active listening involves more than attending and paying attention. Active listening involves skills that convey in your response that you understand or are trying to understand. In other words, you are conveying back to the person what you heard and that you respect what they have said. This skill of actively working to see the situation from the other's point of view is **empathy**.

Active listening and empathic responses all rest on one's ability to suspend one's own needs to control situations. Often in relationships we make decisions, prior to working together, about that outcome based on our wants and needs. If we begin at this point, there is no hope for resolution. For example, if we begin a conference by presenting our wants and needs and not finding out the parents' wants and needs, the conference may doomed before it begins. By first giving the parent an opportunity to express their needs, wants, and concerns a positive tone can be set. Observing nonverbals, listening, and reflecting with empathy all improve the chances for a productive conference.

Using Questions Appropriately

A large part of a teacher's day requires the use of questioning to determine if a student has mastered a concept. This section focuses on how one can use questions to develop a relationship and take interactions to a more personal level. This approach to questioning can be effective with students, parents, and colleagues.

If you ask a question and receive a response, it is usually better to paraphrase what you heard before you ask another question. This helps the interaction remain conversational and avoids giving the feeling of being "grilled." Asking many questions in rapid succession can turn a person off or shut them down totally. Ideally, you will get better responses when the person answering the questions feels heard and knows that you understood their message. This demonstrates empathy and that you are trying to understand.

Phrasing a question so that it is open-ended can lead to a more open and meaningful response. The word used to start a question can have a significant impact on the response you will receive. Questions that start with why tend to put people on the defensive. For example, *"Why are you late?"* comes across differently than *"I notice that you are running late today. What happened?"* Think about which question you would prefer to hear from your principal on a rough morning. Your students will have a similar answer. Questions that begin with what, when, where, who, and how will typically get you more information because they are considered open-ended. Closed-ended questions will get you a yes or a no (and usually a little more frustrated). For example:

Instead of . . .
Q: *Do you have homework today?*
A: *No.*

Try . . .

Q: *What homework do you have today?*
A: *I completed the summary of the reading assignment.*

Instead of . . .

Q: *Can I read your summary?*
A: *No.*

Try . . .

Q: *What did you write about?*
A: *It was a compare and contrast paper about the presidential candidates.*

Even open-ended questions have the potential to come across as "grilling" if they are not coupled with statements that show you are hearing what the person is saying. The next section presents some ways to get the answers you want without having to use a single question mark.

Empathizing

Empathy responses show you are trying to understand how a person feels and what is contributing to the feeling. The usual sentence stems for empathy responses include *"You feel (feeling word)"* or *"You feel (feeling word) because/when (the reason for the feeling)."* It is appropriate to complete the sentence stems with pleasant and unpleasant feeling words because that more adequately encompasses the range of human experiences. People are not born with a feeling word vocabulary and talking about feelings and the causes of them is not an innate reflex and is sometimes discouraged in some environments.

The great news is that anyone benefits from being understood emotionally. Simply saying to a colleague *"You're really frustrated and tired today"* does not usually change a situation, but it can decrease the intensity of the feelings and stress level. That is good for morale and contributes to better problem solving. Having an expansive feeling word vocabulary that attends to different categories and intensities of feelings is necessary to use empathy responses most effectively. See **Figure 4.1** for more ideas about the different categories and intensities of feeling words.

Figure 4.1   Feeling Words by Category and Intensity

Levels of Intensity	Happy	Sad	Angry	Scared	Confused	Strong	Weak
High	Excited Elated Overjoyed	Hopeless Depressed Devas- tated	Furious Seething Enraged	Fearful Afraid Threatened	Bewildered Trapped Troubled	Potent Super Powerful	Overwhelmed Impotent Vulnerable
Medium	Cheerful Up Good	Upset Distressed Sorry	Agitated Frustrated Irritated	Edgy Insecure Uneasy	Disorganized Mixed-up Awkward	Energetic Confident Capable	Incapable Helpless Insecure
Low	Glad Content Satisfied	Down Loyal Bad	Uptight Dismayed Annoyed	Timid Unsure Nervous	Bothered Uncomfort- able Undecided	Sure Secure Solid	Shaky Unsure Bored

From: Carkhuff, R.R. (2000). *The art of helping in the 21st century* (8th ed.). Amherst, MA: Human Resource Development Press.

Encouraging

Encouragement responses develop "I can do it" attitudes and approaches to problem solving. Encouragement returns responsibility to the individual and helps them become more independent. These statements focus on effort rather than end results, which can be helpful when a teacher is working with a student who is making small steps toward a goal. Encouragement does not require completion or perfection. It is a skill that can be used throughout the day and in a variety of educational situations. Encouragement also offers a person the power to decide, which is person-centered. It empowers people to try new approaches to problem solving, which is a key to trying new things like learning. Encouragement focuses on the effort rather than the product. Discouragement has a stifling influence on learning behaviors and encouragement, used properly and liberally, is part of the antidote. The difference between praise and encouragement is presented in **Figure 4.2**. While praise needs a finished project, encouragement can be used whenever you observe positive behavior.

Figure 4.2   Praise vs. Encouragement

Praise	*Encouragement*
Praise recognizes the doer. *"You got an A!"*	Encouragement recognizes the effort of the doer. *"You worked really hard to get your grade."*
Praise is control from the outside. *"You are worthwhile when you do what I want."*	Encouragement is faith that the child can control herself. *"You are a responsible, capable person."*
Praise is evaluation by others. *"You did a good job. Therefore, you are a worthwhile person because you please me."*	Encouragement promotes self-evaluation. *"Your own evaluation of yourself is most important."*
Praise focuses on the finished, well-done task. *"You are worthwhile because you completed the job and did what I expected."*	Encouragement emphasizes effort and progress of a task. *"Look at the improvements you have made."*
Praise emphasizes personal gains. *"You won. Therefore, you are worthwhile."*	Encouragement emphasizes appreciation of contributions and assets. *"Your efforts helped us go for the championship."*

Using Interpersonal Skills in Group Situations

Today problem solving typically takes place in large or small group settings. For example, parent conferences and team meetings all require two or more participants. Educators need effective communication skills to successfully negotiate the vast array of interpersonal interactions they will encounter on a daily basis in these group settings. This section demonstrates how several communication skills can be used simultaneously in real life educational moments like consultations between colleagues, teacher-student interactions in the classroom, parent conferences, and interdisciplinary team meetings.

Interacting with Colleagues

Mrs. Bernard: *I am worried I might have gotten off on the wrong foot with Joshua's grandmother.*

Mr. Flynn: *Sounds like Joshua's grandmother is his primary caretaker. What are your specific concerns?*

Mrs. Bernard:	*Well, she came in late for the conference, and I was feeling kind of annoyed about that. It seemed like she was in a bad mood, too, so I didn't even ask about that. I just focused on his academic progress and got through it as fast as I could. I think she was pretty upset when she left.*
Mr. Flynn:	*I'm hearing that you've had several stressful interactions with Joshua or his grandmother. I wonder if you felt kind of worn out and unsure about how to approach your concerns with his grandmother.*
Mrs. Bernard:	*I do feel worn out when it comes to Joshua, but I regret not talking with his grandmother about my concerns because I care about him and want things to be better for Joshua. I just didn't want to make her angrier than she already was.*
Mr. Flynn:	*You really care about him. Let's see if we can find some ways to effectively discuss your concerns with her that won't make her more upset.*
Mrs. Bernard:	*Let's start with Joshua since I'll see him in 25 minutes.*

In this dialogue between two teachers, helpful communication skills occur everywhere. In a short amount of time, Mrs. Bernard feels comfortable to open up to Mr. Flynn because he uses listening skills to rephrase what he hears Mrs. Bernard saying. When he shows that he is trying to understand her perspective, he conveys empathy, which establishes rapport and builds relationships. This type of relating works well with parents, teachers, and students. Mr. Flynn also attempted to notice how Mrs. Bernard was feeling (e.g., concerned, worn out), which enabled Mrs. Bernard to explore her feelings more thoroughly when she added the feelings of worried and annoyed.

Mrs. Bernard had a concern about making Joshua's grandmother angrier. Mr. Flynn's skill of acknowledging how she might be feeling and why she might be feeling that way is a skill that works well with people who are upset. Many times noticing a feeling and the reason for the feeling can de-escalate potentially volatile feelings. With practice, one can learn how to effectively reduce tension, respond warmly and calmly to others, and even help a stressed out colleague using this skill.

Mr. Flynn also used open-ended questions effectively. He avoided questions that required a yes or no response. Open-ended questions increase sharing and exploration rather than cut it off. He also used questions sparingly. He only asked two, and both led to more exploration on behalf of Mrs. Bernard. His responses to her answers were not immediate additional questions. He paraphrased what he heard her say to convey that he was trying to understand. His statement allowed her to open up and contributed to the development of their working relationship.

Interacting with Parents and Caregivers

After Mrs. Bernard had several successful classroom experiences with Joshua, she wanted to use her improved communication skills in a parent conference with Joshua's grandmother. Mrs. Bernard is hopeful that she will be able to build a better rapport and develop a more positive working relationship with her.

Mrs. Bernard:	*Thanks for coming back. I have lots of great work to share with you.*
Grandmother:	*(raises eyebrows) You do?*
Mrs. Bernard:	*Joshua has been working very hard in his writing journal. Here are some examples of his writing (lays writing journal in front of grandmother).*
Grandmother:	*I can't get him to do any work at home. I'm sorry about that.*

Mrs. Bernard:	*That can be frustrating. I had a tough time getting Joshua started, too, but I have figured out a few things that seem to work.*
Grandmother:	*This is amazing. I was starting to worry that he wasn't doing enough work to pass first grade.*
Mrs. Bernard:	*When Joshua feels like he has a little power, he often makes helpful decisions in the classroom and gets his work done. I have noticed that when I say, "You can choose to write in your journal first or draw your journal picture first," he will often start working immediately on one or the other. Once he starts, I try to notice that he's started and how hard he's working. That is often enough to keep him going through the picture and the writing. As you can see, his work speaks for itself.*
Grandmother:	*(with tears in eyes) I have never heard a positive thing about Joshua from school. He's had such a hard time.*
Mrs. Bernard:	*Seems like you're feeling encouraged by what you're seeing. What else can you tell me about his hard times?*
Grandmother:	*Joshua came to live with me when his mom went to jail. She has struggled with drugs for a long time. He's confused with the on again/off again relationship he has with his mom.*
Mrs. Bernard:	*It sounds like it has been difficult for everyone.*
Grandmother:	*Yeah, it has.*

Mrs. Bernard began this parent-teacher interaction by setting a positive tone from the start. Beginning interactions with positives puts parents at ease. Childrearing is an intensely stressful endeavor that can be discouraging to parents, especially when they are bombarded (often unintentionally) with all negative information about their child's deficits, delays, and misdeeds. By starting with what was going well, Mrs. Bernard changed the momentum of her interaction and relationship with Joshua's grandmother.

When Mrs. Bernard conveyed that she was paying attention, listening, and trying to understand Joshua's grandmother, she sent the message that she cares. Making guesses about how his grandmother felt showed empathy and helped deepen the interaction and strengthen the relationship. Mrs. Bernard paid attention to the words she chose when she spoke about Joshua. Language can have a powerful impact on interpersonal interactions in the short term and relationships in the long term. You can probably recall people in your own education that used encouraging or discouraging language in their interactions with you. For more information on using language effectively and respectfully in parent-teacher conferences, please consult **Figure 4.3**.

In conferences with parents, colleagues, or students, how we say things is as important as what we say. The words we use to describe the behavior can be either encouaging or discoraging. By using respectful descriptions during these interactions we can identify behaviors that interfere with learning and explore positive goal setting (encouraging). (Adapted from LaFountain & Garner, 1998.)

Interacting as a Team Member

As a result of Mrs. Bernard's positive interactions with her fellow teacher and her ongoing concerns about Joshua reading below grade level, she decided to sign up to have a "kid talk" with members of the first grade team, a reading specialist, an assistant principal, and the counselor. Interdisciplinary team meetings have always been an option for teachers at Mrs. Bernard's school (and may be in your school as well), but she has felt worried about show-

Figure 4.3	How to Describe Student Behaviors in Conferences
Discouraging Labels	**Respectful Descriptions**
Lazy	Is capable of more when he tries
Troublemaker	Disturbs the class
Uncooperative	Needs to learn to work with others
Cheats	Depends on others to do her work
Below average	Working below grade level
Stubborn	Enjoys having his way
Wastes time	Has a hard time starting/finishing tasks
Clumsy	Struggles with motor control/coordination
Show off	Seeks attention from others
Insolent	Speaks out in class
Bashful	Does not speak up in class
Hyperactive	Has a lot of energy

casing her flaws as a teacher and avoided it until now. Thankfully, she feels less anxious and more informed about the process after talking to other teachers who have used this approach to problem solving. Let's see how this interaction goes.

AP: *Mrs. Bernard, your paperwork says that you would like to discuss your concerns about Joshua. The group would like to hear more about how he's doing from your point of view. What can you tell us?*

Mrs. Bernard: *Recently, a lot better in many areas. I have been able to get him off to a better start in the morning, which has a huge impact on his day.*

Counselor: *It sounds like you have figured out some strategies that are working already. What are you doing differently?*

Mrs. Bernard: *I have. I give him choices whenever I can, and I try to encourage him whenever I see him on task. I also notice that he really likes to have a job in the classroom and works hard to be able to run errands for me at the end of the day.*

Teacher: *Wow! I bet you feel relieved that his behavior has improved so much.*

Mrs. Bernard: *I do, but it has also helped me figure out the areas where he is still struggling because I am not seeing much improvement there.*

AP: *What's giving him the most trouble?*

Mrs. Bernard: *Reading. He's still behind, and I notice that he has a hard time getting started and sticking with it even when I use choices and encouragement.*

Reading Specialist: *It sounds like reading is his biggest struggle right now. Would a reading evaluation help at this point?*

In an interdisciplinary team meeting the participants have different lenses through which they hear the information and a unique way of contributing. These meetings enjoy their best outcomes when the members bring their specific knowledge areas with them and their communication skills. In the example above, Mrs. Bernard was interacting with different professionals in her school. Not only did members use open-ended questions, but they also remembered to show that they were listening by paraphrasing what they heard. It is imperative that members use observation, attending, and listening skills, so they can accurately understand the other members' perspectives. This type of interaction where the members take turns, ask questions, and show understanding enables them to develop a plan to help Joshua with his reading that is based on factual information rather than emotion or misconception. The next time you have an opportunity to participate in an interdisciplinary team meeting try to notice what is helping the group and what is keeping the group from reaching its goals. For additional information on team building skills and collaboration in schools, see "Collaborative Teaming" (Snell & Janney, 2005) or "Restructuring for Caring and Effective Education" (Villa & Thousand, 2000).

Future Challenges and Perspectives

Collaboration can be a meaningful process for accomplishing positive interactions among professionals and family members for the good of a student with disabilities. It involves time and effort on the part of all involved but can be effective and well worth the time and energy involved. As our society continues to change, school personnel will continue to face challenges in implementing a collaborative model with families. For example, scheduling meetings outside of regular school hours may become even more challenging as the number of students raised by single parents and working parents continues to grow. As more families become familiar with and participate in early intervention programs, they will have more experience in family-centered services and will expect to continue to actively participate in programming decisions for their children with special needs once they enter the public school system. As teachers continue to face challenges, it is important to remember that change is essential for meeting the needs of all students with disabilities.

Summary

This chapter discussed the role of the family and school professionals in providing educational services to students with disabilities. Emphasis has been placed on developing a collaborative model of interaction. Collaboration in the schools is defined as an interactive process that enables people with diverse experiences and expertise to mutually develop goals, define problems, and create solutions. Discussion has focused on the impact of a child with a disability on the family and the family's role in decision making for their child with special needs. Finally, ideas for fostering successful collaboration among families and school personnel have been discussed, including ways to become an effective communicator.

Classroom Application Activities

1. As individuals or groups, discuss why a team or club of which you were a member was "collaborative" or not.

2. Take a moment and jot down a description of your family as you were growing up. Now take a moment and describe another family in your neighborhood. How were the two families similar? How were they different?

3. Role-play one of the barriers to family participation outlined in the chapter. Describe suggested solutions to overcome the barrier.

4. What are five strategies you could use as a teacher to foster communication between yourself and the families of students in your class?

5. Think about a time when an interpersonal interaction with a teacher discouraged your learning. What behaviors contributed to your feelings of discouragement?

6. Think about a time when an interpersonal interaction with a teacher encouraged your learning. What behaviors contributed to your feelings of encouragement?

7. Brainstorm behaviors you hope to see students exhibiting in your classroom. Write the list on the board. Next to each behavior, develop an encouraging statement rather than a praise statement. Discuss your reactions to the process.

8. Break into small groups to discuss your reactions to the communication skills presented in this chapter. Come back to the larger group and explore what steps you will take in the future to develop these skills and attitudes toward others.

Internet Resources

Center for Effective Collaboration and Practice
http://cecp.air.org

Center on School, Family, and Community Partnerships
http://www.csos.jhu.edu/p2000/center.htm

Children, Youth, and Family Consortium Electronic Clearinghouse
http://cyfc.umn/edu

Directory of Parent Centers
http://www.fesn.org/ptis/ptilist.htm

Early Intervention Family Alliance (EIFA)
www.eifamilyalliance.org

Family Village
http://familyvillage.wisc.edu

Family Voices
http://www.familyvoices.org

Federation of Families for Children's Mental Health
http://www.ffcmh.org

National Center for Children in Poverty
www.nccp.org

National Center on Secondary Education and Transition (NCSET)
www.ncset.org

National Coalition for Parent Involvement in Education
http://www.ncpie.org

National Dissemination Center for Children with Disabilities
www.nichcy.org

Parent Advocacy Coalition for Educational Rights (PACER)
http://www.pacer.org

Parents Helping Parents
http://php.com

Partnership for Family Involvement in Education (PFIE)
http://www.ed.gov/pubs/whoweare/index.html

Teacher-to-Teacher Collaboration
http://teachnet.edb.utexas.edu

The Beach Center on Disability
www.beachcenter.org

The Sibling Support Project
www.siblingsupport.org

Yale Child Study Center—Comer School Development Program
http://www.med.yale.edu/comer/

Online Study Centers

The Family Involvement Network of Educators (FINE)
http://www.gse.harvard.edu/hfrp/projects/fine.html

Family Involvement in Children's Education: Successful Local Approaches
http://www.ed.gov/pubs/FamInvolve/index.html

National Network of Partnership Schools
http://www.csos.jhu.edu/p2000/

References

Bateman, B.D., & Linden, M.A. (1998). *Better IEPs*. Longmont, CO: Sopris West.

Carkhuff, R.R. (2000). *The art of helping in the 21st century* (8th ed.). Amherst, MA: Human Resource Development Press.

Correa, V., Jones, H., Thomas, C., & Morsink, C. (2005). *Interactive teaming: Enhancing programs for students with special needs.* Upper Saddle River, NJ: Pearson Prentice Hall.

Coufal, K. (1993). Collaborative consultation for speech-language pathologists. *Topics in Language Disorders, 14*(1), 1–14.

Dettmer, P., Thurston, L.P., & Dyck, N. (1993). *Consultation, collaboration, and team work.* Boston: Allyn & Bacon.

Dunst. C., Trivette, C., & Deal, A. (1988). *Enabling and empowering families.* Cambridge, MA: Brookline Books.

Epstein, J.L. (1989). Building parent-teacher partnerships in inner-city schools. *Family Resource Coalition Report, 8, 7.*

Falvey, M.A. (2005). *Believe in my child with special needs: Helping children achieve their potential in school.* Baltimore: Brookes Publishing.

Fewell, R.R., & Vadasy, P.F. (1986). *Families of handicapped children: Needs and supports across the life span.* Austin, TX: PRO-ED.

Friend, M., & Cook, L. (2007). *Interactions: Collaboration skills for school professionals* (5th ed., pp. 1–26, 68–69). Boston: Pearson Education.

Gallagher, P.A., Fialka, J., Rhodes, C., & Arceneaux, C. (2002). Working with families: Rethinking Denial. *Young Exceptional Children, 5*(2), 11–17.

Gallagher, P.A., Powell, T.H., & Rhodes, CA (2006). *Brothers and sisters: A special part of exceptional families* (3rd ed.). Baltimore: Brookes Publishing.

Henderson, A.T. (1987). *The evidence continues to grow: Parent involvement improves student achievement.* Silver Spring, MD: National Citizens Committee in Education.

Hill, R. (1949). *Families under stress: Adjustment to the crisis of war and separation.* New York: Harper & Row.

Hill, R. (1958). Social stress in the family. *Social Casework, 39, 139*–150.

Johnson, L.J., Pugach, M.C., & Hawkins, A. (2004). School-family collaboration: A partnership. *Focus on Exceptional Children, 36*(4), 1–12.

Kottler, J.A, & Kottler, E. (2007). *Counseling skills for teachers.* Thousand Oaks, CA: Corwin Press.

Kroth, R.L., & Scholl, G.T. (1978). *Getting schools involved with parents.* Arlington, VA: Council for Exceptional Children.

Kubler-Ross, E. (1969). *On death and dying.* New York: Macmillan.

LaFountain, R.M., & Garner, N.E. (1998). *A school with solutions: Implementing a solution-focused/Adlerian-based comprehensive school counseling program.* Alexandria, VA: American School Counselor Association.

Murphy, A.G. (1981). *Special children, special parents: Personal issues with handicapped children.* Englewood Cliffs, NJ: Prentice Hall.

National Center for Children in Poverty. (2012). *The changing demographics of low-income families and their children.* (Research Brief No. 2). New York: National Center for Children in Poverty. From www.nccp.org.

Pagett, R. (2006). Best ways to involve parents. *Education Digest: Essential Readings Condensed for Quick Review, 72*(3), 44–45.

Parish, S.L. (2007, January). *Material hardship in families raising children with disabilities: Evidence beyond the federal poverty level.* Paper presented at the annual meeting of the Society for Social Work and Research, San Francisco, CA. From http://sswr.confex.com/sswr/2007/techprograms/P7033.htm.

Patrikakou, E., Weissberg, R., Hancock, M., Rubenstein, M., & Zeisz, J. (1997). *Positive communication between parents and teachers.* Philadelphia: Laboratory for Student Success (LSS). From http://www.temple.edu/LSS.

Pugach, M.C., & Johnson, L.J. (2002). *Collaborative practitioners; collaborative schools* (2nd ed.). Denver, CO: Love.

Rugg, M. (2008). *Building on the hopes and dteams of families.* From http://www.ihdd.uga.edu.

Singer, G.H.S. (2002). Suggestions for a pragmatic program of research on families and disability. *Journal of Special Education, 36*(3), 148–154.

Snell, M.E., & Janney, R. (2005). *Collaborative teaming* (2nd ed.). Baltimore: Brookes Publishing.

Strickland, B.B., & Turnbull, A.P. (1993). *Developing and implementing Individualized Education Programs.* New York: Macmillan.

Summer, J., Gavin, K., & Purnell-Hall, T. (2003). Family and school partnerships: Building bridges in general and special education. *Advances in Special Education, 15,* 417–444.

Test, D., Mason, C., Hughes, C., Konrad, M., Neale, M., & Wood, W. (2004). Student involvement in individualized education program meetings. *Exceptional Children, 70*(4), 391–412.

Turnbull, A.P., Brotherson, M.J., & Summers, J.A. (1985). The impact of deinstitutionalization on families: A family systems approach. In R. H. Bruininks & K. C. Lakin (Eds.), *Living and learning in the least restrictive environment* (pp. 115–140). Baltimore: Paul H. Brookes.

Turnbull, A.P., Summers, J.A., & Brotherson, M.J. (1984). *Working with families with disabled members: A family systems approach.* Lawrence, KS: University of Kansas, Kansas University Affiliated Facility.

Turnbull, A.P., & Turnbull, H.R. III. (2001). *Families, professionals, and exceptionality* (4th ed.). Columbus, OH: Merrill.

Turnbull, A., Turnbull, R., Erwin, E., & Soodak, L. (2006). *Families, professionals, and exceptionality* (5th ed.). Upper Saddle River, NJ: Pearson/Merrill Prentice Hall.

U.S. Department of Education, Office of Special Education Programs. (2006). From http://IDEA.ed.gov

Villa, R.A., & Thousand, J.S. (2000). *Restructuring for caring and effective education: Piecing the puzzle together* (2nd ed.). Baltimore: Brookes Publishing.

CHAPTER FIVE

Cultural and Linguistic Diversity: Issues in Education

Nicole Patton Terry and Miles Anthony Irving

CHAPTER OBJECTIVES

- to introduce terminology associated with cultural, racial/ethnic, and language diversity;
- to explore factors related to the academic achievement of culturally and linguistically diverse students;
- to explore issues related to identifying and educating children who need special education services in a diverse society;
- to understand how learning styles influence the learning process for students; and
- to develop effective strategies for teaching culturally and linguistically diverse students.

KEY TERMS

culture • culturally diverse students • social class • socioeconomic status (SES) • ethnicity • race • language • linguistically diverse students • learning style • metacognition • culturally relevant pedagogy

We live in a world with an abundant array of diversity. Diversity is evident in people, the environment, and all forms of life. Advancements in technology have made the world seem smaller and increased the interaction between people from different cultures. The world's economy has become increasingly globalized, fueling the rapid expansion of immigration to industrialized countries over the last 60 years. Today, in the United States, it is not unusual to find classrooms where three or four different languages and cultures are represented. In order to educate the future generations of our society effectively, the education system must be successful teaching all children to communicate and interact with people from different backgrounds and with different abilities. In addition, if we are to maintain a country where social mobility and opportunity are viable possibilities, educators must find ways to offer an excellent education to all students regardless of their background. The purpose of this chapter is to discuss several issues related to educating children in a diverse society.

Characterizing Diversity

Diversity is a fundamental aspect of our world and a defining characteristic of the field of special education. This chapter concerns the education of students from diverse cultural and linguistic backgrounds who may or may not have disabilities that require special education services. For culturally and linguistically diverse (CLD) students, issues of diversity, difference, and disability can be quite complex and challenging for classroom teachers. In order to better discuss these challenges, specific terms common in discussions of diversity require explanation.

Culture and Cultural Diversity

Culture is a broad and comprehensive concept that includes all the ways of being. Culture is learned throughout life as one participates in family and social networks (Gollnick & Chin, 2006). Cultures have several components, including values and behavioral styles; language and dialects; nonverbal communications; and perspectives, worldviews, and frames of reference (Banks, 2006). Cultural practices are shared within a specific group and may or may not be shared across groups. It is important to recognize that cultures are always changing because individuals, groups, and the surrounding environment are always changing. Therefore, it is difficult to develop a single, permanent definition of a culture.

In every culture, subgroups may form. Subgroups can differ by any of the components of culture, including ethnicity, language, class, religion, and geography. These subgroups can be very different from each other, even though they share some traits and values. Often members of the dominant society or subgroup of a culture view their culture as correct and all others as incorrect or even inferior. Historically, the mainstream culture in the United States has been Western European, deriving from political, economic, and language systems in Great Britain (Taylor & Whittaker, 2009). The United States also has a history of limited full access to mainstream culture for those members of society who are not racially white or Caucasian.

In this chapter, the term culturally diverse students is used to refer to "students who may be distinguished [from the mainstream culture] by ethnicity, social class, and/or language" (Perez, 1998, p. 6). As such, this term may refer to students who are from racial/ethnic minority groups, students whose primary language is not English, and students who are from low-income or poor households. However, it is also important to remember that all students are culturally diverse regardless of their ethnicity, race, or socioeconomic status. We limit our definition along lines of ethnicity, social class, and race because of the historic and current marginalization these groups have experienced and how these experiences have resulted in inequitable schooling practices.

In the United States, CLD students are disproportionately overrepresented among poor and low-income households. Therefore, the relationship between culture and social class is relevant to discussions surrounding the education of CLD students. Often the terms social class and socioeconomic status (SES) are used interchangeably and refer to "distinctions not only in income but also in property ownership, occupation, education, personal and family life, and education of children" (Taylor, 1986, p. 22). American institutions, including schools, tend to adopt what are typically thought of as "middle class" ideologies to guide practice. These ideologies are associated with the quality of life of society's economically and socially privileged. Although these ideologies are not exclusively middle class, they are culturally influenced and may manifest in different ways for families from diverse backgrounds.

Race, Ethnicity, and Racial/Ethnic Diversity

Race and ethnicity are often used interchangeably, but they are different. Race is a term that attempts to categorize human beings into distinct groups according to phenotypes or physical traits (e.g., skin color, eye shape). Throughout history, race has been used as a social, cultural, and biological construct to group people (Taylor & Whittaker, 2009). The concept of race has changed over time and continues to be difficult to define because our current knowledge of biological science does not support the idea that there are meaningful biological differences between races. Therefore race is best thought of as a socially constructed category.

Ethnicity is defined by group membership based on heritage, national origin, ancestry, and culture. Ethnicity is understood by the values and cultural norms practiced and maintained by the group. It is defined by the practices, behaviors, and beliefs that support group membership and identification. Ethnicity is not clearly demarcated by the boundaries of race. Meaning, a person who is racially Asian may see themself and be accepted as a member of the Latino ethnic group.

Language and Language Diversity

Language can be defined as a means of communication that shapes cultural and personal identity and socializes one into a cultural group (Gollnick & Chinn, 2006). Language can be nonverbal (e.g., facial expressions, gestures) and verbal (e.g., actual speech used in conversations). Language also includes both oral (i.e., listening and speaking) and written (i.e., reading and writing) components. It is impossible to separate language and culture. One cannot be defined without the other. In order to participate fully in a culture, one must learn that culture's language. Conversely, in order to be fluent in a language, one must learn the culture that language represents.

Students from diverse language backgrounds encounter this difficulty every day in schools. Because language and culture are so intertwined, language minority students are expected to learn and use a new language and new cultural dispositions effectively. Often this new language and culture is different from what they have learned at home. In this chapter, the term linguistically diverse students is used to refer to "students whose first language is either a language other than English or a language other than the middle class, mainstream English used in schools" (Perez, 1998, p. 5). As such, this term refers to students who are second language learners, limited English proficient, bilingual, language minority students, and nonmainstream dialect speakers.

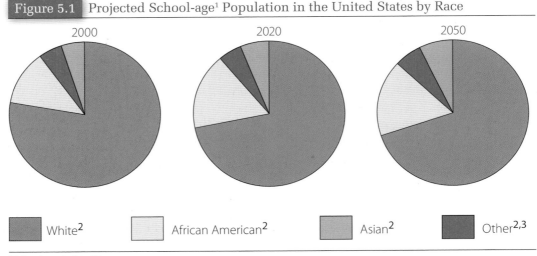

Figure 5.1   Projected School-age[1] Population in the United States by Race

| White[2] | African American[2] | Asian[2] | Other[2,3] |

[1]School age is 5 to 17 years.

[2]Includes individuals of Hispanic and non-Hispanic ethnic origin.

[3]Other includes American Indian/Alaska Natives, Native Hawaiian/other Pacific Islanders, and individuals identified as being of two or more races.

Source: U.S. Census Bureau (2004). *U.S. interim projections by age, sex, race, and Hispanic origin*, http://www.census.gov/ipc/www/usinterimproj/.

Diversity in Schools Today

The changing ethnic, racial, and cultural composition of the United States is well documented. Census data from 2000 indicate several trends toward a more culturally and linguistically diverse society (Hobbs & Stoops, 2002). For instance, one indicator of the changing face of America is that, although the birthrate in the United States is decreasing, the proportion of children from non-white and non-English speaking backgrounds is increasing. In addition, over the last 20 years, the Hispanic population in the United States has doubled. It is estimated that one in every four people in the United States is from a racial or ethnic background other than white. Obviously, these trends are reflected in school populations. Census data from 2000 indicate that the school-aged population is comprised of approximately 1% Indian/Alaskan Native students, 4% Asian/Pacific Islander students, 16% black (non-Hispanic) students, 15% Hispanic students, and 63% white (non-Hispanic) students. As can be seen in **Figure 5.1**, national trends suggest that this diversity will only increase in the coming years. Therefore, teachers must be aware of diversity in their classrooms and how it may impact student achievement.

Teachers must be aware of diversity in their classrooms and how it may impact student achievement.

Factors Influencing the Achievement of Culturally and Linguistically Diverse Students

There is extensive evidence suggesting that students from culturally and linguistically diverse backgrounds experience poorer educational outcomes than their peers (Bennett et al., 2004;

Conchas & Noguera, 2004; Sanders, 2000). Whether examining achievement test scores, grade promotion rates, graduation rates, or other common indicators of school success, CLD students, as a group, tend to perform worse than their peers. The U.S. Department of Education has examined the academic achievement of CLD students with data from the National Assessment of Educational Progress (NAEP). The NAEP is a measure of academic achievement given regularly to students in fourth, eighth, and twelfth grades in public and private schools throughout the United States. The NAEP assesses several academic areas, including reading, math, science, and writing.

The most recent NAEP reports show that white and Asian/Pacific Islander students score higher, on average, than black, Hispanic, and American Indian students in reading and math in fourth and eighth grades (NAEP, 2007a, 2007b; National Center for Education Statistics [NCES], 2011). The same trend was reported for English language learners, who performed more poorly on average than their peers in reading and math in fourth and eighth grades (NAEP, 2007a, 2007b; NCES, 2011). In 2011, among fourth graders who performed the poorest on the reading test, 25% were black, 35% were Hispanic, 74% were from low-income households, and 24% were English language learners. Conversely, among the highest performers, only 7% were black, 11% were Hispanic, 23% were from low-income households, and 2% were English language learners.

Progress in closing the achievement gap between racial/ethnic groups and SES groups has also been explored with the NAEP because it has been administered several times since 1992. The U.S. Department of Education has reported that the achievement gap between white and black students on the NAEP in reading in fourth grade was significantly smaller than that observed when the test was given in 1992 and 2005 (NAEP, 2007b). However, the white–black achievement gap did not change for students in eighth grade. The gap between white and Hispanic students in fourth and eighth grades also did not change from 1992 or 2005 (NAEP, 2007b). **Figure 5.2** shows NAEP reading scores for African American, Hispanic, and white children in fourth grade from 1998 to 2011.

Figure 5.2 Average Scale Scores in Reading on the Fourth Grade National Assessment of Educational Progress, by African American, Hispanic, and White Children

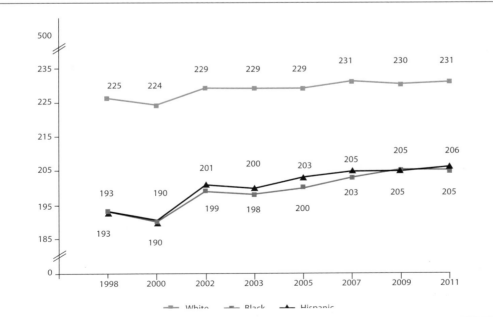

Source: National Center for Education Statistics (2011). *The Nation's Report Card: Reading 2011*(NCES 2012–457). Institute of Education Sciences, U.S. Department of Education, Washington, DC.

Figure 5.3   Average Scale Scores in Reading on the Fourth Grade National Assessment of Educational Progress, by Eligibility for Free or Reduced Price School Lunch Programs.

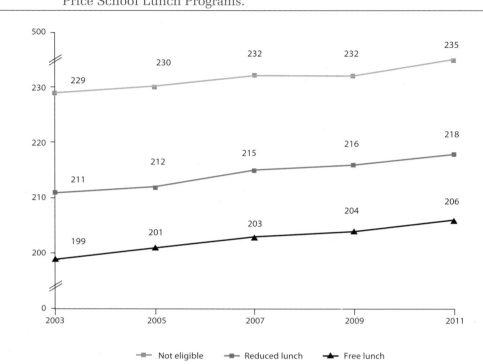

Source: National Center for Education Statistics (2011). *The Nation's Report Card: Reading 2011* (NCES 2012–457). Institute of Education Sciences, U.S. Department of Education, Washington, DC.

Overall, these data indicate that CLD students are struggling in gaining academic skills. Moreover, schools are struggling to provide CLD students with effective instruction to increase their skills. The challenge of uncovering why so many CLD students experience such difficulty in school has been daunting. In fact, it is likely that no one factor can account for why a student or group of students does not perform well in school. The following factors appear to be particularly relevant to the educational success of CLD students.

Socioeconomic Status

On average, children from low SES backgrounds tend to perform poorly on achievement measures. As shown in **Figure 5.3**, this trend has been noted in the NAEP data. The most recent reports from the U.S. Department of Education show that children eligible to participate in federal free and reduced lunch programs (only children from low-income households qualify) performed more poorly than their peers in reading and in math in fourth and eighth grade (NAEP, 2007a, 2007b; NCES, 2011). With the exception of Asian American children, CLD children are represented disproportionately among poor and low-income households. As shown in **Figure 5.4**, whereas 18% of children nationwide lived in poverty in 2009, the rates were 12% for white children, 15% for Asian children, 33% for Hispanic children, 34% for American Indian children, and 36% for black children (Wright, Chau, & Aratani, 2011).

Low Teacher Expectations

Several studies have shown that teachers' expectations of their students were related to student performance and teacher–student interactions in the classroom. Students for whom

Figure 5.4   Rate of Children Who Live in Poverty in 2009, by Race

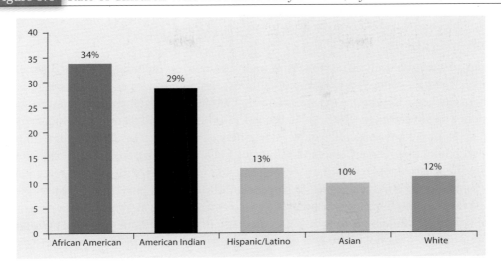

Source: Wright, V. R., Chau, M., & Aratani, Y. (2011). *Who are America's poor children?: The official story*. New York: National Center for Children in Poverty www.nccp.org, Columbia University.

the teacher held lower expectations were called on in class less often, received less positive feedback from the teacher, and received less direct instruction and interaction with the teacher (Entwisle & Alexander, 1988; Ferguson, 1998; Rist, 2000). This differential treatment has obvious implications for student's motivation and behavior in the classroom, both of which are also related to academic achievement.

These low expectations may arise from teachers' personal biases or prejudices against students from different backgrounds. However, low expectations may also arise from teachers' assumptions about the impact of certain student characteristics (e.g., behavior, language use, SES) on academic performance. For instance, a teacher might assume that because a student is from a low-income household, they have fewer books at home and are thus at risk for poor reading achievement. Therefore, the teacher places the student in the low-performance group in their classroom, does not present challenging questions to the student in class, explicitly corrects the student's errors while reading, and teaches less advanced reading skills to the student. Although these behaviors are well intentioned, the teacher's interactions with the student have now changed the quality of instruction the student has received, which may influence the student's reading skill as much as the student's own innate ability. Therefore, teacher expectations are considered to be critical influences on CLD student achievement.

Standardized Test Bias

Considerable research has focused on bias in standardized testing with CLD students, particularly African American children (Jencks & Philips, 1998). As noted above, CLD students tend to perform poorly on such measures. Most tests are now designed to reduce bias between groups. However, their design implies that standardizing administration or scoring will allow one to measure a skill or behavior accurately. Skills and behaviors do not exist apart from contextual and cultural variables, such as prior knowledge, language style differences, or family and home variables (Forman, Minick, & Stone, 1993; Washington, 2001). Although many standardized tests may be statistically unbiased, their administration and the interpretation of the results may not consider cultural or linguistic differences that CLD students may bring to the task. Therefore, test bias continues to be cited as an explanation of apparent poor academic performance among CLD students.

Teacher Quality

In order to function well, schools require many resources, including qualified personnel, adequate financial support, and working facilities. Among schools' most valuable resources are their teachers. Researchers have found that student achievement is related to teacher experience and knowledge (Darling-Hammond, 2000). However, many CLD students attend schools with less knowledgeable and less experienced teachers. For instance, in a study that included school districts in Cleveland, Chicago, and Milwaukee, researchers found that less qualified teachers were more likely to be assigned to schools with a high percentage of minority and poor children (Peske & Haycock, 2006). Others have found that children in high-poverty and high-minority schools are twice as likely to be assigned to less experienced teachers (Mayer, Mullens, & Moore, 2000). Because many CLD students attend high-poverty and high-minority schools with less qualified teachers, teacher quality may partly explain their poor academic performance.

Home–School Mismatch

It is widely accepted that the home environment contributes significantly to student achievement in school. For CLD students, considerable inquiry has focused on whether there are significant mismatches between their home and school environments that may also influence achievement. These mismatches are often attributed to a lack of social or cultural capital—the various linguistic and cultural competencies that schools require for educational success. However, these competencies are not explicitly taught in school, and children may or may not acquire these skills at home.

Consider, for instance, children's storytelling, or narrative, ability. Children's proficiency with narratives is important for reading comprehension and written composition skills. In school, students typically are taught to use *decontextualized* language to tell stories independently, by either retelling events that have occurred or relating their stories to other more familiar stories. Conversely, the storytelling traditions in many African American homes include highly *contextualized* language, joint storytelling with other children, and creative embellishing of events that may or may not have occurred (Vernon-Feagans, Hammer, Miccio, & Manlove, 2002). Schools typically do not place high value in this form of cultural capital (i.e., contextualized storytelling). This mismatch in narrative styles may be reflected in classrooms and on assessments. African American children may be perceived to tell stories less effectively than their peers or they may perform more poorly on assessments that require proficiency with decontextualized language skills. Although these differences in narrative styles may be related to student achievement in school, they do not indicate that African American families place less value on narrative abilities or the importance of decontextualized language for reading success.

Surely, most parents want their children to succeed in school, and this value is likely to be shared between the mainstream culture and CLD families. However, it cannot be assumed that shared values manifest as shared practices. Because differences like these appear to have implications for student achievement, home–school mismatches are often cited as explanations for poor academic performance among CLD students.

Diversity and Special Education

Given the increasing diversity in our society and the complex issues surrounding the academic success of CLD students, teachers must take care when interpreting student performance. Educators must ensure that cultural or linguistic differences are not mistaken for disabilities that affect academic performance. CLD students have been disproportionately placed in special education since its inception. Even after many lawsuits (typically involving African American and Hispanic students) and the passage of legislation designed to guarantee that students are educated and evaluated with culturally fair and nondiscriminatory practices, data from the U.S. Department of Education continues to show that CLD students are misrepresented in special education (Artiles & Trent, 2000; Gollnick & Chin, 2006; Heller, Holtzman, & Messick, 1982; Markowitz, Garcia, & Eichelberger, 1997; National Research Council, 2002).

The percentage of students in special education programs from minority groups is disproportionately high given their percentage in the school age (6–21 years old) population. **Table 5.1** shows the percentage of students, ages 6 to 21, receiving special education services by disability and race/ethnicity in 2007 (Aud, Fox, & KewalRamani, 2010). The distributions are similar to those of previous years. In 2007, 9% of all school age children were served under IDEA. Yet, although American Indian students only constitute 1.2% of the total school age population, they represent nearly 15% of students receiving special education services. The same discrepancies can be seen among African American and Hispanic children. Among all school age children, 14% of American Indian students, 12% of black students, 9% of Hispanic students, 8% of white students, and 5% of Asian students are served under IDEA. Overall, these data suggest that African American, Hispanic, and American Indian students are overrepresented in special education. This misrepresentation of students is also evident by specific disability categories. It is also important to note that CLD students, in particular African American, Hispanic, and Native American students, are underrepresented in gifted and talented programs (Hosp & Reschly, 2004; National Research Council, 2002).

TABLE 5.1

Percentage of Students Ages 6 to 21 served by IDEA, by Disability and Race/Ethnicity, in 2007

Disability	Total School Population	American Indian/ Alaska Native	Asian/ Pacific Islander	Black (non-Hispanic)	Hispanic	White (non-Hispanic)
Total School Population	—	1.20	4.80	17.0	21.20	55.80
All disabilities[a]	8.96	14.38	4.85	12.15	8.51	8.47
Specific learning disability	3.89	7.09	1.60	5.32	4.55	3.42
Speech/language impairment	1.65	2.49	1.34	1.76	1.67	1.74
Mental retardation	0.74	1.01	0.39	1.56	0.59	0.60
Emotional disturbance	0.67	1.11	0.18	1.27	0.41	0.62
Autism	0.12	0.30	0.51	0.36	0.25	0.43
Hearing impairment	0.11	0.14	0.13	0.12	0.13	0.10
Visual impairment	0.04	0.05	0.04	0.04	0.04	0.04

[a] Includes all disability categories served by IDEA, including those not shown on the table.

Source: Aud, S., Fox, M., and KewalRamani, A. (2010). *Status and Trends in the Education of Racial and Ethnic Groups* (NCES 2010-015). U.S. Department of Education, National Center for Education Statistics. Washington, DC: U.S. Government Printing Office.

Diversity presents a unique challenge for educators; especially in the areas of assessment, instruction, and socialization.

This under- and overrepresentation of CLD students in special education programs raises considerable concerns about the denial of access to equal educational opportunity and discrimination on the basis of race, ethnicity, culture, and language. Inappropriate placement in special education programs has significant negative consequences for students' educational outcomes and, ultimately, their quality of life. When students are pulled out of the general education classroom to receive special services, they miss part of the core curriculum and receive instruction that is qualitatively and quantitatively different from that in the general education classroom. Moreover, if it is determined that the student does have a disability and should receive special education services, educators must ensure that the student is receiving culturally and linguistically appropriate intervention and support. Whether a student does or does not have a disability, receiving instruction that is not commensurate with one's ability can lead to low academic achievement, low expectations, decreased motivation and involvement in school, increased placement in lower or vocational tracks, and, ultimately, limited post-secondary education and employment opportunities.

As cultural and linguistic diversity increases in the population at large, so too does it increase in the population of individuals with and without disabilities in schools. As such, diversity presents a unique challenge for educators, especially in the areas of assessment, instruction, and socialization. If differences in culture or language are not considered when administering and interpreting assessments or selecting instructional strategies and social activities, then the result may be academic failure, social isolation, inappropriate referral to special education, or inadequate special education services for students who are culturally or linguistically different.

Educators must also be mindful of the families of students diagnosed with disabilities. It is difficult for any family to accept and adjust to having a child with special needs. The family's attitude toward disabilities and their resultant behavior can be a major factor in the identification of the disorder and the implementation of an intervention program. Families from diverse cultural backgrounds may have beliefs about disabilities that differ significantly from the beliefs of the majority culture. In addition, language differences between the family and school personnel may inhibit the communication of test results and recommendations as well as the expression of parental questions and concerns. Language differences often cause problems in the identification of students who are from diverse cultural or linguistic groups. Educators must be sure to involve the parents of CLD students in the referral, identification, and placement processes in a manner that is sensitive to cultural and linguistic differences. See Chapter 14 for additional suggestions on how to involve families in these processes.

Diversity in Learning

One of the most important things to remember about CLD students is that difference does not mean deficient. Human beings are all different. By just looking at families, it is evident that people look different, think and respond differently, and like different things. People everywhere learn differently, process information in different ways, and look to different external cues for understanding the world. By understanding learning styles, educators can become more aware of how they teach. Moreover, being more reflective and aware of how people learn can improve learning and increase the teacher effectiveness for diverse learners.

Learning Styles

A learning style refers to the way people learn new information. It includes how information is processed and how study habits differ. For example, some students prefer to sit in the front of the class and listen intently to everything the teacher is saying; other students prefer it when teachers use graphs or visual representations of the material. The preferences are associated with which senses a learner uses when learning. Scholars have proposed that students use different perceptual strengths when learning (Kolb, 1984). As noted in **Table 5.2**, these strengths can be auditory (hearing), visual, or kinesthetic (active) in nature. Research on learning styles began to expand in the early 1970s. Today many models and various measures of learning styles exist. It is not clear whether one's learning style is flexible or fixed. However, many people are aware that they have preferences when it comes to the way they learn and study.

This self-awareness of how one learns is related to the concept of metacognition. Metacognition is awareness about one's own cognitive system and includes thoughts about what one knows or does not know. This metacognitive awareness operates as a preliminary skill to regulating learning. Metacognition, which essentially means thinking about thinking, involves a self-reflection process that allows individuals to understand more about how their mind works. It sets the framework for students to have more control over their study strategies by being more effective in regulating their behavior. For example, if a student is aware that he retains information best when he sits in the front of the classroom, then the student has the necessary knowledge to actually regulate his behavior and sit in the front of the class. That basic knowledge or awareness of how one learns best is metacognition. Teachers should also be aware that their students may have learning preferences and develop lesson plans and deliver instruction in a way that actively engages a variety of different learning styles or preferences. Examples of this would include learning by doing (kinesthetic learning), taking the time to explain things clearly (auditory learning), and using charts or handouts (visual learning).

A teacher's understanding that their students may process information differently or may have different strategies for solving problems will allow classroom instruction to more effectively meet the needs of all students. Essentially, by developing this understanding, teachers

TABLE 5.2

Different Types of Learning Styles and the Corresponding Student Learning Preferences and Effective Teaching Practices

Learning Style	Learning Preferences	Teaching Example
Auditory	Listening, talking	Explain things clearly, give verbal examples
Visual	Focusing on handouts and illustrations	Use the overhead projector and handouts with charts and graphs
Active (kinesthetic)	Taking notes and interactive projects	Give hands-on creative assignments, allow the student to interact in different activity centers in the classroom

will begin to learn more about the students in their classrooms. This understanding is critical for developing a relationship with the student that is based on who the student is. Students in our classrooms represent a complex milieu of internal differences and social experiences. By becoming sensitive to the diversity in learning represented among students, teachers can be more effective in generating positive educational outcomes for all students.

Teaching Culturally and Linguistically Diverse Students

Scholars have referred to the way culture plays itself out in the classroom as the hidden curriculum (Jay, 2003). The cultural norms that govern classroom interaction are largely based on white or European American middle-class values. Often there is an implicit expectation that all students will use these norms, even though they are not explicitly taught in the classroom. Educators must recognize that CLD students also have cultural norms and values that they bring into the classroom that may conflict with the teacher's expectations. Teachers are in the perfect position to learn about the culture, norms, and values of their CLD students. By taking an interest in who students are, where they come from, and what their worldview is, teachers can illustrate to them that they care about who they are and not just who they can become.

Attitudes related to power, privilege, and status can make it challenging for some educators to value diversity among their students. For instance, students who may be economically disadvantaged, members of a marginalized racial group, or speak English as a second language are often labeled as at risk, disadvantaged, poor, or underprivileged. Historically, these labels and the perspective associated with them have been referred to as the deficit model (Solorzano & Yosso, 2001). The deficit model is a perspective that characterizes CLD students with a series of negative attributes (e.g., lazy, illiterate, rebellious, violent, and anti-intellectual). This model gained prominence in social science research in the 1960s and 1970s and became associated with culture of poverty theories that are still present today (Gorski, 2008). More recently, deficit theories have been critiqued for blaming the victim, promoting stereotypes, and ignoring classism and institutional causes for poverty and educational underachievement. Nonetheless, such negative attitudes continue to permeate issues related to the education of CLD students.

Instead of focusing on what students cannot do, teachers are encouraged to understand more about their students' strengths and abilities. However, focusing on what children know requires learning more about their culture and the experiences that they bring into the classroom. Educators can then use this knowledge of students' background, interests, and experiences to develop culturally relevant pedagogy. **Culturally relevant pedagogy** is an effective instructional practice and theoretical model that promotes student achievement, supports students' cultural identity, and helps students to develop the critical perspectives needed to challenge inequities in schools and society (Ladson-Billings, 1995). Culturally relevant pedagogy is a healthy model of education that allows children to utilize their strengths (e.g., home language skills, personal interests) as the mechanism for overcoming challenges. For example, many students love to listen to music. They learn about their peer culture through music and use it as a lens to understand their world and themselves. A teacher might employ culturally relevant pedagogy by incorporating music into the classroom. This would allow the students to inject an aspect of their developing identity into their classroom experience, and also allow the teacher to use something the students have interest and expertise in to develop knowledge about math, science, and other traditional academic subjects.

There are school districts in the United States in which over 70 different languages and cultures are represented. A single classroom can have 10 different cultures and 7 different languages represented. It is not realistic to expect teachers to learn the language and everything about the culture of all of their students. Given that every year the student body is constantly changing, it would be virtually impossible to keep up with all of the cultures in some classrooms. What teachers can do is create assignments, lessons, and learning activities that allow the students to share their language and culture with others in the classroom.

Teaching is most effective when the teacher and learner have a healthy relationship. The foundation of a healthy relationship is built as teachers take time to learn about students. Although all educators agree that students need to learn the curriculum, educators can do a much better job of learning about students. By learning about students' interests, cultures, and experiences, educators will be in

When a teacher takes time to learn about students' interests, cultures, and experiences, he/she can apply this understanding to the development of highly educational lesson plans.

a position to develop lesson plans that are exciting, fun, relevant, and, most important, highly educational. Allowing students to infuse aspects of their culture and home language in the classroom will contribute to some students feeling more connected and comfortable with their learning process and assignments.

However, it is important to remember not to single out students who speak a different language or have a different culture. Fitting in is important for many young people, and the last thing they want is to feel as if they are different from everyone else. When interacting with CLD students, teachers are encouraged to be aware of and sensitive to the complex process of adjusting to a new culture or environment. That adjustment to a new environment usually happens most easily when individuals are made to feel a part of the group and welcomed based on their commonalities with the group, not their differences. Using shared commonalities to explore our language, cultural, and individual uniqueness is a wonderful way to celebrate and learn about diversity in a more inclusive manner. See **Figure 5.5** for a case study of Ms. Thompson's third grade classroom. What would you do if Carlos, Rafael, and Kimesha were in your classroom? As a teacher, what kind of individual attention and support would you offer to these students?

Below are some recommendations regarding effective teacher dispositions and practices when working with CLD students:

- Be clear that everyone has cultural biases;
- Be aware of how personal cultural biases may affect your teaching and relationship with students;
- Consider making a home visit to show the student that you are willing to go the extra mile to learn about them;
- Be aware that cultural differences do exist;
- Embrace students' cultural differences;
- Understand that differences are not deficits;
- Do not automatically attribute a student's difficulty to upbringing, low income, or environment;
- Take a positive approach and always build on the student's strengths;
- Do not treat CLD students differently from other students when in a group;

- Use a variety of instructional practices (e.g., cooperative learning, interactive learning, project-based learning); and
- Develop lessons that incorporate the student's culture in the learning process.

Figure 5.5 A Case Study of a Culturally Diverse Classroom

Carlos, Rafeal, and Kimesha are all third grade students in Ms. Thompson's classroom. Carlos is a first generation immigrant to the United States from Brazil. His family moved here with him when he was only 6 years old. Neither he nor his family spoke any English when they arrived, and today Carlos is the most proficient English speaker in his family. At home, Carlos's family only speaks Portuguese. Carlos can understand most of what he hears in English, but he still has a hard time finding words in English when he speaks. Even though Carlos enjoys school, he is very quiet in the classroom and usually only speaks when called upon. The teacher and other students think that Carlos is shy, but at home he is a gregarious and outspoken 9-year-old.

Rafael is also a first generation immigrant. His family moved to the United States from Spain when he was 4 years old. Both of his parents are college educated and speak English. Rafael is fluent in both English and Spanish, and he enjoys art and working with his hands. Rafael also enjoys school, but he is a struggling reader. He is only reading on the first grade level and often has difficulty paying attention during classtime.

Kimesha is an African American girl who was born and raised in the United States. She lives in poverty with both of her parents who are underemployed and struggle to make ends meet. Kimesha is an avid reader and often goes to the library to get books; she is reading on the third grade level. However, Kimesha is constantly clashing with Ms. Thompson in the classroom. Ms. Thompson has sent Kimesha to the principal's office on multiple occasions, and Kimesha has been suspended from school for pushing her books on the floor and talking back to the teacher. Even though Ms. Thompson has a class of 24 students who all need encouragement and attention, Carlos, Rafeal, and Kimesha present unique educational and emotional needs typical of today's students. All three of these students could be referred for special education services. On the surface, Carlos and Rafael could be referred for a special education evaluation for their academic struggles and Kimesha for behavioral problems. However, only one of these children may actually have a disability.

Summary

Our world is remarkably diverse, and this diversity has implications in work, community, and educational contexts. Issues of diversity, difference, and disability can be quite complex and challenging for culturally and linguistically diverse (CLD) students and their classroom teachers. The era of the No Child Left Behind legislation and high-stakes testing discussed in Chapter 2 has left many teachers and educational administrators feeling anxious and overwhelmed with the pressure of school accountability. For some, the joy, creativity, and passion that were once part of teaching have been replaced with testing, accountability, and more testing. The added complexity of diversity in today's schools can make the pressure of delivering an excellent education to students feel overwhelming and arduous for some teachers. Although teaching can be difficult and challenging, it is imperative that teachers find ways to bring wonder, joy, and passion into the classroom. By taking time to connect with and learn about students, teachers have an opportunity to stay connected with the rewards of teaching. These rewards are reciprocal: when the teacher is having fun and enjoying teaching, the students will have fun and enjoy learning.

Classroom Application Activities

1. Define and discuss the differences between the following terms: culture, race, ethnicity, and language.

2. List and discuss two factors that may be relevant to the academic achievement of culturally and linguistically diverse students.

3. Discuss how socioeconomic status is related to the academic achievement of culturally and linguistically diverse students.

4. List one disability category in which students in the following racial/ethnic groups are overrepresented and underrepresented. Discuss why students might be over- or underrepresented in that particular disability category.

    a. American Indian/Alaska Native

        i. Overrepresented:

        ii. Underrepresented:

    b. Asian/Pacific Islander

        i. Overrepresented:

        ii. Underrepresented:

    c. Black (non-Hispanic)

        i. Overrepresented:

        ii. Underrepresented:

    d. Hispanic

        i.   Overrepresented:

        ii. Underrepresented:

    e. White (non-Hispanic)

        i.   Overrepresented:

        ii. Underrepresented:

5. Go to http://www.learning-styles-online.com/inventory/ and take the learning styles inventory to graphically illustrate your learning style.

6. Take some time to engage in some metacognitive self-reflection. Write down five aspects of how your brain works that reflect the way you think. For everything you write, develop a study recommendation that might enhance the way you learn.

7. Complete the following Cultural Artifact Activity (*Note: This activity was adapted from Wilkins, R. [2006]. Cultural Artifact Activity. Originally developed for the University of Georgia Board of Regents On-Line Resource Repository.*)

Description

As a homework assignment, students are instructed to bring an artifact to class that represents their culture. During the next class period, the instructor will first display these artifacts anonymously and ask the students to identify to whom each artifact belongs. Each student will then describe his or her own artifact to the class and explain why this symbolizes his or her culture. The students will engage in a discussion about their personal connection to their own culture and how certain cultural symbols may or may not be related to their concepts of identity.

Suggested Procedures for Instructor

1. *Defining culture.* Engage students in a discussion of the various definitions of culture. Ask them to reflect on their own culture and list general aspects considered when identifying a person's culture. Allow time for students to go beyond the surface and tangible characteristics to more abstract and internal concepts. Also discuss how they believe culture influences their identity.

2. As homework, pass out a lunch-sized brown paper bag to each student and instruct the students to bring in an item, artifact, symbol, etc. that represents the culture with which they most closely identify. The item must fit completely within the paper bag. Tell the students *not* to reveal the contents of their bag when they bring it in.

3. During the next class, students will be asked to identify which item belongs to which student. This should be done with groups of 6 to 10 students. Decide how you want to group the students for the activity and instruct them to place their bags at various locations on the desk or table by group. For example, have the first six students in the class put their bags on one side of the table, the next six in the center, etc. Another separation scheme is to color code the bags by group with small colored dots.

4. Ask the students to gather around the group of bags that includes their own. They can now remove the contents and display each object side by side. Students have only 1 or 2 minutes (depending on the size of the group) to identify which artifact belongs to each student in the group. Have them write their answers down on a piece of paper.

5. After revealing the owners, have each student speak briefly about the object, indicating what it means to them and how it reflects their culture. (For large classes, students can share in groups.)

    a. Did the cultural artifact you brought to class represent aspects of your personal identity, your socially "assigned" cultural designation (Asian, Muslim, African American), or both?

    b. What three cultural aspects would provide the clearest representation of your concept of self in relation to your culture?

    c. What level or component of culture is normally used to understand or define a person's culture in society? in schools?

    d. How will you as an educator create multicultural environments that go beyond "heroes and holidays" in your classroom?

Materials needed: Pen, paper, and brown lunch-sized paper bags, 5/8 inch round color dots from office supply store (optional).

Internet Resources

National Association of Multicultural Educators:
http://www.nameorg.org

Learning-Styles-Online.com:
http://www.learning-styles-online.com/inventory/

National Black Association of Speech-Language and Hearing:
http://www.nbaslh.org

National Center for Children in Poverty:
http://www.nccp.org

U.S. Census Bureau:
http://www.census.gov

Culturally Situated Mathematic Examples:
http://www.rpi.edu/~eglash/csdt.html

National Association for the Education of African American Children with Learning Disabilities
http://www.aacld.org

National Association for Latino Arts and Culture:
http://www.nalac.org

References

Artiles, A.J., & Trent, S.C. (2000). Representation of culturally/linguistically diverse students. In C.R. Reynolds & E. Fletcher-Jantzen (Eds.), *Encyclopedia of special education, Volume 1* (2nd ed., pp. 513–517). New York: John Wiley & Sons.

Aud, S., Fox, M., & KewalRamani, A. (2010). *Status and trends in the education of racial and ethnic groups* (NCES 2010–015). U.S. Department of Education, National Center for Education Statistics. Washington, DC: U.S. Government Printing Office.

Banks, J.A. (2006). *Cultural diversity and education: Foundations, curriculum, and teaching* (5th ed.). Boston: Allyn and Bacon.

Bennett, A., Bridglall, B.L., Cauce, A.M., Everson, H.T., Gordon, E.W., Lee, C.D., Mendoza-Denton, R., Renzulli, J.S., & Stewart, J.K. (2004). *All students reaching the top: Strategies for closing academic achievement gap.* Naperville, IL: North Central Regional Educational Laboratory.

Conchas, G.Q., & Noguera, P.A. (2004). Understanding the exceptions: How small schools support the achievement of academically successful black boys. In N. Way & J.Y. Chu (Eds.), *Adolescent boys: Exploring diverse cultures of boyhood* (pp. 317–337). New York: New York University Press.

Darling-Hammond, L. (2000). Teacher quality and student achievement: A review of state policy evidence. *Education Policy Analysis Archives, 8*(1). From http://epaa.asu.edu/epaa/v8n1/.

Entwisle, D.R., & Alexander, K.L. (1988). Factors affecting achievement test scores and marks of Black and White first graders. *The Elementary School Journal, 88,* 449–472.

Ferguson, R.F. (1998). Teacher's perceptions and expectations and the Black–White test score gap. In C. Jencks & M. Phillips (Eds.), *The Black-White test score gap* (pp. 273–317). Washington, DC.: Brookings Institute.

Forman, E.A., Minick, N., & Stone, C.A. (1993). *Contexts for learning: Sociocultural dynamics in children's development.* New York: Oxford University Press.

Gollnick, D.M., & Chinn, P.C. (2006). *Multicultural education in a pluralist society* (7th ed.). Upper Saddle River, NJ: Pearson.

Gorski, P.C. (2008). Peddling poverty for profit: Elements of oppression in Ruby Payne's framework. *Equity & Excellence in Education, 41*(1), 130–148.

Heller, K.A., Holtzman, W.H., & Messick, S. (1982). *Placing children in special education: A strategy for equity.* Washington, DC: National Academy Press.

Hobbs, F., & Stoops, N. (2002). *Demographic trends in the 20th century: Census 2000 special reports.* Washington, DC: U.S. Census Bureau, U.S. Government Printing Office.

Hosp, J.L., & Reschly, D.J. (2004). Disproportionate representation of minority students in special education: Academic, demographic, and economic predictors. *Exceptional Children, 70,* 185–199.

Jay, M. (2003). Critical race theory, multicultural education, and the hidden curriculum of hegemony. *Multicultural Perspectives, 5*(4), 3–9.

Jencks, C., & Philips, M. (1998). *The Black-White test score gap*. Washington, DC: Brookings Institution.

Kolb, D.A. (1984). *Experiential learning: Experience as the source of learning and development*. Englewood Cliffs, NJ: Prentice Hall.

Ladson-Billings, G. (1995). Toward a theory of culturally relevant pedagogy. *American Educational Research Journal, 32*(3), 465–491.

Markowitz, J., Garcia, S.B., & Eichelberger, J. (1997). *Addressing the disproportionate representation of students from racial and ethnic minority groups in special education: A resource document*. Alexandria, VA: Project FORUM at the National Association of State Directors of Special Education.

Mayer, D.P., Mullens, J.E., & Moore, M.T. (2000). *Monitoring school quality: An indicators report*. Washington, DC: U.S. Department of Education, National Center for Education Statistics.

National Assessment of Educational Progress. (2007a). *The nation's report card: Math*. Washington, DC: U.S. Department of Education, National Center for Educational Statistics, Institute of Education Sciences.

National Assessment of Educational Progress. (2007b). *The nation's report card: Reading*. Washington, DC: U.S. Department of Education, National Center for Educational Statistics, Institute of Education Sciences.

National Center for Education Statistics. (2011). *The nation's report card: reading 2011* (NCES 2012–457). Washington, DC: Institute of Education Sciences, U.S. Department of Education.

National Research Council (2002). *Minority students in special and gifted education*. Committee on Minority Representation in Special Education, Division of Behavioral and Social Sciences and Education. Washington, DC: National Academy Press.

Perez, B. (1998). *Sociocultural contexts of language and literacy*. Mahwah, NJ: Lawrence Erlbaum.

Peske, G., & Haycock, K. (2006). *Teaching inequality: How poor and minority students are shortchanged on teacher quality*. Washington, D.C.: The Education Trust.

Rist, R.C. (2000). HER classic: Student social class and teacher expectations: The self-fulfilling prophecy in ghetto education. *Harvard Educational Review, 70*(3), 257–301.

Sanders, M.G. (Ed.). (2000). *Schooling students placed at risk: Research, policy, and practice in the education of poor and minority adolescents*. Mahwah, NJ: Erlbaum.

Solorzano, D.G., & Yosso, T.J. (2001). From racial stereotyping and deficit discourse toward a critical race theory in teacher education. *Multicultural Education, 9*(1), 2–8.

Taylor, O.L. (1986). *Nature of communication disorders in culturally and linguistically diverse populations*. San Diego, CA: College-Hill Press.

Taylor, L.S., & Whittaker, C.R. (2009). *Bridging multiple worlds: Case studies of diverse educational communities* (2nd ed.). Boston: Pearson.

U.S. Census Bureau. (2004). *U.S. interim projections by age, sex, race, and Hispanic origin*. From http://www.census.gov/ipc/www/usinterimproj/.

Vernon-Feagans, L., Hammer, C.S., Miccio, A., & Manlove, E. (2002). Early language and literacy skills in low-income African American and Hispanic children. In S.B. Neuman & D.K. Dickinson (Eds.), *Handbook of early literacy research* (pp. 192–210). New York: Guilford Press.

Washington, J.A. (2001). Early literacy skills in African-American children: Research considerations. *Learning Disabilities Research and Practice, 16*, 213–221.

Wright, V.R., Chau, M., & Aratani, Y. (2011). *Who are America's poor children?: The official story*. New York: National Center for Children in Poverty.

CHAPTER SIX

Students with Learning Differences Affecting Achievement

Nicole Patton Terry and Melissa A. Leontovich

CHAPTER OBJECTIVES

- to describe the warning signs and characteristics of students with the following disabilities:
  - Specific Learning Disabilities (SLD),
  - Mild Intellectual Disabilities (MID);
- to provide information regarding special considerations for Response to Intervention (RTI);
- to introduce IDEA definitions and unique aspects of determining eligibility; and
- to discuss educational issues related to students with learning challenges.

KEY TERMS

basic psychological processes · significantly subaverage intellectual functioning · mean · standard deviation · adaptive behavior · significant deficits · functional skill

Teachers may not be able to tell that students have challenges in learning by looking at them. However, these students' challenges will become apparent as the students struggle to process verbal information and have difficulty with higher-order thinking skills such as making inferences, drawing conclusions, or predicting outcomes. Teachers should watch for students whose performance on assignments and tests indicate they are having problems processing and demonstrating the knowledge and skills being taught. The majority of students with learning challenges will be successful in school if teachers understand their unique learning needs and adjust the environment, instruction, and assignments accordingly.

As a part of the adjustments to be made, teachers need to monitor their own behavior. Teachers' expectations have a strong influence on the way they respond to students (Van Acker, Grant, & Henry, 1996). If teachers expect students to know an answer, they will wait longer for students to respond. If teachers expect students to fail, the pause for response will be shorter and the teachers' nonverbal communication will be more negative (Sadker, Sadker, Fox, & Salenta, 1994). Effective teachers make sure to use language that the students understand and check their comprehension. For example, the teacher in a sixth grade class told her students to "edit" their work. It was not until one of the more capable students explained to his peers that this meant "fix their mistakes" that the students were able to comply. Kounin (1970) identified specific teacher behaviors that can negatively affect student learning. Teachers who are boring, disorganized, unprepared, or easily side-tracked, as well as those who present material too fast or too slow, will unintentionally cause students to stop attending. To increase student attention and learning, effective teachers will demonstrate the following skills:

- Maintain a comfortable classroom pace,
- Establish a strong sense of purpose,
- Set high expectations for achievement,
- Talk only as much as necessary,
- Focus on academic tasks,
- Structure transitions, and
- Maximize instructional time (keep distractions to a minimum).

Students who demonstrate differences in the way they learn may have difficulty benefiting from typical instructional presentations. Sometimes a change in the way material is presented and emphasized is sufficient to facilitate learning. For example, some individuals learn best when presented with visuals, such as pictures and printed material, to illustrate new information. However, some learning differences cannot be accommodated simply by changing the manner of presentation. Although it is recognized that individualized and intensive instruction may be necessary to promote academic and social achievement for students with learning challenges, it is not known if the instructional strategies vary according to the different eligibilities (Sabornie, Cullinan, Osborne, & Brock, 2005). What is known is that without intervention, individuals with learning challenges have a poor prognosis for success in post-school environments (Luftig & Muthert, 2005; Walker, Ramsey, & Gresham, 2004). For students with mild disabilities, a critical determinant of post-school success is proficiency with the general education curriculum. Indeed, the mandates of the No Child Left Behind Act of 2001 (NCLB) require that the majority of students with learning challenges participate in general education assessments as a part of each school's accountability measure. To promote student achievement, teachers must understand the differences between the categories of learning challenges and must become proficient in implementing instructional strategies shown to be effective across the range of mild disabilities.

This chapter provides an overview of students whose learning needs require differentiated instruction for successful skill development. These students include those with specific learning disabilities (SLD) and mild intellectual disabilities (MID). Both of the disabilities are discussed by first describing the warning signs and characteristics associated with the disability with particular attention paid to how the characteristics may differ across diverse populations. The Response to Intervention (RTI) process, discussed in Chapter 3, is applied to students with characteristics that place them at risk for being identified with a disability in learning. If the RTI process is insufficient for promoting students' learning and achievement, the students may be referred for special education evaluation and deemed eligible for special education services. The assessment process and criteria dictated by IDEA, which must be met for determining eligibility, is described. Finally, issues for the classroom teacher are discussed, covering specific concerns and recommendations that should be considered when working with students with these disabilities.

Specific Learning Disabilities (SLD)

Society places a high emphasis on quick, efficient thought and reactions. For some individuals, the ability to interpret symbols (as in language) and nuances (occurring in social situations) is inhibited. Although of normal or superior intelligence, such individuals are at a disadvantage because of their inability to decode symbols or perceive meaning. If this disadvantage causes a significant impairment, the individual may have difficulty learning the things that are expected at school. Such students are considered to have a specific learning disability (SLD). Often a teacher cannot discern a student with SLD from other students until the student is asked to complete an academic task. Students with SLD may be indistinguishable from same-age peers when they are playing or interacting but may be unable to read aloud when asked. This situation is further complicated by the fact that a student can have a learning disability related to one area, such as reading, and yet perform as expected in another area, such as math. Students with SLD account for the largest percentage of students receiving special education services and also are the most diverse group of students because the disability can affect specific areas of learning and perception which are unique to the individual. **Figure 6.1** provides activities to simulate a learning disability.

SLDs affect an individual's ability to understand and use language and to discriminate differences in visual and auditory stimuli. If you think about it, you'll realize that almost every school task incorporates language. Listening, thinking, speaking, reading, writing, and spelling all involve language. Even calculations must be taught using language. Understanding SLDs has been as challenging for teachers and parents as for the students themselves. Terms that have been used in the past to describe learning disabilities include perceptual handicaps, brain injury, minimal brain dysfunction, dyslexia, central processing disorder, word blindness, and developmental aphasia. The term "specific learning disabilities" has replaced these and other terms.

Characteristics

Students with SLD can have deficits in any or all of the following basic psychological processes: short- or long-term memory; auditory, visual, and haptic discrimination; sequencing; attention; organization; psychomotor skills/visual–motor integration; conceptualization/reasoning; and social perception. These deficits can appear in the classroom as problems of thinking, listening, writing, reading, or speaking and may interfere with any school subject. Even if the student is on grade level in reading, there may be specific failures in mathematics, writing, or in any activity that requires using the deficient skill. For example, oral instructions may be misunderstood, although written instructions are comprehended easily.

Figure 6.1	Activities to Simulate a Specific Learning Disability

To imagine what it would be like to have SLD related to decoding written symbols, read the following two paragraphs. Try to read them aloud while maintaining the same even flow you typically use with reading.

In mobern soceity an inbivibual's ytiliba to be self-sufficient is usually encouraqed fron childhood. By eht tine we are adults, we are ussposed to have learmed to debend upon ourselves, to de as puick on the ward as the next persom and to be ready to dolh our own in a more of less ilesoht world.

Inbequenbence is also comsidered inbortamt so that eno is mot a durben on srehto. This atttiued quts tremendous pressure no the norimyiit mith disapilitiez. Trying to keep threi self-respect im a society that equates inbequenbemce with physical well-being nakes an already tluciffid situation almost elbarelotni, for the bersom with a disahility thinks the sane way. Me neeb to chanqe this boint of viem. It's inportamt to realize that on individual can really tsixe alone. We are all interbeqendent, amd at best, physical deinpendence is variable. Everyome experiences sdoirep of debenqence: illness and dlo age are undiscrinimating. Moral inqebendence, on the other hand, is elbitcurtsedni. (Hale, 1979)

To envision what it might be like to have SLD related to math, here is a simple equation. The math symbol rules are: "÷" means subtract; "+" means to multiply; "−" means to divide; and "×" means to add. Now, cover the rules and find the solution.

$$6 \div 2 + 1 \times 4 - 2 = ?$$

Did you arrive at four as the answer? Well that's wrong. The rules changed again while you were working. Also, that first number is a 9. For some individuals with SLD, it appears as if the rules are constantly changing and that symbols are fluid.

The reverse may be the case for other students with SLD: oral understanding may be intact but there is difficulty in comprehending written instruction. Some specific examples of classroom problems students may exhibit and can be warning signs of SLD are presented in **Table 6.1**.

Teachers must keep in mind that all children may experience difficulty in one or more of these areas at some point in their school careers. For the student with SLD, these problems persist across time and typically are more severe than those of the other students in the class. Students should be assessed for special education services if their problems in these specific areas are not remediated in the Response to Intervention (RTI) process.

By far the most distinguishing characteristic of individuals with SLD is academic under-achievement. Students with SLD may show deficits in one or more of the following skill areas: oral expression, listening comprehension, written expression, basic reading skills, reading comprehension, mathematics computation, and mathematics problem solving. Each of these areas is defined and classroom indicators and instructional supports are provided in **Table 6.2**.

Teachers must also be mindful of the diverse experiences children bring to school and how they may influence performance. Students from diverse backgrounds may exhibit characteristics of SLD that are in fact culturally or linguistically based differences. For example, bilingual and Limited English Proficient individuals may experience great difficulty reading and spelling English words. Further, their difficulties may persist for several years after quality literacy instruction. Teachers must be careful in determining whether these students' performances are reflective of SLD, language differences, or both.

Students with SLD may become frustrated with their own inability to perform as well as their peers who seem to be able to learn so easily. Frustration often translates into anger, nervousness, impulsiveness, and hyperactivity. Students may choose to act out rather than call attention to their inability to complete a task. Or they may choose the opposite route and withdraw from the learning situation by sleeping, daydreaming, or losing interest. Such students often are misunderstood by their teachers and may be accused of being lazy or

TABLE 6.1

Classroom Indicators of Basic Psychological Processing Deficits

Basic Psychological Process	Classroom Indicators
Memory (Short- and Long-Term)	• Makes excuses for things not remembered • Can't recall facts about stories read or TV programs • Can't remember a sequence of letters or numbers • Can't remember where he or she stopped, if interrupted • Overly attentive to detail • Unable to recall sight vocabulary • Can't repeat sentences, numbers, or letters
Auditory Discrimination	• Doesn't pay attention to speech • Unable to locate source of sound • Difficulty assigning voices to people • Can't identify common environmental sounds • Can't discriminate between similar speech sounds • Can't follow oral directions • Can't do oral math problems • Doesn't spell phonetically • Confuses meaning of similar words • Can't blend or sequence speech sounds • Requests things to be repeated
Visual Discrimination	• Reverses, inverts, and confuses letters and words • Omits words and lines while reading • Disregards punctuation • Focuses attention on minor details • Unable to trace designs • Unable to catch a ball • Unable to match shapes and symbols
Haptic Discrimination	• Difficulty locating body parts • Lacks rhythm • Poor handwriting • Can't manipulate scissors, utensils, etc. • Poor athletic ability • Constantly in motion • Slow motor responses
Sequencing	• Cannot correctly sequence items along a dimension such as smallest to largest, lightest to darkest • Cannot follow directions in sequence • Cannot retell a story in sequence • Has poor sense of time
Attention	• Can't concentrate • Shifts attention at inappropriate times • Doesn't finish work on time • Unable to block out background activity • Can't respond to multiple commands or directions • Can't shift from one activity to another • Daydreams

(continued on next page)

TABLE 6.1

Classroom Indicators of Basic Psychological Processing Deficits (*continued*)

Basic Psychological Process	Classroom Indicators
Organization	<ul><li>Sloppy</li><li>Attends to irrelevant details</li><li>Difficulty recognizing missing parts</li><li>Poor directional concepts</li><li>Loses things</li><li>Unable to "get ready" for a task</li><li>Careless</li><li>"Jumps in" before thinking</li><li>Reads word-by-word</li></ul>
Psychomotor Skills/ Visual-Motor Integration	<ul><li>Can't copy from the blackboard</li><li>Can't trace or copy designs</li><li>Appears clumsy</li><li>Can't write or draw between lines</li><li>Grips pencil awkwardly</li><li>Hand trembles with fine motor tasks</li><li>Unable to align numbers or letters vertically or horizontally</li><li>Improper orientation of words or drawings on a page</li><li>Difficulty in running, hopping, skipping</li></ul>
Conceptualization/Reasoning	<ul><li>Lacks vocabulary</li><li>Can't follow directions</li><li>Talks in incomplete sentences</li><li>Can't grasp the main ideas of paragraphs</li><li>Doesn't see things as a whole</li><li>Doesn't recognize cause-effect relationships</li><li>Can't draw conclusions or infer</li><li>Poor sense of time</li></ul>
Social Perceptions	<ul><li>Misinterprets the behavior of his peers</li><li>Misinterprets the meaning of gestures and facial expressions</li><li>Unable to size up social situations</li><li>Unable to make decisions</li><li>Lacks common sense</li></ul>

TABLE 6.2

Academic Skill Deficit Areas for Students with Specific Learning Disabilities

Area	Definition	Classroom Indicators	Instructional Support
Oral Expression	Ability to use spoken language to communicate ideas (as opposed to speech disorders)	• Difficulty labeling • Difficulty relating information in sequence • Difficulty exchanging meaningful conversation	• Use word webs and conceptual maps to visually represent how words and concepts go together
Listening Comprehension	Ability to understand spoken language at a level that is age appropriate	• Difficulty defining words that are used correctly in conversation • Difficulty following basic and multi-step directions • Difficulty retaining what someone has just said • Difficulty recalling information from orally read stories • Difficulty recalling information from oral lectures • Difficulty understanding humor	• Provide student-friendly notes about content in books, stories, and lectures
Basic Reading Skills	Ability to use word attack and sequencing skills in the process of decoding written symbols	• Difficulty remembering what sounds are made by different letters • Difficulty breaking words into component parts • Difficulty recognizing words in isolation • Difficulty in discriminating similar words (e.g., what/that)	• Practice identifying, blending, and segmenting sounds in words (e.g., *What's the first sound in man? Say all of the sounds in mmmmaaannnn*) • Teach students how to sound out words while reading words • Practice reading in sentences and leveled texts (texts that have specific word types that the student has been learning to read)
Reading Fluency Skills	Ability to read connected text accurately and automatically with appropriate expression	• Slow reading rate • Difficulty reading words in connected text that can be read in isolation • Difficulty reading with appropriate prosody and intonation	• Establish a goal for reading a correct number of words per minute, and then let students practice reading the same passage three times to meet that goal • Help students practice reading various kinds of texts • Allow students to practice reading texts with a partner who can model good reading fluency
Reading Comprehension	Ability to process and understand the meaning of written language	• Difficulty remembering what has been read • Difficulty retelling stories in sequence • Difficulty answering questions about material that has been read	• Provide graphic organizers to help students visually represent the content of what they've read • Explicitly teach comprehension strategies (e.g., prediction, sequencing, summarization) • Explicitly teach story grammar (e.g., that all stories have a beginning, middle, and end with characters, setting, plot, conflict, and resolution) • Before reading the text, do picture and word walks through the text, pointing out specific vocabulary and asking students to predict what the story will be about • Model good comprehension monitoring practices by asking questions aloud while reading with students

(continued on next page)

TABLE 6.2

Academic Skill Deficit Areas for Students with Specific Learning Disabilities (*continued*)

Area	Definition	Classroom Indicators	Instructional Support
Math Calculation	Ability to process numerical symbols to derive results, including spatial awareness of symbol placements and sequence algorithms for operations	• Difficulty recognizing numbers • Difficulty remembering basic facts • Difficulty with place value • Difficulty with column alignment • Difficulty with remembering steps in algorithm (e.g., regrouping, long division)	• Provide manipulatives (e.g., counting beads, place value sticks) to use when solving problems • Use graphing paper to write problems, so that all place values are aligned correctly • Place a number line on the student's desk for easy reference
Math Reasoning	Ability to understand logical relationships between mathematical concepts and operations, including correct sequencing and spatial and symbolic representation	• Difficulty determining if solution is correct • Difficulty determining which operation to use in word problems • Difficulty judging the size of objects • Difficulty reading maps and diagrams • Difficulty with time, money, and measurement concepts	• Show students how to represent the problem in drawings or with manipulatives • Teach students key mathematical terms used in word problems (e.g., *difference* means *subtract*; *how many more* means *add*) • Explicitly teach time, money, measurement, volume, and shape concepts
Written Expression	Ability to communicate ideas in writing with appropriate language and formulation skills	• Difficulty with idea organization, organization, and structure of ideas in compositions • Difficulty with writing mechanics (e.g., punctuation) • Difficulty writing grammatically correct sentences • Difficulty applying basic letter-sound correspondences and orthographic rules to spell words • Inconsistent or incorrect size, spacing, alignment, and/or formation when writing letters, words, and numbers • Slow, labored, messy, and often illegible writing products	• Use key words to explicitly teach letter–sound correspondences (e.g., B—boy—/buh/) • Explicitly teach orthographic rules (e.g., the magic E rule) • Provide story starters to help students generate ideas • Explicitly teach grammar, capitalization, and punctuation rules • Provide graphic organizers to help students plan the content of their writing • Use mnemonic strategies like COPS (Always check Capitalization, Organization, Punctuation, and Spelling)

unmotivated. Unfortunately, they have real learning problems that are much more complicated than a lack of motivation.

Students with SLD learn to compensate, but they cannot outgrow or be cured of their disabilities. Fortunately, there are more post-secondary options for students with SLD than ever before. Attendance at colleges and universities has become possible as federal statutes protect the rights of individuals with SLD to enroll and receive appropriate accommodations. Persons with SLD must contact the institution's office of disability services and identify themselves as having a disability. Once this step is taken, the office is responsible for assisting the student and faculty regarding required accommodations within federal guidelines.

Documenting Response to Intervention (RTI)

Much of the research on and implementation of RTI processes like those described in Chapter 3 have involved students with SLD. In fact, many problem-solving models like RTI arose out of two primary concerns for the education of students with SLD. First, many researchers, professional educators, and advocates were concerned that many students diagnosed with SLD did not actually have the disorder (Kavale & Forness, 2003). Rather, these students had "instructional" disabilities and were victims of poor instruction. The second major concern was that many students with SLD were diagnosed too late. These students had experienced failure in school for many years before they were able to receive services. Yet research has shown that the earlier students receive intervention for their learning differences, the more effective those interventions are in remediating and even preventing future learning problems (Snow, Burns, & Griffin, 1998).

In response to these concerns, problem-solving models like RTI have emerged and are now a part of regulations stated in IDEA for SLD. The RTI process emphasizes the student's response to instruction. Therefore, the quality of instruction that the student has experienced in both general education classes (Tier 1) and specialized interventions (Tiers 2 and 3) is critical in determining if the student has SLD and should be evaluated for special education services. As is discussed in the Assessment for Eligibility section, students should not be diagnosed with SLD without sufficient evidence that their learning problems are not due to poor or inappropriate instruction. Further, this evidence must include frequent assessment of the students' progress with the instruction they are receiving. These assessments monitor not only the students' achievement, but also the quality of the instruction they are receiving and whether or not it is effective in alleviating their learning challenges.

Definition

The federal definition of SLD from IDEA is as follows:

Specific learning disability means a disorder in one or more of the basic psychological processes involved in understanding or in using language, spoken or written, that may manifest itself in the imperfect ability to listen, think, speak, read, write, spell, or to do mathematical calculations, including conditions such as perceptual disabilities, brain injury, minimal brain dysfunction, dyslexia, and developmental aphasia. Specific learning disability does not include learning problems that are primarily the result of visual, hearing or motor disabilities, of mental retardation, of emotional disturbance, or of environmental, cultural, or economic disadvantage. [34 CFR 300.8(c) (10)]

The federal definition of SLD includes three critical elements. First, it emphasizes the language-based nature of SLD, noting that deficits in psychological processes underlying language use and comprehension appear to characterize individuals with SLD. Second, the specific academic skill areas affected by SLD are listed in the definition. Third, the definition includes exclusionary criteria, distinguishing SLD from other causes of academic underachievement.

Significant controversy has surrounded the creation of an acceptable definition for SLD. Individuals with SLD represent a heterogeneous population. Because there are so many characteristics of SLD, the disorder can manifest in various ways for different people. One individual may have difficulty reading words, whereas another may only have difficulty understanding the words he can read, and yet another may have difficulty both reading and understanding words. All three of these individuals may have SLD that requires very different types of intervention. This heterogeneity alone makes SLD difficult to define.

Many researchers, professional educators, and advocacy groups have raised several concerns about the current federal definition. For instance, many believe the definition is too vague because it contains terminology (e.g., "psychological processes") that is not clearly defined and can be interpreted in various ways. Consequently, the process of determining eligibility differs across states, resulting in situations where students may qualify for SLD in one school district but not another. Others are concerned that the definition does not reflect the fact that learning disabilities persist into adulthood. Many are also concerned about the definition's implied insistence that SLD cannot coexist with sensory impairments, emotional disturbances, or distinct disadvantages. Finally, the definition does not clearly distinguish between students who have SLD and those whose learning difficulties may be due to poor instruction.

Although there is general recognition that students can have SLD that affects their learning and socialization, it has been difficult to formulate one definition. RTI and new regulations in IDEA, both designed to more clearly determine eligibility for SLD based on both student achievement and instructional quality, may help to clarify the definition of SLD.

Assessment for Eligibility

Under the new regulations outlined in IDEA, students may be found eligible to receive special education services for SLD once three primary conditions have been met. First, a multidisciplinary team of individuals must be convened to determine eligibility as described in Chapter 3.

Second, the team must have sufficient evidence that, even when provided with appropriate instruction, the student has not achieved adequately for his age or grade level in one or more of the following skill areas: oral expression, listening comprehension, written expression, basic reading skills, reading fluency skills, reading comprehension, mathematics calculation, and mathematics problem solving. IDEA states that this evidence may be observational and assessment data gathered from two sources: an RTI process showing the student's unresponsiveness to a scientific, research-based intervention or multiple diagnostic evaluations (e.g., academic or cognitive assessments) showing a pattern of strengths and weaknesses in achievement relative to the student's age, grade level, or IQ.

It is important to note that, irrespective of the data used to show underachievement, IDEA regulates that the school must provide the team with documentation that the student has received appropriate instruction by qualified teachers. If it is determined that the student's learning difficulties might be attributed to poor or inappropriate instruction, then the student should not receive special education services for SLD. Rather, the student must then be provided with quality instruction in general education classes and/or scientific, research-based interventions with qualified personnel. Further, the student's progress must be evaluated with frequent assessments in order to determine the effectiveness of the instruction.

IDEA regulates that the school must provide the team with documentation that the student has received appropriate instruction by qualified teachers.

Finally, the team must determine that the student's underachievement is not primarily the result of other conditions or circumstances, including a visual, hearing, or motor disability; intellectual disabilities; emotional disturbance; cultural factors; environmental or economic disadvantage; or limited English proficiency. Once these conditions have been met, and it is determined that the student's learning problems are due to SLD, the team may determine the services the student should receive.

Issues for the Classroom Teacher

Often the classroom teacher is the first person to notice a student's learning problem because SLD generally is not identified before the child enters the academic setting. During the kindergarten year, many of these problems are thought to be related to lack of maturation. The student may begin to struggle when the demands of reading are increased in subsequent grades. The transition into middle school or junior high is another difficult time period for students with SLD. Often the changes of classes and teachers during the day can be over-whelming. Teachers at all grade levels should be observant of their students in order to refer a student at any grade.

Teachers must be aware of some of the signs of SLD. Common classroom signs of deficits in psychological processes are presented in Table 6.1, and academic deficits are presented in Table 6.2. Teachers should closely observe students who demonstrate persistent and severe problems in one or more of these areas. The RTI process may need to be documented for these students who, after Tier 3, may be referred for eligibility assessment for SLD. Again, many students will exhibit deficits in one or more of these areas at some point in their school careers; care must be taken to avoid inappropriately referring students whose problems are minor and/or transitory.

Students with SLD are typically educated in general education settings. During elementary and middle school years, students tend to receive more support from a core group of teachers who are familiar with their learning differences. As students move into high school, the curricular expectations become more stringent as end-of-term tests, graduation tests, and Carnegie units needed for graduation become priority concerns. With NCLB, the emphasis on having content-specific teachers provide instruction tends to create a focus on acquisition of content rather than the acquisition of learning strategies. Unfortunately, the emphasis on content acquisition and the threat of high-stakes testing can shift the emphasis away from the unique challenges experienced by students with SLD. Many students with SLD will have

Teachers need to be aware of possible problems in the social interactions of students, as some students with SLD fail to understand social cues and nuances.

been exposed to strategy instruction in previous grades but may have difficulty applying those skills in the rigorous curriculum. In the high school setting, difficulties with basic learning strategies such as note-taking can have a detrimental effect on the comprehension and retention of content information. High school students with SLD may need assistance in understanding how to apply basic learning strategies such as reading in content areas, note taking, test taking, and written expression across content areas in order to promote their academic achievement (Boyle & Weishaar, 2001).

There are a number of strategies teachers can use to enhance the performance of students with SLD. Providing a highly structured environment will help students develop routines, and the habits involved with following the routines will provide boundaries for their behavior. Another teaching strategy involves creating modified time schedules so that teachers are checking the students' progress more frequently and reminding them of what needs to be done next. In addition, teachers need to be aware of possible problems in social interactions as some students with SLD fail to understand social cues and nuances. These students may benefit from specific social skills training.

To summarize, students with SLD may benefit from the following strategies:

- Structured environments,
- Predictable routines,
- More frequent progress checks,
- Structured methods of reminding students of what happens next,
- Direct teaching of social skills and learning strategies, and
- Academic accommodations specific to the area of disability (e.g., computers for composing/writing, spell checkers, books on tape, calculators).

The issue of "fairness" in the use of accommodations for students with SLD often is difficult for the general education teacher. Because SLDs are "hidden disabilities," other students in the classroom may believe that the teacher is being "unfair" by making such accommodations. Addressing this in the classroom can be difficult. Teachers must approach this issue mindful of the importance of confidentiality; teachers should never justify the use of accommodations with students by revealing that the students have SLD. Effective teachers differentiate instruction for all students, not just those with identified disabilities. Teachers can remind students that their job is to facilitate learning based on individual need and then turn the focus back to the students who cried "unfair" to ensure that their needs are being met. Specific strategies for remediating the academic problems of students with SLD are presented in Chapter 7. **Figure 6.2** presents a case study of a student with SLD.

Mild Intellectual Disabilities (MID)

There are many labels used in referring to students with mental retardation, such as "students with intellectual disabilities" or "students with developmental disabilities." At this time, the term "mental retardation" is used in the definition found in IDEA (2004); however, advocates prefer and promote the use of the term "intellectual disabilities." Unless referring specifically to IDEA, the term intellectual disabilities is used in this text. Students with Mild Intellectual Disabilities (MID) are described in this chapter. Chapter 12 provides an in-depth look at students with moderate to severe intellectual disabilities.

| Figure 6.2 | Case Study of a Student with SLD |

Nia is a 9-year-old student in fourth grade. She is a good student who behaves well in class and enjoys socializing with her friends. She has excellent reading, spelling, and math skills. However, she began to struggle with writing last year. Nia often had difficulty finishing writing assignments. Although she was able to talk about her ideas for writing, she was unable to put those ideas down on paper. She also had difficulty using paragraph structure in her writing. Her paragraphs did not always have a main idea sentence. Sometimes she added too many supporting details, and other times she did not add enough. Moreover, the supporting details were often just lists of ideas and lacked cohesion. Although her paragraphs lacked structure and cohesion, her sentence structure, spelling, and vocabulary usage were appropriate. Still, Nia was shy about her writing and did not participate fully in writing lessons in class. At the end of her third grade year, Nia was diagnosed with a specific learning disability and began to receive special education services for written expression. With co-teaching support, Nia's ability to write one-paragraph essays improved. She continues to receive this support in fourth grade.

Now in fourth grade, Nia's teacher, Mr. Jarrett, was concerned about Nia's performance in his classroom. Her classmates were learning to write three- and five-paragraph essays. Also, Mr. Jarrett was teaching his students how to write in different genres (e.g., narrative, expository, persuasive), all of which had different text structures. Mr. Jarrett began to worry that Nia could not benefit from writing instruction in his classroom. Mr. Jarrett met with Ms. Walker, the special education teacher, to discuss his concerns. With her support, Mr. Jarrett began to incorporate several learning strategies in his classroom with Nia and with all of his students. For instance, Mr. Jarrett used different kinds of graphic organizers to help students organize their ideas and allowed his students to choose which graphic organizer worked best for them. Ms. Walker also suggested he use sentence and story starters to help the students develop their writing ideas. Mr. Jarrett also decided to teach only one writing genre at a time, beginning with expository writing. Because there are several types of expository products, Mr. Jarrett was able to differentiate instruction so that some of his more advanced students could write book reports while others could write descriptive essays. Meanwhile, Ms. Walker would co-teach the class during writing lessons to help all of the students with their writing. She co-taught a lesson on how to use a graphic organizer specifically designed for three-paragraph essays. In addition, Mr. Jarrett allowed Nia to continue writing one-paragraph essays for classroom assignments, but encouraged her to write two- and three-paragraph essays in her journal writing.

Within a few weeks, Mr. Jarrett began to notice improvement in all of his students' writing skills. Although Nia still struggled with three-paragraph writing, she was able to write one-paragraph essays well and was working on two-paragraph essays. With the help of graphic organizers, she was able to come up with more cohesive ideas for her essays. Nia was also attempting to write various kinds of expository writing in her journals and classroom assignments. She even contributed articles to the classroom newspaper. Mr. Jarrett noticed that Nia participated in the writing lessons in his classroom more often. She contributed ideas, offered to edit her classmates' papers, and generally appeared to enjoy writing time.

Characteristics

The majority of students with MID will begin school in the general education setting. There are a number of warning signs that general education teachers will notice early in the school year. Young children in kindergarten and first grade who are unable to verbalize their thoughts and label common objects easily and who may be difficult to understand due to articulation problems tend to quickly catch the attention of early childhood teachers. Additional language cues might include difficulty in answering questions, providing descriptions, or learning new words. Other warning signs will include the students struggling academically due to poor memory, poor reasoning, and poor comprehension. Not only will teachers notice these students struggling with academic tasks, but they will also notice students having difficulty at mealtimes with their utensils or struggling with managing their needs in the restroom. Teachers want to document these differences as they notice them and begin thinking about interventions for the RTI process.

Physical characteristics of students with MID typically do not distinguish them from the general population. Most often, teachers will be unable to suspect MID by looking at the physical appearance of the student. Beirne-Smith, Patton, and Ittenbach (1994) report some differences in motor development, growth rate, and sensory defects. Because the cause of the disability will be unknown for the majority of students with MID, there is no distinctive pattern of physical characteristics. However, students diagnosed with specific syndromes, genetic conditions, or chromosomal abnormalities such as Down syndrome, Fetal Alcohol syndrome, or Fragile X syndrome will have distinct physical features and related medical problems (Batshaw & Perret, 1992). Students with specific syndromes may be classified as having MID, or the syndrome may result in the presence of moderate to severe levels of intellectual disabilities.

There are strong trends in the demographic characteristics of students with MID. More males than females have MID. This can be attributed to factors such as syndromes associated with sex-linked genetic disorders, role expectations of male students, and the behavior of male students in the school setting that results in referral for special education services. Students from minority cultures and low socioeconomic backgrounds are overrepresented in the population of students with MID (Oswald, Coutinho, Best, & Nguyen, 2001).

The unique characteristics of students with MID will differ from students who are developing typically in terms of their cognitive development, learning, communication, motivation, and adaptive behavior. These differences can lead to challenges in the classroom for both the teacher and student. **Table 6.3** delineates some of these differences.

TABLE 6.3

Characteristics of Mild Intellectual Disabilities

Characteristics	Definition/Description	Classroom Indicators	Instructional Support
Cognitive Development	The ability to perceive, understand, and process information within an academic and functional setting. Cognition develops at a slower rate and a lower level than same age peers.	• Performs best in concrete operations rather than abstract operations. • Reads significantly below grade level. • Can perform basic math calculations of addition, subtraction, multiplication, and division up to three digits. • Understands the basic concepts of science and social studies. • Comprehension of written information and abstract concepts are extremely difficult.	• Provide hands-on activities • Provide repeated practice • Direct instruction for phonics and reading • Read content material while listening to audio textbook
Learning	The ability to process information in an attempt to gain new information or skills. Significant learning problems in many areas.		
• Attention	Inability to discriminate relevant from irrelevant information.	• Difficulty recognizing color, size, or shape of objects and symbols (letters and numbers). In a functional setting does not recognize the size or color of a key to match the door lock.	• Highlight important features with highlighter • Allow frequent breaks
	Short attention span.	• Difficulty concentrating for entire class sessions.	

TABLE 6.3

Characteristics of Mild Intellectual Disabilities (*continued*)

Characteristics	Definition/Description	Classroom Indicators	Instructional Support
● Mediation	Inability to cognitively sort or evaluate alternatives in learning new information.	● Difficulty organizing, creating images, attaching meaning, and classifying new information (e.g., fails to use the technique of crunching together into groups the first three and second four digits in a phone number or not using addition to correct subtraction).	● Provide graphic organizers with pictures ● Visual and auditory prompts
● Memory	Problems of storing information in the brain's short-term memory.	● Forgetting facts and other information within seconds after the presentation—using repetition and additional practice increases the likelihood of storing information in long-term memory.	● Repeated practice of important information ● Provide information in written form such as guided notes
● Generaliz-ation	Difficulty taking skills and information and applying them in new situations.	● Problems calculating the discount percentage price in the classroom versus calculating it in the local clothing store.	● Use calculator ● Teach across a variety of classroom and community settings
Comunication	The ability to send and receive messages with others. Communication skills are significantly below age peers.	● Fifty percent of the students have an articulation problem noticed when pronouncing their words during conversation. ● May not follow directions or use vocabulary that is adequate to the lesson. Other examples would include the use of shorter sentences, speaking infrequently, and misunderstanding questions.	● Use short sentences and simple vocabulary ● Repeat questions and instructions ● Encourage students to speak in class
Motivational	Factors that affect the use of skills and knowledge to learn or function in society. Poor motivation interferes with learning.	● Tend to have an external locus of control so that they will blame others or situations without realizing their responsibility or role (e.g., "My Mom worked late last night so I couldn't do my homework") ● A debilitating fear of failure prevents students from attempting new activities. What appears to be a lazy student is often covering for a "Why try, I'll only fail the task" attitude. ● A sense of outer-directedness causes students to distrust themselves and look to others to tell them what to do.	● Teach self-monitoring skills ● Provide high levels of positive verbal encouragement ● Rewards for a job well done

(continued on next page)

TABLE 6.3

Characteristics of Mild Intellectual Disabilities (*continued*)

Characteristics	Definition/Description	Classroom Indicators	Instructional Support
Adaptive Behavior	The ability to meet the expectations of one's age, gender, culture, and environment including school, home, and, community. Significant deficits in two or more of the following areas:		
	communication	• Difficulty communicating personal information when lost or in need of help.	• Provide identification cards
	self-care	• Lack the skills to meet hygiene standards such as wearing appropriate clothing that is clean and neat or maintaining the cleanliness of their body and hair.	• Explicit instruction in self-care skills.
	home living	• Difficulty in managing the financial aspects and maintenance of a home like paying bills, cooking nutritional meals, and organizing clutter.	• Task analyze skills and teach each step.
	social skills	• Typically have poor social skills that cause them to be socially isolated by behaving like a young child using temper tantrums or crying to control the situation.	• Provide social skills instruction and behavior intervention plan.
	community use	• Utilizing community resources such as the bank, mall, library, laundry, recreational facilities, etc., create a significant challenge due to the requirements of traveling independently and continuous decisions that must be made.	• Provide instruction in the community setting.
	self direction	• Determining life goals and projecting the necessary skills to meet those goals is an ongoing struggle.	• Provide instruction in self-determination. • Assist students to identify post-school support.
	health and safety	• Knowledge of basic first aid, accessing medical assistance, and maintaining good health becomes overwhelming and may create risky situations.	• Provide instruction in health and personal safety such as seeking help.

TABLE 6.3

Characteristics of Mild Intellectual Disabilities (*continued*)

Characteristics	Definition/Description	Classroom Indicators	Instructional Support
	functional academics	• Applying basic math skills to money management, time, and measurement are difficult. Reading the newspaper, mail, email, contracts, applying concepts such as directionality remain a lifelong challenge.	• Direct instruction for reading and math. • Provide instruction in money management skills such as debit card use.
	leisure	• Participation in, being a spectator at, or just understanding the rules of various sports; learning skills and obtaining equipment or materials needed for a hobby; and financing activities such as going to the movies or out to eat become a barrier to the quality of life.	• Provide direct instruction in low-cost leisure skills such as board games.

As adults, persons with MID are capable of holding down jobs, living independently, marrying, raising families, and enjoying recreational and leisure activities within the community (Seltzer et al., 2005). Job placements often include repetitive factory work, maintenance, and service in fast food restaurants. Many adults with MID live independently with supervision provided by social workers or family members on an as-needed basis. Other adults need more closely supervised living arrangements and live in supervised apartments or group homes. Limitations to adult endeavors are imposed by the lack of community support and not by the characteristics of these individuals. However, adults with MID continue to be unemployed or underemployed, with fewer opportunities for independent living, community involvement, and social interactions (Keogh, Bernheimer, & Guthrie, 2004; Luftig & Muthert, 2005).

Documenting Response to Intervention

When teachers observe students having difficulty communicating, struggling to learn new concepts and skills, and being frustrated by the demands of daily living skills such as eating, toileting, dressing, and interacting with peers, necessary steps should be taken to begin a Response to Intervention (RTI). During the Tier 1 interventions, specific skills may need to be taught to the class or a group of students in the class. Students may not have experience with books or know how to look at the pictures and talk about what they see. A lack of exposure to written text, verbal interactions, or games and songs about the alphabet may cause a child to lack communication and learning skills. Classroom instruction specifically targeting exposure and opportunity for language development would be needed. Teaching rituals and routines during lunchtime or bathroom breaks may provide sufficient intervention for students struggling with the tasks of daily living. Some students may need to be taught to eat with certain utensils they have not used before. A major part of Tier 1 interventions is collecting data to indicate how easily and quickly a student learns the needed skills. It is imperative that Tier 1 interventions include physical, hearing, and vision screenings to determine if problems identified in any of these areas need to be addressed.

Looking closely at the data for individual students will determine the need for more intensive intervention. Students whose data indicate they are making progress in developing the skills that at first appeared to be a warning sign may just need reminders and continued practice. Students whose data indicate they are not making progress or they are very slow in making progress will need Tier 2 interventions. For students struggling with developing language, small group lessons that utilize explicit instruction can target specific sentence structures (e.g., subject-verb) or vocabulary development for the concepts (e.g., big/small). Groups may be taught 2 days a week by the general education teacher or a reading or math specialist, or individuals may require one-on-one instruction for brief periods. Targeting behaviors such as how to take turns or using a fork may require individual attention with constant reminders and reinforcement and may require the support of a paraprofessional. Students who enter school lacking a certain level of maturity may require targeted intervention or more time to develop academic skills and appropriate social skills. Constant attention to the data that indicate progress toward student goals is necessary to determine the need for more intensive intervention.

Tier 3 intervention may be delivered in small groups or with individual students.

Students who continue to make very little progress or very slow progress toward academic or social/behavioral skill attainment will need Tier 3 interventions. Students requiring this level of support will be identified by data that indicate their achievement and behavior are well below what is expected for their age/grade level. This intensive intervention may be delivered in small groups or with individual students several days a week or for longer periods of time. Research-based academic programs and materials may be used by a reading or math specialist. Students who are unable to meet the goals that have been identified for them after Tier 3 interventions should be referred for a complete psychological evaluation contingent on parental permission.

Definition

Mental retardation (intellectual disability) is defined in IDEA as follows:

> Mental retardation means significantly subaverage general intellectual functioning, existing concurrently with deficits in adaptive behavior and manifested during the developmental period that adversely affects a child's educational performance.

The term **significantly subaverage intellectual functioning** describes information regarding a person's intelligence. This information is typically assessed using a standardized intelligence test such as the *Wechsler Intelligence Scale for Children–Third Edition (WISC-III)* or the *Stanford Binet IV.* After years of testing thousands of individuals, researchers found that scores from these tests fell along a continuum and created a bell-shaped curve. **Figure 6.3** displays the distribution of scores from intelligence testing and the percentages of the population that fall within these ranges. The calculations of means and standard deviations are made using statistical procedures during the development of the various tests.

Significantly subaverage intellectual functioning is defined as two or more standard deviations from the numerical **mean** of an individualized intelligence test. The mean is the

Figure 6.3 Normal Distribution of IQ Scores

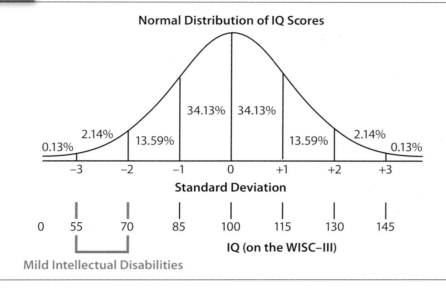

average score obtained when all the scores are added together and divided by the number of people who took the test. The most commonly used intelligence tests have a mean of 100 with a **standard deviation** of 15 or 16. A standard deviation is a unit of measure that indicates how much an individual score differs from the mean. For example, the Wechsler tests have a mean of 100 and a standard deviation of 15. A score of 85 would be one standard deviation below the mean, and a score of 70 would be two standard deviations below the mean. Standard deviations also go above the mean. A score of 115 would be one standard deviation above the mean, and a score of 130 would be two standard deviations above the mean. Standard deviations above the mean are considered when assessing a student's needs for gifted programs. However, to be considered for eligibility under the category of intellectual disability, the score on the Wechsler would have to be 70 or below. As shown in Figure 6.3, students who score between two and three standard deviations below the mean (55–70) could be considered for eligibility as having MID.

According to the American Association on Mental Retardation (AAMR, 1992; now called the American Association on Intellectual and Developmental Disability [AAIDD]), it is critical that the student have significant deficits in adaptive behavior in addition to the significantly subaverage intellectual functioning. **Adaptive behavior** is defined by Grossman (1983) as "the effectiveness or degree with which individuals meet the standards of personal independence and social responsibility expected for age and cultural group" (p. 1). According to the AAMR (1992), skill areas included in adaptive behavior are as follows:

- Communication,
- Self-care,
- Home living,
- Social skills,
- Community use,
- Self-direction,
- Health and safety,
- Functional academics,
- Leisure, and
- Work.

Deficits in adaptive behavior indicate the student's difficulty in communicating, taking care of personal needs such as hygiene and dressing appropriately, functioning in the home and social setting, utilizing community agencies and services, planning and carrying out personal plans, managing their health and other safety issues, using academics in daily living applications such as purchasing clothing, and participating in leisure, recreational, and work activities.

Assessment for Eligibility

Students who continue to struggle after Tier 3 interventions should be recommended for a complete psychological evaluation to determine their eligibility for special education services. All information and data collected during the RTI process will be used by a team of professionals to guide their decisions regarding the types and specific tests that best match the student's needs. Students who are suspected of having MID will be assessed by a multidisciplinary team of professionals, with additional information obtained from parents and teachers. This team generally will consist of a psychologist, educational diagnostician, speech-language pathologist, and others if needed, given the nature of the student's problems. Specific information regarding the student's intellectual abilities, academic achievement, adaptive behavior, and speech-language skills will be obtained.

The assessment of students for MID focuses on two major areas: intellectual abilities and adaptive behavior. **Significant deficits** must be found in both areas. In the area of intellectual abilities, a psychologist will administer an individual intelligence test that results in numerical scores. To be eligible for services in the category of MID, the student must score 55–70 on the intelligence test. A five-point standard error of measurement allows for some variation, meaning that the eligibility team could determine a student eligible for MID services with an IQ up to 75.

A significant deficit in intellectual abilities alone will not qualify a student as having MID. There must be significant deficits in adaptive behavior as well. For years, students who had significant deficits in their academics were placed in special education programs for students with intellectual disabilities. However, these students functioned without problems in the community and at home. More often than not, these students were overrepresented from culturally and linguistically diverse populations. Early awareness of this inequity led to the 1972 court case *Larry P. v. Riles,* which required the use of culturally nonbiased assessments in California. This requirement was incorporated into Public Law 94-142 as it was signed in 1975. States continue to work toward ensuring that students from culturally and linguistically diverse groups are not overrepresented in special education (Skiba, Poloni-Staudinger, Gallini, Simmons, & Feggins-Azziz, 2006).

Deficits that focus on the student's ability to function outside of the school setting are measured using tests that assess how the student is performing in various areas of adaptive behavior. This information is obtained through interviewing the student's parents and teachers. Typically, the interviewer will ask the informant to describe how the student performs certain tasks. For example, parents would be asked to describe how their child eats a slice of roast beef. The interviewer would be listening to determine if the student had specific skills such as using a fork, cutting with a knife, and so forth to score this item. The scores are calculated according to the various test directions to determine if significant deficits are found compared to the norm for the student's age.

Additional assessment in the areas of speech, language, academic achievement, and any motor or physical concerns are completed to identify additional strengths and weaknesses of the student. Deficits in language and speech articulation often coexist with MID. Speech-language pathologists will identify various structures in a student's communication pattern to determine intervention needs. Speech articulation assessments focus on the way words are pronounced and identify sounds that require intervention. For certain students, a physical therapist and/or occupational therapist will assess the student's motor functioning in relation to the school setting (such as their gait, position of pencil, dressing skills, etc.). This information will be used to further document eligibility and assist in planning the student's individual educational program (IEP).

Issues for the Classroom Teacher

Inclusion of students with MID continues to challenge educators (Smith, 2007). Students with MID will have deficits in language, cognition, and adaptive behavior that will make it difficult for them to access grade-level curricula as dictated by NCLB. General education and special education teachers continually struggle with determining appropriate curriculum objectives in the effort to reconcile students' needs with federal mandates. At the elementary level, students with MID often receive instruction in academic content areas in general education settings (Taylor & Larson, 2000). Given the mandates of IDEA and NCLB, students with MID will be expected to participate in the general curriculum and high-stakes testing as they grow older.

Teachers must decide the specific outcomes of a lesson that are critical for students with MID in terms of their performance on the assessments as well as their long-term prognosis as independent adults. To enable students with MID to acquire important information, general education and special education teachers must adapt materials and teaching strategies. Planning for appropriate instruction requires teachers to discuss accommodations and/or modifications for students with MID. Careful consideration must be given to determine if the content should be accommodated or modified. Once content is modified, the student has been taken off the state performance standards and an expectation for successful completion of grade-level state assessments has been greatly lowered. It is important to remember that special education services should not be an automatic modification to ensure that students with MID make high grades. A well earned "C" on work that has been accommodated is far more beneficial than an "A" on work that has been modified. For example, teachers must identify the basic essential information needed to discriminate between vertebrate and invertebrate animals for fifth grade students in the general education setting. Although students without disabilities expand on the discrimination with in-depth detail of the content, students with MID may be taught to focus on the essential differences and are exposed to repetition of the information in various modalities such as lecture, video, and hands-on activities. Appropriate accommodations on high-stakes testing related to vertebrates and invertebrates will allow students with MID to demonstrate their mastery of the content and promote school success in meeting adequate yearly progress. Such adaptations can be time-consuming as well as procedurally difficult for teachers. Use of technology and collaboration strategies discussed in later chapters may be helpful in addressing some of these procedural challenges.

With higher academic expectations for students with disabilities under NCLB, there has been a dramatic shift in curricular expectations in regard to reading and math instruction for students with MID (Cole, Waldron, & Majd, 2004; Conners, Atwell, Rosenquist, & Sligh, 2001). The emphasis has moved from teaching basic sight words to a phonetic approach to decoding. Developmentally, students with MID may have difficulty acquiring phonetic understanding in kindergarten and first grade, but they may be more capable of accomplishing the task if it is introduced later. Unfortunately, by the time students with MID are ready to benefit from a phonetic approach, it is no longer being taught as a part of the general curriculum. Consideration may need to be given to retaining students with MID in early grades to allow exposure to instruction that will be beneficial for subsequent acquisition of reading skills.

At the high school level, expectations for students with MID heavily emphasize the goal of obtaining a general education diploma. The majority of students with MID are educated in the general education classroom with the co-teaching model. This allows the student access to the general education curriculum necessary to pass the high-stakes graduation tests while receiving specialized instruction from the special education teacher in the general education classroom.

In addressing the issues of academic standards and social inclusion, the classroom teacher must decide how to grade the student with MID. Often this issue is embedded in the teacher's sense of fairness. Questions concerning the meeting of curriculum standards, adapting the requirements for the student with MID, or altering the grading procedures by allowing things such as retesting, effort, or using pass-fail instead of numerical/letter grades may depend on the teacher's understanding of the disability (Bursuck, Polloway, Plante, Epstein, Jayanthi, & McConeghy, 1996). For students with MID to succeed in the general education class, there is no question that accommodations must be made. How teachers make these decisions is highly dependent on collaboration among general education and special education teachers, parents, and the student at the IEP meeting.

Another major concern for the classroom teacher is the social inclusion of the student with MID. Cognitive and behavioral characteristics interfere with making and sustaining friendships, which can result in students being socially isolated. In general, students with MID act immaturely, and it would not be uncommon for students with MID to pout when things do not go their way or act silly when it is time to be focused. Such behaviors create challenges for teachers trying to integrate the students and maintain the respect and dignity of everyone in the class (Cullinan, Sabornie, & Crossland, 1992). Often parents of other students in the class are concerned with the impact this student may have on the behaviors of their children. Social integration of the student with MID requires that students, parents, and teachers use problem-solving techniques to create a variety of strategies for success.

In addition to the general education classes, students with MID require electives that will prepare them for the adult working world. Such electives will focus on job training and functional skills. A **functional skill** is one that is required for living an independent and productive adult life. Secondary reading instruction should focus on applying skills already learned to enable the person to live as independently as possible. For example, being able to read signs that provide directions, letters or email that contain information, and notes from relatives would be functional in contrast to reading novels that can now be purchased in audio format. In math, the outcome for students with MID is to be able to calculate measurement, costs of items and wages, as well as to manage money. At the high school level, an emphasis on post-school employment shifts the priority toward inclusive vocational instruction in order to promote independent living, community involvement, and social interactions (Luftig & Murhert, 2000).

General education and special education teachers must work together to meet the educational needs of students with MID. Through appropriate accommodations and modifications, students with MID will have access to the general education curriculum and vocational/technical training necessary to ensure independent and productive post-school functioning. This is the ultimate goal of IDEA and NCLB. **Figure 6.4** presents a case study of a student with MID.

| Figure 6.4 | Case Study of a Student with Mild Intellectual Disabilities |

Melvin entered the world with a bang! His mother had been in labor for less than 2 hours and had received very little prenatal care. A beautiful baby boy, Melvin weighed slightly less than 6 pounds and struggled to keep his breathing at a constant pace. The day after his arrival, Melvin went home to be welcomed by his three older brothers and two sisters. Life in a three-bedroom house with one bathroom was chaotic at best with two adults and six children.

During his early childhood, Melvin hit the developmental milestones but much later than his older siblings. When he finally learned to walk, he took off and enjoyed following everyone outside to play. Melvin was 4 when he was finally toilet trained, and his older sisters had to help him dress each morning while Mom was cooking breakfast. No one in the family really thought much about the fact that Melvin didn't talk much. It was hard to understand what he was saying anyway, and his brother closest in age to Melvin had to interpret what he was saying for people outside the family.

At age 4, Melvin attended the Head Start program just three blocks from his house. The Head Start bus picked him up just after the other siblings caught their bus for school. The teachers at Head Start noticed that Melvin did not talk as well as the other children. During center time, he was not interested in doing any of the academically related tasks. When given a choice, Melvin headed to the toys in the back of the class and played with them in an immature way; everything was an object to be thrown. When discussing their concerns with Melvin's mom, the teachers decided that his behaviors and lack of interest in academic activities were related to being the baby of such a large family. As the year progressed, Melvin made little progress in his language or behavior development.

The next year brought a big change in Melvin's life. Being in kindergarten was really different. The school was big, and there were so many locations to go to during the day, including the classroom, gym, cafeteria, media center, music room, and art room. Melvin felt lost for a big part of the day. In class, everyone was expected to sit for long periods of time, and the teacher expected Melvin to be working on something or looking at a book. Giving all the students a chance to settle into the routines of kindergarten, Melvin's teacher decided to wait and see if after the first month of school Melvin would engage more in the learning activities. When October came, Melvin's teacher scheduled a conference with his mom to talk about the kinds of behaviors she noticed in the classroom. During the conference, Melvin's mom shared the concerns of his teachers at Head Start and how she had noticed that he had always been slower to develop than his siblings. They agreed to work together to help Melvin develop appropriate kindergarten skills. At school, Melvin's teacher began to use a timer and reinforced Melvin for sitting in his chair during table time. Books were carefully selected based on things that Melvin was interested in during his group's reading time. During activity time, the paraprofessional sat next to Melvin and reminded him of the tasks he needed to complete.

At the end of October, Melvin's mom came back for a conference with his teacher and together they looked at how he was progressing. He was sitting for longer periods of time, but he still could not answer questions about a story that had been read aloud. Academic tasks remained a mystery to him. It was determined that Melvin needed more support through Tier 2 interventions. The goals would be for him to answer who and what questions about a story, identify the letters in his name, and name his body parts. Melvin would be grouped with three other students with the Title 1 reading specialist providing instruction 2 hours per week. Melvin's mom planned to attend the weekly parent make-and-take sessions that provided activities to do at home. After 6 weeks of working on specific targets with the Title 1 teacher, Melvin had learned the first letter of his name and 4 of the 10 body parts. He could answer who and what questions with 25% accuracy. After conferencing, it was determined that Melvin required Tier 3 interventions.

For 6 weeks, Melvin continued to work on his goals and gained skills in counting to 5 and identifying math concepts such as long/short, more/less, and big/little. In mid-March, the student support team had an in-depth conference and Melvin's mom, teacher, Title 1 teachers, the assistant principal for instruction, and the special education teacher carefully reviewed the data from the beginning of the school year. Melvin had not made the progress that was expected, and he was far behind his peers in academic knowledge and skills. He continued to get lost at school and while playing with friends in the neighborhood. In the mornings, he was unable to dress himself, and mealtime was always messy. It was decided that Melvin should be referred for a comprehensive evaluation. His mom quickly gave her signed permission as she was fully confident that his teachers and the school had Melvin's best interests in mind and had kept her informed and considered her concerns.

Melvin was evaluated by a team of professionals. His mom was interviewed by a psychologist to determine how he functioned at home and in the community. The psychologist also gave Melvin a standardized intelligence test. The speech-language pathologist evaluated Melvin's language and speech (articulation, fluency, voice) skills. The special education evaluator completed several achievement tests to determine Melvin's current level of performance. To address the difficulties Melvin had with writing and eating, the occupational therapist administered a battery of assessments to determine strength and coordination in Melvin's hands. Once the assessment information was compiled, the evaluation team determined that Melvin was eligible for special education services by meeting eligibility requirements for mild intellectual disabilities. It was also determined that Melvin required additional speech and language services and occupational therapy.

At the placement meeting, it was decided that Melvin would continue to receive his special education services and support services in the general education classroom. Special education services would be provided by a special education teacher for 10 segments per week. Both speech-language and occupational therapy would be provided in the general education classroom during activity time. The IEP was written, and services began immediately.

In May, another conference was held, and it was decided that Melvin would repeat kindergarten with all services remaining in place. During the next year, Melvin began to identify letters and name all his body parts. He could write his name, but his letters were very large. Lunchtime was a little less messy, and he could dress himself but could not tie his shoes. Melvin began to speak in short sentences, and he could answer who and what questions with 50% accuracy. At the end of the year, Melvin was promoted to first grade with all services continuing. In first grade, Melvin was taught to sight read with the Edmark reading program. He used the program for 2 years and could read on a first grade level. During the third grade, Melvin's special education teacher used the Reading Mastery program with him. He continues to improve his reading skills, and although reading comprehension is difficult for him, he can predict what might happen in a simple story.

Summary

Students with learning challenges, such as those who are identified as having SLD or MID, can benefit from appropriately planned educational services in general education classrooms. Federal legislation reflects an awareness that the most promising post-school outcomes are associated with an education that aligns with the general education curriculum. IDEA and NCLB mandate that students with learning challenges receive their education in the same settings as their peers without disabilities to the maximum extent appropriate and participate in the same assessments. With few exceptions, students with mild disabilities are required to participate in the same high-stakes testing as their peers without disabilities and earn a high school diploma (Johnson, Stodden, Emanuel, Luecking, & Mack, 2002). The federal mandate for evaluating a student's response to intervention (RTI) emphasizes the importance of documenting use of evidence-based practices in general education settings prior to considering eligibility for special education services.

Teachers may be overwhelmed at first when faced with some of the unique needs presented by students with learning challenges. Students identified with SLD present a unique profile of strengths and weaknesses that create as much frustration for teachers as they do for the students. The inconsistent and sporadic mastery of tasks evident in students with SLD creates daily challenges in instruction. Students with MID, with their limitations in intellectual functioning and adaptive behavior, may need a high degree of support and accommodation and modifications to be successful in general education classrooms. Teachers may need to be vigilant about recognizing social altercations among some of their students without disabilities and those with mild disabilities, because students with SLD and MID are more likely to be victims of teasing and bullying.

All students with mild disabilities will participate to some degree in general education settings and have academic goals aligned with the general education curriculum. Understanding the differences among the categories of mild disability will enable teachers to be more aware of the behavior and learning differences of all students. Although initially an intimidating prospect, general education teachers possess the content knowledge and pedagogy to successfully educate students with mild disabilities. Incorporating instructional strategies effective for students with mild disabilities will likely produce benefit for all students in the general education classroom. All students with mild disabilities as per IDEA will receive some level of additional support. Collaboration between general education teachers and special education teachers is the key to the most favorable post-school prognosis for students with SLD and MID.

Classroom Application Activities

1. Examine the list of skills that Kounin (1970) ascribed to effective teachers. In contemplating your own personality and style, which of these will present a challenge for you, and how will you plan to become more proficient in these skills to support the attention and learning of all students in your classroom?

2. Individually or in groups, compare and contrast the characteristics and eligibility requirements of students with SLD and MID. Which academic, social, and behavioral characteristics will be similar, and which will be specific to each category?

3. Individually or in groups, identify two behaviors that a teacher might see in the classroom for both of the following disabilities. Describe implications specific to these behaviors:

    a. SLD

b. MID

4. Individually or in groups, describe three characteristics of a student with SLD and MID and give two critical components that will support the student's learning in your classroom.

5. Interview a general education teacher in your preferred content area (e.g., secondary biology, elementary art, early childhood) and ask about accommodations that are used for students with learning challenges.

6. Compare and contrast the Tier 1, 2, and 3 interventions used to document RTI in the case studies presented for Nia and Melvin.

7. Locate an adult who has SLD or MID. If you do not already know someone with one of these disabilities, you can ask your instructor for recommendations or go through a local agency supporting individuals with mild disabilities. Interview the adult to find out where the person works and the types of things she does for fun. Ask about experiences in school and find out who her favorite teacher was and why.

Internet Resources

American Association on Intellectual and Developmental Disabilities
http://www.aamr.org

Intervention Central
http://www.interventioncentral.org

LD On-Line
http://www.ldonline.org

Learning Disabilities Association of America
http://www.ldanatl.org

Response to Intervention Action Network
http://www.rtinetwork.org

The Arc (Association for Intellectual and Developmental Disabilities)
http://www.thearc.org

References

American Association on Mental Retardation. (1992). *Mental retardation: Definition, classification, and systems of supports* (9th ed.). Washington, DC: Author.

Batshaw, M., & Perret, Y. (1992). *Children with disabilities: A medical primer.* Baltimore, MD: Paul H. Brookes.

Beirne-Smith, M., Patton, J., & Ittenbach, R. (1994). *Mental Retardation.* New York: Merrill.

Boyle, J.R., & Weishaar, M. (2001). The effects of strategic notetaking on the recall and comprehension of lecture information for high school students with learning disabilities. *Learning Disabilities Research and Practice, 16,* 133–141.

Bursuck, W., Polloway, E.A., Plante, L., Epstein, M.H., Jayanthi, M., & McConeghy, J. (1996). Report card grading and adaptations: A national survey of classroom practices. *Exceptional Children, 62*(4), 301–318.

Cole, C., Waldron, N., & Majd, M. (2004). Academic progress of students across inclusive and traditional settings. *Mental Retardation, 42,* 136–144.

Conners, F.A., Atwell, J.A., Rosenquist, C.J. & Sligh, A.C. (2001). Abilities underlying decoding differences in children with intellectual disability. *Journal of Intellectual Disability Research, 45*(4), 292–299.

Cullinan, D., Sabornie, E.J., & Crossland, C.L. (1992). Social mainstreaming of mildly handicapped students. *The Elementary School Journal, 92,* 339–352.

Drews, C.D., Yeargin-Allsopp, M., Decoufle, P., & Murphy, C.C. (1995). Variation in the influence of selected sociodemographic risk factors for mental retardation. *American Journal of Public Health, 85*(3), 329–334.

Epstein, L.J., Taubman, M.T., & Lovaas, O.I. (1985). Changes in self-stimulatory behaviors with treatment. *Journal of Abnormal Child Psychology, 13,* 281–294.

Fletcher, J.M., Morris, R.D., & Lyon, G.R. (2003). Classification and definition of learning disabilities: An integrative approach. In H.L. Swanson, K.R. Harris, & S. Graham (Eds.), *Handbook of learning disabilities* (pp. 30–56). New York: Guilford Press.

Grossman, H.J. (Ed.). (1983). *Classification in mental retardation.* Washington, DC: American Association on Mental Deficiency.

IDEA: Individuals with Disabilities Education Act of 1990, 15, 20 U.S.C. 1401 (1990).

Individuals with Disabilities Education Improvement Act of 2004, 20 U.S.C. §1400 et seq. (2004) (reauthorization of the Individuals with Disabilities Act of 1990)

Johnson, D., Stodden, R., Emanuel, E., Luecking, R., & Mack, M. (2002). Current challenges facing secondary education and transition services: What research tells us. *Exceptional Children, 68,* 519–531.

Kavale, K.A., & Forness, S.R. (2003). Learning disability as a discipline. In H.L. Swanson, K.R. Harris, & S. Graham (Eds.), *Handbook of learning disabilities* (pp. 76–93). New York: Guilford Press.

Keogh, B., Bernheimer, L.P. & Guthrie, D. (2004). Children with developmental delays twenty years later: Where are they? How are they? *American Journal on Mental Retardation, 109,* 219–230.

Kounin, J. (1970). Discipline and group management in classrooms. New York: Holt, Rinehart and Winston.

Luftig, R.L., & Muthert, D. (2005). Patterns of employment and independent living of adult graduates with learning disabilities and mental retardation of an inclusionary high school vocational program. *Research in Developmental Disabilities, 26,* 317–325.

No Child Left Behind Act of 2001, 20 U.S.C. 70 § 6301 *et seq.* (2002)

Oswald, D.P., Coutinho, M.J., Best, A.M., & Nguyen, N. (2001). Impact of sociodemographic characteristics on the identification rates of minority students as having mental retardation. *Mental Retardation, 39,* 351–367.

Sabornie, E.J., Cullinan, D., Osborne, S. & Brock. L. (2005). Intellectual, academic, and behavioral functioning of students with high-incidence disabilities: A cross-categorical meta-analysis. *Exceptional Children, 72,* 47–63.

Sadker, M., Sadker, D., Fox, L., & Salata, M. (1994). Gender equity in the classroom: The unfinished agenda. *College Board Review, 170,* 14–21.

Seltzer, M., Floyd, F., Greensberg, J., Lounds, J., Lindstromon, M., & Hong, J. (2005). Life course impacts of mild intellectual deficits. *American Journal on Mental Retardation, 110,* 451–468.

Skiba, R.J., Poloni-Staudinger, L., Gallini, S., Simmons, A.B., & Feggins-Azziz, R. (2006). Disparate access: The disproportionality of African American students with disabilities across educational environments. *Exceptional Children, 72,* 411–424.

Smith, M.D. (1995). *A guide to successful employment for individuals with autism.* Baltimore: Paul H. Brookes.

Smith, P. (2007). Have we made any progress? Including students with intellectual disabilities in regular education classrooms. *Intellectual and Developmental Disabilities, 45,* 297–309.

Snow, C.E., Burns, M.S., & Griffin, P. (Eds.). (1998). *Preventing reading difficulties in young children.* Washington, DC: National Academy Press.

Van Acker, R., Grant, S.B., & Henry, D. (1996). Teacher and student behavior as a function of risk for aggression. *Education and Treatment of Children, 19,* 316–334.

Walker, H.M., Ramsey, E., & Gresham, F.M. (2004). *Antisocial behavior in school: Evidence-based practices* (2nd ed.). Belmont, CA: Wadsworth.

CHAPTER SEVEN

Approaches to Instruction for Students with Learning Differences

Kimberly Viel-Ruma, Nicole Patton Terry, and Adrienne Stuckey

CHAPTER OBJECTIVES

- to identify appropriate assessment procedures that document student achievement and progress, and to describe the role of assessment in designing instruction;

- to describe the environmental foundations of academic learning time, the zone of proximal development, and differentiation of instruction and their impact on student achievement;

- to describe the components and sequence of general models of effective instruction; and

- to identify, describe, and provide examples of the multiple ways instruction can be delivered, including teacher-directed and student-directed approaches.

KEY TERMS

allocated learning time · engaged learning time · differentiation · zone of proximal development (ZPD) · teacher-directed approaches · student-directed approaches · explicit instruction · implicit instruction · direct instruction · advance organizers · mnemonic devices · concept map · Venn diagram · cooperative learning

Over half of all students with disabilities spend the majority of their school days and receive instruction in general education classrooms (U.S. Department of Education, 2011). Most of these students have high-incidence disabilities (e.g., specific learning disabilities, speech-language impairments, or emotional disturbances). In Chapter 6, it was presented that regardless of disability category, many students with disabilities have learning differences. Given the likelihood of having students with disabilities in their general education classrooms, it is critical for general education teachers to have practical knowledge of a wide variety of research-based approaches to instruction to maximize student opportunities for success.

The purpose of this chapter is to identify a variety of approaches to instruction and to examine specific strategies that can be implemented across numerous content areas and in multiple instructional settings. General approaches are described followed by specific strategies that support performance in the areas of reading, writing, and math.

The chapter is organized around several principles on which teachers can rely to successfully design instruction for all students (see **Figure 7.1**). The first principle is to ensure teachers fully comprehend the academic content that they are mandated to cover within their courses. Chemistry teachers require a different set of core content knowledge than language arts teachers; therefore, training programs for teachers vary across the disciplines. The second principle is to utilize assessment to better understand students' academic skills and deficit areas. Teachers cannot know how to proceed with instruction without knowledge of their students' prerequisite skills and current levels of performance. The third principle is to ensure the classroom environment is focused on learning. Class time and structure must maximize students' learning opportunities. The fourth principle is to select effective approaches to instruction and procedures to successfully teach the content. Last, teachers must not rely on a single teaching strategy, but should differentiate the instructional strategies they use based on the needs of students.

Step 1: Understand the Academic Content for Students with Learning Differences

Students with learning differences often exhibit difficulties accessing the course content in the same manner that students without learning difficulties do. **Table 7.1** lists some of the common critiques of conventional curriculum design and identifies several short- and long-term solutions to these issues. Some material in many content area textbooks may be inappropriate, both in design and content, for many students with such learning differences (Rose, 2001). The material may be too abstract or students may lack the learning strategies needed to access and comprehend the material. It is not uncommon, for example, to encounter a student in ninth grade who is reading at a fifth grade level. This student likely lacks the foundational skills necessary to read and understand a ninth grade level text. The challenge for both the general education and special education teacher is to help the student master

Figure 7.1   Principles of Successful Instruction

STEP 1.	Understand the academic content you want to teach
STEP 2.	Assess students' skills and deficits in that content
STEP 3.	Establish a learning-focused environment
STEP 4.	Select effective approaches to instruction and procedures to teach the content
STEP 5.	Differentiate instruction

TABLE 7.1
Design Problems in Curriculum Materials and Possible Solutions

Design Problem	Short-Term Design Adaptation	Long-Term Instructional Goal
1. Abstractness. The content appears too conceptual, hypothetical, and impractical.	Provide students with more concrete examples, analogies, interpretations, or experiences.	Teach students how to seek more examples, explanations, and interpretations through questioning and research.
2. Organization. The organization is not clear or is poorly structured.	Make the organization explicit for students by creating graphic organizer and reading guides and inserting cues that focus attention.	Teach students how to survey materials and identify text organization, read to confirm organization of ideas, and reorganize information for personal understanding and use.
3. Relevance. The information does not appear to have any relationship to students or their lives.	Make the connections between the information and students' lives explicit by building rationales and tying information to student experiences.	Teach students to ask appropriate questions about relevance, search for personal connections, and explore ways to make content relevant when given material that appears irrelevant to their lives.
4. Interest. The information or presentation of the information is boring.	Present information of an assignment in ways that build on students' attention spans, participation, strengths, and interests.	Teach students self-management strategies for controlling attention in boring situations and how to take advantage of options and choices provided in assignments to make work more interesting.
5. Skills. The information is written at a level that assumes and requires skills beyond those possessed by students.	Present information in ways that use the skills students have.	Provide intensive instruction in basic skills required for basic literacy to middle-school students who are unprepared for secondary school content.
6. Strategies. The information is presented in ways that assume that students know how to approach tasks effectively and efficiently in strategic ways.	Provide instruction in learning strategies to students who do not know how to approach and complete tasks.	Cue and guide students in how to approach and complete learning and performance tasks by leading them through complex tasks.
7. Background. Understanding information usually requires critical background knowledge, but students often lack the experiences and concepts (or cannot make connections to personal background experiences) to make new information meaningful.	Present information in ways that provide background experiences or make background linkages clear.	Teach students how to become consumers of information from a variety of information sources and how to ask questions of these sources to gain background knowledge and insights.
8. Complexity. The information or associated tasks have many parts or layers.	Break down the information or tasks and present them explicitly and in different ways so that students can learn and perform.	Teach students how to "chunk" tasks, represent complex information graphically, ask clarifying questions, and work collaboratively in teams to attack complex tasks.
9. Quantity. There is a lot of difficult or complex information that is crucial to remember.	Present the information in ways that facilitate remembering.	Teach strategies for chunking, organizing, and remembering information.

(continued on next page)

TABLE 7.1

Design Problems in Curriculum Materials and Possible Solutions (continued)

Design Problem	Short-Term Design Adaptation	Long-Term Instructional Goal
10. Activities. The instructional activities and sequences provided do not lead to understanding or mastery.	Provide students with scaffold learning experiences that include additional or alternative instructional activities, activity sequences, or practice experiences to ensure mastery at each level of learning before instruction continues.	Teach students to independently check and redo work, review information, seek help, ask clarifying questions, and inform others when they need more or different types of instruction before instruction in more content begins.
11. Outcomes. The information does not cue students how to think about or study information to meet intended outcomes.	Inform students about expectations for their learning and performance.	Teach students how to identify expectations and goals embedded in materials or to create and adjust goals based on previous experiences with similar materials.
12. Responses. The material does not provide options for students to demonstrate competence in different ways.	Provide opportunities to students to demonstrate what they know in different ways.	Teach students how they can best demonstrate competence, identify and take advantage of performance options and choice when they are offered, and request appropriate adaptations of tests and competency evaluations.

Taken from Lenz, B.K. & Schumaker, J.B. (1999). *Adapting language arts, social studies, and science materials for the inclusive classroom*, pp. 12–13. Reston, VA: Council for Exceptional Children.

not only the ninth grade content but also the foundational skills necessary to be successful in accessing the ninth grade curriculum. The reason for this is that these foundational skills are critical to the success of students with learning differences, and all students must master several foundational skills to succeed in these areas as well as in their other content area classes. However, because students with learning differences may not be performing at grade level expectations, teachers may need to teach or re-teach skills that are not specified in state curriculum or the classroom textbooks. In order for these students to be successful in school, they may need instruction in several foundational skills and the classroom content. Ample research evidence is available about what reading, writing, and math skills to teach, and about how best to teach them to students who have learning differences. **Table 7.2** briefly introduces skills identified as critical for students with learning differences in the areas of reading, writing, and math. What should be evident from this table is that reading, writing, and math are complex processes. However, a necessary first step is assessing which skills the student has mastered and which skills still require instruction.

Step 2: Assess the Students' Skills and Deficits Areas

Students' instructional needs cannot be met until those needs have been identified. There are several types of assessment used in educational settings for a variety of different purposes. There are screening assessments that are used to identify potential areas of strength and weakness for groups of students. Screenings are regularly administered, broad-field tests given to the entire school body that may or may not be connected to the curriculum. These screening tests are frequently given schoolwide group-administered achievement or benchmark assessments. Although classroom teachers often proctor these exams and review the results, they do not develop them. These assessments are typically used to identify students

TABLE 7.2

Critical Areas of Reading, Writing, and Math Instruction

Skill Area:	Brief Definition and Characteristics	Potential Grades for Instruction	
		Typical Students	Students with Learning Differences
Reading:			
Print Knowledge	Knowledge of the forms, functions, and uses of print • Reading from left to right • Knowing the difference between pictures, symbols, letters, numbers, and punctuation marks • Mechanics (capitalization and punctuation rules)	Preschool Kindergarten–3rd Grade	Preschool Kindergarten–12th Grade
Alphabet Knowledge	Knowledge of letter names, sounds, and formation • Knowing letter names • Knowing letter sounds • Writing letters	Preschool Kindergarten	Preschool Kindergarten–3rd Grade
Phonological Awareness	Playing with and manipulating sounds in words • Rhyming • Identifying, blending, and segmenting sounds in words (e.g., tell me the 1st sound in "bat")	Preschool Kindergarten–1st Grade	Preschool Kindergarten–5th Grade
Alphabetic Principal (Phonics and Spelling)	Understanding that letters map onto sounds and using that knowledge to "sound out", read, and spell words. • Matching letters and letter combinations to their sounds (e.g., B says "buh"; EE says "eeee") • Reading and spelling one syllable and multisyllabic words	Kindergarten–5th Grade	Kindergarten–12th Grade
Reading Fluency	Reading text quickly and correctly with appropriate expression • Reading at an appropriate rate with few errors • Reading with an appropriate tone and prosody	3rd–5th Grade	3rd–12th Grade
Vocabulary	Understanding and using words to form meaning orally and in texts. • Knowing a lot of words (breadth) or a lot about a single word (depth) • Linking known and unknown words • Multiple meaning of words	Preschool Kindergarten–12th Grade	Preschool Kindergarten–12th Grade
Reading Comprehension	Gaining meaning from text by both extracting knowledge and constructing new knowledge • Using background knowledge and life experiences to understand text • Predicting what will happen next • Inferring what the author meant	3rd–5th Grade	3rd–12th Grade
Writing:			
Handwriting	Writing print, shapes, and other forms with appropriate formation, size, alignment, and spacing • Writing letters and numbers • Lining up numbers in a math problem • Producing geometrical shapes	Preschool Kindergarten–1st Grade	Preschool Kindergarten–5th Grade

(continued on next page)

TABLE 7.2

Critical Areas of Reading, Writing, and Math Instruction *(continued)*

Skill Area:	Brief Definition and Characteristics	Potential Grades for Instruction	
		Typical Students	Students with Learning Differences
Text/Genre Composition	Understanding the principles of writing texts and the structure of different kinds of texts • Understanding paragraph structure (e.g., main idea sentence, supporting sentences, conclusion sentence) • Knowing the characteristics of narrative, persuasive, and expository texts (e.g., all narratives have characters, setting, plot, conflict resolution) • Planning, drafting, and revising texts	3rd–12th Grade	3rd–12th Grade
Math:			
Math Awareness	Understanding math concepts and associating them in concrete, semi-concrete, and abstract representations • Understanding number, measurement, space, time, temperature, volume, etc. • Classifying or ordering objects by size, number, etc. • Counting and place value	Grades K–12 for all Students Math content proceeds in a hierarchy, such that each skill area may be included at any grade level across the following content: 1. Counting 2. Addition 3. Multiplication 4. Problem Solving 5. Decimals 6. Telling Time 7. Measurement 8. Study Skills (e.g., graphing) 9. Geometry 10. Symbol identification and place value 11. Subtraction 12. Division 13. Fractions 14. Percent and ratio 15. Money 16. Estimation 17. Probability 18. Statistics 19. Math reasoning 20. Communication of math ideas For example, students may learn about addition for single digit problems in 1st grade (1+1) or for algebra in 8th grade ($a + 5 = 8$). However, students with learning differences in 8th grade may continue to need support in math awareness, concepts, fluency, language, and application associated with addition that was taught in 1st–8th grades.	

who might qualify for special education and/or gifted services. Conversely, diagnostic assessments are usually administered to individual students and they target specific areas of performance. They are not given to the entire student body. Students who are identified for special education and/or gifted programs are usually administered diagnostic assessments based on the results of the screening test. Classroom teachers generally are not involved in this diagnostic procedure.

Different from both of these types of assessment is progress monitoring, which is conducted by giving teacher-made tests. For most classroom teachers progress monitoring is used to determine whether or not the students in their classes have mastered the content. These results inform teachers about whether or not their instruction has been successful. Student progress can be measured by any form of teacher-made test such as weekly spelling tests, timed math fact quizzes, or essay questions comparing the character flaws of Hamlet and Macbeth. **Table 7.3** lists different types of assessments and their use.

The first step in determining whether or not instruction is effective, and whether or not any adjustment to instruction is warranted, is through the effective use of assessment. If students are regularly making adequate progress on valid classroom measures, there can be

TABLE 7.3

Types of Assessment

Type of Assessment:	Purpose:	Characteristics:	Example:	Locating the Assessment:
Screening	• To determine participation in grade level programs • To identify students who are at-risk for academic difficulty	• Brief • Given 1-3 times a year • Universal, not specifically linked to curriculum	Fluency probes (e.g., mad-math minute; oral reading fluency; DOLCH sight word list)	• Easy CBM http://easycbm.com • DIBELS https://dibels.uoregon.edu • Get it! Got it! Go! http://ggg.umn.edu • Really Great Reading Co. http://www.rgrco.com • Get Ready to Read! http://www.getreadytoread.org
Progress Monitoring	• To monitor students' performance • To determine if students are making progress toward instructional goals and objectives.	• Brief • Given frequently (weekly or monthly) • Linked to curriculum (often teacher made) • Results used to make adjustments to instruction	Curriculum-based Measurement (e.g., weekly spelling test; state curriculum tests)	• Intervention Central http://www.interventioncentral.org • AIMSWEB http://www.aimsweb.com
Diagnostic	• To provide in-depth information on a wider range of specific skills • To determine if a disability is present for students who do not respond to effective instruction	• Lengthy • Given infrequently, as a part of a diagnostic process • Chosen specifically for the individual student • Results used to diagnose	Norm-referenced standardized achievement tests	School psychologists

Broad-field tests are administered to screen the student body.

some confidence that the instructional methods in current use are effective. However, if assessment results routinely indicate that students are not making progress or fail to achieve mastery after instruction has occurred, approaches to instruction and procedures should be examined.

Curriculum-based measures (CBMs) are a form of assessment that allows teachers to measure the effectiveness of their instructional interventions by monitoring student progress over time (Deno, 1985). CBMs differ from the standardized achievement tests frequently given in schools in that standardized tests are generally given just once a year or less frequently, and the results of these tests are used to compare students across a population of similar students. CBMs also differ from progress monitored by teacher-made tests because they measure the same skills over and over and are aligned to the curriculum. Student performance on CBMs is monitored on an ongoing basis and allows teachers to receive timely feedback in order to evaluate student performance on specific skills throughout the instructional unit to determine if changes to instruction are required. The use of CBMs is preferable to the use of standardized tests when measuring student performance because CBMs are:

1. directly connected to the curriculum or skill being studied,
2. short in duration so they can be frequently administered, and
3. sensitive to small improvements in achievement (Jenkins, Deno, & Mirkin, 1979).

Because the use of CBMs is an assessment technique and not a specific type of exam, CBMs can be created and used as efficient measures of general achievement in all academic areas. Based on the results of student CBMs, instructors can then begin to make informed choices about their approaches to providing instruction.

Step 3: Establish a Learning-Focused Environment

Once teachers are comfortable with the content to be taught and have determined students' learning strengths and weakness through the use of assessment, it is important that they ensure their classroom is focused on learning. There are some basic concepts that teachers must understand and consider as they begin to think about effective instruction. One of the concepts is time management. All teachers must maximize the time they have with students in order to optimize instruction. Another important concept for understanding students' levels of readiness to learn is the zone of proximal development. Assessments will ensure that teachers proceed with instruction at the appropriate learning levels or zones of their students. Last, teachers must be aware of a variety of instructional methods, whether they are teacher directed or student directed, to deliver content in a manner that can best support their students' acquisition and retention of that content.

Emphasizing Learning Time

Prioritizing the time that students spend learning may seem an obvious way to positively impact student achievement, but research suggests that there are many tasks competing with learning in the classroom. Allocated learning time is the amount of time that an instructor assigns for instructional tasks, but it is not necessarily the amount of time that students spend learning. It has been suggested that only approximately 70% of the school day is allocated for learning (Archer & Hughes, 2011). This percent is well below 100% because basic activities that are part of classroom management (e.g., distributing materials, taking attendance, making announcements) reduce the amount of time that is authentically spent on instruction and learning. To minimize these intrusions, it is important for teachers to employ efficient classroom procedures and classroom management strategies that protect instructional time.

A related concept, engaged learning time, is the amount of time that students spend immersed in learning activities. Activities like note taking, listening to the teacher, and reading are examples of what occurs during engaged learning time, and such activities are reported to comprise less than 50% of students' days (Anderson & Wahlberg, 1994). Although these "engaged" activities are instructional in nature, they do not necessarily require students to interact with or be responsive to the material, and they can often be rather passive.

Engaged learning time includes the time that students spend listening to the teacher.

In contrast, academic learning time is the amount of time students spend attending to relevant academic tasks while interacting with and performing those tasks with a high rate of success. This means that students have to be engaging in activities that are at the appropriate instructional level so that opportunities exist for them to respond with a high level of success (Berliner, 1987; Caldwell, Huitt, & Graeber, 1982). For learning to occur, the ability to attend is critical. Many students with learning difficulties may need to learn attending strategies before academic learning will occur. It has been suggested that students are engaged in academic learning time approximately 20% of the school day (Fisher et al., 1978). Because there is a correlation between the amount of academic learning time and student achievement, it is important for teachers to focus on increasing academic learning time. **Figure 7.2** describes learning time and ways to increase it.

Increasing Academic Learning Time

In preparing to work with students with learning differences, one key to promoting achievement among this group is increasing academic learning time (ALT) (Berliner, 1987). The emphasis during planning and teaching is on having students produce as many active, correct responses as possible to maximize academic achievement. With some students, specific

Figure 7.2	Learning Time	
	What is it?	*How can I increase it?*
Allocated Time	Amount of time scheduled for academic subjects.	Make certain there is sufficient time scheduled for academic knowledge and skills.
Engaged Time	Proportion of scheduled time in which students are on task.	Increase instructional efficiency through routines and management strategies.
Academic Learning Time	Portion of the time on task during which students make correct responses.	Maximize student success through briskly paced direct instruction.

instructional approaches are needed to help them in making a high rate of correct responses. These approaches may be appropriate for all students in general education settings.

Before mentioning strategies, the first way to increase ALT is to assure that appropriate allocated learning time has been scheduled for the academic skill area of concern. When planning the presentation of new material or even the review of previously acquired content, it is important to schedule enough time in the lesson to adequately cover the material in the depth that is required to support student mastery. Skimping on the amount of planned instructional time due to outside intrusions like school assemblies or testing schedules should be avoided. Introducing the concept of division during a shortened instructional period should be counterintuitive; however, as previously noted, in many classrooms nonacademic activities (e.g., activity periods, lunch counts, announcements, planning for nonacademic school activities) take away from the time allocated for academics (Baker & Zigmond, 1990). When the additional instructional needs of students with academic problems are considered, the limited amount of instructional time that is provided in most classrooms assures that these students will probably never catch up (Haynes & Jenkins, 1986; Simmons, Chard, & Kame'enui, 1995). Classrooms that have an academic focus in which teachers actively instruct, frequently test, and hold students responsible for their work tend to result in higher achievement (Rosenshine, 1997).

With the current emphasis on inclusion in the general education setting for students with learning differences, once the appropriate amount of time is allocated for ALT, teachers must implement appropriate strategies to increase it. Montague, Bergeron, and Lago-Delello (1997) recommend the following strategies to increase academic learning time for students with special needs:

1. provide direct instruction prior to task assignment to ensure the student understands the task directions;
2. provide frequent positive and corrective feedback during academic activities to monitor students' progress;
3. reduce task requirements and assign academic tasks that are commensurate with the students' ability levels to increase academic success and task completion; and
4. reinforce and reward students for task completion.

Zone of Proximal Development

Increasing ALT requires increased opportunities for correct responses. This means that all instruction should be directed at levels that are neither too advanced nor too simplistic. Presenting instructional material that is too complex or beyond the comprehension level of students leads to student frustration, which can have a negative impact on learning. Such a scenario results in wasted instructional time because the student does not have the prerequisite skills needed to master the new task. Clearly, if a student has not mastered addition facts, it will be difficult to progress to multiplication. Similarly, presenting information that has already been learned and mastered can lead to frustration in students. This scenario also represents a waste of instructional time as new learning will not occur as the newly presented information has already been acquired. For this reason, it is important for teachers to have some understanding of the zone of proximal development (ZPD) of their students, and to adjust their instruction to these levels (Vygotsky 1978).

The ZPD, as shown in **Figure 7.3,** is the difference between the levels at which a student can perform independently and the levels at which support from an adult or more competent peer are required (Vygotsky, 1978). If students are presented with already acquired informa-

Figure 7.3   The Zone of Proximal Development (ZPD)

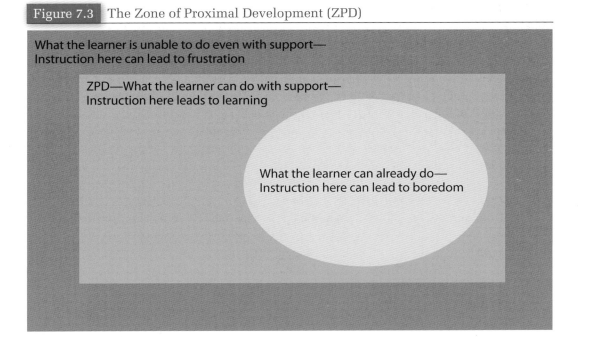

What the learner is unable to do even with support—
Instruction here can lead to frustration

ZPD—What the learner can do with support—
Instruction here leads to learning

What the learner can already do—
Instruction here can lead to boredom

tion, they may become bored. If the information is too complex, they may become confused. When students are in the ZPD, they can achieve the next stage of mastery with some instructional coaching or prodding. Many students with learning difficulties who are being served in general education classrooms may find themselves slipping in and out of their ZPDs throughout the academic year in any given class as the demands of the curriculum change. When students are in their ZPDs, some Tier 1 instructional approaches may serve as appropriate methods to assist them in reaching mastery.

If instructors determine that students are spending adequate amounts of engaged time on task, and that they are working within their ZPDs, and assessment results continue to yield poor results, the method of the delivery of instruction can then be examined. There are many ways to deliver material to students so if one method is not effective then another method can be used. It is important to note that not any one method of instruction has been demonstrated to be the best or most effective for any population of students. Although many methods of instruction have been established as effective approaches to presenting content material to a variety of populations, overreliance on any one method may not provide optimum results across students, settings, and content area. For this reason, it is imperative that teachers learn many approaches to delivering their instructional content.

Step 4: Select Effective Approaches to Instruction

In order to provide variety in their instruction, teachers must be familiar with a number of methods of content delivery. Several of these approaches are described in this section. The extent to which general educators use these approaches in their classrooms is based primarily on how well the teachers view this instruction as fitting into the day-to-day classroom routine with the required course content (Gersten & Woodward, 1990; Whinnery, Fuchs, & Fuchs, 1991). A variety of factors can impact this view and those factors and strategies are discussed.

When making the decision about how to approach their instruction, teachers have many options. One of the first questions a teacher may ask himself in this process is whether or not the lesson's activities will use more teacher-focused instruction or more student-focused instruction. Teacher-focused instruction exists when the instructor is at the center of the lesson's content by being the primary agent of delivery for that content. In this model, the instructor is, for the most part, wholly responsible for providing all of the lesson's information, and most of the interaction in the class is between the instructor and the students (with little to no exchange among the students). Also, in this model, the instruction is generally highly explicit. **Explicit instruction** is the systematic approach to introducing new content that includes three main components:

1. Demonstration—modeling the skill,
2. Guided practice—assisting students to produce correct responses multiple times, and
3. Independent practice—allowing students the opportunity to complete the task without assistance.

Explicit instruction within the context of a teacher-centered approach is frequently used for introducing new skills and topics.

Alternatively, student-focused instruction exists when the students themselves adopt greater responsibility for mastering the content of the lesson by becoming more active agents in the discovery process of learning. In this model, students may not receive as much specific guidance regarding the exact steps that should be taken to lead to lesson mastery, and much of the interaction during the lesson is among the students (possibly with instructor support and prompting). The instruction is often highly implicit. **Implicit instruction** is a less structured approach that emphasizes the use of inquiry, hypothesis-testing, and problem solving on the part of the students. It is important to remember that the decision to use teacher-focused (more explicit) or student-focused (more implicit) instruction is not an either/or prospect. Any combination of these approaches can be appropriate for all students depending on the nature of the content and the learning needs of the students.

Typically the most effective approach for students with learning problems is to start with more teacher-directed instruction. Then move to more student-directed learning. The research evidence shows that teacher-directed methods are powerful tools for teaching and managing students with learning and behavior problems (Gersten, 1998). These must be included in the arsenal of techniques used in inclusive settings. There also is a complementary role for student-directed techniques. Teacher-directed instruction emphasizes how teachers think about, adapt, and present critical content to all students in a learner-friendly approach with the teacher playing a central role in delivering and managing the content. Student-directed instruction includes the skills and strategies needed to learn the content, but allows students and their peers to have greater control over the delivery of the content (Deshler et al., 2001). When practice beyond initial mastery and generalization to other tasks is important, student-directed techniques are a viable option for providing focused practice and drill. Peer tutoring, technology-mediated instruction, and self-regulation strategies offer useful procedures that incorporate a student-centered focus.

Educators should be guided in their selection of these tools by their knowledge of the instructional principles that have proven to be effective for students with disabilities. For example, a review of validated practices for teaching students with mild disabilities by Swanson and Hoskyn (2001) provides an excellent foundation for examining and selecting instructional procedures for promoting learning in inclusive settings. These authors identified validated inclusive instructional approaches that benefit most, if not all, students in a class, which can be embedded within the general education curriculum, and are practical in terms of time and implementation. Many of these approaches are addressed in the next section. The effective approaches to instruction that are described include both teacher-directed and student-directed programs and self-management strategies.

Teacher-Directed Approaches to Instruction

There are many teacher-directed approaches that have been demonstrated to be effective for students both with and without learning differences. This section reviews interventions that may be appropriately used in general education classrooms. The approaches reviewed here may be implemented either with the whole class or in small groups depending on the learning task.

Direct Instruction

One of the more effective means of teaching students with learning differences is by using direct instruction, a form of explicit instruction (Hudson, Miller, & Butler, 2006). Direct instruction is a systematic form of instruction that includes explicit step-by-step teaching procedures that account for student mastery, immediate student feedback, student practice, and gradual fading of teaching direction. According to Strickland and Maccini (2010), the components of direct instruction are the use of advance organizers, teacher demonstration, guided practice, independent practice, cumulative practice, and progress monitoring. Direct instruction includes frequent checks for understanding and ensuring that every student participates (Maccini, Strickland, Gagnon, & Malmgren, 2008).

Direct instruction involves four or five teacher-directed phases. First is the use of an advance organizer designed to activate prior knowledge and to focus students on the goal of the lesson. At this introductory phase, a teacher who is introducing decimals may introduce the lesson by connecting the new content to previously learned material about fractions. Second is a demonstration phase including explanation, modeling of the task by the teacher, questioning the students to check for understanding, and adjusting instruction based on feedback from that questioning. In this second phase, the teacher would provide several examples in which she demonstrates the conversion of fractions to decimals. Third is guided practice, or opportunities for student practice. Guided practice begins with high levels of verbal or written prompts that are gradually faded as students demonstrate increased mastery. Students at this stage might be given an opportunity to practice the newly learned decimal skill using a practice worksheet or computer application. The fourth phase is independent practice with corrective feedback (Hudson, Miller, & Butler, 2006; Maccini, Mulcahy, & Wilson, 2007; Miller & Hudson, 2007). Miller and Hudson (2007) include a fifth stage of checking for maintenance of skills at some point in time after mastery has occurred. The purpose of

Direct instruction involves four or five teacher-directed phases.

this stage is to ensure that students have retained the instructed skills over time. Direct instruction is an effective approach to teaching mathematics to learners with learning differences in math because it results in increased automaticity of basic skills and increased skill in problem-solving (Kroesbergen & van Luit, 2003). Direct instruction has also been shown to be highly effective in teaching reading to students who are struggling with literacy skills. Although direct instructional approaches are often associated with packaged curricula, the features of direct instruction do not require the use of specialized program materials.

© 2013 Lorraine Swanson. Under license from Shutterstock, Inc.

Teaching Strategies

Teaching strategy is the term used to describe what the teacher does to present the content to students. The teacher decides how best to present the content to the students in a way that they are most likely to understand and remember the information. Teachers need to use a well-designed instructional approach to mastering an academic task (Schumaker & Deshler, 2003). Often instruction is more explicit at the beginning, but as learning progresses, greater emphasis is placed on more implicit techniques (Deshler et al., 2001) due to the following reasons:

1. students with learning differences often exhibit processing deficits that require more structure for learning to take place;
2. steps are taught using task analysis and are, therefore, not as confusing as initial general exposure to the overall process; and
3. students with learning differences frequently experience failure, and the success attained at each step of instruction allows students to develop a feeling of achievement (Schumaker & Deshler, 2003).

There are a number of teaching strategies that can aid in preparing students for learning and in the acquisition and retention of the content material. Most strategies can be adapted across grade level and curriculum so that they can be used in some form with all age groups and in all subjects. Effective strategies can include advance organizers, mnemonic devices, and graphic representations.

An **advance organizer** is a tool that is used to assist students in recalling and transferring previously learned information to the new information that is being presented (Ausubel, 1960). The purpose of using an advance organizer is to activate previously learned information in order to attach new information with the advance organizer itself serving as that anchor. Students with disabilities can use advance organizers to gain more access to the curriculum by connecting new information to information that has already been retained. This can aid in the acquisition of the new material. It is a verbal or written technique used to provide students with an overview or preview of material to be presented. When teachers use advance organizers there is an increase in comprehension of critical concepts during content area instruction (Darch & Gersten, 1986). An effective advance organizer:

*   informs the student of the purpose of the organizer;
*   clarifies the actions of both the teacher and student;
*   identifies and explains the topics;
*   identifies subtopics and concepts that need to be addressed;
*   provides background information;
*   provides rationales for teaching the lesson;
*   introduces unfamiliar terms or words;
*   provides an organizational framework; and
*   states the desired results of the lesson.

Advance organizers may be either verbal or written. For example, when introducing a unit on safety in the home, one teacher might use a verbal advance organizer as follows:

"Today, we will begin a unit on safety in the home. We will talk about several different topics: first, we'll talk about common household accidents and how to prevent them; second, we'll talk about ways to keep your home safe from intruders; and

finally we'll discuss safe ways to exit your home in case of a fire. During each topic area, you'll apply the information we discuss to your own house. At the end of the unit, you will have a household safety manual specifically designed for your own home."

Another teacher might provide the advance organizer in the form of an outline of main topics. Students fill in the outline with information gained from the lectures and discussions. Another type of advance organizer is the KWL Chart. In this chart, students begin the lesson by listing information that they already know (K) and what (W) they would like to know, and they end the lesson by describing what they actually learned (L). **Figure 7.4** provides a model for developing a KWL chart.

Mnemonic devices are memory aids that serve to assist students in recalling information, particularly lists or specific facts. Mnemonics may use phrases or sentences where the first letter of each word spells out a difficult word or aids in remembering a long list of other words. For example, *A rat in Tom's house may eat Tom's ice cream*, assists in the spelling of the word arithmetic. Some mnemonics may involve rhymes. The rhyming sentence *In fourteen hundred and ninety-two, Columbus sailed the ocean blue* helps us remember when Columbus landed in America. Such devices provide students with disabilities greater access to the general education curriculum by providing them with the necessary tools to both acquire and retrieve information. Students with disabilities have shown increased performance using mnemonic devices (Forness, Kavale, Blum, & Lloyd, 1997; Swanson, 2001; Uberti, Scruggs, & Mastropieri, 2003). There are many types of mnemonics and, in each, students associate new information with differing prompts as shown in **Table 7.4**.

A graphic representation can consist of symbols, pictures, or words that represent concepts, and it structures those symbols and pictures within a framework that is designed to aid students in retaining the new concepts. What differentiates this strategy from others is the use of the schematic diagram within which new information is presented (Jitendra, 2002). The graphic display of the information may improve performance and provide students with more access to the general curriculum by organizing the information graphically. This might allow them to better focus on analyzing and synthesizing the information (Gersten, Chard, & Jayanthi, 2008).

Figure 7.4 KWL Chart

Topic_____

What I Know	What I Want to Know	What I Learned

TABLE 7.4

Types of Mnemonics Devices

For information involving key words	**Acrostic**—Create a sentence in which the first letter of each word is a cue to an idea you need to remember.	**EVERY GOOD BOY DOES FINE** is an acrostic to remember the order of the G-clef notes on sheet music—E,G,B,D,F.
For information involving key words	**Acronym**—Form a word through a combination of the first letters of the words you want to remember.	**HOMES** is the acronym used to remember the names of the Great Lakes; Huron, Ontario, Michigan, Erie, and Superior.
For ordered or unordered lists	**Rhyme-Keys**—a 2-step memory process: 1. Memorize key words that can correspond with numbers (two-moo); 2. Come up with an image of the items you need to remember with key words. (A cow that is mooing will remind me of meat, fish, and poultry.)	**Food groups:** 1. Dairy products: one-bun-cheese melted on a hamburger bun. 2. Meat, fish, and poultry: two-moo-cow mooing. 3. Grains: three-bee-a bee flying around in a wheat field. 4. Fruit and vegetables: four-store-envisioning a grocery store display of fruits and vegetables.
For approximately twenty items	**Loci Method**—Think about placing the items you want to remember in certain areas in a room that is familiar to you.	To remember **presidents:** Place a five dollar bill (Abraham Lincoln) on the floor. Go into the room and see Roosevelt sitting on a chair and Kennedy looking in the cupboards.
For foreign language vocabulary	**Keyword Method**—Choose what foreign words you must remember and determine what English word sounds like the foreign one. Create a picture in your mind that puts together the key word with the English meaning of the foreign word.	The Spanish word for phone booth is "cabina." Think about a cab attempting to drive into a phone booth. Every time you see the word "cabina" your memory should think of the image you created and cause you to remember "phone booth."
For remembering names	**Image-Name Technique**—Create a relationship between the person's name and their physical characteristics.	**Shirley Temple**—her temples are framed by curly (rhymes with Shirley) blonde hair.
For ordered or unordered lists	**Chaining**—Invent a story where each word or idea brings up the next idea you need to remember.	**Ben Franklin, eye, ocean, Great Britain** Story: **Ben Franklin** kept his **eye** on the **ocean** to watch for the **British** to come.
For rote information or rules	**Ode or Rhyme**—Put the information you want to remember in the form of a story	**"I before e, except after c"** **"In 1492, Columbus sailed the ocean blue."**

Adapted from web site developed by Meg Keeley and the Special Populations Office at Bucks County Community College with funding from the Carl D. Perkins Vocational and Applied Technology Education Act found at http://www.bucks.edu/media/bcccmedialibrary/pdf/studentservices/pass/Mnemonics.pdf.

A **concept map** is a graphical representation designed to indicate the relationships that exist within a framework of concepts or ideas. Rather than presenting ideas in a linear fashion (as is the case in a traditional outline), the concept map allows students to view the information in a more spatial format. The concepts and ideas are generally boxed and lines are drawn to indicate the connections that exist between the varying terms. Often concept maps are hierarchical with the most important information occurring at the top of the map, and frequently linking words that further define the relationship between two concepts are included on the lines that connect those concepts (see **Figure 7.5**).

Venn diagrams are graphical representations that are used to display compare-contrast relationships between ideas. Generally consisting of two overlapping circles (although they can contain more circles depending on the number of compared ideas), similarities are indicated in the space that is shared by the two circles. Differences are written in the independent spaces on the circles. **Figure 7.6** presents a Venn diagram.

Figure 7.5 Organized Reading Using a Science Concept Map

Definition: A mammal is a warm-blooded vertebrate that has hair and nurses its young

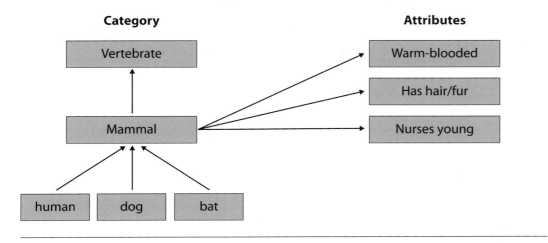

Figure 7.6 Example of a Venn Diagram

Forty pet owners are surveyed. Of the 40, 27 have dogs as pets. Eighteen have cats. In the group, there are 12 owners who have both a dog and a cat. Label the diagram with the correct numbers if A represents dog owners and B represents cat owners.

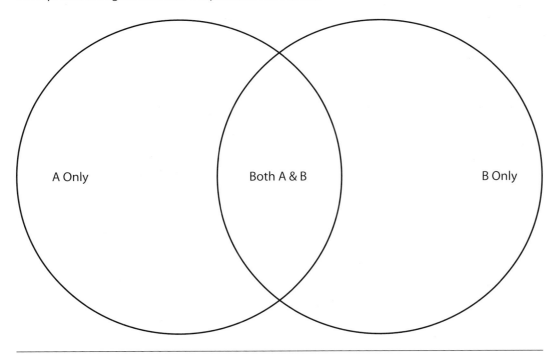

Both concept maps and Venn diagrams can be used across a variety of subject areas. Additionally, concept mapping and graphic organizers are useful in helping students with learning differences demonstrate knowledge while requiring fewer verbal skills.

Student-Directed Approaches to Instruction

In contrast to teacher-directed interventions, student-directed interventions focus on helping students learn to plan and evaluate the effectiveness of their classroom performance. Student-directed interventions emphasize implicit instruction. Implicit instruction is a self-regulated instructional approach where students are viewed as learners who actively set their own goals, monitor their classroom progress, use learning strategies, and reflect on and evaluate their progress and learning effectiveness. Learning strategy is the term used to describe what the teacher teaches the student to do independently to remember the content taught. Students with learning differences often have never developed effective ways to learn and retain new information. They need instruction regarding how and when to use a learning strategy.

Factors that contribute to the success of student-directed and implicit instruction are the ability to set realistic goals and plans, to deal with frustration, to overcome problems, and to be persistent. These are also related to successful post-school adjustment (Spekman, Goldberg, & Herman, 1992; Werner, 1993). To assist students in developing a more self-directed outlook, educators and students might consider the following recommendations:

- begin by focusing on a content area that the student is committed to improving;
- establish with the student a well-defined goal that is easily monitored;
- emphasize self-monitoring some part of behavior related to the goal;
- establish and teach a routine for working on the goal that includes responses that are correct with abundant repetition to promote early success;
- assist students in over-learning the steps of the routine to ensure application;
- teach routines that are content specific with clear applications to the student problem to ensure the likelihood of generalization;
- reduce the content difficulty during the initial stages of establishing the program so the student can focus on aspects of self-regulation, such as self-monitoring and self-instruction, rather than the curriculum; and
- include a focus on attribution from the beginning of the student's work by emphasizing the link between commitment, effort, and progress (Schunk, 2000).

Teachers can select from a variety of instructional strategies that have been designed to be more student-focused. Again, these approaches can be used in combination with one another and in conjunction with the more teacher-focused strategies discussed in the previous section.

Student-Regulated Instruction

Student-regulated instruction, a type of implicit instruction, is a teaching approach with the goal of transferring control and responsibility of learning from the teacher to the student gradually through a variety of self-regulation and self-management strategies. Although student-regulated and teacher-directed strategies are more similar than different (e.g., they both tend to follow the same general sequence of instruction described earlier), important differences exist. Whereas teacher-directed instruction is typically viewed as a *bottom-up* teaching strategy that focuses on basic skill acquisition (e.g., learning letter sounds), student-regulated instruction is generally thought of as a *top-down* teaching process that focuses on rules and the generalization of these rules to other settings (Swanson & Hoskyn, 2001). Although teacher-directed instruction (such as direct instruction) focuses on the acquisition of progressively more difficult skills, student-regulated instruction (like the teaching of learning strategies) focuses on learning a variety of self-regulated strategies that can be applied generally to a variety of skill areas.

With student-regulated instruction, learners are viewed as active constructors of their own knowledge, self-managers of academic goals, self-monitors of academic progress, and self-evaluators of their work. Because student-regulated instruction dovetails with our broader educational goals of independence of thought and generalization of learning to all aspects of life, and because it transfers control and responsibility of learning to students, this approach can be a valuable tool for teachers. Importantly, student-regulated instruction has proven to be effective in increasing the academic skills of students with learning difficulties (Swanson & Hoskyn, 2001).

Graham and Harris (1994) developed a comprehensive approach to making instruction more student-directed called the Self-Regulated Strategy Instruction (SRSD) model. It has been evolving over the last 20 years. Drawing on years of research with students with learning differences, this model not only makes allowances for the critical components of effective instruction (i.e., demonstration/modeling, guided practice, and independent practice), but it also considers the motivational, cognitive, and academic characteristics of students with learning difficulties (Lienemann & Reid, 2006). Divided into six stages, the SRSD model serves as a step-by-step guide for the self-regulated use of any learning strategy.

The first stage is *developing and activating background knowledge*. It involves task-analyzing the selected strategy by breaking the strategy down into its smaller prerequisite subskills and then linking these older skills to the new material. Although developing and activating background knowledge may seem obvious to many advanced teachers, in practice it is often overlooked (Lienemann & Reid, 2006). Before introducing a strategy (or any skill or concept), it is essential that teachers identify the critical subskills and determine if their students have the requisite skills to accommodate the new information.

The second stage is *discussing the strategy* and it involves a motivational component. Here teachers "sell" the strategy and persuade students that the strategy will help them in the future. Teachers discuss the relevance of the strategy to students' lives (e.g., it would be needed for success in the present class, future classes, in balancing a checkbook, and in buying and returning items from stores). After earning this "buy-in" from students, the final part of this stage is to discuss the steps of the strategy and to instill in students the belief that success (or failure) with the strategy results from effort and not innate ability.

Modeling the strategy is the third stage of SRSD. It is common to most effective instructional practices and plays a critical role in subsequent learning outcomes. Lienemann and Reid (2006) recommend that teachers model the strategy by using a "think aloud" technique. The teacher being the expert model can have a powerful instructional effect on students' strategy acquisition using a thoughtful "think-aloud."

The fourth stage is *memorizing the strategy*. Because students with learning difficulties do not typically internalize strategy steps independently, it is critically important that they memorize the steps of the strategy. This memorization of steps may free up working memory resources during later strategy application, thus increasing the likelihood they will use the strategy correctly both now and in the future.

Supporting the strategy is the fifth stage. In this stage, guided practice is used. Guided practice enables successful learning outcomes by having expert models (i.e., the teacher) guide students toward goal completion with the use of scaffolds, or instructional supports. With scaffolding, teachers first demonstrate the skill as students watch and then offer supports (i.e., scaffolds) in a variety of ways, including gradually increasing the difficulty of the material or publicly posting prompt sheets or posters of the strategy's steps. Gradually, these scaffolds are taken away, and the student is ready to attempt the strategy independently.

The final stage of SRSD allows for *independent performance* to take place. At this point, a student's ability to independently use the strategy should be evident. In effect, the control and responsibility of applying the strategy has been transferred from the teacher to the student. An approach such as SRSD is important for several reasons. First, it is a systematic strategy that is introduced and taught within a general education classroom in the context of the general education curriculum. Second, students with disabilities and their peers without disabilities have shown improvements in academic performance. Third, the self-regulation skills and strategy are taught within a content area so that no separate instruction is needed to apply these skills in an isolated instruction context.

Teachers using SRSD have been successful at promoting the goal of systematically moving from effective teacher-directed instruction to student-directed instruction. When teaching writing, teachers begin by explicitly modeling and teaching how to write, teaching strategy use, correcting written work, and gradually withdrawing direct teacher instruction as students become increasingly independent with each part of the writing process (Graham & Harris, 1994). The process moves from an emphasis on teacher-directed multiple opportunities for correct responses and students memorizing steps in the strategy to student-directed strategy implementation and self-monitoring.

There are a number of other student-regulated learning strategies within general education that can effectively promote the achievement of students with learning difficulties. Strategies such as IT FITS, PLEASE, RPV-HECC, and TELLS Fact or Fiction can all be taught using the SRSD model. Brief descriptions of these learning strategies follow.

An example of applying strategies to content areas is called IT FITS. This strategy has been used to help students in special education learn science terms and definitions when using the keyword mnemonic approach IT FITS. Groups of students are taught to:

- I (Identify the term),
- T (Tell the definition of the term),
- F (Find a keyword),
- I (Imagine the definition by doing something with the keyword),
- T (Think about the definition doing something with the keyword), and
- S (Study what you imagined until you know the definition).

Students learn and retain more definitions when taught the terms and definitions in a systematic manner (King-Sears, Mercer, & Sindelar, 1992).

The PLEASE strategy is used to improve students' ability to write paragraphs (Welch, 1992). This strategy is effective in increasing understanding of written expression for students with learning difficulties. The strategy teaches students to:

- P (Pick a topic, audience, and appropriate textual format);
- L (List ideas concerning the topic);
- E (Evaluate the list);
- A (Activate the paragraph using a topic sentence);
- S (Supply sentences to support the topic);
- E (End the paragraph with a concluding sentence) and E (Evaluate the finished product).

A different view of training self-regulation skills comes from research on developing strategies for solving problems in mathematics and shows that middle school students can successfully use the strategy to solve multiple-step word problems. The cognitive strategy RPV-HECC includes direct instruction on these steps:

- **Read** (for understanding),
- **Paraphrase** (your own words),
- **Visualize** (a picture or diagram),
- **Hypothesize** (a plan to solve the problem),
- **Estimate** (predict the number),
- **Compute** (do arithmetic),
- **Check** (make sure everything is right).

TELLS Fact or Fiction is a guided comprehension tool used to prepare students for approaching reading assignments. In teaching students to use TELLS Fact or Fiction, the teacher trains them to study these elements:

- **T** (Title);
- **E** (Examine the text to determine the theme);
- **L** (Look for words that appear to be important);
- **L** (Look for words that appear to be difficult);
- **S** (Identify the Setting);
- and, finally, decide whether the story is **Fact or Fiction.**

For example, before reading a passage, the teacher might have the students answer a question concerning one of the previous steps, such as "What does the title tell you about the story?" The teacher continues in this fashion until each step is completed. According to Sorrell (1990), a teacher may need to reserve approximately 15 minutes for this portion of the lesson.

Teaching students to problem-solve is essential if they are to be successful in applying their skills to the real world. Problem-solving is usually difficult for students. It requires them to understand vocabulary, sequence data, discriminate between the relevant and irrelevant, isolate key information within problems, apply computational skills, understand similarities and differences, apply the correct strategy to solve the problem, and think abstractly (Bley, 2001). The more hypothetical and abstract the problems, the more difficult they are for students. If students with math difficulties are to be successful problem solvers, they need incremental practice at all grade levels and explicit instruction in solving problems.

According to Montague (2007), students should be taught explicit steps to solve problems. She suggests teachers instruct students to use the following eight-step strategy:

1. *Read the problem aloud.* Assistance is provided to the student with unfamiliar vocabulary. The problem can be read out loud to the student if necessary.
2. *Paraphrase the problem aloud.* The student rephrases the problem verbally.
3. *Visualize.* The student draws a representation of the problem.
4. *State the problem.* The student verbally states, "I have . . . I want to find . . ." Students can underline keywords in the problem.
5. *Hypothesize.* The student verbally states, "If I . . . then . . ."
6. *Estimate.* The student estimates the potential answer and underlines it. Rounding and estimating skills are emphasized here.
7. *Calculate.* The student calculates the answer and circles it.
8. *Self-check.* The student examines each step involved in solving the problem then asks herself, "Is this answer logical?" Computation calculations are checked.

Cooperative Learning Strategies

Cooperative learning models offer a way to promote the progress of individual students. These models have students of heterogeneous achievement levels assigned to groups of four or five for the purpose of promoting the learning of all group members as they work toward a common goal, such as passing the test at the end of the chapter. There are group rewards for evidence of progress in learning by the members of the group, as opposed to only rewarding top individual students in traditional classrooms. Cooperative learning models have been recommended for use to include students with diverse backgrounds and to promote the achievement of students with academic difficulties (Johnson & Johnson, 1994; Slavin, 1996). Several cooperative learning strategies are reviewed.

One example of a cooperative learning tool that uses cooperative groups is the Student Teams-Achievement Division model (Slavin, 1990). After a traditional presentation of the material, students meet in assigned groups to review the material as a means of preparing for a quiz. In cooperative learning situations, students have to rely on each other to achieve a common goal, thus rewards are based on group performance (Peck, 1989).

Jigsaw is a cooperative learning strategy in which students are responsible for a portion of the learning and teaching. Students are asked to independently research a particular portion of the lesson and be prepared to share with their classmates (Brown, 1994). In this way, each student shares responsibility for a piece of the puzzle. Before presenting the Jigsaw lesson, Brown (1994) suggests that teachers work closely with specialists within the domain of interest. After selecting a topic, it is divided into subtopics and distributed among members of each group. Each member is responsible for becoming an "expert" in the assigned area. The students later regroup and share their findings. For example, the teacher may assign a topic on life in Brazil. One member of the group may choose to research the sports and recreational activities found in Brazil. Another student may choose to learn about the types of food found in Brazil. A third student may learn about the traditions and cultures of Brazil. After the students obtain the necessary information, they share the information with the rest of the group members. If absenteeism is a concern, students may work in pairs to ensure the work is completed. Johnson and Johnson (1994) modified the Jigsaw format to create interdependence among the group members. In the Johnson model the teacher assigns specific students within the group to assume the role of the "checker," "recorder," "observer," etc. The purpose of the roles is to encourage teambuilding to help one another succeed.

Peer tutoring is another form of cooperative learning in which one student serves as a teacher/monitor of another student who needs additional instruction or practice. Students with learning problems can benefit from the help given by a peer tutor, as well as benefit from serving as a tutor for a younger student who might be having difficulty (Scruggs, Mastropieri, & Rickter, 1985). Peer tutors are effective when used to provide drill and practice after the teacher has given the initial instruction. Peer tutors must have clearly defined roles, and they should be trained to follow a well-defined instructional procedure, give corrective feedback when an error is made, reinforce correct responses, and keep track of their pupil's progress (Keel, Dangel, & Owens, 1999).

Classwide peer tutoring (CWPT) is an instructional strategy that provides both an increase in practice opportunities with immediate feedback and delivery of instruction in small groups. CWPT is a system in which all class members are organized in tutor-tutee pairs that work

Peer tutoring provides extended individual instructional support and increased opportunities to respond.

together (Greenwood & Delquadri, 1995). Unlike other types of peer tutoring, which involve upper-grade or higher-skilled students from other classes, CWPT is implemented within an intact classroom. Classroom peers tutor one another in a reciprocal fashion on academic skills. Structured, teacher-directed lessons are presented to students prior to the implementation of CWPT. During a CWPT session, students work in pairs and tutor one another on the same material presented by the teacher for 15 to 30 minutes. Students are provided instruction on proper reinforcement procedures for correct responses and for correcting errors. Instructional procedures include an explicit presentation format, contingent point earning, error correction procedures, and public display of student products.

CWPT is considered an effective instructional procedure because of the many benefits associated with using the procedures. First, the structured interaction between a well-trained tutor and a tutee promotes positive classroom management, and also increases efficient use of academic time. Second, peer tutoring encourages teachers to design lessons that follow clear, specific procedures. It also encourages active monitoring of students' progress and understanding. Finally, peer tutoring provides extended individual instructional support and increased opportunities to respond. **Figure 7.7** presents student grouping options that enhance collaborative learning models.

Figure 7.7 Student Grouping Options

Instructional Delivery	Advantages	Disadvantages
Whole class grouping	Easiest way to teach. Sense of teacher control.	Least effective, especially for students with learning difficulty.
Collaborative student groups	More effective in promoting student learning than whole class teaching.	Must train students in how to collaborate. Classroom is more active and noisy.
Peer Tutoring (one-to-one students)	More learning, especially for students with learning difficulties. Better able to monitor student progress.	Requires training of tutors. Is most effective in learning skills subjects, e.g., reading words, math facts.
One-to-one teacher-directed grouping	Maximizes probability of student learning, especially students with learning difficulties.	Very inefficient. Shifts teacher's time away from more capable learners.

Teaching Self-Management

Using effective teacher-directed and student-directed instructional approaches involve skills related to having students stay on task and complete their work. Although some students may be adept at staying focused and motivated, others will need instruction and strategies to ensure they acquire these skills. These self-management or self-regulated skills fall into five areas:

1. goal setting,
2. self-management,
3. self-instruction,
4. self-monitoring or self-recording, and
5. self-reinforcement (Maag, 2005).

Figure 7.8 summarizes strategies for each of these skills.

Figure 7.8   Self-regulated Skills and Strategies

Self-regulated Skills	Strategies
Goal setting	• Students are given the option of setting personal goals for accuracy and often prioritize objectives. • For example, "My goal is to improve from 65% to 80% correct on the weekly spelling test."
Self-management	• Students organize themselves by identifying elements that are difficult and easy. • For example, "I think I know all 6 times tables, but I need to practice the 7 times tables some more."
Self-instruction	• Students use "self-talk" steps in learning how to do a procedure. • For example, "To help me follow directions, first I read the directions to myself, then I underline the words that tell me what to do, then when I finish, I check to be sure that I did it correctly."
Self-monitoring and recording	• Students identify the frequency with which target behaviors occur and use charts and graphs to show changes in performance. • For example, "I will color in the bar graph that shows the number of facts I got correct on my timed math drill."
Self-reinforcement	• Students accept responsibility for rewarding themselves for the occurrence of target behaviors. • For example, "Because I met my goal of 80% on the spelling test, I will choose to do my new words on the computer."

In self-regulation a key aspect of what a student learns to do is to postpone an immediate reward in return for a more appropriate (and hopefully more satisfying) reward at a later time. This involves identifying behavioral alternatives (continuing to work), choosing reinforcers for the behavioral alternatives, and managing the delivery of delayed consequences (teacher praise or a good grade). Students begin with setting goals for their performance or behavior. They then use any of the self-management and self-instruction strategies as described in the student-directed approach to instruction. The next step is self-monitoring and self-recording followed by self-reinforcement

Self-monitoring and self-recording have been demonstrated in a number of studies to improve classroom behavior of students in special education programs. For example, self-monitoring has been shown to increase on-task behavior of students served in programs for mild disabilities (Blick & Test, 1987). The efficacy of a self-recording strategy has been demonstrated when applied to a broader array of behaviors. Four middle school students who were receiving special educational services in a resource room were taught to use a self-recording procedure to promote a set of discrete behaviors (Clees, 1994–95). General education mathematics teachers identified the students as not meeting the teachers' expectations for appropriate behavior and having deficient organization skills. Specific target behaviors were developed with the assistance of general educators in social studies and science and included on a brief checklist:

• Brings necessary materials to class,

• Begins class on task,

• Turns in completed homework,

• Completes all class work, and

• Writes homework in assignment book.

Students were trained to self-record whether their behavior in class had met the teacher's expectation statement. Students were instructed to keep track of what they needed to do by taking the form containing the schedule of teachers' expectations to each class and completing it and turning it in to the special education teacher at the end of the day. Students simply marked "yes" or "no" as to whether each of the five expectations was met. The attractiveness of this self-recording approach is its effectiveness and efficiency. Not only did the students' behavior improve across general education classes on behaviors that the general educators themselves identified as problems, but the procedure also required little training time, maintained the behavior change after the intervention was ended, and required only minimal participation by general educators.

Self-monitoring, self-evaluation/self-reinforcement, and self-instruction have been used to reduce inappropriate verbalizations with junior high students. Self-monitoring involved making tally marks on one side of an index card for appropriate verbalizations and on the other side for inappropriate verbalizations. The self-evaluation/self-reinforcement strategy required students to ask, "How is this working out? How am I doing?" When students thought they were doing well, they were instructed to tell themselves, "I'm doing a great job." Self-instruction training involved the teacher first demonstrating for students and then having students overtly and then covertly repeat a series of self-instruction commands (i.e., "Do I understand what I'm working on? What don't I understand? Should I raise my hand or talk out loud?"). The resultant drop in inappropriate verbalizations indicated the training was effective. Combining self-monitoring and self-instruction enhanced the improvement for these students (DiGangi & Maag, 1992).

Self-monitoring also can be used to improve academic performance. For example, students with learning differences used a student-directed intervention to improve spelling in a general education class. They listened to their spelling words using cassette players with headsets while they looked at the words printed in a column. Their scores in spelling improved and the students indicated they preferred this approach to the traditional method of study (Wirtz, Gardner, Weber, & Bullara, 1996). See **Figure 7.9** for sample self-monitoring charts.

Figure 7.9   Sample Self-monitoring Charts

Did I remember to:	Mon	Tue	Wed	Thu	Fri
Arrive at class on time?	✓	✓	✓		
Bring my books and pencil?	✓	—	✓		
Complete my homework?	✓	✓	✓		
Sit in my assigned seat?	—	✓	✓		
(Your choice)					

In doing my math did I . . .	Yes
Check the operation sign before starting?	✓
Line up the numbers in my columns?	✓
Begin solving in the ones column?	✓
Check my work?	—
Write my numbers neatly?	✓

In addition to self-monitoring, students can record and chart the results of their work to show themselves (and their teacher) the progress they have made in working toward their goal. Charts might show the number of things a student remembered to do, the number of words spelled correctly, or the percent of problems answered correctly. Once taught, these strategies also should assist students to function more independently in the regular education classroom.

Step 5: Differentiate Instruction

Differentiation of instruction is an approach to instruction that is firmly anchored in the notion that all instructional methods should be adjusted and adapted to the diverse individual learning needs of students (Tomlinson, 2001). The underlying premise is that all students, not just those with disabilities, learn in different ways. It is a process that requires that teachers examine the curriculum and develop a variety of ways to present the content of that curriculum to students. Again, it is essential for teachers to understand that there is no one preferred method for delivering content, but instead to acknowledge that a variety of research-based methods exist for delivering the content of that curriculum. With this in mind, it is possible to envision a classroom that incorporates student-directed and teacher-directed approaches to instruction within the same class setting. Such a classroom could allow for many opportunities for cooperative learning, but would also provide time for individual practice. One class session might start with a KWL chart, but the next might incorporate a story map to kick off instruction. It would also allow for co-teachers to play different roles at different times within the classroom depending on the needs of the students within that classroom.

Co-teaching is an effective model for providing differentiated instruction. It is an approach to serving students of multiple ability levels in one classroom. In this service delivery model, there is generally one general educator and one special educator who act as instructional specialists in the classroom. There is a shared responsibility between the teachers for the planning, delivery, and assessment of the instruction. Just as there are several approaches to delivering instruction, there are also several models of co-teaching. These approaches are:

1. one teach/one support,
2. station teaching,
3. parallel teaching,
4. alternative teaching, and
5. team teaching (Friend, 2006).

In the one teach/one support model, one teacher handles the bulk of the instruction and lesson presentation while the other teacher circulates among the students to ensure that they are on task and that they comprehend the material by offering individual support during the instruction. This model is frequently used by co-teachers who are new to the experience and who have not yet learned to integrate their contributions to the class.

For station teaching, several centers are positioned around the classroom, and one element of the lesson is the focus at each of the designated centers. In this model, both teachers are responsible for instructing. Both may circulate around the centers, or both may be responsible for leading one of the centers. These roles are agreed upon during the planning phase of the lesson. In parallel teaching, students are heterogeneously grouped together in similarly sized groups. The two teachers are then responsible for teaching the same content to each group. This approach allows for a reduced student-to-teacher ratio during active instruction.

With an alternative teaching model, flexible grouping is utilized to ensure that students are receiving instruction in the area in which it is most needed. One teacher interacts with a larger group while the other teacher works with a smaller group, and the content of that instruction is not the same and is dependent upon the learning needs of the students in the respective groups. In team teaching, the general educator and the special educator lead the lesson together adeptly transitioning throughout the lesson from one leading the instruction to the other.

Differentiating instruction allows teachers to meet a multitude of students' needs when serving students of multiple ability levels in the same classroom. It assumes that all of the students are at differing readiness levels due to differences in their background knowledge, learning styles, and interest levels. It is important to emphasize that differentiation is not a change in the curriculum or the learning objective, but rather it is a variation in the delivery of the content. With so many general education classrooms serving as the setting for meeting the educational needs of students with and without disabilities, it is critical that teachers embrace differentiation as they approach their instruction. When differentiating their instruction in any content area, in addition to implementing a variety of instructional methods, teachers must also be aware of the underlying factors that impact student receptiveness to those methods. In math, deficits in reading and attention, and a lack of corrective feedback can make some strategies more effective than others in different classrooms. **Figure 7.10** applies the principles for differentiating instruction in math.

Figure 7.10   Four Principles for Differentiating Instruction When Teaching Students with Math Difficulties

Be Alert to the Impact of Reading Difficulties
Teachers need to be alert to whether their students with math learning differences also have reading difficulties, and they will need to take this into account when teaching their classes how to read and comprehend math text. This is especially true because math directions involve specialized vocabulary that often uses everyday words in alternate ways that are specific to the field of math. This can lead to frustration, inaccuracy, and student responses that are confusing to interpret.

Be Alert to the Impact of Attention
Students with math learning differences struggle with directing their attention to the right place or operation in a math problem at the necessary moment, in the necessary sequence (Miller & Hudson, 2007). For teachers and co-teachers, therefore, an essential part of instruction is to use instructional methods that effectively grab the attention of students with math difficulties and direct it to the important visual information in a problem.

Be Alert to the Need for Corrective Feedback
Many students with learning differences experience difficulty in identifying errors in their own work and the work of others. For example, young children with math learning differences have greater difficulties than their peers when identifying errors made by others in counting (Murphy, Mazzocco, Hanich, & Early, 2007), which may persist into older ages. Math instructors should include immediate, corrective feedback on student responses because these students cannot afford to persist in using ineffective or inaccurate procedures. Such corrective feedback is essential so teachers and co-teachers can quickly locate and address student misunderstanding and reteach immediately.

Summary

Today's teachers will have students of varying ability levels in their classes. Some of those students may have been identified as having a specific disability, whereas others may simply be struggling with certain content. In striving to maximize student opportunities for success, teachers must first fully comprehend the academic content that they will be teaching. They then need to understand how to use assessment to better understand their students' academic skills and deficit areas. After ensuring their classroom environment is focused on learning, teachers must select research-based effective approaches to instruction to successfully teach the content. Lastly, it is critical that teachers not rely on a single teaching strategy, but use a variety of instructional strategies according to the needs of their students. The approaches to instruction and specific strategies presented in this chapter can be implemented across numerous content areas and in multiple instructional settings with all students, not just those with disabilities.

Classroom Application Activities

1. Think about the information presented and the structure of one of the class periods in this course. Design an advance organizer that indicates (a) the goals of the class period, (b) the main points that were covered, (c) the activities that took place during the class period, and (d) the expectations the instructor had for the students.

2. Select five terms and definitions in the content area of your choice. Follow the IT FITS Keyword Mnemonic method to develop picture cards using the keyword method in learning vocabulary words. The picture cards should include all of the components of the IT FITS method.

3. Interview a classroom teacher who has one or more students with learning differences. What instructional approaches does the classroom teacher use with her students? Why does she think that these methods are effective?

4. Observe a classroom in which peer tutoring is taking place. What skills are being taught or practiced? Is the peer tutoring providing reinforcement for correct answers? Corrective feedback for errors? What is the teacher doing while peer tutoring is occurring? Ask the teacher what was done to train tutors to work with other students.

5. Examine the co-teaching models described in this chapter. As you imagine your classroom (current or in the future), which two models do you believe you will use most frequently? Explain why these two approaches are your preferred methods.

Internet Resources

World Wide Web sites for teachers
Education World
http://www.education-world.com

The Educator's Reference Desk
http://www.eduref.org

Home page of the Council for Exceptional Children
http://www.cec.sped.org

Office of English Language Acquisition, Language Enhancement, and Academic Achievement for Limited English Proficient Students
http://www.ncela.gwu.edu

School-wide resources
http://school.aol.com

Strategies for teaching students with disabilities
http://curry.edschool.virginia.edu/go/specialed

What Works Clearinghouse
http://ies.ed.gov/ncee/wwc

Federal Government Resources for Teachers
http://www.ed.gov/free

Web-based resources on research on teaching
http://www.idea.uoregon.edu/~ncite/
http://cftl.org

Web-based resources for teachers and parents of students with learning disabilities
http://www.ldonline.org

Center for Applied Special Technology
http://www.cast.org

References

Anderson, L.W., & Wahlberg, H.J. (1994). *Time piece: Extending and enhancing learning time*. Reston, VA: NASSP.

Archer, A., & Hughes, C. (2011). *Explicit instruction: Efficient and effective teaching*. New York: Guilford Publications.

Ausubel, D. (1960). The use of advance organizers in the learning and retention of meaningful verbal material. *Journal of Educational Psychology, 51*, 267–272.

Baker, J.M., & Zigmond, N. (1990). Are regular education classes equipped to accommodate students with learning disabilities? *Exceptional Children, 56*, 515–526.

Berliner, D.C. (1987, January). *Effective classroom teaching*. Paper presented at the Fourth Annual School Effectiveness Workshop, Phoenix, AZ.

Bley, N.S. (2001). *Teaching mathematics to students with learning disabilities* (4th ed.). Austin, TX: Pro-Ed.

Blick, D.W., & Test, W. (1987). Effects of self-recording on high-school students' on-task behavior. *Learning Disability Quarterly, 10*, 203–213.

Brown, A.L. (1994). The advancement of learning. *Educational Researcher, 23*(8), 4–12.

Caldwell, J., Huitt, W., & Graeber, A.O. (1982). Time spent in learning: Implications from research. *The Elementary School Journal, 82*, 471–480.

Clees, T. (1994–95). Self-Recording of students' daily schedules of teachers' expectancies: Perspectives on reactivity, stimulus control, and generalization. *Exceptionality, 5*, 113–129.

Darch, C., & Gersten, R. (1986). Direction-setting activities in reading comprehension: A comparison of two approaches. *Learning Disability Quarterly, 9*, 235–243.

Deno, S. (1985). The nature and development of curriculum-based measurement. *Preventing School Failure, 2*, 5–11.

Deshler, D.D., Schumaker, J.B., Lenz, B.K., Bulgren, J.A., Hock, M.E, Knight, J., & Ehren, B. (2001). Ensuring content-area learning by secondary students with learning disabilities. *Learning Disabilities Research & Practice, 16,* 96–108.

DiGangi, S., & Maag, J. (1992). A component analysis of self-management training with behaviorally disordered youth. *Behavioral Disorders, 17,* 281–290.

Fisher, C.W., Filby, N.N., Marliave, R.S., Cahen, L.S., Dishaw, M.M., Moore, J.E., & Berliner, D. (1978). *Teaching behaviors, academic learning time, and student achievement. Final report of Phase III-B. Beginning Teacher Evaluation Study.* San Francisco: Far West Laboratory of Educational Research and Development.

Forness, S.R., Kavale, K.A., Blum, I., & Lloyd, T. (1997). Mega-analysis of meta-analysis: What works in special education and related services. *Teaching Exceptional Children, 29,* 4–9.

Friend, M. (2006). The coteaching partnership. *Educational Leadership, 64,* 48–52.

Gersten, R. (1998). Recent advances in instructional research for students with learning disabilities: An overview. *Learning Disabilities Research and Practice, 13,* 162–170.

Gersten, R., Chard, D., & Jayanthi, M. (2008). *Mathematics instruction for students with learning disabilities or difficulty learning mathematics: A synthesis of the intervention research.* Portsmouth, NH: RMC. Research Corporation, Center on Instruction.

Gersten, R., & Woodward, J. (1990). Rethinking the regular education initiative: Focus on the classroom teacher. *Remedial and Special Education, 11,* 7–16.

Graham, S., & Harris, K. (1994). The role and development of self-regulation in the writing process. In D.H. Schunk and B.J. Zimmerman (Eds.), *Self-regulation of learning and performance: Issues and educational applications* (pp. 203–228). Hillsdale, NJ: Erlbaum.

Greenwood, C.R., & Delquadri, J. (1995). Classwide peer tutoring and the prevention of school failure. *Preventing School Failure, 39,* 21–26.

Haynes, M.C., & Jenkins, J.R. (1986). Reading instruction in special education resource rooms. *American Educational Research Journal, 23,* 161–190.

Hudson, P., Miller, S.P., & Butler, F. (2006). Adapting and merging explicit instruction within reform based mathematics classrooms. *American Secondary Education, 35*(1), 19–32.

Jenkins, J., Deno, S., & Mirkin, P. (1979). Measuring pupil progress toward the least restrictive environment. *Learning Disability Quarterly, 2,* 81–92.

Jitendra, A.K. (2002). Teaching students math problem solving through graphic representations. *Teaching Exceptional Children, 34,* 348–390.

Johnson, D.W., & Johnson, R.T. (1994). *Learning together and alone: Cooperative, competitive, and individualistic learning* (4th ed.). Boston: Allyn & Bacon.

Keel, M.C., Dangel, H.L., & Owens, S.H. (1999). Selecting instructional interventions for students with mild disabilities in inclusive classrooms. *Focus on Exceptional Children, 31,* 1–16.

King-Sears, M.E., Mercer, C.D., & Sindelar, P.T. (1992). Toward independence with keyword mnemonics: A strategy for science vocabulary instruction. *Intervention in School and Clinic, 13,* 22–33.

Kroesbergen, E.H., & van Luit, J.E.H. (2003). Mathematics interventions for children with special educational needs: A meta-analysis. *Remedial and Special Education, 24*(2), 97–114.

Lenz, B.K. & Schumaker, J.B. (1999). *Adapting language arts, social studies, and science materials for the inclusive classroom.* Reston, VA: Council for Exceptional Children.

Lienemann, T., & Reid, R. (2006). Self-regulated strategy development for students with learning disabilities. *Teacher Education and Special Education, 29(1),* 3–11.

Maag, J.W. (2005). Social skills training for youth with emotional and behavioral disorders and learning disabilities: Problems, conclusions, and suggestions. *Exceptionality, 13,* 155–172.

Maccini, P., Mulcahy, C.A., & Wilson, M.G. (2007). A follow-up of mathematics interventions for secondary students with learning disabilities. *Learning Disabilities Research & Practice, 22*(1), 58–74.

Maccini, P., Strickland, T., Gagnon, J.C., & Malmgren, K. (2008). Accessing the general education math curriculum for secondary students with high-incidence disabilities. *Focus on Exceptional Children, 40,* 1–9.

Miller, S.P., & Hudson, P.J. (2007). Using evidence-based practices to build mathematics competence related to conceptual, procedural, and declarative knowledge. *Learning Disabilities Research & Practice, 22*(1), 47–57.

Montague, M (2007). Self-regulation and mathematics instruction. *Learning Disabilities Research & Practice, 22*(1), 75–83.

Montague, M., Bergeron, J., & Lago-Delello, E. (1997). Using prevention strategies in general education. *Focus on Exceptional Children, 19*(8), 1–12.

Murphy, M.M., Mazzocco, M.M., Hanich, L.B., & Early, M.C. (2007). Cognitive characteristics of children with mathematics learning disability (MLD) vary as a function of the cutoff criterion used to define MLD. *Journal of Learning Disabilities, 40*(5), 458–478.

Nelson, B. (2011). *Memory Techniques.* From www.iss.stthomas.edu/studyguides/memory.htm.

Peck, G. (1989). Facilitating cooperative learning: A forgotten tool gets it started. *Academic Therapy, 25,* 145–150.

Rose, D.H. (2001). Universal Design for Learning: Deriving guiding principles from networks that learn. *Journal of Special Education Technology 16*(1), 66–70.

Rosenshine, B.V. (1997). Advances in research on instruction. In J.W. Lloyd, E.J. Kame'enui & D. Chard (Eds.), *Issues in educating students with disabilities.* Mahwah, NJ: Lawrence Erlbaum.

Schumaker, J.B., & Deshler, D.D. (2003). Can students with LD become competent writers? *Learning Disability Quarterly, 26,* 129–141.

Schunk, D. (2000). Learning theories: An educational perspective (3rd ed.). Upper Saddle River, NJ: Prentice-Hall.

Scruggs, T.E., Mastropieri, M.A., & Rickter, L. (1985). Peer tutoring with behaviorally disordered students: Social and academic benefits. *Behavioral Disorders, 10,* 283–294.

Simmons, D.C., Chard, D., & Kame'enui, E.J. (1995). Translating research into basal reading programs: Applications of curriculum design. *LD Forum, 19(4),* 9–13.

Slavin, R.E. (1990). *Cooperative learning: Theory, research and practice.* Englewood Cliffs, NJ: Prentice-Hall.

Slavin, R.E. (1996). Research on cooperative learning and achievement: What we know, what we need to know. *Contemporary Educational Psychology, 21,* 43–69.

Sorrell, A.L. (1990). Three reading comprehension strategies: TELLS, story mapping, and QARs. *Academic Therapy, 25,* 359–368.

Spekman, N.J., Goldberg, R.J., & Herman, K.L. (1992). Learning disabled children grow up: A search for factors related to success in the young adult years. *Learning Disabilities Research and Practice, 7,* 161–170.

Strickland, T.K., & Maccini, P. (2010). Strategies for teaching algebra to students with learning disabilities: Making research to practice connections. *Intervention in School and Clinic, 46*(1), 38–45.

Swanson, H.L. (2001). Searching for the best model for instructing students with disabilities. *Focus on Exceptional Children, 34*(2), 1–15.

Swanson, H.C., & Hoskyn, M. (2001). Instructing adolescents with learning disabilities: A component and composite reality. *Learning Disabilities Research & Practice, 16,* 109–119.

Tomlinson, C.A. (2001). *How to differentiate instruction in mixed-ability classrooms* (2nd ed.). Alexandria, VA: ASCD.

Uberti, H., Scruggs, T.E., & Mastropieri, M.A. (2003). Keywords make the difference! Mnemonic instruction in inclusive classrooms. *Teaching Exceptional Children, 10,* 56–61.

U.S. Department of Education. (2011). Data Accountability Center. From https://www.ideadata.org.

Vygotsky, L. (1978). Interaction between learning and development. In *Mind and society* (pp. 79–91). Cambridge, MA: Harvard University Press.

Welch, M. (1992). The PLEASE strategy: A metacognitive learning strategy for improving the paragraph writing of students with learning disabilities. *Learning Disabilities Quarterly, 15,* 119–128.

Werner, E. (1993). Risk, resilience, and recovery: Perspectives from the Kauai Longitudinal Study. *Development & Psychopathology, 5,* 503–515.

Whinnery, K.W., Fuchs, L.S., & Fuchs, D. (1991). General, special, and remedial teachers' acceptance of behavioral and instructional strategies for mainstreaming students with mild handicaps. *Remedial and Special Education, 12*(4), 6–17.

Wirtz, C.L., Gardner, R., Weber, K., & Bullara, D. (1996). Using self-correction to improve the spelling performance of low-achieving third graders. *Remedial and Special Education, 17,* 48–59.

CHAPTER EIGHT

Students with Behavior Differences Affecting Achievement

L. Juane Heflin and Ginny L. Van Rie

CHAPTER OBJECTIVES

- to provide a brief overview of the two systems for classifying behavioral differences;
- to discuss Response to Intervention (RTI) for students with social and behavioral challenges;
- to describe the warning signs and characteristics of students with the following disabilities:
  - Attention Deficit/Hyperactivity Disorder (ADHD)
  - Emotional Disturbance (ED) or Emotional/Behavioral Disorders (EBD)
  - Traumatic Brain Injury (TBI)
- to introduce IDEA definitions and unique aspects of determining eligibility; and
- to discuss educational issues related to students identified with ADHD, ED, and TBI.

KEY TERMS

depression · oppositional defiant disorder · bipolar disorder · conduct disorders · schizophrenia · inattention · impulsivity · hyperactivity · motivation · emotional/behavioral disorders (EBD) · externalizing behavior disorders · internalizing behavior disorders · traumatic brain injury

This chapter provides an overview of students whose behavioral challenges may necessitate specialized management in order for them to be successful in the classroom. This includes students with attention deficit/hyperactivity disorder (ADHD), emotional/behavioral disorders (EBD), and traumatic brain injury (TBI). General factors influencing perceptions of behavior, including cultural diversity, are discussed. Because students with behavioral challenges, regardless of the subtype, require similar supports across the tiers of intervention, the unique applications for this population in documenting Response to Intervention (RTI) (discussed in Chapter 3) are described. Then the warning signs and characteristics associated with each of the disabilities are discussed with particular attention paid to how the characteristics may differ across diverse populations. If the RTI process is insufficient for promoting students' academic and social learning, the students may be deemed eligible for special education services. The assessment process and criteria dictated by Individuals with Disabilities Education Improvement Act of 2004 (IDEA 2004) for determining eligibility are described. Finally, issues for the classroom teacher are discussed, covering specific concerns and recommendations that should be considered when working with students with ADHD, EBD, and TBI.

Understanding Behavior

As discussed in Chapter 5, the culture in which we are raised and live plays a powerful role in shaping how we perceive and respond to the world around us (Chavis, 2012; Salett & Koslow, 1994). Each culture defines what is deviant (different from the norm) and expectations for people who are labeled as deviant (Lai, Luk, Leung, Wong, Law, & Ho, 2010; Scheff, 1966). In addition to cultural variations in determining acceptable behavior, culture can even dictate when conditions require intervention. Weisz, Suwanlert, Chaiyasit, and Weiss (1988) demonstrated that Thais do not consider extreme shyness or frequent fighting as problematic and believe that such behaviors will improve over time. In contrast, Americans rated these behaviors as serious enough to warrant professional help. Cultural socialization also may contribute to under- or overdiagnosis of students from different racial and ethnic groups. Contributing factors may include intentional or unintentional bias of professionals determining eligibility, mismatch between the values and behaviors of teachers and the students they serve, or institutional discrimination (Osher et al., 2004). Epstein et al. (2005) determined that teachers did not give biased ratings of students with ADHD from different ethnic groups; direct observation revealed that the children behaved differently, but the differences were related to socioeconomic status rather than ethnicity. At higher socioeconomic levels, African American males are overrepresented as having mental retardation whereas Asian females are least likely to be identified with mental retardation (Oswald, Coutinho, Best, & Nguyen, 2001). Similarly, African American students are overrepresented in the category of emotional disturbance whereas Asian, Pacific Islander, and Hispanic students are disproportionately underrepresented (Cullinan & Kauffman, 2005).

Culturally sanctioned behaviors that differ from what schools or teachers expect may present challenges. For example, some individuals are culturally socialized to keep their emotions to themselves, whereas other cultures encourage the expression of emotions (Rotheram-Borus, 1993). Some teachers will be intolerant of the "call-response" behavior (i.e., students making comments as teachers present information) preferred by some African American students (Weinstein, Tomlinson-Clarke, & Curran, 2004, p. 26). Or teachers may become upset when some Southeast Asian students smile when they are being reprimanded (not realizing that the student is smiling to show he knows he's guilty; Brown, 2003). These differences can contribute to the emergence of behavior problems.

Every teacher has a set of expectations for how students should behave for teaching to occur. Some teachers expect students to stay seated at all times, work individually, and speak only after they have raised their hands and been called on. Other teachers allow students to move around the room as necessary in order to gather materials for completing work and allow students to talk without raising their hands. When students demonstrate behaviors that differ from those expected by teachers, special consideration will have to be given to their management. Before developing management strategies, teachers should consider two key factors that influence students' behavior. The first factor is that all behavior happens for a reason. The second factor is that students' behaviors are inextricably linked to what is happening in the classroom.

Behavioral learning theory (Skinner, 1953) emphasizes that individuals engage in behaviors that allow them to either get something they want or avoid something they do not want. For example, college students who want to get a good grade in class will attend class meetings, study for tests, and demonstrate good social skills with the instructor. College students know to exhibit these behaviors in order to get a desired outcome (a good class grade). Likewise, most adults have learned to brush their teeth in order to avoid having the dentist fill cavities. Children and youth are quick to learn which behaviors help them get something they want or avoid something they do not want. If students come from chaotic and deprived home environments, they may have learned that the only way they can have food to eat is to take it from someone else. It should come as no surprise then that they demonstrate the same behaviors in school. Students also learn that if they want to avoid doing math, all they need to do is pick a fight with a peer right before math class, and they will spend the period in the principal's office, rather than in the dreaded math class. Or they may have learned to act "helpless" so that someone else will do their lab assignment for them. Students may learn to give up and act disinterested instead of attempting an assignment that they have not been able to do in the past. After all, who wants to put effort into something that has been graded "wrong" in the past? In particular, students who have experienced a traumatic brain injury (TBI) may be unable to adjust their behavior so that they get what they want or avoid what they do not want in a socially appropriate manner. Teachers should routinely ask themselves, "What is this student getting or avoiding with this behavior?" (A systematic way of conducting a functional behavior assessment [FBA] to answer this question is presented in Chapter 9.)

In addition to understanding that all behavior is demonstrated to get something or to avoid something, effective teachers recognize that behavior is related to the context in which it occurs. For example, there is a clear association between academic underachievement and behavior problems (Scott, Nelson, & Liaupsin, 2001). This association suggests curricula factors may influence behavior. Failure to individualize curricula can result in assignments that are too difficult or too easy, promoting misbehavior (Moore & Edwards, 2003; Umbreit, Lane, & Dejud, 2004). When students react to inappropriate curricula by behaving inappropriately, they typically are removed from the learning situation and consequently do not acquire the knowledge or skills being presented. This tends to cause the students to fall further behind in their learning which, in turn, increases the likelihood that they will demonstrate inappropriate behaviors because they are frustrated by the academic demands. Often the educational experiences of students with behavior challenges will be confounded by the emergence of learning challenges. Students with behavior challenges tend to have learning difficulties, and students with learning difficulties tend to demonstrate challenging behavior. When two or more disabilities occur in an individual, they are said to be coexisting. When individuals have coexisting disabilities, the primary or most pronounced disability will be listed first in the eligibility determination and given priority when determining appropriate educational services. For example, if a student has both learning disabilities and behavioral disorders, the student's eligibility team will decide which of the disabilities is most severe, will designate that as the primary disability, and will make educational programming decisions that reflect the primary disability. However, the secondary disabilities also will need to be considered when writing goals and determining needed services.

Classifying Differences in Behavior

Teachers can effectively manage most of the behavioral challenges in their classrooms by modifying the environment and expectations based on why they think a student is misbehaving and how the instructional demands are causing the behavior. A few students may have behavioral issues that are severe enough to warrant consideration for one or both of the following outcomes: (a) a professional diagnosis and (b) consideration of eligibility for special education services. The two are not the same, and each provides the potential for unique support.

A professional diagnosis is given based on the *Diagnostic and Statistical Manual of Mental Disorders* (American Psychiatric Association [APA], 2000) which contains an approach to classifying disorders that is widely used by medical and mental health professionals. The unique support that comes with a *DSM-IV* diagnosis is access to financial resources via insurance companies and government agencies. Insurance companies will not provide reimbursement for therapies to treat behavioral issues unless a qualified professional can document a *DSM* diagnosis. Similarly, individuals need a diagnosis to access the services offered by some government agencies. A physician, psychologist, psychiatrist, or specially licensed counselor gives a diagnosis based on the time frames and criteria established in the *DSM-IV*. Educational personnel (with the possible exception of a school psychologist with licensure) cannot give *DSM-IV* diagnoses. The *DSM-IV* differentiates among many behavioral conditions that IDEA 2004 collapses into the eligibility category of emotional disturbance (ED). There are *DSM-IV* criteria for depression, oppositional defiant disorder, bipolar disorder, and conduct disorders, among many others. All of these are subsumed under ED in IDEA 2004. Indeed, 76% of students who meet eligibility criteria for ED had at least one of the disorders contained in the *DSM* with approximately 65% of them taking prescription psychiatric medications (Hall, Bowman, Ley, & Frankenberger, 2006). Making distinctions among the various types of ED can help physicians and psychiatrists decide the best course of treatment, including the use of medications, for managing the disorders. Diagnoses enable professionals to speak a common language, plan treatments, and make insurance claims. However, a *DSM-IV* diagnosis does not qualify a student for special education services and actually may exclude the student from services (e.g., a *DSM-IV* diagnosis of conduct disorder specifically excludes a student from special education services in many states). *DSM-IV* diagnoses are frequently irrelevant for educational purposes, and teachers must be cautious when encountering a *DSM-IV* diagnosis because these diagnoses are not reviewed annually, unlike the eligibilities under IDEA. However, because the *DSM-IV* is widely used among noneducational agencies and must be used for diagnosing certain conditions such as attention deficit/hyperactivity disorder (ADHD), schizophrenia, and bipolar disorder, this classification system is referenced during the discussions of behavior challenges.

Another way of defining differences in behavior comes from federal law. As presented in Chapter 1, students in educational settings are classified according to categories defined in IDEA. Each state uses federal definitions as guidelines to develop specific eligibility criteria for each of the categories of disability. All of the definitions include the necessity for the disability to adversely affect educational performance before a student may be considered eligible for special education services. For example, students with mild learning disabilities may not be identified during kindergarten because the disabilities have not affected their ability to benefit from educational opportunities. However, as these students encounter more demanding academic tasks, it may become apparent that the disabilities are affecting learning and the students are not being helped by the multitiered interventions provided in general education settings. At this point, a referral to assess for special education eligibility would be appropriate. Federal law also provides a mechanism for identifying students in need of specialized support services even if they do not meet eligibility requirements for IDEA. Section 504 of the Rehabilitation Act requires the provision of support services if a condition affects an individual's functioning in major life areas (not just academic performance). Indeed, many students with attention deficit/hyperactivity disorder (ADHD) will be supported in schools under 504 plans rather than IEPs.

Response to Intervention for Students with Behavioral Challenges

Response to intervention (RTI) was introduced in IDEA 2004 to help identify students with learning disabilities (Sugai, 2008). The inclusion of RTI in the federal law emerged from the realization that the previously used model requiring documentation of a "discrepancy" between ability and achievement was not capturing the possibility that these discrepancies could occur because of inadequate teaching. The premise behind RTI is to ensure that evidence-based practices are used when implementing interventions and adapting instructional methods prior to referring a student for a full evaluation for special education eligibility (McCook, 2006). "RTI is defined as an inadequate change in target behaviors as a function of intervention" (Gresham, 2005, p. 331). The use of RTI ensures that evidence-based interventions are implemented and requires careful documentation of lack of improvement in the student's behavior prior to referring the student for a full evaluation. Implemented correctly, RTI may prevent behavior differences that affect learning from becoming disabilities (Greenwood & Kim, 2012).

Although RTI was introduced in IDEA 2004 specific to the category of learning disabilities, many states are now requiring that the RTI process be used in the determination of students with all types of disabilities, including those with behavior problems (Fairbanks, Sugai, Guardino, & Lathrop, 2007; Gresham, 2005, 2007). A word of caution is in order before describing how the RTI process could be used for students with behavior differences affecting achievement. Although RTI requires the use of empirically validated interventions, RTI itself has not been scientifically demonstrated to be effective for students with learning disabilities, let alone any other type of disability. Researchers may discover that RTI does not adequately identify students with learning disabilities but in fact may identify some students as having learning disabilities when they really do not, or RTI may not identify some students who really do have learning disabilities. This also could be the case for all other types of disabilities. Additionally, some districts are establishing guidelines for how long the interventions should be tried in each tier, with 4 weeks per tier being common. Because the research base to support the use of RTI is lacking and district requirements could lead to a 3-month delay in evaluating a student for eligibility consideration, IDEA 2004 contains a provision to bypass the process. Parents can write a request to skip the RTI process in order to get an immediate evaluation once a disability is suspected. Similarly, school districts can waive the need to document RTI for students with EBD if there is compelling evidence that the disability is not a result of inadequate opportunity to learn. However, because RTI has the potential to improve educational experience for all students by emphasizing the use of high-quality evidence-based instruction in general education classrooms (Gresham, 2007), possible applications for students with behavior difficulties are discussed.

Research is emerging that supports the use of RTI to reduce both the frequency and intensity of inappropriate behaviors displayed by students in general education classrooms (Benner, Nelson, Sanders, & Ralston, 2012). Another promising benefit of RTI is the ability to help reduce the overrepresentation of students from culturally and linguistically diverse populations who are receiving special education services for EBD (Cartledge et al., 2008). The RTI process removes the subjectivity that can result in disproportionate representation in EBD of children and youth from diverse populations (Harris-Murri et al., 2006). When the RTI tiers are followed correctly and data on the students are collected accurately, RTI has the potential to truly benefit students with various difficulties, including behavioral problems. RTI gives teachers the opportunity to intervene appropriately with behavioral problems in their classrooms instead of just observing or reporting the problems to someone else (Gresham, 2005).

The most common approach to RTI uses a tiered system that allows for consistency as well as permits interventions to be implemented based on the individual academic and behavioral needs of particular students (McCook, 2006). The process generates a pyramid. Tier 1 is the foundation of the pyramid and involves evidence-based classroom instruction and classroom management that is designed to meet the needs of all students. The implementation of a "Positive Behavior Support" model (see Chapter 9) is critical to the success of Tier 1 interventions for students with challenging behavior (Bradley, Doolittle, & Bartolotta, 2008). Tier 2, the middle of the pyramid, includes scientifically based supplemental instruction for students who require additional academic or behavioral support to keep pace with their peers. Tier 3 is the most intensive and individualized level of intervention. Students who do not respond favorably to the interventions and supports provided through all three tiers are referred for evaluation for eligibility for special education services. **Figure 8.1**

Figure 8.1   Interventions by Tier for Students with Behavioral Challenges

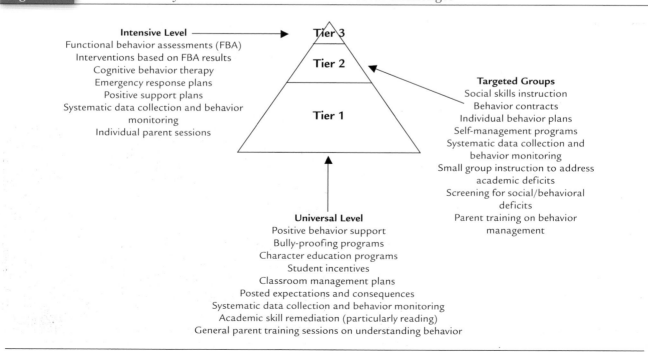

contains examples of interventions that may be helpful at each tier for students who have behavior differences affecting achievement.

Specific to supporting students with behavioral challenges, Tier 1 interventions could include schoolwide behavior expectations being explicitly taught to all students, school-based character education and anti-bullying programs, and structured classroom management plans implemented by the teacher (Fairbanks et al., 2007; Lane et al., 2007; Sugai, 2008). Because behavioral challenges often result in academic struggles, Tier 1 interventions must ensure that students can perform as expected on academic tasks (Kamps et al., 2003). This may be particularly important for students from underperforming schools containing high percentages of students who are culturally and linguistically diverse (Cartledge, Singh, & Gibson, 2008). Evaluating and remediating deficits in decoding and comprehension of written material is a critical Tier 1 intervention (Lane et al., 2002).

Students who continue to demonstrate challenging behavior after Tier 1 efforts would need to receive Tier 2, or targeted behavior interventions. This level of intervention is usually conducted using small, flexible, homogeneous groupings of students having similar problems within the same class or grade level (Fairbanks et al., 2007; Lane et al., 2007; McCook, 2006). Behavior interventions for Tier 2 could include behavior checklists, token economies, more frequent reinforcement for appropriate behavior, social skills instruction, conflict resolution training, self-management plans, and behavior contracts. Continuing to remember that academic deficits and misbehavior are highly correlated, Tier 2 interventions may need to include more intensive remediation of academic deficits.

Tier 3 is reserved for students whose behavior differences do not respond sufficiently to interventions used during the first two tiers. These students may require truly individualized instruction or behavior plans to help them succeed (Fairbanks et al., 2007; Lane et al., 2007; McCook, 2006; Sugai, 2008). Interventions used during the third tier could include a functional behavior assessment, behavior plans implemented based on the function of the behavior, cognitive behavior therapy, and emergency response plans. Some Tier 3 interventions will need to be implemented by someone with specialized training or expertise. Finally, students whose behaviors do not change sufficiently for them to experience academic success should be referred for a full evaluation to determine eligibility for special education services. If the behavior differences continue to take priority over learning differences, then students may be evaluated for eligibility under the categories of ED and TBI. Although ADHD is not a discrete category in IDEA, students with this disorder may meet criteria for other disability categories or may be served under the category of Other Health Impaired (OHI).

Attention Deficit/Hyperactivity Disorder (ADHD)

Children naturally vary in such things as activity level, impulse control, and ability for sustained attention. As they grow older, most children develop an increased ability to inhibit and control their activity level, impulsivity, and attention. However, a small group of children have extreme problems in managing all three. Such children exhibit inattention, impulsivity, and overactivity. Many exhibit problems in learning and may not exhibit acceptable behaviors in most social situations, especially in school. Estimates of the prevalence of ADHD vary widely, but the Centers for Disease Control and Prevention (2010) suggest that approximately 9.5% of students between 4 and 17 years of age have been

Inattention is an inability to focus or concentrate for age-appropriate amounts of time.

diagnosed by a licensed professional using *DSM-IV* criteria as having ADHD, making ADHD the most commonly diagnosed neurobehavioral childhood disorder.

Characteristics

There are three major characteristics present in children with ADHD: inattention, impulsivity, and hyperactivity. Inattention is defined as an inability to focus or concentrate for age-appropriate amounts of time. It is indicated by chronic difficulty in sustaining attention to tasks or play, chronic careless mistakes in schoolwork, not listening when spoken to directly, not following directions, having cluttered and disorganized materials, losing books and other materials, and being easily distracted by external stimuli not affecting other students. Setley (1995) discusses the misnaming of attention deficit disorder and suggests other possibilities such as "Attention Focusing Disorder," "Attention Fluctuation Disorder," or "Attention Surplus Disorder." Impulsivity is the inability to control one's behaviors and reactions on a reflective level. It is characterized by a tendency to blurt out answers, answering a question before the question is completely asked, not waiting for turns, chronically interrupting others, and failing to finish work. Teachers may describe impulsivity as a tendency to act first and think later. Hyperactivity is defined as excessive motor movement. It includes such behaviors as excessive fidgeting, squirming in seat, leaving seat while others remain seated, running about and climbing when such activity is clearly inappropriate, and seeming to be continuously in motion. Bloomingdale, Swanson, Barkley, and Satterfield (1991) describe hyperactivity as an excess of activity that is not task related, and others have suggested that this overactivity has erroneously been the focus of adult concern when the other components have more negative implications for learning (DuPaul, Guevremont, & Barkley, 1991). In addition, research indicates that individuals with ADHD not only have difficulties with inattention, impulsivity, and hyperactivity, but also have deficits in motivation (Barkley, 1990). Deficits in motivation explain why students with ADHD have difficulty focusing on school or social tasks but seem to have little difficulty playing video games for prolonged periods of time.

More than half of students labeled as having ADHD also exhibit conduct disorders or oppositional defiant disorder (Conner, Steeber, & McBurnett, 2010). Students with conduct disorders (CD) exhibit aggression toward people or animals, destruction of property, stealing, chronic lying, and severe rule violations. Oppositional defiant disorder (ODD) involves "a recurrent pattern of negativistic, defiant, disobedient, and hostile behavior toward authority figures that persists for at least 6 months" (APA, 2000, p. 100). Clearly, ADHD, CD, and ODD can coexist, creating a condition where a student may be at risk of engaging in anti-social behavior. In fact, studies show a significantly higher prevalence of involvement with the law by youth with coexisting ADHD and CD (Crowley, Milkulich, MacDonald, Young, & Zerbe, 1998). Yet it should be noted that not all students with ADHD have antisocial tendencies.

In addition to ever-increasing numbers of children being identified as having ADHD, more adults are being diagnosed with the disorder. Individuals with ADHD typically do not outgrow the disability (CDC, 2010). Due to the growing awareness that adults can have the disorder, one of the large parent and professional organizations, Children with Attention Deficit Disorder (CH.A.D.D.), had changed its name to "*Children and Adults* with Attention Deficit Disorders." Although school systems are responsible for identifying all students with disabilities, adults with disabilities, such as those with ADHD, must self-identify in order to receive accommodations in post-secondary education or the workplace according to the Americans with Disabilities Act (ADA).

Definition

Because IDEA does not define ADHD, the assessment team must turn to the psychiatric classification system to establish a diagnosis. As mentioned previously, the *Diagnostic and Statistical Manual of Mental Disorders* (DSM; APA, 2000) contains criteria for a number of disability conditions, including ADHD. The *DSM-IV* definition of ADHD specifies that the condition requires evidence of inattention, hyperactivity, and impulsivity, as defined by the presence of a certain number of symptoms. The *DSM-IV* lists the specific symptoms that must be present. The symptoms must have been apparent before age 7, have occurred for at least 6 months, and be inconsistent with the child's developmental level. The behaviors must be present in two or more settings (e.g., school and home). In addition, the student must show significant impairment in social and academic functioning. Finally, the *DSM-IV* (APA, 2000, p. 93) requires the following:

> The symptoms do not occur exclusively during the course of a Pervasive Developmental Disorder, Schizophrenia, or other Psychotic Disorder and are not better accounted for by another mental disorder (e.g., Mood Disorder, Anxiety Disorder, Dissociative Disorder, or a Personality Disorder).

DSM-IV criteria classifies students with ADHD into the following categories:

- Predominantly inattentive;
- Predominantly hyperactive/impulsive; and
- Combined type with inattentive and hyperactive.

According to the first category, an individual with ADHD can have problems with sustained attention without demonstrating hyperactivity (excessive motor movements). For example, students with the predominantly inattentive type of ADHD may be able to sit at their desks and look at the teacher, giving the appearance of listening to directions, but will fail to carry out the assignment given by the teacher. In contrast, students with the predominantly hyperactive/impulsive type of ADHD may fidget with their shoes, lean over the desk to talk to another student, and jump up to sharpen a pencil. Neither student will complete the assignment. Although differences in the diagnosis of ADHD relate to the level of hyperactivity, the educational outcomes are basically the same in that the students will not complete their assignments. In addition, students who demonstrate highly active behavioral levels create challenges for teachers who are trying to establish orderly, focused learning environments.

Various definitions of ADHD include the characteristics of inattention, impulsivity, motor restlessness, and differences in motivation. Parent and advocacy groups for ADHD lobbied to have ADHD as a discrete definition and category during the 1990 reauthorization of IDEA, but the issue was controversial. Some parents of children with ADHD think the current disability categories are insufficient to include their children. Many professionals believe that these children can be served by existing programs and that creating too many categories would be counterproductive (Forness, 1993).

As a result of the efforts of advocates, the IDEA description of Other Health Impairment (OHI) includes considerations for differences in attention. ADHD is listed as one of the chronic or acute health problems that could lead to an OHI eligibility. As stated in the law:

> Other health impairment means having limited strength, vitality or alertness, including a heightened alertness to environmental stimuli, that results in limited alertness with respect to the educational environment, that:
>
> (i) Is due to chronic or acute health problems such as asthma, attention deficit disorder or attention deficit hyperactivity disorder, diabetes, epilepsy, a heart

condition, hemophilia, lead poisoning, leukemia, nephritis, rheumatic fever, and sickle cell anemia; and

(ii) Adversely affects a child's educational performance.

Some students with ADHD will be found eligible for special education services under the category of OHI. Some students with ADHD will be served under another category of eligibility, such as ED or SLD, as determined by the eligibility team to reflect the most pronounced coexisting disability. Students with ADHD who do not qualify for special education services under one of the specific IDEA categories can receive accommodations under Section 504 of the Rehabilitation Act (1973). Indeed, most students with ADHD will be served according to the guidelines of Section 504, and a written plan will identify specific types of accommodations to allow them to benefit from their educational opportunities.

Assessment for Eligibility

A noneducational diagnosis of ADHD by someone such as a psychologist or psychiatrist, using the *DSM-IV*, can lead to a student being deemed eligible for special services under Section 504. Students with ADHD who need accommodations as guaranteed by Section 504 will receive those services in the general education classroom. Students with ADHD who are eligible for services under IDEA will have an IEP that specifies the support they will need to benefit from their educational opportunities.

Behavior rating scales are often used to document the symptoms of ADHD. Both parents and teachers use methods of direct observation and different rating scales to support the existence of symptoms across settings. **Figure 8.2** provides examples of the teacher version and the parent version of the Conners' Rating Scales (Conners, 1993).

Issues for the Classroom Teacher

There is general agreement that students with ADHD require highly structured home and school environments. In addition, a significant number of students with ADHD have been prescribed a variety of medications to help improve academics and enhance social functioning. Stimulant medications such as Ritalin, Dexadrine, and Cylert are prescribed by physicians, with Ritalin being the most common. When stimulant medications were first prescribed for students, they were described as having a paradoxical effect. The paradox occurs because a stimulant would excite an adult but has the opposite effect on children. We now know that this is untrue. Stimulants stimulate children just as they do adults. However, our understanding of ADHD has changed considerably. It is now believed that the parts of the brain that control motivation, attention, and inhibition are underactive in persons with ADHD. Therefore, the stimulants do what they should: stimulate the understimulated parts of the brain, resulting in greater attention and control of behavior.

As with all human behavior, the relationship between medication and improvement, or lack thereof, appears to be complex. Medication alone constitutes an inadequate form of intervention. Academic and environmental modifications definitely will be needed for students receiving stimulant medication. Teachers working with students who demonstrate the characteristics associated with ADHD must create carefully structured environments which incorporate behavior management techniques as described in Chapter 9.

To conclude, IDEA does not contain a discrete eligibility category for students with ADHD, although provisions have been made for students with the disability to be served under the label OHI if a medical professional has diagnosed the presence of the condition. Stimulant medications have been found to be helpful for reducing the motor activity of students with ADHD, but the use of such drugs has been controversial. Teachers will be

Figure 8.2 Samples of Rating Scales to Document ADHD

Conners' Teacher Rating Scale - Revised (S)
by C. Keith Conners, Ph.D.

Child's Name:_____ Gender: M   F

Birthdate:____/____/____   Age:_____   School Grade:_____
           Month   Day   Year

Teacher's Name:_____   Today's Date:____/____/____
                                                      Month   Day   Year

Instructions: Below are a number of common problems that children have in school. Please rate each item according to how much of a problem it has been in the last month. For each item, ask yourself, "How much of a problem has this been in the last month?", and circle the best answer for each one. If none, not at all, seldom, or very infrequently, you would circle 0. If very much true, or it occurs very often or frequently, you would circle 3. You would circle 1 or 2 for ratings in between. Please respond to each item.

	NOT TRUE AT ALL (Never, Seldom)	JUST A LITTLE TRUE (Occasionally)	PRETTY MUCH TRUE (Often, Quite a Bit)	VERY MUCH TRUE (Very Often, Very Frequent)
1. Inattentive, easily distracted	0	1	2	3
2. Defiant	0	1	2	3
3. Restless in the "squirmy" sense	0	1	2	3
4. Forgets things he/she has already learned	0	1	2	3
5. Disturbs other children	0	1	2	3
6. Actively defies or refuses to comply with adults' requests	0	1	2	3

Conners' Parent Rating Scale - Revised (S)
by C. Keith Conners, Ph.D.

Child's Name:_____ Gender: M   F

Birthdate:____/____/____   Age:_____   School Grade:_____
           Month   Day   Year

Parent's Name:_____   Today's Date:____/____/____
                                                     Month   Day   Year

Instructions: Below are a number of common problems that children have. Please rate each item according to your child's behavior in the last month. For each item, ask yourself, "How much of a problem has this been in the last month?", and circle the best answer for each one. If none, not at all, seldom, or very infrequently, you would circle 0. If very much true, or it occurs very often or frequently, you would circle 3. You would circle 1 or 2 for ratings in between. Please respond to each item.

	NOT TRUE AT ALL (Never, Seldom)	JUST A LITTLE TRUE (Occasionally)	PRETTY MUCH TRUE (Often, Quite a Bit)	VERY MUCH TRUE (Very Often, Very Frequent)
1. Inattentive, easily distracted	0	1	2	3
2. Angry and resentful	0	1	2	3
3. Difficulty doing or completing homework	0	1	2	3
4. Is always "on the go" or acts as if driven by a motor	0	1	2	3
5. Short attention span	0	1	2	3
6. Argues with adults	0	1	2	3

challenged to structure the environment and academic tasks so that students with ADHD will be able to succeed in school. **Figures 8.3A** and **8.3B** provide examples of the performance on a spelling test of a 10-year-old boy diagnosed with ADHD. The sample in Figure 8.3A was written while the student was not taking medication. Notice that he did not begin

| Figure 8.3A | Spelling Test of a Student with ADHD While Not on Medication |

the test until the teacher was on number seven. The test in Figure 8.3B reflects his performance after medication was initiated. **Figure 8.4** presents a description of a student with ADHD.

Emotional Disturbance (ED)

All teachers will encounter students with challenging behaviors. Students come to class with many personal issues and needs. Most of these will spill over into the classroom and affect the student's potential for learning. Not all challenging behaviors will be extreme. Teachers are accustomed to working with students who sulk or who are less than thrilled about an assignment. It is developmentally appropriate for students to go through phases where they orchestrate mini-rebellions (*"At 11:00, everyone drop your pencil"*) or are more interested in interacting with their peers than they are in complying with adult directives. However, some students' inappropriate behaviors and emotional reactions occur with greater intensity and frequency than the behaviors and reactions of their peers. These students' behaviors may differ so significantly that they are labeled as having emotional disturbances (ED). Most researchers and authors in the field use the term emotional/behavioral disorders (EBD) rather than ED in recognition that emotional and behavioral disorders coexist. Although state eligibilities must be based on the federal definition, the category label can vary. The preferable term, EBD, is used throughout this section.

Figure 8.3B   Spelling Test of the Same Student as in Figure 8.3A While on Medication

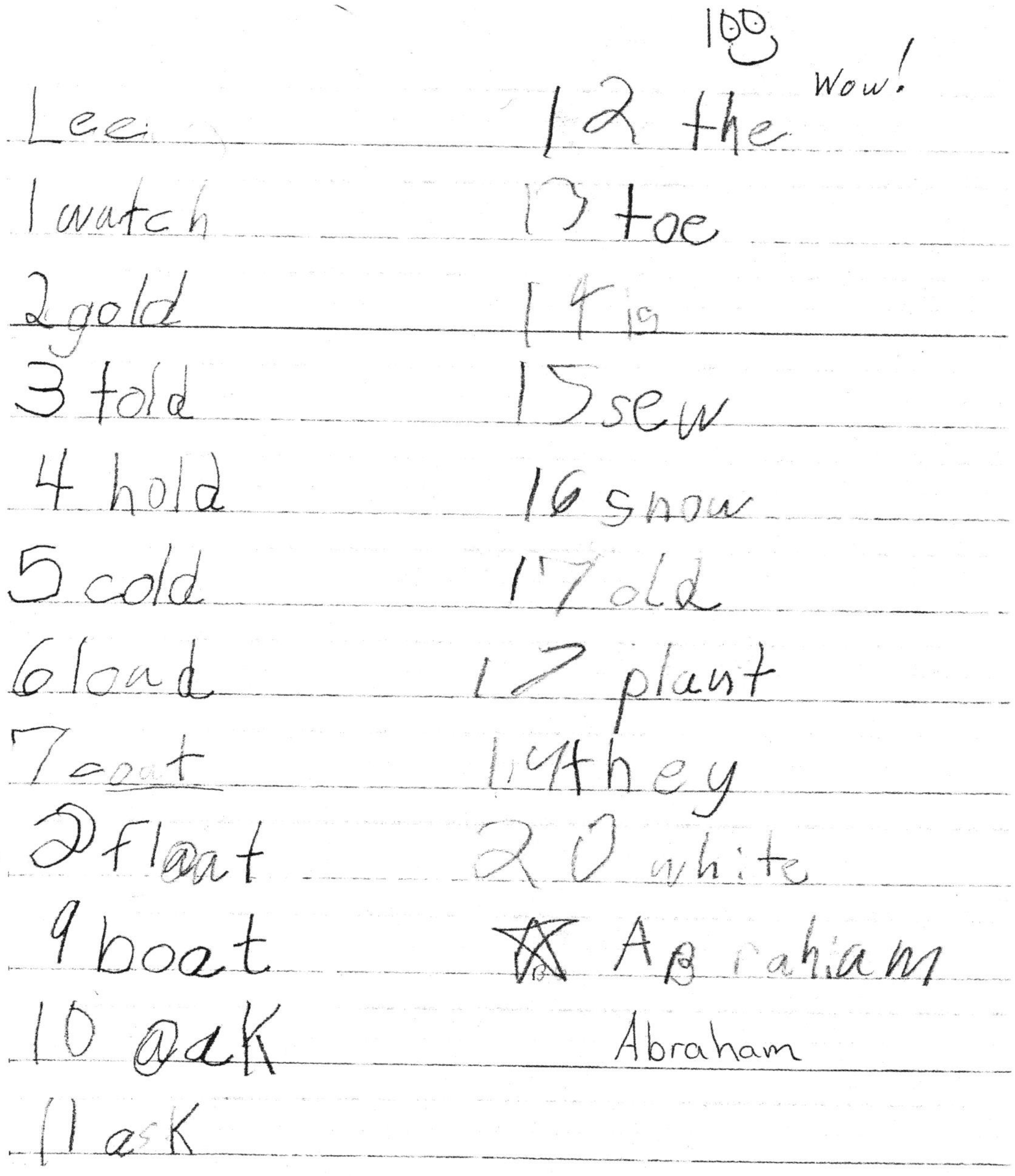

Characteristics

Emotional/behavioral differences may be directed outward, as in the case of students who are verbally or physically aggressive, or may be directed inward, as in the case of students who become depressed or develop extreme fears (phobias). The behaviors and emotions that are directed outward are called externalizing, and the ones directed inward are called internalizing (Quay, 1986). Students with EBD can demonstrate externalizing behavior disorders, internalizing behavior disorders, or a combination of both. Because students with externalizing behavior disorders are those who act out, educators tend to notice them before

Figure 8.4	Case Study of a Student with ADHD

Jessie's parents married later in life than most of their friends. They also waited until the perfect time to have children. It had taken quite a long time and many doctors' visits before Jessie was conceived. The birth of a healthy boy was a joyous and celebrated occasion. The baby was the center of attention, and attention he demanded! Feeding an infant on demand and giving the long-awaited only child that attention didn't seem out of line to his doting parents.

During his preschool years, Jessie was demanding, easily frustrated, and often destructive. When other children began to make friends and invite each other over, Jessie was left out. Around other children, Jessie's behavior became intolerable. He was possessive, reckless, and never satisfied. Special occasions, such as birthdays or parties, became a nightmare for anyone around Jessie. He would become overstimulated, scream, cry, and throw tantrums.

The preschool teacher talked at length to Jessie's parents about his behavior. His language skills and memory were advanced when compared to his peers. However, his fine motor skills were below expectation for his age; he had great difficulty cutting and coloring. During activities, Jessie would demand his turn, then rush through carelessly, and race to whatever caught his eye.

Jessie's parents, agreeing with the teacher's assessment, scheduled an appointment with their pediatrician. Dr. Smalley had a personal interest in ADHD and had received additional training in the identification and treatment of this disability. Dr. Smalley recommended several behavioral techniques for managing Jessie's behavior. Although the strategies could not stop Jessie's behavior, his parents gained valuable insight into minimizing his out-of-control behaviors. His parents also became more comfortable managing Jessie's behavior by using unemotional and consistent responses.

In school, additional problems began to appear. Jessie knew all the answers to the questions his teacher posed to the class and did not hesitate to blurt out his response, even when the inquiry was made to a reading group of which he was not a member. Jessie spent a great deal of time at the pencil sharpener, the window, and in time out. His papers were almost impossible to read due to his illegible handwriting, erasures, and the way he rushed through the task. At school, an RTI process was implemented, and his teacher began to use incentives to get him to complete his assignments. A classroom management plan was developed with behavioral expectations and consequences posted on the wall. Jessie's teacher collected data on out-of-seat behavior, completion of assignments, and altercations with peers.

The Tier 1 interventions had a positive effect on the overall class. However, Jessie's data continued to show high frequencies of out-of-seat behavior, incomplete assignments, and altercations with peers. A Tier 2 intervention was implemented in which his parents and teacher wrote a behavioral contract with Jessie that stipulated when he completed 75% of his assignments during the school day, he would be allowed to play with his Wii in the evening. The data indicated mixed results; Jessie did better some days than others.

His parents continued to consult with Dr. Smalley and provided him with information regarding Jessie's classroom behavior. It was decided that an in-depth evaluation needed to be done. Jessie's parents and his teacher completed questionnaires specific to his behavior. Additional tests were given to assess his cognitive abilities, language skills, and academic achievement levels. After reviewing all the documentation, Dr. Smalley diagnosed Jessie as having ADHD. Before prescribing medication, Dr. Smalley instructed both the parents and the teacher to collect information for 2 weeks. At home, his parents were told to record food intake, number of hours sleeping, and outbursts of screaming and crying. At school, the teacher continued to record the number of times Jessie was out of his seat, how many papers he completed legibly, altercations with his peers such as pushing incidents, shouting out of answers, and overall classroom participation. After the 2-week observation period, Dr. Smalley prescribed Concerta. Jessie's parents and his teacher were requested to continue collecting information on Jessie's behavior, food intake, and sleep patterns to determine if the medication was beneficial for supporting his academic and social behavior. The parents and teacher also monitored for potential adverse side effects. Because the environmental supports and medication were helpful, the school team determined that Jessie could be provided accommodations and adaptations under Section 504.

After many years of continued medication and behavior management, Jessie is now in middle school. His grades are excellent, and he exceeds academically. His behavior remains a challenge to everyone: teachers, parents, grandparents, scout leaders, and friends. He has not overcome his compulsive need to be first, interrupt conversations, have his say, or tell others what to do. Interactions are difficult because of his lack of control, and he does not have many friends. Although he always will have difficulty with relationships, Jessie will be able to earn a college degree and select a career that he finds rewarding. Jessie's ADHD can be managed, but it will look different as he grows into adulthood.

they notice students with internalizing behavior disorders. Students with internalizing behavior disorders may be withdrawn and call little attention to themselves, but they may need specialized interventions just as much as the students who are acting out (Bucy, 1994).

Quay and Peterson (1987) categorize behaviors using a behavioral dimensions classification system. According to their system, emotional/behavioral disorders may be divided into six classifications. These classifications and examples of typical behaviors are as follows:

1. Conduct Disorder (CD): antisocial, acting out, disruptive, temper tantrums, uncooperative, negative, argumentative, bully, blames others, selfish, cruel.
2. Socialized Aggression (SA): also called socialized delinquents; associates with "bad" companions, may belong to a gang, steals, cheats, lies, is truant, runs away from home, thinks highly of others who break laws or violate moral codes.
3. Attention Problems–Immaturity (AP): short attention span, distractible, impulsive, inattentive, acts younger than they are, has trouble following directions.
4. Anxiety–Withdrawal (AW): anxious, avoids, self-conscious, sensitive, depressed, fearful, believes they will always fail, difficulty making decisions, complains of feeling sick.
5. Psychotic Behavior (PB): difficulty differentiating between reality and fantasy, hallucinations, delusional thinking, e.g., childhood schizophrenia.
6. Motor Excess (ME): hyperactive, difficulty sitting still, fidgety, appears nervous, jumpy.

These six categories of behavior are useful in describing students who have emotional behavioral disorders. These six categories are grouped to create two behavioral profiles (undersocialized aggressive and socialized aggressive) and one emotional profile. The difference between the two behavioral profiles is awareness. Students who fit the profile of having an undersocialized aggressive conduct disorder appear to be unaware of behavioral expectations and do not appear to be aware of how to behave. These are students who demonstrate behaviors that fit in the categories of CD, AP, and ME. On the other hand, students who fit the profile of having a socialized aggressive conduct disorder appear to be aware that their behaviors are inappropriate and try to hide them or engage in them secretly. These are students who demonstrate behaviors described in the second category, socialized aggression (SA) (Quay, 1986). Whereas undersocialized aggression and socialized aggression are behavioral disorders, the behaviors described in the fourth category, anxiety-withdrawal (AW), are considered emotional disorders. Psychotic behaviors (PB) also may result from emotional disorders and are included in that profile. Although this distinction between behavioral and emotional disorders seems fairly clear-cut, the difficulty comes when one attempts to separate the emotions from the behavior or vice versa (Tankersley, 1993). **Table 8.1** provides a depiction of the types of EBD and their corresponding Quay and Peterson (1987) categories.

Note that using the classification system provided by Quay and Peterson (1987) or the classifications provided in the *DSM-IV* may actually prevent a student from being deemed eligible for special education services. Specifically, if he is classified as having a conduct disorder (CD) according to either source, the student will be automatically excluded from special education eligibility according to IDEA 2004. In addition, classifying a student as demonstrating socialized aggression according to Quay and Peterson often creates barriers for being able to consider whether or not the student is eligible for special education because of the perceived association with social maladjustment.

Two specific types of EBD warrant attention due to their increasing prevalence among school-age children and youth: bipolar disorder and schizophrenia. Bipolar disorder and schizophrenia are diagnosed using *DSM-IV* criteria by a professional who is qualified by

TABLE 8.1	
Categories of Emotional Behavioral Disorders According to Quay and Peterson	
Behavioral Disorders (externalizing)	*Emotional Disorders (internalizing)*

Undersocialized Aggressive Conduct Disorder

- Conduct Disorder
- Attention Problems—Immaturity
- Motor Excess

- Anxiety-withdrawal
- Psychotic behavior

Socialized Aggressive Conduct Disorder

- Socialized Aggression

training and license. These diagnoses may be useful for explaining a lack of responsiveness to intervention and documenting a need for special education services.

Bipolar Disorder. Bipolar disorder is a mood disorder that affects the brain as well as the nervous system and causes extreme mood swings from severe depression involving suicidal thoughts or actions to mania or elation (Walden & Grunze, 2004; Waltz, 2000). There can be a few days between the episodes or several years. However, children and adolescents with bipolar disorder can cycle from depression to mania several times in a day (Wilkinson, Taylor, & Holt, 2002). Children and adolescents with bipolar disorder are often incorrectly diagnosed as having attention deficit hyperactivity disorder, conduct disorder, oppositional defiant disorder, or anxiety disorders (Bardick & Bernes, 2005). Until recently children and adolescents were rarely diagnosed with bipolar disorder despite a large number of adults with bipolar disorder who reported they had their first manic or depressed episode prior to the age of 19 (Waltz, 2000).

There are several types of bipolar disorder, but the defining characteristic for all of them is extreme mood swings that negatively affect an individual's life (Waltz, 2000). All forms of bipolar disorder include one or more of the following moods: depression, hypomania, and mania. Clinical depression in reference to bipolar disorder involves a depressed state that lasts over a week and usually lasts about 2 months (Walden & Grunze, 2004). Some of the symptoms of clinical depression include prolonged sadness, uncontrollable crying, anger, irritability, anxiety, lack of energy, change in appetite, and withdrawal from social situations. Clinical mania is when individuals have manic thoughts and behavior that continue over a period of time and negatively affect their daily functioning. Symptoms of a manic phase include abnormal euphoria or optimism, exaggerated sense of self-confidence, aggression, talking really fast, impulsiveness, poor judgment, decreased need for sleep, and irritability. Hypomania is described as a milder version of a manic episode and is usually shorter in duration. During a hypomanic episode, individuals experience increased energy and creative ideas and require less sleep, but unlike in a manic episode, they are still able to control their behavior and appear to be socially acceptable. Finally, when individuals experience a mixed state, they have symptoms of both mania and depression.

Bipolar I (BPI) disorder used to be referred to as "manic depression." Individuals with BPI have at least one manic phase and may or may not have depressed or mixed states as well (Waltz, 2000). BPI is considered the most severe form of bipolar disorder but tends to be easier to treat because the mood swings tend to be wider, farther apart, and more predictable. Bipolar II (BPII) is characterized by recurrent depression with hypomania, without manic or mixed states. Cyclothymic disorder (cyclothymia) is usually diagnosed in children with chronic mood disturbances that include both depressed and hypomanic moods, but not major depressive, manic, or mixed episodes, and the symptoms must be present for at least one year. Finally, a doctor can diagnose a child with "mood disorder not otherwise specified" if the child has characteristics of BPI, BPII, or cyclothymic disorder but does not meet the requirements for a diagnosis.

A few behavioral characteristics of children with bipolar disorder include: irritability, hyperactivity, outbursts, hypersexuality, suicidal thoughts, self-centeredness, and oppositional, defiant, risky, or dangerous behavior (Bardick & Bernes, 2005). Often children and adolescents with bipolar disorders have sensitivity to physical stimuli such as pockets, clothing labels, and wrinkles in their socks (Wilkinson et al., 2002). They overreact to certain smells and noises, as well as either hot or cold temperatures. Some children and adolescents with bipolar disorders have extreme cravings for carbohydrates and sweet foods. **Table 8.2** provides some of the characteristics that may be displayed by children and adolescents with bipolar disorder (Bardick & Bernes, 2006; Wilkinson et al., 2002).

Bipolar disorder is a medical condition and beyond the control of the individual (Walden & Grunze, 2004; Waltz, 2000). However, environmental factors such as neglect, abuse, or an extremely emotional event such as the loss of a loved one can initiate the first manic or depressed episode or exacerbate the course of bipolar disorders. Bipolar disorders affect males and females equally. Bipolar disorders are diagnosed by a physician or psychiatrist using a process referred to as differential diagnosis or process of elimination (Wilkinson et al., 2002). The doctor or psychiatrist has to ensure that the symptoms are abnormal for the individual and that the mood swings are not caused by another disorder or the use of illegal or prescription drugs. A strong indicator of bipolar disorder in children is a family history of mood disorders or substance abuse (Walden & Grunze, 2004; Wilkinson et al., 2002). A major concern for parents, teachers, and physicians is that if children and adolescents with bipolar disorders go undiagnosed or without treatment, they may resort to the use of illegal drugs to help stabilize their moods or commit suicide.

Schizophrenia. Researchers hypothesize that a combination of genetic and environmental factors result in the expression of schizophrenia. Male children are diagnosed with schizophrenia two times more often than female children, but both males and females appear to develop psychotic symptoms around the same age (Gonthier & Lyon, 2004). In order to be diagnosed with schizophrenia, individuals must have two or more of the following symptoms during a 1-month period: delusions, hallucinations, disorganized speech, grossly disorganized or catatonic behavior, flat affect, deficiency of speech, or lack of resolve (Findling & Schulz, 2005). A child who has schizophrenia will demonstrate symptoms that add unusual behaviors as well as symptoms that reflect the absence of typical behavior. Symptoms that add behavior include hallucinations and delusions. The absence of typical behavior results in flat affect, loss of speech or concentrated thought, disorganized speech, bizarre behavior, and poor attention. Many children with schizophrenia demonstrate language delays, motor develop-

TABLE 8.2

Characteristics of Children and Adolescents with Bipolar Disorder

Irritability	Outbursts	Irregular sleep patterns (days and nights reversed)	Unable to display empathy
Destructive rage	Oppositional		Loss of cognitive ability
Tyrannical	Defiance	Combative	Unable to focus
Akathesia (restless inner tensions)	Anxiety	Self-centered	Difficulty controlling thoughts
	Hyperactive (especially at night)	Impulsive	
Risky/dangerous behavior		Hypersexual	Suicidal thoughts

TABLE 8.3
Characteristics of Children and Adolescents with Schizophrenia

Added Behaviors		*Absence of Typical Behavior*	
Hallucinations	Delusions	Flat affect	Lack of speech
		Lack of concentrated thought	Disorganized speech
		Bizarre behavior	Poor attention
		Unresponsive	Inappropriate emotional responses

ment delays, and inappropriate peer relationships (Gonthier & Lyon, 2004). The majority of children with schizophrenia have IQs in the normal range, but cognitive functioning is negatively affected once the child starts cycling through the four phases of the disorder. **Table 8.3** presents the behaviors characteristic of schizophrenia (Gonthier & Lyon, 2004).

Children with schizophrenia cycle through four phases and get progressively worse during each cycle (Findling & Schulz, 2005; Gonthier & Lyon, 2004). The four phases are the promordal phase, acute phase, recuperative or recovery phase, and the residual phase. During the promordal phase, children experience functional deterioration before they begin having psychotic symptoms. The acute phase produces significant decreases in social and cognitive functioning as well as the appearance of symptoms such as hallucinations and delusions. Children usually have to be treated in a hospital setting during this phase to ensure their safety and to monitor their reaction to medications used to treat their hallucinations and delusions. During the recuperative or recovery phase, children usually return home and to school and the hallucinations and delusions stop. However, poor attention and abnormal behavior usually persist. Finally, during the fourth stage (residual phase), children continue to be free of the hallucinations and delusions but are still impaired by flat affect, problems concentrating, disorganized speech, bizarre behavior, and poor attention (although these will have decreased).

The five main areas of focus when determining treatment for children with schizophrenia include pharmacological therapy, cognitive strategies, family interventions, educational interventions, and environmental manipulations (Gonthier & Lyon, 2004). Pharmacological therapy involves antipsychotic medication and close monitoring by a physician. Cognitive strategies include education about schizophrenia and treatment options, problem-solving skills, social skills training, and relapse prevention. Family therapy helps the family understand schizophrenia, treatment options, and coping strategies as well as communication skills. Environmental manipulations can include special education services as well as day treatment or residential settings, depending on the severity of the disorder. All five areas need to be considered and addressed when a child is diagnosed with schizophrenia.

Students with schizophrenia can benefit from the three tiers of interventions provided in the general education classroom, such as shortened assignments, large tasks broken into smaller tasks, tutoring, direct instruction, and instruction in functional life skills (Gonthier & Lyon, 2004). However, the severity of their disability may require evaluation for special education services in order to access smaller class sizes and experienced teachers knowledgeable in the area of EBD. Students with schizophrenia respond best to environments that are structured with consistent routines with teachers who are sensitive to the student's individual needs.

IDEA Definition for ED

Until IDEA 97, the federal category for students who met the eligibility being discussed here was "serious emotional disturbances" (SED). The legislative concession to the ongoing pressure to change the definition of SED was to drop the word "serious." IDEA 97 specified that the term "emotional disturbances" (ED) would be used instead of SED. Nothing was changed in the actual definition for ED.

The federal definition of ED was taken from the work of Bower (1960) who was designing criteria to determine which California school children were in need of mental health services. Bower's criteria were incorporated, with some critical changes, into the definition that became a part of IDEA. According to federal law, ED is defined as:

(i) The term means a condition exhibiting one or more of the following characteristics over a long period of time and to a marked degree, which adversely affects educational performance:
  (A) An inability to learn which cannot be explained by intellectual, sensory, or other health factors
  (B) An inability to build or maintain satisfactory interpersonal relationships with peers and teachers
  (C) Inappropriate types of behavior or feelings under normal circumstances
  (D) A general, pervasive mood of unhappiness or depression
  (E) A tendency to develop physical symptoms or fears associated with personal or school problems
(ii) Emotional disturbances includes schizophrenia. The term does not apply to children who are socially maladjusted unless it is determined that they have an emotional disturbance.

The definition in Public Law 94-142 (1975) originally included children with autism under section (ii), but autism was moved into the category of "Other Health Impaired" in 1981 and finally established as a discrete category under IDEA in 1990.

The federal definition of ED contains components that are controversial and inhibit the provision of services to students with challenging behaviors and emotional disorders. Questions have been raised as to what is meant by "a marked degree" and "a long period of time" and how that should be measured. The exclusion of students who are socially maladjusted seems to contradict criteria (B) and has led to the conclusion that we should be able to differentiate between students who are making a choice to act out and those whose behavior is not under their control (Weinberg, 1992). This conclusion has been challenged repeatedly (Merrell & Walker, 2004). Some cite lack of remorse as evidence against eligibility for EBD (Gacono & Hughes, 2004) because emotion is not involved. However, lack of remorse should be viewed as one of the strongest indicators of a disturbance in emotion. Additionally, social maladjustment is comorbid with internalizing disorders such as depression (Davis, Sheeber, & Hops, 2002). Finally, Nelson, Rutherford, Center, and Walker (1991) argue that the public schools have an obligation to serve all students, including those with social maladjustments, and that it is in society's best interest to serve these students and hopefully prevent many of them from becoming a social burden.

Assessment for Eligibility

Determining the eligibility of students who might have emotional behavioral disorders can be difficult. This is the most subjective of all disability areas in that it relates directly to teacher tolerance and cultural expectations (White & Renk, 2012). Teachers who expect

Determining eligibility of students who may have emotional behavioral disorders is the most subjective of all disability areas.

rigid conformity to a set of permissible behaviors as they have defined them will refer more students for consideration of EBD than will teachers who have a high tolerance for behavioral variations (Kauffman & Wong, 1991; Nelson, 1991). For example, teachers who expect students to stay in their seats unless given permission to do otherwise, raise their hands before speaking, and work quietly on an assignment until it is finished will experience a higher number of students who do not behave "appropriately" than will the teacher who allows students to speak at will, move about the classroom, and make decisions about the order in which tasks are to be completed. Teacher tolerance relates not only to the rules established in a classroom, but also to a teacher's preferences. Some teachers do not mind higher noise levels or students balancing back on two legs of a chair. These same behaviors will be so distracting to other teachers that they will spend large amounts of time and energy trying to change these behaviors. Some behaviors, such as fighting, verbal assault, and sexual acting out, are clearly unacceptable in school environments and will be perceived by all teachers as intolerable.

Once unacceptable behaviors have been identified, professionals will need to document their occurrence. Direct observation may be used in which the teacher counts the number of times a behavior occurs (frequency) and/or how long a behavior lasts (duration). Simple tallying may be used to record the frequency of a behavior, such as when a teacher makes a mark on a piece of paper or clicks a golf-counter whenever a student talks without raising her hand. The duration of time that a student is out of his seat and wandering around the room may be measured by using a stopwatch or the second hand on a wall clock. It also is important to determine if there is a pattern in when the behavior occurs (e.g., only during math class).

Another method of determining the degree of inappropriateness of a student's behavior is to assess the student on a behavior rating scale. There are several behavior rating scales available for use. To use a rating scale, someone who knows the student fairly well will mark behavioral items by indicating if they are characteristic of the student being rated. For example, one item on a rating scale might be "Fights." The rater would decide if fighting is not a problem, a mild problem, or a severe problem for the student being rated (Quay & Peterson, 1987). Some scales ask the observer to rate a student on a continuum between two opposite behaviors. For example, the observer would rate the student between "outgoing" and "withdrawn" (Bullock & Wilson, 1989). There are no right or wrong answers on rating scales; they simply indicate how students behave in relation to their peers. Once a student has been rated on a scale, the rater will follow the directions on the scale to determine a score. The score will indicate how different from the norm the student's behavior is and usually will provide scores in different subscale areas to help identify where the student has the most behavioral trouble. For example, the Revised Behavior Problem Checklist (RBPC) (Quay & Peterson, 1987) provides subscale scores in Conduct Disorders, Socialized Aggression, Attention Problems, Anxiety–Withdrawal, Psychotic Behavior, and Motor Excess. A student's subscale scores may indicate that the student has little problem with psychotic behavior, but significant problems with socialized aggression. The Behavior Dimensions Rating Scale (BDRS) (Bullock & Wilson, 1989) provides subscale scores in Aggressive/

Acting Out, Irresponsible/Inattentive, Socially Withdrawn, and Fearful/Anxious. **Figure 8.5** provides excerpts from the RBPC and the BDRS. Behavioral rating scales and/or direct observation may be used to substantiate the five criteria for EBD as specified in the law in order to help determine eligibility.

In addition to evaluating a student's behavior to determine eligibility, multidisciplinary school personnel must evaluate cognitive development, academic performance, physical abilities, and communication skills. To be eligible for classification as having an EBD, students must have an IQ test with a score above 70. With an IQ score below 70, the student probably will be considered eligible for special education services under the category of mental retardation. In addition, physical abilities must include adequate vision and hearing, or the student would be considered for eligibility as having a visual or hearing impairment. The presence of health conditions (such as diabetes, narcolepsy, and seizures) might force the consideration of the student as having a health impairment (OHI) and exclude the consideration for classification as EBD. Although most professionals agree that disability conditions can coexist, EBD will not be the preferred eligibility if any other condition is present. Professionals will use another eligibility (e.g., OHI, MR) if it applies because EBD is considered the most stigmatizing of all disability conditions (Osher et al., 2004).

Figure 8.5 Samples of Behavior Rating Scales

Behavior Dimensions Rating Scale (Bullock & Wilson, 1989)

1. hurts others	★ ★ ★ ★ ★ ★ ★	praises others 1.
2. self-conscious	★ ★ ★ ★ ★ ★ ★	confident 2.
3. short attention span	★ ★ ★ ★ ★ ★ ★	long attention span 3.
4. nondisruptive	★ ★ ★ ★ ★ ★ ★	disruptive 4.
5. outgoing	★ ★ ★ ★ ★ ★ ★	withdrawn 5.
6. possessive	★ ★ ★ ★ ★ ★ ★	sharing 6.
7. talkative	★ ★ ★ ★ ★ ★ ★	quiet 7.
8. shy	★ ★ ★ ★ ★ ★ ★	sociable 8.
9. likes classmates	★ ★ ★ ★ ★ ★ ★	dislikes classmates 9.
10. observes rules	★ ★ ★ ★ ★ ★ ★	breaks rules 10.
11. distractible	★ ★ ★ ★ ★ ★ ★	stays on task 11.
12. tense	★ ★ ★ ★ ★ ★ ★	tranquil 12.
13. bold	★ ★ ★ ★ ★ ★ ★	timid 13.

Revised Behavior Problem Checklist (Quay & Peterson, 1987)

1. Restless; unable to sit still	0 1 2
2. Seeks attention; "shows-off"	0 1 2
3. Stays out late at night	0 1 2
4. Self-conscious; easily embarrassed	0 1 2
5. Disruptive; annoys and bothers others	0 1 2
6. Feels inferior	0 1 2
7. Steals in company with others	0 1 2
8. Preoccupied; "in a world of his own;" stares into space	0 1 2
9. Shy, bashful	0 1 2
10. Withdraws; prefers solitary activities	0 1 2
11. Belongs to a gang	0 1 2
12. Repetitive speech; says same thing over and over	0 1 2
13. Short attention span; poor concentration	0 1 2
14. Lacks self-confidence	0 1 2
15. Inattentive to what others say	0 1 2
16. Incoherent speech, what is said doesn't make sense	0 1 2

In states requiring the use of an RTI model, teachers will need to document that they have tried a number of strategies in the general education classroom and that these strategies have been unsuccessful. In states that do not require RTI for students who might have an EBD, it is still worthwhile to ensure that environmental and instructional factors are meeting the needs of students before referring them for an eligibility evaluation. Prereferral strategies are described fully in Chapter 3 of this book and might include establishing a behavioral management plan, seating the student in an area free from distraction, and reducing the potential for frustration (which often leads to acting out) by shortening assignments, giving tests orally, and providing students with their own copies of material so that they do not have to copy from the board. Strategies such as those provided in three-tiered Figure 8.1 also may be useful for adequately supporting the needs of students with behavior differences affecting achievement.

Issues for the Classroom Teacher

One of the most challenging issues for classroom teachers who are working with students with EBD is the management of distracting and disruptive behaviors. Teachers who implement a sound classroom management plan for the entire class will reduce the number of challenging behaviors they have to address (Emmer & Stough, 2001). Chapter 9 describes considerations for creating a positive, focused atmosphere that encourages appropriate behaviors and discourages inappropriate behaviors.

Most teachers can relate to the challenges associated with managing disruptive behavior, but an emerging management issue for teachers is how to help students with internalizing disorders. These are the students who are depressed, anxious, possibly suicidal, and who may engage in self-destructive behaviors (anorexia, bulimia, substance abuse). Often these students do not want to attract the attention of an adult and will be extraordinarily obedient and compliant in school, even though their disorders are just as serious as the disorders of students who act out. Teachers should be aware of the telltale signs of depression and potential suicide as well as the indicators of self-destructive behaviors. **Table 8.4** lists some of the common signs that students are depressed and may be experiencing suicidal ideation (thoughts about ending one's life). School counselors are trained to recognize the signs and indicators and are a good resource for teachers.

TABLE 8.4

Warning Signs of Depression and Potential Suicide

1. Verbal threats
2. Changes in behavior (withdrawal, aggression, hyperactivity) including mood swings
3. Unusual purchases (items used in suicide attempts OR bizarre, out of character items)
4. Difficulty concentrating and staying on task (includes indecisiveness)
5. Changes in appetite, sleep, weight, or affect
6. School problems (drop in grades, absences, tardies, disruptions, cheating)
7. Final arrangements (giving away prized possessions, making a will, cleaning out room)
8. Death themes in conversation, writings, drawings, etc.
9. Use of drugs or alcohol
10. Sudden, unexpected happiness (relief, energy)
11. Frequent accidents
12. Prolonged grief after a loss
13. Neglect of personal hygiene and appearance
14. Previous suicide attempts

The most dangerous thing that educators do is ignore the warning signs, thinking that the youth will grow out of a "stage." All too often, educators who think that the student is just going through a phase or who see the suicide threats as attention-seeking behavior end up attending a funeral wondering what went wrong. The most helpful thing that educators can do is support the student without minimizing the depth of the student's experience. For example, rather than tell a student that "it's not the end of the world," empathize with and actively listen to the student's perceptions. Attempts to convince the student that suicide is morally wrong are usually counterproductive. Never promise that you will not tell anyone. Rather, promise the student that you will be very selective about who you tell and that you will only tell the people who need to know in order to help. Being supportive also includes helping students recognize what they have to look forward to, not only in life, but also in the near future. A game, concert, or holiday can be more motivational for withstanding daily dilemmas than the promise of a career. Finally, for students who are suicidal, never leave them alone, especially when they say they "just need to go to the bathroom." Teachers are not usually trained as counselors, but they can actively listen to a student until trained help arrives.

There are several ways teachers can help students with bipolar disorder or schizophrenia. First teachers need to be patient with the student and communicate concerns regarding a student's behavior with the parents and school officials (Bardick & Bernes, 2005). Teachers should be educated regarding bipolar disorder and schizophrenia and refer families to local support groups and community resources. They need to communicate with the parents the importance of an accurate diagnosis and the variety of support services available through the school system. Teachers should create activities and programs for students to teach appropriate social skills and self-management skills. Teachers can share their knowledge regarding bipolar disorders and/or mood disorders. Teachers should work to eliminate the stigma associated with mental illness and mood disorders by educating parents, peers, and children about the disorder and that the disorder is not shameful. Finally, teachers must take every threat of suicide seriously and inform both the family as well as the school officials to ensure the student's safety.

Another issue facing teachers is how to manage students who have gone beyond disruptive and distracting behaviors and are demonstrating behaviors that threaten the safety of others. Violence in the classroom has become one of the major issues impacting education (Sautter, 1995) with 38% of schools involving police for one or more episodes of violence in the 2005–2006 school year (U.S. Department of Education and Justice, 2009). In an attempt to reduce the number of violent incidents, schools have taken measures such as installing metal detectors and hiring security officers. Schools also are developing anti-violence curricula which emphasize problem-solving and peaceful alternatives to violent behavior. Just as with students who are threatening suicide, students who are threatening to harm someone else must be taken very seriously. Each school should develop a set of procedures for how to address threats of violence. The most ineffective actions that a school can take in addressing threats of violence are to suspend or expel the student. If the student has threatened violence in order to get kicked out of school, it worked. The student got exactly what was desired. Guess what the student will do again when the suspension is up? If the student has threatened violence in order to get attention, it worked again. The student not only got the attention from school staff when the violence was threatened but probably got some sort of peer attention and approval while out of school. The procedures developed by a school to address threats of violence must take into consideration what life events have brought the student to this action and how more effective problem-solving strategies can be taught so the student does not resort to the same threats in the future. For the morale of the intended victim(s), students who make threats should be considered for placement in alternate environments that can provide additional supervision, structure, and instruction in peaceful problem-solving. If the student is receiving special education services, it will be up to the IEP team to decide which alternatives are most appropriate. **Figure 8.6** describes a student who exhibits EBD characteristics.

Figure 8.6 Case Study of a Student with EBD

Jenny was born to an upper-middle-class family in a suburban area. As their firstborn, Jenny's parents had high expectations for her and reinforced her for perfect performance in all areas. Although they did not punish her when her performance was less than perfect, Jenny could sense that her parents were disappointed, which made her feel bad about herself. Frequently, Jenny would work on tasks much longer than necessary until the finished product met her standards.

Jenny did well in school until her third grade year. As the work became more challenging, Jenny discovered that she could not complete assignments perfectly within the given amount of time. Her previous teachers had provided Jenny with multiple copies of handouts so that her assignments would be turned in with no mistakes or erasures. Her third grade teacher, Ms. Jones, refused to give her extra copies of worksheets so that she could have a perfect product and expected her to finish her work in the same amount of time that it took the other students to finish. In addition, Jenny's tolerance for the mistakes made by her peers diminished, and she openly criticized their efforts.

As the year progressed, Jenny became more and more anxious about making mistakes and felt physically ill when her teacher gave an assignment. She attempted to structure herself so that there was little deviation in her routines and kept her desk and locker highly ordered as a way to cope with her anxiety.

Tired of her criticism and what they perceived to be an attitude of superiority, her peers began to torment her by moving things in her desk and "accidentally" marking on her papers. Jenny rarely spoke to anyone and bottled her turmoil inside of her until one day she exploded.

As Ms. Jones was passing back test papers, Jenny was thinking about her current unfinished assignment, full of erasures and mistakes, wadded up in her bookbag. She was further dismayed to see the 87 that glared at her in red ink at the top of her test. At the same time, one of her peers bumped her desk on the way back to his seat and laughed. Jenny grabbed her pencil and lunged at the boy, stabbing him in the arm.

When her mother arrived to pick her up from the principal's office, Ms. Jones described Jenny as uncontrollably violent. When Jenny returned to school following a brief suspension, her interactions with peers and teachers became increasingly aggressive and abusive. It was a relief to Jenny to be sent to the principal's office instead of staying in class where her peers taunted her and she was faced with the prospect of being rushed to turn in imperfect work. Ms. Jones started noticing a pattern in Jenny's eruptions—they came just as an assignment was being given. Ms. Jones implemented several Tier 1 interventions to address the situation. After consulting with Jenny's second grade teacher, Ms. Jones decided to give Jenny extra time to complete her work and gave Jenny blank assignment sheets to record her final answers. Most class periods ended with some downtime that Jenny could use to keep working or she could finish her work at lunch. Simultaneously, Ms. Jones asked the school counselor to come to her class to launch the "Bully Proof" program being implemented in several other classes. The counselor came in weekly and discussed the need for tolerance of individual differences, what the students could do to advocate for themselves if they were being victimized, and alternatives to bullying behavior. The counselor set up an incentive system for students to "catch" their peers being nice so that the class could work toward earning a pizza party. Ms. Jones's documentation of Jenny's behavior indicated that she was having fewer meltdowns but that the number was still unacceptable.

With the data to support that the Tier 1 interventions hadn't been completely effective, and realizing that Jenny was going to have to learn to accept imperfections, Ms. Jones implemented some Tier 2 strategies. She talked to the school counselor who invited Jenny to join his weekly social skills group to enhance her social competence and help her manage her anger. Ms. Jones contacted a local university and asked if any play therapists-in-training needed intern hours. Getting an affirmative response, Ms. Jones talked to Jenny's mother who willingly agreed to take Jenny to the university once a week after school. Ms. Jones, the school counselor, and Jenny's parents also met to talk about how to best help Jenny address her irrational thinking about perfectionism. They wanted to make sure they were all responding the same way and giving Jenny the same message. Ms. Jones tried implementing a self-monitoring system with Jenny in the classroom, but the number and intensity of Jenny's explosions increased, and Ms. Jones realized that asking Jenny to record her own behavior caused too much additional stress.

After a month of implementing the Tier 2 interventions, Ms. Jones analyzed the data on Jenny's assignment completion, duration of working, and peer interactions. The number of assignments completed had increased, but so had her duration of working. Apparently, Jenny was spending every minute at school working on her assignments, which was not allowing her much opportunity to apply the social skills she was learning. Her peer interactions were still problematic, although none of the other students taunted her any longer. It seemed that most of the peers simply ignored Jenny as if she didn't exist. Jenny's explosions had been reduced to one per day, but she also spent more time crying in class and seemed depressed.

Tier 3 interventions were implemented. Jenny started meeting individually with the school counselor every morning to talk about the day ahead. He checked on Jenny again at the end of the day to see how her day had gone. Ms. Jones started reducing the number of questions/problems that Jenny needed to complete for her assignments. A behavior specialist from the district was called to collect observational data on Jenny's outbursts. The function of the behavior was determined to be escape; Jenny lashed out to either get the peers to leave her alone or to get sent out of the room. The behavior specialist worked with Ms. Jones to develop a behavior intervention plan to modify the antecedents occasioning the behavior and to teach Jenny a replacement behavior. Even with these supports in place, data revealed that Jenny was still struggling to interact appropriately. Her grades, which had been slipping all year, also documented that her emotional and behavioral challenges were affecting her educational performance. Jenny's parents decided to initiate a referral for special education as it finally became apparent that Jenny's long-standing beliefs were interfering with her ability to be a part of and benefit from the general education environment.

Traumatic Brain Injury (TBI)

With the addition of the category of traumatic brain injury (TBI) to IDEA in 1990, an increase in attention and research has been given to the challenge of educating students with TBI (Bergland & Hoffbauer, 1996). This disability is unique because in addition to the rehabilitation of the injury, the student, family, friends, and teachers must adapt and cope with the sudden onset of the disability, as well as the changes in the student after the injury.

TBI is the most common cause of death and injury in the United States, with approximately 1.7 million brain injury cases reported annually (Coronado et al., 2011). Three major causes of traumatic brain injury are the following (Hooper et al., 2004):

- Accidents;
- Sports; and
- Violence/abuse.

Vehicle-related accidents are the most common cause of TBI, especially among adolescents. According to statistics, young children are more likely to be injured in a fall. Also in the United States, there is an increase in the number of gunshot wounds causing TBI in the younger population. Although technology has allowed us to protect students involved in sports with padding and helmets, a significant number of closed head injuries continue to occur during sporting events.

Nontraumatic brain injuries can be caused in a number of ways. Anoxic injuries occur due to a lack of oxygen to the brain. Possible causes of anoxic injuries include drownings, strangulation, and choking. Infections such as encephalitis and meningitis also are possible causes of nontraumatic brain injuries as are strokes, poisonings, and metabolic disorders (Savage & Ross, 1994).

Traumatic brain injuries continue to be a puzzle to the medical profession. Children who suffer such an injury rehabilitate differently than adults with the same type of injury. Due to the fact that the brain of a child or adolescent is not fully developed when the injury occurs, the outcome can be affected by the continuing development of the brain. Other factors that contribute to the outcome include the severity of the injury and whether the injury affects a specific area of the brain or if it is global in nature (Savage & Ross, 1994).

Characteristics

Students with TBI often exhibit variable outcomes and deficits in several major areas of functioning (Taylor, 2004). These include physical abilities, cognitive processes, language skills, behavioral and emotional conduct, and social relations (Kelly & Filley, 1994; Lehr, 1990). Often the degree of disability is related to the severity of the brain injury, the length of time spent in a coma following the injury, and the specific area of the brain that was injured (Voogt & Voogt, 1994). Neuropsychologists describe recovery from a brain injury as a process that continues to present challenges over time. Problems that emerge immediately after a brain injury evolve during the maturation of the student and may actually become worse over time, particularly in terms of behavior (Taylor, 2004). TBI that occurs at an earlier age often results in greater impact and deficits than brain injuries occurring in older students (Gil, 2003). According to Bergland and Hoffbauer (1996), Hooper et al. (2004), Kelley and Filley (1994), and Sosin, Sniezek, and Thurman (1991), unique characteristics of students with traumatic brain injury include the following:

- Typically male;
- Member of ethnic/racial minority from urban settings;
- Under age 10 and between ages 15 and 24;
- Often with prior history of special education services (ADHD and BD most common);
- Sudden onset of the disability;
- Loss of prior abilities or functions;
- Inability to learn due to cognitive or processing deficits;
- Inappropriate behavior resulting in a disruption of socialization.

In cases of mild TBI, students complain of headaches, fatigue, and sleep disorders long after the injury has occurred (Hooper et al., 2004). Possible physical problems associated with moderate and severe TBI include loss of consciousness; fine and gross motor problems involving activities such as walking, talking, running, and writing; seizures; hydrocephaly; and paralysis, among others. Depending on the specific area of the injury, the student may have sensory impairments that include vision and hearing problems. These impairments will affect the future educational needs of the student. Motor problems may affect speed and coordination, particularly when the task is complex (Lehr, 1990). Often physical impairments have a good prognosis for remediation with intensive rehabilitation programs (Tate et al., 2006).

In the area of cognitive processes, TBI may produce effects on concentration, memory, and executive functioning. Impairments in concentration and attention may make the student appear easily distracted or off task. This in turn will significantly slow down the student's ability to process information. Memory deficits most often affect long-term storage and retrieval, particularly of verbal material. Because memory skills are, to a large extent, developmental, the effects of TBI on memory may vary, depending on the age at which a head injury occurs. Executive functioning deficits interfere with students' ability to organize, plan, and carry out their plans (Keyser-Marcus et al., 2002).

Although language impairments generally are less severe in children than in adults with brain injuries, there may be effects on speech and articulation as well as subtle effects on language functioning. The impact on language functioning most likely will be evident in academic performances involving written language. Some initial problems with language may be an inability to recall names or bits of information, mutism (not talking), and/or not initiating conversation. According to Lehr (1990), there are great expectations for a positive recovery of language and speech skills unless the injury has damaged the specific area of the brain that controls language and speech functioning.

In general, the effects on behavior may include an increase in the variability of behavior and an exaggeration of behavior patterns already present at the time of injury. The overall appearance is a reduced level of control over behavior that makes the student's behaviors appear less predictable. Specific effects that might be observed include hyperactivity (overly active) or hypoactivity (underactive), less frustration tolerance, an increase in irritability, aggressiveness and impulsiveness, a greater susceptibility to fatigue, emotional immaturity, egocentrism, sexual acting out, and a reduction in motivation (Ganesalingham et al., 2011; Ylrisaker et al., 2007).

In the area of social/emotional behavior, deficits are described by family, teachers, and friends as a change in the student's personality. There may be a reduction in social perception and judgment, exaggerated emotional expression, social ineptitude and social insensitivity, an increase in demands on others, and a decrease in compliance with the demands of others. Students may describe themselves as feeling out of control. It is possible that these inappropriate behaviors are rooted in the student's anger or in a perception of who they used to be.

Definition

Traumatic brain injury (TBI) is defined in IDEA as follows:

> Traumatic brain injury means an acquired injury to the brain caused by an external physical force, resulting in total or partial functional disability or psychosocial impairment, or both, that adversely affects a child's educational performance. Traumatic brain injury applies to open or closed head injuries resulting in impairments in one or more areas, such as cognition; language; memory; attention; reasoning; abstract thinking; judgment; problem solving; sensory, perceptual, and motor abilities; psychosocial behavior; physical functions; information processing; and speech. Traumatic brain injury does not apply to brain injuries that are congenital or degenerative, or brain injuries induced by birth trauma.

The definition of TBI focuses on students who have sustained an injury caused by an external force. These injuries typically fall into two categories. A closed head injury occurs when the trauma does not cause a puncture to the skull or protective covering of the brain. It might be caused by hitting a windshield during an accident or when an infant is shaken violently. An open head injury causes some type of puncture to the protective covering of the brain, such as a gunshot wound. Students can experience traumatic and nontraumatic head injuries. Nontraumatic head injuries include brain damage from a stroke or near drowning. Students with nontraumatic head injuries are served under other disability categories according to their specific needs (Kelly & Filley, 1994; Savage & Ross, 1994).

Assessment for Eligibility

The actual diagnosis of a traumatic brain injury is made by a physician. However, for educational purposes, assessment of students with traumatic brain injury requires a multidisciplinary team composed of professionals from a variety of areas, as well as family, teachers, and friends of the student (Keyser-Marcus et al., 2002). When possible, a pediatric neurologist completes a comprehensive neurological examination. Other professionals such as the speech-language pathologist, occupational therapist, physical therapist, and educational diagnostician will assess their specific areas of concern. It is critical that the family, teachers, and friends contribute information concerning how the student functioned before the injury, and how the student is currently functioning in the home, school, and community environments (Lehr, 1990; Savage & Ross, 1994).

During the assessment process, it is important to obtain information about the abilities of the student before the injury occurred, as well as the student's current strengths and weaknesses. Previous learning skills will give the team members insight as to the strengths and particular ways of learning the student used previously. Recommendations for future programming will take this information into account in the rebuilding of lost skills. For example, if the student was a strong auditory learner (i.e., learned quickly when listening to lectures), the use of materials with an auditory component may be a way to regain information that was lost.

Professionals will assess the student using many of the standardized test instruments available. Typically, an intelligence test and other achievement tests will be given. These tests will provide information regarding how the student solves problems, organizes information, and recalls information, and will determine specific reading, math, and writing skills. Several speech and language tests will be administered by the speech-language pathologist to obtain information concerning the student's expressive and receptive language, as well as the student's speech production. The occupational and physical therapists will conduct an assessment of the student's fine and gross motor skills, providing information on the student's motor abilities such as balance, gait, movement, and dressing, as well as the ability to use utensils such as a pencil or fork. Behavioral/personality tests will be given to assess the student's current social behavior, including activity levels, self-control, interactions, and emotionality (Kelly & Filley, 1994; Keyser-Marcus et al., 2002; Lehr, 1990; Savage & Ross, 1994).

An assessment of a student with TBI always should include observation of how the student functions in the home, school, and community settings (Savage & Ross, 1994). The standardized test information is important, but it is limited in regard to how the student performs in daily living situations. Because appropriate performance in everyday settings is the ultimate goal, information regarding how the student processes information or behaves in the school, home, and community is critical. Gil (2003) recommends ongoing educational assessments as students with TBI continue to develop. Family, teachers, and friends play an important role in observing and reporting this information.

Issues for the Classroom Teacher

A major issue related to the disability of traumatic brain injury is the adjustment of the student, family, teachers, and friends to the loss of the student's skills and the change in personality (Fowler & McCabe, 2011). By the time the student returns to school, the medical aspects of the injury will be resolved so that the person "looks" the same as before. When learning, behavioral, and social problems occur, it is difficult for teachers and peers to understand because the expectation is that the student is the same as before. More often than not, students with TBI remember how they were before the injury and feel frustration and anxiety, which only adds to the problems. Family, teachers, and friends also become frustrated with the situation, adding to the difficulties. Another major challenge for students with traumatic brain injuries occurs as they continue to grow and develop. There is ample research to support the positive recovery of physical, cognitive, language, and behavior skills in students with TBI; however, as the student develops, additional problems may occur and cause a developmental lag (Gil, 2003). This is especially true of behavioral and emotional characteristics. As social demands increase with adolescence, new behavioral problems may appear. A functional behavior assessment (see Chapter 9) may be critical for addressing behavioral challenges (Bowen, 2005).

With regard to the actual teaching of students with traumatic brain injury, the technology, teaching strategies, and behavior management techniques discussed in other chapters assists in planning and implementing day-to-day instruction. The use of personal digital assistants, color coding, graphic organizers, and mnemonic strategies can assist students with TBI in organizing and retaining information (Keyser-Marcus et al., 2002). Close attention to noise, light, and activity will be important (Bowen, 2005). Knowledge of the specific strengths and weaknesses of the student will allow the teacher to select the appropriate technology, strategies, and techniques that will enhance the success of the student with a TBI. It would be beneficial for the teacher to obtain information regarding the specific type of brain injury that the student has experienced. This will allow the teacher to better understand what to expect in regard to behavior and learning. Current written information, direct contact with the student's physician, or contact with one of the national organizations listed at the end of this chapter will be beneficial to the teacher.

Information gained from these sources will aid in the teacher's understanding of the need to revise the IEP more frequently during the first few years following the injury. Progress in all of the areas of concern may render the IEP out of date before the typical annual revision is needed. Also, the issue of transition should be a major focus of the IEP due to the fact that transitions and change often trigger a need for additional support for the student with a TBI. **Figure 8.7** contains a case study of a student with a TBI.

Figure 8.7 Case Study of a Student with a Traumatic Brain Injury

Rauol really enjoyed all sports but was not particularly great at any one sport. His favorite afternoon activity was a basketball game on the driveway. His grades were above average, and his favorite class was science. He looked forward to the days when there was an experiment to conduct in the science lab. One time the teacher had instructed the students to dissect a cow's eye. Now that was a great class!

It was a typical Saturday evening as a group of the guys gathered to drive around town and find where everyone was hanging out. It was 6 weeks before Rauol's sixteenth birthday and the rite of passage into adulthood when he would receive his driver's license. This was the first opportunity for Rauol's best friend to drive the guys around in the old pickup truck his father had saved for him. When the guys arrived at the mall where everyone had gathered, they stopped to visit the girls. After a brief visit, it was decided that everyone would ride over to the drag strip for some fun. Everyone piled in, and the truck sped off. Just as the truck made its lunge forward, Rauol tumbled off the tailgate and landed on his head.

It was months later before Rauol emerged from the rehabilitation center. He had spent 3 weeks in a coma and 2 months in the intensive care unit. From there it was hours and hours of physical therapy, occupational therapy, and speech-language therapy. It was a slow and painful process, and although Rauol regained his ability to walk and talk, it was not a total recovery. It was obvious when he walked that Rauol's gait was abnormal, and when he talked his speech was slurred. But Rauol and his family were ecstatic with his recovery.

Upon returning to school, it was a shock to find that so much of what he knew before the accident was gone or fragmented. It was impossible to start where he had left off at the time of his accident. Documentation of the severity of his TBI and his frustration in class during his first day back at school was sufficient to document RTI. Rauol received intensive instructional services in pull-out and general education settings in the eleventh grade. Rauol could learn; it just took him longer. He did not take notes but listened intently to the information being presented. Often the information would have to be repeated or explained in a different way. He needed to have his tests read aloud but was able to pass them. These changes required a tremendous emotional adjustment for Rauol and his friends.

Progress continued at a slow pace, and it took an additional 2 years for Rauol to graduate. It was a great accomplishment, but his social life was never what one would expect for a teenager. Often Rauol's interactions were inappropriate. His questions to females were out of line, and he would attempt to touch them inappropriately. He was unable to perceive subtle hints regarding typical interactions. This would result in peers rejecting him.

Rauol completed college, majoring in rehabilitation counseling. It has been a long and difficult road, but his hard work has paid off. However, his social interactions continue to be depressing and frustrating for him. What is so difficult is that Rauol remembers and realizes the way he used to be, but he cannot change the way he is.

Summary

The majority of students with behavior differences affecting achievement will be educated in general education classrooms. Some of these students will have needs that require the provision of specialized services outside of general education settings. Students with ADHD, who may be eligible for special education support under the category of OHI, will have difficulty sustaining attention on the relevant aspects of instruction and may also exhibit problems controlling their impulses. Students with EBD may demonstrate behaviors that interfere with their learning and the learning of others in the instructional environment. Although few students will be identified with TBI, the sudden discrepancy between their current functioning and how they functioned prior to the injury creates psychological and practical challenges for teachers, the students, their peers, and the students' families. Students with TBI present additional challenges as their functioning is not stable but continues to change over the course of their recovery and development. Students with behavioral challenges frequently will be under the care of a physician or psychiatrist who will prescribe medication to help manage their disabilities. Teachers are in an important position to report on the benefits as well as the unwanted side effects of these medications.

Given increases in class sizes and numbers of teachers encountered, educational systems are structured so that students are expected to demonstrate more and more control over their own behavior as they get older. Students with behavioral challenges may not respond well to the decreasing levels of external control in middle and high school settings and may be more likely to get into trouble at school. Walker, Colvin, and Ramsey (1995) indicate that students who continue to be aggressive, disruptive, and antisocial after the third grade will probably need ongoing support to manage their behavior. They draw the analogy that chronic antisocial behavior is similar to chronic health conditions such as diabetes—it cannot be cured but must be managed daily. EBD affects not only teachers, peers, and family members of those affected, but also has a negative impact on the students themselves. Sacks and Kern (2008) found that adolescents with EBD were more dissatisfied with themselves and their relationships than were their peers without EBD. Ongoing behavioral challenges and diminished quality of life converge so that the social and academic outcomes of students with EBD are worse than all other disability categories, and 56% of students with EBD will drop out of school before graduating (Bradley et al., 2008). More than 50% of students with EBD will be arrested even if they do graduate, but 70% of those who drop out will get in trouble with the law (Quinn as cited in Sacks & Kern, 2008). Of those who graduate, only 20% will enroll in colleges or technical schools, and only about 30% can find and maintain employment (Wagner, Kutash, Duchnowski, & Epstein, 2005). At least 33% of all students will experience EBD at some point in their school careers, with only the most severely affected receiving special education services (Forness, Freeman, Paparella, Kauffman, & Walker, 2012). Teachers who effectively provide positive behavior supports while maintaining a focus on ensuring academic success for all students may help reduce the severity and duration of EBD (Bradshaw, Mitchell, & Leaf, 2010). However, behavioral challenges extend beyond the school environment, making it even more critical that parents, teachers, medical practitioners, and administrators collaborate effectively to promote learning and social behavior for students with ADHD, EBD, and TBI in the school, home, and community.

Classroom Application Activities

1. What are the differences between the **DSM-IV** classification of disabilities and the eligibility categories in IDEA? Why are there two different systems?

2. Individually or in groups, compare and contrast the characteristics and eligibility requirements of students with attention deficit/hyperactivity disorder, emotional/behavioral disorders, and traumatic brain injuries. Which academic and behavioral characteristics will be similar, and which will be specific to each category?

3. Individually or in groups, identify five behaviors that a teacher might see in the classroom for each of the following disabilities. Describe implications specific to these behaviors.

    a. ADHD

    b. EBD

    c. TBI

4. Individually or in groups, consider the eligibility issues regarding students with ADHD. In what situations would a student with ADHD qualify for special education services?

5. Individually or in groups, identify the possible associated difficulties for students with TBI and their families. What are the implications for supporting the students with TBI in your classroom?

6. Interview a general education teacher in your preferred content area (e.g., secondary biology, elementary art, early childhood) and ask about accommodations that are used for students with behavior differences affecting achievement.

7. Talk with an administrator of a local school and ask what the procedures are for the following:

   a. Intervening with students who have suicidal ideation

   b. Handling students who threaten school personnel

   c. Reporting suspected abuse or neglect

8. Locate a **Physician's Desk Reference** and look up the following medications that are commonly prescribed to children with behavior challenges. Write down the reasons for prescribing, the impact on learning/behavior, and associated side effects for each medication.

   a. Ritalin

   b. Dexedrine

   c. Cylert

   d. Concerta

   e. Abilify

   f. Seroquel

   g. Anafranil

   h. Risperdal/Risperidone

Internet Resources

American Academy of Child and Adolescent Psychiatry
http://aacap.org

Balanced Mind Foundation (family resources for children with mood disorders)
http://www.thebalancedmind.org

Brain Injury Association of America
http://www.biausa.org

CH.A.D.D. (Children and Adults with Attention Deficit/Hyperactivity Disorders)
http://www.chadd.org

Council for Children with Behavioral Disorders
http://www.ccbd.net

Depression and Bipolar Support Alliance
http://www.ndmda.org

Intervention Central
http://www.interventioncentral.org

National Center on Response to Intervention
http://www.rti4success.org

National Institute of Mental Health on Bipolar Disorder
http://www.nimh.nih.gov/health/publications/bipolar-disorder/complete-publication.shtml

Response to Intervention Action Network
http://www.rtinetwork.org

Traumatic Brain Injury Resource Center
http://www.braininjuryresources.org

What Works Clearinghouse (contains strategies for each tier of RTI)
http://ies.ed.gov/ncee/wwc

References

American Psychiatric Association. (2000). *Diagnostic and statistical manual of mental disorders* (4th ed., text revision). Washington, DC: Author.

Bardick, A.D., & Bernes, K.B. (2005). A closer examination of bipolar disorder in school-age children. *Professional School Counseling, 9,* 72–78.

Barkley, R.A. (1990). *Attention-deficit hyperactivity disorder: A handbook for diagnosis and treatment.* New York: Guilford Press.

Benner, G.J., Nelson, J., Sanders, E.A., & Ralston, N.C. (2012). Behavior intervention for students with externalizing behavior problems: Primary-level standard protocol. *Exceptional Children, 78,* 181–198.

Bergland, M., & Hoffbauer, D. (1996). New Opportunities for Students with Traumatic Brain Injuries: Transition to Postsecondary Education. *Teaching Exceptional Children, 28*(2), 54–56.

Bloomingdale, L., Swanson, J.M., Barkley, R.A., & Satterfield, J. (1991, March). *Response to the ADD Notice of Inquiry by the Professional Group for ADD and Related Disorders.* Scarsdale, NY: Professional Group for ADD and Related Disorders.

Bowen, J.M. (2005). Classroom interventions for students with traumatic brain injuries. *Preventing School Failure, 49,* 34–41.

Bower, E.M. (1960). *Early identification of emotionally handicapped children in the schools.* Springfield, IL: Charles E. Thomas.

Bradley, R., Doolittle, J., & Bartolotta, R. (2008). Building on the data and adding to the discussion: The experiences and outcomes of students with emotional disturbance. *Journal of Behavioral Education, 17,* 4–23.

Bradshaw, C.P., Mitchell, M.M., & Leaf, P.J. (2010). Examining the effects of schoolwide positive behavioral interventions and supports on student outcomes. *Journal of Positive Behavior Interventions, 12,* 133–148.

Brown, D.F. (2003). Urban teachers' use of culturally responsive management strategies. *Theory into Practice, 42,* 277–282.

Bucy, J.E. (1994). Internalizing affective disorders. In R.J. Simeonsson (Ed.), *Risk resilience and prevention: Promoting the well-being of all children.* Baltimore, MD: Paul H. Brookes.

Bullock, L.M., & Wilson, M.J. (1989). *BDRS: Behavior dimensions rating scale*. Chicago, IL: Riverside.

Cartledge, G., Singh, A., & Gibson, L. (2008). Practical behavior-management techniques to close the accessibility gap for students who are culturally and linguistically diverse. *Preventing School Failure, 52*, 29–38.

Centers for Disease Control and Prevention. (2010). Increasing prevalence of parent-reported attention-deficit/hyperactivity disorder among children—United States, 2003 and 2007. *Morbidity and Mortality Weekly Report, 59*(44), 1439–1443.

Chavis, A. (2012). Social learning theory and behavioral therapy: Considering human behaviors within the social and cultural context of individuals and families. *Journal of Human Behavior in the Social Environment, 22*, 54–64.

Connor, D.F., Steeber, J., & McBurnett, K. (2010). A review of attention-deficit/hyperactivity disorder complicated by symptoms of oppositional defiant disorder or conduct disorder. *Journal of Developmental and Behavioral Pediatrics, 31*, 427–440.

Conners, C. (1993). *Attention Deficit Hyperactivity Disorder*. North Tonawanda, NY: Multi-Health Systems.

Coronado, V.G., Xu, L., Basavaraju, S.V., McGuire, L.C., Wald, M.M., Faul, M.D., Guzman, B.R., & Hemphill, J.D. (2011). Surveillance for traumatic brain injury-related deaths: United States, 1997–2007. *Morbidity and Mortality Weekly Report, 60*(SS05), 1–32.

Crowley, T.J., Milkulich, S.K., MacDonald, M., Young, S.E., & Zerbe, G.O. (1998). Substance-dependent, conduct-disordered adolescent males: Severity of diagnosis predicts 2-year outcomes. *Drug & Alcohol Dependence, 49*, 225–237.

Cullinan, D., & Kauffman, J.M. (2005). Do race of student and race of teacher influence ratings of emotional and behavioral problem characteristics of students with emotional disturbance? *Behavioral Disorders, 30*, 393–402.

Davis, B., Sheeber, L., & Hops, H. (2002). Coercive family processes and adolescent depression. In J.B. Reid, G.R. Patterson, & J.J. Snyder (Eds.), *Antisocial behavior in children and adolescents: A developmental analysis and model for intervention* (pp. 173–192). Washington, DC: American Psychological Association.

DuPaul, G.J., Guevremont, D.C., & Barkley, R.A. (1991). Attention-deficit hyperactivity disorder. In T.R. Kratochwill & R.J. Morris (Eds.), *The practice of child therapy* (2nd ed., pp. 115–144). New York: Pergamon.

Emmer, E.T., & Stough, L.M. (2001). Classroom management: A critical part of educational psychology, with implications for teacher education. *Educational Psychologist, 36*, 103–112.

Epstein, J.N., Willoughby, M., Valencia, E.Y., Tonev, S.T., Abikoff, H.B., Arnold, L., & Hinshaw, S.P. (2005). The role of children's ethnicity in the relationship between teacher ratings of attention-deficit/hyperactivity disorder and observed classroom behavior. *Journal of Consulting and Clinical Psychology, 73*, 424–434.

Fairbanks, S., Sugai, G., Guardino, D., & Lathrop, M. (2007). Response to intervention: Examining classroom behavior support in second grade. *Exceptional Children, 73*, 288–310.

Findling, R.L., & Schulz, S.C. (Eds.). (2005). *Juvenile-onset schizophrenia: Assessment, neurobiology, and treatment*. Baltimore: Johns Hopkins University Press.

Forness, S. (1993, November). *The Balkanization of Special Education*. Paper presented at the meeting of the Severe Behavior Disorders Conference, Tempe, AZ.

Forness, S.M., Freeman, S., Paparella, T., Kauffman, J.M., & Walker, H.M. (2012). Special education implications of point and cumulative prevalence for children with emotional or behavioral disorders. *Journal of Emotional and Behavioral Disorders, 20*, 4–18.

Fowler, M., & McCabe, P.C. (2011). Traumatic brain injury and personality change. *Communique, 39*(7), 4, 6, 8, 10.

Gacono, C.B., & Hughes, T.L. (2004). Differentiating emotional disturbance from social maladjustment: Assessing psychopathy in aggressive youth. *Psychology in the Schools, 41*, 849–860.

Ganesalingam, K., Yeates, K., Taylor, H., Walz, N., Stancin, T., & Wade, S. (2011). Executive functions and social competence in young children 6 months following traumatic brain injury. *Neuropsychology, 25*, 466–476.

Gil, A.M. (2003). Neurocognitive outcomes following pediatric brain injury: A developmental approach. *Journal of School Psychology, 41*, 337–353.

Gonthier, M., & Lyon, M.A. (2004). Childhood-onset schizophrenia: An overview. *Psychology in the School, 41*, 803–811.

Greenwood, C.R., & Kim, J. (2012). Response to Intervention (RTI) services: An ecobehavioral perspective. *Journal of Educational and Psychological Consultation, 22*, 79–105.

Gresham, F.M. (2005). Response to intervention: An alternative means of identifying students as emotionally disturbed. *Education and Treatment of Children, 28*, 328–344.

Gresham, F.M. (2007). Response to intervention and emotional behavioral disorders: Best practices in assessment for intervention. *Assessment for Effective Intervention, 32*, 214–222.

Harris-Murri, N., King, K., & Rostenberg, D. (2006). Reducing disproportionate minority representation in special education programs for students with emotional disturbances: Toward a culturally responsive response to intervention model. *Education and Treatment of Children, 29*, 779–799.

Hooper, S.R., Alexander, J., Moore, D., Sasser, H., Laurent, S., King, J., Bartel, S., & Callahan, B. (2004). Caregiver reports of common symptoms in children following a traumatic brain injury. *NeuroRehabilitation, 19*, 175–189.

Individuals with Disabilities Education Improvement Act of 2004, 20 U.S.C. § 1400 *et seq.* (2004) (reauthorization of the Individuals with Disabilities Act of 1990).

Kamps, D.M., Wills, H.P., Greenwood, C.R., Thorne, S., Lazo, J.R., Crocket, J.L. et al. (2003). Curriculum influences on growth in early reading fluency for students with academic and behavioral risks: A descriptive study. *Journal of Emotional and Behavioral Disorders, 11,* 211–224.

Kauffman, J.M., & Wong, K.L. (1991). Effective teachers of students with behavioral disorders: Are generic teaching skills enough? *Behavioral Disorders, 16,* 225–237.

Kelly, J.P., & Filley, C.M. (1994). Traumatic brain injury in children. In C. Simkins (Ed.), *Analysis, Understanding and Presentation of Cases Involving Traumatic Brain Injury* (pp. 37–52). Washington, DC: National Head Injury Foundation.

Keyser-Marcus, L., Briel, L., Sherron-Targett, P., Yasuda, S., Johnson, S., & Wehman, P. (2002). Enhancing the schooling of students with traumatic brain injury. *Teaching Exceptional Children 34,* 62–67.

Lai et al. 2010.

Lane, K.L., Rogers, L.A., Parks, R.J., Weisenbach, J.L., Mau, A.C., Merwin, M.T. et al. (2007). Function-based interventions for students who are nonresponsive to primary and secondary prevention efforts: Illustrations at the elementary and middle school levels. *Journal of Emotional and Behavioral Disorders, 15,* 169–183.

Lane, K.L., Wehby, J.H., Menzies, H.M., Gregg, R.M., Doukas, G.L., & Munton, S.M. (2002). Early literacy instruction for first-grade students at-risk for antisocial behavior. *Education and Treatment of Children, 25,* 438–458.

Lehr, E. (1990). *Psychological management of traumatic brain injuries in children and adolescents.* Rockville, MD: Aspen.

McCook, J.E. (2006). *The RTI guide: Developing and implementing a model in your schools.* Horsham, PA: LRP Productions.

Merrell, K.W., & Walker, H.M. (2004). Deconstructing a definition: Social maladjustment versus emotional disturbance and moving the EBD field forward. *Psychology in the Schools, 41,* 899–910.

Moore, J.W., & Edwards, R.P. (2003). An analysis of aversive stimuli in classroom demand contexts. *Journal of Applied Behavior Analysis, 36,* 339–348.

Nelson, C.M. (1991). Serving troubled youth in a troubled society: A reply to Maag and Howell. *Exceptional Children, 58,* 77–79.

Nelson, C., Rutherford, R., Center, D., & Walker, H. (1991). Do public schools have an obligation to serve troubled children and youth? *Exceptional Children, 58(1),* 406–415.

No Child Left Behind Act of 2001, 20 U.S.C. 70 § 6301 *et seq.* (2002).

Osher, D., Cartledge, G., Oswald, D., Sutherland, K.S., Artiles, A.J., & Coutinho, M. (2004). Issues of cultural and linguistic competency in disproportionate representation. In R.B. Rutherford, M.M. Quinn, & S.R. Mathur (Eds.), *Handbook of research in emotional and behavioral disorders* (pp. 54–77). New York: Guilford.

Oswald, D.P., Coutinho, M.J., Best, A.M. & Nguyen, N. (2001). Impact of sociodemographic characteristics on the identification rates of minority students as having mental retardation. *Mental Retardation, 39,* 351–367.

Quay, H. (1986). Classification. In H.C. Quay & J.S. Werry (Eds.), *Psychopathological disorders of childhood* (3rd. ed.). New York: Wiley.

Quay, H.C., & Peterson, D.R. (1987). *Manual for the revised behavior problem checklist.* Odessa, FL: Psychological Assessment Resources.

Rotheram-Borus, M. (1993). Multicultural issues in the delivery of group interventions. *Special Services in the Schools, 8(1),* 179–188.

Sacks, G., & Kern, L. (2008). A comparison of the quality of life variables for students with emotional and behavioral disorders and students without disabilities. *Journal of Behavioral Education, 17,* 111–127.

Salett, E.P., & Koslow, D.R. (Eds.). (1994). *Race, ethnicity, and self: Identity in multicultural perspective.* Washington, DC: National Multicultural Institute.

Sautter, R.C. (1995). Standing up to violence. *Phi Delta Kappan, 76,* K1–K12.

Savage, R.C., & Ross, B. (1994). School-age children with traumatic brain injuries. In C. Simkins (Ed.), *Analysis, understanding and presentation of cases involving traumatic brain injury* (pp. 53–64). Washington, DC: National Head Injury Foundation.

Scheff, T. (1966). *Being mentally ill.* Chicago, IL: Aldine.

Scott, T.M., Nelson, C.M., & Liaupsin, C.J. (2001). Effective instruction: The forgotten component in preventing school violence. *Education and Treatment of Children, 24,* 309–322.

Setley, S. (1995). *Taming the dragons: Real help for real school problems.* St. Louis, MO: Starfish.

Skinner, B.F. (1953). *Science and human behavior.* New York: Macmillan.

Sosin, D.M., Sniezek, J.E., & Thurman, D.J. (1991). Incidence of mild and moderate brain injury in the United States. *Brain Injury, 10,* 47–54.

Sugai, G. (2008). *School-Wide Positive Behavior Support and Response to Intervention.* From http://www.rtinetwork.org/Learn/Behavior/ar/SchoolwideBehavior.

Tankersley, M. (1993). Classification and identification of internalizing behavioral subtypes (behavioral disorders, emotional disorders). *Dissertation Abstracts International, 54(06),* 2118. (University Microfilms No. AAC 9324904).

Tate et al. 2006.

Taylor, H.G. (2004). Research on outcomes of pediatric traumatic brain injury: Current advances and future directions. *Developmental Neuropsychology, 25,* 199–225.

Umbreit, J., Lane, K.L., & Dejud, C. (2004). Improving classroom behavior by modifying task difficulty: Effects of increasing the difficulty of too-easy tasks. *Journal of Positive Behavior Interventions, 6,* 13–20.

U.S. Department of Education. (1991). *Clarification of policy to address the needs of children with attention deficit disorders within general and/or special education.* Washington, DC: Author.

Voogt, R.D., & Voogt, K.R. (1994). Emotions and traumatic brain injury. In C. Simkins (Ed.), *Analysis, understanding and presentation of cases involving traumatic brain injury* (pp. 23–35). Washington, DC: National Head Injury Foundation.

Wagner, M., Kutach, K., Duchnowski, A.J., & Epstein, M.H. (2005). The Special Education Elementary Longitudinal Study and the National Longitudinal Transition Study: Study designs and implications for children and youth with emotional disturbance. *Journal of Emotional and Behavioral Disorders, 3,* 25–41.

Walden, J., & Grunze, H. (2004). *Bipolar affective disorders: Etiology and treatment* (2nd ed.). New York: Georg Thieme Verlag Stuttgart.

Walker, H.M., Colvin, G., & Ramsey, E. (1995). *Antisocial behavior in school: Strategies and best practices.* Pacific Grove, CA: Brooks/Cole.

Waltz, M. (2000). *Bipolar disorders: A guide to helping children & adolescents.* Paris: O'Reilly.

Weinberg, L.A. (1992). The relevance of choice in distinguishing seriously emotionally disturbed from social maladjusted students. *Behavioral Disorders, 17,* 99–106.

Weinstein, C.S., Tomlinson-Clarke, S., & Curran, M. (2004). Toward a conception of culturally responsive classroom management. *Journal of Teacher Education, 55,* 25–38.

Weisz, J., Suwanlert, S., Chaiyasit, W., & Weiss, B. (1988). Thai and American perspectives on over and undercontrolled child behavior problems: Exploring the threshold model among parents, teachers and psychologists. *Journal of Consulting and Clinical Psychology, 56*(4), 601–609.

Ylvisaker et al. 2007Wilkinson, G.B., Taylor, P., & Holt, J.R. (2002). Bipolar disorder in adolescence: Diagnosis and treatment. *Journal of Mental Health Counseling, 24,* 348–357.

CHAPTER NINE

Managing Behavior for Effective Learning

L. Juane Heflin and Kristine Jolivette

CHAPTER OBJECTIVES

- to discuss the influence of teachers' perspectives and students' perspectives on classroom behavior;

- to identify basic classroom components that affect whether students behave appropriately or inappropriately, including the use of a comprehensive instructional approach for addressing inappropriate behavior;

- to describe a variety of evidence-based strategies that teachers can use to effectively manage behavior so all students can learn; and

- to provide information on systematically analyzing chronic problem behavior that is not responsive to general strategies by conducting a Functional Behavior Assessment (FBA) that will lead to the development of a Behavior Intervention Plan (BIP).

KEY TERMS

authoritarian · permissive · authoritative · warm demander · reinforcement · punishment · decontamination · proximity control · insistence · precision requests · withitness · student accountability · CLOCS-RAM · opportunities to respond (OTR) · independent group contingencies · dependent group contingencies · interdependent group contingency · behavior pairs · A-B-C model · antecedent · consequence · positive behavioral interventions and supports (PBIS)

Most individuals who enter the teaching profession imagine themselves dispensing knowledge and information to groups of students who are paying attention and complying with instructions out of respect for the adult who obviously knows much more than they do. Although this will be true of some students, other students will use their behavior to communicate reluctance to be in the classroom and refuse to comply with teacher directives. About 50% of teachers leave the profession within their first 5 years of employment (Alliance for Excellent Education, 2005) and the behavioral climate of the school has been strongly linked to teachers quitting their jobs (Kukla-Acevedo, 2009). Student misbehavior is cited as having a negative effect on teacher satisfaction (National Center for Education Statistics, 1997). Teachers who constantly struggle to maintain classroom control are more likely to perceive themselves as ineffective and be dissatisfied with their jobs. Teachers may be well-prepared to provide content instruction but ill-prepared to deal with students' challenging behavior, just as the students whose behaviors are challenging may be ill-equipped to deal with the academic and social demands of school. The most effective teachers are those who use culturally responsive management strategies in order to meet the needs of increasingly diverse student populations (Brown, 2003).

Unfortunately, happy memories of their favorite teachers and fond intentions of making a difference in the lives of students are quickly overshadowed by a sense of not being in control of their classrooms as teachers discover that they are spending more time trying to restore order than they are teaching (Goodlad, 2004). There is an alternative. This chapter:

- Describes two perspectives that come together to affect learning environments (teacher and student);
- Establishes the foundation for management and learning that includes setting up physical environments that minimize misbehavior, establishing classroom expectations, linking teachers' directions to those expectations, evaluating instructional variables under teachers' control, and developing a comprehensive instructional approach for teaching both academic and social skills;
- Identifies evidence-based tools for management and learning that have been found to be effective across environments and diverse student populations and give examples of each;
- Describes approaches to address more severe behavioral problems within the classroom; and
- Presents a cycle of success for teachers and students.

A True Story

Ms. Connell sat wearily in her chair as the bell rang and her class fled the room noisily. It had happened again. She had prepared a good lesson and really thought she would get the students engaged in the learning opportunity. But she did not even get a chance to introduce the lesson. Milo struck again. He came into the room, announcing his intention to sit by Roger that day. After a failed negotiation to get Milo to sit in his regular seat, Ms. Connell gave up when other students started changing their seats. Trying to get the focus on the lesson, Ms. Connell used her most winsome tone to ask, "Who can remember what we were talking about yesterday?" Milo and Roger began talking about what they were going to do after school and the students who might have answered Ms. Connell slouched in their chairs, unwilling to compete with the boys' animated discussion. Recognizing the futility of continuing, Ms. Connell tried again to get Milo to go to his typical seat. After that, things are fuzzy in her memory. She remembers moving toward Milo, warning him that if he did not go sit in his seat he would not need after school plans as he would be sitting in detention. As she approached, Milo stood up quickly, knocking over his desk. Ms. Connell told him to pick up the desk and, instead, he knocked over another desk. Ms. Connell told another student to go get the principal as Milo began to yell at her for being a terrible teacher, using colorful and wholly unacceptable language for the school environment. Other students started laughing. Ms. Connell tried to reason with Milo, citing her credentials and her years of experience. But, by this time, Milo was revved up and, with a captive audience, expounded upon Ms. Connell's shortcomings until the principal appeared in the doorway. At the sight of the principal, Milo stopped as quickly as he had begun, gathered his books, and followed the principal out the door. Shaking, Ms. Connell proceeded with the lesson, but her heart was not in it. What was she doing wrong? Was she as bad a teacher as Milo said?

Because she is overwhelmed, Ms. Connell is not stopping to think about the smaller pieces that come together that contribute to an orderly learning environment in which the focus is on instruction and not on dealing with escalating misbehavior. Ms. Connell needs to stop and think about the proactive things she can do to reduce misbehavior including simple things like how she arranges the classroom, establishes classroom expectations, and uses general behavior management strategies as well as how she presents academic content. Then Ms. Connell needs to think about how she responds to misbehavior, making sure she uses effective behavior management strategies including those designed to handle more disruptive and chronic behavior challenges. Before discussing the basic strategies that create the foundation for effective classroom management, it is important to recognize that whether a behavior is perceived as acceptable or unacceptable has a lot to do with the perspective from which the behavior is being evaluated.

Perspectives in the Classroom

Teaching is a social endeavor in that it involves at least two individuals interacting as a learner (student) and a facilitator of learning (teacher). When multiple individuals interact, they bring their own unique perspectives to the experience. Teachers' personalities, expectations, and tolerance levels influence their ability to facilitate learning, just as students' previous experiences with school success and failure and personal goals influence their ability to learn. This section discusses these two perspectives that affect how harmoniously students and teachers will get along.

Teacher Perspective

As would be predicted, teachers tend to respond negatively to interruptions, disruptions, and insubordination from students. However, why is it that some teachers seem to have better control over their classrooms than others? Why do some teachers send more students to an administrator's office for discipline than others? The answers to these questions may partially depend upon unique characteristics of the teacher, such as personality, tolerance levels, and expectations.

A teacher's personality may have a profound impact on reactions to students, colleagues, and parents. Indeed, classroom management styles (Martin, 1998), patterns of interaction between teachers and students (Fisher & Kent, 1998), and even student achievement (Lessen & Frankiewicz, 1992) have been correlated with individual personality profiles. Individuals who choose to enter teaching tend to be more interested in others and tend to rely on objective data to come to logical conclusions than those who choose other fields of study (Thornton, Peltier, & Hill, 2005).

Teachers' personalities influence their expectations and levels of tolerance for student behavior. Teacher tolerance is affected by personal preference as teachers decide which behaviors are acceptable in their classrooms and which are unacceptable (Vitaro, Tremblay, & Gagnon, 1995). For example, some teachers are not bothered by students moving around classrooms whereas other teachers insist that students remain seated. These are two different reactions to the same behavior. Teachers often expect students to act and think just like they do. This sets the stage for constant conflict and power struggles. Instead, teachers need to focus on the ways the students learn best and adjust expectations accordingly. Weinstein, Tomlinson-Clarke, and Curran (2004, p. 26) discuss the problems that can occur when some African American students use "call-response" behaviors (e.g., teacher asks a question and students call out answers; students call out comments while teacher is providing instruction) to actively engage in classroom instruction when their teachers would prefer that they listen quietly. African American students may learn best from conversational instruction (Brown, 2003). Similarly, teachers may not realize that competitive instructional activities are going to be at odds with the upbringing of some Pacific Islander students who will be reluctant to participate. Or teachers may become upset when some Southeast Asian students smile when they are being reprimanded (not realizing that the student is smiling to show he knows he's guilty). Teachers need to be aware that their tolerance for specific behavior is firmly entrenched in their own cultural upbringing and work diligently to recognize cultural differences in behavior. There are some behaviors that are unacceptable in all cultures, but there are many more whose acceptability is dictated by culture. For example, "teachers are likely to view African American children's overlapping speech as disrespect, play fighting as authentic aggression, and ritualized humor as valid insults" (Cartledge, Singh, & Gibson, 2008). Identifying a behavior as indicative of a cultural difference creates opportunities to adjust tolerance or to teach alternative behaviors (Bondy, Ross, Galligane, & Hambacher, 2007).

Personalities also influence teaching styles. Teaching styles can be compared to three parenting styles that were defined by Baumrind (1966) as authoritarian, permissive, and authoritative. The first of these styles, **authoritarian**, is characterized by adults who expect conformity and obedience, are often unrealistic with their expectations, and use disciplinary approaches that are punitive and coercive. The second style, **permissive** (originally called "laissez-faire"), is a style in which adults are overly responsive to students, imposing few expectations or sanctions for inappropriate behavior. The last style is **authoritative** and is characterized by adults who have realistic expectations for students and are responsive to individual needs while using positive approaches to discipline. Students who are culturally and linguistically diverse appear to respond better to teachers who use an authoritative teaching style (Ware, 2006). Students respect authoritative teachers because the teachers establish reasonable rules and are direct in telling the students what they need to do to succeed. Authoritative teachers respond immediately to inappropriate behavior. Students who are culturally and linguistically diverse may be more motivated to change their behavior if the authoritative teacher discusses the negative effects on the well-being of the group rather than trying to coerce students to respond to an authority figure. Pellerin (2005) found that beneficial outcomes for high school students were associated with the authoritative teaching style whereas schools in which professionals relied on the authoritarian style have higher drop-out rates. In the same study, the lowest rates of engagement occurred in schools in which professionals adopted the permissive style. To get an idea of your own teaching style, complete the questionnaire in the Appendix. The questionnaire gives examples of how each style manifests in classrooms.

Teacher expectations have been shown to have a dramatic effect on how they interact with students. Teacher expectations for student success may be linked to socioeconomic status (Rumberger & Palardy, 2005) as well as expectations for student misbehavior (Van Acker, Grant, & Henry, 1996). Teachers tend to perceive students who are culturally and linguistically diverse as being less capable (Good & Nichols, 2001). Rosenthal and Jacobson (1968) demonstrated that teacher expectations for students' achievement can become a self-fulfilling prophecy. Students who had been identified as bright and capable were found to perform significantly better during assessments than those whom teachers had been told were not very bright. The remarkable feature of this outcome is that the researchers misled the teachers by telling them that the lowest performing students were bright and the highest performing students were not capable of learning. In the end, the test results confirmed teachers' expectations, inciting a critical analysis of how teachers behave based on their expectations, since clearly the students' actual abilities had been misrepresented. The work of Rosenthal and Jacobson along with that of Van Acker et al. (1996) and Good and Brophy (1978) suggest that teachers interact differently with students for whom they have higher expectations. **Figure 9.1** provides a comparison of how teachers behave differently based on expectations for student achievement and appropriate behavior.

Teachers may avoid interacting with students who demonstrate negative and aggressive behavior so that they do not have to address the misbehavior. In this way, the student's inappropriate behavior modifies the teacher's behavior as the teacher seeks to avoid having to deal with the negative behavior. Teachers may react to the potential for problem behavior by not asking the students to do their work or by assigning work they think the students will find easy or fun (Carr, Taylor, & Robinson, 1991). Referred to as the "curriculum of non-instruction," teachers learn to modify their demands to avoid dealing with disruptive behavior while students learn to behave badly so that the teachers do not give them work they would rather not do (Gunter, Jack, DePaepe, Reed, & Harrison, 1994, p. 36).

The ways teachers communicate with students, particularly those who are beginning to engage in undesirable behavior, may result in the behavior stopping or getting worse. Nonverbal communication constitutes the majority of any message sent to students. Angry or judgmental expressions and closed body language (e.g., arms crossed across the chest) can send the message that the teacher is frustrated by or even disinterested in the student. Paraverbal aspects of communication also influence messages sent to students. Paraverbal aspects are those related to how words are said. Paraverbal includes the tone, inflection, volume, and cadence of the spoken message. Teachers who get angry or frustrated tend to talk louder and more quickly. A good rule of thumb is: Low, Slow, and Soft. In particular, when interacting with agitated students, teachers should lower the pitch of their voice, speak more slowly, and speak quietly. It is difficult for students to continue to argue with someone who is speaking low, slow, and soft. Teachers should not allow the tone of their voice to become sarcastic or demeaning. Both of these qualities tend to make student behavior worse. Teachers who are culturally responsive have found that using a kind but firm tone and conveying requests with warmth are highly effective (Bondy et al., 2007). Kleinfeld (1975) used the term **warm demander** to describe teachers who are effective with Eskimo and Native American students.

Figure 9.1	Teacher Behavior Based on Expectations

Teachers who have low expectations for student success tend to:	Teachers who have high expectations for student success tend to:
— Give more criticism	— Do the opposite of those with low expectations PLUS
— Ask fewer questions	— Get in closer proximity to the student
— Provide less prompting	— Engage in more face to face interaction
— Give more negative feedback (including reprimands)	— Provide more praise and signs of positive approval
— Provide less positive feedback (if any given)	—Give redirection rather than reprimands

This term has been used to describe exemplary teachers of African American students as well (Ware, 2006) and characterizes teachers who challenge students to do their best and hold them accountable for their behavior. The actual words constitute only a small percentage of the message sent. When interacting with students, teachers are encouraged to keep their sentences brief and direct while avoiding giving advice or insinuating judgments. Most importantly, they need to carefully modulate nonverbal and paraverbal communication.

In addition to teachers' personalities, interaction styles, expectations, and the monitoring of nonverbal and paraverbal aspects of communication, other aspects of the school environment can increase the risk that students will misbehave. The comfort, safety, and maintenance of the physical environment can affect student behavior (Kozol, 1991). Students in run-down school buildings that are considered unsafe tend to engage in more misbehavior. The appropriateness of the curriculum and difficulty of assigned tasks can influence student behavior (Dunlap, Dunlap, Clarke, & Robbins, 1991). If teachers ask students to complete assignments that seem irrelevant to their lives and are either boring or too hard, students tend to misbehave more. Schools that rely on punitive consequences for inappropriate behavior, including suspension and expulsion, experience higher levels of misbehavior (Walker, Ramsey, & Gresham, 2004). Aggressive behaviors are more likely to emerge when there is no system in place to recognize and reward good behavior (Wehby, Symons, & Shores, 1995). A variety of factors related to teachers and schools can set the stage for the appearance of behavior that disrupts the learning environment. There also are a number of factors related to the students that may make them more likely to misbehave.

Student Perspective

Why do some students display inappropriate or challenging behavior during class and even in non-academic environments like the cafeteria and hallways? Many environmental factors contribute to whether or not a student engages in inappropriate behavior at school. These factors include those found in the home, school, community, and interpersonally. Any factor that negatively influences an individual's life is considered a "risk" factor. For example, home risk factors may include ineffective parental discipline, lack of parental involvement, and abuse or neglect (Walker, Stieber, Ramsey, & O'Neill, 1991). Coercive family interactions, in which the child and the parents try to out-intimidate each other, are strongly correlated with the development of aggression in children and youth (Patterson, Reid, & Dishion, 1992). School risk factors can include academic and/or social failure, not enough time devoted to instructional tasks, and the expectation that all students are the same and will learn by listening quietly (Guerra & Williams, 1996). Community risk factors may include limited opportunities to engage in socially appropriate recreation activities and few post-school employment options (Walker & Sprague, 1999). Interpersonally, individuals who are aggressive tend to distort events and think that other people are out to get them. These individuals may believe that others interact with malice of intent and that even accidents, such as bumping into someone in the hall, are deliberate acts of hostility (Dodge, Price, Bachorowski, & Newman, 1990). Intelligence

It is important for teachers to understand their students' risk factors in order to plan ahead to encourage students to succeed.

levels and achievement are other interpersonal factors that may influence aggressive behavior (Huesmann, Eron, & Yarmel, 1987). Students who have been told that they are not very bright or who have not been successful at school may act out in order to hide the fact that they cannot do the assignments.

Each student will present various risk factors but no single risk factor is known to cause inappropriate behavior. It is important for teachers to understand their students' risk factors in order to plan ahead to encourage students to succeed. However, teachers should focus on school risk factors since those are the ones over which they have the most control.

Students who have been exposed to multiple risk factors in school, home, and community settings may not automatically display inappropriate behavior at school. Some students become resilient to the risk factors present in their lives. Resiliency is often referred to as individuals' abilities to grow up well-adjusted with appropriate social skills even when they have experienced numerous risk factors. A number of strategies that teachers can use in schools have been shown to promote resilience (Walker et al., 1996). Students who behave inappropriately often say that they feel like they do not belong and that school has nothing to offer them (Catalano, Loeber, & McKinney, 1999). The most important step in fostering resilience is to establish a caring relationship with students. Caring relationships may help students overcome adversities and are recognized as a critical component in culturally responsive management and as necessary for being successful in urban settings (Brown, 2003). Teachers can make time to get to know the students personally, show interest in their outside activities, and establish the classroom as a safe and supportive environment. Teachers must exhibit genuine warmth and interest to establish the emotional climate. Teaching skills in cooperation, negotiation, and conflict resolution as well as fostering student interactions during instruction can create a strong social climate. As a part of a caring relationship, teachers can mentor students. This mentorship could increase students' sense of belongingness when teachers: (a) spend additional time during the school day with the student by using a check-in process whereby the teacher can ask the student how things are going and what they can do to help, as well as praise the student's accomplishments; and (b) provide guidance in selecting school-related activities for the student to engage in where success is likely based on student strengths and areas of interest.

Another method teachers can employ to promote resiliency is to become educational advocates for students for both academic and social purposes (Furlong & Morrison, 2000). As an advocate, the teacher could support the student through various methods: (a) by frequently monitoring the student's academic progress and assessing areas where reteaching, adaptations, and/or accommodations in instructional practices may be required; (b) by frequently monitoring the student's social progress for predictable patterns or areas where social skills instruction or conflict resolution strategies may be needed or consequences altered; (c) by talking with the student's other teachers to discuss what is working effectively or not working and providing suggestions and resources for the teachers to use; and (d) by providing feedback to teachers regarding student progress as a means of positively affecting the academic and social expectations the teachers have for the student. Overall, no matter which risk factors are present or whether or not those factors negatively affect the student's school behavior, there are many opportunities for a teacher to promote student resiliency.

Although it is important for teachers to recognize that students who come to their classrooms may be experiencing many risk factors, it is just as important to recognize misbehavior for what it is: behavior. As such, teachers must remember that behavior is not arbitrary or incidental but purposeful and effective for accomplishing desired goals. Termed the "functions" of behavior (Iwata, Dorsey, Slifer, Bauman, & Richman, 1982/1994), the goals of behavior are either to get the individual something that is desired or to enable the individual to avoid something that is not desired. For example, college students attend class in order to gain knowledge as well as grades so that they can earn degrees and get jobs. College students also will attend class in order to avoid failing. Gaining and avoiding are powerful determinants of behavior. Toward that end, teachers should examine students' behaviors to identify what the behavior is getting the student and/or helping the student avoid.

When students get what they want or avoid what they do not want, they are reinforced for their behavior. **Reinforcement** is a key concept in effective classroom management that will appear throughout the chapter so it needs to be defined. Anything that happens after a behavior is a consequence. For example, students who turn in their work on time are likely to get a grade. The grade is a consequence for the behavior. If the grade is one the student wants and makes the student want to turn in assignments in the future, the consequence is reinforcement. If the grade is one the student does not want and the student gives up and stops turning in assignments, then the consequence is punishment. There are no consequences that are universally reinforcing or punishing. The only way to tell if something is reinforcing or punishing is to look at subsequent behavior. If a teacher yells at a student who is talking to her neighbor and the student continues to talk to her neighbor throughout the day, then the yelling is reinforcing. Punishing consequences may stop a behavior temporarily. However, the most effective classroom management will be based on reinforcement. Sometimes the challenge for teachers is in identifying what is reinforcing for their students.

To illustrate the functions of behavior (get or avoid) and the powerful effects of reinforcement, consider students who have difficulty completing assignments or getting along with others and who may misbehave in order to hide the fact that they are behind their peers in academic or social skills (Scott, Nelson, & Liaupsin, 2001). When these students are presented with academic and/or social tasks they think are hard or that they do not want to do, they may misbehave in order to avoid the task. These students may become noncompliant, aggressive, destructive, or run out of the room. In response, teachers typically remove students from the setting by sending them to an administrator's office or to an alternative learning environment like detention or an "opportunity room." The students are reinforced for their behavior because it kept them from doing work they did not want to do. Teachers are reinforced for sending the students out of the room because now they do not have to deal with them. However, removal from class deprives the students of needed instruction, resulting in them falling further behind in the academic or social skills needed to be successful. So, the work becomes more difficult, leading to continued use of behavior that students have learned will get them removed from class (misbehavior), allowing them to temporarily avoid failure (reinforcement) but which results in even less chance that they will ever catch up academically or socially. The vicious cycle continues, showing the strong connection between academics, and specifically academic failure, and behavior (Casillas et al., 2012). The cycle may be seen even in achieving students who are absent for a few weeks due to illness. When they return, their behavior may communicate the frustration experienced when they discover they have fallen behind their peers in learning. **Figure 9.2** depicts the damaging cycle between misbehavior and academic failure (Scott et al., 2001).

In order to intervene effectively, the cycle must be broken. Students need instruction targeted at their learning levels that will improve their skill acquisition and promote academic achievement. They also will need social skills instruction to learn how to handle frustration and challenging situations. Breaking the cycle that perpetuates academic and behavioral failure increases the chances that students will be successful in school and after they graduate.

| Figure 9.2 | Cycle of Failure |

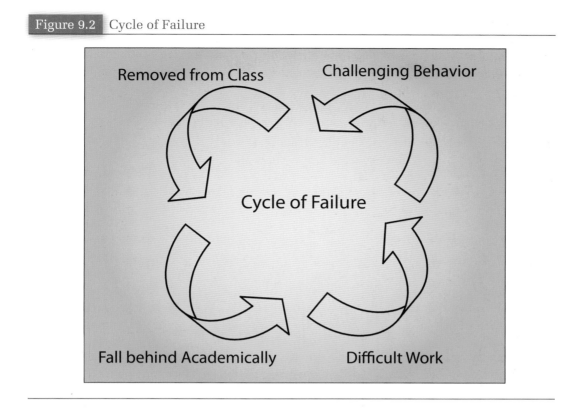

Foundation for Management and Learning

Students may be using misbehavior to get something they want or to avoid something they do not want in a given environment. In this way, behavioral problems may be interpreted as problems with the environment (Witt, VanDerHeyden, & Gilbertson, 2004). So, teachers must look closely at school environments, including classrooms and non-academic settings like the bus areas and gymnasiums. The critical difference between effective and ineffective teachers is not how they try to punish problem behavior but how well they change the environment to reduce the likelihood the problem behaviors will occur (McKee & Witt, 1990). Important environmental considerations include creating an environment conducive to learning, establishing clear expectations, using precision requests, analyzing instructional variables, and adopting a comprehensive instructional approach.

Creating an Environment Conducive to Learning

The physical structure of a classroom establishes the basic foundation for the learning space and can have a tremendous influence on student behavior. The way the classroom is arranged promotes or hinders students' ability to pay attention. Although teachers may not have much choice about how their classrooms have been built, simple decisions about how the environment is arranged can make a difference in whether or not teachers spend more time teaching or more time trying to squelch disruptive behavior. These simple decisions include:

1. Which way should desks face? Desks that face windows invite students to attend to things other than the teacher. Desks that face doors offer the same invitation. The desks should be positioned so that students have a clear view of chalk or dry erase boards and the teacher.

2. Where are the pencil sharpener, trash can, areas for storing personal belongings, and areas for submitting work? All of these are considered "high traffic" areas and tend to be the spots with high levels of misbehavior, particularly if out of the teacher's sight. The area for storing personal belongings should be away from the door or there will be a perpetual traffic jam during arrival, dismissal, and transitions (e.g., going to lunch or other areas) as students try to get their belongings in the same place where other students are lining up. Additionally, behavior problems may be prevented if teachers send students to get personal belongings in stages (e.g., "Group 4, can get their lunches or lunch money. . . ." followed by Group 2 and so forth). Pencil sharpeners, trash cans, and areas for submitting work should be separated by space and not in the front of the room. Most teachers allow students to go to those areas as needed and it can be distracting to other students if the pencil sharpener is behind the teacher and a student gets up to sharpen his pencil during the lesson.

3. Are distractions minimized? Also called **decontamination**, the careful storage of obvious distracters such as athletic equipment, DVDs, art materials, magazines, and so forth can help students focus on the teacher and their assignments. Cages with gerbils or other animals should be at the back of the room and not up front next to the teacher. Teachers will need to balance the amount of student work displayed and classroom decoration with the students' abilities to pay attention. The classroom also needs to be decontaminated to eliminate any items that are potential weapons. For example, years ago, teachers frequently had what looked like a nail on a base that was used to spear pieces of paper to hold them in one place. Classrooms were decontaminated by removing such dangerous memo holders. The same is true of letter openers that look like knives. Today, preschools typically require that scissors have rounded tips. In classrooms for older students who have a history of violence, sharp scissors may be kept in a secured location. Teachers will need to carefully examine their classrooms to make sure distracting items are removed or covered and potentially dangerous items are eliminated or secured.

Once teachers have examined their classrooms to identify high traffic areas and the potential for distractions, they can decide how to arrange desks and other instructional areas. Arrangements that cluster students close together can result in problem behavior. Spacing needs are influenced by culture and mood. Some students will be more comfortable with greater distances between themselves and others, particularly when agitated or frustrated. Classroom arrangements also should allow teachers to circulate throughout the room and be close to students. This physical closeness, also known as teacher proximity to students, has a positive affect on behavior and learning (Lampi, Fenty, & Beaunae, 2005). This allows for what is called **proximity control**. When teachers can move easily among the students' desks/tables, they can use their presence to remind students of the expectations by moving closer to students who are off-task. When teachers move closer to two students who are talking, the talking typically stops. If the desks are arranged in tight rows, with student materials on the floor between the desks, teachers will not be able to use proximity control. Teacher proximity to students also has been shown to increase student participation in instruction. Additionally, when students start to argue or fight, teachers need to be able to get to the students quickly, further highlighting the need to arrange the desks/tables in ways that allow easy access to all students. **Figure 9.3** provides several possible arrangements of desks that allow for maximum proximity control.

Space constraints and class size may prevent teachers from arranging the learning space to maximize proximity control. In such situations, teachers will have to rely on other strategies to promote desirable behavior. The classroom arrangement may need to be flexible in order to accommodate a variety of instructional activities. For example, following a group

Figure 9.3　Desk Arrangements That Maximize Proximity Control

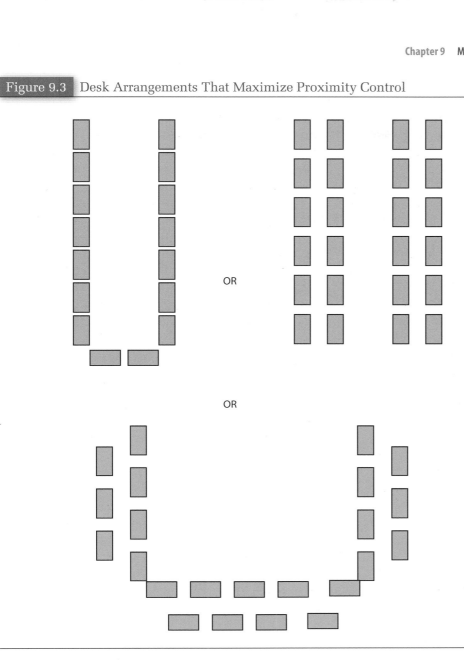

OR

OR

lesson, teachers may want students to get in groups of four to work together. Desks will have to be rearranged to accommodate the activity.

Once the learning space is decontaminated and arranged to allow for proximity control, teachers must face the dilemma of whether to assign or not to assign seats. Deliberation should not take too long as decisions about seating arrangements have been described as the cheapest form of classroom management (Jones, 2000). Allowing students to choose their own seats will result in seating choices that are good for the students and typically bad for teachers. Many teachers will start the school year by assigning seats alphabetically (unless information provided by previous teachers would suggest otherwise). Teachers can change assigned seats at any time, although it can become confusing for students if seat assignments change too frequently. (Most college students will sit in the same seat throughout a term although seating was not assigned.) Reassignment will be based on teachers' observations that current seating is not resulting in students spending the majority of their time doing what is expected. When reassigning seats, teachers are encouraged to reassign all seats, so as not to point out (and potentially reinforce) students with problem behavior.

In addition to the important influence of the classroom arrangement, teachers will be faced with fewer problem behaviors when students know what they are expected to do during frequently occurring non-instructional tasks such as turning in assignments, submitting homework, borrowing supplies, collecting money, collecting permission slips for field trips, and so forth (Emmer & Stough, 2001). Teachers will need to identify what they expect the students to do during routines, teach the students what is expected, and have them practice the routines prior to actually using them. As an example, teachers need to create routines for transitions such as moving from one content area to another (e.g., stop math, start science) and from one classroom to another. Students should be taught the signals for a transition, what they must do during the transition, and how to know when the transition is over. They need to be supervised during the transition and praised or reinforced for quick completion.

Teachers have control over a number of variables related to their classrooms. Teachers make simple but critical decisions about the basic parameters of working within the space they are assigned, keeping students close enough but not too close to each other, making sure they can move around to use proximity control, and assigning seats to reduce the possibility that students will misbehave. These variables, along with carefully describing, teaching, and reinforcing compliance to basic routines, can have a noticeable effect on student behavior. Once the physical environment is conducive for learning, teachers are ready to establish the behavioral and psychological climate of their classrooms by developing the expectations that will govern the classroom.

Establishing Clear Expectations

Until the expectations are clear, no one in a classroom will know what they should and should not do. Years ago, the development of rules was not as important to teachers because students behaved appropriately or were not allowed in school. Now, all children and youth must attend school, even if their behavior is inappropriate, and teachers must devote time teaching students how to behave. The most successful way to start a school year is to assume that none of the students know what to do and begin by teaching the expectations. The expectations should apply equally to adults and students. For example, if students are not allowed to chew gum in class, neither should the teacher. The basic guidelines for creating, teaching, and monitoring classroom rules and expectations are as follows:

a. three to five positively stated rules and expectations;
b. teaching and modeling of the rules and expectations with rationales provided;
c. reinforcement for following the rules and displaying the expectations;
d. consistent and fair application of the rules and expectations;
e. immediate corrective feedback for breaking the rules; and
f. equitable consequences for rule violations.

Teachers should consider the needs of the students when identifying important classroom rules. These needs include aspects of age-appropriateness, links to overall schoolwide expectations, and the short- and long-term goals for student behavior. When creating classroom rules and expectations, the focus is on preventing students from displaying inappropriate behavior. Such prevention can be linked to different types of rules such as those that focus on student compliance, preparation, verbalizations, engagement, and transition. Students will be more likely to follow class rules if they have a role in creating them. On the first day of class (and anytime misbehavior increases), teachers can lead discussions of the rules necessary for everyone to learn. This approach also can help create a sense of common community that has been identified as critical for students who are culturally and linguistically diverse (Bondy et al., 2007). For example, the teacher of an out-of-control group of Mexican students had each write one criticism about the class. The teacher then read the criticisms aloud, and the class discussed changes that could be made. After the students were given a chance to provide their suggestions for improving the learning environment, they began to participate in the instructional activities (Weinstein et al., 2004).

An analysis of culturally responsive management emphasizes the importance of reviewing classroom expectations many times during the first weeks of school. In a study of three teachers working in public schools where more than 90% of the students received free or reduced-price lunch and more than 90% of the student body was African American, Bondy et al. (2007) identified five strategies that the teachers used in establishing classroom expectations. These are presented in **Figure 9.4.** (Note: The teachers are named by their grade level assignment. For example, "Ms. Second" is a second-grade teacher.)

In addition to teaching the rules and expectations, teachers must consistently enforce the rules. This means recognizing students who are complying with the rules and using insistence to address rule violations. Teachers who are effective with students who are culturally and linguistically diverse are described as using insistence (Bondy et al., 2007, p. 341). Using insistence means just what the word implies: teachers continue to insist that students demonstrate the appropriate behavior until they comply. The important component of insistence is that teachers do not punish students for failing to meet expectations; they simply require students to do what is expected. In insisting that the students perform as expected, teachers must be calm, firm, and positive while never using a sarcastic or threatening tone. Insistence has been found to be critical for creating a predictable, respectful, and caring environment in urban settings (Ware, 2006). Inconsistent enforcement of the rules will undermine the sense of community in the classroom and may lead to perceptions of racial discrimination (Bullara, 1993; Weinstein et al., 2004).

To illustrate, students in Mr. Bloomquist's sixth grade science classroom have an agreed upon set of classroom rules with specific behavioral expectations. Mr. Bloomquist teaches students with and without disabilities, including many students who engage in inappropriate behavior. At the beginning of the school year, he decided on three core classroom rules. They are (1) respect yourself, (2) respect others, and (3) respect property. Mr. Bloomquist based these rules on his prior experiences teaching students at this middle school. During the first week of school, he presented these three positively stated rules to the students, provided a rationale for why he selected them, and provided a generic example of what each rule might

Figure 9.4   Varied Strategies for Establishing Rules and Procedures

Providing nonexamples	[Said with energy and humor] If I'm walking by and someone starts tapping, tapping on me. Ooooooo, it drives me crazy for someone to do that! You don't need to tap me; just raise your hand, and I will get to you. (Ms. Second)
Requiring demonstration	Okay, [let's pretend] we're getting ready for lunch. . . . Row two? Row one? Row four? Row three?. . . . Excellent. (Ms. Fifth)
Asking for choral response	Repeat after me! I will treat my friends like I want to be treated! (Ms. Second)
Using humor	To use the restroom, you have to raise your hand and hold your fingers like this [middle finger over the index finger]; kind of looks like you're crossing your legs [she demonstrates] 'cause you have to go! (Ms. Third)
Using "what ifs"	What about those kids who say, "You can take away my free time, I don't care. "What should I do? (Ms. Fifth)

From: Bondy, E., Ross, D.D., Gallingane, C., & Hambacher, E. (2007). Creating environments of success and resilience. *Urban Education, 42,* 339.

look like in his classroom. To increase student buy-in with the classroom rules, he had the class engage in an activity called a "chalk and talk." During this activity, the students wrote examples of what the three rules would look like to them. Students wrote: be prepared, be on time, and give your best effort as examples for "respect yourself"; raise your hand, accept correction gracefully, and follow directions as examples for "respect others"; and ask before borrowing and using materials and keep your science station clean as examples for "respect property." Mr. Bloomquist praised his students' ideas and added another example for each rule (listen during instruction, keep hands and feet to self, and return supplies where found). Then, he taught and modeled examples (what the students wrote) and non-examples of each classroom rule and discussed the consequences for violating those rules. As a class, the students practiced modeling the expected behaviors while Mr. Bloomquist provided corrective feedback and praise. In addition, Mr. Bloomquist told the class that he would randomly reinforce students who engaged in the three rules by giving out homework passes, "sit where you want" passes, and "work with whom you want" passes. As the school year progressed and based on student feedback and performance, Mr. Bloomquist retaught the three rules, what they looked like, and reviewed the reinforcers available for following the rules and the consequences that would occur if the rules were violated.

Using Precision Requests

Establishing a set of behavioral expectations via the classroom rules allows teachers to positively recognize students who are meeting the expectations. The emphasis should always be on the positive consequences that occur when the rules are followed. There will be students who violate the classroom expectations or fail to respond to teachers' directions. In these situations, an empirically based strategy called **precision requests** (Neville & Jenson, 1984) gives teachers a structured way to intervene and is reflective of culturally responsive management (Cartledge et al., 2008). To make a precision request, the teacher should be close to the student (but not in an intimidating manner), make eye contact with the student, and deliver the request with a calm, unemotional tone. The teacher gives the brief and clear request and then waits 5 seconds. If the student complies, the teacher provides reinforcing consequences. If the student has not complied within 5 seconds, the same request is given a second time. If the student complies the second time, the teacher praises the student. If the student does not reply a second time, the teacher implements a behavior reduction strategy (described more fully later).

Ms. Mozart has found that precision requests help her have more time for instruction and reduce the amount of time she spends trying to manage misbehavior. When, during a lesson, Allison begins to draw on her book, Ms. Mozart tells the class to silently identify the three main points in the next paragraph and moves close to Allison. Ms. Mozart quietly says, "Writing in your book is not respecting property. You need to stop writing in your book and look for the three main points in this (pointing) paragraph or you'll need to finish it during free time." Ms. Mozart moves away from Allison to talk quietly with the next student, but counts to five in her head. At the count of five, she looks back over at Allison who appears to be studying her book intently. Ms. Mozart goes back to Allison and says, again quietly so that only Allison hears, "Good choice for respecting property, Allison!" and then asks loudly, so that the entire class can hear, "Who has found one of the main points?"

The strategy of precision requests provides teachers with a specific sequence to follow in the event of rule violations and other inappropriate behavior. Teacher behavior within the exchange can influence the effectiveness of the request (Kauffman, Mostert, Trent, & Pullen, 2006). To avoid engaging in arguments with students in the process of the precision request, teachers should:

- Stay calm and not show any external manifestation of being upset;

- Clearly restate the expectation or response one time. In restating the expectation, remind the student of the positive consequences of meeting the expectation and the negative consequences for failing to meet the expectation;

- Move away from the student, allowing time for the student to calm down or respond appropriately;

- Ignore the student's efforts at saving face (e.g., most students will roll their eyes, mutter under their breath, or make faces as the teacher moves away). These behaviors can be addressed privately at a later time; and

- Respond immediately with a positive consequence when the student begins to engage in the expected behavior.

Analyzing Instructional Variables

Decades of research have demonstrated that engaging students in instruction is the most effective method of reducing problem behavior in classrooms. Student engagement can be increased (and misbehavior decreased) when teachers demonstrate specific behaviors, use effective instructional practices, and make sure that curricula are appropriate for the students. Over 30 years ago, Kounin (1970) identified teacher behaviors that were critical for increasing engagement and reducing inappropriate behavior. The behaviors include:

- **Withitness,** which indicates that teachers are aware of what is going on at all times in all parts of the classroom.

- **Momentum,** describing the teacher's ability to keep a lesson moving at a fairly brisk pace, make efficient transitions among the activities, and bring the lesson to a clear conclusion. Teachers may use general management strategies (e.g., moving close to a student who is getting distracted; calling attention to a relevant point; asking students questions when attention starts to wander) to prevent potential problems.

- **Group Alerting,** which means that the teacher uses strategies to keep all students alerted to the task and involves capturing students' attention, clarifying expectations, and effectively drawing disengaged students into the lesson.

- **Student Accountability,** describing the use of strategies that evoke answers, demonstrations, and explanations from students and increase levels of engagement.

- **Overlapping,** which requires that teachers juggle a variety of activities at the same time (i.e., checking on students doing independent work while conducting a lesson with a group of students and redirecting another student to the assigned task).

Several of the behaviors that Kounin identifies as critical to creating a positive learning climate are subsumed in the culturally responsive management strategy known as insistence. Teachers' **withitness** allows them to immediately spot students who are not meeting expectations and they use **student accountability** to ask the students to try again and perform correctly. By asking individuals or groups of students to demonstrate the correct behavior, the teachers also provide *group alerting* to remind everyone of the expectations.

To be culturally responsive, teachers will add "being assertive and acting with authority" (Brown, 2003, p. 279) to Kounin's list of critical teacher behaviors. Students who are culturally and linguistically diverse are reported to respond better to teachers who act with authority (Bondy et al., 2007). Assertive teachers who act with authority are those who promote clear academic expectations for learning along with explicit rules of conduct. These teachers hold students responsible for meeting the expectations and are quick to engage the support of the students' caregivers if students do not learn or behave appropriately. Being assertive also means that teachers use direct verbal commands to tell students what to do. Students in urban settings may be unresponsive to commands expressed indirectly or as questions. For example, saying "It's time to get ready for class" is an indirect way of telling students to get out their books. Saying, "Are you ready for math?" is not only using a question to occasion a behavior but is also likely to elicit a hearty "No!" from some students. Instead of being indirect or using questions, culturally responsive teachers will tell the students what to do in a very direct manner (e.g., "Open your math book to page 173"). Assertive teachers behave as if they are confident that students will cooperate with requests.

In addition to specific teacher behaviors, there are particular instructional practices that influence student engagement in lessons and directly influence the amount of misbehavior with which teachers will have to contend. The effective instructional practices have been summarized in an acronym, CLOCS-RAM, and are presented in **Figure 9.5.** Teachers are encouraged to evaluate their lessons according to the instructional practices represented by CLOCS-RAM.

In addition to effective instructional practices, other variables that have an effect on behavior include curricula being used and the expectations for academic performance. If the assignment does not match the student's ability level, misbehavior is more likely to occur. This holds true for work that is too easy (Umbreit, Lane, & Dejud, 2004), as well as for work that is too difficult (Lee, Wehmeyer, Soukup, & Palmer, 2010). Difficult tasks probably increase levels of off-task and disruptive behavior because students are trying to get out of work they know they cannot do (Moore & Edwards, 2003). Teachers must know students are able to do the work assigned or they will need to provide additional support. Work that is too easy can be supplemented with challenging extension tasks. In addition to ensuring assignments match students' instructional levels, relatively simple techniques have been found to have a marked effect on engagement and behavior. Students can be given a choice among acceptable alternatives for completing assignments. For example, students may be able to complete tasks involving writing by choosing to use paper and pencil, a computer,

---

Figure 9.5	Effective Instructional Practices

Keys to offering effective instruction:

1. **Clarity:** The student must know exactly what to do (i.e., have no doubt about what is expected).
2. **Level:** The student must be able to do the task with a high degree of accuracy (i.e., be able to get at least 80% correct), but the task must be challenging (i.e., the student should not easily get 100% correct repeatedly).
3. **Opportunities:** The student must have frequent opportunities to respond (i.e., be actively engaged in the task a high percentage of the time).
4. **Consequences:** The student must receive a meaningful reward for correct performance (i.e., the consequences of correct performance must be frequent and perceived as desirable by the student).
5. **Sequence:** The tasks must be presented in logical sequence so that the student gets the big idea (i.e., steps must be presented and learned in order that the knowledge or skill is built on a logical progression or framework of ideas, which is a systematic curriculum).
6. **Relevance:** The task is relevant to the student's life and, if possible, the student understands how and why it is useful (i.e., the teacher attempts to help the student see why in his or her culture the task is important).
7. **Application:** The teacher helps the student learn how to learn and remember by teaching memory and learning strategies and applying knowledge and skills to everyday problems (i.e., teaches generalization, not just isolated skills, and honors the student's culture).
8. **Monitoring:** The teacher continuously monitors student progress (i.e., records and charts progress, always knows and can show what the student has mastered and the student's place or level in a curriculum or sequence of tasks).

Source: Kauffman, J. M., Mostert, M. P., Trent, S. C., & Pullen, P. L. (2006). *Managing classroom behavior: A reflective case-based approach* (4th ed., p. 17). Boston, MA: Allyn & Bacon.

or by dictating into a tape recorder (Kern, Delaney, Clarke, Dunlap, & Childs, 2001). Amazingly enough, students will sometimes select the paper and pencil option, even though that was the one that resulted in high levels of problem behavior previously. As discussed in a later section, the option to make choices can have a positive influence on overall student behavior.

Adapting curricula by incorporating high interest activities can promote higher levels of engagement and reduce disruptive behavior. In addition to giving students choices of which medium to use to complete a written assignment, Kern et al. (2001) adapted the curriculum by allowing students to copy passages from a Sega Genesis game booklet rather than the sentences in the traditional handwriting book. To teach the American voting process, a teacher of African American students had them select, campaign for, and vote for their favorite rap artist (Ware, 2006). Curricula that do not match students' ability levels, interests, or expectations for production can result in misbehavior. As a part of instructional considerations, teachers will need to examine these variables as a proactive means of providing an orderly learning environment. Chapter 7 contains additional suggestions for providing effective instruction.

Adopting a Comprehensive Instructional Approach

> Behavior problems are teaching problems.
>
> —Sigfried Engelmann

Teachers who have set up their classrooms appropriately, developed and taught the classroom rules, are good at giving precision requests, and carefully consider instructional variables influencing student engagement will discover that most minor misbehavior is eliminated. These proactive strategies help maintain focus on teaching and reinforcing behavior conducive to learning. Unfortunately, there will be some students who have already developed fairly ingrained patterns of inappropriate behavior. Teachers must remember that some of these students' behavioral patterns have become automatic. Without conscious thought, students have learned that inappropriate behaviors allow them to get what they want and avoid what they do not want. Van Acker and Talbott (1999) draw an analogy between these students' disruptive behaviors and driving ability. When first learning to drive, most individuals have to concentrate on each step of the process and proceed slowly. After a few times, the behaviors required to drive become more familiar and over time they become quite automatic. Few experienced drivers have to stop and think through the steps for driving a car. Indeed, most drivers do so quite automatically, thinking of many things other than driving and even engaging in other behaviors like talking on cell phones. The inappropriate behaviors of students with chronic problem behavior occur just as automatically. When a teacher corrects a student, the student may start yelling without thinking that the teacher is trying to help. Indeed, it would take considerable effort for the student not to respond automatically.

Rather than discourage, this awareness should provide reassurance to teachers. Students who are misbehaving are doing so because that is how they know to behave—it is nothing personal about the teacher. Students who are misbehaving must be taught better ways to behave—and teaching is what teachers do best. Teachers who approach classroom management proactively and plan instruction for behavioral deficits just like they do for academic learning may have fewer disruptive behaviors to address and more time and energy for the important job of teaching content (Clunies-Ross, Little, & Kienhuis, 2008). Unfortunately, most teachers do not think of teaching behavior like they teach academic content. When teaching academic skills, teachers assume students are trying hard and will view student errors as honest mistakes. When students make academic errors, teachers provide corrective feedback and observe as the student attempts the task again, being ready and willing to provide additional assistance. In stark contrast, when dealing with errors in behavior, teachers tend to assume that the student is not trying or is engaged in willful disobedience. Teachers then try to punish the student, which often involves sending the student out of the class. Teachers do not provide instruction or practice in the expected behavior, and carry the delusion that the student will do better in the future.

Students will not learn to behave more appropriately unless they are taught to do so. Classrooms are well managed when teachers identify and teach desirable behavior (Emmer & Stough, 2001). The comprehensive instructional approach recognizes that chronic behavior problems must be addressed just like chronic academic problems. **Figure 9.6** depicts the five steps for addressing chronic academic problems and the corresponding five steps for intervening with chronic behavior problems. The strategies mentioned for addressing chronic behavior problems are described later in this chapter.

Evidence-Based Tools for Management and Learning

When the only tool you own is a hammer, every problem begins to resemble a nail.

—Abraham Maslow

As has been described, effective classroom management is proactive rather than reactive (Emmer & Stough, 2001). Rather than wait for students to misbehave and then react, teachers create highly engaging lessons by examining expectations and supporting students so that they can meet the expectations. Such proactive strategies include adopting a compre-

Figure 9.6   Comparison of Procedures to Remediate Chronic Academic Problems and Chronic Behavior Problems

	Chronic Academic Problem	Chronic Behavior Problem
STEP 1	Identify the error pattern or misrule.	Identify functional relationships between behavior and environment.
STEP 2	Identify rule.	Identify expected or acceptable behaviors.
STEP 3	Modify examples and presentations to provide clearer focus on rule and provide less opportunity for practice of misrule.	Modify environment to allow practice of expected behaviors and remove stimuli that are likely to occasion the inappropriate behavior.
STEP 4	Provide differential feedback so that more accurate responses are more strongly reinforced.	Provide differential reinforcement so that direction of correct responding is reinforced.
STEP 5	Shape context toward target context, provide review and integrate skill with other skills.	Move toward least restrictive environment program for generalization and maintenance.

Source: Colvin, G., & Sugai, G.M. (1988). Proactive strategies for managing social behavior problems: An instructional approach. *Education and Treatment of Children, 11*, p. 347.

hensive approach to instruction in which behavioral errors are treated like learning errors. By implementing proactive systems of support in which expected behaviors are identified, defined, taught, and recognized, 80% to 90% of students in school will demonstrate appropriate behavior (Lewis & Sugai, 1999). The more intensive interventions needed for the other 10% of the students will be more effective if the school environment supports the positive behavior of all students (Eber, Sugai, Smith, & Scott, 2002).

The most obvious feature of proactive interventions is reliance on positive supports to build appropriate behavior. Students are told exactly what is expected and have opportunities to practice and receive recognition when they perform as expected. This is in sharp contrast to punitive methods of control in which expectations are vague and variable and the only time students are recognized by teachers is when they have done something wrong, as in the case of negative "demerit" systems. In those negative systems, students learn they have to misbehave in order to be noticed.

Interventions that help students build repertoires of appropriate behavior exist on a continuum. **Figure 9.7** provides a diagram of this continuum. The continuum ranges from relatively easy interventions that are not intrusive to those that require more time to develop and are more intrusive. The continuum depicts a variety of tools that teachers can use to manage their classrooms. It is important to choose the tool that is appropriate for a given behavior and student. The continuum is depicted as a pyramid to stress that interventions selected from the upper levels will be less effective unless the more positive interventions on the lower levels are tried first.

All of the interventions depicted on the pyramid are considered evidence-based, meaning research supports their implementation in specific situations. The first three levels of the

Figure 9.7   Pyramid of Evidence-Based Interventions

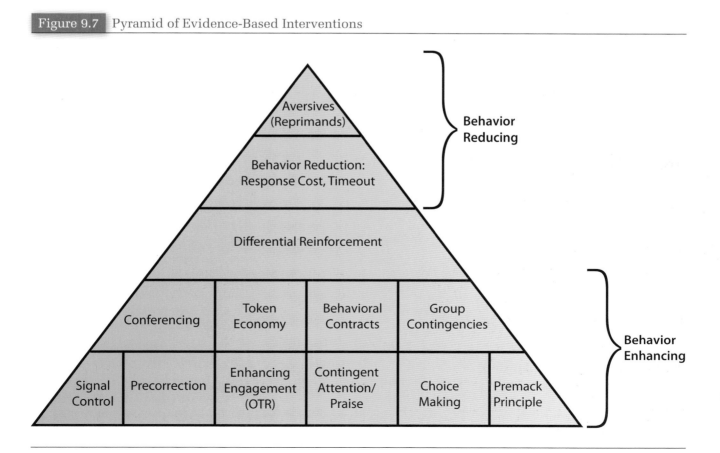

pyramid contain interventions that have been found universally effective and are recommended as tools that teachers can choose based on their preferences and the needs of their students. These interventions are considered *behavior enhancing* as they are positive in nature and recognize students who are behaving appropriately. The interventions on the top two levels of the pyramid are considered *behavior reducing* as they focus on providing punishing consequences for students who misbehave. Given how automatically some misbehavior occurs, behavior reducing strategies may be necessary to get students who chronically misbehave to stop and think about what they are doing. However, behavior reduction strategies do not build behavior—they are intended to stop behavior. Behavior reduction strategies must be used in conjunction with behavior enhancing strategies so that students learn behaviors to be more successful in school as well as after they graduate. The description of each of the behavior enhancing and behavior reducing strategies follows with examples of classroom application.

Behavior Enhancement Strategies

As shown in the pyramid in Figure 9.7, there are a wide variety of tools available that enable teachers to help students demonstrate appropriate behavior. The emphasis with behavior enhancement strategies is to teach students what is expected and then recognize them when they behave appropriately. The strategies listed on the pyramid do not include all of the behavior enhancing strategies but are inclusive of the more commonly used strategies. These include signal control, precorrection, enhancing engagement, contingent attention/praise, choice making, Premack Principle, conferencing, token economy, behavioral contracts, group contingencies, and differential reinforcement.

Signal Control

Signals are the audible, verbal, and visual behaviors taught to students that prompt them to engage in specific behavior. Examples of audible signals include timer bells, chimes, music, whistles, and clapping. Verbal signals are phrases such as "Listen up" or the use of directions and questions. Flipping the lights off and on, holding up a certain number of fingers, changing colors on "traffic signals," and displaying written signs are all examples of visual signals. (Do not use flipping the lights off and on in classes with students with seizure disorders.) The signals notify students that certain behaviors are expected. However, the signals will not cue students' behavior unless the signals are systematically taught with opportunities to practice and the students are reinforced for behaving as expected. See how this is done in the following example.

> *Ms. Dennis realized she was losing instructional time because her students did not stop talking when it was time for the lesson to begin. Ms. Dennis knew that there would be noise as the students entered the room, chattering, retrieved their materials, and took their seats. She needed an effective way to signal the students when it was time for them to stop what they were doing and listen to her. Ms. Dennis had a small pair of chimes at home that made a pleasant but clearly audible noise when they moved. She brought the chimes to school and suspended them from the ceiling so that they hung over the area where she typically stood to teach. The next class period, after most of the students had settled, Ms. Dennis ran her hands across the chimes. Many students looked up curiously and conversations quickly faded away. Ms. Dennis told the students that she wanted to do everything she could to make sure they were prepared for the end of course exam and given how much information they needed to cover, she was going to have to use every minute of instructional time available. She then said that when the students heard the chimes, they should stop talking immediately and look at her. She informed them that each time the entire class responded by getting quiet within*

2 seconds of the signal, she would write one of the letters of "homework" on the board. Ms. Dennis told the students that she would not assign homework on the day that the word "homework" was spelled in entirety. Ms. Dennis had the students practice by engaging in conversations with their neighbors, and after waiting a few seconds she made the chimes sound. Everyone was instantly quiet so Ms. Dennis wrote an "h" on the board. They practiced two more times and had "hom" written on the board the first day. Ms. Dennis continued to use the system and was pleased at how quickly the students responded to the signal. She noticed that many of the students even stopped talking when she moved toward the chimes to make them sound. Clearly, signal control had been established.

Precorrection

Teachers do not want students to fail academically or socially. Precorrection is one evidence-based strategy that can be used as a tool to prevent student failure (Lampi et al., 2005). Precorrection occurs when a teacher provides the student with a very clear cue or prompt of how to perform an expected behavior before the student displays a predictable inappropriate behavior. For example, prior to lining up for recess, the teacher says, "When you line up, please walk quietly and keep your hands to yourself," knowing that the students had a tendency to run and push each other. Precorrection typically includes seven distinct steps (Mercer & Mercer, 2005):

1. identify the context for the predictable behavior to occur;
2. explicitly identify the expected behavior;
3. modify the environment;
4. conduct a behavior rehearsal;
5. provide an effective reinforcer for expected behavior;
6. prompt the student to engage in the expected behavior; and
7. monitor the plan.

Ms. Schmidt uses precorrection with Jameson who has difficulty transitioning from whole class reading instruction to independent reading activities. The seven steps Ms. Schmidt used for Jameson included: (1) Identifying that Jameson was noncompliant and disruptive to other students during this transition; (2) Specifying that Jameson should get his reading text, a pencil, and a piece of paper and then begin working within 1 minute after the direction to begin the next activity; (3) Modifying the environment so that she stood by Jameson's desk and gave the class very clear instructions about how to transition to the next activity; (4) Rehearsing the behavior by having Jameson and another peer be the class models as she guided them through going from whole class reading instruction to independent reading activity time; (5) Reminding the students that whoever begins the independent reading activity within 1 minute of her prompt will receive bonus points which can be used to get items from their class store and then privately tells Jameson that he will receive additional bonus points if she does not have to remind him to begin; (6) Prompting the expected behavior by saying to the class "It's time to change activities" and giving bonus points to those students who begin the transition as instructed; and (7) Recording how many bonus points Jameson received, the number of points his peers received, and how long it took Jameson and the class to transition. In the above example, Ms. Schmidt used precorrection as a proactive strategy to teach, model, and reinforce Jameson and his peers to transition appropriately from one activity to the next instead of waiting for Jameson or his peers to engage in the predictable inappropriate transition behaviors.

Enhancing Engagement

Engagement, the amount of time that students spend actively participating in learning activities, has consistently been identified as critical for achievement (Dotterer & Lowe, 2011). Student engagement in learning tasks is directly related to teachers, providing students with opportunities to respond (OTR). Teachers use a variety of strategies to increase OTR (Conroy, Sutherland, Snyder & Marsh, 2008). Research suggests the maximum OTR are present when students are engaged in producing something (e.g., written product, project); the fewest OTR occur during teacher lectures and group discussions. Examples of strategies that increase OTR include introducing interesting materials, providing prompts (e.g., the capital of Kentucky starts with the letter "F"), and asking questions. Strategies to increase the number of opportunities to respond during lecture and group discussions include the use of choral responding and response cards.

Response cards (RC) are a teacher-mediated strategy that provides all students in the class with multiple OTR throughout an instructional lesson. RC is a method allowing all students to participate silently, and can encourage those not wanting to be "wrong" to be engaged. With RC, teachers can quickly and efficiently scan the class to determine who is participating and who is responding accurately. Teachers can adjust the content of the lesson if students are not accurate in their responses. This strategy has been used successfully to increase engagement (Christle & Schuster, 2003; George, 2010) and reduce disruptive behaviors (Lambert, Cartledge, Heward, & Lo, 2006). RC may be used with a whole class or small groups and is amenable to a variety of class settings, academic areas, and grade levels. At its simplest, RC can be prepared and used in four steps.

First, the teacher selects a lesson and group of students to implement RC with emphasis on the content of the lesson. For example based on lesson content, the teacher decides if OTR will be embedded in the lesson in multiple choice, true/false, yes/no, or open-ended formats.

Second, the teacher creates the RC. To keep RC an affordable, efficient, durable, and flexible classroom strategy, the teacher may use commercial white erase boards, laminated card stock, or pieces of white paper inserted into a sheet protector along with dry erase markers and erasers, paper towels, or socks. Once the medium for the RC is selected, the teacher prepares the RC to match the OTR format. For example, for a multiple choice format, the RC would have an A, B, C, D written vertically on separate lines; for a true/false format, the word "true" would be written on the top of the paper and the word "false" written upside down on the bottom of the paper; for a yes/no format, the word "yes" would be written on the top of the paper and the word "no" would be written upside down on the bottom of the paper; and for an open-ended format, the page would be left blank and each student would be provided with a dry erase marker (note: the other formats do not require a dry erase marker).

Third, the teacher would need to teach, model, and reinforce the students on how to use the RC prior to actually implementing the strategy during instruction. This needs to be pre-planned and well-constructed to maximize appropriate student use of the RC. To teach and model the use of RC, the teacher: (a) introduces the materials to the students; (b) explicitly teaches and models the cues (e.g., teacher asks a question and states "select an answer on your card, put your finger on it, and keep it on your desk"), wait time (e.g., teacher waits 3 to 5 seconds after the cue is provided), and behavior (e.g., cards remain on the desk until the signal is given for them to be held up over their heads); and (c) reinforces students' appropriate use of the RCs (e.g., providing behavior-specific praise statements).

Fourth, after explicitly teaching the students how to use RC the teacher is ready to implement RC as a strategy to improve engagement and appropriate behaviors. The RC materials should be disseminated to the students prior to use and precorrection used to remind students of how and when they are to use the RC throughout the lesson.

Ms. Powell and her co-teacher teach middle school academic classes containing students with and without disabilities and some at-risk for academic failure. Both teachers have noticed that several students, some with disabilities and some without, are not actively engaged during whole class instruction when new material is being taught and synthesized with review materials. They notice some students with their heads on their desks or students sleeping, students staring into space, students asking off-topic questions, and students asking for content to be repeated. Ms. Powell decides to use a combination of choral responding and RC with the class (having previously explained, modeled, and practiced both strategies). About every 3 minutes during her instruction, she asks a recall question about something she has just described. She prefaces the question by saying, "OK, this is for everyone to answer . . ." She has taught the students that this means they all should call out the answer simultaneously (i.e., choral responding). Beginning at the middle portion of her lesson, she instructs students to use their RC to determine if individual students are mastering the material. Ms. Powell previously decided to use both multiple-choice and true/false question formats for this lesson and put options A, B, C, D on one side of laminated paper with true and false on the other side. The co-teacher distributes the RC to each student and provides a precorrection statement: "When Ms. Powell asks a question, put your finger on your response, keep the card on your table, and only hold the card above your head when she gives you the thumbs-up sign." Ms. Powell then provides a few review-type OTR for the class to practice using their RC and provides any redirection needed (e.g., "remember to hold up the card only after I give the signal"). Ms. Powell then continues with her lesson providing the OTR she embedded within the lesson, scans the room to determine which students are providing accurate responses, provides verbal reinforcement for accurate responses and correct use of the RC, and reteaches concepts in which the class is not providing accurate responses. The combination of choral responding and RC interjected throughout the lesson give each student ample opportunities to respond, thereby increasing engagement and promoting learning. In addition to increasing the number of OTR, engagement can be facilitated through briskly paced guided practice, alternating easier with more difficult tasks, and following non-preferred activities with high-interest activities.

Contingent Attention

Contingent attention is a low-cost and effective strategy teachers can implement in the classroom with students at any time. Specifically, contingent attention occurs when teachers provide immediate and genuine attention to students who have or are engaging in appropriate forms of behavior (Walker et al., 2004). For example, if a student is on-task, completes a task with high accuracy, or attempts new tasks, the teacher may provide the student with attention by: (a) taking time to talk with the student and providing feedback, (b) giving the student a "thumbs-up," (c) looking at the student and smiling, or (d) providing the student with praise. Most students desire their teachers' attention. In a study of four African American students with extremely disruptive behavior, it was determined that they were acting out to get their teachers to attend to them (Lo & Cartledge, 2006). Once the students were taught an appropriate way to recruit attention from the teachers, they no longer engaged in the disruptive behavior.

Praise is probably the most common form of contingent attention used by classroom teachers. Generically, praise is a positive statement ("good job," "nicely done," "super") provided in verbal or written form to the student. Some argue that such generic statements, although positive, are not adequate for some students who may have difficulty understanding what behavior is being praised (e.g., good job for what? what did I do that was nicely done?).

Behavior-specific praise, in which the teacher describes the desirable social or academic behavior, can be more effective than general praise statements (Reinke, Lewis-Palmer, & Martin, 2007; Sutherland, Wehby, & Copeland, 2000). For example, rather than saying "Excellent work," the teacher can make the praise behavior-specific by saying, "Excellent work finishing your assignment on time and with 90% correct!"

Student characteristics can influence the effectiveness of teacher praise and attention (Hawkins & Heflin, 2011). Culturally responsive management suggests that some students will respond better to praise for their individual effort or ability whereas other students will respond better to praise that recognizes their contribution to the group's functioning (Weinstein et al., 2004). Younger students tend to view their peers who are praised by the teacher as capable and smart whereas older students may believe that peers praised by the teacher are less competent (Miller & Hom, 1997). Males may prefer behavior-specific praise for effort whereas females may respond better to praise for their ability (Burnett, 2001).

Mr. Quincy is working with Anthony on his noise-making behavior during whole class instruction. During instruction, Anthony makes a clicking noise with his tongue and lips that was distracting to his peers and Mr. Quincy. Mr. Quincy typically reprimanded Anthony or would stop his instruction and engage in discussions about the inappropriate behavior. Mr. Quincy realized that Anthony would make the inappropriate noise as soon as he began teaching again or stopped talking to Anthony. Using praise statements, Mr. Quincy began verbally attending to Anthony during instruction when he was not making the noises. This attention was provided immediately, frequently, and enthusiastically. For instance, Mr. Quincy would say "Anthony, I like the way you are sitting quietly and paying attention to the lesson" or "Anthony, I appreciate how you are quietly concentrating on your work." In addition, Mr. Quincy made a card to remind him to provide Anthony with some one-on-one time (additional attention) at the end of a lesson in which he was able to provide multiple specific praise statements. After using behavior-specific praise with Anthony for a few days, Mr. Quincy observed a decrease in his noise making. In addition, the interactions between teacher and student were more positive as Anthony made fewer noises.

Choice Making

Making choices is a fundamental skill that can have positive effects on students' academic and social performance within the classroom (Jolivette, Wehby, Canale, & Massey, 2001; Ramsey, Jolivette, Puckett Patterson, & Kennedy, 2010). A choice making opportunity occurs when a teacher selects two or more options from which the student may choose. The number of options should be based on student age and ability and on the objectives the teacher has set for the student. For example, a young child in a preschool setting who displays challenging behaviors when dropped off by her mother may be provided with two options whereas a middle school aged student who is noncompliant with teacher requests may be offered a choice of three or four options. Another example may include a high school student who is provided with the choice of either completing an assignment by herself or with a partner and also the choice of selecting the topic. No matter the number of options, teachers should provide only options they are willing for the students to select. In addition, teachers can use choice making opportunities before, during, or after a specific task or activity in which they can predict inappropriate patterns of student behavior.

Mr. Hooper can predict that Tye will be verbally aggressive, noncompliant, and out of seat when prompted to get ready for math class. Mr. Hooper decides to provide Tye with opportunities to make choices immediately after his prompt. He says, "Tye, after you finish math class without any problems would you like to take Jerome, Steve, or Marilyn with you to the computer lab?" At first, this opportunity for Tye to make a choice was effective in that he went to math and actively and appropriately participated without incident. However, Mr. Hooper noticed that after about 5 weeks Tye's inappropriate behavior was occurring during math and he overheard Tye tell a friend that he really liked his new erasable pen. So, after the whole class math instruction occurred and students were getting ready to work on independent activities, Mr. Hooper praised Tye for his appropriate behavior during the lesson and then asked Tye if he would like to use a pencil or his erasable pen to complete the worksheet. Whereas Tye used to misbehave during math class, by giving Tye choices before and during the activity Mr. Hooper now observed appropriate behaviors from Tye.

Premack Principle

The Premack (1959) Principle is frequently used to encourage students to engage in tasks and activities they usually would rather not do. Premack is a statement that pairs the display of an appropriate behavior with a reinforcer sought by the student and is usually phrased as "if . . . then . . ." or "after . . . then . . ."

Parents may use the Premack Principle on Saturday mornings by saying "*If* you clean your room by making your bed, putting your laundry away, and putting your toys in the basket, *then* you can go outside and play with your friends." Knowing what is expected and knowing what will happen after the expectations are fulfilled promotes compliance.

Conferencing typically involves only the student and the teacher. The goal is to help students see connections between their behavior and the outcomes.

In his classroom, Mr. Scott decided to use the Premack Principle with Travis, a fourth grade student who refused to legibly copy items written on the board (e.g., math problems, spelling words). When such activities took place, Mr. Scott found himself pleading with Travis to "get busy" and nagging him to do his work. Mr. Scott realized these strategies were not helping Travis get to work and were creating negative interactions between himself and Travis. Mr. Scott knew that Travis enjoyed working on the computer. The next time Travis was expected to copy his spelling words from the board, Mr. Scott discretely said to Travis "If you copy all 15 of your spelling words using your best handwriting, then you can use the computer to type in your math homework problems." Mr. Scott found that by clearly describing the behavior he expected from Travis (i.e., legibly writing all 15 spelling words) and what Travis was to get by engaging in the expected behavior (i.e., computer time), he was more focused on positive behavior, he decreased the likelihood of negatively interacting with Travis, and Travis was doing more work.

Conferencing

Teachers will need to talk to students who are stuck in automatic misbehavior. The purpose of the conference is not to lecture students or try to make them feel bad about their behavior but rather to help students see connections between their behavior and the outcomes. Conferencing provides students with a supported opportunity to think of alternatives for their misbehavior and for teachers to secure commitments from the students that they will try the alternatives. The time to conference with a student is not in the midst of misbehavior. To have a productive conference, everyone must be calm. Conferencing is usually conducted one-on-one, with just the student and teacher. Teachers should be ready for students' attempts to divert the focus of the conference. Following is an example of a productive conference:

Mr. Powell: *Tell me what happened that got you sent to the principal's office.*

Sylvester: *It wasn't my fault. Stupid Derrick started it.*

Mr. Powell: *What happened first?*

Sylvester: *When we were working on the project, Derrick started making fun of the way I was writing. That's what happened. See it's all Derrick's fault and you should be talking to him instead of me.*

Mr. Powell: *What did Derrick do to make fun of your writing?*

Sylvester: *He started telling me that I write like a girl and that we were not going to get finished and it was all my fault 'cause I was writing so slow. Then he started laughing and singing, "Sylvester writes like a girl. Just like his sister the retard."*

Mr. Powell: *So Derrick tried to insult you by telling you that you write like a girl and then made a crack about your sister. That's pretty hard to hear. Derrick needs to stop doing stuff like that. What happened after he said all that stuff?*

Sylvester: *I made a big "X" across our project and told him that he could just finish it himself. He started yelling at me again, calling me "stupid" and "idiot" and so I tore the project in half. And then we both started yelling at each other and that's when you jumped in.*

Mr. Powell: *Yeah, you two were disturbing the entire class. And you didn't calm down when I asked you. Remember, we call that "belligerence." What's the rule when you're belligerent?*

Sylvester: *You have to go to the principal's office.*

Mr. Powell: *That's right, you go to the principal's office and he calls your parents.*

Sylvester: *But that wasn't fair because I didn't start it! Derrick started it and I was just defending myself. I have to be able to defend myself, you know!*

Mr. Powell: *The rule is that belligerence lands you in the principal's office, no matter who starts it.*

Sylvester: *That's not fair because I didn't start it. Derrick was mean and I had to stop him.*

Mr. Powell: *I know you wanted to stop him from saying those things and I probably would, too. But what could you do besides tear up your project when someone tries to insult you?*

Sylvester: *There's nothing else to do. I had to get his attention to make him stop.*

Mr. Powell: *But it didn't make him stop. What are some things we've talked about that you can do when someone teases you?*

Sylvester: *Oh, you mean like ignore him? Well, I couldn't do that because then he would get away with it.*

Mr. Powell: *Right! Ignoring him and pretending like you didn't hear a word he said is a good alternative. It will be hard but you could teach yourself to do it and then you wouldn't get in trouble.*

Sylvester: *But then Derrick gets away with it and he's mean.*

Mr. Powell: *You're right. Derrick needs to learn not to do those things. But when you react like you did, what happens?*

Sylvester: *I mess up a project we've been working on and then my parents get called. But I don't care. It was a stupid project anyway.*

Mr. Powell: *Right. When you react to someone's teasing by tearing up your project, then you're not going to get a good grade either. How can we work on your not losing your cool?*

Sylvester: *You could send Derrick to another class and make him stop being mean.*

Mr. Powell: *Well I can't help Derrick if he is in another class and we all need to work on respecting other people. Now, what can you and I do so that you don't lose your cool?*

Sylvester: *You could make Derrick shut up when he starts talking like that.*

Mr. Powell: *How will I know when he's trying to insult you? I couldn't hear him when you two were working on your project.*

Sylvester: *I can tell you when he's being mean.*

Mr. Powell: *Right, you can tell me. What would you do? Would you just yell, "Mr. Powell, Derrick is being mean!" or what? How about you walk away from Derrick and come toward me and give me a signal?*

Sylvester: *Like what?*

Mr. Powell: *You could come toward me and hold up your index finger, like this. Then I would know that you are walking away from someone who is teasing you.*

Sylvester: *I think it would be better if I just told him to shut up.*

Mr. Powell: *Well, you can certainly try that first. If it doesn't work, then you could walk away and give me the signal, and then your parents won't have to be called and you'll get your assignment finished. Can we try this?*

Sylvester: *I'm not sure it's going to work, but we can try.*

Mr. Powell: *Great. We'll give it a try.*

In this conference, Mr. Powell connected what happened to Sylvester's behavior, helped Sylvester think of alternative behaviors that would have better outcomes, and secured a commitment from Sylvester to try the alternative. Mr. Powell did not respond to any of Sylvester's provocative statements or attempts to change the topic to anything other than Sylvester's behavior. Mr. Powell was empathetic and applauded Sylvester's good ideas. The conference is relatively brief, focused, and positive which will enable students to move toward more adaptive solutions to problems.

Token Economy

Token economies allow teachers to provide structured feedback for behavior and academic achievement in a systematic fashion (Kazdin, 1977). Tokens are things that are given as a consequence of behavior. They provide tangible proof that students are performing as expected. Tokens have no intrinsic value but become valuable because of how they can be used, which is to trade them for something that is valuable to the individual. Tokens include such things as grades, check marks, poker chips, tickets, marbles, and so forth. Tokens selected for use will depend upon the developmental age of the students (e.g., check marks for older students and marbles for younger students). A prime example of a token economy is teacher salary. Teachers sign a contract that they will receive a certain amount of money if they perform their duties as expected. The money is not meaningful in and of itself but is quite meaningful in terms of what it allows teachers to purchase. Similarly, grades have no intrinsic value but can be accumulated and later exchanged for a diploma or degree.

In classrooms, token economies are linked to behavioral and academic expectations. Teachers decide if students are to receive tokens in a structured or spontaneous way. To use a token economy in a structured way, teachers determine an interval that is appropriate for students. Young children and older students with poor ability to delay gratification may need to have the structured feedback given more frequently. For example, young children may earn a smiley face after each activity. The teacher will quickly talk to each child after an activity and draw or place a sticker of a smiley face in the box representing that activity on a chart. Some older students may receive tokens only at the end of the day or the end of the week.

To use a token economy in a more spontaneous fashion, teachers may intermittently award tokens when they observe students performing as expected. As with structured token economies, when awarding tokens spontaneously, teachers need to clearly describe the behavior reflecting the class rules that are being reinforced. There are many variations on spontaneous awarding of tokens. Teachers may set a timer for an undisclosed amount of time and when the timer goes off, each student who is on-task will receive a token. In another variation, students who are acknowledged for behaving as expected are given a slip of paper on which to write their names. The slips of paper are then put into a container and at the end of the day (or week) a slip is drawn and the student whose name is on the paper gets to do something special (e.g., eat lunch with teacher, get a "no homework" ticket) or receives something special (e.g., pizza coupon, bonus points). Teachers also may use token economies for the entire class. When the teacher praises the entire class for appropriate behavior or meeting an academic criteria (e.g., everyone scored above 80% on the math quiz), a token is awarded (e.g., marble placed in a container, check mark on the board) and after the accumulation of a predetermined number of tokens, the entire group gets to do or receive something special.

The keys to a token economy include that students receive feedback in the form of tokens frequently enough to make it meaningful to them and that the items for which the tokens are exchanged are things that the students want. In order to promote an understanding that the tokens are meaningful, the frequency of exchange, similar to the frequency of feedback, must match students' ability to delay gratification. In terms of the exchange items, many teachers using a token economy will have a store in which they have a variety of items with corresponding costs. The items available for the student to acquire will be determined by how many tokens the student has earned. The items available in the store do not have to be expensive or even purchased by the teacher. These items can be donated by parents, donated by the schools' business partners, or accumulated through friends (e.g., toys that come in children's meals at many fast food restaurants are popular with young children). The store also may contain activity items like passes for extra time on the computer, lunch with the principal, ice cream at lunch, 5 minutes in the gym to play basketball with a peer of choice, and so forth. The cost of each item will be based on how desirable it is and how much effort should be required to earn. For example, small items like candy may be priced very low. Big ticket items like a football or pizza coupon may be priced higher. In some schools, the price for eating lunch with the janitor may be higher than the price for eating lunch with the teacher. Teachers may need to identify special interests to motivate reluctant students to participate. For example, adding a popular music CD to the class store may greatly increase the motivation of a particular student to participate.

An interesting example of a token economy is described by Cook (1999). In this token economy, the teacher duplicated enlarged photocopies of $1, $5, and $10 "behavior bucks." Students who were ready with all materials needed for the lesson (i.e., books, papers, and pencils) received behavior bucks. Raising the hand and waiting to be called on earned behavior bucks as did completed work. Students engaged in banking activities at the end of the day, completing deposit slips to bank their bucks. Students graphed their 5-day earning totals. They could write checks to purchase preferred items. In this study, the items included: hockey cards, extra computer time, time out of class to work with the librarian or custodian, special projects with the secretary to answer the phone or operate the photocopier, or extra time in the gym with a fifth grade teacher. The time in the gym with the fifth grade teacher was the big ticket item and cost $200. The token economy not only emphasized the literal value of appropriate behavior but also provided opportunities for students to learn banking, saving, and purchasing skills.

The interesting aspect of this token economy is that after a few months, the students agreed to collectively raise $10,000 in behavior bucks and use that money to help needy families. A local department store agreed to exchange the $10,000 in behavior bucks for $1,000 of store credit. Four families (not in the school community) were adopted by the class. Although their identities were never revealed, the students knew how many adults were in the family as well as the number and ages of children. After accumulating the targeted goal, the class made a field trip to the store and worked collaboratively to equitably spend the store credit to purchase items such as clothing, toys, and house wares for their adopted families. This extension of the token economy provided an opportunity to develop empathy and altruism.

Token economies will succeed only if the students' abilities are considered in terms of how often the tokens should be awarded and exchanged and if the exchange items available are things the students want. Ideas for high interest items include soda, candy bars, late to class pass, coupon to get out of detention, coupon for $2 off Friday morning breakfast, and chips of choice on Tuesday (Kehle, Bray, Theodore, Jenson, & Clark, 2000). Anticipation of reinforcement can be heightened by adding a surprise element. For example, teachers can make a pie chart with preferred items and activities written on each slice and then add a spinner. Students who meet criteria spin to discover what they have earned. Or, the preferred items and activities may be written on individual slips of paper and placed in a container for drawing when students have earned the opportunity. Unless students' behaviors warrant, token economies should not be used as a permanent strategy in a classroom for routine tasks (Van Acker, 2006). Teachers should fade the use of the artificial reinforcers used in token economies and rely as much as possible on natural reinforcers such as praise and grades. However, a token economy can be a good way to bring a classroom under control and can be used to emphasize the importance of following the class rules.

Behavioral Contracts

Some students who misbehave or who do not do their work respond positively to a written and/or verbal agreement with the teacher. Such an agreement is commonly referred to as a behavioral contract. A behavioral contract is a tool in which the teacher states which appropriate behavior the student is to display and the student identifies which reinforcer he would like to earn for displaying this behavior. Some negotiation may occur. A typical sequence of steps is followed to create a behavioral contract.

1. Based on the data the teacher has collected and what other strategies have been tried, the teacher identifies a positive academic or social behavior the student needs to demonstrate.
2. The teacher approaches the student and both discuss the behavior of concern.
3. Both the teacher and student discuss the appropriate behavior the student will display. During this discussion, the appropriate behavior needs to be clearly defined. The definition will include: (a) under what conditions the student should display the behavior, (b) what cues or prompts the teacher may provide to the student, and (c) when the student should not display the behavior (e.g., it would not be appropriate for a student to raise her hand on the playground to receive a turn on the slide).

4. The teacher will ask the student what type of reinforcer is preferred for when the appropriate behavior is displayed. If a student cannot name a reinforcer or the reinforcer is not appropriate (too big or costly), the teacher can ask the student to list a variety of reinforcers and then select from that list. During this discussion, the teacher and student decide how many times or how long the student needs to display the appropriate behavior before the reinforcer is given. The time element will be based on the student's age and difficulty of the behavior to be displayed. For example, some contracts may be written each day whereas others may span a week or more. In addition, how and by whom the reinforcer will be provided needs to be discussed. For example, will the teacher or principal deliver the reinforcement to the student at the end of the school day or as soon as the behavior is displayed?

5. At this point, the teacher and student review the appropriate behavior the student is to display, the reinforcer the student will receive for the behavior, and the time frame for delivery of the reinforcer. This step is for purposes of negotiation and detailing both the teacher and student responsibilities. If both the teacher and student are in agreement of the terms of the contract, they are ready for step 6.

6. Depending on the abilities of the student, either the student or the teacher will write the contract. The complexity of the contract will vary but it is best to keep it simple. Based on the discussion in the proceeding steps, the following are written: (a) the student's and teacher's names; (b) the behavior the student is to display along with the number of times and under what conditions; (c) what the teacher will do to support the student; (d) what the reinforcer is and when, how, and by whom it will be delivered; (e) a start and end date for the contract; and (f) signature lines for both the student and teacher. It is important that all aspects of the contract be written in positive terms.

Behavioral contracting can be a powerful yet simple strategy to use with students who misbehave as you can see in the following example.

Mr. Landis is concerned about Jason's inconsistent and often inaccurate homework completion which is negatively affecting his grades. In the past, Mr. Landis has provided Jason with reinforcers for turning in his homework but realized that it did not mean Jason had completed the assignment accurately. In addition, when Mr. Landis prompted students to turn in their homework, he and Jason often got in an argument. Mr. Landis decided to try a behavioral contract with Jason. They met privately in the back of the classroom while the other students worked on independent assignments. Mr. Landis discussed his concern regarding Jason's homework and its effect on his grades. Both agreed that homework needed to be turned in each time it was given and that Jason would receive a reinforcer (e.g., weekend homework pass, computer time) if he turned it in with 80% or higher accuracy. They decided that the duration of the contract would be 1 week and he had to display the appropriate behavior all 5 days to earn his reinforcer. A note was added to the contract that each Monday, they would sign a new contract and if Jason had earned the previous week's "weekend homework pass" that he had to display the appropriate behavior Tuesday through Friday (since he would not be turning in homework on Monday). They wrote the contract and both signed it. For the past 6 weeks, Jason has met his contract goal four times. Mr. Landis is pleased with Jason's goal attainment and he has seen an increase in Jason's grades as well as a positive change in his relationship with Jason during their morning routine when homework is due. If Jason was not meeting the requirements of the contract, Mr. Landis would need to reconvene a meeting with Jason to discuss changing aspects of the contract (e.g., the selected appropriate behavior, reinforcement schedule) to promote student success.

Group Contingencies

Group contingencies are programs that make getting something reinforcing dependent on the behavior of a group. Often these are expansions of token economies that use the behavior of a group as the determining factor in whether or not tokens, and ultimately, reinforcement will be given. Group contingencies can create a focus on expected behavior and students have a vested interest in prompting and encouraging appropriate behavior from their peers. In addition to being useful for getting peers involved in supporting each other, group contingencies tend to reduce students' tolerance for others who do not behave as expected, which can remove peer reinforcement of misbehavior. There are three types of group contingencies: independent, dependent, and interdependent.

In using **independent group contingencies**, the same criteria are used for all students but each student is able to access reinforcement individually. For example, the teacher may say that everyone who scores above 80% on an assignment can engage in a 5-minute free time period for talking with their friends at the end of class. The contingency applies to the entire class and each student who meets the criteria has access to the reinforcement. This type of group contingency does little to get peers to encourage each other to perform as expected since the criteria must be met individually.

With **dependent group contingencies**, the class is allowed access to a token or reinforcer based on the behavior of one individual or a small group of individuals. Modifying the example just given to be a dependent group contingency, the teacher would inform the class that if Robert earns 80% or better on his assignment, the entire class will get 5-minutes of free time to talk with their friends at the end of the class period. In this way, maximum peer pressure is exerted and students can become "heroes" in the classroom. On the other hand, the targeted student may be yelled at and snubbed if the group does not get the reinforcement. One unique variation of the dependent group contingency is evident when the teacher does not tell the class the identity of the targeted student. The teacher writes the name of a student on a piece of paper, folds it, and places it in plain sight. The "mystery" student is not revealed until the end of the class period. At this point, the teacher makes the decision whether or not to reveal the identity of the mystery hero based on possible reactions from the class. Students may be motivated to meet the stated criteria in case they are revealed as the mystery student and peer encouragement is spread across the class rather than concentrated on Robert. Again, however, it is possible that if the mystery student does not earn the reinforcement for the group that others will be unkind.

The third type of group contingency is an **interdependent group contingency**. In an interdependent contingency, access to a token or reinforcement depends upon the combined performance of members of a group. The group may be an entire class or subset groups within the class. Use of subsets within a classroom adds the element of competition. Not every team will earn the reinforcement—only the team with the highest (or lowest) number of points. The competitive angle of interdependent contingencies can create high levels of animosity among classmates and should be used with caution and only when students in the class are mature enough to handle the competitive aspect.

More commonly, interdependent group contingencies are developed based on the behavior of the class as a whole. Examples of interdependent group contingencies have already appeared as parts of examples for other strategies. In the description of signal control, Ms. Dennis wrote one of the letters from the word "homework" on the board each time the entire class was quiet within 2 seconds of hearing the chime. In the discussion of the token economy using "behavior bucks" the students worked together toward a group contingency of $10,000. Lohrmann and Talerico (2004) describe an interdependent group contingency called "Anchor the Boat." In this group contingency, at the end of every 42-minute class period, if the number of students who got out of their seats + the number of students who did not complete the assignment + the number of students who called out was less than a specified number, a paper clip was added to the chain suspended between a picture of a boat that had been placed on the wall and the picture of an anchor that was 20 inches away (it took ten 2-inch paper clips to connect the boat to the anchor). When the boat was anchored, students could choose items from a treasure chest that included toys, bookmarks, and games. For students in middle and high school, earning a specific number of tally marks on the board for appropriate behavior may result in 5 minutes to sleep, visit, read, or primp. As with any contingency, after students become proficient at achieving the goal, variables can be modified to promote development of increasingly responsible behavior. In the anchor the boat game, the criteria could be systematically lowered until it was zero. Or, the anchor could be moved farther away from the boat. Or small paper clips could be substituted for the large ones. In terms of the three types of group contingencies, dependent and interdependent group contingencies have been found to be more effective for increasing appropriate behavior than independent group contingencies (Pappas, Skinner, & Skinner, 2010).

Differential Reinforcement

Differential reinforcement must be discussed separately and appears on the third level of the pyramid because it takes a little more teacher effort to implement than strategies in which students simply earn reinforcement. As discussed previously, behaviors are followed by consequences and if the consequences result in the behavior continuing, then the consequence is reinforcing. If the consequence results in the student no longer demonstrating the behavior, then the consequence is punishing. Teachers who say, "His behavior was getting worse even though I was reinforcing him with candy" do not understand the concept of reinforcement. If the candy resulted in behavior getting worse, then it was a punisher, not a reinforcer. Some students find teacher attention and praise reinforcing, others do not. Students who continue to misbehave even though they are consistently sent to the office must be finding the trips to the office reinforcing. Some students even seem to be reinforced by teachers reprimanding them since the misbehavior continues to occur. To use differential reinforcement, teachers must first identify what the student finds reinforcing (e.g., praise, going to the office, reprimands). Then, differential reinforcement occurs when teachers reinforce appropriate behavior but withhold reinforcement when students misbehave. This is why differential reinforcement is a little harder to implement. Teachers must get very good at noticing and reinforcing appropriate behavior but must resist the urge to notice or reinforce misbehavior. Consider the example of Ms. Long.

One of Ms. Long's students, Michelle, wanders around the room, asks the teacher and peers questions usually not on-topic, and looks out the window when Ms. Long is trying to teach the class. This out-of-seat behavior is interfering with Michelle's ability to learn as well as the other students' learning because Ms. Long finds herself interrupting her teaching to redirect Michelle back to her seat, answering her off-topic questions, and pleading with her to sit down. The behavior stops only when Ms. Long, totally exasperated, sends Michelle to the principal's office. Ms. Long's data suggested that Michelle spends more time out-of-seat during math class than any other class. Since math class lasts 25 minutes, Ms. Long made a data recording sheet with five squares and if Michelle was in her seat for the entire 5 minute segment, Ms. Long recorded a "+" and verbally reinforced Michelle (e.g., "You've earned a "+" for sitting in your seat"). Most importantly, Ms. Long ignored Michelle's out-of-seat behavior and did not interrupt her instruction to answer Michelle's questions. She also used a group contingency and put a check on the board whenever other students ignored Michelle's questions, having told the class that when they got 10 checks, they would not get math homework that day. By using differential reinforcement, Ms. Long ignored

Michelle's misbehavior and reinforced her for staying in her seat. When Michelle earned 10 "+" marks, she was allowed to go to the principal's office for a visit.

The use of behavior enhancement strategies, such as the 11 described in this text, helps teachers stay focused on the positive behaviors they want students to display and allows students to receive systematic reinforcement for engaging in appropriate behavior. Teachers will find that students demonstrate less misbehavior when the emphasis is on performing as expected. Unfortunately, some students will have high levels of chronic automatic misbehavior that respond only partially to behavior enhancement strategies. For these students, teachers may have to consider temporarily adding behavior reduction strategies.

Behavior Reduction Strategies

Behavior reduction strategies, including response cost, timeout, reprimands, and aversives, may be effective but must be used with great caution because of two predictable outcomes. First, most behavior reduction strategies result in unwanted reactions from students (Sidman, 1989). Students may comply with teacher directives when faced with the prospect of punishment, but will do so grudgingly and their resentment will show in other types of resistant behavior, both overt (e.g., verbal or physical aggression) and covert (e.g., vandalism, truancy). Indeed, the use of punishment is associated with increased rates of misbehavior (Way, 2011) as students may want to be suspended or go to detention instead of doing their work (Atkins et al., 2002). The use of corporal punishment (an aversive) has not been shown to be effective in reducing misbehavior (Robinson, Funk, Beth, & Bush, 2005) and may actually lead to depression in adulthood (Turner & Muller, 2004).

Second, although behavior reduction strategies may stop misbehavior, they do nothing to teach the student what should be done instead. As has been discussed previously, errors in behavior need to be treated like errors in academics and the student should be taught the appropriate response and reinforced when it is demonstrated. Punishment does not teach, it simply suppresses, leaving a behavioral vacuum and a strong likelihood that students will repeat the misbehavior when faced with the same situation because they do not know what to do instead.

With these two cautions in mind, some behavior management plans combine strategies designed to teach appropriate behavior with those designed to reduce misbehavior. The guiding concept is to think in terms of **behavior pairs** (Kauffman et al., 2006, p. 26) in which the opposite or acceptable alternative for the misbehavior is identified. For example, if a student is out of his seat frequently and this is a problem, what is the behavior that the teacher wants to see? The behavior pair for being out of seat would be sitting in the seat. Strategies used to address the behavior should focus on increasing the time the student spends in his seat, similar to the example given of Ms. Long and differential reinforcement. If the strategies are not effective after a reasonable effort, then the teacher may want to continue to focus on motivating the student to stay in his seat but may add strategies designed to discourage him from getting out of his seat without permission. The behavior reduction strategies discussed here include response cost and timeout. Aversive consequences also are discussed in order to highlight why such commonly used strategies are rarely effective for long-term behavioral change.

Response Cost

Response cost procedures involve the removal or loss of something following the misbehavior in the hopes that the misbehavior will be less likely to occur in the future (Azrin & Holz, 1966). A cost is associated with the behavior. A common example of response cost is what happens when individuals are caught driving too fast. The behavior (speeding) costs something, usually literally, as the individual has to pay the speeding ticket. Response cost procedures rarely involve money in school settings. Instead, misbehavior costs students things such as lost tokens, lost privileges, lost possessions, or loss of the ability to participate in extracurricular activities. Whatever is taken away from the student must be valued by the student or the response cost procedure will not be effective.

Ms. Demming recognized that Jerry's talking out in class was disrupting his learning and the learning of other students. She and Jerry wrote a behavioral contract that specified he would earn 1 minute of extra time on the computer for every 5 minutes in which he raised his hand and waited to be called on before talking during instruction. The strategy was somewhat effective, as Jerry did earn a few extra minutes on the computer for several days. However, his talking out was still a problem. Ms. Demming met with Jerry and modified his contract to include a loss of 1 minute of computer time for each instance of talking out. After Jerry experienced 1 day where he did not get to use the computer during free time because the response cost procedure resulted in the loss of the available minutes, the instances of talking out were reduced to near zero. In combination, the reinforcement for raising his hand and waiting, along with the loss of minutes for talking out, was effective for reducing the misbehavior and increasing the amount of instructional time for everyone.

Timeout

Timeout is one of the most often used and, unfortunately, misused consequences for misbehavior in schools (see the CCBD's position summary on the use of seclusion in school settings; Peterson, Albrecht, Johns, & CCBD, 2009a). The term "timeout" refers to several strategies, all of which separate students from reinforcement when they demonstrate inappropriate behavior. If timeout is effective, students will stop demonstrating the behaviors that resulted in the timeout. As described by Ryan, Sander, Katsiyannis, and Yell (2007), three commonly used types of timeout follow:

Exclusion timeout occurs when students are removed from the group so they cannot observe instruction and their peers cannot see them.

1. Inclusion timeout occurs when reinforcement is taken away from the student. Students are still part of the group, but they may be ignored by all others in the classroom for a brief period of time for inappropriate behavior. In one variation of inclusion timeout, materials may be removed. For example, teachers take pencils away from students who are tapping them on their desks. In another variation of inclusion timeout, students may be moved away from the group and told they need to watch but are not allowed to participate. These forms of inclusion timeout provide a consequence for inappropriate behavior, but students can still see and hear instruction.

2. Exclusion timeout occurs when students are removed from the group so that they can no longer observe instruction and their peers can no longer see them. To implement exclusion timeout, teachers may have students sit in a separate area of the classroom, behind a divider, or move them to the hallway or another classroom.

3. Seclusion timeout occurs when students are isolated in a room where they must stay for a specified amount of time. To use seclusion timeout, teachers need specialized training and must follow district policies. The policies typically dictate the features of the room

as well as the paperwork that must be completed to document adequate supervision during timeout. There is scant evidence to support the use of seclusion timeout and numerous cases to challenge its legality (Knoster, Wells, & McDowell, 2003), so very few teachers use this form of timeout.

In order for timeout to be effective in reducing inappropriate behavior, teachers have to remember the full name for the strategy. "Timeout" is short for "timeout from reinforcement." Therefore, classroom activities and interactions have to be enjoyable and interesting to the student. Unfortunately, some students may prefer to be excluded from the group or sent out of the classroom rather than participate in instructional activities. Rather than being "timeout from reinforcement," the strategy becomes "timeout to reinforcement" as students misbehave in order to avoid staying in the classroom or doing their work.

To use timeout effectively, teachers must be sure the academic and social demands placed on students are within their ability so that students are not misbehaving to avoid the demands (Knoster et al., 2003). Instruction should include high levels of reinforcement in the form of positive feedback and should be engaging to students. The foundations for management and learning described in this chapter need to be in place. Strategies from the lower three tiers of the evidence-based intervention (see Figure 9.7) should have been consistently implemented. A functional behavioral assessment (FBA; discussed in the next section) needs to demonstrate that the behavior is being exhibited for attention in order for timeout to be effective.

If all these precursors are in place, there are guidelines for using timeout effectively. The length of time spent in timeout should be brief and based on the student's developmental age. The commonly used rule is no more than a minute for each year of the student's age (Ryan et al., 2007). Students need to be taught how to behave while they are in the different types of timeout. They also need to complete the activity that was going on when they were given a timeout; otherwise they will be reinforced for using misbehavior to get out of tasks. Teachers need to keep data on how frequently timeout strategies are used and come to the logical conclusion that it is not working if students receive timeout multiple times a week. At that point, teachers should stop using timeout as a strategy for those students and consider alternatives. Teachers must remember that timeout is only one strategy to be used in conjunction with other strategies, particularly those that teach acceptable behaviors to students (Knoster et al., 2003).

Mr. Carlson was concerned about Andrew's use of threats and intimidation with his peers. These seemed to occur most often when Andrew thought the other students were making fun of him or not letting him have his way. Mr. Carlson implemented social skills training for the entire class during the Social Studies block. The class discussed historical and current events in which aggression erupted as a result of misunderstanding or intimidation. They then spent several days role-playing how to handle teasing and several more days addressing the steps for negotiation and compromise. Mr. Carlson was quick to encourage students to demonstrate their developing skills when opportunities presented themselves at other times during the day. Mr. Carlson commended the students whenever he saw students using the skills.

The number of threats and intimidating comments Andrew made were reduced but still occurred two or three times per week. Knowing that Andrew was reinforced by engaging in group activities, Mr. Carlson decided to implement exclusion timeout with Andrew and met with him privately. He knew inclusion timeout would be ineffective because it would be too easy for Andrew to continue to make eye contact with and taunt his peers. Having Andrew move to a separate area of the class creates physical separation and gives Andrew something specific to do to interrupt the inappropriate verbal behavior. He discussed with Andrew the potential consequences for his behavior in terms of the effect on friendships and negative implications for future employment. Mr. Carlson told Andrew that if he made a threat or intimidating comment, he would be told to remove himself to a designated area and set the timer for 5 minutes. At the end of 5 minutes, Andrew could return to the group. They also discussed the consequences if Andrew refused to go to timeout and the consequences if Andrew continued to make intimidating or threatening comments while he was in timeout. Over the next few weeks, the number of times Andrew was sent to timeout decreased to zero, reflecting that Andrew was no longer making intimidating or threatening comments in class. Mr. Carlson continued to commend Andrew for using the social skills the class had learned.

Aversives

Aversive consequences cause physical or psychological pain to reduce future occurrence of a behavior. Reprimands are the most commonly used aversive procedure in schools and consist of statements informing students that they need to stop what they are doing. When Ms. Lewis is distracted by a side conversation, she might reprimand the student by saying, "William, stop talking to Hannah." Cultural differences are evident in reprimands used. According to Weinstein et al. (2004), European American teachers typically use reprimands that label students' internal states (e.g., "Even though you're upset . . .") and emphasize logical outcomes (e.g., "If you talk in class, you won't hear the information that will be on the test"). Effective teachers of children who are culturally and linguistically diverse tend to emphasize their concern for the students (e.g., "I like you and want you to do your best") while appealing to their sense of community and less immediate consequences (e.g., "Other people need to be able to hear, too. I'm sure your mother would be disappointed if she saw you talking in class"). Culturally responsive management dictates that teachers cannot reprimand students for behaviors that the teachers have not specifically taught (Cartledge et al., 2008).

As with all behavior reduction strategies, reprimands should be used sparingly because they do not teach appropriate behavior. In the rare instances that reprimands are used, teachers also will need to use strategies that teach the behavior pair (i.e., the opposite of the inappropriate behavior). Reprimands cannot be delivered without giving students attention, which is another reason to use them sparingly. There are some students who seek any attention, even if it is in the form of a reprimand. If reprimands are not reducing problem behavior, they may be serving as reinforcement rather than punishment. Finally, teachers who overuse reprimands are focusing on students who are misbehaving rather than those who are behaving appropriately (Shores et al., 1993). This can actually lead to higher rates of misbehavior. Instead, teachers should concentrate on reinforcing students for appropriate behavior. Rather than reprimand misbehavior, teachers can use *insistence* (as discussed earlier) to have students practice the correct behavior.

In addition to reprimands, the category of aversives includes other consequences that are given or applied to reduce behavior. Aversives include corporal punishment (i.e., spanking), forced activity, physical restraint, and delivery of noxious substances (e.g., hot sauce on tongue). The use of aversive procedures to reduce inappropriate behavior is rarely sanctioned in schools and then only under extenuating circumstances, after all other strategies have failed. Permission to use aversives must be given by multiple individuals including parents and district personnel (see the CCBD's position summary on the use of physical restraint procedures in school settings; Peterson, Albrecht, Johns, & CCBD, 2009b). It is important to discuss the use of aversives other than reprimands, however, because some teachers use them unwittingly. For example, the teacher who makes students write "I will not talk in class" 500 times is using an aversive procedure intended to produce fatigue. The same is true for a coach who has students run laps or do push-ups as a consequence for misbehavior. Or the teacher who has a student stand-up for 10 minutes to punish him for being out of his seat. Historically, some teachers made students sit in the corner wearing a dunce cap. This is aversive because it is intended to cause humiliation and social ostracization. All of these are examples of aversives that violate the students' rights, generate unwanted side effects, and are not effective for behavioral change. Federal and state regulations limit the use of aversive procedures (Weiss, 2005) and teachers should recognize if they are using aversives and discontinue use of unsanctioned aversive procedures.

Addressing More Severe Behavioral Problems

Functional Behavior Assessment (FBA)

For more severe misbehaviors displayed by students during academic and/or social instruction, an additional set of strategies may be employed. For students who engage in chronic or predictable misbehavior, who have a history of displaying such behavior, or when placement changes are considered due to behavior, a functional behavior assessment (FBA) may need to be conducted to determine the variables contributing to the occurrence of misbehavior. An FBA consists of four core processes and is conducted by a multidisciplinary team that contains members who know the student and who have expertise in academic and social student difficulties (Moreno, 2011). The first process, *defining the problem,* consists of the team: (a) discussing the problem behavior; (b) collecting data through archival records reviews, direct observations, and interviews to determine the environments where the problem behaviors are occurring and in which environments the student behaves appropriately; and (c) reframing the problem into a measurable, observable, and objective behavior.

Mr. Carter has growing concerns about Cecil's consistent inappropriate behavior in class. Mr. Carter approaches his grade level support team to discuss Cecil's behavior and the negative impact the behavior is having on Cecil's learning as well as the learning of his peers. This grade level support team meets once a month to give teachers a forum to discuss the academic and social progress of students as well as to get assistance with problem-solving behavioral challenges. At the meeting, Mr. Carter shares his growing concerns about Cecil by stating the problem behavior. In this case, Mr. Carter states that Cecil is noncompliant. The team asks what Mr. Carter means by noncompliance as that term can mean many different things in different contexts. Mr. Carter defines noncompliance in measurable and observable terms by stating that when Cecil is given a simple or complex direction (e.g., "Get out your Social Studies book"), Cecil (a) typically says, "You can't make me," (b) continues with what he was doing prior to the prompt, and (c) sometimes will comply with the direction about 15 minutes after it was given. Once the team understands the specific problem of noncompliance, they discuss with the other team members who have Cecil in class whether this behavior is being observed across subject areas. There is consensus that Cecil is engaging in noncompliance across the school day, and based on office referral data, there also are records of this behavior occurring during lunch and dismissal.

Because several team members are not convinced that this behavior is severe enough to warrant an FBA, the team decides to collect better documentation that Cecil is displaying noncompliant behaviors across the school day in both instructional and noninstructional settings. One team member volunteers to interview two of Cecil's teachers from last year to determine if this behavior occurred previously or is something new this school year. Additionally, the team asks each teacher who has Cecil to keep anecdotal records of incidents of the noncompliance as well as incidents of when he is compliant. Finally, the team has the behavior specialist visit several of Cecil's classes to conduct direct observations. The team reviews the definition of the problem behavior and commits to reconvene in 1 week to review these data.

To accomplish the second process in conducting an FBA, the team *identifies the predictable sequences of the problem behavior*. The team analyzes the data collected in terms of an observable and predictable pattern or A-B-C model. The "A" is the antecedent or what happens immediately prior to the problem behavior, the "B" is the defined problem behavior, and the "C" is the consequence or what happens immediately after the problem behavior. Based on the combination of anecdotal records, interviews, and behavioral observations, a predictable pattern emerges for Cecil's noncompliance. By looking at the data, the team realizes that the A-B-C sequence occurs 10 to 15 times per 90-minute block.

Cecil's predictable pattern is as follows:

- Antecedent: Specific direction given by the teacher to Cecil individually or to the class as a whole;
- Behavior: Noncompliance within the expected timeframe (typically 10–25 seconds); and
- Consequence: Teachers continue to teach the other students, and Cecil is allowed to do what he wants.

Based on these data, the entire team is convinced that Cecil's noncompliance is negatively impacting his learning (e.g., lower grades) and that of his peers (e.g., interfering with their learning). Some members of the team who teach Cecil express some surprise that they do not pursue the task demand with Cecil.

For the third process, the team summarizes all the data collected, reviewed, and analyzed thus far and *creates a hypothesis*. A hypothesis includes the conditions (the antecedents) when the student misbehaves and what usually happens after the behavior (the consequences). After summarizing all the data, the team develops the following hypothesis for Cecil: During academic settings when the teacher gives a direction, Cecil does not comply with the task demand within the expected time frame or not at all, and then the teacher removes the task demand.

Fourth, the data from the three prior processes are used by the team to *state the function* of the student's inappropriate behavior. As discussed previously, behavior always occurs for a reason, and students are achieving a goal through their behavior. Students who misbehave during instruction typically do so to either get something or to avoid something. Identifying the function is essential in allowing the team to select interventions for the student that will be effective. Scott and Kamps (2007) note that "intervention is not based on behavior—it is based on the function of that behavior" (p. 151). **Figure 9.8** provides typical classroom examples of what students may try to get or avoid.

The team decides that Cecil's noncompliant behavior is being used to escape or avoid the work and demands Mr. Carter and other teachers are giving. The team quickly reviews the data one more time to be confident that the functional hypothesis is accurate. The team had no data, whether archival, anecdotal, interviews, or direct observations, that contradicted the pattern of problem behavior. For example, the team discusses how Mr. Carter and the other teachers leave Cecil alone when they see that he is not going to do what was requested. This lets Cecil avoid any task demands he does not like. Although Cecil's team was confident they had accurately analyzed the data, any team that is not confident would need to repeat the second through fourth processes or experimentally confirm the function. To experimentally confirm the function, the team could present the same "A" (a direction to Cecil) and if the same "B" (noncompliance) was observed, either ignore the "B" ("C": let Cecil do what he wants) or change the "C" and present Cecil with another "A" to see if the hypothesis and

Figure 9.8   Classroom Examples of the Get and Escape Functions

Function	Classroom Examples
Get	
Attention from teacher	Student yells "I need help" and teacher walks over and helps.
Attention from peers	Student calls another student a "pig" and the other students sitting at the table laugh and encourage the student to continue being inappropriate.
Access to privileges	Student pushes other student so she can be at the front of the lunch line and the teacher lets her be first.
Access to items	Student grabs a puzzle box from another student during free time and the teacher allows that student to play with the puzzle.
Escape	
Avoid teacher	When the student sees Ms. Connely walking toward her desk, student says "I hate you" and Ms. Connely walks away.
Avoid peers	Student is assigned to work with a partner, student hits her partner, and student is told to work independently.
Avoid task demands	Student is asked to begin a worksheet but refuses and the teacher does not ask the student again to complete the assignment.
Avoid activities	A few minutes before the weekly timed math test, student pushes items off desk and is sent to the office.

function would remain. In this case, the team's confidence in the FBA data collected, summarized, and analyzed through the four processes lends itself to the next stage.

Behavior Intervention Plan (BIP)

Once an FBA has been conducted, the team has the necessary data to write a behavior intervention plan (BIP) which details the strategies the teachers can use to address the student's inappropriate behavior during academic and social instruction. The team uses the data collected from the FBA as a means to guide the development of the BIP. In writing a BIP, the team will follow six steps. First, the team *decides what appropriate behaviors or replacement behaviors* the student should be displaying instead of the problem behavior. These replacement behaviors should be those that will be recognized and reinforced by the student's teachers and peers across multiple environments. Such behaviors need to be more relevant, efficient, and effective for the student than the initial inappropriate behavior. As previously discussed, behavioral pairing is the identification of an appropriate behavior that could replace the inappropriate behavior.

In Cecil's case, the team discusses multiple possible replacement behaviors. The team first thought of having task completion be the replacement behavior; however, as the discussion proceeded, it was determined that noncompliance could still occur because Cecil was not compliant within the expected time frame (e.g., he might finish the task, but the allocated time for that activity had already passed and now he was missing the next activity). The team also discussed task engagement as a replacement behavior. That, too, was not supported in the end because the team thought Cecil may be engaged in aspects of a task but may not respond quickly to the actual teacher request. In the end, the team decided the behavioral pair was compliance instead of noncompliance. Mr. Carter and Cecil's other teachers want Cecil to increase his compliance to requests and to do so in a timely fashion within the expected time frame.

Second, the team will *discuss environmental signals* that will remind the student to engage in the replacement behaviors. Typically, these signals are provided verbally, visually, or gesturally by the teacher to the student in some clear manner and no longer used when the student independently engages in the replacement behaviors. As part of Cecil's BIP, the team agrees that when Mr. Carter and the other teachers give a direction, they will give it to the entire class and then place a 5-minute card on Cecil's desk. The card is a visual cue to remind Cecil that he has 5 minutes to comply. The 5-minute card is replaced on Cecil's desk every minute, the next card showing "4 minutes," the next "3 minutes" and so on to "1 minute." The card provides an additional prompt for Cecil to begin the task and decreases the likelihood that he and his teachers will get into an argument or that Cecil will be allowed to avoid the task demands. The team decided that the visual cue was the least intrusive disruption to the overall learning environment and kept the teacher who gave the task demand positively engaged with Cecil.

Third, the team *describes any barriers that may make it hard for the student to display the replacement behavior.* Once barriers have been identified, the team will need to develop ways to get around the barriers. During the team discussion, several team members who are Cecil's teachers and who would be implementing the BIP noted several potential barriers. The team discussed how consistency across and within classrooms would be critical. To address this concern, the team decided that all of Cecil's teachers would use the same intervention procedures so that consistency in expectations for compliance to task requests is as clear as possible. In terms of consistency within each classroom, some team members stated that they may forget to provide the visual cue cards and/or reinforce Cecil when he engages in the replacement behavior. As a means to address this concern, the team made each teacher a set of written prompts on sticky notes to post on their lesson plans and in areas of the room where task requests are frequently provided. In addition, extra minute cards were placed near Cecil's desk and in areas from which the teachers teach. The team also discussed the importance of avoiding "verbally nagging" Cecil as that could increase the likelihood of the problem behavior. To address this, the sticky notes also had the phrase "minute cards, not verbal prompts, once a task request is given." This extra phrase prompted the teachers to use the visual cue cards instead of verbal exchanges that could be perceived by Cecil as an unintended reinforcer (e.g., verbal exchanges also allowed him to avoid the initial task request).

Fourth, the team *agrees upon the consequences for the student engaging or not engaging in the replacement behaviors.* At this time, the team also will need to agree upon the short- and long-term goals and objectives related to the student and the academic and/or social behavior. With Cecil, the team agrees that if he engages in the replacement behavior (follows his teachers' directions within 5 minutes), he can earn opportunities to take a break from activities and can get homework passes. That is, Cecil can appropriately avoid work contingent upon following his teachers' directions. The team also agrees that when Cecil does not follow directions, his teachers will not argue with Cecil but give a natural consequence. For Cecil, if he does not do his work in class, then that assignment becomes homework. Thus, Cecil will no longer be reinforced with the removal of a work when he does not follow directions. A crisis management plan may be necessary for students who display extreme and unsafe challenging behavior (e.g., prolonged aggression). Each school district has a set of policies to deal with unsafe behavior and such policies should be known to all classroom teachers. If this is a concern, teachers should seek assistance and support from their school administration.

Fifth the team *creates a data collection system* and sixth a *monitoring plan* to determine if the student's BIP is working to reduce the problem behavior and increase use of the replacement behavior. Data are reviewed and the plan is monitored frequently and purposely as related to the long- and short-term objectives. If the student is not behaving better or if changes in the student's behavior are not occurring to the degree the team wants, the plan is modified. Embedded within the BIP process are the strategies used by the teacher to enhance student engagement, including the effective instructional practices and curricular accommodations described previously in this chapter.

With Cecil, the team decides to collect both the frequency (number of times) and latency (time between a task demand and student engagement) of Cecil's noncompliance. Using the definition of noncompliance from the first step of the FBA process, Cecil's teachers can record each time Cecil is noncompliant to their requests. In addition, the teachers can record how long it takes for Cecil to comply with their requests. The team has planned to meet in 2 weeks to see if Cecil's BIP is effective in producing the change desired. Two weeks later, team members bring their data. For example, Mr. Carter shares data from his classroom with the team. Prior to the implementation of the BIP, Cecil was noncompliant an average of 15 times per day and spent on average 45 minutes per day not engaged in the tasks asked of him. Since implementing the BIP, Cecil has been noncompliant an average of 6 times per day and spent on average 15 minutes per day not engaged in the tasks. The team is initially pleased with these data which suggest that Cecil has decreased his noncompliant behavior and, when he is noncompliant, he is quicker to engage in the task. Mr. Carter reported that Cecil is motivated by earning homework passes and short breaks from tasks. In addition, Mr. Carter stated that he is praising Cecil more often and he has heard Cecil say "I might as well do this dumb thing so I don't have to do it tonight at home." Cecil's other teachers report similar data patterns, comments, and observations. The behavior specialist who observed Cecil in these classes during the intervention also observed fewer instances of noncompliance and stated that the intervention was being implemented as written by the team. The team decides to continue monitoring Cecil's BIP by reconvening in another 2 weeks. If Cecil's data suggest that the BIP is no longer effective (e.g., increases in noncompliance, the reinforcers are longer as powerful) adaptations to the plan will be made.

The above example illustrates how the data from an FBA can be linked directly to the interventions selected, implemented, and monitored in a BIP. As Scott and Kamps (2007) state, "the purpose . . . is to understand the relationship between behavior and the surrounding environment, thereby contributing to improved services and intervention" (p. 147). In Cecil's case, the team collected, summarized, and analyzed multiple sources of data related to Cecil's noncompliance and then discussed various interventions as well as barriers and possible solutions to the barriers to effectively and efficiently improve Cecil's behavior. Some people think that once the first process of the FBA (defining the problem) occurs that a team is ready to write a BIP. That, however, is faulty reasoning as teams need to use sound data decision-making processes. Skimping on the data processes provides a weak foundation for the team to select, implement, and monitor subsequent behavioral strategies (Scott & Kamps, 2007), and may in fact result in higher occurrences of misbehavior if non function-based interventions were implemented (Payne, Scott, & Conroy, 2007).

Positive Behaviorial Interventions and Supports (PBIS)

Positive behaviorial interventions and support (PBIS) is a nationally recognized model in which administrators and teachers can proactively, effectively, and efficiently teach, model, and reinforce appropriate academic and social behaviors. Students are reinforced for engagement in the expected behaviors, and teachers are reinforced for implementation of the model (Lewis & Sugai, 1999; see the Technical Assistance Center on Positive Behavioral Interventions and Supports website for training modules and materials: http://www.pbis.org). The PBIS model has been successfully implemented in more than 5,000 Head Start programs, elementary, middle, and high schools as well as alternative programs, residential schools, and juvenile justice settings (U.S. Department of Education, 2005). The PBIS model contains multiple core elements and is typified by a three-tiered triangle (Lewis & Sugai, 2007). **Figure 9.9** displays the commonly referenced triangle.

The base of the triangle is the universal tier. At this tier, the same behavioral instruction is provided to all students in the school by administrators, teachers, and support staff. The primary objective of this tier is consistency of expectations and equitability for reinforcement so that 80 to 90% of student misbehavior is addressed proactively. As previously discussed, it is important to have clearly and positively stated classroom rules as a means to promote appropriate student behavior. As such, it also is important for schools to adapt three to five positively stated rules, which all students are to follow. For example, a school may link their PBIS rules to their school mascot—EAGLE is *E*nter quietly, *A*ccept responsibility, *G*row academically, *L*ead by example, *E*xit quietly. This set of rules is taught in all instructional and noninstructional environments by administrators, teachers, and support staff using shared lesson plans. As part of this teaching, the students are shown examples and nonexamples of the rules (e.g., what does it mean to lead by example in the classroom, restroom, hallway?), and taught what to expect when they engage in the rules (e.g., GOTCHAs given to students whereby they can then cash in the GOTCHAs for some school privilege, school supplies,

Figure 9.9 Triangle of Continuum of Positive Behaviorial Interventions and Supports

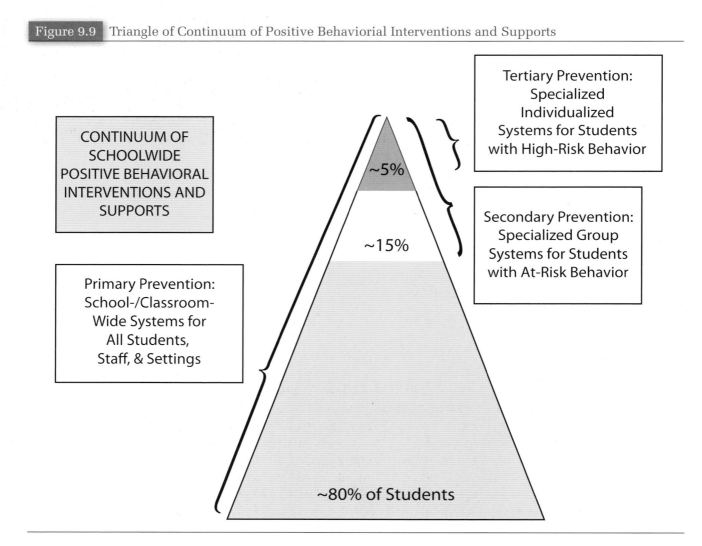

CONTINUUM OF SCHOOLWIDE POSITIVE BEHAVIORAL INTERVENTIONS AND SUPPORTS

Primary Prevention: School-/Classroom-Wide Systems for All Students, Staff, & Settings

Tertiary Prevention: Specialized Individualized Systems for Students with High-Risk Behavior

Secondary Prevention: Specialized Group Systems for Students with At-Risk Behavior

~5%

~15%

~80% of Students

or small tangible item) or break a rule (e.g., office discipline referral). In terms of the effectiveness of the universal tier on the behaviors displayed by students, the school will need to monitor the data (e.g., office discipline referrals by total number, student, location, type of behavior, and time) and make changes necessary based on the data (e.g., if the data suggest more referrals are happening at dismissal, then what could be changed within that environment to improve student behavior in terms of changing supervision patterns or expectations, reteaching, or increasing reinforcement opportunities?). It is important to remember that the PBIS universal tier needs to be visible (e.g., posters with the rules displayed, teachers giving students GOTCHAs), tangible (e.g., students reinforced for compliance), and agreed upon (e.g., at least 80% of all staff must agree to and implement the model as defined by the school team).

The second level of the triangle is the targeted tier. At this tier, approximately 5% to 10% of the students who did not respond to the universal strategies will need more targeted strategies to address misbehavior. These targeted strategies can take place in both instructional (e.g., the classroom, gym, library) and noninstructional (e.g., hallways, bathroom, cafeteria) environments depending on the data (location of the office discipline referrals). For example, data may suggest that a few students are having difficulties managing their behavior when around specific peers. The school counselor may work with these students on conflict resolution skills and social skills that can be used when those peers are present. A few other students may be identified as needing extra adult support to get through the day without incident. For those students, adult mentors may be identified so the mentors can use the Check-In/Check-Out program (Crone, Horner, & Hawken, 2004) in which they briefly meet with the student in the morning before classes and at the end of the day to review behavior, provide feedback and encouragement, and set future behavioral goals. When targeted strategies are required, they are implemented in addition to the universal strategies.

The top level of the triangle is the intensive tier. This tier is for approximately 1% to 5% of the students who have not responded to either the universal or targeted tier strategies. These students demonstrate chronic and intense misbehaviors above and beyond their peers. For example, data on these students may reflect high frequencies of office discipline referrals across school environments, frequent use of in- or out-of-school suspension as consequences, and poor grades. These students may need FBAs to determine the variables within the environment that are supporting the misbehavior and then need written BIPs to support appropriate behavior. These students also may need daily or weekly contact with the school counselor to address specific, individualized issues or may require a team to provide wrap-around services (e.g., social services, counselors, academic remediation).

Cycle of Success

Teachers can adapt their instructional practices within classrooms in order to be proactive in reducing the possibility of student misbehavior. Teachers have many skills and tools they can use to break the cycle of failure illustrated at the beginning of the chapter in Figure 9.2. Examples of just a few of the interventions that can be used are depicted in **Figure 9.10**.

Teachers can evaluate students' academic and social strengths to determine if students are behind their same-age peers. Teachers can modify which assignments are given and how they are presented by embedding strategies such as precorrection, the model-lead-test approach, choices, and curricular modification. Teachers can implement a comprehensive set of instructional, classroom, and behavioral strategies to address misbehavior. The encouraging message is that teachers can intervene in students' cycles of failure at various points and implement a wide variety of instructional and behavioral strategies that have been proven to be effective.

Figure 9.10   Cycle of Success

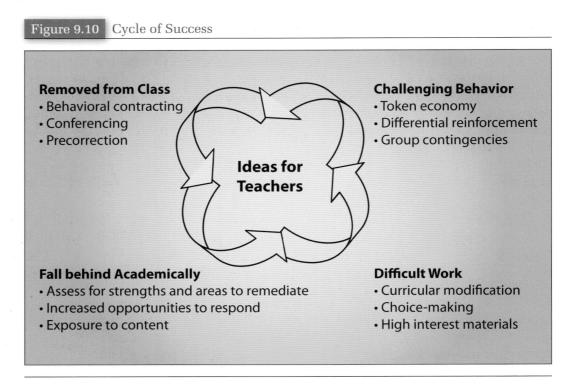

Removed from Class
- Behavioral contracting
- Conferencing
- Precorrection

Challenging Behavior
- Token economy
- Differential reinforcement
- Group contingencies

Ideas for Teachers

Fall behind Academically
- Assess for strengths and areas to remediate
- Increased opportunities to respond
- Exposure to content

Difficult Work
- Curricular modification
- Choice-making
- High interest materials

Legal Issues Related to Managing Behavior

Since its inception as the Education for the Handicapped Act of 1975, the Individuals with Disabilities Education Act (IDEA) has contained provisions to ensure that students with disabilities who also have challenging behaviors continue to receive a free, appropriate education (FAPE) at public expense. FAPE must be provided, no matter where students receive educational services. Although the federal law is described comprehensively in Chapter 2, the topics of manifestation determination and interim alternative educational setting (IAES) are highlighted briefly.

Manifestation Determination. The purpose of manifestation determination is to ensure that school personnel do not circumvent due process safeguards when students with disabilities engage in inappropriate behavior. The *stay-put* provision requires that students with disabilities remain in their current placements to avoid wrongful removal while teams decide how and where to provide educational services to the students. In fact, IDEA stresses the importance of schools being proactive and preventative in the educational programming provided to students with disabilities when behavioral challenges may be an issue. Under IDEA, when students display inappropriate behavior and the team decides that the inappropriate behavior is a manifestation of their disabilities, then an FBA needs to be conducted and a BIP written and implemented. If an FBA and BIP already exist, the team is to review, modify, and re-implement the BIP. If the team decides that a student's inappropriate behavior was not a manifestation of the disability, then FAPE needs to be provided; however, the team can place the student in an IAES. With these changes, the classroom teacher will want to make sure that an FBA is conducted and a BIP written and implemented for students who have a history of inappropriate behavior, display consistent inappropriate behavior, or have the potential to display inappropriate behavior. Of note, IDEA does not provide a specific process for teams to follow when conducting FBAs and writing BIPs. However, by following the research-based FBA and BIP processes described in this chapter, teachers will be better able to address the challenging behaviors presented by some students with disabilities as well as decrease future occurrence of such behavior.

Interim Alternative Educational Setting (IAES). Under IDEA, if a student causes serious bodily injury or brings drugs or weapons to school or school functions, the student can be placed in an IAES for up to 45 school days regardless of whether or not the student's behavior is a manifestation of the disability. IDEA gives greater authority to school personnel to temporarily change a student's placement to an IAES for 10 or fewer school days if the student violates the school code of conduct.

Summary

Instructional strategies, classroom management, and behavioral strategies in combination with effective teaching practices and the positive behavioral interventions and supports model, afford classroom teachers multiple opportunities to support the needs of diverse student populations in both general and special education settings (Stough & Palmer, 2003). Such support can be provided as preventative and proactive management or to address specific academic and/or behavioral issues presented by students who misbehave during instruction. The strategies discussed in this chapter are the components that come together to allow teachers to create environments conducive to learning.

The first area, *instructional strategies,* is directly linked to teacher behavior. In this area, teachers adapt and/or alter their current teaching methods to better meet the needs of all students, including students with and without disabilities and/or challenging behaviors. Teachers use precision requests, incorporate CLOCS-RAM, and may alter the specificity and length of their oral requests when noncompliance is observed. Teachers use specific requests ("Take out your math text, turn to page 32, and touch problem 1") which have been found to be more effective for students who are culturally and linguistically diverse, as opposed to generic requests ("Get ready for math class"). Teachers exhibit behaviors consistent with having high expectations for students by providing more prompting, giving less criticism, asking more questions, and giving more praise. Behavior-specific praise is used instead of generic praise, and praise for contributions to group functioning is emphasized with students who are culturally and linguistically diverse. Teachers adopt an authoritative style in their classrooms and use "insistence" to communicate that they expect students to succeed.

In the second area, *classroom management,* teachers make subtle adaptations to their existing overall classroom management strategies to directly benefit the student experiencing academic and/or social challenges. Teachers set up their classrooms so that students are better able to attend and adopt a comprehensive instructional approach to addressing behavioral errors. Behavioral expectations are defined, taught, and reviewed regularly. Teachers may alter the "cash-in" date for the classwide token economy system for a student who needs more frequent reinforcement by allowing that student to cash their tokens in on Wednesday as well as Friday along with their peers. Other classroom management strategies that could be used include group contingencies and proximity.

Due to the automaticity of some students' chronic behavior problems, teachers may need to incorporate the third area, *behavioral strategies,* in which they add specific strategies and methods to individually meet the needs of the student engaged in challenging behavior, whether the student has a BIP or not. Often teachers want to skip to this third area without making changes to their instructional behavior and current classroom management strategies. By skipping the first two areas, teachers are missing an opportunity to positively affect their own teaching behaviors and management because teacher behavior can positively and/or negatively affect the behavior of the student. For example, teachers may have one student in their classes who consistently fails to come to class with the materials necessary to fully and actively participate so a behavioral contract may be written. Other behavioral strategies that could be used include choice-making, differential reinforcement, and the Premack Principle. The combination of all three areas (instructional, classroom management, and behavioral) should create a classroom environment conducive to ongoing learning and appropriate behavior for all students and lead to the acquisition of skills necessary for post-school success.

Classroom Application Activities

1. Develop three to five positively stated behavioral expectations for your classroom. Give three examples and three non-examples for each of the expectations. Describe how you would teach the expectations to your students.

2. Give an example of how each of the elements of CLOCS-RAM has been (or could be) incorporated into an instructional lesson.

3. Describe how you would use signal control in your classroom.

4. Reflect on your personality. What aspects of your personality are well-suited to being a teacher? What aspects of your personality could interfere with your effectiveness as a teacher? According to the styles described by Baumrind (authoritative, authoritarian, permissive), which one best describes your approach to teaching? What student behaviors are you likely to find the most annoying? What behaviors do you think others might find annoying that would not be troublesome for you? Compare your descriptions and lists to those of other teachers.

5. With respect to behavior pairs, identify at least one appropriate behavior to pair with the following misbehaviors:
    —gets out of seat without permission

        —calls out in class

        —interrupts others

—does not come to class on time

—fails to bring necessary materials to class

—sleeps during class

—writes on desk

—hits others

—bites others

—leaves class without permission

—does not turn in homework

—makes inappropriate comments to peers and teachers

6. Develop a behavioral contract to increase the appropriate behavior from one of the behavior pairs created in #5.

7. Create a group contingency plan for elementary age students who are not turning in their homework and one for high school students who are talking during instruction.

8. Go to the Technical Assistance Center on Positive Behavioral Interventions and Supports website at http://www. pbis.org. Then develop a PBIS model for your school.

9. Think of a student who is demonstrating inappropriate behavior. How would you modify your instructional strategies, classroom management, and behavioral strategies to promote the demonstration of more appropriate behavior?

10. Considering the academic-behavior failure cycle, identify one proactive and preventative action you could take to interrupt the cycle at each of the four points.

Internet Resources

Websites

Council for Children with Behavioral Disorders
www.ccbd.net

The National Technical Center on Positive Behavioral Interventions and Supports
www.pbis.org

The National Center on Education, Disability, and Juvenile Justice
www.edjj.org

Oregon Social Learning Center
www.OSLC.org

What Works Clearinghouse
www.whatworks.ed.gov

Midwest Symposium for Leadership in Behavior Disorders
http://www.mslbd.org

Intervention Central
http://www.interventioncentral.org

The Really Big List of Classroom Management Resources
http://drwilliampmartin.tripod.com/classm.html

Teacher Vision
http://www.Teachervision.fen.com

Center for Effective Collaboration and Practice [American Institutes for Research]
http://cecp.air.org

Early Childhood Behavior Project—University of Minnesota
http://cehd.umn.edu/ceed/projects/preschoolbehavior/default.html

Center for the Prevention of Violence—Colorado
http://www.colorado.edu/cspv

Behavior Homepage—Kentucky
http://www.state.ky.us/agencies/behave/homepage.html

Florida Department of Education Facilitator's Guide to Positive Behavior Supports
http://www.apbs.org/files/PBSwhole.pdf

Printed Resources

Alberto, P.A., & Troutman, A.C. (2009). *Applied behavior analysis for teachers* (8th ed.). Upper Saddle River, NJ: Pearson.

Jenson, W.R., Rhode, G., Reavis, H.K. (1995). *The tough kid tool box.* Longmont, CO: Sopris West.

Kerr, M.M., & Nelson, C.M. (2006). *Strategies for addressing behavior problems in the classroom* (5th ed.). Upper Saddle River, NJ: Pearson.

Liaupsin, C.J., Scott, T.M., & Nelson, C.M. (2000). *Functional behavioral assessment: An interactive training module.* Longmont, CO: Sopris West.

O'Neill, R.E., Horner, R.H., Albin, R.W., Sprague, J.R., Storey, K., & Newton, J.S. (1997). *Functional assessment and program development for problem behavior: A practical handbook* (2nd ed.). Pacific Grove, CA: Brooks/Cole Publishing.

Rhode, G., Jenson, W.R., & Reavis, H.K. (1996). *The tough kid book: Practical classroom management strategies.* Longmont, CO: Sopris West.

Scott, T.M., Liaupsin, C.J., & Nelson, C.M. (2001). *Behavior intervention planning.* Longmont, CO: Sopris West.

Scott, T.M., Liaupsin, C., & Nelson, C.M. (2006). *Functional behavior assessment and planning.* Longmont, CO: Sopris West.

References

Alliance for Excellent Education. (2005). *Teacher attrition: A costly loss to the nation and to the states.* Washington, DC: Author.

Atkins, M.S., McKay, M.M., Frazier, S.L., Jakobsons, L.J., Arvanitis, P., Cunningham, T., Brown, C., & Lambrecht, L. (2002). Suspensions and detentions in an urban, low-income school: Punishment or reward? *Journal of Abnormal Child Psychology, 30,* 361–371.

Azrin, N.H., & Holz, W.C. (1966). Punishment. In W.K. Honig (Ed.), *Operant Behavior: Areas of Research and Applications* (pp. 380–447). New York: Appleton-Century-Crofts.

Baumrind, D. (1966). Effects of authoritative parental control on child behavior. *Child Development, 37,* 887–907.

Bondy, E., Ross, D.D., Galligane, C., & Hambacher, E. (2007). Creating environments of success and resilience. *Urban Education, 42,* 326–348.

Brown, D.F. (2003). Urban teachers' use of culturally responsive management strategies. *Theory into Practice, 42,* 277–282.

Bullara, D.T. (1993). Classroom management strategies to reduce racially-biased treatment of students. *Journal of Educational and Psychological Consultation, 4,* 357–368.

Burnett, P.C. (2001). Elementary students' preferences for teacher praise. *Journal of Classroom Interaction, 36,* 16–23.

Carr, E.G., Taylor, J.C., & Robinson, S. (1991). The effects of severe behavior problems in children on the teaching behavior of adults. *Journal of Applied Behavior Analysis, 24,* 523–535.

Cartledge, G., Singh, A., & Gibson, L. (2008). Practical behavior-management techniques to close the accessibility gap for students who are culturally and linguistically diverse. *Preventing School Failure, 52,* 29–38.

Catalano, R.F., Loeber, R., & McKinney, K.C. (1999). School and community interventions to prevent serious and violent offending. *Juvenile Justice Bulletin,* 1–12.

Casillas, A., Robbins, S., Allen, J., Kuo, Y.-L., Hanson, M.A., & Schmeiser, C. (2012). Predicting early academic failure in high school from prior academic achievement, psychosocial characteristics, and behavior. *Journal of Educational Psychology, 104*(2), 407–420.

Christle, C.A., & Schuster, J.W. (2003). The effects of using response cards on student participation, academic achievement, and on-task behavior during whole-class math instruction. *Journal of Behavioral Education, 12,* 147–165.

Clunies-Ross, P., Little, E., & Kienhuis, M. (2008). Self-reported and actual use of proactive and reactive classroom management strategies and their relationship with teacher stress and student behaviour. *Educational Psychology, 28,* 693–710.

Colvin, G., & Sugai, G.M. (1988). Proactive strategies for managing social behavior problems: An instructional approach. *Education and Treatment of Children, 11,* 341–348.

Conroy, M.A., Sutherland, K.S., Snyder, A.L., & Marsh, S. (2008). Classwide interventions: Effective instruction makes a difference. *Teaching Exceptional Children, 40,* 24–30.

Cook, D. (1999). Behavior bucks: A unique motivational program. *Intervention in School & Clinic, 34,* 307–309.

Crone, D.A., Horner, R.H., & Hawken, L.S. (2004). *Responding to problem behavior in schools: The behavior education program.* New York: Guilford Press.

Dodge, K.A., Price, J.M., Bachorowski, J., & Newman, J.P. (1990). Hostile attributional biases in severely aggressive adolescents. *Journal of Abnormal Psychology, 99,* 385–392.

Dotterer, A.M., & Lowe, K. (2011). Classroom context, school engagement, and academic achievement in early adolescence. *Journal of Youth and Adolescence, 40,* 1649–1660.

Dunlap, G., Dunlap, L.K., Clarke, S., & Robbins, F.R. (1991). Functional assessment, curricular revision, and severe behavior problems. *Journal of Applied Behavior Analysis, 24,* 387–397.

Eber, L., Sugai, G., Smith, C.R., & Scott, T.M. (2002). Wraparound and positive behavioral interventions and supports in the schools. *Journal of Emotional and Behavioral Disorders, 10,* 171–180.

Emmer, E.T., & Stough, L.M. (2001). Classroom management: A critical part of educational psychology, with implications for teacher education. *Educational Psychology, 36,* 103–112.

Fisher, D., & Kent, H. (1998). Associations between teacher personality and classroom environment. *Journal of Classroom Interaction, 33,* 5–13.

Furlong, M., & Morrison, G. (2000). The school in school violence: Definitions and facts. *Journal of Emotional and Behavioral Disorders, 8,* 71–82.

George, C.L. (2010). Effects of response cards on performance and participation in social studies for middle school students with emotional and behavioral disorders. *Behavioral Disorders, 35,* 214–228.

Good, T., & Brophy, J. (1978). *Looking in classrooms.* New York: Harper and Row.

Good, T.L., & Nichols, S.L. (2001). Expectancy effects in the classroom: A special focus on improving the reading performance of minority students in first-grade classrooms. *Educational Psychologist, 36,* 113–126.

Goodlad, J.I. (2004). *A place called school: Twentieth Anniversary Edition.* New York: McGraw-Hill.

Guerra, N.G., & Williams, K.R. (1996). *A program planning guide for youth violence prevention.* Boulder, CO: Center for the Study and Prevention of Violence.

Gunter, P.L., Jack, S.L., DePaepe, P., Reed, T.M., & Harrison, J. (1994). Effects of challenging behaviors of students with EBD on teacher instructional behavior. *Preventing School Failure, 38,* 35–39.

Hawkins, S.M., & Heflin, L. (2011). Increasing secondary teachers' behavior-specific praise using a video self-modeling and visual performance feedback intervention. *Journal of Positive Behavior Interventions, 13,* 97–108.

Huesmann, L.R., Eron, L.D., & Yarmel, P. (1987). Intellectual functioning and aggression. *Journal of Personality and Social Psychology, 52,* 232–240.

Individuals with Disabilities Education Improvement Act of 2004, 20 U.S.C. § 1400 *et seq.* (2004) (reauthorization of the Individuals with Disabilities Act of 1990)

Iwata, B.A., Dorsey, M.F., Slifer, K.J., Bauman, K.E., & Richman, G.S. (1982/1994). Toward a functional analysis of self-injury. *Journal of Applied Behavior Analysis, 27,* 197–209.

Jolivette, K., Wehby, J.H., Canale, J., & Massey, N.G. (2001). Effects of choice making opportunities on the behaviors of students with emotional and behavioral disorders. *Behavioral Disorders, 26,* 131–145.

Jones, F.H. (2000). *Tools for teaching: Discipline-instruction-motivation.* Santa Cruz, CA: Fredric H. Jones & Associates.

Kauffman, J.M., Mostert, M.P., Trent, S.C., & Pullen, P.L. (2006). *Managing classroom behavior: A reflective case-based approach* (4th ed.). Boston, MA: Allyn & Bacon.

Kazdin, A.E. (1977). *The token economy.* New York: Plenum Press.

Kehle, T.J., Bray, M.A., Theodore, L.A., Jenson, W.R., & Clark, E. (2000). A multi-component intervention designed to reduce disruptive classroom behavior. *Psychology in the Schools, 37,* 475–481.

Kern, L., Delaney, B., Clarke, S., Dunlap, G., & Childs, K. (2001). Improving the classroom behavior of students with emotional and behavioral disorders using individualized curricular modifications. *Journal of Emotional & Behavioral Disorders, 9,* 239–247.

Kleinfeld, J. (1975). Effective teachers of Eskimo and Indian students. *School Review, 83,* 301–344.

Knoster, T., Wells, T., & McDowell, K.C. (2003). *Using timeout in an effective and ethical manner.* Available from Iowa Department of Education, Bureau of Family Support Services, Grimes State Office Building, Des Moines, IA 50319-0146.

Kounin, J.S. (1970). *Discipline and group management in classrooms.* New York: Holt, Rinehart, & Winston.

Kozol, J. (1991). *Savage inequalities: Children in America's schools.* New York: Crown.

Kukla-Acevedo, S. (2009). Leavers, movers, and stayers: The role of workplace conditions in teacher mobility decisions. *The Journal of Educational Research, 102,* 443–452.

Lambert, M.C., Cartleges, G., Heward, W.L., & Lo, Y. (2006). Effects of response cards on disruptive behavior and academic responding during math lessons by fourth grade urban students. *Journal of Positive Behavioral Interventions, 8,* 88–99.

Lampi, A.R., Fenty, N.S., & Beaunae, C. (2005). Making the three Ps easier: Praise, proximity, and precorrection. *Beyond Behavior, 15,* 8–12.

Lee, S., Wehmeyer, M.L., Soukup, J.H., & Palmer, S.B. (2010). Impact of curriculum modifications on access to the general education curriculum for students with disabilities. *Exceptional Children, 76,* 213–233.

Lessen, E., & Frankiewicz, L. (1992). Personal attributes and characteristics of effective special education teachers: Considerations for teacher educators. *Teacher Education and Special Education, 15,* 124–32.

Lewis, T.J., & Sugai, G. (1999). Effective behavior support: A systems approach to proactive school-wide management. *Focus on Exceptional Children, 31*(6), 1–24.

Lo, Y., & Cartledge, G. (2006). FBA and BIP: Increasing the behavior adjustment of African American boys in schools. *Behavioral Disorders, 31,* 147–161.

Lohrmann, S., & Talerico, J. (2004). Anchor the boat: A classwide intervention to reduce problem behavior. *Journal of Positive Behavior Intervention, 6,* 113–120.

Martin, N. (1998). Construct validation of the attitudes & beliefs on classroom control inventory. *Journal of Classroom Interaction, 33,* 6–15.

McKee, W.T., & Witt, J.C. (1990). Effective teaching: A review of instructional, and environmental variables. In T.B. Gutkin & C.R. Reynolds (Eds.), *The handbook of school psychology* (pp. 823–847). New York: John Wiley & Sons.

Mercer, C.D., & Mercer, A.R. (2005). *Teaching students with learning problems* (7th ed.). Upper Saddle River, NJ: Pearson.

Miller, A.T., & Hom, Jr., H.L. (1997). Conceptions of ability and the interpretation of praise, blame, and material rewards. *Journal of Experimental Education, 65,* 163–177.

Moore, J.W., & Edwards, R.P. (2003). An analysis of aversive stimuli in classroom demand contexts. *Journal of Applied Behavior Analysis, 36,* 339–348.

Moreno, G. (2011). Addressing challenging behaviours in the general education setting: Conducting a teacher-based functional behavioural assessment (FBA). *Education 3–13, 39,* 363–371.

National Center for Education Statistics. (1997). *Job satisfaction among America's teachers: Effects of workplace conditions, background characteristics, and teacher compensation.* Washington, DC: Author.

Neville, M.H., & Jenson, W.R. (1984). Precision command and the "Sure I will" program: A quick and efficient compliance training sequence. *Child & Family Behavior Therapy, 6,* 61–65.

Pappas, D.N., Skinner, C.H., & Skinner, A.L. (2010). Supplementing accelerated reading with classwide interdependent group-oriented contingencies. *Psychology in the Schools, 47*, 887–902.

Patterson, G.R., Reid, J.B., & Dishion, T.J. (1992). *Antisocial boys.* Eugene, OR: Castalia Press.

Payne, L.D., Scott, T.M., & Conroy, M. (2007). A school-based examination of the efficacy of function-based intervention. *Behavioral Disorders, 32*, 158–174.

Pellerin, L.A. (2005). Applying Baumrind's parenting typology to high schools: Toward a middle-range theory of authoritative socialization. *Social Science Research, 34*, 283–303.

Peterson, R., Albrecht, S., Johns, B., & CCBD. (2009a). CCBD's position summary on the use of seclusion in school settings. *Behavioral Disorders, 34*, 235–243.

Peterson, R., Albrecht, S., Johns, B., & CCBD. (2009b). CCBD's position summary on the use of physical restraint procedures in school settings. *Behavioral Disorders, 34*, 223–234.

Premack, D. (1959). Toward empirical behavior laws: I. Positive reinforcement. *Psychological Review, 66*, 219–233.

Ramsey, M.L., Jolivette, K., Puckett Patterson, D., & Kennedy, C. (2010). Using choice to increase time on-task, task completion, and accuracy for students with emotional/behavioral disorders in a residential facility. *Education and Treatment of Children, 33*, 1–21.

Reinke, W.M., Lewis-Palmer, T., & Martin, E. (2007). The effect of visual performance feedback on teacher use of behavior-specific praise. *Behavior Modification, 31*, 247–263.

Robinson, D.H., Funk, D.C., Beth, A., & Bush, A.M. (2005). Changing beliefs about corporal punishment: Increasing knowledge about ineffectiveness to build more consistent moral and informational beliefs. *Journal of Behavioral Education, 14*, 117–139.

Rosenthal, R., & Jacobson, L. (1968). *Pygmalion in the classroom: Teacher expectation and pupils' intellectual development.* New York: Holt, Rinehart & Winston.

Rumberger, R.W., & Palardy, G.J. (2005). Does segregation still matter? The impact of student composition on academic achievement in high school. *Teachers College Record, 107*, 1999–2045.

Ryan, J.B., Sanders, S., Katsiyannis, A., & Yell, M.L. (2007). Using time-out effectively in the classroom. *Teaching Exceptional Children, 39*, 60–67.

Scott, T.M., & Kamps, D.M. (2007). The future of functional behavior assessment in school settings. *Behavioral Disorders, 32*, 146–157.

Scott, T.M., Nelson, C.M., & Liaupsin, C.J. (2001). Effective instruction: The forgotten component in preventing school violence. *Education and Treatment of Children, 24*, 309–322.

Shores, R.E., Jack, S.L., Gunter, P.L., Ellis, D.N., DeBriere, T.J., & Wehby, J.H. (1993). Classroom interactions of children with behavior disorders. *Journal of Emotional and Behavioral Disorders, 1*, 27–29.

Sidman, M. (1989). *Coercion and its fall-out.* Boston: Authors Cooperative.

Stough, L.M., & Palmer, D.J. (2003). Special thinking in special settings: A qualitative study of expert special educators. *The Journal of Special Education, 36*, 206–222.

Sutherland, K.S., Wehby, J.H., & Copeland, S.R. (2000). Effect of varying rates of behavior-specific praise on the on-task behavior of students with emotional and behavioral disorders. *Journal of Emotional and Behavioral Disorders, 8*, 2–8.

Thornton, B., Peltier, G., & Hill, G. (2005). Do future teachers choose wisely: A study of pre-service teachers' personality preference profiles. *College Student Journal, 39*, 489–496.

Turner, H.A., & Muller, P.A. (2004). Long-term effects of child corporal punishment on depressive symptoms in young adults: Potential moderators and mediators. *Journal of Family Issues, 25*, 761–782.

Umbreit, J., Lane, K.L., & Dejud, C. (2004). Improving classroom behavior by modifying task difficulty: Effects of increasing the difficulty of too-easy tasks. *Journal of Positive Behavioral Intervention, 6*, 13–20.

U.S. Department of Education, Office of Special Education Programs. (2005). *Technical Assistance Center on Positive Behavioral Interventions and Supports: Final Report.* Washington, DC: Author.

Van Acker, R. (2006). Effective classroom-level disciplinary practices: Redefining the classroom environment to support student and teacher success. In L.M. Bullock, R.A. Gable, and K.J. Melloy (Eds.), *Effective disciplinary practices: Strategies for maintaining safe schools and positive learning environments for students with challenging behaviors* (pp. 23–31). Arlington, VA: Council for Exceptional Children.

Van Acker, R., Grant, S.B., & Henry, D. (1996). Teacher and student behavior as a function of risk for aggression. *Education and Treatment of Children, 19*, 316–334.

Van Acker, R., & Talbott, E. (1999). The school context and risk for aggression: Implications for school-based prevention and intervention efforts. *Preventing School Failure, 44*, 12–20.

Vitaro, F., Tremblay, R.E., & Gagnon, C. (1995). Teacher ratings of children's behaviors and teachers' management styles: A research note. *Journal of Child Psychology & Psychiatry & Allied Disciplines, 36*, 887–898.

Walker, H.M., Horner, R.H., Sugai, G., Bullis, M., Sprague, J.R., Bricker, D., & Kaufman, M.J. (1996). Integrated approaches to preventing antisocial behavior patterns among school-age children and youth. *Journal of Emotional and Behavioral Disorders, 4*, 194–209.

Walker, H.M., Ramsey, E., & Gresham, F.M. (2004). *Antisocial behavior in school: Evidence-based practices.* Belmont, CA: Wadsworth/Thomson Learning.

Walker, H.M., & Sprague, J.R. (1999). Longitudinal research and functional behavioral assessment issues. *Behavioral Disorders, 24,* 335–337.

Walker, H.M., Stieber, S., Ramsey, E., & O'Neill, R.E. (1991). Longitudinal prediction of the school achievement, adjustment, and delinquency of antisocial versus at-risk boys. *Remediation and Special Education, 12,* 43–51.

Ware, F. (2006). Warm demander pedagogy: Culturally responsive teaching that supports a culture of achievement for African American students. *Urban Education, 41,* 427–456.

Way, S.M. (2011). School discipline and disruptive classroom behavior: The moderating effects of student perceptions. *Sociological Quarterly, 52,* 346–375.

Wehby, J.H., Symons, F.J., & Shores, R.E. (1995). A descriptive analysis of aggressive behavior in classrooms for children with emotional and behavioral disorders. *Behavioral Disorders, 20,* 87–105.

Weinstein, C.S., Tomlinson-Clarke, S., & Curran, M. (2004). Toward a conception of culturally responsive classroom management. *Journal of Teacher Education, 55,* 25–38.

Weiss, N.R. (2005). Eliminating the use of behavioral techniques that are cruel and dehumanizing. *Exceptional Parent, 35*(10), 42–43.

Witt, J.C., VanDerHeyden, A.M., & Gilbertson, D. (2004). Troubleshooting behavioral interventions: A systematic process for finding and eliminating problems. *School Psychology Review, 33,* 363–383.

CHAPTER TEN

Students with Autism Spectrum Disorders

L. Juane Heflin and Kelle M. Laushey

CHAPTER OBJECTIVES

- to explain the neurological basis for Autism Spectrum Disorders (ASD);
- to describe the characteristics commonly associated with ASD;
- to discuss diagnosis and classification of ASD;
- to examine factors that are contributing to the increasing prevalence of ASD;
- to provide information regarding special considerations for Response to Intervention (RTI) for students with ASD;
- to introduce IDEA definitions and unique aspects of determining eligibility for students with ASD; and
- to discuss educational issues related to students with learning challenges due to ASD.

KEY TERMS

de novo mutations • neurotypical • pervasive developmental disorders (PDD) • echolalia • perseveration • self-stimulating • self-injurious behaviors • prevalence • incidence • total communication approach • aberrant behavior • dysregulated • emotional self-regulation

Students are being identified with autism spectrum disorders (ASD) at an alarmingly high rate (Baio, 2012), sufficiently high to be confident that ALL teachers will have students with ASD in their classrooms at some point in their careers. Although individuals with ASD may be some of the most delightful students you have a chance to teach, they also may be some of the most challenging students you will ever teach. How can a student who knows every detail about train engines not be able to understand that he cannot always be first in line?

A student with ASD may be delightful, but also may pose big challenges in the classroom.

Does the student who quotes baseball statistics for hours really understand that a question such as "Can you look it up in the dictionary?" means he is supposed to do just that? Can a student who is told not to scrape a pencil against the edge of the desk really not understand that means she should not scrape a ruler against the edge of the desk either? Students with ASD range on a spectrum from those who are extremely intelligent about fact-based subjects (and can talk for hours about their topic of interest), but are clueless about how to behave in a group, to students with intellectual disability who do not speak at all and who prefer to be left alone to engage in repetitive actions of their own choosing (such as sifting sand through their fingers). The sheer number of students demonstrating the characteristics of ASD makes it critical to devote a full chapter to understanding why they behave the way that they do and how teachers can support their learning needs in school. An understanding of the behaviors that are characteristic of ASD is facilitated by information about the underlying neurological differences in individuals with ASD. Once neurological differences are recognized, the characteristics of individuals with ASD will seem logical and necessary for defining the disability. Discussion of characteristics of ASD includes how the behaviors common to this population are assessed for determining eligibility for special educational services. Once the characteristic behaviors seem logical, issues for the classroom teacher become apparent and it is a straightforward matter to discuss how instructional environments can be structured to support the unique learning needs of students with ASD. Finally, examination of ASD would not be complete without considering why the prevalence is increasing so dramatically.

Etiology of ASD

It may be a bit deceptive to portend to discuss the etiology of ASD because researchers do not know what causes ASD. However, the validity of possible etiological theories can be discussed, followed by descriptions of neurological differences of unknown etiology identified in the population. Researchers cannot explain *what* causes autism, but they can document *why* individuals with ASD demonstrate the behaviors characteristic of the disability. When autism was first being identified and defined (circa 1943), medical personnel believed it to be a type of emotional disturbance caused by a child's reaction to a cold, unloving mother (hence the term *refrigerator mother*; Bettleheim, 1967). Many of the mothers of the first 11 children identified with autism (Kanner, 1943) had careers outside the home, including some university professors. Freud's influence led to the psychoanalytic conclusion that the mothers resented the babies during pregnancy and after birth because the children were impediments to their careers. Indeed, the earliest intervention for children with ASD involved putting their mothers through intensive psychotherapy to uncover why they did not want their children. Of course, many of these mothers had other children who were developing typically, so the notion of a child singled out to be unloved was patently ludicrous.

The "refrigerator mother" theory was followed by the notion of *deprived environments*. This theory of the cause of autism also was psychoanalytic in nature. Infants sensed they were in environments devoid of the stimulation necessary for growth and development, and so therefore turned inward, ignoring the world around them. A parallel has been made to infants placed in orphanages where their basic needs to be fed and clean were met, but the overworked caregivers did not have the time to provide sufficient pleasant, affective interactions to stimulate the brain in prosocial ways (Gindis, 2008). Rutter et al. (1999) followed a group of infants placed in institutional orphanages, but adopted as young children by British citizens, and documented that early social deprivation resulted in children who had cognitive, motor, and language delays, and rarely cried, but did engage in high rates of repetitive, stereotyped behavior—all characteristics that can be descriptive of ASD.

Interestingly, this theory actually has some merit, but not for the obvious reasons, as shall be explained. Currently, researchers document that ASD results from *differences in the neurological system* (structure and functioning of the nervous system, including neurochemicals). As such, the brains of infants who later will be diagnosed as having an ASD are not hardwired for social interaction as are the brains of most infants. Instead the structure and functioning of the nervous system of infants later diagnosed with ASD places a premium on inanimate objects (Ozonoff et al., 2008). After the developing brain is deprived of stimuli related to social interactions, the brain becomes more specialized in terms of the world of objects. So the external environment is not deprived. It is the neurological system of infants later diagnosed with autism that deprives itself by focusing on stimuli related to inanimate objects and excluding incoming stimuli related to social interactions. This has subsequent implications for atypical neurological development. For these reasons, the American Academy of Pediatrics (2008, p. 1) stated "Autism is not a specific disease, but rather a collection of disorders of brain development called 'autism spectrum disorders' or ASD."

The question that emerges from this realization is: What makes the brain develop so differently in individuals with ASD? Researchers conclude that the neurological differences in ASD are genetically based. This does NOT mean individuals inherit ASD. Inherited traits also are genetically based (eye color, height, facial features, etc.). However, the genetics that lead to the neurological differences underlying ASD occur primarily through mutations after the human embryo has been formed (O'Roak et al., 2011). Researchers do not know what causes these **de novo mutations**, but are studiously attempting to determine which combination of chromosomes are involved and most susceptible to mutations (Wassink, Brzustowicz, Bartlett, & Szatmari, 2004). It has long been suspected that ASD had a genetic component, since a little over four times as many boys as girls are diagnosed with an ASD (Baio, 2012). Whereas the XX chromosomes that produce a girl allow for the genetic redundancy necessary to protect against mutations, the XY chromosomes that produce a boy cannot protect each other against mutations on one of the chromosomes. In copious genetic studies, researchers have determined that 90% of ASD are heritable (Caglayan, 2010), resulting in the differences in brain development. In contrast, individuals without ASD who do not experience the critical genetic mutations, are considered to have a typical neurological system, and are referred to as **neurotypical**.

Although a neurological system functions as an integrated, interconnected unit, making it difficult to draw conclusions based on differences in any one area of the brain, specific subsystems have been investigated to determine how they contribute to the behaviors demonstrated by individuals with ASD. These include the brainstem, the cerebellum, and the limbic system. A brief analysis of each will illustrate their roles in the emergence of ASD.

Brainstem. Among its many interconnected functions, the brainstem controls the basic mechanisms necessary for survival, such as breathing, digestion, and sleep. The brainstem also helps regulate sensory input and motor output, as occurs in reflexes, and contains the basic conduit for processing auditory stimuli. In a postmortem analysis of the brainstem of a woman with autism, researchers realized that the brainstem was shorter than the brainstem of controls who were neurotypical, with defective and missing elements (Rodier, 2000). These brainstem differences would result in disorders in sleeping, problems with reflexes, difficulty controlling facial expressions (possibly leading to "blank" expressions; Kanner, 1943), and a delayed processing of auditory information. Sleep disorders are common in individuals with ASD—many sleeping for only a few hours a day (Sivertsen, Posserud, Gillberg, Lundervold, & Hysing, 2012). Preschool and kindergarten teachers, who schedule "naptime" during school hours, are urged to keep children with ASD awake during that time if parents report the children do not sleep at night. Problems with reflexes may emerge as one of several early indicators of an ASD diagnosis, as those infants fail to put their hands out reflexively to protect themselves when falling, and fail to use a smooth corkscrew motion when rolling over from their backs to their stomachs (Teitelbaum et al., 2004). The delay in processing auditory information (O'Connor, 2012) means those students with an ASD will need additional time to respond to verbal directives. For example, after asking a student with an ASD to get out a book, teachers should allow 15–30 additional seconds for the student to process the auditory information. Teachers who try to be helpful by repeating the direction or stating components of the direction (e.g., Stand up, go to your locker…) will only be bombarding the student with more auditory information that needs to be processed.

Cerebellum. The cerebellum plays many important roles in interconnected brain functioning, including controlling balance and coordination, filtering sensory stimuli, modulating attention, and allowing us to anticipate and predict experiences. Via brain scans and microscopic analyses, researchers have identified differences from the typical in the shape and density of the cerebellum in individuals with an ASD (Courschesne et al., 1994). These differences are associated with the clumsiness often seen in individuals on the higher functioning end of the autism spectrum (Goh & Peterson, 2012). The filtering system deficit in individuals with ASD (Kemper & Bauman, 1998) leads to an inability to filter relevant from irrelevant stimuli. For example as you are reading these words, your intact filtering system is allowing you to concentrate on the text while filtering out the buzz of florescent lights, sight of objects close by, noises of cars driving outside, smell of food cooking, and even the awareness that a waistband is exerting mild pressure on your stomach. In contrast, individuals with an ASD experience all sensory stimuli (e.g., sounds, smells, sights, touch) as equally relevant, and even overwhelming to the point of being painful (Grandin, 2009). Without an intact filtering system, students with an ASD will be unable to maintain focus on relevant stimuli if other stimuli are present, since they cannot be filtered out.

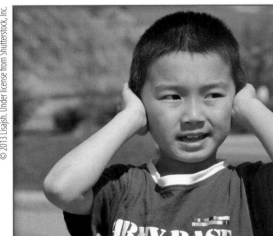

Individuals with ASD may experience all sensory stimuli as overwhelming to the point of being painful.

An intact cerebellum allows neurotypicals to predict upcoming events and anticipate that changes can still be a part of those events. Neurotypicals have developed schema for how the world operates. For example, infants quickly learn that if they drop something over the edge of their highchairs, it will fall to the ground, and someone will have to pick it up and hand it to them before they will get it back. After sufficient repetition, neurotypical infants who drop something may attempt to recruit someone's attention to retrieve the item and hand it back to them. In contrast, infants with compromised cerebellums may not develop that schema and it will take them much longer to understand what happens when something is dropped. This inability to predict can result in highly anxious behavior as individuals with ASD constantly struggle to understand what will happen next. Many teachers have reported that students with high-functioning autism continue to ask every morning if lunch will be at 11:40, even though they have gone to the cafeteria at that time every day for several months. All it takes is one day when lunch is early due to an early release, or one day when lunch is late due to testing, for students with ASD to doubt that they can predict its occurrence; therefore, the majority of their cognitive effort is spent trying to figure out what is happening. Think of the cognitive effort that is required when you are driving to work and encounter an obstacle, perhaps a road closure due to construction. Whereas you typically drive to work while listening to music, talking on your cell phone, and eating a snack, the inability to follow your habitual and predictable route leads to the need for concentrated effort to determine an alternate route. You may end the call, turn off the music, and put the snack aside as you consider the various options to get where you are going. The level of concentration will be heightened if you already are running late and are under pressure to be on time. Many students with ASD experience multiple obstacles every day, as they desperately try to consider possible alternatives and predict what happens next. Added to this is the strong pressure to perform as quickly as their neurotypical peers while they are still trying to process what they need to do. It is no wonder that these students have meltdowns as differences in their cerebella cause them to struggle to anticipate and predict behaviors and expectations.

Limbic System. The limbic system is responsible for facilitating all aspects of social and emotional behavior. As such, the limbic system influences drive, motivation, and affect. The limbic system also supports development of representational memory. Given that the core deficit in ASD is socialization (Laushey & Heflin, 2000), neurological differences in the limbic system play a key role in the manifestation of ASD. Klin, Jones, Schultz, Volkmar, and Cohen (2002) have used sophisticated eye-tracking devices to document that individuals with an ASD, even those as young as 20 months (Shic, Bradshaw, Klin, Scassellati, & Chawarska, 2011), are preoccupied with nonsocial stimuli, such as light switches and lamps, and fail to recognize the information conveyed via facial expressions. Researchers (Klin, 1992) have found that individuals with an ASD prefer nonhuman noise to the sound of human voices, orienting toward nonhuman noises and ignoring people who are speaking to them, even during the first year of life (Dawson, Osterling, Meltzoff, & Kuhl, 2000). As discussed previously, this neurologically predisposed preference for the inanimate can become more deeply ingrained, unless the child is encouraged to interact with the social world. An interesting speculation is that modern society's reliance on personal devices, such as smart phones, electronic tablets, and handheld electronic games, is shaping everyone's brains to be more object focused, and may be leading to evolutionary changes in our brains. To facilitate prosocial neurological systems, all young children should be encouraged to participate in social interactions with humans, with minimal amounts of time spent focusing on electronic devices, including televisions.

For many, animal studies explain why children born with ASD do not demonstrate the associated behaviors until around 2 years of age. Of particular interest are the animal studies related to the effect of early versus late damage on subsequent behaviors in animal models of ASD (Bachevalier, 1991, 1994; Bachevalier & Vargha-Khadem, 2005; Green & Schwartzbaum, 1968; Kimble, 1963; Mishkin & Aggleton, 1981; Murray & Mishkin, 1985). From these animal models, we can infer that human infants who are born with neurological differences in the limbic system may not demonstrate behavioral manifestations until 2 or 3 years of age.

Neurochemistry. In addition to the intensively studied differences in major brain structures, researchers also have examined the role of neurotransmitters (e.g., serotonin, dopamine) in the manifestation of characteristics associated with ASD. To date, neurochemical differences appear to relate more to associated conditions (e.g., anxiety, depression) than to the core features of ASD. The good news is that the judicial and carefully monitored prescription of psychotropic medications can greatly alleviate some of the symptoms of neurochemical imbalances that may occur in individuals with ASD (Palermo & Curatolo, 2004). In particular, risperidone and aripiprazole have been found to reduce behavioral challenges and some repetitive behavior; however, unwanted side effects must be carefully considered to determine benefit (McPheeters et al., 2011).

Functional Differences. Researchers examining the neurological differences in individuals with ASD have considered not only brain structures and chemicals, but also how those components function as a unit. Of particular interest are the documented deficits in executive functioning, including poor problem solving, inability to organize, and failure to generate alternative options when something changes (Endedijk, Denessen, & Hendriks, 2011). Scrutiny of mirror neurons has exposed their role in the development of empathy, along with speculation that this functional component may be missing in individuals with an ASD (Enticott et al., 2012). Via mirror neurons, brain waves in neurotypical individuals respond as if the person is actually experiencing something he is only watching (di Pellegrino, Fadiga, Fogassi, Gallese, & Rizzolatti, 1992). For example, when watching a video of a hand opening and closing, brain waves assume patterns that occur when the person opens and closes his own hand. In contrast, the brain waves of individuals with ASD are not affected by watching a video of a hand opening and closing. Similarly, individuals who are neurotypical will feel sadness if they observe others being sad—individuals with ASD do not have this same reaction. The inability of the mirror neurons in individuals with ASD to register similar emotions makes it impossible for them to empathize and assume another person's perspective. Problems with executive functioning and failed mirror neurons may be at the heart of socialization difficulties for individuals with ASD.

In summary, ASD is a genetically based disability. Although researchers have not discovered what causes de novo gene mutations or even the specific chromosomes involved, these mutations lead to differences in the way the neurological system develops and functions. Some of the neurological differences become self-perpetuating (Amaral, Schumann, & Nordahl, 2008), such as when preoccupations with objects interfere with social development, which becomes cumulative, making socialization even more difficult. Brain structures, including the brainstem, the cerebellum, and the limbic system, have been studied extensively, as have neurochemicals and neurological functioning, in order to understand the behaviors characteristic of individuals with an ASD. **Table 10.1** contains a synopsis of a few of the behavioral manifestations related to neurological differences in specific subsystems. In the next section we elaborate on the common characteristics associated with ASD.

Characteristics of Individuals with ASD

Coming from the Greek root "autos" (which means "self"), Kanner (1943) used the term "autism" to characterize the behaviors of a group of children who he thought to be so self-centered that they could not relate to the world around them. The *Diagnostic and Statistical Manual of Mental Disorders (DSM-IV)* (APA, 2000), includes autism under a broader umbrella category of pervasive developmental disorder (PDD). Other autism-related

TABLE 10.1

Neurological Subsystems and Manifestations of Differences

Subsystem	General Roles	Manifestations of Differences
Brainstem	• controls basic functions (e.g., breathing, sleeping, reflexes) • regulates sensory input/output • conduit for sensory stimuli • controls facial muscles	• sleep disorders • inadequate reflexes • increased stereotypic behavior • unusual and/or "blank" expressions • auditory processing lag; may be slow to respond to directions and become more confused if additional auditory directions given
Cerebellum	• controls motor coordination • contains sensory filters • contains preparatory system to enable ability to anticipate and predict • modulates attention	• clumsy and awkward movement • inability to filter relevant from irrelevant stimuli, leading to hyper- and hypo-sensory sensitivities • difficulty maintaining attention in presence of competing stimuli • inability to anticipate and predict flow of events • prefers an established routine that does not vary • resists changes • perseverates
Limbic System	• orchestrates all aspects of social and emotional behavior • attaches meaning to events • influences drive, motivation, and affect • supports representational memory	• has greater interest in objects than in people • unresponsive to typical systems of motivation • difficulty understanding cause/effect • problems with generalization
Neurochemistry	• transports signals and messages in the brain	• depression • anxiety • obsessive-compulsive disorder • ADHD • Bipolar Disorder
Neurological Functioning	• supports executive functioning and information processing • activates mirror neurons	• emergence of seizure disorders • disorganized • poor problem solving • challenges with motor planning • inability to empathize or relate to others' experiences

disorders that fall under the category of PDD in the DSM-IV are Rett syndrome, childhood disintegrative disorder (CDD), Asperger syndrome, and PDD-Not Otherwise Specified. Each of these subtypes of PDD has differentiating diagnostic criteria. However, there is so much overlap among the subtypes that it can be difficult to distinguish among them. The term "autism spectrum disorders" (ASD) has emerged as the preferred term for referring to the various subtypes of PDD without having to distinguish among them. Reference to a "spectrum" recognizes that ASD range from mild to severe (Lord, Cook, Leventhal, & Amaral, 2000). This means that some people may demonstrate extreme forms of the behaviors characteristic of autism whereas others may be only mildly affected. To acknowledge the dramatic differences among individuals on the autism spectrum, an oft repeated saying is "if you've seen one child with autism . . . you've seen one child with autism" (rather than being able to say you've seen them all). The commonality among individuals with ASD is that their disabilities will affect three major areas of functioning: communication, socialization, and interests.

Communication. Individuals with ASD demonstrate communication patterns that are different from what is expected (Wetherby et al., 2004). They typically fail to make eye contact and instead may prefer to use peripheral vision. Lack of eye contact makes it hard to initiate and maintain communication. Infants with ASD may not turn toward someone calling their names or even orient to human voices. They may point at something that want or "lead" a person to get something for them, but will not point to call attention to something they find interesting. In addition, some individuals with autism fail to develop spoken language or may not use it even if it has developed. The speech of individuals with ASD who develop spoken language may have unusual intonation or pitch and may sound like machine-generated speech (Kanner, 1943). The exception to machine-sounding speech occurs when individuals with ASD repeat something they have heard. The repetition of others' oral speech may sound like an echo and is called **echolalia**. During echolalia, the speech may mimic exactly the original speaker, including the intonation and pitch. Echolalia may occur right after the original words are spoken (e.g., when asked *What's your name?* the person with ASD may say *What's your* name? *Your name?* or simply *'Name?'*) or the echolalia may be delayed as when a TV program heard the previous night or months prior is repeated verbatim. Individuals with ASD may talk to themselves, demonstrating that they can speak (Volden & Lord, 1991), but may have difficulty using verbal communication in an interactive manner.

Individuals with ASD typically fail to make eye contact.

Socialization. In addition to the lack of interactive communication, individuals with autism have difficulty socializing with others. Infants with ASD may not be cuddly and may actively resist being held. As these infants grow older, they may not seek out others for interactions and may not go to another person even for comfort or help when hurt. Individuals with ASD may appear to be oblivious to the feelings of others and may not acknowledge the presence of another person. Those functioning on the lower end of the autism spectrum may appear to be disinterested in interacting with others whereas those functioning on the higher end of the autism spectrum may be very interested in interacting with others but they do not know how to do so appropriately. Related to challenges in understanding the social world, individuals with ASD may display emotions that do not fit the situation. For example, they may laugh when others around them are sad or may cry for no reason related to the immediate context. Individuals with ASD have difficulty developing reciprocal relationships.

Interests. Due to the neurological differences that cause ASD, affected individuals appear to be more interested in objects than in people (Klin et al., 2002) and may use objects in unusual ways. For example, rather than rolling a toy truck across the floor, a child with ASD may turn the toy over and spin the wheels. Rather than playing a xylophone, a child with ASD may flip the string that is attached to the front of the toy. Individuals with ASD may not show fear about things that typically produce fear (e.g., heavy traffic) but they may express terror at things that usually are not fear-producing (e.g., flushing toilets, noise from fish aquariums). Individuals with ASD tend to have an extremely narrow range of interests. Individuals functioning on the low end of the spectrum may want only to line up objects or to look at the same books. Individuals functioning on the higher end of the spectrum may talk constantly about a topic of special interest and appear to be unable to talk about anything else.

Differences in the three core areas of communication, socialization, and interests lead to challenges in learning and frustration in interacting with the world. These challenges and

© 2013 Zurijeta. Under license from Shutterstock, Inc.

frustrations result in the behaviors that are characteristic of ASD. Individuals with ASD are characterized by an inability to adapt to change. They may insist that appearances and routines are always the same. For example, if a chair is moved from one place to another or if a different route is taken when driving to the store, individuals with ASD may be noticeably upset. Resistance to change can be seen when a student with ASD insists on wearing a t-shirt without a coat even when the temperature drops below freezing or insists on sitting in the same seat every day. When this insistence on sameness extends into activities it is called **perseveration**. Individuals with ASD may perseverate on one activity, such as spinning coins or memorizing baseball statistics, for hours at a time. An individual with autism may demonstrate perseveration by repeating the same word over and over or by engaging in the same motor motion, such as touching each floor tile once, for extended periods of time. Because of their insistence on sameness and their tendency to perseverate, individuals with ASD are not very adaptable. In fact, the insistence on sameness and perseveration may lead to behaviors that appear almost ritualistic. For example, one young girl with autism always started her school day by taking barrettes out of a baggie that she brought from home and lining them up in one corner of the room. If she was prevented from engaging in this activity (e.g., a piece of heavy equipment had been placed in that particular corner of the room) or was interrupted during this activity (e.g., if there was a fire drill or another student took one of her barrettes), she would become upset and throw a tantrum. It can be challenging to work with a student who wants everything to stay the same and insists on engaging in specific activities at specific times.

Challenges in learning as well as frustration interacting with the world can be seen in **self-stimulating** or self-injurious behaviors. Self-stimulating behaviors, also called "stimming," are repetitious actions that serve no apparent purpose. For example, individuals with ASD may "stim" by rocking back and forth on their heels, finger flicking, tapping objects, and so forth (DiGennaro Reed, Hirst, & Hyman, 2012). Interestingly, infants between 9 and 12 months of age with developmental delays may demonstrate higher rates of self-stimulatory behavior than infants who are later diagnosed with ASD (Baranek, 1999). Although self-stimulating behaviors do not appear to serve a useful purpose, researchers indicate that such behaviors are biologically necessary and actually may decrease stress levels while increasing awareness. For these reasons, all humans engage in self-stimulating behaviors, even college students (Rago & Case, 1978). The difference is that individuals without ASD learn to self-stimulate in socially acceptable ways. For example, most college students will flip their feet, twist their hair, or doodle on papers to increase their awareness and stay awake when they get bored in class. In contrast, individuals with ASD who get bored or upset may jump up and down, flap their arms, or blow on their fingers to self-stimulate. When individuals without ASD get upset, they self-stimulate by walking, eating, or rubbing the back of their necks, which serves to lower stress levels. Those with ASD may rock, pace, bite their own hands, or repeat scripts from movies when they get stressed. Deficits in socialization make it difficult for individuals with ASD to recognize or adhere to social conventions.

Self-injurious behaviors (SIBs) are those behaviors that seem to be directed at causing injury to a person's own body. SIBs include banging one's head against a wall, hitting oneself in the ear, and biting or scratching oneself (Richards, Oliver, Nelson, & Moss, 2012). These behaviors become serious when they are repeated over and over, posing a threat of tissue damage, brain damage, and even death. It is believed that SIBs are committed for one of two reasons. One reason is to exert control over the environment, and the other is as a response to a biologic defect (de Catanzaro, 1978; Guess & Carr, 1991). Most SIBs will be demonstrated in order to control the environment by manipulating others. For example, a student may have learned that if he screams, the teacher will give up trying to make him write his name on a paper. At some point, however, the student who is screaming to get out of the task will encounter someone who does not care if he screams. Then the student will have to do something more drastic, such as scream and roll around on the floor, in order to get out of the task. This behavioral progression will continue until the student is demonstrating SIBs to manipulate others and control events in the environment. Once the student learns that banging his head against the wall is effective for getting him something he wants or helping him avoid something he does not want, the student will choose the SIB as the quickest means of getting a desired outcome and will not even bother starting with the lesser behavior, screaming.

In a smaller percentage of cases SIBs will occur, not to manipulate the environment, but as a result of a biological defect that causes a need for deep pressure or results in uncontrollable motor activity (Bakke, 1990; Baumeister, 1991; Cataldo & Harris, 1982). Individuals with disorders other than ASD may engage in high rates of SIBs. SIBs are seen in persons with Lesch-Nyhan syndrome (Zirpoli & Lloyd, 1987), intellectual disability (Kobe, 1994), and Tourette syndrome (Muehlmann & Lewis, 2012), as well as other disabilities.

Before leaving this discussion of the characteristics of ASD, it is important to point out that individuals can demonstrate any of the behaviors mentioned and not have ASD. For example, individuals with severe intellectual disability will engage in self-stimulating and self-injurious behavior. Many people insist on sameness by sitting in the same seat in a classroom or theater. An infant with a difficult temperament may not want to be cuddled (Chess & Thomas, 1987). In order to diagnose autism a clear pattern must exist across behaviors and the specific criteria, as mentioned in DSM-IV, must be met. **Table 10.2** summarizes the characteristics associated with ASD.

TABLE 10.2

Behavioral Characteristics Commonly Associated with Autism Spectrum Disorders

- difficulty relating to others
  - may not demonstrate typical patterns of affection
  - may not initiate social interaction
  - oblivious to other's feelings/mood
- difficulty relating to objects
  - unusual attachments (collects sticks, straws, gum wrappers, etc.)
  - odd play that goes on and on (picks fuzz off chairs, arranges items in a line, etc.)
- unusual reactions to events
  - insistence on sameness
- unusual communication
  - little direct eye contact
  - delayed language
  - use of behaviors to communicate
  - unusual intonation and pitch when language present
  - echolalia
- abnormal responses to sensations
  - hyper- or hyposensitive to touch, smell, taste, sound
  - affect does not match situation
- self-stimulation (stims)
- self-injurious behaviors (SIBs)

Diagnosis of ASD

DSM-IV clusters the behaviors associated with ASD into three categories: communication, socialization, and restricted and repetitive patterns of behaviors and interests. There are two major problems with this categorization system. One is that the criteria listed in the category of communication are of limited relevance until children develop language. The real issue is how individuals of any age attempt to interact with others (or fail to do so). The second major problem is that professionals have become quite adept at identifying who has a Pervasive Developmental Disorder (PDD) and who does not; however, there can be considerable disagreement as to the type of PDD identified (i.e., autistic disorder, Asperger disorder, childhood disintegrative disorder, PDD-Not Otherwise Specified). For these reasons among others, the group of professionals charged with revising the definition and criteria for PDD for the next version of the DSM (which will be DSM-V, and is slated to be published in 2013 or 2014) is proposing major changes (Wing, Gould, & Gillberg, 2011). First, acquiescing to popular nomenclature, the name of the disorder will change from pervasive developmental disorders to autism spectrum disorders. Then, instead of having subtypes (e.g., autism, Asperger's), the disability will be characterized by severity of impairment (i.e., mild, moderate, severe). The number of categories that define the disorder will change from three to two, with the social and communication categories combined into one. **Figure 10.1** provides a graphic representation of the differences between the current categorization of criteria and the proposed revision.

Although the change in name certainly defers to the terminology preferred by most people, other proposed changes are being questioned. For example, removal of the subtypes, particularly Asperger's, has generated considerable outcry. Although some argue that classification by level of impairment is more useful in understanding the disability, others fear the loss of identity, as they consider themselves "Aspies" (i.e., Asperger's). Since the criteria are changing slightly, some fear that a percentage of individuals on the higher functioning end of the autism spectrum will no longer qualify for the diagnosis (Mattila et al., 2011), whereas others speculate that individuals on the lower functioning end of the spectrum may not be diagnosed with ASD (Worley & Matson, 2012). Considerable work and effort have

Figure 10.1   Changes in the *DSM* Concepts of ASD

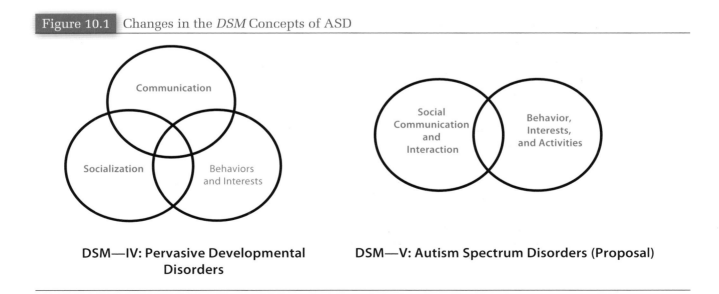

DSM—IV: Pervasive Developmental Disorders

DSM—V: Autism Spectrum Disorders (Proposal)

gone into the creating the next edition of the DSM and, as of the time of this printing, the final outcomes are still unknown.

Differences in the neurological system of individuals with ASD manifest into behaviors that are characteristic of the disability. These characteristics have been organized into diagnostic criteria by the DSM. Since ASD are pervasive disorders that are evident at a young age, the diagnosis usually is made by a pediatrician or multidisciplinary team working in a medical context. ASD diagnoses given by professionals licensed to do so, using the criteria in the DSM-IV, do not automatically qualify students for special education services in their local school systems. Such a diagnosis can contribute to an understanding of the student, but according to IDEA, the school system has to undertake its own evaluation process to determine if the disability is adversely affecting the student's educational performance. As discussed in Chapter 3, for some students determining eligibility for special education will begin with documenting that failure to achieve is related to the disability and not to poor teaching or inadequate opportunity.

Prevalence of ASD

Two constructs provide an indication of quantity: prevalence and incidence. Unfortunately used interchangeably, the two constructs have very different meanings. Prevalence refers to the proportion or ratio of a given phenomenon in a specified population. For example, you could determine the prevalence of people wearing sandals at your family reunion in 2011. If 28 of 47 people at your family reunion this year were wearing sandals, the prevalence is 60% or 1.6 people wearing sandals for every 1 person who is not (1.6:1). You know the phenomenon (wearing sandals) and you know the population (people who are at your family reunion in a given year). What you do not know is the incidence, or number of new cases of sandal wearing at reunions in your family across time. Incidence rates have never been calculated for ASD because it has been impossible to measure the same phenomenon across time. However, we have seen the prevalence rates rise, from 1 in 110 (Rice & Centers for Disease Control and Prevention, 2009) to 1 in 88 (Baio, 2012). Since there is no way to calculate incidence, it is unclear if the increase is based on new cases, or simply identifying more people in a given population. There are several reasons to believe that the latter is true, and they are as follows:

- Definitional changes
- Better diagnostics
- Diagnostic substitution
- Differences in study methodology
- Over-identification

Definitional changes. There is no doubt that the first 11 children Kanner (1943) identified as having autism are very different from the majority of individuals today who are identified as being on the autism spectrum. Kanner's original conceptualization of autism was restricted to individuals with little to no language, absence of social awareness, and severe self-preoccupation. Additionally, Kanner believed that individuals with autism could not have any co-occurring conditions. Today, we have an autism "spectrum" that encompasses the children Kanner described, as well as individuals who are higher functioning, and those with co-occurring disabilities such as tuberous sclerosis, fragile X (Fombonne, 2005), obsessive compulsive disorder, anxiety disorder, conduct disorders, and major depressive disorders (Amr et al., 2012). The clearest example of definitional changes can been in the publications of the Autism Society of America. In the November/December 1996 the *Advocate*, autism was defined as "a severely incapacitating lifelong" disability affecting "approximately 15 out of every 10,000 births." The behavioral criteria are paraphrased from the DSM, and sound clinical. The concluding statement of the 1996 definition is that "Special educational programs using behavioral methods have proved to be the most helpful treatment for persons with autism" with early diagnosis and intervention leading to the best prognosis.

In the very next issue of the *Advocate* (January/February 1997), a new definition appears that is shorter as the clinical behavioral manifestations have been replaced with description that is more generic. Instead of being "severely incapacitating" and "lifelong," autism is described simply as a "developmental disability." The prevalence is still listed at 15 out of every 10,000, but the definition also contains an estimate that 400,000 people in the United States have autism. Dishearteningly, the definition concludes with the statement that "the majority of the public and professionals are clueless as to how to effectively work with individuals with autism."

The next time a new definition appeared in the *Advocate* was 19 months later in the September/October 1998 issue. The definition was shorter yet, with the behavioral symptoms becoming more ambiguous and concise. In this definition, autism is referred to as a "complex developmental disability" affecting 1 in 500 people, bringing the estimate to "over one half million people in the U.S." Rather than the "majority" not knowing how to effectively intervene with autism, the definition was softened to assert that "most of the public" was unaware of effective interventions for individuals with autism.

This focused scrutiny of how the definition of autism, provided by the leading advocacy agency for those affected by autism and their families, changed dramatically over less than a 2-year period. Similar substantial changes occurred in the definitions appearing in evolving versions of the DSM, starting from the earliest version (1952) in which autism was described as a "schizophrenic reaction, childhood type," to the DSM-III (1980) in which "pervasive developmental disorders" become the category, and criteria were provided for "infantile autism," "child onset Pervasive Developmental Disorder (PDD)," and "atypical PDD," to the DSM-IV (1994) containing the five subtypes mentioned previously.

Some of the precipitous increase in the prevalence of ASD must be attributed to changes in the way an ASD is defined. Kanner's (1943) definition would have included only individuals who were more severely affected, whereas more recent definitions are broader and more inclusive. A large percentage of individuals who are identified as functioning on the higher end of the autism spectrum would not have been diagnosed with the disability in years past (Wing & Potter, 2002).

Better diagnostics. Another factor propelling the increase in the numbers of individuals with ASD is that we have become much more proficient at identifying the presence of the constellation of behaviors indicative of autism. As awareness of ASD has increased, so have the methods used to distinguish individuals who have the disability from those who do not (Fombonne, 2005). The American Academy of Neurology published a brief list of warning signs that should alert medical professionals that further screening is needed to identify underlying conditions, possibly ASD (Filipek et al, 2000). This was followed by the American Academy of Pediatrics (Plauché-Johnson et al., 2007) calling for universal screening for ASD of all young children at their 18- and 24-month well-baby checkups. People are more aware of the existence of ASD and seek diagnostic evaluations that are specific to and accurate for identifying the presence of ASD.

The driving impetus behind improved diagnostics is the increase in the number and types of services available for the population of individuals with ASD (Gillberg, Cederlund, Lamberg, & Zeijlon, 2006; Nassar et al., 2009). If there were no services available, there would be no need to identify individuals with conditions that would qualify them for the services;

however, with services available, there is a real need to identify those who are eligible to receive them. Williams, MacDermott, Ridley, Glasson, and Wray (2008) conducted a comprehensive analysis in the states and territories of Australia and found that prevalence varied significantly between areas with services available and those without services for individuals with ASD. Researchers have found that clinicians are willing to give diagnoses on the autism spectrum, even in the presence of questionable characteristics, if they believe the diagnoses enable the children to receive services.

Diagnostic substitution. Along with increased awareness and better diagnostics comes the ability to differentially identify individuals with an ASD. As mentioned previously, there was no special education eligibility for students with ASD prior to 1990. Those with ASD could not receive specialized instruction and support unless they were found eligible for another disability, the most commonly used being Other Health Impairments, Emotional Disturbance, and Learning Disabilities. Once autism became available as an eligibility category, during the re-evaluation process, IEP teams began to substitute "autism" for the eligibility used previously to access special education services. Shattuck (2006) analyzed U.S. special education statistics for children ages 6 to 11 years across the school years from 1984–2003, and found that the increase in the number of students being served under an autism eligibility was almost exactly the same as the decrease in the number of students being served under the categories of Intellectual Disabilities and Learning Disabilities— diagnostic substitution accounted for all of the increase in the number of students being served as having autism in half of the states. Bishop, Whitehouse, Watt, and Line (2008) found that individuals who were identified as having developmental language disorders between 1986 and 2003 would now be classified as having ASD. Eagle (2004) noted that students formerly diagnosed with Attention Deficit Hyperactivity Disorder, Obsessive Compulsive Disorder, Oppositional Defiant Disorder, anxiety disorder, and learning disabilities were being reclassified as having high-functioning autism or Asperger's. Definitional changes to include a broader spectrum, along with the availability of services and better diagnostics, are resulting in substitution of less accurate diagnoses and eligibilities for more accurate classification on the autism spectrum.

Differences in study methodology. One of the greatest barriers to determining accurate prevalence rates is that there are multiple ways to calculate the number of people with an ASD. Prevalence rates vary based on the definition being used. There are a variety of definitions for ASD available. Given the population of the world, it would be impossible to count all of the individuals who have an ASD and verify, via a consistent evaluation, that all of the individuals really have an ASD as reported. This leaves the task of determining prevalence to indirect methods. Some researchers look at records (not people) from health agencies, whereas others look at records from educational agencies. A higher prevalence will be found by researchers who look at school eligibility and health records combined (Pinborough-Zimmerman et al., 2012). Kogan et al. (2009) used a random telephone survey to 78,037 homes in the United States to query if a child in the home between the ages of 3 and 17 years had ever been identified as having an ASD. Analysis of results revealed that parents reported an ASD in 1.1% of the survey population, equivalent to a prevalence of 1 in 91 children 3 to 17 years old with current identification as having an ASD. Of particular interest in this phone survey was that 40% of the parents reported their children previously, but no longer, had an ASD. Obviously, it is difficult to draw conclusions from parent- or self-reported diagnoses, particularly when such a large percentage no longer met criteria for an ASD.

The most common method of determining prevalence from records, and that employed by the Centers for Disease Control and Prevention, is to have trained people first go through records to look for indications that individuals have received a diagnosis of an ASD or have received specialized services by meeting eligibility for autism. For records that do not contain an ASD diagnosis or eligibility, trained observers will "abstract" the files—they look at narrative descriptions and clinical notes written about the person in the file and write down indicators they believe might indicate the presence of an ASD. Once files have been reviewed, the abstracts are evaluated by clinicians, who give their impressions about whether or not the individuals have an ASD.

Of particular concern with this methodology is that there are no behaviors unique to ASD. As discussed previously, we all demonstrate echolalia, that is how we learn to talk. We all go through periods of social withdrawal when we are too tired, ill, or distracted to want to socialize. Individuals with intellectual disability and those with extreme forms of emotional disturbance will engage in self-stimulatory behavior, possibly even those that are self-injurious. An abstract containing descriptors such as "does not like change," "needs things in a particular order" may just as well describe someone with obsessive/compulsive disorder but not an ASD. Clearly, use of records to abstract and evaluate potential for ASD is highly likely to result in over-identification, and artificial inflation of prevalence.

Over-identification. As broad as the ASD definitions have become, there also is a real danger that individuals who do not have an ASD are being told (or telling others) that they have an ASD. Conducting searches on the worldwide Web reveals an explosion in the number of blogs, chat rooms, and Web pages authored by adults who are retrospectively diagnosing themselves as having an ASD. Given that most did not receive specialized support in school, and have gone on to train for and maintain a career, it is possible that they are self-identifying inaccurately (Ketelaars et al., 2008). The ready availability of services in most locations for individuals who have been identified with an ASD may motivate parents to seek the diagnosis so that children receive special support, although there may be a difference of opinion as to whether or not the child actually has an ASD. Widespread awareness plus availability of certain services that require an ASD diagnosis are probably factors leading to the ever-expanding prevalence numbers in ASD. Additionally, as mentioned previously, there are no behaviors unique to ASD—every behavior demonstrated by someone with ASD has been demonstrated by individuals without an ASD. Grandin (2002), a woman who was diagnosed with autism as a child, and who has provided exceptional "insider" information into the disability, states it best when she wonders about the distinction between a computer nerd and someone with Asperger's. The blurred edges of ASD may invite over-identification of the disability.

Documenting Response to Intervention

The process of documenting Response to Intervention (RTI) for students with ASD will be more applicable to some students than to others. With the emphasis on early intervention (National Research Council [NRC], 2001) and universal infant and toddler screening (Plau-ché-Johnson, Myers, & Council on Children with Disabilities, 2007), many children with ASD are being diagnosed at very young ages. Most parents will provide documentation from a physician when they enroll their children in school. Many of these parents will expect that the outside diagnosis of ASD will guarantee that their child receive specialized supports and services. School personnel will probably agree with this expectation for students functioning on the low end of the autism spectrum, as their learning and behavioral differences may require interventions more intensive and specialized than those which can be provided in general education classrooms.

Students functioning on the higher end of the autism spectrum may benefit from universal (Tier 1), targeted (Tier 2), and intensive (Tier 3) interventions. Indeed, these students are fully capable of mastering the general curriculum, and tend to score the highest on classroom and district assessments. In Tier 1, students with ASD will respond well to teachers who use explicit instruction (e.g., direct instruction) and visuals to illustrate abstract concepts. Students with ASD may be motivated to complete assignments and demonstrate their competence if the topics match their personal interests. For example, a student with ASD may be more cooperative in learning about paragraph construction and punctuation when allowed to write about his special interest in cryptozoology. Typically, documentation of Tier 1 interventions relies on calculating the frequency and percentage of correct answers on academic assignments.

Unique social and communication needs may require Tier 2 and Tier 3 interventions as students with ASD will need instruction targeted at helping them understand social convention and to enhance their social competence. Students with ASD will need targeted instruction in understanding nonliteral language such as metaphors and idioms, as well as nonverbal language, such as deciphering facial expressions and interpreting intonation. Documenting the outcome of Tier 2 interventions aimed at ameliorating social and communication deficits may involve collecting observational data on the number of positive peer interactions, number of facial expressions correctly identified, ability to accurately infer emotional states, and so forth. **Figure 10.2** presents examples of interventions that may be helpful at each tier for students with ASD. The figure does not include all possible strategies at each tier but only a sample of interventions that may be useful. The unique learning challenges presented by the student with ASD will dictate the relevance of the strategies listed as well as other potential interventions to be considered.

Figure 10.2   Interventions by Tier for Autism Spectrum Disorders

Tier 3:

- Functional assessment of challenging behavior
- Task analyze ongoing academic and social errors
- Increase frequency and duration of targeted interventions

Tier 2:

- Social skills instruction
- Instruction in pragmatic and non-verbal communication
- Teach students to monitor and modulate emotional reactions
- Check-in with support staff
- Specific instruction to enhance comprehension of written and spoken material
- Facilitate understanding of concepts

Tier 1:

- Incorporate topics of fascination into assignments
- Evaluate sensory stimuli in environment and modify as needed
- Structured routines for completing tasks and transitioning
- Use visual and concrete supports to illustrate lecture, discussion, and expectations
- Explicit instruction and direct teaching of academic skills and behavioral expectations
- Close contact with families to identify unique adaptations used at home
- Professional development for teachers regarding the characteristics and learning styles in ASD

IDEA Definition of ASD

Although the characteristics of persons with autism have remained surprisingly constant since Kanner's (1943) original description, the definition has changed considerably. Much of the changes in definition have occurred as a clearer understanding of the etiology has evolved. When P.L. 94-142 (1975) was signed, the prevailing belief was that autism was an emotional disturbance, so it was included within the Serious Emotional Disturbance (SED) category. Due to the efforts of advocacy groups, autism was moved out of SED and into Other Health Impairments (OHI) in 1981 in an attempt to contradict the myth that autism was an emotional disturbance. The inclusion of autism under OHI, although believed to be less stigmatizing by some advocates, did little to help clarify the nature of the disability or the types of interventions that would be appropriate. In 1990, during the reauthorization of P.L. 94-142, autism was again moved, this time out of OHI and into its own discrete category. According to IDEA 2004:

> Autism means a developmental disability significantly affecting verbal and nonverbal communication and social interaction, generally evident before age 3, that adversely affects educational performance. Other characteristics often associated with autism are engagement in repetitive activities and stereotyped movements, resistance to environmental change or changes in daily routines, and unusual responses to sensory experiences. Autism does not apply if a child's educational performance is adversely affected primarily because the child has a serious emotional disturbance. A child who manifests the characteristics of autism after age three could be identified as having autism if the criteria . . . are satisfied.

This definition reminds us that autism is a developmental disability (it occurs during the developmental years) and must be evident before 3 years of age (APA, 2000). Although parents may not realize that their child has unusual patterns of behavior until the child is 4 years of age or older, parents must be able to document unusual behaviors prior to the age of 3 for a diagnosis of autism. Many state definitions of autism specify that a diagnosis of or characteristics related to any of the Pervasive Developmental Disorder (PDD) subtypes (i.e., Asperger syndrome, Childhood Disintegrative Disorder [CDD], Rett syndrome, PDD-Not Otherwise Specified) are included under the IDEA category of autism.

Assessment for Eligibility for Special Education Services

To determine eligibility, school system personnel across a number of disciplines will conduct a variety of evaluations. Parents may provide the results of independent assessments, including DSM-IV diagnoses, if available. Many of the younger students will arrive at school with diagnoses of autism, CDD, Rett syndrome, or PDD-NOS. A diagnosis of Asperger syndrome is usually not given until around 11 years of age (Howlin, 2003), so school systems may be integrally involved in providing documentation that may lead to that diagnosis.

There are a number of assessments specifically designed to evaluate behavior characteristics of students with ASD. For example, the *Autism Diagnostic Observation Schedule* (ADOS) (Lord, Risi, et al., 2000) provides a standardized protocol for observation of social and communicative behavior and is considered to be the best of the diagnostic tools. In addition to collecting data using instruments designed to identify the presence or absence of ASD, school psychologists or other diagnosticians will attempt to measure IQ/cognitive functioning/developmental level, academic level, and adaptive behavior. Speech-language pathologists (SLPs) will conduct assessments of language and communication, including articulation, oral-motor coordination, language comprehension, expressive language, and conventional and nonconventional nonverbal behavior. Occupational therapists may be needed to assess the students' functional adaptations and evaluate their sensory performance. Physical therapists, education specialists, and others also may conduct evaluations as necessary. Many districts have personnel who are specialists in ASD and they may supervise specialized assessments.

Each of the professionals is trained to know which assessments are necessary and most likely to provide valid and reliable information for eligibility determination and identification of present levels of performance. The choice of which evaluations to conduct depends on the unique needs of the student. The school system's purpose for conducting the evaluations is to get as accurate a picture as possible of the child's current level of functioning and areas of need in order to determine eligibility and develop an appropriate program.

Supporting Students with ASD in Instructional Environments

Classroom teachers will be challenged to address the unusual learning styles of students with ASD. Teachers will need to be aware of their students' strengths and preferences and incorporate them into the daily routine. Most students with ASD benefit from high levels of structure and routine in the class setting. Establishing a consistent routine and delineating appropriate expectations will help reduce disruptive and distracting behaviors. Once the student can function within an established routine, the teacher will be able to carefully plan the introduction of deviations into the schedule. Therefore, critical educational components for promoting appropriate learning opportunities for students with ASD include:

- employing visual and concrete systems and structure
- addressing restrictive and repetitive patterns of interests and behaviors
- implementing strategies to address social skills
- delivering strategies to address communication
- modifying the environment to accommodate sensory needs
- dealing with aberrant behavior

Most students with ASD benefit from high levels of structure and routine in the class setting.

Visual and Concrete Systems and Structure

In order for teachers to meet the needs of individuals with ASD, they must incorporate visual and concrete systems for learning and structure their classroom to provide predictable routines. Providing predictable routines will help students better understand expectations for behavior within those routines. The majority of individuals with ASD are visual learners (Tissot & Evans, 2003); therefore, using visual systems for instruction is critical. Additionally, language (including language processing) is difficult for most students with ASD. Supporting language with visual cues will assist in the ability to process spoken language. For younger students, this may involve the use of pictures. For older students who can read, this may simply involve written words as the visual cues. **Figure 10.3** contains visual cues for helping a student with ASD make appropriate choices when she gets frustrated. Graphic organizers, guided notes, PowerPoint slides, and written rules/expectations are all helpful for supporting language processing in students with ASD. **Figure 10.4** contains an example of a checklist used to support transitioning between classes for a student functioning on the higher end of the autism spectrum.

Structuring the environment requires consideration of the way the classroom is organized in terms of both the physical layout as well as the daily schedule. The physical layout of the room should incorporate physical boundaries to help students understand the context for instruction and learning. In an early elementary classroom, having furniture separate sections in the room will help students to better understand expectations during calendar time or group time versus individual work time. Many teachers use carpet squares or a large, patterned rug to help students understand where they are to be during group time. Students may have individual desks or sectioned off areas at a larger table to indicate where they are to be during independent work. They are then taught the expectations for behavior during both of those times. Older students may sit in the same area for both large group and independent work. This makes it especially important for the teacher to review

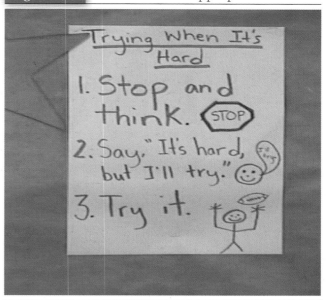

Figure 10.3   Visual Cues for Appropriate Behavior

Figure 10.4   Checklist to Support Transitioning between Classes

TO DO 5 minutes before the bell rings to change classes:

	Tasks	Check when Done
QUIETLY put away all materials used in class	Book, pencil, and notebook go in backpack Completed work goes in "finished" box Other items are put back where they belong (if any used)	
QUIETLY leave the room	Stand still by desk and look at teacher When teacher looks at me, nod and wave Walk out door, closing it softly	
Get materials for next class	Go to locker and open Take book and notebook just used out of backpack and put in locker Get book and notebook for next class and put in backpack Close locker and spin dial	
Go to next class	Walk to next class and stand against wall beside door until the bell rings Wait for students to leave the room Go inside and say "Hi" to the teacher Sit down at my desk and get materials for class out of my backpack	

I'm ready for a great class!!

group or individual expectations to help students understand the context and expectations. Since many students have language processing deficits, it will be important that all expectations are stated using positive terms (i.e., tell them what to do, not what NOT to do) and posted in a conspicuous place. For example if one of the expectations is for the student to raise his hand and wait to be called on before speaking, that is how the rule should be written. If the rule is "do not call out," students with ASD who struggle to process language may miss the "do not" portion of the directions. It may also be helpful to explicitly state the rationales for rules, since these may not be inferred by students with ASD. **Figure 10.5** contains a list of rules posted in a classroom for younger students.

Addressing Restrictive and Repetitive Patterns of Interests and Behaviors

The daily schedule for individuals with ASD should incorporate their strengths and preferences into the daily routine. One of the characteristics of ASD is that individuals have restricted and repetitive patterns of behavior and interests. Incorporating these interests into the routine can be a strong motivator for a student with ASD (Winter-Messiers et al., 2007). Likewise, many individuals with ASD become experts in their field of interests as adults. Therefore, it is typically not necessary to extinguish those interests. However, there will be many times during the day when focusing on those interests is not best for the student's learning nor is it feasible. By using a visual schedule to structure the day or class period, students with ASD will be able to understand how long they need to work to accomplish tasks that may not be as motivating for them. Additionally, by using a visual first/then schedule, students are more motivated to complete a nonpreferred task when they know that it will be followed by a preferred task or interest. Additionally, there will be many times

Figure 10.5 Positively Stated Rules with Rationales

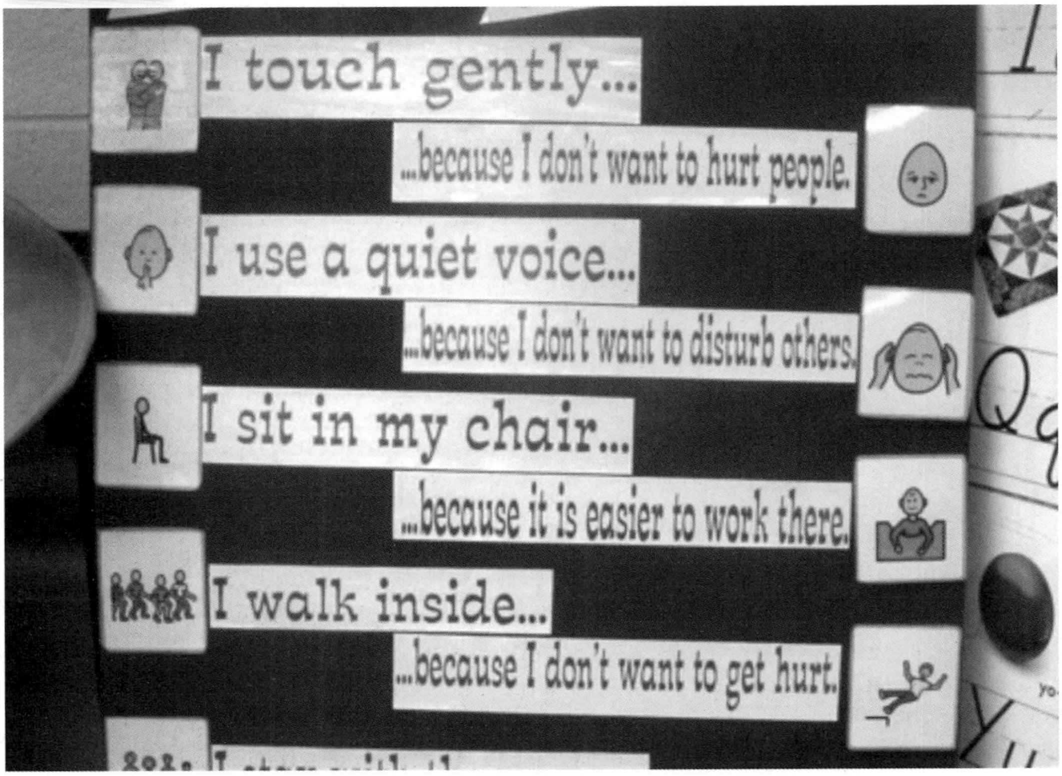

when including a student's particular interest into the instruction of a nonpreferred subject or task will assist him in understanding and increase motivation to learn the nonpreferred task or subject. For example, if a student with ASD does not enjoy word problems in math but he loves trains, writing word problems dealing with trains may make word problems more palatable and interesting to him.

For some students including a visual schedule or using first/then is not enough as the task that they are being asked to do does not have a clear ending or is too difficult for them to attend to for long periods of time. In this case, breaking the task down into smaller portions will help them achieve success. This may involve a schedule within a schedule. For example, with early elementary students, calendar time may not have a clear enough beginning and ending for students with ASD. If this activity is not something they enjoy, it may be difficult for them to sit and attend without understanding how long they are expected to sit and attend. Therefore, visually breaking calendar time down into its individual sections and allowing the student to follow along and either physically or mentally check off each section will help them sit and attend throughout calendar time. For older students, the use of a PowerPoint or guided notes will help them understand how long a lecture will last. Guided notes are often better than simply having a PowerPoint, because it encourages students to attend and fill in the notes as the teacher lectures. Students with ASD may need a difficult task broken down into more manageable components. Some students also may need to earn tokens or points for completing a certain portion of their tasks. Once they have earned a certain number of tokens or points, they can earn time to spend doing a preferred activity.

Another way to break the schedule down so that students understand beginning and ending of work time in an activity involves the use of the timer. When students are engaged in a nonpreferred task, the ding of a timer can be a welcome relief. Note that for some students with ASD, task completion itself is essential for them to be able to transition to another task regardless of the ding of a timer—they may not want to stop working if the task is not finished. If this is the case, the teacher may need to manipulate the timer so that it matches a student's completion or the teacher may need to break the student's work down into even smaller components. For preferred activities, the timer is often a necessary cue to let the student know that it is time to go back to work. The timer is often a more palatable cue for the student than a teacher letting the student know that it is once again work time. This also keeps the student from getting mad at the teacher for telling him his preferred task is over. Instead, the enjoyment is finished simply because "the timer went off." This also lessens power struggles between students and teachers when it comes to beginning work. However, a verbal warning from the teacher that time is almost over during a preferred task is often necessary to assist the student in transitioning from his preferred task to his nonpreferred task.

Strategies to Address Social Skills

Another one of the core characteristics of ASD includes deficits in socialization. Therefore, it is critical that social skills goals are included in Individualized Education Plans (IEPs) and specifically taught to individuals with ASD. Social skills interventions are used to instruct students to engage in the necessary social interaction to develop and maintain relationships with others (Cappadocia & Weiss, 2010). Many social skills strategies have been used effectively to teach individuals with ASD. According to a recent meta analysis on social skills instruction for individuals with ASD, the most notable social improvements and generalization of skills occur when the intervention dosage is high, the instruction is provided in the child's natural setting, and the intervention strategy is determined based on the individual student's deficit areas and needs (Bellini, Petters, Benner, & Hoph, 2007). Some of the most common and research-based social skills interventions include peer mediated interventions, social skills instruction, script fading procedures, pivotal response training, video modeling, and strategies that include reinforcement for evoking instructed social skills, as well as a combination of those strategies.

Peer mediated interventions involve selecting and teaching the typically developing peers in the class to instruct and facilitate social interaction of the children with ASD (Hundert & Houghton, 1992). Social skills instruction consists of directly teaching specific social skills to a small group of children. Sometimes the groups have children with and without ASD in them so the students with ASD have appropriate models in the group. Other social skills groups involve teaching only individuals with social deficits. Within the social skills group, effectiveness is determined based on the learning and demonstration of the specific skills taught (Flyn & Healey, 2012). In the school setting, social skills groups often take place during lunch time with a teacher instructing and facilitating the skills group while the students participate and eat their lunches, which is a natural time to display social skills.

Script fading procedures involve teaching the student with ASD to follow a particular social script such as that involved in greeting peers, then fading the prompt of the script. With script fading, it is important for the student also to be taught how to respond if her peer does not respond according to the script. Often peer mediation is initially included within script fading so that peers are instructed to respond in a predictable manner. Pivotal Response Training (PRT) is a technique used to teach students with ASD key social skills that then generalize to other social skills. Peer mediation is often a feature of PRT in that typically developing students assist their peer with ASD in attending to and maintaining social interactions such as gaining and maintaining attention, exchanging communication, taking turns, and so forth (Koegel, Vernon, & Koegel, 2009).

Video modeling involves showing a videotape of a person or a group of people demonstrating the target social skill to the individual with ASD. Teachers often create their own videos utilizing typically developing peers in the classroom to tailor social skills instruction for the individual with ASD. Additionally, prepackaged programs are available. For example, *Story Movies* is a video modeling program that has taken the popular strategy of Social Stories™ and has turned it into video modeling (Lindblad, 2006). Social Stories teach social concepts via a teacher-created story to address the student's particular social need. Although it is a popular strategy due to its ease of use, most of the supporting research comes from single-case and case study methodology, showing it to be promising but requiring more research to determine efficacy. **Figure 10.6** contains the text from a Social Story to help a student understand why he cannot always be first in line. Social Stories also typically contain illustrations (e.g., photos, line drawings, student-generated art).

Finally, reinforcement-based procedures, often involving a treatment package that consists of any or all of the strategies of direct instruction, self-management, and prompting procedures paired with reinforcement, have been found to be effective to teaching specific social skills (Flyn & Healey, 2012).

Although social skills instruction is paramount for students with ASD, teachers have increasing demands to be sure that they are meeting all of the core academic standards and they often struggle with determining a time in the school day to teach social skills. The most generalizable skills are taught in naturalistic settings. As mentioned earlier, lunch is a natural social time in which social skills instruction can be taught. Additionally center time or recess (during preschool and elementary years) is a natural time for students to learn and practice social skills. As students become older, social skills can be taught and reinforced during cooperative learning groups. Some students with ASD are provided with the academic work that they will practice during cooperative learning groups the day prior to the group activity.

| Figure 10.6 | Social Story to Promote Understanding of a Social Convention |

Since a group of people have to take turns, they need to stand in a line.

People stand in line at the grocery store to wait for their turn to buy food and other things they need.

People stand in line at the movie theatre to wait their turn to buy a ticket and go inside.

When my Dad took me to the Monster Truck Rally, we had to stand in line to wait to have our tickets checked to go inside. I like Tom Meents. His truck, Maximum Destruction, is AWESOME!

I stand in line at school, too. We walk in lines to go to the cafeteria, to the gym, and to other places in the school building.

One student gets to be the first in a line, and another person gets to be the last in the line. Everyone else is in a line between the first and last person. That is why it is called a "line."

I really like to be first in line. Other students like to be the first in line, too. It would not be fair if the same kid was first in line every time.

Our teacher lets us take turns being the first in line. That way everybody gets a chance to be first, last, and somewhere in between.

It does not matter if I am the first student in line, the last student in line, or somewhere in between. We will all get to where we're going!

Just like all the kids in my class, I will get a turn to be first in line. It is OK when it is not my turn to be first in line. I will stand somewhere else in the line, maybe a different place every day. That will be fun!

They complete the assignment as homework so that they can simply focus on practicing specific social skills during the cooperative learning group activity rather than try to focus on social skills and content. Additionally, in the upper grades, the instruction of social and study skills has become content for an elective or required course for all students. Furthermore, in the upper grades, there are extracurricular clubs and activities that may be of particular interest to students with ASD in which their social skills also can be practiced. There is no correct or incorrect time to teach social skills as long as they are taught. Teachers have been and continue to be creative in their approaches to teaching these skills and most teachers find that teaching and reinforcing social skills is important for all of their students and not just those with ASD.

Strategies to Address Communication

Another characteristic of those with ASD is a deficit or difference in communication. Communication includes both receptive language and expressive language. Receptive language is what is understood and expressive language is produced. For those with ASD who struggle receptively, using sign language and picture cues can provide another modality to help them understand speech. However, much of what is communicated often does not involve speech. The vast majority of the messages we send when we communicate relates to para- and nonverbal communication in the form of grunts, intonations, facial expressions, and body language (Mehrabian, 1981). Understanding information conveyed by gestures, intonation, expressions, and so forth falls under the category of pragmatic language, which can be taught using some of the strategies mentioned in the previous section. Teaching students with ASD to appropriately use and understand facial expressions and body language is an important pragmatic skill. Additionally, helping students understand meaning in language depending upon intonation is a basis for helping them understand meaning in language. Take for example the following sentences. Each sentence contains exactly the same words, but the meaning conveyed is very different depending on which word is stressed.

> **_I_** *didn't say she was late.* (meaning someone else said it)
> *I **_didn't_** say she was late.* (meaning she was not late)
> *I didn't **_say_** she was late.* (but it was implied)
> *I didn't say **_she_** was late.* (meaning someone else was late)
> *I didn't say she was **_late_**.* (meaning she was something other than late)

Individuals with ASD may hear the five words exactly the same in each sentence, or at least the fact that one word is stressed will not convey the same message to them that it does to someone who is neurotypical.

Likewise when communicating, people often use stress on words to express sarcasm. Sarcasm is particularly difficult for individuals with ASD to understand. Often teachers find it funny to use sarcasm or rhetorical questions with students. Sarcasm not only makes victims out of students but the meaning is most often completely lost of those with ASD. For example, if someone sarcastically says, *"Oh don't you look nice today,"* individuals with ASD will reply *"Thank you"* rather than realize that someone was being rude. Social autopsies, or an adult breaking down and reviewing a social situation by pointing out relevant aspects, have been successfully used with some individuals with ASD to teach them to understand sarcasm; however, this continues to be a difficult receptive pragmatic skill for those with ASD to comprehend. To expand further, individuals with ASD are very literal in their understanding of language. We often speak in idioms, which can be quite confusing for those with ASD. Teachers use phrases such as "all eyes on me" and "hop to it." When we really think about those words, we should not be surprised when one of our students with ASD either looks puzzled or tries to follow the directions. Our world is fraught with idioms so teachers should not completely stop using them. However, teachers must be careful to make sure that students with ASD understand what is meant by the idioms.

Some students with ASD not only struggle with receptive language, but many also struggle to express speech. Some use idiosyncratic speech in a sing-song sounding way and some demonstrate immediate and/or delayed echolalia, often from favorite television shows or movies. However, it may be difficult for them to respond verbally to simple questions. In order to teach speech, it is often necessary for students with ASD to first understand the social reciprocity or give and take of speech. This means that students must first learn the power of their speech. Many individuals with ASD can produce the speech, but they struggle with the social issues around the speech, and are not motivated to speak. In order to facilitate speech production in children with ASD, several strategies have proven successful. Picture Exchange Communication system (PECS), sign language, and augmentative/assistive devices have the most research support. Some teachers and speech-language pathologists use all of these strategies together along with a speech model to facilitate speech/communication. This combination is termed a **total communication approach**. Some parents have expressed concerns that if their nonverbal or minimally verbal children with ASD uses any of the approaches in total communication, their children will not learn to speak. This has not proven to be the case. In fact, rather than hinder speech, using other approaches teaches the give and take of language that encourages speech production.

One of the unique features of PECS is that it teaches children with ASD a means of communicating within a social context (Bondy & Frost, 1994). When using PECS the student actually exchanges or hands a communication partner a picture. There are six phases in PECS. The only prerequisite to beginning PECS is knowledge of what a student really likes.

If the teacher does not know what the student likes, this can be determined by placing an array of objects on a table and observing what the student picks up and either plays with or eats. Once the teacher knows what the student wants, the desired item is placed in front of the student. In Phase I of PECS, it is best if two people can work with the student, one in front of and one behind the student. When the student reaches for the object, the person behind the student places a card with a picture that resembles the object in the student's hand, and then guides the student to hand the card to the person in front of him. This is done to teach the student the act of the exchange. Once the person has been given the card, she immediately provides the student with the object and says something like, *"Oh, you want the cookie? Here it is!"* acting as if the student verbalized his request for a cookie rather than exchanged a card. This begins the process of teaching a student how to request his wants or needs. Receipt of the desired object reinforces and teaches the student that his communication with others earns him his requests. Phase I is continued until the student can pick a card up off a table and hand it to the teacher without assistance from anyone behind that student and without any cues from the teacher in front of him. In Phase II, the student learns to communicate with the teacher when neither the teacher nor the picture card is directly in front of him, forcing him to be more persistent in communicative attempts with the teacher. By moving the picture card farther away from the student, the teacher is teaching the student to spontaneously request. During Phase III, the student is taught to discriminate between two or more pictures. During Phase IV of PECS, the student begins working on sentence structure to ask for his desires. During Phase V, the student is taught to respond directly to the question *"What do you want?"* and by the end of Phase V, the student can spontaneously request desired objects or actions, and answer questions throughout daily activities. In Phase VI, the student is taught to label items and actions. The trainer teaches the student to use the sentence *"I see"* to label items in his environment. One of the benefits of PECS is that the majority of students either develop speech as their sole form of communication or use a combination of speech and pictures (Bondy & Frost, 1994).

Another technique used to teach communication to individuals with ASD who are either nonverbal or minimally verbal is sign language. One of the pros to using sign language is that students always have their means of communication with them. One of the cons is that many of the signs used by students are approximations and those who do not understand those approximations will not understand the communicative attempts made by the student with ASD. Kostantareas and Leibovitz (as cited in Toth, 2009) suggest that sign language increases the spontaneity of speech as well as signs as students learn to speak.

Various types of assistive devices also have been used to help facilitate speech in students with ASD. One caveat to using an augmentative communication device is that there is not a physical exchange and oftentimes the student becomes more focused on the computerized output of the device than the communication opportunities it provides. However, when devices are individualized according to the student's needs, they can provide a purposeful and functional means of communication for individuals with ASD.

Sensory Needs

Although sensory differences have not been listed in definitions of autism, including the criteria found in DSM-IV, individuals with ASD have been very forthcoming about their challenges with sensory stimuli. Some individuals with ASD have discussed their sensory perceptions in terms of too much stimulation or insufficient stimulation. Some have expressed their difficulty processing information when in noisy environments. Others are hypersensitive or hyposensitive to tactile stimulation. This is often witnessed by teachers who state that their students cannot stand to get anything on their hands or others who state that their students are constantly using their hands to explore their surroundings. Some are sensitive to the textures that they eat and some put everything in their mouths whether edible or not. Some are bothered when they are lightly touched, especially when they cannot see to anticipate the touch, such as someone touching them from behind. They express that a firm touch is less aversive than a very light touch. Some also are bothered by seams or tags in clothing or even clothing that is made out of certain materials.

Individuals with ASD have explained that many of these sensory stimuli are actually painful to them—making it almost impossible to concentrate on what they should be learning. It is notable that although individuals with ASD express differences in sensory sensations, the sensory challenges are unique to the individual. Therefore, the classroom teacher must become knowledgeable about the individual sensory needs of the students with ASD in her classroom and help adjust the environment as much as possible to help them process information and learn. For example, if florescent lights are painful to students with ASD, being placed in a classroom with natural lighting can help reduce the intrusive stimuli. Even changing out the bulbs frequently can cut down on the flicker. If that is not possible, dimming the lights and using lamps or even allowing the student to take a break away from the lights to regroup will be helpful. Likewise, if noisy environments lead to agitation in students with ASD, then providing more support such as headphones with music to drown out the noise during the bus ride, PE, and lunch may allow them to better handle the noise. Being aware of students' sensory needs will help teachers be creative in coming up with ways to support the students throughout the school day. This also lessens the anxiety that many individuals with ASD express when it comes to the school environment.

Aberrant Behavior

Some students with ASD develop inappropriate behaviors that interfere with their learning and the learning of others. Termed aberrant behavior, many of the behaviors are due to overstimulation, miscommunication, or lack of functional communication. Therefore, many of the strategies discussed previously in this chapter are proactive strategies to keep aberrant behaviors from occurring in the classroom. However, if a student with ASD engages in aberrant behaviors, it will be important to define the behavior then document what is occurring before the behavior and after the behavior. This will help determine why the behavior is occurring. All behavior serves some sort of a function. If the student is in an aversive environment or situation, the behavior may serve the function of helping him escape that environment. It may also serve the function of gaining attention from the teacher or other students or the function of obtaining a desired object or activity. Once the teacher can determine the function of the aberrant behavior, she can begin to teach a replacement behavior that is appropriate while serving that same function. A mistake would be to jump straight to administering a consequence without first trying to understand why the behavior occurs. For example, many teachers have the standard consequence of time out regardless of the behavior or the reason for the behavior. Yet if the child is engaging in aberrant behavior in order to escape an undesirable activity, then timeout will actually increase the likelihood that the aberrant behavior will be displayed again in another situation. If the teacher cannot determine the function of the behavior, most school systems have behavior specialists who can come in and help determine the function of the behavior to develop a positive behavior support plan for the student. For teachers, it is important to note that students with ASD are typically not engaging in behaviors to be obstinate; they are just getting some need met and teachers need to try and teach them more acceptable ways of getting those needs met. Chapter 9 contains a description of the process used to determine behavioral function and use that information to develop a behavior intervention plan. The message here is that teachers always need to consider the messages being communicated via behavior, even aberrant behavior, before they attempt to intervene.

Sometimes aberrant behaviors communicate that the student has become so overwhelmed that she has lost control. Given the impact of sensory processing problems, coupled with a lack of understanding of what is happening or will happen, students with ASD become **dysregulated**. They become so overwhelmed that they lose control of their behavior. It is critical to note that this loss of control is not a choice the student is making—the student is not being willful. For this reason, one of the most important concepts students with ASD need to learn is that of **emotional self-regulation** (Bieberich, & Morgan, 2004). Individuals who are neurotypical tend to learn to keep their cool and calm themselves down by observing others or by hearing about how others stay regulated. Individuals with ASD will need to be explicitly taught these essential skills. In order to stay emotionally regulated, they need to be taught how to identify the signs that they are becoming dysregulated (e.g., clenching fists, feels like head will explode), and learn to label those signs as emotions. Once students with ASD can label their emotions, they can be taught to tell an adult how they are feeling, and work with the adult to develop strategies to manage those feelings before they become overpowering. **Figure 10.7** contains a simple visual cue to help a student functioning on the low end of the autism spectrum recognize when he is getting angry. Notice that the clipboard contains a smaller icon depicting frustration that the student can remove and give to a staff member who will then take him to a quieter area to calm down.

For a student functioning on the higher end of the autism spectrum, but who had difficulty recognizing the appropriateness of his own behavior, a teacher created a 1 to 5 rating system, and associated the ratings with stoplight colors. The teacher took the rating system and made a portable ring with each behavior on a slip of paper (see **Figure 10.8**). Two types of the behavior (i.e., informal social behaviors and responsible behaviors) were acceptable

Figure 10.7   Simple Visual Cue for Recognizing Anger

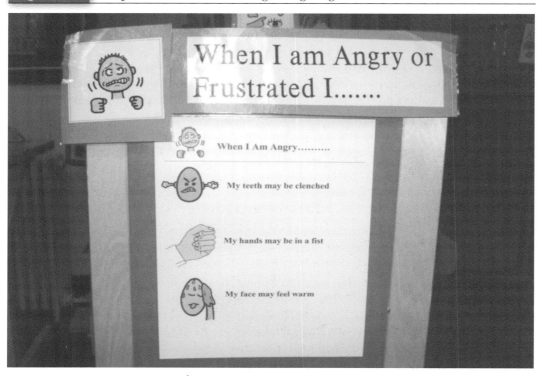

Figure 10.8 Portable Ring of Behavior Ratings and Suggested Actions

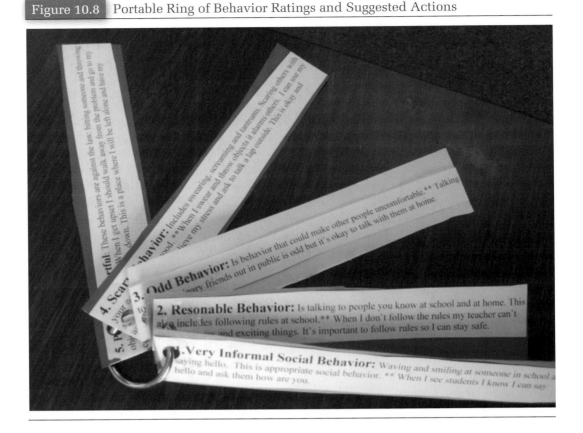

in all situations and so were pasted on green paper. One type of behavior (i.e., odd) bordered on unacceptable and was pasted on yellow, the color of warnings and caution. Two types of behavior (i.e., scary and physically harmful) were never appropriate and so were pasted onto red paper. Each piece of red paper also contained directions that would enable the student to calm down. For "scary" behavior, the student was directed to use a stress ball and ask to take a lap outside. For "harmful" behavior, the student was directed to walk away from the problem and go to his comfortable place to calm down. The comfortable place had been established in advance. When the teacher observed the student behaving in ways consistent with the ratings, she gave the student feedback by calling out the numeral associated with the behavior (e.g., *"Nice 1!"* or *"4"*). This prompted the student to look at the behavior ring to mentally register his behavior and follow directions if the number was a 4 or 5.

Additional Issues for the Classroom Teacher

Classroom teachers may become involved in the controversy surrounding differing opinions regarding the best method to educate persons with ASD. A number of options are available and all have been found to be successful with at least a few students with ASD. For school systems, the choice of intervention approaches must be made according to which approach has a substantial research base (NRC, 2001). Some approaches, such as the one promoted by Ivar Lovaas at UCLA, require intensive one-on-one instruction using specially trained persons over a long period of time (Lovaas, 1987) and are therefore difficult to implement in school settings (Chambliss & Doughty, 1994). In addition, the one-on-one therapy is not compatible with the trend toward inclusive education. Other approaches incorporate techniques that make exaggerated claims about their effectiveness, yet have not been proven effective (Shute, 2010; Warren et al., 2011). Educators need to be aware of current fads in the treatment of ASD so that they do not seem uninformed when parents request a particular intervention. However, researchers support that the most effective programs are those that involve the family in the development of an individually tailored plan providing systematic instruction within structured environments that take a functional approach to addressing problem behavior (Iovannone, Dunlap, Huber, & Kincaid, 2003). School programs need to incorporate relevant curricula which include functional academics, vocational preparation, and the explicit teaching of necessary life skills (Berkell, 2005).

Developing IEP goals and objectives that are individualized for students with ASD is critical. Students with ASD need to have an IEP written for them which emphasizes their greatest areas of need: communication and socialization. Unfortunately, this clarity of need often is clouded when IEP teams focus on the student's "splinter skills." Splinter skills are defined as those skills that seem to indicate specific areas of competence or ability. For example, it is not uncommon for students with autism to demonstrate hyperlexia, the ability to decode any print material. Students with hyperlexia can read aloud almost anything that is placed in front of them and can usually spell and reproduce words, even difficult words. However, this is a splinter skill. The students have no comprehension of what they are reading and writing. The tendency is then for IEP teams to capitalize on this special skill in writing goals and objectives. It is not unusual to see a goal written that an 8-year-old child will improve his decoding ability from the 11th to the 12th grade level. This is unfortunate as such a goal ignores the student's more pressing needs: the ability to initiate interactions, the ability to communicate needs and wants, and even the ability to demonstrate comprehension at the first grade level. A very real issue for classroom teachers is how to promote the writing of chronologically age-appropriate goals and objectives that focus on communication and socialization (the two major deficit areas in autism) when others on the IEP team may be wanting to place the child in algebra or calculus.

With awareness of the neurological differences underlying ASD, and the ability to extract implications for instruction from that knowledge, classroom teachers will be better prepared to promote positive outcomes for their students with ASD. As mentioned at the beginning of this chapter, being prepared to educate students with ASD is important since the number of students being identified with ASD has increased dramatically in the last decade, with no indication that the trend is slowing.

Figure 10.9   Case Study of a Student with ASD

Similar to most parents of children with ASD, Mr. and Ms. Murrillo knew that something was "wrong" with Ian during his infancy. His mother described him as a "good" baby, in fact almost too good. He rarely cried unless he was hungry, and they couldn't believe their luck when he slept through the night almost as soon as they brought him home. When Ian was about 6 months old, Mr. Murrillo reported that he realized Ian wasn't actually sleeping through the night. Surprised to find him awake, Mr. Murrillo discovered that Ian was lying in his crib staring at the moving ceiling fan illuminated by the night light. Ms. Murrillo reported that Ian's comfort object was his father's calculator, rather than a blanket or stuffed animal. Ian would not go to sleep unless he was holding the calculator. But it wasn't until Ian failed to start talking that his parents became really concerned. After examining Ian, their pediatrician said that he was fine and probably wasn't talking because of the older sister in the home who did most of his talking for him.

Ian's parents felt much better the day Ian started talking when he was almost 4 years old. They were so relieved that he was talking that it didn't really register to them that he was talking in complete sentences. Nor did they pay much attention to the fact that he would talk only about cars. In fact, Mr. Murrillo encouraged the topic by buying books about cars, watching TV shows about cars and trucks with Ian, and taking Ian to car shows. Ian was reading the books by himself when he was 5 years old. Their friends were impressed that Ian knew so much about cars, and he frequently engaged in lively conversations with the adults about cars. No one noticed that he never talked to children his own age about cars, or about anything else for that matter. The family quickly learned to avoid Ian's often violent meltdowns by sticking to a tight routine (e.g., frozen waffles for breakfast, dinner at 6 P.M. sharp, bath without bubbles at 8:30). However, the day-care centers Ian attended couldn't be as regimented, and he was kicked out of one after another with the staff complaining that Ian was inflexible and explosive. His parents breathed a sigh of relief when he started kindergarten, believing that the school staff would be better trained and able to handle Ian. Unfortunately, he continued to demand that the schedule and peers' behavior comply with his expectations and raged against whoever did not conform. Subsequently, Ian spent much of his school day in an administrator's office. In desperation, his parents took Ian to a psychiatrist who diagnosed him with Oppositional-Defiant Disorder (ODD) and started him on risperdal. The medication seemed to take the edge off things for Ian, and he did much better in school as the structure increased in environment and curricula with each passing grade.

Early in his fourth grade year, Ian's language arts teacher, Ms. Watiu, emailed Ms. Murrillo to let her know that Ian had changed the settings on her computer. When Ms. Watiu asked the class who had changed the settings, a smiling Ian raised his hand. He then looked horribly confused and upset when Ms. Watiu reprimanded him. Ms. Watiu said she was emailing Ms. Murrillo to let her know that Ian was still upset when he left school.

When Ian got home, Ms. Murrillo told him she had received the email from Ms. Watiu and asked him why he changed the settings on her computer. Ian again looked confused and said that Steve told him that Ms. Watiu would think it was funny if he changed the computer settings. Ian was obviously upset that the outcome had not been what he was led to believe would happen. Ms. Murrillo told Ian he should never change someone else's computer settings without permission and made an appointment to talk to Ms. Watiu the next afternoon. At their meeting, Ms. Murrillo told Ms. Watiu what Ian had said. Ms. Watiu said she did not doubt Ian's explanation and reported being surprised the previous day when she saw Steve and Ian talking as Ian rarely spoke to any of the students in class. Ms. Murrillo's dismay to learn that Ian did not talk to his peers (when he was so chatty at home) worsened as Ms. Watiu explained how she knew Ian was honest. During the first week of school, Ms. Watiu described how she had run to the office for a minute and left the class with specific instructions to keep working quietly. When she returned to the room, Ian raised his hand and named all the students who had left their seats in her absence and told exactly what each student did. Naturally, the other students were irritated by Ian's telling, but Ian seemed more satisfied that order had been restored to the classroom than upset by his peers' chagrin. Since that time, Ms. Watiu said she always left Ian "in charge" if she had to leave the room. She knew he was an accurate reporter and also very honest because one day he told her that a particular outfit made her look fat.

Although pleased that Ms. Watiu viewed Ian as honest and dependable, Ms. Murrillo was devastated that Ian apparently had no friends and was seen as the class narc. He also appeared to be unable to discern when his peers were lying to him. Ms. Watiu asked the school counselor to come to her room while Ms. Murrillo was still there so the three of them could talk about Ian's social concerns. The counselor had spoken to Ian numerous times because of their shared interest in cars and so was able to reflect that Ian was much less socially competent than other boys his age. His affect was unusual, and he got confused when the counselor used metaphors and idioms. The counselor remembered asking Ian about a trip to the stock car races, and Ian had reported statistics to him but could not tell him about the experience or if he enjoyed the trip. When the counselor gave an example of something else Ian had trouble comprehending, Ms. Watiu remarked that Ian had started struggling with the comprehension of the stories they were reading in class. She knew he could read well above the fourth grade level but said his comprehension abilities were similar to those of a child in second grade unless the topic was cars. Then his extensive background on the topic helped support his comprehension. His problems with comprehension were beginning to affect his grades, and Ms. Watiu urged Ms. Murrillo to keep on eye on the papers that were sent home.

A troubled Ms. Murrillo took the information home to her husband. They realized that there was something more than ODD affecting Ian. Together they wrote a request for a full special education assessment. By submitting a written request for assessment, parents can circumvent the need to complete the full RTI process. A multidisciplinary team was assembled that included a school psychologist, the counselor who knew Ian well, a speech-language pathologist to evaluate pragmatic language, and an occupational therapist to consider his almost illegible handwriting, lack of coordination, and unusual reactions to sensory stimuli. Ms. Watiu and the parents completed the team. In addition to using standardized assessments, the speech-language pathologist also observed Ian interacting with his peers in the classroom and in the cafeteria. After interacting with Ian to evaluate his intelligence, the school psychologist asked that he be allowed to invite the autism specialist for the district to join the team. The rest of the team, including the Murrillos, agreed. The autism specialist interviewed the Murrillos to get a complete developmental history and then had the parents and a few of Ian's teachers complete screening instruments to check for autism and Asperger syndrome.

Based on the results of the comprehensive assessments, the team decided that Ian met the eligibility criteria for an autism spectrum disorder. They wrote several goals targeting Ian's comprehension, social skills, and pragmatic language ability. Ian stayed in his general education settings for most of the school day but received pull-out services to get specialized instruction in study and organizational skills, reading and listening comprehension, and pragmatic language skills. His general education teachers were given specific strategies to use that included more visual supports and longer processing times. Ian joined a social skills group conducted by the counselor that met three times a week. The social skills training included lessons to teach Ian to learn how to monitor and regulate his own behavior. The Murrillos realize that Ian will always struggle to fit into social situations, but they are confident that his intelligence and his sustained interest in certain topics will allow him to find a job and be self-sufficient.

Summary

Having a student with ASD in the classroom can be a tremendously rewarding experience as these students challenge individuals without ASD to consider the world from a different perspective. Given the increasing prevalence of ASD, the chances are high that every teacher will work with several students with ASD during their careers. Remembering to focus on structure, routine, predictability, and clear visual signals will help all students, not just those who meet the eligibility requirements for ASD. Emphasizing effective communication and appropriate socialization also will be important for all students and will facilitate their post-school independence and self-determination.

Post-school outcomes for persons with ASD once were described as extremely poor, as the majority of adults with autism were unable to live independently or productively and required residential care. This outlook has changed considerably due to more appropriate school programming and a heightened awareness of the needs of individuals with ASD. Programs that emphasize the acquisition of useful skills in the vocational, recreational, and social realms and the provision of supported employment opportunities have demonstrated positive outcomes for adults with ASD (Smith, 1995). Individuals functioning at the higher end of the autism spectrum tend to readily acquire the knowledge and skills necessary to do a job. However, these individuals are notoriously underemployed and unemployed because their social and communication deficits affect their ability to maintain a job (Lewis, Woodyatt, & Murdoch, 2008). For example, these individuals need to be taught that it is inappropriate to tell their bosses, *That's a stupid idea*. Although the idea may be stupid, employees tend to get fired for that type of comment. Providing instruction that facilitates academic achievement while emphasizing development of social and communication skills will generate the best prognosis for personal and professional success among individuals with ASD. **Figure 10.9** presents a case study of a student with ASD.

Classroom Application Activities

1. Interview the parents of a child or adolescent with an ASD. Solicit information in the following categories. The * is where you would use the child's name. Please be advised that parents of young children and parents of children with severe impairments may not want to talk about D (Future); please do not press them.

    A. Development and Awareness
        Tell me about *'s developmental history.
        When/how did you know you had a child with special needs?
        Was the diagnosis a surprise for you?
        Tell me about how the diagnosis affected you.
        How did you tell other family members about *'s diagnosis?
        How did they react?
        What did you think about their reactions?

    B. Daily Life
        How does * communicate with you?
        Tell me about unique behaviors that * might have.
        What do you like most about *?
        In what activities or hobbies does * like to engage?
        What and who does * like to play with?
        How many siblings are there?
        Do any of the siblings have special needs? If so, please describe.
        How do the siblings get along together?
        Describe the following daily activities:

            Getting ready for school
            Weekends
            Mealtime
            Bedtime
            Vacation
            Community involvement

        Tell me about any particular routines or preferences * might have.
        How do you prepare for changes in *'s routine (for example, guests in the home, medical appointments)?
        What kinds of things are helpful for *?
        How do people react when they met * for the first time?
        When do you get a break? What do you do to relax?
        Where do you go for outside help?
        Tell me about experiences with baby sitters.

    C. Education
        Tell me about your child's educational experiences.
        What kind of different interventions have you tried?
        If you could create the perfect teacher, describe that teacher?
        What do you think about the current special education laws?

    D. Future
        What expectations and hopes do you have for your child?
        If you could no longer care for *, what would happen?

2. Create a single-page handout that you could give to teachers and administrators in a school setting that would help them understand how neurological differences affect the way individuals with ASD react to and interact with the world.

3. Individually or in groups, identify two behaviors that a teacher might see in the classroom related to students with ASD. Describe implications specific to these behaviors.

4. Individually or in groups, describe three characteristics of a student with ASD and give two critical components that will support the student's learning in your classroom.

5. Interview a general education teacher in your preferred content area (e.g., secondary biology, elementary art, early childhood) and ask about accommodations that are used for students with ASD.

6. Obtain a copy of the most current edition of the *Diagnostic and Statistical Manual of Mental Disorders* published by the American Psychiatric Association (available in most libraries). For each of the criteria listed for autism, identify which aspect of neurology might be involved. Discuss how the criteria may differ by age and severity of functioning.

7. Locate an adult who has ASD. If you do not already know someone with ASD, you can ask your instructor for recommendations or go through a local agency supporting individuals with ASD (e.g., local chapter of the Autism Society of America). Interview the adult to find out where the individual works and the types of things that person does for fun. Ask about experiences in school and find out who the favorite teacher was and why.

8. Go to the website for the Autism Society of America (www.autism-society.org) and find what services and resources are available in your state and the city where you live.

Internet Resources

ABA Educational Resources
www.abaresources.com

Autism Network
www.autismnetwork.org

Autism Services Center
www.autismservicescenter.org

Autism Society of America
www.autism-society.org

Autism Speaks
http://www.autismspeaks.org

Autism Spot
www.AutismSpot.com

Division TEACCH
(Treatment and Education of Autistic and related Communication-handicapped Children)
www.teacch.com

Ohio Center for Autism and Low Incidence
http://www.ocali.org

Teacher Resources
www.do2learn.com

References

Amaral, D.G., Schumann, C., & Nordahl, C. (2008). Neuroanatomy of autism. *Trends in Neurosciences, 31,* 137–145.

Amr, M., Raddad, D., El-Mehesh, F., Bakr, A., Sallam, K., & Amin, T. (2012). Comorbid psychiatric disorders in Arab children with autism spectrum disorders. *Research in Autism Spectrum Disorders, 6,* 240–248.

American Academy of Pediatrics. (2008). *Facts for parents about autism and vaccine safety: From the American Academy of Pediatrics (AAP).* Elk Grove Village, IL: Author.

American Psychiatric Association. (2000). *Diagnostic and statistical manual of mental disorders* (4th ed., text revision). Washington, DC: Author.

Bachevalier, J. (1991). An animal model for childhood autism: Memory loss and socioemotional disturbances following neonatal damage to the limbic system in monkeys. In C.A. Tamminga & S.C. Schultz (Eds.), *Advances in neuropsychiatry and psychopharmacology: Schizophrenia research* (pp. 129–140). New York: Raven Press.

Bachevalier, J. (1994). The contribution of medial temporal lobe structures in infantile autism: A neurobehavioral study in primates. In M.L. Bauman & T.L. Kemper (Eds.), *The neurobiology of autism* (pp. 146–169). Baltimore, MD: Johns Hopkins University Press.

Bachevalier, J., & Vargha-Khadem, F. (2005). The primate hippocampus: Ontogeny, early insult and memory. *Current Opinion in Neurobiology, 15,* 168–174.

Baio, J. (2012). Prevalence of autism spectrum disorders: Autism and developmental disabilities monitoring network, 14 Sites, United States, 2008. *Morbidity and Mortality Weekly Report (MMWR), 61*(SS03), 1–19.

Bakke, B.L. (1990). *Self-injury: Answers to questions for parents, teachers, and caregivers.* Minneapolis, MN: Minnesota University Institute for Disabilities Studies.

Baranek, G.T. (1999). Autism during infancy: A retrospective video analysis of sensory-motor and social behaviors at 9–12 months of age. *Journal of Autism and Developmental Disorders, 29,* 213–224.

Baumeister, A.A. (1991). Expanded theories of stereotype and self-injurious responding: Commentary on "Emergence and maintenance of stereotype and self-injury." *American Journal on Mental Retardation, 96,* 321–323.

Bellini, S., Peters, J.K., Benner, L., & Hoph, A. (2007). A meta-analysis of school-based social skills interventions for children with autism spectrum disorders. *Remedial and Special Education, 28,* 153–162.

Berkell, D.E. (2005). *Autism: Identification, education, and treatment.* (2nd ed.) Hillsdale, NJ: Erlbaum.

Bettleheim, B. (1967). *The empty fortress: Infantile autism and the birth of the self.* New York: Free Press.

Bieberich, A.A., & Morgan, S.B. (2004). Self-regulation and affective expression during play in children with autism or Down syndrome: A short-term longitudinal study. *Journal of Autism and Developmental Disorders, 34*, 439–448.

Bishop, D.M., Whitehouse, A.O., Watt, H.J., & Line, E.A. (2008). Autism and diagnostic substitution: Evidence from a study of adults with a history of developmental language disorder. *Developmental Medicine & Child Neurology, 50*, 341–345.

Bondy, A.S., & Frost L.A. (1994). The picture exchange communication system. *Focus on Autistic Behavior, 9*(3), 1–19.

Caglayan, A.O. (2010). Genetic causes of syndromic and non-syndromic autism. *Developmental Medicine and Child Neurology, 52*, 130–138.

Cappadocia, M.C., & Weiss, J.A. (2010). Review of social skills training groups for youth with Asperger syndrome and high functioning autism. *Research in Autism Spectrum Disorders, 5*, 70–78.

Cataldo, M.R., & Harris, J. (1982). The biological basis for self-injury in the mentally retarded. *Analysis and Intervention in Developmental Disabilities, 2*, 21–40.

Chambliss, C., & Doughty, R.J. (1994). *Parental response to Lovaas treatment of childhood autism.* Paper presented at the 9th Annual University of Scranton Psychology Conference, Scranton, PA. (ERIC Document Reproduction Service No. ED 370 340.)

Chess, S., & Thomas, A. (1987). *Origins and evolution of behavior disorders: From infancy to early adult life.* Cambridge, MA: Harvard University Press.

Courchesne, E., Saitoh, O., Yeung-Courchesne, R., Press, G., Lincoln, A., Haas, R., & Schreibman, L. (1994). Abnormality of cerebellar vermian lobules VI and VII in patients with infantile autism: Identification of hypoplastic and hyperplastic subgroups with MR imaging. *American Journal of Roentgenology, 162*, 123–130.

Dawson, G., Osterling, J., Meltzoff, A., & Kuhl, P. (2000). Case study of the development of an infant with autism from birth to 2 years of age. *Journal of Applied Developmental Psychology, 21*, 299–313.

de Catanzaro, D.A. (1978). Self-injurious behavior: A biological analysis. *Motivation and Emotion, 2*, 45–65.

DiGennaro Reed, F.D., Hirst, J.M., & Hyman, S.R. (2012). Assessment and treatment of stereotypic behavior in children with autism and other developmental disabilities: A thirty year review. *Research in Autism Spectrum Disorders, 6*, 422–430.

di Pellegrino, G., Fadiga, L., Fogassi, L., Gallese, V., & Rizzolatti, G. (1992). Understanding motor events: A neurophysiological study. *Experimental Brain Research, 91*, 176–180.

Eagle, R.S. (2004). Commentary: Further commentary on the debate regarding increase in autism in California. *Journal of Autism and Developmental Disorders, 34*, 87–88.

Endedijk, H., Denessen, E., & Hendriks, A.W. (2011). Relationships between executive functioning and homework difficulties in students with and without autism spectrum disorder: An analysis of student- and parent-reports. *Learning and Individual Differences, 21*, 765–770.

Enticott, P.G., Kennedy, H.A., Rinehart, N.J., Tonge, B.J., Bradshaw, J.L., Taffe, J.R., Daskalakis, Z.J., & Fitzgerald, P.B. (2012). Mirror neuron activity associated with social impairments but not age in autism spectrum disorder. *Biological Psychiatry, 71*, 427–433.

Filipek, P.A., Accardo, P.J., Ashwal, S., Baranek, G.T., Cook, Jr., E.H., Dawson, G., Gordon, B., Gravel, J.S., Johnson, C.P., Kallen, R.J., Levy, S.E., Minshew, N.J., Ozonoff, S., Prizant, B.M., Rapin, I., Rogers, S.J., Stone, W.L., Teplin, S.W., Tuchman, R.F., & Volkmar, F.R. (2000). Practice parameter: Screening and diagnosis of autism: Report of the Quality Standards Subcommittee of the American Academy of Neurology and the Child Neurology Society. *Neurology, 55*, 468–479.

Flyn, L., & Healey, O. (2012). A review of treatments for deficits in social skills and self-help skills in autism spectrum disorder. *Research in Autism Spectrum Disorders, 6*, 431–441.

Fombonne, E. (2005). The changing epidemiology of autism. *Journal of Applied Research in Intellectual Disabilities, 18*, 281–294.

Gillberg, C., Cederlund, M., Lamberg, K., & Zeijlon, L. (2006). Brief report: "The autism epidemic." The registered prevalence of autism in a Swedish urban area. *Journal of Autism and Developmental Disorders, 3*, 429–435.

Gindis, B. (2008). "Institutional autism" in children adopted internationally: Myth or reality? *International Journal of Special Education, 23*, 118–123.

Goh, S., & Peterson, B. (2012). Imaging evidence for disturbances in multiple learning and memory systems in persons with autism spectrum disorders. *Developmental Medicine and Child Neurology, 54*, 208–213.

Grandin, T. (2002). The autism continuum. Presentation given at the Southeastern Super Conference on Autism/Asperger's sponsored by Future Horizons, Atlanta, GA.

Grandin, T. (2009). Visual abilities and sensory differences in a person with autism. *Biological Psychiatry, 65*, 15–16.

Green, R.H., & Schwartzbaum, J.S. (1968). Effects of unilateral septal lesions on avoidance behavior, discrimination reversal, and hipppocampal EEG. *Journal of Comparative and Physiological Psychology, 65*, 388–396.

Guess, D., & Carr, E. (1991). Emergence and maintenance of stereotype and self-injury. *American Journal on Mental Retardation, 96*, 299–319.

Howlin, P. (2003). Outcome in high-functioning adults with Autism with and without early language delays: Implications for the differentiation between Autism and Asperger syndrome. *Journal of Autism and Developmental Disorders, 33*, 3–13.

Hundert, J., & Haughton, A. (1992). Promoting social interaction of children with disabilities in integrated preschools: A failure to generalize. *Exceptional Children, 58*, 311–320.

IDEA: Individuals with Disabilities Education Act of 1990, 15, 20 U.S.C. 1401 (1990).

Individuals with Disabilities Education Improvement Act of 2004, 20 U.S.C. §1400 et seq. (2004) (reauthorization of the Individuals with Disabilities Act of 1990).

Iovannone, R., Dunlap, G., Huber, H., & Kincaid, D. (2003). Effective educational practices for students with autism spectrum disorders. *Focus on Autism and Other Developmental Disabilities, 18,* 150–165.

Kanner, L. (1943). Autistic disturbances of affective contact. *The Nervous Child, 2,* 217–250.

Kemper, T.L., & Bauman, M. (1998). Neuropathology of infantile autism. *Journal of Neuropathology and Experimental Neurology, 57,* 645–652.

Ketelaars, C., Horwitz, E., Sytema, S., Bos, J., Wiersma, D., Minderaa, R., & Hartman, C.A. (2008). Brief report: Adults with mild autism spectrum disorders (ASD): Scores on the Autism Spectrum Quotient (AQ) and comorbid psychopathology. *Journal of Autism and Developmental Disorders, 38,* 176–180.

Kimble, D.P. (1963). The effects of bilateral hippocampal lesions in rats. *Journal of Physiological Psychology, 56,* 273–283.

Klin, A. (1992). Listening preference in regard to speech: A possible characterization of the symptom of social withdrawal. *Journal of Autism and Developmental Disorders, 21,* 29–42.

Klin, A., Jones, W., Schultz, R., Volkmar, F., & Cohen, D. (2002). Defining and quantifying the social phenotype in autism. *The American Journal of Psychiatry, 159,* 895–908.

Kobe, F. (1994). Nonambulatory persons with profound mental retardation: Physical, developmental, and behavioral characteristics. *Research in Developmental Disabilities, 15,* 413–424.

Koegel. R.L., Vernon, T.W., & Koegel, L.K. (2009). Improving social initiations in young children with autism using reinforcers with embedded social interactions. *Journal of Autism and Developmental Disorders. 39,* 1240–1251

Kogan, M.D., Blumberg, S.J., Schieve, L.A., Boyle, C.A., Perrin, J.M., Ghandour, R.M., Singh, G.K., Strickland, B.B., Trevathan, E., & van Dyck, P. C. (2009). Prevalence of parent-reported diagnosis of autism spectrum disorder among children in the US, 2007. *Pediatrics, 124,* 1395–1403.

Laushey, K.M. & Heflin, L.J. (2000). Enhancing social skills of kindergarten children with autism through the training of multiple peers as tutors. *Journal of Autism and Developmental Disorders, 30,* 183–193.

Lewis, F.M., Woodyatt, G.C., & Murdoch, B.E. (2008). Linguistic and pragmatic language skills in adults with autism spectrum disorder: A pilot study. *Research in Autism Spectrum Disorders, 2,* 176–187.

Lindblad, T. (2006). Story movies: A review. *Journal of Speech Language Pathology and Applied Behavior Analysis.* From http://www.baojournal.com/SLP-ABA%20WEBSITE/SLP-ABA-VOL-1/SLP-ABA-1-4--2-1.pdf.

Lord, C., Cook, E.H., Leventhal, B., & Amaral, D.G. (2000). Autism spectrum disorders. *Neuron, 28,* 355–363.

Lord, C., Risi, S., Lambrecht, L., Cook, E.H., Leventhal, B.L., DiLavore, P.C., Pickles, A., & Rutter, M. (2000). The Autism Diagnostic Observation Schedule–Generic: A standard measure of social and communication deficits associated with the spectrum of autism. *Journal of Autism and Developmental Disorders, 30,* 205–223.

Lorimer, P.A., Simpson, R.L., Myles, B.S., & Ganz, J.B. (2002). The use of social stories as a preventative behavioral intervention in a home setting with a child with autism. *Journal of Positive Behavior Interventions, 4,* 53–60.

Lovaas, O. (1987). Behavioral treatment and normal educational and intellectual functioning in young autistic children. *Journal of Consulting and Clinical Psychology, 55,* 3–9.

Mattila, M., Kielinen, M., Linna, S., Jussila, K., Ebeling, H., Bloigu, R., Joseph, R.M., & Moilanen, I. (2011). Autism spectrum disorders according to DSM-IV-TR and comparison with DSM-5 draft criteria: An epidemiological study. *Journal of the American Academy of Child and Adolescent Psychiatry, 50,* 583–592.

McPheeters, M.L., Warren, Z., Sathe, N., Bruzek, J.L., Krishnaswami, S., Jerome, R.N., & Veenstra-VanderWeele, J. (2011). A systematic review of medical treatments for children with autism spectrum disorders. *Pediatrics, 127,* e1312–e1321.

Mehrabian, A. (1981). *Silent messages* (2nd ed.). Belmont, CA: Wadsworth.

Mishkin, M., & Aggleton, J.P. (1981). Multiple functional contributors of the amygdala in the monkey from the amygdaloid complex. In Y. Ben-Ari (Ed.), *INSERM Symposium, No. 20.* Amsterdam: Elsevier/North Holland Biomedical Press.

Muehlmann, A.M., & Lewis, M.H. (2012). Abnormal repetitive behaviours: Shared phenomenology and pathophysiology. *Journal of Intellectual Disability Research, 56,* 427–440.

Murray, E.A., & Mishkin, M. (1985). Amygdaloidectomy impairs crossmodal association in monkeys. *Science, 228,* 604–606.

Nassar, N., Dixon, G., Bourke, J., Bower, C., Glasson, E., de Klerk, N., & Leonard, H. (2009). Autism spectrum disorders in young children: Effect of changes in diagnostic practices. *International Journal of Epidemiology, 38,* 1245–1254.

National Research Council. (2001). *Educating children with autism.* Committee on Educational Interventions for Children with Autism. Division of Behavioral and Social Sciences and Education. Washington, DC: National Academy Press.

O'Connor, K.K. (2012). Auditory processing in autism spectrum disorder: A review. *Neuroscience and Biobehavioral Reviews, 36,* 836–854.

O'Roak, B.J., Deriziotis, P., Lee, C., Vives, L., Schwartz, J.J., Girirajan, S., Karakoc, E., MacKenzie, A.P., Ng, S.B., Baker, C., Rieder, M.J., Nickerson, D.A., Bernier, R., Fisher, S.E., Shendure, J. & Eichler, E. E. (2011). Exome sequencing in sporadic autism spectrum disorders identifies severe de novo mutations. *Nature Genetics, 43*, 585–589.

Ozonoff, S., Macari, S., Young, G.S., Goldring, S., Thompson, M., & Rogers, S.J. (2008). Atypical object exploration at 12 months of age is associated with autism in a prospective sample. *Autism: The International Journal of Research and Practice, 12*, 457–472.

Palermo, M.T., & Curatolo, P. (2004). Pharmacologic treatment of autism. *Journal of Child Neurology, 19*, 155–164.

Pinborough-Zimmerman, J., Bakian, A.V., Fombonne, E., Bilder, D., Taylor, J., & McMahon, W.M. (2012). Changes in the administrative prevalence of autism spectrum disorders: Contribution of special education and health from 2002–2008. *Journal of Autism and Developmental Disorders, 42*, 521–530.

Plauché-Johnson, C., Myers, S.M., & the Council on Children with Disabilities. (2007). Identification and evaluation of children with autism spectrum disorders. *Pediatrics, 120*, 1183–1215.

Rago, W., & Case, J. (1978). Stereotyped behavior in special education teachers. *Exceptional Children, 44*, 342–344.

Rice, C., & Centers for Disease Control and Prevention. (2009). Prevalence of autism spectrum disorders: Autism and Developmental Disabilities Monitoring Network, United States, 2006. *Morbidity and Mortality Weekly Report, 58*, SS–10.

Richards, C.C., Oliver, C.C., Nelson, L.L., & Moss, J.J. (2012). Self-injurious behaviour in individuals with autism spectrum disorder and intellectual disability. *Journal of Intellectual Disability Research, 56*, 476–489.

Rodier, P.M. (2000). The early origins of autism. *Scientific American, 282*, 56–63.

Rutter, M., Andersen-Wood, L., Beckett, C., Bredenkamp, D., Castle, J., Grootheus, C., Kreppner, J., Keaveney, L., Lord, C., & O'Connor, T.G. (1999). Quasi-autistic patterns following severe early global privation. *Journal Child Psychology Psychiatry, 40*, 537–549.

Shattuck, P. (2006). The contribution of diagnostic substitution to the growing administrative prevalence of autism in US special education. *Pediatrics, 117*, 1028–1037.

Shic, F., Bradshaw, J., Klin, A., Scassellati, B., & Chawarska, K. (2011). Limited activity monitoring in toddlers with autism spectrum disorder. *Brain Research, 138*, 246–254.

Shute, N. (2010). Desperate for an autism cure. *Scientific American, 303*, 80–85.

Sivertsen, B., Posserud, M., Gillberg, C., Lundervold, A., & Hysing, M. (2012). Sleep problems in children with autism spectrum problems: A longitudinal population-based study. *Autism: The International Journal of Research and Practice, 16*, 139–150.

Smith, M.D. (1995). *A guide to successful employment for individuals with autism.* Baltimore, MD: Paul H. Brookes.

Teitelbaum, O., Benton, T., Shah, P., Prince, A., Kelly, J., & Teitelbaum, P. (2004). Eshkol-Wachman movement notation in diagnosis: The early detection of Asperger's syndrome. *Proceedings of the National Academy of Sciences of the United States of America, 101*, 11909–11914.

Tissot, C., & Evans, R. (2003). Visual teaching strategies for children with autism. *Early Child Development and Care, 173*, 425–433.

Toth, A. (2009). Bridge of signs: Can sign language empower non-deaf children to triumph over their communication disabilities? *American Annals of the Deaf, 154*, 85–95.

Volden, J., & Lord, C. (1991). Neologisms and idiosyncratic language in autistic speakers. *Journal of Autism and Developmental Disorders, 21*, 109–130.

Warren, Z., McPheeters, M.L., Sathe, N., Foss-Feig, J.H., Glasser, A., & Veenstra-VanderWeele, J. (2011). A systematic review of early intensive intervention for autism spectrum disorders. *Pediatrics, 127*, e1303–e1311.

Wassink, T.H., Brzustowicz, L.M., Bartlett, C.W., & Szatmari, P. (2004). The search for autism disease genes. *Mental Retardation and Developmental Disabilities Research Reviews, 10*, 272–283.

Wetherby, A.M., Woods, J., Allen, L., Cleary, J., Dickinson, H., & Lord, C. (2004). Early indicators of autism spectrum disorders in the second year of life. *Journal of Autism and Developmental Disorders, 34*, 473–493.

Williams, K., MacDermott, S., Ridley, G., Glasson, E.J., & Wray, J.A. (2008). The prevalence of autism in Australia. Can it be established from existing data? *Journal of Paediatrics and Child Health, 44*, 504–510.

Wing, L., Gould, J., & Gillberg, C. (2011). Autism spectrum disorders in the DSM-V: Better or worse than the DSM-IV? *Research in Developmental Disabilities, 32*, 768–773.

Wing, L., & Potter, D. (2002). The epidemiology of autistic spectrum disorders: Is the prevalence rising? *Mental Retardation and Developmental Disabilities Research Reviews, 8*, 151–161.

Winter-Messiers, M., Herr, C.M., Wood, C.E., Brooks, A.P., Gates, M.M., Houston, T.L., & Tingstad, K.I. (2007). How far can Brian ride the Daylight 4449 Express?: A strength-based model of Asperger syndrome based on special interest areas. *Focus on Autism and Other Developmental Disabilities, 22*, 67–79.

Worley, J.A., & Matson, J.L. (2012). Comparing symptoms of autism spectrum disorders using the current DSM-IV-TR diagnostic criteria and the proposed DSM-V diagnostic criteria. *Research in Autism Spectrum Disorders, 6*, 965–970.

Zirpoli, T.J., & Lloyd, J.W. (1987). Understanding and managing self-injurious behavior. *Remedial and Special Education, 8*(5), 46–57.

CHAPTER ELEVEN

Students with Sensory, Communication, Physical, and Health Impairments

Kathryn Wolff Heller and Debra Schober-Peterson

CHAPTER OBJECTIVES

- to describe the most common etiologies of sensory, communication, physical, and health impairments;
- to provide an overview of each of these types of disorders;
- to define and describe the educational impact of visual impairments, hearing impairments, communication disorders, physical impairments, and health impairments; and
- to discuss effective management strategies for classroom teachers and special educators when teaching students with these disabilities.

KEY TERMS

etiologies · TORCH · visual acuity · low vision exam · functional vision exam · low vision devices · braille · hearing impairments · hard-of-hearing · deaf · total communication system · American Sign Language (ASL) · cochlear implant · FM (frequency modulated) system · communication disorder · expressive language · receptive language · speech disorders · language disorders · speech sound disorder · articulation disorders · phonological disorder · voice disorders · fluency disorders · physical impairments · orthopedic impairments · health impairments

Many students with sensory, communication, physical, or health impairments can be found in general education classes, following the general academic curriculum. In some instances, the disability may not be noticeable. In other cases, it results in severe limitations regarding sensory input, communication, movement, and/or activity. In either case, the impairment typically results in the need for the classroom teacher to plan collaboratively with a special education teacher for the use of assistive devices and teaching adaptations to allow the student to learn effectively.

Knowing the characteristics associated with these disabilities will give the classroom teacher the foundation to provide appropriate education. Students with vision or hearing loss often miss vital information due to the impact of the sensory impairment. Students with communication disorders may be unable to ask questions effectively. Students with physical impairments often have difficulty accessing material due to physical limitations. Students with health impairments may have conditions that affect stamina, resulting in fatigue during the school day. When teachers are responsible for the education of students with these types of disabilities, an understanding of the impairment and its implications will allow them to make the appropriate adaptations for school success. This chapter provides an overview of sensory, communication, physical, and health impairments to assist teachers in understanding these disabilities and their educational implications.

Etiologies

There are numerous causes (etiologies) of sensory, communication, physical, and health impairments. These disabilities typically are due to either biologic factors or environmental factors which can occur anytime from before birth through adulthood. The etiologies can be divided as occurring during three time periods:

(a)   prenatally (before birth),

(b)   perinatally (during or shortly after birth),

(c)   postnatally (after birth).

There are several prenatal factors that can result in sensory, communication, physical, or health impairments. During prenatal development, the fetus may acquire chromosomal or genetic defects that result in a variety of disorders, such as muscular dystrophy and sickle cell anemia. The developing fetus may also be exposed to a prenatal infection that can result in severe disabilities. The most common of these are referred to as TORCH infections. TORCH refers to toxoplasmosis, other, rubella, cytomegalovirus, and herpes (Boyer & Boyer, 2004). Other prenatal factors, such as congenital abnormalities (e.g., limb deficiency) or adverse environmental factors (e.g., fetal exposure to radiation or drugs), can occur.

Perinatal factors and postnatal factors also may result in various impairments. During birth the infant may be exposed to infection, trauma, or a lack of oxygen, all of which may cause disability. After birth, the infant, child, or adolescent may have an accident or an infection that can result in such conditions as vision loss, hearing loss, communication disorders, or physical disability. Environmental causes, such as malnutrition, also may result in disability.

Identification and Eligibility for Services

Due to the visibility of many sensory, communication, physical, and health impairments, most students will be identified as having these impairments before they enter school. However, the teacher needs to be alert to some of the milder forms of these impairments or other impairments that may not manifest themselves until the school years. The teacher may be the first person to recognize that the student has a vision or hearing impairment. Physical impairments, such as scoliosis, often are detected in school during routine screening exams. Health impairments such as seizures also may be detected initially by a teacher. Knowing the characteristics of these conditions will assist the teacher in identifying possible impairments and referring the student for further assessment.

Assessments documenting a sensory, communication, physical, or health impairment usually involve medical personnel. However, when a sensory, communication, physical, or health impairment is diagnosed and documented, it does not automatically qualify a student for special education services. The impairment must impact on the student's educational performance for the student to be eligible for services in the school setting.

A team of professionals is needed to ensure that these students receive appropriate services. The special education teacher has knowledge and expertise in providing instructional strategies, adaptations, and modifications for students. In many states special education teachers are certified in specific disability areas, such as visual impairments, hearing impairments, or physical and health disabilities. As seen in **Table 11.1**, special education teachers who are certified in specific disability areas have specialized knowledge regarding the education of students with particular disabilities.

There may be several additional members of the educational team, such as an orientation and mobility instructor, optometrist, nurse, or physician. An orientation and mobility (O & M) instructor has specialized training in mobility and travel for students with visual impairments. Instruction may include learning to use a cane and/or electronic mobility device. An optometrist may be part of the team when low-vision devices (e.g., magnifiers and telescopes) have been prescribed for students. A nurse can be a valuable information source for the educational team concerning a student's physical or medical condition and its effects on

TABLE 11.1

Specific Types of Special Education Teachers

Teachers Certified in Visual Impairments
- Special education teachers who are certified in visual impairments (VI Teachers) have knowledge of the educational implications of visual impairments and blindness and appropriate teaching strategies needed to serve this population. Some of the areas of expertise include adapting material, enhancing visual functioning, conducting educationally oriented functional vision exams and learning media assessments, teaching the use of assistive devices, teaching computer use with voice output or screen enlargement and keyboard skills, teaching reading and writing braille, teaching social skills, teaching the use of low vision devices, promoting concept development, and instruction in academic and nonacademic areas.

Teachers Certified in Hearing Impairments
- Special education teachers who are certified in hearing impairments (HI Teachers) have specific knowledge in hearing impairments and deafness. Some areas of expertise include teaching sign language, teaching concept development, adapting materials and instruction, selection and use of assistive devices, teaching the use of residual hearing, and teaching academic and nonacademic areas.

Teachers Certified in Physical and Health Disabilities (also known as Orthopedic Impairments)
- Special education teachers who are certified in physical and health disabilities specialize in meeting the unique needs of students who have physical disabilities. Some areas of expertise include adaptations to instruction and material to accommodate for limitations in physical movement, selection and implementation of assistive devices, knowledge of educational implications of physical impairments, training in physical health care procedures, promoting communication through the use of augmentative and alternative communication systems, feeding techniques, positioning and handling techniques, and teaching academic and nonacademic skills.

the student's educational program. In addition, nurses may perform specialized healthcare procedures such as tube feedings and catheterizations, and they may train others to perform these procedures.

Visual Impairments

Students with visual impairments comprise a small percentage (0.5%) of the students receiving special education services. They vary as to the type of vision loss, the severity of the loss, and the impact this sensory loss has on functioning. Certain types of visual impairments will affect how clearly a student sees whereas others may affect how much a student can see at one time. Having an understanding of the common terms used in this field, the common conditions causing visual impairments and general characteristics of students with visual impairments will assist the teacher in better understanding the effects of visual impairments.

In the educational setting, visual impairment is defined by its impact on educational performance. Under IDEA, a student is defined as having a visual disability if the visual impairment, even with correction, adversely affects educational performance. There are several specific terms used to describe visual impairments.

- **Visual Impairment.** This term covers a wide range of vision loss which can include any visual deficit.

- **Blind.** Individuals who are totally without vision or who have light perception only are said to be blind. In education, this term refers to students who use other senses (i.e., hearing and touch) as primary channels for learning or receiving information.

- **Legal Blindness.** A person who is legally blind has a visual acuity of 20/200 or less in the better eye with correction or a visual field that is no greater than 20 degrees. The term visual acuity refers to the finest detail that the eye can distinguish. In this definition, the term 20/200 means that the person with the visual impairment can see an object or symbol at 20 feet that a person with unimpaired vision can see at 200 feet. Field of vision refers to the ability to see objects in the periphery of one's vision when looking straight ahead. Individuals with unimpaired vision can see objects within a 180 degree arc when looking straight ahead.

- **Low Vision (partially sighted or partial vision).** This term refers to individuals who have significant visual impairments with best correction, but still have usable vision. Vision is used as the primary channel for learning or receiving information. Visual functioning may increase with the use of low vision devices, environmental modifications, and/or training (Corn, DePriest, & Erin, 2000). Less used terms include partially sighted or partial vision which tend to refer exclusively to distance vision with an acuity between 20/70 and 20/200.

Impairments Affecting Visual Functioning

When there is a visual impairment, the functioning of the eye may be affected in several different ways. These include: (a) poor visual acuity, (b) visual field deficits, (c) eye movement abnormalities, (d) light and color reception impairments, and (e) abnormalities of visual perception and brain functions (Corn, DePriest, & Erin, 2000); Heller, Easterbrooks, McJannet, & Swinehart-Jones, 2009).

Poor Visual Acuity

Visual acuity refers to how clear or sharp an image appears. Poor visual acuity may occur from refractory errors (e.g., nearsightedness) that are usually correctable with glasses or surgery. Poor visual acuity may also occur from medical abnormalities of the visual system (e.g., retinitis pigmentosa) that may not be correctable and result in blurry vision (Chang, 2007).

Visual Field Deficits

A person's field of vision is the entire area that can be seen without shifting one's gaze. Defects in visual fields may occur in a person's central field of vision, peripheral field of vision, or both as shown in **Figure 11.1**.

Figure 11.1   Field of Vision Deficits

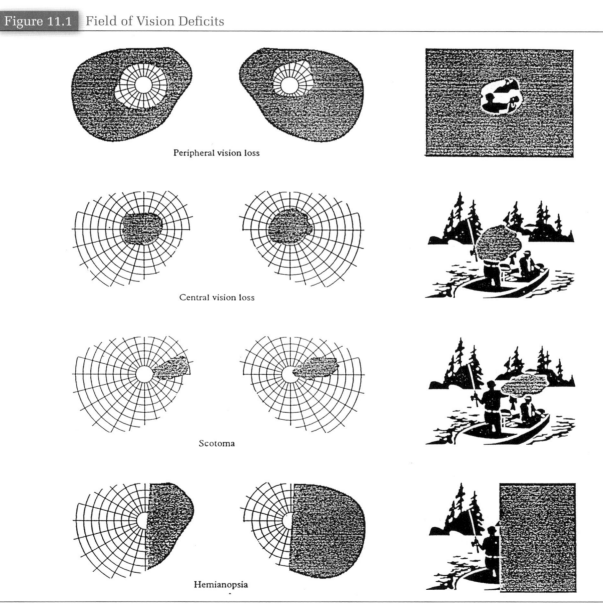

Peripheral vision loss

Central vision loss

Scotoma

Hemianopsia

From Heller, K.W., Easterbrooks, S., McJannet, D., & Swinehart-Jones, D. (2009). Vision loss, hearing loss, and deaf–blindness. In K.W. Heller, P.E. Forney, P.A. Alberto, A.J. Best, & M.N. Schwartzman (Eds.), *Understanding physical, health, and multiple disabilities, 2nd ed.* (p. 196). Upper Saddle River, NJ: Merrill/Pearson.

Central vision refers to the direct line of vision (Chang, 2007). When a central vision loss is present, students may not be able to see items directly in front of them. Instead, they may direct their gaze off to the side to see the desired item using their peripheral (side) vision (which is known as eccentric viewing). Since central vision is important for discerning details, students with this type of visual loss will have difficulty seeing print and may benefit from having print and other materials enlarged.

Peripheral vision refers to the ability to perceive the presence of objects outside the direct line of vision. When a peripheral field loss exists, the student is unable to see objects in part or all of the peripheral vision. One of the common types of peripheral vision losses involves the loss of vision in a ring shape along the periphery which results in a narrower visual field (i.e., like looking through a tunnel as depicted in the term "tunnel vision"). A peripheral field loss may be accompanied by loss of night vision. Other field deficits include blind spots (non-seeing area in the visual field) or loss of entire sections of the field of vision (e.g., loss of one half of the visual field).

Eye Movement Abnormalities

Problems in eye movement may occur from abnormalities of the six muscles surrounding each eye, the nerves innervating these muscles, or the brain. Three common impairments associated with problems in eye movement are strabismus, amblyopia, and nystagmus.

Strabismus is an unequal pull of the muscles surrounding the eye in which the eyes are not aligned and may look "cross-eyed." This can usually be corrected with surgery. In amblyopia, also known as lazy eye, the brain suppresses the vision in one eye because one eye has very poor acuity or there is double vision. To correct amblyopia, the good eye may be patched to force the use of the "weak" eye. Nystagmus is an involuntary rhythmic eye movement. Individuals with nystagmus usually will perceive objects as stationary, with the brain adjusting perceptually for the movement. However, students may lose their place while reading and often can benefit from using an index card or typoscope (paper with rectangular hole cut out of it) to help keep their place.

Impairment in Color and Light Reception

The primary impairment in color reception is color blindness. Students who are color blind usually cannot see certain colors due to missing or damaged color receptors in the eye. For example, in a red-green color defect, red and green appear the same color.

Lighting conditions also may impact on a student's visual functioning. Some students may be sensitive to light (photophobia); they may be uncomfortable in normal lighting conditions and need to wear sunglasses or a visor (or cap) indoors. Other students may need increased lighting to improve visual functioning. Still other students may be unable to see in dim light and may have difficulty going from the bright sunlight to a darkened hallway.

Abnormalities of Visual Perception and Brain Function

Students with a normal eye exam, but who have damage to areas of the brain affecting vision, may have multiple visual problems. Some visual issues may occur with depth perception, estimating distances, spontaneous visual learning, inability to see or perceive items, difficulty with fixation, smooth pursuit of a moving target, and difficulty keeping visual attention and visual communication (Alimovic & Mejaski-Bosnjak, 2011; Ward, 2000).

Common Eye Conditions

There are several eye conditions that may result in poor visual acuity, visual field deficits, eye movement abnormalities, light and color reception impairments, and abnormalities of visual perception and brain functions. It is important to know the type of eye impairment a student has and possible educational implications of the condition. **Table 11.2** provides examples of conditions affecting different parts of the eye as well as general educational implications of each condition.

Visual Assessment

There are several different types of assessments to evaluate a student's visual functioning. Assessments can be divided into various categories: visual screening, ophthalmologic or eye exam, low vision exam, and functional vision exam.

Some students will display certain behaviors that may indicate a visual problem as shown in **Table 11.3.** Teachers need to be alert for possible vision problems and refer the student for further testing if a vision impairment is suspected. To help detect a vision problem, schools use routine screening exams. These usually are performed by a school nurse or other trained personnel. Often they include reading an eye chart and visually locating objects. Typically this type of screening only detects problems in how clearly someone sees (acuity) from a distance and can miss other types of impairments.

TABLE 11.2

Examples of Eye Conditions

Glaucoma
- Glaucoma is an abnormal increase in intraocular pressure in one or both eyes which can damage the eye. If left untreated, the increase in pressure causes damage to the optic nerve fibers in the back of the eye. This results in restricted visual fields and eventual blindness. It is treated by medication and/or surgery. Low vision devices and sunglasses may be prescribed since photophobia and decreased visual acuity occur in glaucoma.

Cataract
- A cataract is clouding of the lens of the eye. A cataract's effect on vision varies depending on the size, position, and density of the cloudy area. Some cataracts involve pinpoint areas that do not interfere with vision whereas others may be centrally located and so dense that blindness results. Often decreased visual acuity and difficulty seeing in bright light is present. Cataracts typically are treated by surgical removal of the lens. Special glasses may be worn after surgery or artificial lenses may be implanted in the eye. If the cataract has not been surgically treated, lighting may be adjusted to reduce glare. Also, if the cataract is positioned centrally in the lens, unusual head positions may be observed, since the person is "looking around the cataract." Occasionally magnification may be helpful to improve vision.

Congenital Macular Dystrophies
- Macular dystrophies refer to a wide variety of disorders in which there are abnormalities of the part of the eye responsible for central vision and clear, distinct vision. Macular dystrophies range in severity from a reduction of visual acuity to a loss of central vision. There is no effective treatment at this time; however, to improve visual functioning, some individuals may use eccentric viewing or magnification.

Retinitis Pigmentosa
- In retinitis pigmentosa, there is a gradual loss of vision, beginning in the periphery and progressing toward the center of the field of vision. The condition begins with a peripheral field loss and night blindness. As it progresses, tunnel vision results and eventually central vision may be affected as well. There is no effective treatment at this time for retinitis pigmentosa. To assist with visual functioning, several optical devices may be helpful, such as magnifiers, hand telescopes, closed circuit television, and infrared devices for use at night.

Cortical Visual Impairment
- Cortical visual impairment (CVI) refers to damage to the visual pathways or cortex of the brain. The resulting visual impairment may range from poor visual acuity to blindness, depending on the cause, the location, and the severity of the damage. Visual functioning may fluctuate during the day resulting in the student sometimes being able to see an object while other times not being able to see it. There is no specific medical treatment at this time, except treating underlying causes when possible. In individual students, it is difficult to determine whether visual functioning will improve or remain the same.

TABLE 11.3

Screening Checklist for Visual Impairments

A. Eye Appearance

_____ Eyes red

_____ One eye turns in, out, up, or down

_____ Eyes in constant motion (nystagmus)

_____ Tears excessively

_____ Eyelid crusted

B. Visual Abilities

_____ No blink reflex

_____ Pupils do not react to light

_____ Does not fixate on object

_____ Cannot track object

_____ Does not scan for object

_____ Cannot follow moving object toward nose (converge eyes)

C. Behaviors

_____ Rubs eyes frequently

_____ Squints eyes

_____ Blinks frequently

_____ Closes one eye doing certain tasks

_____ Does not look straight at an object (looks from side)

_____ Turns or tilts head

_____ Approaches items by touch rather than sight

_____ Holds items (e.g., book) too close or too far

D. Verbal Complaints

_____ Complains of eye pain, headaches

_____ Complains of seeing double

_____ Complains of not being able to see well

E. Academic Work

_____ Cannot copy off the blackboard

_____ Makes frequent errors reading letters that are shaped similarly

_____ Rereads or skips words or lines when reading

_____ Uses hand to keep place

_____ Writes uphill or downhill on paper

From *Understanding Physical, Health and Multiple Disabilities* (2009) by Heller, Forney, Alberto, Best and Schwartzman (Eds.) p. 192. Copyright Merrill/Pearson. Reprinted by permission.

An eye exam by an ophthalmologist or optometrist is designed to detect eye disease and problems in visual functioning. Eye disease is detected through close examination of the structure of the eye using a variety of instruments, as well as various tests.

A low vision exam is performed by an optometrist trained in low vision. The primary purpose of this exam is to determine if the person would benefit from low vision devices. Low vision devices include such items as magnifiers (which are used for reading print) and telescopes (which are used for seeing distant items).

An educationally oriented functional vision exam usually is performed by the teacher certified in visual impairment (VI teacher). The focus of this exam is to determine how well the student is using vision and what modifications or teaching strategies are needed. A learning media assessment is also performed which determines the best instructional media for students who have visual impairments (e.g., large print, braille, auditory media) (McKenzie, 2007).

Management of Visual Impairments

Students with visual impairments comprise a diverse group of individuals who will need various amounts and types of adaptations to assist them in school. The educational team, with the lead of the vision teacher, will determine the types of adaptations needed. Adaptations for students with visual impairments can be divided into seven main areas:

1. Use of assistive technology,
2. Use of a person,
3. Changes in the physical environment,
4. Changes in student response,
5. Changes in teacher instruction,
6. Alteration in material, and
7. Alteration in activities and/or curriculum (See **Table 11.4**).

Students with visual impairments often will require assistive technology. **Low vision devices** are a type of assistive technology that has been found to be effective in improving children's visual performance and hence maximizing their educational performance (Labib, Sada, Mohamed, Sabra, & Aleen, 2009). These consist of such items as magnifiers, which enlarge print which is close to the student, and telescopes, which enlarge items at a distance. Machines such as CCTV (closed circuit televisions) enlarge books and other materials onto a large screen for the student to see. Other types of assistive devices include those for mobility. Canes, guide dogs, braille compasses, and electronic mobility devices may be used to assist the student in moving from one location to another. Students with visual impairments may also use various types of assistive technology to provide access to school activities,

TABLE 11.4

Managing Visual Impairments

	Visual Impairment
Assistive Technology	• Low vision devices (e.g., magnifier)
Use of Person	• Peer teaming
Physical Environment	• Position student in relation to activities
	• Lighting
	• Contrast
Student Response	• Alternate response forms (e.g., braille)
	• More time
Teacher Instruction	• Use of verbal description
Alter Material	• Alter material so student can use it regardless of visual loss (e.g., enlarge material, use tactile models)
Alter Activity	• Modify activity to compensate for sensory loss
Alter Curriculum	• Learn additional specialized skills (e.g., mobility training)

including computer use (e.g., voice output word processors, braille printers [embossers], screen reading software).

A second type of adaptation involves using another person. Peer assistance may be used in which a peer assists the student in activities that require additional description or assistance in locating certain items. Peer teaming or working in groups also may be used. This not only allows additional assistance to the student with the visual impairment, but also provides this student the opportunity to assist peers on parts of the tasks that do not require a visual component.

Student Using a CCTV to Read. Students with visual impairments often require assistive technology.

The third type of adaptation is arrangement of the physical environment. Some students with visual impairment may need to be seated near the front of the room in order to see the board. Other options may be placing the student where there is less glare or where the lighting is appropriate for the student's needs. Sometimes there may be so much visual clutter in the room that it is difficult for the student to see what is important. In this case the teacher will need to make some changes regarding what is on the classroom walls.

A fourth adaptation is student response. Some students with visual impairments will be using **braille** as their primary form of written communication and may do some of their classwork in braille. The teacher certified in visual impairments will be able to translate the braille into print for the teacher. Other response modifications include extending time limits for assignments or tests since reading braille or large print requires more time than reading standard print.

A fifth adaptation is teacher instruction. The teacher typically will not need to change the instructional strategies used in the class. However, it is important that the teacher provides ample verbal description of what is being displayed or demonstrated so that the student with a visual impairment will understand and follow the discussion.

A sixth adaptation is adapting the material. Students with visual impairments or blindness may need material in braille, large print, or on CD. The special education teacher will assist in obtaining large print books or braille books as well as putting material into braille. It also is important that the student be provided with concrete objects and tactile models representing what is being taught. For example, when teaching counting the students would benefit from using concrete objects to count. In geometry class it will be important to use models of the geometric shapes. When teaching anatomy in biology class, anatomical models that can be touched by the student are helpful.

In some instances an activity or curriculum adaptation is needed for the student with a visual impairment. Due to the lack of the most important distance sense used for learning, the student with a visual impairment may have several incomplete or incorrect concepts. A student who has only touched part of a fire truck may not fully understand its size or shape. Providing activities in which the student may touch and experience the concept being taught will promote a better understanding of the material. Additional areas may be added to the student's curriculum, such as teaching braille, mobility, and vocational and independent living skills, in order to meet the student's needs. See **Figure 11.2** for a case study of Rachel, a student with a visual impairment.

| Figure 11.2 | Description of Rachel, a High School Student with a Visual Impairment |

Rachel is a 16-year-old student who attends her local high school. She was born with retinitis pigmentosa and is legally blind. She receives special education services from a teacher certified in visual impairments and an orientation and mobility teacher. Rachel is unable to see fine detail; however, she is able to see large items, although they are blurry. In the classroom, she sits in the front of the room, and her teachers are careful to provide visual descriptions of what they are doing. According to Rachel's learning media assessment, braille is her best media, and her textbooks and written materials are provided in braille. The vision teacher also converts maps and figures from her textbooks into tactual graphics or provides verbal descriptions. Rachel takes notes in class using a braille note taker. She is able to move around the school using her cane. The orientation and mobility instructor is teaching her to use public transportation. With these services and adaptations, Rachel is on the road to success in school and independent living.

Hearing Impairments

Just like students with visual impairments, students with **hearing impairments** are considered low incidence since they comprise only 1.5% of the population of students receiving special education services. Over 86% of students who are deaf and hard-of-hearing will spend time in the general education classroom. They will vary as to the type of hearing loss, the severity of the loss, and the impact the loss has on their ability to communicate and learn. Knowledge of the terminology associated with hearing loss, types of hearing loss, and characteristics of students with hearing impairment will increase the teacher's understanding of the effects of hearing impairment.

The term hearing impairment is a general term that includes all amounts and types of hearing loss, from mild, temporary hearing losses to profound, permanent losses. Individuals with a hearing impairment often are categorized as either deaf or hard-of-hearing. Under IDEA, the terms are defined as follows:

> Deaf: a hearing impairment which is so severe that the child is impaired in processing linguistic information through hearing, with or without amplification, which adversely affects educational performance.
>
> Hard-of-hearing: a hearing impairment, whether permanent or fluctuating, which adversely affects a child's educational performance, but which is not included under the definition of "deaf."

Books and handouts can be translated to braille for students with severe visual impairments.

Braille

Individuals who are **hard-of-hearing** have sufficient auditory acuity and skills to learn speech and language through hearing when assisted by amplification devices. Like individuals with normal hearing, persons who are hard-of-hearing rely on hearing and listening for communicating and learning. In contrast, individuals who are **deaf** have such limited auditory acuity and skills that they generally must rely on systems other than their hearing for communicating and learning. They will use systems that are visually based and use sign language as their primary mode of communication. Individuals who are deaf also can be classified as **Deaf** or **deaf**. The use of the capital "D" indicates an identification with deaf culture and use of American Sign Language whereas the small "d" indicates individuals who primarily use oral communication.

Hearing Assessment

There are different assessments that may be done to evaluate a student's hearing. These assessments can be divided into screenings and diagnostic evaluations. Many newborn infants who have hearing loss are now being identified through Universal Newborn Hearing Screening programs. Other children who acquire hearing loss in infancy or as toddlers may be identified by their parents if the child does not respond to noises in the environment and/ or is not developing speech and language as expected. The parents often seek help from their pediatrician or community health clinic. The family is then referred to an audiologist for testing and to a physician who specializes in the ear (otologist) for the diagnosis of the problem.

Many students with less severe hearing losses, or hearing losses that are fluctuating in nature, are not identified as having a hearing loss until school age. Their losses may be identified first in schoolwide hearing screening or by astute classroom teachers. **Table 11.5** summarizes some of the student behaviors teachers might observe that could indicate a hearing loss.

If these behaviors are noted, the teacher should refer the student for a hearing screening. The screening typically is performed in the school by a speech-language pathologist, nurse, or other trained personnel. When students fail the hearing screening, they will be referred to the audiologist for a complete hearing evaluation to determine both the degree and type of hearing loss. Depending on the results of the assessment, the student may be referred to an otologist for medical evaluation and treatment.

Degree of Hearing Loss

The degree or amount of hearing loss is determined by measuring an individual's hearing acuity to a series of tones of various pitches. The results are recorded on an audiogram, a graph that plots the faintest intensity levels (as measured in decibels), at which a person can hear tones of specific pitches or frequencies (as measured in Hertz or Hz). **Figure 11.3** presents an audiogram with familiar sounds displayed on it according to their loudness and pitch. **Table 11.6** shows a commonly used classification system for degree of hearing loss and the psychosocial and educational impact of the loss.

Types of Hearing Loss

Hearing loss can result from damage to any part of the auditory system. If the hearing loss is the result of damage to the outer or middle ear, the loss is called conductive. For example, wax or an object trapped in the ear canal, or a hole in the eardrum could all result in a conductive hearing loss. Most conductive type hearing losses are not permanent; they can be treated and, in most cases, hearing will be restored. The most common cause of conductive hearing loss in children is middle ear infection (otitis media).

If a hearing loss is the result of damage to the sensory cells or nerve fibers in the ear (inner ear damage), the loss is called sensory (or sensorineural). If the loss is due to injury to the auditory cortex of the brain, or the brainstem pathways leading to the brain, the term central hearing loss may be used to describe it. Sensory losses can result from many of the conditions or infections noted earlier in the chapter (heredity, TORCH infections, postnatal infections, etc.). Generally, sensory losses are permanent. Once damaged, the sensory cells and/or nerve fibers cannot be restored or repaired. Today there is great concern over the

TABLE 11.5
Screening Checklist for Hearing Impairments

A. Ear Appearance

_____ Discharge or drainage from ear

_____ Outer ear is red or swollen

B. Auditory Abilities

_____ Is unaware of sounds in the environment that others can hear

_____ Cannot localize sound (determine its location by listening)

_____ Does not startle or respond to very loud noises

_____ Does not turn or respond when called

C. Behaviors

_____ Is inattentive

_____ Scratches or pulls at ears frequently

_____ Frowns when listening

_____ Leans toward speaker or turns one ear toward speaker

_____ Concentrates on speaker's face and lip movements

_____ Turns volume on CD players, TV, or radios unusually high

_____ Exhibits delays in speech or language development

_____ Omits sounds at the end of words when speaking

_____ Omits or mispronounces high pitch speech sounds ("s", "t", "sh")

_____ Uses an excessively loud or soft voice

_____ Has frequent colds, allergies, or ear infections

D. Verbal Complaints

_____ Complains of ear aches, pain, tenderness, or itching

_____ Complains of ear noises (ringing or buzzing)

_____ Complains others "mumble" or speak too softly

_____ Complains of not being able to hear well

E. Academic Work

_____ Misinterprets questions or instructions and responds incorrectly

_____ Asks for repetition of information, questions, and directions presented auditorily

_____ Waits to see what classmates are doing before beginning a task or responding

_____ Has difficulty in language arts (especially vocabulary, grammar, reading)

increasing presence of sensory hearing loss in children due to exposure to loud noise from music and recreational activities.

Hearing loss may affect both ears (bilateral) or it may affect only one ear (unilateral). Even unilateral losses can have a significant impact on a student's ability to hear and listen. A hearing loss in one ear makes it difficult to locate the source of sounds (localize) and to listen when background noises are present. In other words, a unilateral hearing loss can make it difficult to hear in typical classroom conditions.

Effects of Hearing Loss

The effects of a hearing loss will depend on many factors: the type and severity of the loss; whether the loss is unilateral or bilateral; the age at which the loss is acquired; the age at which the loss is identified; the hearing status of the parents; and the presence of additional disabilities (intellectual, sensory, or physical). Generally, the more severe the hearing loss,

Figure 11.3   Audiogram of Familiar Sounds

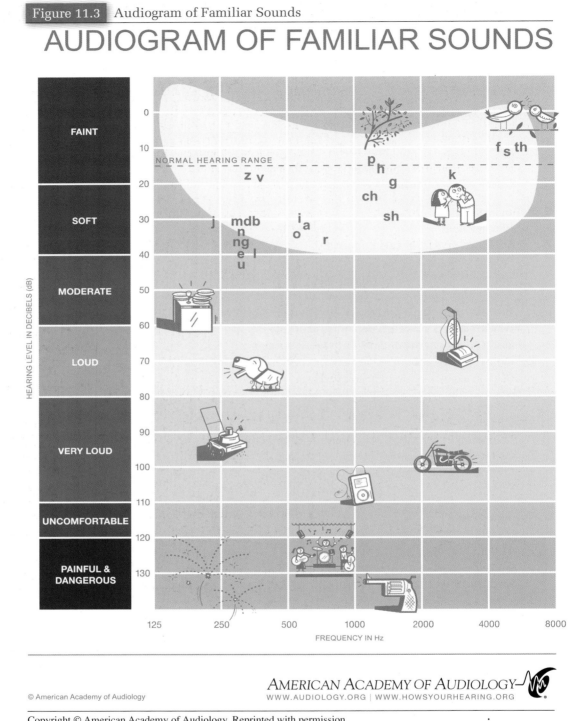

the greater its impact on communication and learning. If a loss is acquired before the development of language (**prelingual**), significant delays and difficulties are anticipated in speech and language development. When the loss occurs after a child has acquired speech and language (**postlingual**), the child may have the foundation for good oral communication skills. The loss still can have a significant impact on academic performance and social interaction.

TABLE 11.6

Relationship of Hearing Loss to Listening and Learning Needs

26–40 dB Hearing Loss (Mild)		
Possible Impact on the Understanding of Language and Speech	*Possible Social Impact*	*Potential Educational Accommodations and Services*
• Child can "hear" but misses fragments of speech, leading to misunderstanding. • Degree of difficulty experienced in school will depend upon noise level in the classroom, distance from the teacher, and configuration of the hearing loss, even with hearing aids. • Often experiences difficulty learning early reading skills such as letter/sound associations. • Child's ability to understand and succeed in the classroom will be substantially diminished by speaker distance and background noise, especially in the elementary grades.	• Barriers begin to build with negative impact on self-esteem as child is accused of "hearing when he/she wants to," "day-dreaming," or "not paying attention." • Child begins to lose ability for selective listening and has increasing difficulty suppressing background noise, causing the learning environment to be more stressful. • Child is more fatigued due to effort needed to listen.	• Noise in typical class will impede child from full access to teacher instruction. • Will benefit from hearing aid(s) and use of a desktop or ear-level FM system in the classroom. • Needs favorable acoustics, seating, and lighting. • May need attention to auditory skills, speech, language development, speech reading, and/or support in reading and self-esteem. • Teacher in-service on impact of so-called "mild" hearing loss on listening and learning to convey that it is often greater than expected.
41–55 dB Hearing Loss (Moderate)		
Possible Impact on the Understanding of Language and Speech	*Possible Social Impact*	*Potential Educational Accommodations and Services*
• Without amplification, child may understand conversation at a distance of 3 to 5 feet if sentence structure and vocabulary are known. • Without early amplification, the child is likely to have delayed or disordered syntax, limited vocabulary, imperfect speech production, and flat voice quality. • Addition of a visual communication system to supplement audition may be indicated, especially if language delays and/or additional disabilities are present. • Even with hearing aids, child can "hear" but may miss much of what is said if classroom is noisy or reverberant.	• Communication will be significantly compromised with this degree of hearing loss if hearing aids are not worn. • Socialization with peers can be difficult, especially in noisy settings such as cooperative learning situations, lunch, or recess. • May be more fatigued than classmates due to effort needed to listen.	• Consistent use of amplification (hearing aids + FM) is essential. • Needs favorable classroom acoustics, seating, and lighting. • Special academic support necessary if language and educational delays are present. • Attention to growth of oral communication, reading, written language skills, auditory skill development, speech therapy, self-esteem likely. • Teacher in-service required with attention to communication access and peer acceptance.

(continued on next page)

TABLE 11.6

Relationship of Hearing Loss to Listening and Learning Needs *(continued)*

56–70 dB Hearing Loss (Moderately Severe)

Possible Impact on the Understanding of Language and Speech	Possible Social Impact	Potential Educational Accommodations and Services
• Without amplification, conversation must be very loud to be understood. • If hearing loss is not identified before age 1 year and appropriately managed, delayed spoken language, syntax, reduced speech intelligibility, and flat voice quality are likely. • Age when first amplified, consistency of hearing aid use, and early language intervention strongly tied to success of speech, language, and learning development. • Addition of visual communication system often indicated if language delays and/or additional disabilities are present.	• If hearing loss was late-identified and language delay was not prevented, communication interaction with peers will be significantly affected. • Children will have greater difficulty socializing, especially in noisy settings such as lunch, cooperative learning situations, or recess. • Tendency for poorer self-concept and social immaturity may contribute to a sense of rejection; peer in-service helpful.	• Full-time, consistent use of amplification (hearing aids + FM system) is essential. • May require intense support in development of auditory, language, speech, reading, and writing skills. • Consultation/supervision by a specialist in childhood hearing impairment to coordinate services is important. • Use of sign language or a visual communication system by children with substantial language delays or additional learning needs may be useful. • Note-taking, captioned films, etc. often are needed accommodations. • Teacher in-service required.

71–90 dB and 91 + dB Hearing Loss (Severe and Profound)

Possible Impact on the Understanding of Language and Speech	Possible Social Impact	Potential Educational Accommodations and Services
• Without amplification, children with 71–90 dB hearing loss may only hear loud noises about 1 foot from ear. • Individual ability and intensive intervention prior to 6 months of age will determine the degree that sounds detected will be discriminated and understood by the brain. • The child with hearing loss greater than 70 dB may be a candidate for cochlear implant(s) and the child with hearing loss greater than 90 dB will not be able to perceive most speech sounds with traditional hearing aids.	• Socialization with hearing peers may be difficult. • Children in general education classrooms may develop greater dependence on adults due to difficulty perceiving or comprehending oral communication. • Children may be more comfortable interacting with peers who are deaf or hard-of-hearing due to ease of communication.	• There is no one communication system that is right for all hard-of-hearing or deaf children and their families. • Whether a visual communication approach or auditory/oral approach is used, extensive language intervention, full-time consistent amplification use, and constant integration of the communication practices into the family by 6 months of age will highly increase the probability that the child will become a successful learner.

TABLE 11.6

Relationship of Hearing Loss to Listening and Learning Needs *(continued)*

71–90 dB and 91 + dB Hearing Loss (Severe and Profound)		
Possible Impact on the Understanding of Language and Speech	*Possible Social Impact*	*Potential Educational Accommodations and Services*
• For full access to language to be available visually through sign language or cued speech, family members must be involved in child's communication mode from a very young age.	• Relationships with peers and adults who have hearing loss can make positive contributions toward the development of a healthy self-concept and a sense of cultural identity.	• The language gap is difficult to overcome, and the educational program of a child with hearing loss, especially those with language and learning delays secondary to hearing loss, requires the involvement of a teacher with expertise in teaching children with hearing loss. • Note-taking, captioning, captioned films, and other visual enhancement strategies are necessary; training in pragmatic language use and communication repair strategies helpful. • In-service of general education teachers is essential.

Reprinted by permission of Karen L. Anderson, Ph.D.

Students who are deaf and hard-of-hearing often lag behind their normal hearing peers in academic achievement (Bess, Dodd-Murphy, & Parker, 1998; Moores, 2001). Research has demonstrated significant deficits in reading ability, with many secondary students reading only at the fourth grade level (Quigley & Paul, 1989; Schirmer, 2000). These deficits exist despite cognitive abilities comparable to that of individuals with normal hearing. The IQ distribution of the deaf population mirrors that of the hearing population (Marschark, Lang, & Albertini, 2002; Moores, 2001) with the deaf displaying the same diversity in IQ scores and the same average performance IQ score nearly the same (96.89) as the norm. Academic performance, however, relies not only on cognitive abilities, but also on language skills. Most students who are deaf or hard-of-hearing have significant and persistent delays and deficits in language skills. These deficits are exhibited in their language expression (speaking and writing) as well as their language reception (listening and reading). Successful performance in the typical classroom depends on the ability to hear and understand the teacher, follow lectures, understand classroom discussions, and hear questions from peers. It is easy to see why the student who is deaf or hard-of-hearing is at a disadvantage.

Communication Systems

Students with hearing loss will develop and rely on different modes of communication depending on a variety of factors. These factors include, but are not limited to, the amount of hearing loss, the individual's ability to use whatever hearing remains, the age at the onset of the loss, the mode of communication preferred by the family, and the availability of services and training. In general, the communication systems used by students with hearing impairment can be divided into auditory/oral systems, manual systems, and a combined or total communication system. The benefits and limitations of each system have been debated for many years by the advocates of each of the various systems (Moores, 2001). No single system can meet the needs of all students who are deaf and hard-of-hearing. More important than which specific system is used is the development of good communication skills in these students.

Auditory/oral systems focus on the use of residual hearing (the usable hearing an individual has) to develop speech and language. Hearing aids, training in listening skills (auditory training), and lipreading (or speechreading) are used to develop the student's ability to understand and produce spoken English.

Manual systems do not rely on auditory or oral output for communication, but use a system of hand symbols or movements to convey ideas or words. Finger-spelling is a form of manual communication in which each letter of the English alphabet is represented by a single hand and finger position. Words are spelled using this system. American Sign Language (ASL) is another form of manual communication in which whole words and complete thoughts can be expressed by a systematic combination of hand movements. ASL is only one of several sign languages that are used in the world. It is the most widely used manual communication system among deaf adults in this country. It is a unique language with its own structure, grammar, and rules, not a word for word translation of English language.

The third system of communication is referred to as total communication. It is based on the premise that simultaneously using a combination of signs and speech will allow students who are deaf and hard-of-hearing to use whatever mode possible to acquire language. True total communication systems incorporate and emphasize every possible mode for learning language and communication. This includes hearing, speechreading, speech, signing, finger-spelling, reading, and writing. Most public schools report that a total communication system is being used to educate their students who are deaf and hard-of-hearing. The teachers in these schools, however, will admit they do not give equal emphasis and training to all communication modes.

Management of Hearing Impairments

Because hearing loss has a profound impact on the development of speech and language, and on academic performance, special services will be required to assist these students in school. Students who are deaf and hard-of-hearing are a diverse group of individuals and the specific services, adaptations, or modifications needed will vary. These adaptations can be divided into the same seven categories as described earlier for students with visual impairments:

1. Use of assistive technology,
2. Use of a person,
3. Changes in the physical environment,
4. Changes in student response,
5. Changes in teacher instruction,
6. Alteration in material, and
7. Alteration in activities and/or curriculum (see **Table 11.7**).

Students who are deaf and hard-of-hearing typically will use amplification devices to improve their auditory functioning. With the implementation of the Americans with Disabilities Act of 1990, the public is becoming more aware of amplification devices and the assistance available for individuals with hearing loss. Public telephones with amplifiers, televisions with closed captioning, modified alarms and alerting devices, and churches and movie theaters with specialized listening devices are becoming commonplace in our society.

TABLE 11.7

Managing Hearing Impairments

	Hearing Impairment
Assistive Technology	• Amplification and alerting devices
Use of Person	• Peer teaming, interpreter, or notetaker
Physical Environment	• Position student in relation to activities
	• Noise
	• Vision
Student Response	• Use of interpreter
Teacher Instruction	• Repeat announcements, questions from peers
	• Work with speech-language pathologist and teacher certified in hearing impairment
Alter Material	• Use supplemental visual aids
Alter Activity	• Provide written instructions and assignments
Alter Curriculum	• Learn additional specialized skills (e.g., speechreading, manual communication)

Individuals with hearing loss rely on such assistive devices in addition to personal hearing aids to improve their ability to communicate.

Most students who are deaf and hard-of-hearing can benefit from, and will wear, hearing aids or cochlear implants. Hearing aids are personal amplification devices that pick up sound in the environment, amplify it and direct it into the ear of the hearing aid user. Hearing aids come in various forms as shown in **Figure 11.4**. The behind-the-ear aid is the one most often worn by school-age individuals.

A common misperception is that hearing aids can restore normal hearing to the user, much like glasses can restore vision to normal acuity. Hearing aids cannot restore normal hearing. These devices simply increase the loudness of the sound that enters the ear. Individuals with sensory hearing loss are the primary users of hearing aids. For them, sounds not only are inaudible, but also are distorted due to the loss of sensory cells and nerve fibers in the ear. Hearing aids will allow these individuals to detect and hear many sounds that were inaudible without the amplification; however, the sounds often remain distorted. A

Figure 11.4   Types of Hearing Aids: Behind-the-Ear Model (A) and In-the-Ear Model (B)

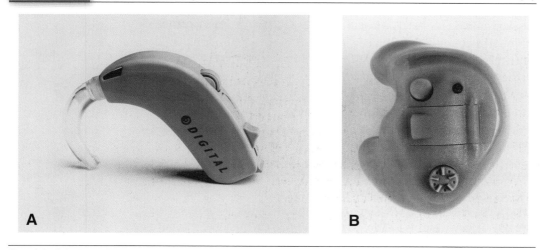

A

B

more recent development in amplification for individuals with severe to profound hearing loss is a device called the **cochlear implant**. This device is described in **Figure 11.5**.

In the classroom setting, students with hearing impairments often utilize an amplification device known as an **FM (frequency modulated) system**. With this system, the classroom teacher wears a small microphone that picks up the teacher's voice. The voice is transmitted via a radio frequency carrier wave to a special receiver worn by the student or students in the class who have a hearing loss. The receiver sends the signal to earphones or to the students' own hearing aids, allowing for improved reception of the teacher's voice in noisy classrooms.

The second category of adaptations, using another person, includes peer teaming and using interpreters and notetakers. Students who are deaf and hard-of-hearing can benefit from cooperative learning strategies that involve peer teaming or group work. Such strategies allow these students to benefit from the assistance of other students on some tasks and to offer assistance to their peers on other tasks. Students who rely on manual communication systems and are placed in the general education classroom often require interpreter support. A certified interpreter will accompany the student to classes to translate the teacher's and peers' spoken English into the manual communication system the student uses. The interpreter also may translate the student's questions and comments into spoken English if the student's speech is not understandable. No matter which communication system students with hearing impairment use, they will be using their visual and/or auditory skills to focus on understanding what is being said to them. They may be unable to take adequate notes in the classroom. For this reason, fellow classmates may serve as notetakers. Notetakers can use two-part, pressure-sensitive paper when taking their own notes, and then provide the additional copy to the student with the hearing loss.

Figure 11.5   Cochlear Implants

The cochlear implant is a device deigned for individuals with severe to profound hearing loss who cannot benefit from the use of conventional hearing aids. This amplification system is shown in the picture. It consists of a microphone and processor worn behind the user's ear which pick up the sounds in the environment and converts them to an electrical signal. The amplified signal is sent to a transmitter, worn behind the ear. The transmitter relays the signal to a receiver that has been surgically implanted in the skull, behind the ear. The signal travels into the inner ear through electrodes that also have been implanted. Thus, the cochlear implant delivers an electrical signal directly to the inner ear, the cochlea.

Some individuals have shown significant improvement in their hearing and speech production abilities through the use of the cochlear implant. However, these devices are a point of great controversy in the medical, audiological, and Deaf communities. Some professionals believe the cochlear implant represents an appropriate use of technology to improve the hearing of individuals who are profoundly deaf, providing them with communication options. Others argue that the cochlear implant is an unnecessary and invasive surgical procedure being used by surgeons and parents who are unfamiliar with the Deaf culture to "cure" the condition of deafness. These opponents do not view deafness as an "illness" or condition that needs to be "cured."

Auria™ sound processor, part of the Bionic Ear System cochlear implant, courtesy of Advanced Bionics Corp.

The third type of adaptation that may be needed for students who are deaf and hard-of-hearing is the modification of the physical environment. These students should be seated where they can maximize the use of auditory and visual input. This generally means away from noisy hallways or windows and in close proximity to the teacher and the interpreter. However, most teachers do not remain stationary when teaching. They present information from different locations in the classroom during different activities. In this case, an exchange of seats between the student with the hearing loss and a peer with normal hearing can be prearranged if needed.

The fourth adaptation, student response, may be needed for students using manual communication systems. If the student's speech skills are limited, the student may sign responses to questions posed by the teacher or by classmates to an interpreter. The interpreter then relays the student's response in spoken English.

Significant adaptations of teacher instruction, or instructional strategies, generally are not needed for students who are deaf and hard-of-hearing. Since these students often rely on speechreading, teachers should remember not to speak when their back is turned to the class (e.g., when writing on the board). In addition, announcements over the public address system or questions and comments from classmates seated behind a student with a hearing loss are difficult, if not impossible, for the student to hear. The teacher will need to repeat these announcements and questions. Many students who are deaf and hard-of-hearing have language skills below their peers and will receive additional services from the speech-language pathologist or the teacher certified in hearing impairment. If the classroom teacher discusses upcoming lessons with these professionals, it will allow them to prepare the students for key concepts and vocabulary words prior to their use in the classroom.

A student using the Nucleus 24 cochlear implant. Picture courtesy of Cochlear Corporation.

Some alteration of the materials used in teaching may be needed by students with hearing loss. These students may miss or not understand information that is presented only auditorily. Using visual aids when teaching (overheads, diagrams, models, handouts, etc.) and being certain videos shown in class are captioned (the text is printed at the bottom of the screen) will help students with hearing loss succeed in the classroom.

Lastly, activity or curriculum adaptations may be needed for the student who is deaf or hard-of-hearing. If the student cannot hear instructions and assignments given orally, the teacher will need to have them available in written form. Additional areas may be added to the student's curriculum depending on the individual's needs. These areas might include instruction in manual communication, auditory training, speechreading, and/or speech and language therapy. This specialized instruction would be provided by the appropriate professionals (the speech-language pathologist, the audiologist, the teacher certified in hearing impairment), and would not be the responsibility of the classroom teacher.

The classroom teacher is the key to the success of students who are deaf and hard-of-hearing. Using assistive devices and other support personnel as well as slightly modifying the environment and adapting teaching strategies can have a significant impact on the academic performance of these students. **Table 11.8** summarizes suggestions for the classroom teacher. See **Figure 11.6** for a description of a student with a hearing loss.

TABLE 11.8

Suggestions for Teachers of Students Who are Deaf and Hard-of-Hearing

1. Know the student's range of hearing and have the student seated close enough to hear you.
2. If the student uses an FM system, ask the audiologist for training on its use and maintenance.
3. Allow the student to change seats with another student if you move to another location in the room during a lesson.
4. If the student uses an interpreter, be sure that person is seated close to both you and the student.
5. Be sure the student has a clear view of your face and of the interpreter.
6. Try to keep your hands, books, and other objects away from your face when speaking. Do not speak while your back is toward the class.
7. Speak naturally; avoid exaggerated lip movements and shouting.
8. Loudspeaker announcements may not be heard by the student. The teacher or a fellow student should inform the student of the announcement.
9. The student may not hear questions, answers, or comments made by other students; be sure to repeat them.
10. Have lesson outlines, vocabulary words, and assignments in writing for the student.
11. Make sure the student has heard and understood instructions.
12. When the student does not understand something you say, rephrase what you have said, changing some of the words you used rather than just repeating what you said.
13. Most students who have a hearing loss are not able to take notes while trying to listen and speechread. They will need to have a note-taker, typically another student in the class.
14. Work with other school personnel who are providing services to the student (e.g., speech-language pathologist, teacher of the deaf, tutor) to preteach key vocabulary words and concepts in the curriculum.
15. Work with the audiologist and the teacher of the deaf to modify the classroom to reduce noise and reverberation whenever possible.

Figure 11.6   A Description of a Student with a Hearing Loss

Marisa (aged 12) has a congenital, bilateral, moderate to severe sensory hearing loss of unknown cause. Her hearing loss was first diagnosed at age 1 month, and she was fitted with behind-the-ear hearing aids at age 3 months. Marisa was enrolled in a parent-infant program at that time and received supplemental speech-language therapy. She was placed in a neighborhood preschool program at age 3 and then attended general education classes with support services (weekly services from the speech-language pathologist and weekly tutoring by a teacher certified in hearing impairment) in elementary and middle school. Marisa gets her hearing tested each year, and her hearing aids have been replaced every 3 to 4 years as needed. Her teachers have been willing to make whatever adaptations have been needed to ensure that Marisa is successful in school.

Marisa has always been a good student and has been able to keep up with her peers academically. In the past few months, however, Marisa's parents and teachers have noticed that her grades have been dropping, and she has not been wearing her hearing aids every day, saying, "Oh, I don't need them anymore." Why might Marisa suddenly not want to wear her hearing aids? What adaptations and additional services might be needed to help Marisa improve her school performance?

Communication Disorders

Among the various disability categories, students with communication disorders, or speech and language impairments, are second in prevalence in the schools only to students with learning disabilities. Because over 88% of students with communication disorders are educated exclusively in the general education classroom (U.S. Department of Education, 2005), it is important for classroom teachers to have an understanding of the nature and impact of these disorders. Although hearing impairments often are considered a type of communication disorder, they are also a type of sensory deficit and have been discussed previously. A **communication disorder** can be defined as follows:

> an impairment in the ability to receive, send, process, and comprehend concepts or verbal, nonverbal and graphic symbols systems (Owens, Metz & Haas, 2011).

Communication disorders may be developmental or acquired and can range from mild to severe. They may be the result of the conditions or infections discussed earlier in the chapter and may accompany other disabilities in students, such as intellectual disabilities, hearing impairment, and physical impairment. But many students with communication disorders have no other disabilities and have the same cognitive, sensory, and physical abilities as their peers. Under IDEA, speech or language impairment means a communication disorder such as stuttering, speech sound disorder, language impairment, or voice impairment that adversely affects a student's educational performance. To understand communication disorders, we first must consider the process of communication.

Communication

The ability to communicate is a skill most of us take for granted. We exchange information, opinions, and feelings by speaking, listening, reading, and writing on a daily basis. Only when the ability to communicate becomes impaired do we realize what an important and complex process it is. Humans communicate in many ways: verbally and nonverbally. The tools for communication can include facial expressions, body posture, hand gestures, even art and music. We will focus on two elements of communication: language and speech.

Language

Language can be defined as a rule-governed symbol system shared by a community which enables those people to communicate (Kuder, 2008). Rules govern language systems and users of any language system must learn to use the rules of their language to communicate effectively. **Expressive language** refers to the sending of information or messages to others, while **receptive language** refers to the receiving of messages from others.

Before considering language disorders, it is important to understand the components or elements of normal language. The components relate to its form (phonology, morphology, and syntax), its content (semantics), and its use (pragmatics). **Phonology** is the sound system of a particular language and the rules for combining sounds. Not all languages use the same sound system. Some sounds used in the spoken English language are not found in other languages, just as other languages use sounds not found in spoken English. These differences in sound systems can make learning and speaking a second language difficult for some students. **Morphology** refers to the rules for the structure of words, for example, the rules that we follow when we convert a word to a plural form or to a past tense. **Syntax** is the rule system that specifies word order for sentence structure. The two sentences "Mark gave Keesha the book" and "Keesha gave Mark the book" have very different meanings. The meaning is determined by the order of the names in the sentences. We understand the meaning of those sentences if we know the syntactical rule to apply when we decipher them. **Semantics** refers to the meanings of words and sentences, the content of the language we use. Many words, phrases, and sentences can have multiple meanings. The sentence "Maria was cold" could mean that Maria was physically cold or that she behaved in an uncaring manner. **Pragmatics** refers to the way language is used rather than the way it is structured. It involves the way we vary our language depending on the audience and the situation. For example, we change our vocabulary, phrasing, and length of sentences depending on whether we are speaking to a friend in a social setting, a supervisor at work, or a child playing.

Speech

Speech is the process of producing the vocal sounds associated with an oral language. Speech production involves several processes. Respiration, the inhalation and exhalation of air, provides the exhaled air stream that powers the voice. The vocal folds, found in the larynx, are set into vibration as air is exhaled during respiration.

This results in phonation, the actual production of voice. Resonation occurs as the vibrating air stream passes through the vocal tract, the cavities above the larynx, and the richness of the sound is enhanced. The tongue, teeth, lips, and palate accomplish the final shaping or articulation of the sound to produce the speech sounds of our language.

The process of producing speech involves the complex coordination of all the structures and muscles of the respiratory system, the larynx, the mouth, and the face. Injury to any of these regions (e.g., lung cancer, laryngitis, cleft palate), or damage to the neurologic systems that control these regions (e.g., cerebral palsy, traumatic brain injury) can have a significant impact on speech production. Some students with severe disabilities may never be able to produce understandable or intelligible speech, and alternative systems of expressive language must be used such as sign language or computerized communication systems.

Communication Disorders Assessment

Some school districts screen students for communication disorders prior to school enrollment whereas others screen selected grades, most commonly the elementary grades. Screenings are conducted by the speech-language pathologist using both informal and formal measures. When students fail a screening, they will be referred for a comprehensive speech and language evaluation. Although screenings are successful in identifying severe communication disorders, they may miss mild speech and language problems. Some students may have communication disorders that are subtle (e.g., difficulty with the appropriate use of language) or variable (e.g., a voice disorder associated with cheerleading). These disorders may be noted only when observed over a period of time by the classroom teacher. For this reason, the speech-language pathologist relies on referrals from classroom teachers regarding potential communication disorders. In some school districts, schoolwide screening programs for communication disorders have been eliminated, and the identification of disorders relies solely on teacher and parent referrals. The speech-language pathologist may provide teachers and parents with a communication skills checklist like the one in **Table 11.9** to assist in the identification of potential disorders.

The classroom teacher is the person most aware of the student's communication abilities and difficulties in the school setting. It is important that teachers and speech-language pathologists work cooperatively in the identification, assessment, and treatment of communication disorders. If the teacher observes difficulty with communication skills, the student should be referred for Response to Intervention (RTI) services. Then, specific evidence-based strategies can be implemented by the classroom teacher to assist the student. If the student makes appropriate improvement in speech and language skills, no referral to special education for a complete evaluation will be needed.

If it is determined that a student needs a comprehensive speech and language assessment, the methods and test materials used will vary depending on the age of the student and the type of suspected disorder. The speech-language pathologist may begin with an examination of the oral speech mechanism, looking for structural abnormalities or muscle incoordination. A hearing screening to detect potential hearing loss generally is included in the evaluation process. Specific tests will be administered to assess the student's production of speech

TABLE 11.9

Teacher Checklist for Communication Disorders

A. Receptive Language (Comprehension)

1. Does the student appear to understand what is heard in conversation and in classroom activities?	Yes	No	N/A
2. Does the student hear sounds (in words) appropriately? (e.g., you say "Wash the dog," and the student hears "Watch the dog")	Yes	No	N/A
3. Does the student follow verbal directions?	Yes	No	N/A
4. Does the student repeat simple sentences verbatim?	Yes	No	N/A
5. Does the student remember what was heard the previous day, week, or month?	Yes	No	N/A
6. Does the student understand basic concepts: opposites, categories, sequencing, etc.?	Yes	No	N/A
7. Does the student generalize knowledge of new concepts in a meaningful way?	Yes	No	N/A

B. Expressive Language

1. Is the student nonverbal (doesn't talk)?	Yes	No	N/A
2. Does the student use a minimum of five words (average) in a sentence during conversation?	Yes	No	N/A
3. Does the student use age-appropriate vocabulary?	Yes	No	N/A
4. Does the student use age-appropriate grammar?	Yes	No	N/A
5. Does the student respond appropriately to questions?	Yes	No	N/A

C. Articulation

1. Is the student who is functioning at the 4-year-old level mispronouncing p, b, t, d, k, g, f, m, n, ng, h, w, or v?	Yes	No	N/A
2. Is the student who is functioning at the 5-year-old level mispronouncing s, z, zh (as in beige), ch, dz (as in joke), l, sh, or any of the sounds listed in number 1?	Yes	No	N/A
3. Is the student who is functioning at the 6-year-old level mispronouncing th (voiceless as in thin and voiced as in then), r (er), or any of the sounds listed in numbers 1 and 2?	Yes	No	N/A
4. Is the student using mainly vowel sounds when talking?	Yes	No	N/A
5. Is the student leaving the final consonant sound off of words?	Yes	No	N/A
6. Is the student concerned about his/her speech?	Yes	No	N/A
7. Are the student's parents concerned about his/her speech?	Yes	No	N/A
8. Are there any physical problems with the oral structures (e.g., cleft palate, missing teeth, etc.)?	Yes	No	N/A

D. Voice

1. Is the student's voice always hoarse?	Yes	No	N/A
2. Is the pitch of the student's voice abnormally high or low?	Yes	No	N/A
3. Is the student's voice breathy?	Yes	No	N/A
4. Is the loudness of the student's voice appropriate?	Yes	No	N/A
5. Does the student abuse his/her voice (loud talking, yelling, singing, excessive throat clearing, etc.)?	Yes	No	N/A
6. Is the student's voice too nasal?	Yes	No	N/A
7. Is the student's voice lacking in nasality?	Yes	No	N/A

(continued on next page)

TABLE 11.9

Teacher Checklist for Communication Disorders *(continued)*

E. Fluency

1. Does the student repeat, hesitate, or draw out sounds?	Yes	No	N/A
2. Does the student repeat, hesitate, or draw out syllables?	Yes	No	N/A
3. Does the student repeat, hesitate, or draw out words?	Yes	No	N/A
4. Does the student repeat, hesitate, or draw out phrases?	Yes	No	N/A
5. When speaking, does the student appear to struggle to get the words out (e.g., clench jaw, blink eyes, tense neck muscles, etc.)?	Yes	No	N/A
6. Is the student concerned about his/her disfluency?	Yes	No	N/A
7. Are the student's parents concerned about his/her disfluency?	Yes	No	N/A

sounds, fluency of speech, voice quality, and language comprehension and expression. Depending on the results of the testing and on the history of the disorder, the speech-language pathologist may recommend additional evaluation by the audiologist, otorhinolaryngologist, psychologist, or special education teacher. Children may qualify to receive speech and language services if their speech-language difficulties significantly impact their educational success.

Common Communication Disorders

Communication disorders can be divided into speech disorders (problems with the production of oral language) and language disorders (problems with the comprehension or use of spoken or written language). These two types of communication disorders are not always discrete disorders; some students exhibit both speech and language disorders.

Speech Disorders

A speech disorder is an impairment of articulation or phonology, voice, or fluency. Of these, speech sound disorders are the most common. Speech sound disorders include problems with articulation or phonological rules. Children with speech sound disorders have difficulty with speech development and will not outgrow their problems without some type of assistance.

An articulation disorder occurs when a child has difficulty moving the structures of the mouth precisely to make a speech sound. For example, a child might substitute a "w" for "r" (saying "wabbit" for "rabbit") or he may produce an "s" that is "slushy" in quality. The ability to correctly articulate the sounds of a language depends on several factors including the student's age and physical abilities. Errors in speech production may be due to abnormalities of the oral structures (e.g., missing teeth or a cleft palate). Errors may also occur when a child has damage to parts of the brain or nerve fibers that control the muscles used for speech (e.g., cerebral palsy or traumatic brain injury). Developmental norms indicate that most children should be able to produce all sounds of English at least some of the time by age 5. By age 8, they should have mastered all speech sounds.

In contrast, a phonological disorder occurs when a child consistently uses patterns of errors that affect a group of sounds or particular parts of words. For example, a child may omit all "friction" sounds like "s, z, sh, and ch" when talking. Similarly, a child might omit all sounds at the ends of words. Phonologic errors are not due to the inability to say particular sounds; instead, they are due to a child's simplification of the rules that govern how sounds are combined into words. Children who have phonological disorders are usually very difficult to understand. Although some children have phonological disorders as a result of frequent ear infections, for many children the cause of their speech sound difficulty is unknown. Research has shown that children who exhibit phonological disorders often demonstrate reading and spelling problems when they get older, so early intervention is crucial.

Voice disorders involve the attributes of the pitch, loudness, resonance, duration, and quality of the voice. Teachers may notice that a student's voice seems too high or too low in pitch. They may consider it abnormally soft or loud, or unusually breathy or harsh. If these characteristics of the voice are significantly different from what is expected given a student's age and gender and are abusive to the larynx or negatively impact on communication, a voice disorder is present. Some voice disorders may be temporary—for example, the hoarseness associated with laryngitis or the lack of nasal resonance due to a cold. Other persistent disorders may be the result of more serious medical problems—for example, growths on the vocal folds, nerve damage resulting in paralysis of the vocal folds, or a cleft palate. A significant number of voice disorders in students are the result of vocal abuse. Frequent loud talking and yelling in school, especially during free time and sports activities, can become a habit for some students. These behaviors can lead to calloused growths on the vocal folds known as vocal nodules. The presence of nodules results in chronic hoarseness of the voice.

Fluency disorders is the third category of speech disorders. As speakers, we all exhibit occasional disfluencies, or interruptions in the flow of our speech. We pause in the middle of expressing a thought, we stumble over a word, we repeat a phrase, we use fillers such as "uh" and "uhm." Some disfluency also is common in young children learning language (Culatta & Leeper, 1987). It is when these disruptions are so frequent that they draw extraordinary attention to the person's speech or interfere with communication that a fluency disorder is present. A fluency disorder can be defined as an interruption in the flow of speaking, involving abnormal rate, rhythm, and repetitions. It may be accompanied by excessive tension and struggle behavior (ASHA, 1993). The most common fluency disorder is stuttering. When stuttering, students may exhibit whole-word repetitions, part-word repetitions (b-b-boy), or prolongations of sounds (mmmmmy). Students may seem to get stuck on sounds, unable to get the sound out. Their speech may be accompanied by struggle behaviors such as gestures, facial contortions, or squinting. Individuals who stutter typically begin to display abnormal disfluency between the ages of 2 and 5 years. Although spontaneous recovery may occur in some children, many will need the assistance of a speech-language pathologist to attain fluent speech. Some individuals never attain fluent speech, continuing to stutter throughout their lives, in spite of attempts at intervention or treatment. Stuttering has many interesting aspects as shown in **Table 11.10**.

Language Disorders

Language disorders can include the absence of language, delayed language development, deviations in language development, and language problems acquired after language has developed. They can range from mild to severe impairments. A language disorder is an impairment in the comprehension and/or use of spoken, written and/or other symbol systems. It may involve the form of language (phonology, morphology, or syntax), the content of language (semantics), and/or the function of language (pragmatics) (ASHA, 1993).

In some students, language disorders may be associated with other disabilities such as intellectual disabilities, learning disabilities, hearing impairment, autism, or emotional disorders. Other language disorders may be acquired after normal language has developed due to brain damage from head injury, tumors, or serious illness. Some students may exhibit

TABLE 11.10

Aspects of Stuttering

- Stuttering is universal. The disorder has existed throughout recorded history and is found among all peoples of the world.
- Stuttering almost always begins in childhood, usually before age 6. Ages 2 to 4 are particularly common periods for the onset of stuttering.
- Stuttering occurs more often among males than females. Reports of sex ratio vary from 3:1 to as high as 6:1.
- Stuttering tends to run in families. Family studies have shown that the risk of stuttering in relatives of a person who stutters is increased over that for the general population. Furthermore, the pattern of transmission in families is consistent with predictions derived from genetic models (Cox, 1988), yet genetic components of stuttering have not been proved.
- The amount of stuttering varies widely with situations. Persons who stutter often report excessive speech difficulties when they are excited or feel under pressure. Saying their name, talking on the telephone, ordering in a restaurant, talking to a person in authority (e.g., a teacher), and talking in front of a group (as in a classroom) also are situations that elicit much stuttering. Additionally, persons who stutter have good days and bad days meaning that the frequency and severity of their stuttering fluctuates.
- Stuttering is reduced or eliminated in a variety of conditions as well. Most affected people report being able to sing, whisper, and talk to themselves or their pets fluently. By talking in a prolonged, slow fashion, most become stutter free. Choral or unison speaking and talking to a rhythmical beat also improve fluency.
- For those who do not outgrow it, stuttering tends to change—and worsen—as the person matures. What began as a speech problem evolves into not only a speech problem, but also a personal-social-psychological problem.
- Stuttering need not hold a person back from achieving full potential. Many famous, brilliant, and talented people stuttered, such as: Winston Churchill, Moses, Marilyn Monroe, Sommerset Maugham, Isaac Newton, Mel Tillis, Bob Newhart, and James Earl Jones.

From *Communication Disorders in the Classroom*, 4th edition by Haynes et al. Copyright 2006 by Jones & Barlett Learning Company. Used with permission.

language disorders that are the result of limited opportunity to learn language, whereas for other students the cause of their language disorder is never determined. No matter what the cause, language disorders can have a significant impact on the academic performance and social skills of students. Language is the foundation of instruction and interaction in the classroom. Students with language disorders may have difficulty following directions, understanding lectures, reading and comprehending their textbooks, asking questions, and participating in conversations.

Children with language disorders may appear to be inattentive or noncompliant when, in fact, they do not understand directions or they have difficulty formulating responses. Speaking, listening to conversation, reading, and writing are all language-based activities. It is common for students who have language disorders to also have difficulty with reading and writing. Classroom teachers and speech-language pathologists often collaborate to address language and literacy issues in the classroom environment.

Certain groups of school-age individuals are considered to be "at risk" for language disorders. These groups include: (a) students with a history of preschool language delay, (b) students with learning and/or reading disabilities, and (c) students who are earning poor grades or are being retained in a grade (Haynes, Moran, & Pindzola, 2006). Classroom teachers should be particularly alert to signs of possible language disorders in these students. In addition to the checklist of communication skills in Table 11.9, the common symptoms of language disorders presented in **Table 11.11** may assist teachers in identifying language problems in the classroom.

Management of Communication Disorders

Most students with speech and/or language impairments benefit from direct services provided by the speech-language pathologist. The specific objectives and treatment approaches will

TABLE 11.11
Common Symptoms of Language Disorders in Older Children

Semantics
- word finding/retrieval deficits
- use of a large number of words in an attempt to explain a concept because the name escapes them (circumlocutions)
- overuse of limited vocabulary
- difficulty recalling names of items in categories (e.g., animals, foods)
- difficulty retrieving verbal opposites
- small vocabulary
- use of words lacking specificity (thing, junk, stuff, etc.)
- inappropriate use of words (selection of wrong word)
- difficulty defining words
- less comprehension of complex words
- failure to grasp double word meanings (e.g., can, file, etc.)

Syntax/Morphology
- use of grammatically incorrect sentence structures
- simple, as opposed to complex, sentences
- less comprehension of complex grammatical structures
- prolonged pauses while constructing sentences
- semantically empty placeholders (e.g., filled pauses, "uh," "er," "um")
- use of many stereotyped phrases that do not require much language skill
- use of "starters" (e.g., "you know")

Pragmatics
- use of redundant expressions and information the listener has already heard
- use of nonspecific vocabulary (e.g., thing, stuff) and the listener cannot tell from prior conversation or physical context what is referred to
- less skill in giving explanations clearly to a listener (lack of detail)
- less skill in explaining something in a proper sequence
- less conversational control in terms of introducing, maintaining, and changing topics (may get off track in conversation and introduce new topics awkwardly)
- rare use of clarification questions (e.g., "I don't understand," "You did what?")
- difficulty shifting conversational style in different social situations (e.g., peer to teacher, child to adult)
- difficulty grasping the "main idea" of a story or lecture (preoccupation with irrelevant details)
- trouble making inferences from material not explicitly stated (e.g., "Sally went outside. She had to put up her umbrella." The inference is that it was raining.)
- difficulties comprehending and using slang
- difficulties in deriving meaning from vocal inflection and prosodic cues (e.g., sarcasm)

From *Communication Disorders in the Classroom*, 4th edition by Haynes et al. Copyright 2006 by Jones and Bartlett Learning Company. Used with permission.

vary depending on the student's age, as well as the type and severity of the disorder. The intervention might focus on improving the articulation of speech sounds or the fluency of speech, changing voice characteristics, or improving language use and understanding. When providing direct services, the speech-language pathologist may work with students in the classroom or in a separate room located in the school building.

The majority of students with communication disorders are educated in the general education classroom. Many are capable of full participation in all instructional activities without major adaptations or modifications. Other students may require adaptations to ensure maximum learning and full participation. Five of the adaptations described for students with sensory deficits (visual and hearing impairments) can be applied to students with communication disorders. These include:

1. Use of assistive technology
2. Use of a person
3. Changes in student response
4. Changes in teacher instruction
5. Alteration in activities and/or curriculum (see **Table 11.12**).

As noted previously, some students with communication disorders may be unable to communicate by talking. These students may use augmentative and alternative communication (AAC). AAC includes any means of communication that enhances the student's current verbal communication or is the student's primary form of communication. Some examples of different types of AAC include: gestures, manual signs, objects, picture notebooks, and communication devices. Communication devices can range from pictures on a piece of cardboard to electronic devices that may contain from one to hundreds of messages. Instead of being restricted by just one type of communication, students will typically learn several different forms of communication (e.g., gestures, facial expressions, vocalizations, and use of a communication device). The educational team will determine the most appropriate forms of communication and should not hesitate to explore AAC options because research has shown that AAC may accelerate the development of spoken communication (Romski & Sevcik, 2005).

Peer teaming and working in groups provide students with communication disorders an opportunity to practice speaking and listening skills. Peers can model appropriate speech, and small groups may be less intimidating to students who are self-conscious about their speech. Students with poor receptive language skills may benefit from a "listening buddy," a classmate who assists with oral instructions and assignments.

Changes in the student response might be needed in some situations. If a student uses an augmentative communication device, it may take longer for that student to respond to a question. Similarly, students with receptive or expressive language disorders may need additional time to process questions and formulate their answers. Students who stutter may be uncomfortable responding in class or may need more time for oral responses.

Students who exhibit speech or language disorders typically do not require significant modifications in teacher instruction. Teachers should be certain the language level of their instruction is appropriate for students who exhibit language disorders. The classroom pro-

TABLE 11.12

Managing Communication Disorders

	Communication Disorders
Assistive Technology	• Augmentative communication devices
Use of Person	• Peer teaming
Student Response	• Allow more time
Teacher Instruction	• Model appropriate speech and language
	• Provide practice opportunities
Alter Activity	• Alter language level of instructions and assignments
Alter Curriculum	• Direct and/or collaborative services from speech-language pathologist

vides natural opportunities for communication and for generalization of the skills being targeted in speech-language therapy. Teachers should model appropriate speech and language and encourage the learning and practice of communication skills. Speech and language impairments can be barriers to social interaction and may have a negative impact on a student's self-esteem. Teachers should strive to promote a positive classroom environment that encourages and facilitates communication. Emphasis on quick responses or competition may cause stress for students with communication disorders and result in decreased participation in the classroom. Small group activities, large group discussions, oral reports, active listening, and role playing are instructional strategies that can benefit all students, including those with speech or language impairments.

Adaptation of activities and/or curriculum may be necessary for some students. If students have limited language skills, the language level of classroom activities and assignments may need to be altered to ensure that students can participate. Direct services from the speech-language pathologist typically are added to the curriculum for students with communication disorders. The speech-language pathologist may ask to observe the student in the classroom to assess more accurately the effectiveness of intervention strategies. Both the classroom teacher and the speech-language pathologist play a role in the development of communication and literacy skills (oral language, vocabulary, reading, writing, etc.). Students with speech and language impairments benefit from the development of curriculum-based goals and the implementation of collaborative treatment programs. Although direct speech-language services are important for many students, collaborative and cooperative service delivery models also are appropriate and important for these students. Speech-language pathologists are spending more time in classrooms, co-teaching with classroom teachers, and; planning and delivering lessons that develop and enhance speech, language, and literacy skills in all students.

Communication Variations

Regional, ethnic, and racial dialects of the English language are common in this country. These dialects are differences in the patterns of speech or the use of language found in a given region of the country, in certain social groups, or in specific cultural/ethnic groups. The linguistic variations may involve any aspect of speech and language, including: vocabulary (calling carbonated beverages *soda, pop,* or *coke*), pronunciation, word order, sentence structure, use of pronouns, and even the cadence of speech. These linguistic variations are considered language differences, not language disorders. For this reason, students who speak a dialectical variation of English generally do not receive direct services from the speech-language pathologist. Some professionals (Delpit, 1988; Foster, 1986) argue that although these students do not have disorders, they must acquire the skills they need to communicate effectively as judged by the dominant culture. If they don't, these students will be denied equal educational and employment opportunities. These professionals advocate that students be allowed, and encouraged, to retain their regional, ethnic, or racial dialects since it is an important part of their culture. Yet, such students also should be taught Standard English to ensure they will have equal social, economic, and educational opportunities.

Physical Impairments

Students with physical impairments, although few in number, comprise one of the most diverse group of exceptional individuals, due to the many types of diseases and disorders that interfere with the normal functioning of the muscles or bones. Physical impairments are also referred to as orthopedic impairments. According to IDEA, orthopedic impairments are defined as follows:

> Orthopedic impairments means a severe orthopedic impairment that adversely affects a child's educational performance. The term includes impairments caused by congenital anomaly (e.g., clubfoot, absence of some member, etc.), impairments caused by disease (e.g., poliomyelitis, bone tuberculosis, etc.), and impairments from other causes (e.g., cerebral palsy, amputations, and fractures or burns that cause contractures). (34 CRF, Ch. III, Sec. 300.7)

Physical Assessment

Most physical impairments are readily apparent and diagnosis will be made by a physician. Usually a physician who specializes in the specific area of disability, such as a neurologist or an orthopedist, will be involved. Physical examination, laboratory tests, and specialized tests for the specific disability will be performed to arrive at a diagnosis.

Further assessment will be made by a physical therapist, occupational therapist, speech-language pathologist, and teacher certified in physical disabilities, as appropriate. The type of support and modifications that the student needs will be decided by the educational team, based on their assessments of the student's physical and academic functioning. Some students with physical impairments will need support from special education whereas others will not.

Common Physical Impairments

Cerebral Palsy

Cerebral palsy refers to a variety of nonprogressive disorders of voluntary movement and posture. It is caused by a malfunction of the motor areas of the brain occurring before birth, during birth, or within the first few years of life (Miller, 2005; Porter, 2011). Students with cerebral palsy typically have abnormal and uncoordinated motor movement. The cerebral palsy may be very mild and result in minimal or no limitation in physical activities. For example, a student's mild cerebral palsy may only be noticeable when running. At the other extreme, the cerebral palsy may be very severe, interfering with the ability to perform activities of daily living. For example, a student with severe spastic cerebral palsy may be unable to make the coordinated arm movements needed for eating, to coordinate legs to walk, and to articulate clearly when talking. Due to the differing limb involvement, cerebral palsy may be classified by which limb is affected as shown in **Table 11.13**. Several different types of cerebral palsy that have differing motor characteristics are described in **Table 11.14**.

Students with cerebral palsy often have additional impairments, such as visual impairments and seizures. Teachers will need to adapt for the physical impairment (e.g., use of adapted pencils or pointing devices) as well as the secondary conditions (e.g., use of low vision devices).

TABLE 11.13

Classification of Cerebral Palsy by Limb Involvement

Monoplegia: one limb is affected
Paraplegia: both legs are affected
Hemiplegla: one arm and one leg on the same side are affected
Triplegia: three limbs are affected (usually two legs and one arm)
Quadriplegia: all four limbs are affected equally
Diplegia: all four limbs are affected with legs more affected

---

TABLE 11.14

Different Types of Cerebral Palsy

Spastic Cerebral Palsy
- In spastic cerebral palsy, affected muscles have increased tone with increased resistance to movement. Movement is often slow and jerky with a decreased range of motion.

Athetoid Cerebral Palsy
- In athetoid cerebral palsy, there is fluctuating muscle tone resulting in slow, abnormal writhing movements in which the limb rotates back and forth. There are usually extra, purposeless movements that make it difficult to move the limb to the intended location.

Ataxia
- In ataxia, there is an incoordination of voluntary muscle movement, with poor balance and equilibrium. Children often walk with feet wide apart, trunk weaving back and forth, and arms held out.

Mixed
- Many individuals with cerebral palsy have a combination of the above types of cerebral palsy.

Spinal Cord Injury

Damage to the spinal cord can be caused by a wide range of disorders (e.g., spinal tumors) and traumatic events (e.g., car accidents). Depending on the location and type of spinal cord injury, the student may have symptoms ranging from weakness of a limb to paralysis of all parts of the body below the neck with ventilator-assisted breathing. The top part of the spinal cord relays nervous impulses to control movement and detect sensation to the arms and upper part of the body. Damage at this level would result in paralysis and loss of sensation from the upper body and arms down to the feet. Damage to the lower portion of the spinal cord may affect only the legs and urinary and bowel function, or only urinary and bowel function (since the nerves affecting bladder and bowel function are below the nerves affecting the legs). Additional problems of pressure sores (skin breakdown from having sustained pressure on a part of the body), respiratory insufficiency (from paralysis of the muscles which aid in breathing), blood clots, urinary complications, loss of speech, and adjustment problems (such as depression) may occur as well (MacBean et al., 2009; Migliorini, Tonge, & Sinclair, 2011; Thietje et al., 2011). Physical and occupational therapies usually are prescribed, and psychological counseling may be of benefit.

Spina Bifida

Spina bifida is a defective closure of the bony spine, occurring in the first 28 days of gestation. Myelomeningocele is the most common type of spina bifida. In this condition, the spinal cord is not completely surrounded by the spine. The infant is born with a sac like protrusion on the back which contains the spinal cord.

Surgery will be performed to remove the sac, but this will not correct the paralysis and lack of sensation that occur below the area of spinal cord damage. The area that is affected will depend upon where the outpouching occurred. In most instances, the myelomeningocele will occur in the lower section of the spinal cord. This results in total or partial leg paralysis, loss of sensation in the legs, and bowel and bladder problems. Adaptations and assistive devices will be needed by the student.

In many students with spina bifida, there may be a blockage in the flow of cerebral spinal fluid in the brain, resulting in a fluid accumulation in the brain, known as hydrocephalus. A shunt (tube) is usually put in place to drain the fluid. Most children who have spina bifida and (shunted) hydrocephalus have low average intelligence with many having learning problems due to deficits in attention, memory, recall, motor reaction times, visual-perceptual skills, or ADHD (Burmeister et al., 2005; Iddon et al., 2004; Jacobs, Northam, & Anderson, 2001).

Muscular Dystrophy

Muscular dystrophy can be defined broadly as a group of inherited diseases characterized by progressive muscle weakness due to primary degeneration of muscle fibers (Finkel, 2002; Heller, Mezei, & Schwartzman, 2009). There are several different types of muscular dystrophy, which vary as to their prognosis and severity. The most common childhood form is Duchenne muscular dystrophy. In this type of muscular dystrophy, weakness begins in the legs and progresses upward. Typically, muscle weakness begins around 3 years of age with difficulty walking, running, or climbing stairs. By age 5, there is a characteristic gait and calf enlargement. Weakness continues to progress, and a wheelchair often is needed by 10 to 12 years of age. Through the teenage years, muscle weakness occurs in the muscles of the arms and upper body. A power wheelchair eventually will be needed. Muscle weakness continues to the point that it is difficult for the adolescent to maintain an upright head position. Due to the weakness of the muscles for breathing and coughing, there is an increased incidence of respiratory infections, and the heart muscle often is affected. Most individuals with Duchenne type muscular dystrophy will die around 20 years of age due to respiratory infections or heart complications (Heller, Mezei, & Schwartzman, 2009). The student with muscular dystrophy will need to be assessed and monitored continually to determine appropriate adaptations and physical assistance as the disease progresses. This disease results in a physical degeneration, not a mental one. Counseling regarding issues of death and dying often are needed to assist the student with a degenerative, terminal illness.

Limb Deficiency

A limb deficiency refers to any number of skeletal abnormalities in which the limbs (arms and legs) are partially or totally missing. Limb deficiencies include those types in which the end part of the limb is missing (such as in an amputation) as well as those that have the middle part of the limb missing (such as when a hand is attached to the shoulder or elbow region). There are several types of prosthetic devices (artificial limbs) that may be used to assist the individual with a limb deficiency in optimum functioning. Artificial legs may be used to walk or run, or a prosthetic hand may be used to pick up items. However, children born with limb deficiencies often are able to compensate for the deficiency by using the remaining part of the limb or by using a different limb. Children missing their arms, for example, may compensate by using their feet for a variety of tasks the missing hands would do (e.g., writing). In these cases, the individual may use a prosthesis for only cosmetic reasons, or may elect not to use one at all.

Management of Orthopedic Impairments

Management of the orthopedic impairment will vary depending upon the type of orthopedic impairment and its severity. The educational team, including the teacher certified in physical disabilities, physical therapist, occupational therapist, speech-language pathologist, family, and other educational personnel will determine the types of modifications needed. Adaptations for students with orthopedic impairments can be divided into six main areas:

1. Use of assistive technology
2. Use of a person
3. Changes in the physical environment

4. Changes in student response
5. Alteration in material
6. Alteration in activities and/or curriculum (See **Table 11.15**) (Heller, Forney, Alberto, Best, & Schwartzman, 2009).

Students with physical disabilities often will need to use assistive technology. There are many different types of assistive technology that may be used. Some of the types of assistive technology address positioning, hand and arm use, communication, mobility, and access to school activities. Proper position is imperative for students with physical impairments in order to optimize the movement and range of motion they have. Several positioning devices may be used, such as special chairs, trays and cut out tables, that optimize the student's ability to move. Assistive devices for hand and arm use may range from a student using a clay wrapped pencil, which can be grasped easily, to using a switch to control a computer, which scans possible selections. Augmentative communication devices also may be used to allow the student to communicate effectively with others. Specialized wheelchairs, scooters, and other mobility devices may be needed to allow the student to move independently or with assistance. Many other assistive technology devices may be used to support computer access (e.g., enlarged keyboard, joysticks) and access to school activities (e.g., Smart Board for note taking).

A second type of adaptation involves using another person. Peer assistance may be used to help the student in activities that require additional physical movement the student is unable to perform. Peer teaming or working in groups also may be used. This not only allows additional assistance to the student with an orthopedic impairment on the parts of the task that require physical movement, but it also provides the student an opportunity to assist peers on parts of the tasks that do not involve a physical component.

The third type of adaptation is arrangement of the physical environment. Aisles may need to be widened to allow a student in a wheelchair to move freely about the classroom. Blackboards, light switches, and bulletin boards may need to be lowered so the student can access them.

A fourth adaptation is student response. Students with severe physical impairments may be unable to write using a pad and paper. They may use a computer to write their responses or answer questions orally. Students may tire easily when their impairment is severe, so homework and tests may need to be shortened to minimize fatigue. Time limits often need

TABLE 11.15

Managing Physical Impairments

	Physical Impairment
Assistive Technology	• Devices to compensate for physical impairment (e.g., clay wrapped pencil, adapted computer)
Use of Person	• Peer teaming
Physical Environment	• Modify to allow access (e.g., wider aisles, lowered chalkboard)
Student Response	• Alternate response forms (e.g., eye gaze response, giving answers orally rather than in writing) • Allow more time
Teacher Instruction	• Allow student to feel material
Alter Material	• Alter material so student can physically use it (e.g., material larger so it can be manipulated, material placed in multiple choice format)
Alter Activity	• Change activity to compensate for physical disability
Alter Curriculum	• Add to curriculum specialized skills (e.g., use of technology)

to be extended for students who are slow due to their impairment or their use of augmentative devices.

A fifth adaptation is teacher instruction. The teacher typically will not need to modify the instructional strategies used in class. However, it is important that the teacher allows the student to feel or touch what is being discussed. Some students with physical impairments may have missed opportunities to feel what the item is like due to limitation in mobility and have incorrect information regarding the item.

A sixth adaptation is adapting the material. Students with physical impairments may provide their answer in any number of ways which will require modifying the material. Material often will need to be rewritten and spaced appropriately for a student to eye-gaze an answer. Students who have limited responses may need items placed in multiple choice format in order to respond. Other students may need material adapted for the computer in order to access it.

In some instances an activity or curriculum modification is needed for the student with a physical impairment. Due to the lack of motor movement, students may need some activities adapted. For example, frog dissection would be possible using a computer program, but not in the laboratory. Additional areas may be added to the student's curriculum, such as teaching the use of adapted devices, teaching the student to independently perform any physical health care procedures such as clean intermittent catheterization, and adaptations to vocational and independent living skills. See **Figure 11.7** for a description of a student with a physical disability.

Health Impairments

There are several different types of **health impairments** that may interfere with a student's functioning at school. When this occurs, the students are classified as having other health impairments (OHI). Other health impairments are defined under IDEA as follows:

The health impairment results in having limited strength, vitality, or alertness, including a heightened awareness of environmental stimuli, that results in limited attentiveness to the educational environment that: (1) is due to chronic or acute health problems such as asthma, attention deficit or attention deficit hyperactivity disorder, diabetes, epilepsy, a heart condition, hemophilia, lead poisoning, leukemia, nephritis, rheumatic fever, and sickle cell anemia, and (2) adversely affects a child's educational performance.

Figure 11.7   A Description of Carlos, a Middle School Student with Cerebral Palsy

Carlos is an 11-year-old boy with severe spastic quadriplegia who sees a teacher certified in physical disabilities in a resource room for two class periods a day and attends general education classes for the remainder of the day. His cerebral palsy interferes with his ability to walk, use his hands, and speak, although he has normal intelligence. Carlos independently uses a power wheelchair to go between classes. His laptop computer has a software program that allows him to use it as an AAC device which stores hundreds of messages for communication. He is able to also use his laptop computer for academic work and accesses it using a joystick and on-screen keyboard. Carlos is behind in reading and writing by a few grade levels due to numerous health problems and fatigue issues. However, he is making good grades in math, science, and social studies. What adaptations might you make to assist Carlos in your classroom?

Assessment of Health Impairments

Health impairments are diagnosed through the use of physical examination, blood work, and specialized tests for the specific type of impairment. Additional assessments may be made by the educational team to determine how the student is performing academically and whether modifications and support from special education are needed. Often these students require few modifications in the classroom. The teacher will need to be knowledgeable about the specific health impairment and any special procedures needed should an emergency situation arise. Based on the student's condition and assessment of the student's needs, a plan of action should be written out by the physician or nurse and known by all the educational staff working with the student in case an emergency occurs.

Common Health Impairments

Epilepsy

A seizure is a brief, temporary change in the normal functioning of the brain's electrical system due to excessive, uncontrolled electrical activity in the brain. Epilepsy refers to a condition in which a person has recurrent seizures. The most common treatment for seizures is medication. However, in some instances medication may not be able to completely stop seizures from occurring, but only decrease their frequency.

There are many different types of seizures with varying characteristics. Some students will see flashing lights or experience some type of sensation immediately prior to the seizure, but many students will have no warning that a seizure is about to occur. Most seizures will involve a loss of consciousness, or altered consciousness, in which the student will miss information and not know what has occurred during the seizure. Some seizures will be very obvious, and others will be subtle. The most obvious type of seizure is the convulsive type known as a **generalized tonic-clonic** seizure. In this seizure, the student loses consciousness, and the body initially becomes very stiff, followed by a rhythmic jerking motion. Other seizures are not as noticeable, such as the **absence** seizure in which the student often stares blankly for a few seconds. Other types of seizures, such as **myoclonic** and **complex partial** seizures, involve very different types of motor movements and may not appear to be a seizure to those unfamiliar with seizure disorders (Heller & Cohen, 2009). **Table 11.16** describes the common types of seizures.

Teachers play a major role in seizure treatment, documentation, and identification. Teachers need to know what type of seizures the student has, and what to do if a seizure occurs. Often no treatment is needed, but for tonic-clonic seizures, the teacher will need to know what steps to take if one occurs as described in **Table 11.17**.

Accurate documentation of the occurrence of seizures (including a description of the seizure, how long it lasted, and time of day it occurred) will assist the physician in diagnosis and treatment. Seizures such as absence seizures are so subtle that teachers are often the first people to suspect that the student is having this type of seizure. Teachers will need to make a medical referral if a seizure is suspected.

Asthma

Asthma is the most common lung disease of childhood. With asthma, there are acute attacks of shortness of breath and wheezing due to airway inflammation and airway obstruction (Porter, 2011). A student with asthma has normal breathing until contact is made with a substance or situation which triggers the asthma attack. There are many different triggers, with some of the most common ones being allergies (including pollen), air pollution, exercise, weather changes, emotional stress, and medications (Goksel, Celik, Erkekol, Gullu, Mungan, & Misirligil, 2009; Washington et al., 2012). When the asthma attack occurs, the

TABLE 11.16

Common Types of Seizures

Tonic-Clonic Seizure (also known as grand mal seizure)
- **Characteristics:** When a tonic-clonic seizure occurs, the student suddenly loses consciousness and falls to the floor (and may be injured during the fall). In the first part of this seizure, the student will become very stiff. This is followed by a rhythmic jerking of the body. During this time, the tongue may be bitten causing blood and saliva to come out of the mouth. Breathing may be shallow which can cause the lips and fingernails to turn a bluish color. The person may lose bowel and/or bladder control during the seizure. Usually the seizure lasts only a few minutes, after which the student regains consciousness. At this time, the student experiences some confusion and is very tired.
- **Actions:** Know the steps to take if one occurs in the classroom (see Table 11.17). Allow the student to rest after the seizure is over.

Absence Seizure (also known as petit mal seizure)
- **Characteristics:** In this seizure, the student suddenly loses consciousness, stops whatever activity was being done, and either stares straight ahead or rolls the eyes upward. There usually is no movement or change in posture, except possibly some eye blinking or mouth twitching. This type of seizure lasts a few seconds, and at its completion, the student will resume the previous activity as if nothing occurred. Absence seizures can occur only a few times a day or as frequently as hundreds of times a day.
- **Actions:** There is no specific first aid for this seizure. However, this type of seizure often interferes with learning since the student is missing information each time the seizure occurs. Pairing the student with another student may be helpful, so that the peer may show the student where they are in the book or lesson after a seizure occurs. Teachers also need to be alert to identify this subtle type of seizure which is often mistaken for daydreaming.

Myoclonic Seizure
- **Characteristics:** This seizure appears as a sudden, uncoordinated body jerk of all or part of the body. Sometimes the student may drop something, fall against something, or fall to the floor.
- **Actions:** There is no specific first aid for this seizure unless injury occurs.

Atonic Seizure (also known as a drop attack)
- **Characteristics:** This seizure involves the student suddenly collapsing or falling. Recovery typically occurs after 10 seconds to 1 minute.
- **Actions:** There is no specific first aid for this seizure unless injury occurs in the fall.

Complex Partial Seizure (also known as psychomotor or temporal lobe seizure)
- **Characteristics:** This seizure consists of random purposeless activity in which the student appears dazed and may walk around, pick up objects, pick at clothes, or perform some other type of complex motor sequence. The student cannot control motor movements and will not remember what happened when the seizure is over.
- **Actions:** The teacher should remain with the student until the seizure is over, guiding the student away from any hazards.

student will have difficulty breathing, as seen by shortness of breath, coughing, wheezing, labored breathing, and complaints of difficulty breathing.

Teachers who have students with asthma need to know how to decrease the occurrence of asthma attacks and what to do when one occurs. Teachers should be aware of the specific causes of an asthma attack for specific students and try to avoid those causes or triggers when possible. For example, if being close to the school rabbit causes an asthma attack or exercising is a factor, then modifications can be made to decrease contact with the rabbit or adapt the exercise program. When an asthma attack occurs, the student needs medication immediately. Medication usually is in the form of a spray that is inhaled and opens up the airway to improve breathing. The teacher needs to be sure the medication is always accessible (e.g., is taken on any field trips) and be familiar with proper administration as well as emergency procedures. Although it is rare for an asthma attack to be fatal, there are approximately 5,000 deaths each year and most could have been prevented with treatment (Beers et al., 2006).

TABLE 11.17

What to Do for a Tonic-Clonic Seizure

1. Stay calm and glance at a watch near the start of a seizure to determine how long it lasts.
2. Put the student in a lying position, move furniture out of the way to avoid injury.
3. Put student on his or her side to allow saliva to drain from mouth and prevent aspiration.
4. Shirt collars can be loosened, and something soft, such as a jacket, should be placed under the student's head.
5. Do not restrain the student's movements and do NOT put anything in the student's mouth since this may cause injury.
6. If seizure continues for more than 5 minutes or there are multiple seizures occurring immediately one after the other, call an ambulance (Epilepsy Foundation, 2001). This is because the student may need intravenous medication to stop the seizure.
7. If the seizure stops, but the student is not breathing, give mouth to mouth resuscitation. (This is very rare.)
8. After the seizure is over, the student will not remember what happened and should be reassured and informed of what occurred.
9. The student should be assessed as to whether any injury occurred. If there was a blow to the head when the student fell, the student should be seen by a nurse or other medical personnel.
10. The student will be exhausted after the seizure and should be allowed to sleep.
11. It is important that the student's dignity be protected during and after the seizure. If the clothes were soiled, arrangements should be made to change them.
12. Document the occurrence of the seizure, including a description of the seizure, the time it occurred, the length of the seizure, if the student fell and had any injuries, what first aid was given (if any), and whether the parents were notified.

Sickle Cell Disease

Sickle cell disease is an inherited disorder in which some of the red blood cells are abnormally shaped like a sickle (crescent) due to the presence of abnormal hemoglobin in the red blood cell. These sickle shaped cells do not survive as long as normal shaped red blood cells survive which results in fewer red blood cells and, hence, anemia. Students with sickle cell disease often experience fatigue due to the anemia. They also may experience "sickling crisis" in which an increased number of cells sickle and become wedged in small capillaries due to their sickle shape. This will stop the flow of oxygen to the tissues below the block, and tissue death will occur. The sickling crisis may be triggered by several factors, such as a decrease in oxygen, dehydration, infection, environmental

It is very important for a student with diabetes to eat lunch and snacks on a regular schedule.

temperature change, excessive exercise, or stress (Brown, 2012). The student will experience pain wherever the blockage is occurring.

The teacher needs to be aware that students with sickle cell disease may experience fatigue and short attention span due to the anemia. Planning more difficult work early in the day or in short segments may be helpful. If the student has a sickling crisis, the main symptom will be pain, and an emergency plan must be followed. Often students with sickle cell disease have frequent or extended absences due to the sickling crisis. The teacher must ensure that arrangements are made to assist the student in making up missed work. See **Figure 11.8** for additional health impairments.

| Figure 11.8 | Additional Health Impairments |

Childhood cancer. Cancer refers to a condition in which certain cells have the trait of unregulated excessive growth. These cells invade tissues and organs of the body and interfere with their normal functioning. There are several types of cancers (e.g., leukemia), and some of these are curable. Depending upon the type of cancer, treatment options include surgery, chemotherapy, and/or radiation. Students being treated for cancer may miss school, have fatigue, and have various side effects of treatment (e.g., hair loss).

Chronic renal failure. Students who have chronic renal failure no longer have functioning kidneys. When the kidneys can no longer effectively filter out waste products from the blood, there can be fluid accumulation, anemia, and electrolyte imbalance. One way to treat this disorder is by having dialysis on a regular basis. When this treatment is used, teachers may need to monitor these students' diets (for adequate intake as well as for any restrictions) as well as their fatigue level. The preferred treatment option is a kidney transplant. Students having this procedure will be more susceptible to infections due to the immunosuppressive medications they must take; hence, the teacher will need to use good infection control measures.

Cystic fibrosis. Cystic fibrosis is a genetic disease in which there is an abnormal excessive secretion of mucus from the exocrine glands, especially affecting the respiratory and gastrointestinal systems. Students need to be encouraged to cough to clear the secretions and may require respiratory medications. They also need to be encouraged to eat (e.g., have extra helpings at lunch) due to the loss of calories that occurs with this condition. Electrolyte abnormalities can occur during excessive exercise and this may require the student to take salt supplementation. Most individuals die of respiratory complications in their mid- to late thirties.

Hemophilia. Hemophilia refers to a group of bleeding disorders in which there are insufficient clotting factors in the blood. The severity of the hemophilia depends upon the percentage of clotting factor that is missing. Students who have severe hemophilia may not only bleed upon sustaining some trauma, but they may bleed spontaneously without any injury. When a bleeding episode occurs, the student will need clotting factor replacement as soon as possible.

Type I diabetes. Type I diabetes is a condition that occurs when the pancreas produces little or no insulin. Treatment consists of monitoring blood glucose, receiving insulin (through injection or a pump), following a meal plan, and a regular exercise regimen.

Management of Health Impairments

A diverse group of conditions comprise the category of other health impairments. Most students will have normal intelligence and may not appear ill. However, in many of these conditions, students will have periodic episodes of extreme distress. The teacher must be alert for these signs of distress and know what to do when they occur. For this reason, a plan of action in emergency situations should be developed with the physician and family, and then shared with the education team. Often students with these conditions have frequent absences due to their health-related problems. The teacher will need to assist the student in making up work. In certain instances, hospital or home bound instruction will be appropriate. In some of these conditions, fatigue and just not feeling well may impact negatively on the student's performance.

Adaptations for students with other health impairments typically fall into four categories:

1. Assistive technology and medical technology
2. Use of a person
3. Modification of physical environment
4. Adaptation to the curriculum (See **Table 11.18**)

Students with other health impairments may require certain health procedures during the school day, such as testing for the level of glucose in the blood to determine insulin dosage. Assistive devices or equipment, such as the glucose monitoring machine and other

TABLE 11.18

Managing Health Impairments

	Health Impairment
Assistive Technology	• Use of items used in health procedures
Use of Person	• Individual may assist student with health procedure
Physical Environment	• Arrange for a private area to perform procedure
Alter Curriculum	• Add to curriculum student learning how to do physical procedure

similar equipment, may be needed for the particular type of health impairment. A person may be required to assist with the procedure. The student should be provided with an appropriate secluded physical environment, such as the nurse's office, to perform the procedure. Lastly, the curriculum may be altered to include teaching the student how to perform the health care procedure, recognize the signs which indicate distress, and understand the actions to take when a health problem occurs. See **Figure 11.9** for a description of a student with a health impairment.

Figure 11.9 A Description of Jamal, an Elementary School Student Who Has Epilepsy

Jamal attends third grade at his local elementary school. He was diagnosed 2 years ago with epilepsy and experiences two types of seizures: tonic-clonic seizures and absence seizures. He takes medication for his epilepsy which has greatly reduced the number of tonic-clonic seizures he has experienced over the past 2 years. Jamal's last tonic-clonic seizure occurred at school 6 months ago. Fortunately, his teachers were trained as to what to do if such a seizure occurred, and they were able to handle the situation well.

Jamal's medication has been less successful in stopping his absence seizures that continue to occur on a weekly basis. To help Jamal find his place after having an absence seizure, he has a student partner who can point to the book or activity when Jamal comes out of the seizure. Jamal's teachers document the frequency of his seizures, as well as other information about them. These records are important to his parents and the physician so they can determine the effectiveness of his medication. Are there other adaptations you would consider if Jamal was placed in your classroom?

Summary

This chapter reviewed a variety of sensory, communication, physical, and health impairments that students may experience. Students with these disabilities may encounter barriers to their success in the classroom that are unique to the disabilities. It is not possible to provide an in-depth discussion of each disability in an introductory textbook; however, it is important that the classroom teacher have a general understanding of these impairments and the adaptations that may be needed. The responsibility for these adaptations should be a shared one, with the classroom teacher playing a major role on the educational team that meets the needs of these students.

Classroom Application Activities

1. When you have a student with a sensory impairment in your general education classroom, what will be the role of the related service staff and special education teachers?

2. A student with a physical disability is going to be placed in your general education classroom. What do you need to know about the student's physical impairment? How will you get this information? (What if the student were to have a health impairment rather than a physical disability?)

3. Currently some Deaf adults are expressing concern that the move toward full inclusion of students with deafness in the general education classroom is not allowing these students to achieve to their fullest academic potential. In addition these students are not provided with an opportunity to learn about the Deaf culture. Advocates are calling for a separate educational system for these students (i.e., separate classes and/or schools). Discuss the pros and cons of a separate educational system for students who are deaf.

4. You teach in an inclusive general education classroom and among your students are several who have sensory, communication, physical, and health impairments. The parents of another student in your class (one who does not have any disability) have called and expressed their displeasure that their child is in your classroom. They are concerned that their child will be held back in her learning because you will have to slow down your teaching and spend so much time with these students who have disabilities. How will you handle this situation?

5. Conduct a short lesson with the students using simulators to determine how much information they miss and what adaptations would be helpful. Vision impairment simulators may be purchased or made. To construct simulators, buy protective goggles (from a hardware store) and place construction paper over them. If construction paper is placed completely over the goggles, this will simulate total vision loss. If a hole is placed in the center of the construction paper, this will simulate a peripheral field loss. Placing only a circle of construction paper over the direct line of vision simulates a central field loss. Placing scotch tape over the goggles, instead of construction paper, will simulate light perception only. It should be stressed that since the college students actually have sight, the simulators do not give them an idea of what it would be like not having vision from birth. The simulators give only a general idea of the types of vision losses, but can prove helpful in understanding how lessons, environments, and materials may need to be modified. Ear plugs can be used to simulate a mild to moderate hearing loss.

6. Have an interpreter, speech-language pathologist, special education teacher, or related service provider (physical therapist, occupational therapist, etc.) come to class and discuss their role in the educational setting.

7. Contact your local school system and make arrangements to observe a teacher of students with visual impairments, a teacher of students with hearing impairments, a speech-language pathologist, an audiologist, a physical therapist, or an occupational therapist as they provide services to students with disabilities.

8. Peter is a 10-year-old boy who enjoys playing computer games and talking with his friends on the Internet. He was born with spastic quadriplegia cerebral palsy and a seizure disorder. Peter later developed asthma which results in frequently missing school in the winter months. He uses a power wheelchair for mobility and is able to maneuver quite well around the school. His speech is not understandable so he uses an augmentative communication device with voice output that he accesses by slowly pointing to the symbols with his right hand. Peter does most of his work on the computer using an adapted keyboard. He is in general education classes for four periods a day and receives special education services for two periods a day. Peter successfully finished third grade last year, although he is one grade level behind in reading. Peter is now entering fourth grade and will be in Ms. Jones's class. Ms. Jones has never had a student with such severe physical and health impairments in her class. Although she understands that Peter has normal or near normal intelligence, she is very concerned about how she will teach him in her class. Prior to the start of school, the special education teacher, Ms. Daniels, has scheduled a meeting with Ms. Jones to discuss Peter.

   a. What does Ms. Jones need to know about Peter's health and physical condition?

   b. What are some possible modifications that you would expect Peter would need?

c.   What are some of the issues that should be covered in the meeting?

d.   What other professionals may be providing services to Peter?

e.   What should be the role of the special education teacher throughout the academic year?

9.   Marsha is a 15-year-old student in tenth grade who has been getting mostly "B" grades and has been very active in sports. She is popular and enjoys socializing with her peers. However, lately she has been doing poorly in her school work. Marsha does not appear to be interested in her classwork and often appears to be daydreaming. Her math teacher attributed this to her age and her interest in boys. However, her basketball coach has found that Marsha is performing poorly in the sport and has noticed that she keeps bumping into her teammates and is not making the easy shots. Mr. Tuttle, Marsha's English Literature teacher, also is concerned about her behavior and noticed that she rubs her eyes frequently, and rereads or skips words or lines when reading. Marsha also seemed to be oblivious to the work on the blackboard when it was not read aloud.

a.   What type of impairment does Mr. Tuttle suspect and what should Mr. Tuttle do?

b.   What type of medical exams should Marsha receive?

c. What would qualify Marsha for special education services?

d. If Marsha qualifies for special education services, what would be the role of the special education teacher?

e. What would Marsha's general education teachers need to know and what type of modifications would be discussed?

Internet Resources

Alexander Graham Bell Association for the Deaf
3417 Volta Place NW
Washington, DC 20007-2778
202-337-5220 (V/TTY)
www.agbell.org

American Speech-Language-Hearing Association
2200 Research Blvd.
Rockville, MD 20850-3289
1-800-638-8255
www.asha.org

Brain Injury Association of America
1608 Spring Hill Road, Suite 110
Vienna, VA 22182
703-761-0750
www.biausa.org

Clerc National Deaf Education Center
At Gallaudet University
800 Florida Ave. NE
Washington, DC 20002
www.clerccenter.gallaudet.edu

The Council for Exceptional Children (CEC)
1110 North Glebe Road, Suite 300
Arlington, VA 22201
703-620-3660
www.cec.sped.org

Epilepsy Foundation of America
4351 Garden City Dr.
Landover, MD 20785-2267
1-800-EFA-1000
www.efa.org

National Association of the Deaf
814 Thayer Ave.
Silver Spring, MD 20910-4500
301-587-1788
301-587-1789 (TTY)
www.nad.org

The National Center for Hearing Assessment and Management at Utah State University
2880 Old Main Hill
Logan, UT 84322
435-797-3584
www.infanthearing.org

The National Organization for Rare Disorders, Inc. (NORD)
P.O. Box 8923
New Fairfield, CT 06812-8923
1-800-999-6673
www.rarediseases.org

National Stuttering Association
119 W. 40th Street
14th floor
New York, NY 10018
800-937-8888
www.nsastutter.org

NIDCD Clearinghouse (National Institute on Deafness and Other Communication Disorders)
1 Communication Ave.
Bethesda, MD 20892-3456
1-800-241-1044
1-800-241-1055 (TTY)
www.nidcd.nih.gov

Stuttering Foundation of America
3100 Walnut Grove Road, Suite 603
P.O. Box 11749
Memphis, TN 38111
800-992-9392
www.stutteringhelp.org

References

Aicardi, J. (2002). What is epilepsy? In B.L. Maria (Ed.), *Current management in child neurology* (pp. 86–89). Hamilton: BC Decker.

Alimovic, S., & Mejaski-Bosnjak, V. (2011). Stimulation of functional vision in children with perinatal brain damage. *Collegium Antropologicum, 35*(Suppl. 1), 3–9.

American Speech-Language-Hearing Association. (1993). Definitions of communication disorders and variations. *Asha, 35*, (Suppl. 10), 40–41.

Andersen, R.A. (2004). *Infections in children: A sourcebook for educators and child care providers.* Austin, TX: Pro-Ed.

Bess, F., Dodd-Murphy, J., & Parker, R. (1998). Children with minimal sensorineural hearing loss: Prevalence, educational performance, and functional status. *Ear and Hearing, 19*(5), 339–354.

Bhatnagar, S.C., & Andy, O. (1995). *Neuroscience for the study of communicative disorders.* Baltimore, MD: Williams & Wilkins.

Boyer, S.G., & Boyer, K.M. (2004). Update on TORCH infections in the newborn infant. *Newborn & Infant Reviews, 4*(1), 70–80.

Brown, M. (2012). Sickle cell disease and thalassemia: Pathophysiology, care and management. In M. Brown & T. J. Cutler (Eds.), *Haematology nursing* (pp. 117–149). Oxford, UK: Wiley-Balckwell.

Burmeister, R., Hanney, H.J., Copeland, K., Fletcher, J.M., Boudousquie, A., & Dennis, M. (2005). Attention problems and executive functions in children with spina bifida and hydrocephalus. *Child Neuropsychology, 11*, 265–283.

Chang, D. (2007). Ophthalmologic exam. In P. Riordan-Eva, J.P. Whitcher, & T. Asbury (Eds.), *Vaughn and Asbury's general ophthalmology* (17th ed., pp. 28–60). New York: Lange/McGraw-Hill Medical.

Corn, A.L., DePriest, L.B., & Erin, J.N. (2000). *Visual efficiency.* In M.C. Holbrook & A.J. Koenig (Eds.), *Foundations in education Volume II: Instructional strategies for teaching children and youths with visual impairments* (2nd ed.). New York: American Foundation for the Blind.

Culatta, R., & Leeper, L. (1987). Disfluency in childhood: It's not always stuttering. *Journal of Childhood Communicative Disorders, 10*, 157–171.

Delpit, L.D. (1988). The silenced dialogue: Power and pedagogy in educating other people's children. *Harvard Educational Review, 58*(3), 280–298.

Epilepsy Foundation. (2001). *First aid for generalized tonic clonic (grand mal) seizures.* Landover, MD: Author.

Finkel, R.S. (2002). Muscular dystrophy and myopathy. In B.L. Maria (Ed.), *Current management in child neurology* (pp. 360–367). Hamilton: BC Decker.

Foster, H.L. (1986). *Ribin', jivin', and playin' the dozens* (2nd ed.). Cambridge, MA: Ballinger.

Gordon, N. (1998). Colour blindness. *Public Health, 112*(2), 81–85.

Goksel, O., Celik, G.E., Erkekol, F.O., Gullu, E., Mungan, D., & Misirligil, Z. (2009). Triggers in adult asthma: Are patients aware of triggers and doing right? *Allergol Immunopathol, 37*, 122–128.

Grundfast, K., & Carney, C.J. (1987). *Ear infections in your child.* Hollywood, FL: Compact Books.

Haynes, W.O., Moran, M.J., & Pindzola, R.H. (2006). *Communication disorders in the classroom: An introduction for professionals in school settings* (4th ed.). Burlington, MA: Jones & Bartlett Learning.

Heller, K.W., & Cohen, E.T. (2009). Seizures and epilepsy. In K.W. Heller, P. Forney, P.A. Alberto, S.J. Best, & M.N. Schwartzman (Eds.), *Understanding physical, health, and multiple disabilities* (2nd ed., pp. 294–315). Upper Saddle River, NJ: Merrill/Pearson.

Heller, K.W., Dangel, H., & Sweatman, L. (1995). Systematic selection of adaptations for students with muscular dystrophy. *Journal of Physical and Developmental Disabilities, 7*(3), 253–265.

Heller, K.W., Easterbrooks, S., McJannet, D., & Swinehart-Jones, D. (2009). Vision loss, hearing loss, and deaf-blindness. In K.W. Heller, P. Forney, P.A. Alberto, S.J. Best, & M.N. Schwartzman (Eds.), *Understanding physical, health, and multiple disabilities* (2nd ed., pp. 191–218). Upper Saddle River, NJ: Merrill/Pearson.

Heller, K.W., Forney, P.E., Alberto, P.A., Best, A.J., & Schwartzman, M.N. (Eds.) (2009). *Understanding physical, health, and multiple disabilities* (2nd ed.). Upper Saddle River, NJ: Merrill/Pearson.

Heller, K.W., Mezei, P., & Schwartzman, M. (2009). Muscular dystrophies. In K.W. Heller, P.E. Forney, P.A. Alberto, A.J. Best, & M.N. Schwartzman (Eds.), *Understanding physical, health, and multiple disabilities* (2nd ed., pp. 232–248). Upper Saddle River, NJ: Merrill/Pearson.

Iddon, J.L., Morgan. D.J., Loveday, C., Sahakian, B.J., & Pickard, J.D. (2004). Neuropsychological profile of young adults with spina bifida with or without hydrocephalus. *Journal of Neurology, Neurosurgery, and Psychiatry, 75*, 1112–1118.

Jacobs, R., Northam, E., & Anderson, V. (2001). Cognitive outcome in children with myeolomeningocele and perinatal hydrocephalus: A longitudinal perspective. *Journal of Developmental and Physical Disabilities, 13*, 389–405.

Kuder, S.J. (2008). *Teaching students with language and communication disabilities* (3rd ed.). Boston: Allyn and Bacon.

Labib, T., Sada, M., Mohamed, B., Sabra, N.M., & Aleen, H.M. (2009). Assessment and management of children with visual impairment. *Middle East African Journal of Ophthalmology, 16*, 64–68.

MacBean, N., Ward, E., Murdoch, B., Cahill, L., Solley, M., Geraghty, T., & Hukins, C. (2009). Optimizing speech production in the ventilator-assisted individual following cervical spinal cord injury: A preliminary investigation. *International Journal of Language & Communication Disorders, 44*, 382–393.

Marschark, M., Lang, H.G., & Albertini, J.A. (2002). *Educating deaf students: From research to practice.* New York: Oxford University Press.

McKenzie, A.R. (2007). The use of learning media assessments with students who are deaf–blind. *Journal of Visual Impairments & Blindness, 101*, 587–600.

Migliorini, C., Tonge, B., & Sinclair, A. (2011). Developing and Piloting ePACT: A flexible psychological treatment for depression in people living with chronic spinal cord injury. *Behaviour Change, 28*, 45–54

Miller, F. (2005). *Cerebral palsy.* New York: Springer.

Moores, D.F. (2001). *Educating the deaf: Psychology, principles, and practices* (5th ed.). Boston: Houghton Mifflin.

Owens, R.E., Metz, D.E., & Haas, A. (2011). *Introduction to communication disorders: A lifespan approach* (4th ed.). Boston: Allyn and Bacon.

Porter, R.S. (2011). *The Merck manual of diagnosis and therapy* (19th ed.). Whitehouse Station, NJ: Merck & Co.

Quigley, S., & Paul, P. (1989). English language development. In M. Wang, M. Reynolds, & H. Walberg (Eds.), *The handbook of special education: Research and practice* (Vol. 3) (pp. 3–21). Oxford, England: Pergamon.

Reynolds, M.C., & Birch, J.W. (1988). *Adaptive mainstreaming: A primer for teachers and principals.* New York: Longman.

Romski, M.A., & Sevcik, R.A. (2005). Augmentative communication and early intervention: Myths and realities. *Infants and Young Children, 18*, 174–185.

Schirmer, B.R. (2000). *Language and literacy development in children who are deaf* (2nd ed.). Boston: Allyn and Bacon.

Singer, H.W. (1998). Movement disorders in children. In J. Jankovic & E. Tolosa (Eds.), *Parkinson's disease and movement disorders* (pp. 729–753). Philadelphia: Lippincott, Williams, & Wilkins.

Stemple, D.A., & Redding, G.J. (1992). Management of acute asthma. *Pediatric Clinics of North America, 39*, 1311–1325.

Thietje, R., Giese, R., Pouw, M., Kaphengst, C., Hosman, A., Kienast, B., Meent, H., & Hirschfeld, S. (2011). How does knowledge about spinal cord injury-related complications develop in subjects with spinal cord injury? A descriptive analysis in 214 patients. *Spinal Cord, 49*, 43–48.

U.S. Congress. (2004). The Individuals with Disabilities Education Improvement Act of 2004. Washington, DC: U.S. Government Printing Office.

U.S. Department of Education. (2005). *Twenty-seventh annual report to Congress on the implementation of the Individuals with Disabilities Education Act.* Washington, DC: Author.

Ward, M. (2000). The visual system. In M.C. Holbrook & A.J. Koenig (Eds.), *Foundations of education, Vol 1. History and theory of teaching children and youths with visual impairments* (pp. 77–110). New York: AFB Press.

Washington, D., Yeatts, K., Sleath, B., Ayala, G.X., Gillette, C., Williams, D., Davis, S., & Tudor, G. (2012). Communication and education about triggers and environmental control strategies during pediatric asthma visits. *Patient Education & Counseling, 86*, 63–9.

CHAPTER TWELVE

Students with Moderate to Severe Intellectual Disabilities

Paul Alberto, Rebecca Waugh, and Desirée Cabrices

CHAPTER OBJECTIVES

- to define the specific learning characteristics of students with moderate to severe intellectual disabilities;
- to provide an overview of an appropriate curriculum model;
- to present effective instructional strategies;
- to explore the relationship between student characteristics, curriculum, and instructional strategies;
- to describe the various settings considered appropriate for instruction; and
- to present a discussion on the post-school options available for individuals with moderate to severe intellectual disabilities.

KEY TERMS

observational learning · developmental delay · functional · community- referenced curriculum · ecological assessment · discrepancy analysis · partial participation · task analysis · forward chaining · backward chaining · total task programming · prompting · inclusion · community-based instruction · community-based vocational instruction

Students functioning at the cognitive level of moderate to severe intellectual disabilities can and do learn. The learning of these students can be substantial, and it is shaped and advanced by instruction in the public schools and community neighborhoods. Since the 1970s, professional journals have documented the acquisition of cognitive, communication, social, motor, self-help, and vocational skills by these students. Years of research and classroom practice make it clear that student learning is a result of systematic direct instruction. Direct instruction is teacher directed through the selection of functional learning objectives. It involves the use of behavioral strategies (e.g., reinforcement, response prompting, shaping, fading, and task analysis), a learning environment which provides opportunities for student errorless responding, and ongoing data collection for program monitoring and adjustment. In addition to learning through direct instruction, observational learning was verified in these students. Observational learning employs modeling, in which correct imitation of a model by the student is reinforced. Learning through observation is one of the reasons for using group instruction. The use of adults, peers, and nondisabled peers as models is effective for social, motor, and some communication and problem solving skills (Snell & Brown, 2011). In both direct and observational learning, instruction is targeted directly to the student. Direct rather than exploratory instructional strategies should be used. These conclusions arise from the learning characteristics of students with moderate to severe intellectual disabilities. Their learning characteristics, along with each student's post-school outcome goals, influence curriculum development to result in graduates who can actively live, work, and participate in an integrated adult community with as great a degree of independence as possible.

Characteristics

The term moderate to severe intellectual disability is descriptive of students functioning at a level significantly lower than that of the typical student. The broad characteristic of students with moderate to severe intellectual disability is developmental delay. Developmental delay implies these students go through the same stages of cognitive, communicative, social, and motor development as nondisabled peers; however, due to their disability, they progress through the stages of development at a slower rate (Zigler, 1969). It needs to be emphasized that slower developmental progress is directly correlated to these students' levels of cognitive functioning. This delay in rate of progress is not a difference in stages. Common across these students are assessed IQ scores below 55 (moderate intellectual disability has an IQ range of 55–40; severe intellectual disability has an IQ range of 40–25, and profound intellectual disability has an IQ below 25; AAMR, 2002). All students with moderate to severe disabilities have as the cause of their disability either brain damage or genetic errors. These etiologies result in a heterogeneous population and in a population of students who are multiply disabled. Significant numbers of these students will have, in addition to their cognitive disability, sensory, physical, and health disabilities. These may include vision and hearing impairments, physical disabilities (e.g., cerebral palsy, spina bifida, seizures), or health impairments (e.g., coronary or respiratory problems). These various potential combinations of disabilities present a significant challenge to our educational technology and creativity.

Although this is a heterogeneous population of students, certain generalizations can be made about their learning characteristics that result from their cognitive deficits. The following characteristics frame the content of curriculum and influence strategies for instruction.

Chapter 12   Students with Moderate to Severe Intellectual Disabilities   395

Skills Learned

Students with moderate to severe intellectual disabilities learn fewer skills within the time available in school, require more instructional opportunities (trials) to learn those skills and therefore more time to learn, and require more time to recoup lost skills (Brown et al., 1989). These learning characteristics require the careful selection of learning objectives and those selected must have a direct effect on the student's life. For example, teaching a student to put together a peg board has little direct effect on a student's life now or in the future. However, teaching a student to set the table for morning snack has an immediate and long-term purpose.

Generalization

One of the most significant learning weaknesses of these students is their inability to apply information learned in one situation to another. This is known as a deficit in generalization (Browder, 1991; Haring, 1988). Deficits in generalization will appear when the student attempts to use newly learned skills in contexts other than the initial learning environment. Thus, they have difficulty using new skills in different settings (e.g., dressing at home and at school), with a variety of people (e.g., giving correct coins to the teacher, a cashier, and a bus driver), with various materials (e.g., learning to clean the floor in a grocery with a broom and a mop), and across time (maintenance of learned skills). Generalization also involves using skills in other environments and situations in different ways. For example, calculators can be used to do addition in situations other than just grocery shopping. Students without intellectual disabilities would determine a variety of ways addition can be used in everyday life whereas students with moderate to severe intellectual disabilities would require explicit instruction (Taylor, Richards, & Brady, 2005). Context and environment are critical factors for instruction (Brown et al., 1989). To the extent possible, instruction should take place in the setting(s) in which skills are to be used with natural materials and with a variety of people.

Memory

Students with moderate to severe intellectual disabilities may have a variety of deficits that will affect their memory ability. These deficits include impaired reception of information due to sensory deficits, inability to attend to and rehearse relevant information for storage, and ineffective grouping of information for retrieval. These deficits result in memory characterized by less reliable information storage, fragmented skill performance, and significant loss of information. This may be due to inadequate initial exposure to the learning condition, insufficient opportunity to practice or use the information or skill, or learning without appropriate context. Skills selected for instruction must be those that occur frequently in the students' lives so that they have repeated opportunities for practice. For example, reading words should be selected from directions and instructions encountered in the community rather than from a basal reader or high-frequency word list. Skills that are used often and in various settings will have natural reoccurrence and, therefore, enhance memory functions (Ellis, 1970; Westling & Fox, 1995).

Attention

Typically, for a student with moderate to severe intellectual disability, the ability to discriminate between relevant and irrelevant stimuli is overwhelmed by the quantity of information in the environment. These students have difficulty learning what in the environment or on what part of an object they should focus to get information to make a correct answer or decision (Zeaman & House, 1979). Therefore, the teacher must employ behavioral instructional strategies such as prompting in order to focus student attention. For example, a teacher would draw a student's attention to the function sign of an addition problem (e.g., 6 + 4 =) by making it larger or a different color; a teacher would draw a student's attention to the label of a sweater by attaching a red ribbon in order for the student to learn "front" and "back" for dressing. Without such prompting, there will be long periods of trial and error by the student.

Synthesizing Information

The ability of these students to synthesize information and skills is limited (Westling & Fox, 1995). They have difficulty perceiving the relationship between parts and a whole. This can be seen in their inability to combine parts to create a story or relate a morning's series of activities. This also is demonstrated in their initial limited ability to perform self-help and vocational skills. They do not initially detect the relationship between one step in a chain and the next. Therefore, there is no anticipation of the next step. For example, during job training after spraying window cleaner, the student would not necessarily anticipate the need for wiping the window. This lack of anticipation is seen across behaviors. As a result, one cannot teach isolated skills and expect them to be organized for use. Skills must be taught within the contexts of the environment and activity in which they will be performed. In addition, the acquisition of skills requires an instructional strategy that breaks down task chains into component steps and skills so each can be taught directly (task analysis).

Communication

The cognitive and physical impairments of students with moderate to severe intellectual disabilities impact their ability to communicate effectively. The two forms of communication used by these students are nonsymbolic and symbolic. Both nonsymbolic and symbolic communication serve the purpose of relaying a message to another individual. Forms of nonsymbolic communication include vocal sounds (e.g., yelling, crying, cooing), facial expressions, behavior (e.g., clapping, hitting, throwing, pushing away), body movement (e.g., leaning toward, pulling away), and gestures. Forms of symbolic communication include use of words, manual sign language, photographs, pictures, and objects to indicate activities (e.g., a ball to indicate time for gym, a spoon to indicate time for lunch). During most communication encounters, individuals incorporate a combination of symbolic and nonsymbolic forms. However, many students with moderate to severe intellectual disabilities are limited to the use of one form of communication.

Nonsymbolic Communication. The majority of children with severe intellectual disability use primarily nonsymbolic forms of communication to express their wants and needs (Mar & Sall, 1999; McLean, Brady, & McLean, 1996; McLean, Brady, McLean, & Behrens, 1999). Their nonsymbolic communication is expressed as vocalizations, body movements, and/or physical behaviors upon objects or persons in an attempt to communicate (e.g., grabs for a toy, pushes away a bowl of food, or strikes out at a teacher when frustrated). For these students their behavior itself is the communication message. McLean et al. (1996) examined the communicative forms of 211 children and adults with severe intellectual disability. Their results indicated that during childhood 57% were nonsymbolic communicators. In a follow-up study, McLean et al. (1999) found that individuals with severe intellectual disability used more gestures with physical contact than gestures made at a distance (e.g., pointing).

Symbolic Communication. Although the majority of children with severe intellectual disability communicate using nonsymbolic forms, the majority of adults with severe intellectual disability use symbolic forms, indicating a continued development and learning of communication abilities into adolescence and adulthood (McLean et al., 1996; McLean et al., 1999). Adults with severe intellectual disability also use more complex forms of symbolic communication by using multiple word phrases and symbols to communicate. Symbolic communication is not limited to speech but may include a variety of behaviors that have a standard meaning. Nonverbal forms of symbolic communication include manual sign language, pictures or photographs, and augmentative and alternative communication (AAC) devices. AAC devices (e.g., electronic and nonelectronic language boards) are used to extend and standardize an individual's ability to communicate. Instruction for these students focuses on access and use of the device, vocabulary selection, and generalization across settings and individuals.

Language development includes various components, including morphology (study of the smallest unit of meaningful language, such as word parts), semantics (study of the meaning of language), syntax (the rules that indicate the order in which words are sequenced), and pragmatics (the social use of language). The language development of individuals with intellectual disabilities across these various components is characterized as delayed development, not different development, indicating these students develop language skills in the same sequential manner as typically developing students but at a slower rate (Pruess, Vadasy, & Fewell, 1987). Their verbal communication is characterized by a limited vocabulary pool, lack of abstractions, shorter sentence length, and simple grammatical structures (no compound or complex sentences). In addition to these language characteristics, a majority of these students have speech disorders (e.g., articulation and voice problems).

Of particular concern for effective communication is the deficit in pragmatics of students with intellectual disabilities. Pragmatics involves the social aspects of communication, including skills such as turn-taking and maintaining the topic of a conversation (McLaughlin, 1998). For students with intellectual disabilities, deficits in pragmatics can significantly impact their relations with their peers. For example, they have difficulty interpreting social cues, such as facial expressions, which impacts their ability to interact or respond appropriately to others (Kasari, Freeman, & Hughes, 2001). They have difficulty adjusting their conversation to the status of the person to whom they are talking, whether it is a peer, family member, teacher, coworker, or employer.

Social Skills

Social relationships are limited by these students' inability to interpret social cues and situations (Kennedy, Horner, & Newton, 1989; Sullivan, Vitrello, & Foster, 1988). Deficits in both communication and physical abilities often lead to social isolation (Gaylord-Ross & Peck, 1984) and fewer opportunities to learn appropriate social skills across individuals and settings. These social skills include conversation skills, eye contact, sharing, and control of physical contact. Systematic instruction of social skills is required to provide varied practice across individuals in integrated school and community settings.

Another influential social characteristic is the students' view that their environment is controlled by someone other than themselves. This is known as having an *external locus of control*. This view results in their waiting for others to initiate social interactions or task engagement, to look to others for cues about the correctness of their performance or behavior, or expect others to make even basic personal choices as what to wear, or to eat, or with what toy to play. In some students this is seen as learned helplessness. This tendency hinders development of a sense of self-determination and independence as the students do not realize they can or should have input into life choices (Hodapp & Zigler, 1997).

The social skills deficits of students with intellectual disabilities significantly impacts the types of interactions they have with nondisabled peers.

The social skills deficits of students with intellectual disabilities significantly impact the types of interactions they have with nondisabled peers. They have difficulty establishing friendships with same-age typical peers. This lack of friendships may be the result of infrequent opportunities to interact with same-age peers and also may be due to their frequent interest in age-inappropriate activities and materials which make friendships difficult to establish. When students with intellectual disabilities are asked to identify friends, they often report adults, such as teachers and administrators, rather than same-age peers (Siperstein & Bak, 1989). The ability for them to establish reciprocal friendships may become more challenging as they grow older. In an attempt to increase meaningful social interactions with nondisabled peers, students with intellectual disabilities often spend segments of the school day in inclusive settings. However, mere physical integration does not directly produce social interaction. It is necessary that students be provided appropriate social skills training, and opportunities for social interaction in various school locations must be arranged.

Challenging Behaviors

Many students with moderate to severe intellectual disabilities exhibit challenging behaviors, especially those students with the most severe disabilities. These behaviors include stereotypic behavior (e.g., repetitive behaviors such as body rocking and hand flapping), self-injurious behaviors (e.g., head banging and hair-pulling), and aggressive behaviors (e.g., hitting others and throwing objects). It is generally accepted that these behaviors are attempts to communicate, resulting from an inability to communicate in a more standard manner (Carr & Durand, 1985). In most instances these behaviors serve the function of gaining a person's attention or a particular object; or escaping from a demanding task or social situation. As indicated by "best professional practice" and required by IDEA, the function of a student's challenging behavior is determined by conducting a Functional Assessment and/or Functional Analysis (Alberto & Troutman, 2003; Iwata, Dorsey, Slifer, Bauman, & Richman, 1982). Instructional implications for addressing these behaviors include instruction of alternative standard forms of communication, simplifying difficult and complex tasks by breaking them down into smaller parts, and scheduling activities that are functional throughout the day.

Figures 12.1 to 12.3 present descriptions of three students with moderate to severe intellectual disabilities. **Figure 12.1** describes Shandra, an elementary student with severe intellectual disability, without a secondary physical disability. **Figure 12.2** describes Ross, a middle school student with moderate intellectual disability. He has Down syndrome. **Figure 12.3** describes Dario, a high school student with severe intellectual disability and cerebral palsy.

Curriculum

The goal of education for students with moderate to severe intellectual disabilities is the same as for nondisabled students. As a result of their years in school, they will live, work, and participate in an integrated community. When typical students graduate, it is expected that they will have a range of vocational and living options, as well as a variety of social associations from which to choose. This is the same expectation for students with moderate to severe intellectual disabilities. The purpose of curriculum is to provide students with the skills necessary to meet this goal. Because of their developmental delay, curriculum for students with moderate to severe disabilities will require significant deviations from the general education core curriculum. These students will require a curriculum based on a functional model rather than one that is developmentally or academically sequenced.

Figure 12.1   Description of Shandra, an Elementary School Student with Severe Intellectual Disability

Shandra is a 7-year-old girl who attends the neighborhood elementary school. She is eligible for special education services for students with severe intellectual disability. She has a reported IQ of 28 with severe deficits in adaptive behavior. Shandra has no sensory disabilities, but she does have grand mal seizures that occur at least twice per week while at school. She is on a toileting schedule of every hour and has few accidents. She can eat with a spoon and eat finger foods. She can put on jackets and pull-over blouses with assistance, and she can put on pants independently. However, she does require assistance with zippers and buttons. Shandra can wash her hands and face independently and is learning to brush her hair and teeth. She can make her needs and wants known through the use of one and two word phrases and gestures. However, most of her communication is responsive; she makes few social communication initiations. She is independently mobile and she likes to ride on a bicycle, but needs physical prompting to push the peddles. Shandra also is learning to play with toys appropriately and to share them with classmates. When she first entered the class, she waited for someone to direct her through her morning arrival routine, regularly laying on the floor. She now has a picture prompt system she follows that gets her through her arrival routine of entering, hanging up her coat, going to the bathroom, and finding her seat and first task. She can match by color (black, white, and red), follow one step directions, understands one-to-one correspondence (she can put one straw with each milk carton and give one cookie to each student), and is beginning to learn to "read" community logos.

Shandra tends to body rock, both when sitting and standing, when she does not know what to do next or is confronted with a task she does not know how to perform. Shandra currently is included with her nondisabled peers in music and math classes two days per week, physical education class one day per week, and the second grade social studies class three days per week.

Figure 12.2   Description of Ross, a Middle School Student with Moderate Intellectual Disability

Ross is a 12-year-old boy who attends the neighborhood middle school. He is eligible for special education services for students with moderate intellectual disability. He has a reported IQ of 50 with moderate deficits in adaptive behavior. Ross has Down syndrome. He has a heart murmur that restricts some of his physical activities, and he wears glasses (when he remembers to bring them to school; sometimes he throws them out the school bus window). He knows when he needs to go to the bathroom and is independent while there. He also can perform all his hygiene, dressing, and eating tasks independently and is independently mobile. He tends to be stubborn when he does not want to do a particular task. He will sit and ignore all requests from the teacher pretending he does not hear. Ross communicates verbally with a limited vocabulary. Ross is very social and has friends in the school with and without disabilities. However, he needs to work on following a conversation without going off on tangents and not monopolizing it. He enjoys participating in group games such as volleyball and T-ball and also can play simple board games with up to two peers. Ross has learned to read on a second grade level through sightwords and some initial sounds. His math skills include double-digit addition using a calculator, counting money to the next dollar, rational counting to 12, and rote counting to 25. He can write names and numbers and provide personal information when requested. One day a week, he and his classmates work at the Red Cross center where he assembles mailing materials and blood donation kits. Ross currently attends exploratory classes, art, and science classes with his nondisabled peers and is an active participant in the after school chorus.

A curriculum is **functional** if its content is derived from the life skills that are performed in the integrated community settings in which these students currently, or ultimately, will live, work, and participate (Brown et al., 1979). Such a content source ensures that the behaviors to be learned are of immediate or future importance and are age appropriate. A skill or behavior is functional if a direct line can be drawn between the skill and its use by the student in an immediate or identifiable future environment. This is more narrowly defined than for the general education student. Knowing the details of grammatic structure may be important if the student goes to college, or knowledge of the economic history of the United

Figure 12.3 Description of Dario, a High School Student with Severe Intellectual Disability

Dario is an 18-year-old boy who attends high school. He is eligible for special education services for students with severe intellectual disability. He has a reported IQ of 38 with severe deficits in adaptive behavior. Dario has cerebral palsy that severely limits his use of his lower extremities and mildly affects his arms and facial muscles. He uses a wheel chair and has use of both arms and hands. He wears Attends, adult undergarments, and needs to be changed at least once per day while at school. He partially participates in dressing and hygiene. Dario uses an electronic communication device to communicate his wants and needs. He has a vocabulary of 434 words which include social vocabulary, but the limited pool of words limits the length of his interactions. Dario uses switches to operate a radio to listen to music and to turn on the television. He recognizes logos, understands the concepts of quantity, can rote count up to 10 and rationally knows up to 5, can match by color and size, and can make one-to-one correspondence, as well as follow two-step directions. He participates in vocational training in a local department store where he unpackages shoes. Both in school and on the job, Dario will engage in face slapping when he feels frustrated by a task or direction. While on the job site he enjoys interacting with coworkers in the break room. At school Dario attends fifth period keyboarding class where he accesses computer games with a peer. He also attends home economics class where he practices his home living, eating (drool control), and arithmetic skills. For school dances he is a member of the ticket-taking staff.

States may make one a more informed voter. However, for students with moderate to severe intellectual disabilities, content must be much less inferential and have more concrete application. A functional curriculum would have students counting or sorting coins to be used in a vending machine rather than pegs to be placed in a pegboard, matching or sorting socks or silverware rather than colored cubes, stringing shoe laces rather than beads, and walking on bleachers in the gym rather than a balance beam. Given its content source, a functional curriculum would have objectives that occur often and naturally and provide opportunities for ongoing practice and improved retention. Further examples are provided in **Figure 12.4**.

A functional curriculum is developed from a "top-down" perspective rather than "bottom-up" (Brown et al., 1979). A top-down curriculum is one in which goals and objectives are defined by the skills needed in the settings in which we want the student to function. These settings include home, school, neighborhood shops and services, leisure facilities, and work settings. A bottom-up curriculum is based on a Developmental Model of learning. It follows the progression of learning of typical students for curriculum objectives. In a developmental curriculum, learning objectives based on chronological age are sequenced for each curriculum area (e.g., language, social, self-help, motor skills). Since students with moderate to severe intellectual disabilities are developmentally delayed, they often are

Figure 12.4 Examples of Functional and Nonfunctional Activities

Steps	Functional Task	Non-Functional Task
Domestic (Elementary)	• Buttoning and unbuttoning jacket for school arrival, departure, and community trips.	• Buttoning and unbuttoning clothes on doll at 9:45, 3 mornings per week for 5 trials.
Leisure (High School)	• Buying a card (birthday, holiday), "signing" and mailing it at the post office.	• Teacher distributes Valentine cards and students mail them in a shoe box in the classroom.
Community (Middle School)	• Identifying the size labels on clothing in Target.	• Sorting 3×5 index cards with "L," "M," "S" on them in the classroom.
Vocational (High School)	• Sorting sets of silverware and rolling them in napkins in the school cafeteria and at a local restaurant.	• Sorting pictures of silverware and paper clipping them to a napkin in the classroom.

chronologically beyond the developmental stages at which they are seen to be performing. This may result in inappropriately teaching 19-year-old students the developmental skills of a 2-year-old. This has the effect of teaching skills and tasks that are chronologically age inappropriate, in inappropriate settings, utilizing materials typically designed for young children. This results in students leaving school without the adolescent or adult skills needed to live somewhere other than their parents' homes or state facilities, to do any kind of work in the real economy, or to participate in age-appropriate community activities.

Because a curriculum based on developmental milestones results in an inappropriate educational focus for students with moderate to severe intellectual disabilities, educators now use a **community-referenced curriculum**. This is a curriculum based on skills needed for functioning in current and future environments. The objectives for a student are taken from the environmental demands of the community in which they live. These environments are those in which the student currently lives and functions and those in which it is projected the student will live. If a high school student is to live in a community group home or supervised apartment and engage in supported employment in a local discount store, the skills needed for entry into these environments are the skills that are taught. Additionally, objectives will focus on those skills needed to function in the student's high school and the current community settings in which the student and family participate. Similarly, for students in middle and elementary schools, objectives are drawn from the requirements of current and future school and community settings.

The process by which functional, community-referenced curriculum content is identified is known as **ecological assessment** (Brown et al., 1979; Falvey, 1989). Ecological assessment is the development of an ecological inventory of sequences of behaviors that reflect the skills necessary to participate in community environments (Brown et al., 1979).

An inventory is done for each of the four curriculum domains: the domestic domain (objectives for personal care and residential care), the community domain (objectives for access to services and commodities), the leisure domain (objectives for individual and group activities in the home and community settings), and the vocational domain (objectives for prevocational education and the development of a vocational training resume for entry into supported or competitive employment).

Identified in each of the domains are environments in which the student must function either now or in the future (e.g., restaurants, stores, transportation, playgrounds, libraries, instructional areas in the school, work settings). For each environment, activities are identified in which the student must engage. For example, in a store, activities include: finding the entrance, finding the cashier, paying, and exiting the store. For each activity, teachers identify the basic skills needed to perform the activity that include communication, motor, mobility, social, and academic skills. For example, to pay for an item in a store, the student must be able to wait in line, attend to the cashier, accept change, take the purchase, and exit the line. **Figure 12.5** provides examples of the steps of an ecological assessment.

Once the list of activities and skills are identified, instructional priorities among them are made by the student's IEP committee. Bases for setting instructional priorities include parent, student, and teacher preferences; the frequency of the activity across environments; safety concerns; age-appropriateness; and/or the time, material, appropriate settings available to teach the skills (Nietupski & Hamre-Nietupski, 1987).

Once the curriculum content is defined and specific activities are selected for instruction and incorporated into the student's IEP, direct assessment of the student's current capability to perform the activity is done. Assessment of student performance is accomplished through a **discrepancy analysis**. The teacher observes the student performing the activity and notes which skills the student can and cannot perform. For those skills the student cannot perform, it may be that he was never exposed to the activity and direct instruction is required. It also

| Figure 12.5 | Steps in an Ecological Assessment |

Domain (Curriculum Area): Community
Environment (Instructional Setting): Store (Target and WalMart)
Subenvironment (Training Site): Men's clothing
Activity (Goal): Locate rack of socks
Skills (Objectives): Scan displays
                          Identify display of socks
                          Walk to display of socks
                          Identify white tube socks
Activity (Goal): Select sock size 10–13
Skills (Objectives):   Pick up pair of socks
                           Identify size on label
                           Identify number 10 (match to prompt card)
                           Place in basket
Domain (Curriculum Area): Domestic-Personal Care
Environment (Instructional Setting): Public Restroom and School Restroom
Subenvironment (Training Site): Sink
Activity (Goal): Wash hands
Skills (Objectives):   Turn on water
                           Pick up soap
                           Wet hands and soap
                           Scrub hands
                           Rinse hands
                           Pull paper towel
                           Dry hands
                           Throw towel away

Adapted from: Falvey, M. (1989). Community skills. In M. Falvey (Ed.), *Community-based curriculum: Instructional strategies for students with severe handicaps* (2nd ed., pp. 100–102), Baltimore, MD: Paul H. Brookes.

may be that an adaptation or alternative performance strategy is needed. A determination is made whether there is a cognitive, physical, or sensory hindrance to the student performing the skills of an activity. If one is identified, the teacher must devise necessary adaptations or alternatives so that the student is able to complete the activity. For example, a young student may need to use a switch to turn on a toy, or a high school student may need to use a switch to turn on a computer.

Developing an Instructional and Evaluation Program

At this point, the teacher takes into consideration the student's learning characteristics, the skills to be learned, and the performance adaptations necessary in order to devise a combination of learning technology necessary for instruction. Often included in instructional planning are related service professionals such as the physical therapist, occupational therapist, and speech-language pathologist. This team determines the nature of assistance or prompting strategies to be employed, the instructional setting, and the materials to be used. In addition, the team must decide how the effectiveness of instruction will be evaluated.

Evaluation of student performance is based on skill acquisition data collected at least twice per week (Farlow & Snell, 1994). Overall, measures are taken of the number of activities, tasks, and skills acquired, maintained, and generalized; the number of settings in which the student participates; the number of social and communicative initiations made by the student; and whether or not the IEP objectives were attained.

When setting criteria for performance, standards for accuracy must be established. Three levels of standards exist from which to choose: degree of participation, functional result, or performance equal to a nondisabled peer. The first level, the degree of participation by the student, sets the amount of an activity or task a student will be expected to perform and the student's degree of independence. For example, for a four-task morning hygiene routine (wash hands, wash face, brush teeth, brush hair) the criterion might include:

1. The number of tasks the student will perform.
2. The number of steps within a task the student will perform.
3. The number of skills within a task step the student will perform.
4. The amount of third-person assistance the student will require.

The second level is the criterion of functional result. That is, can the student achieve the desired outcome of the behavior? For example, does the student's behavior at the counter result in the clerk giving the drink wanted? The third, and strictest, criterion level is performance equal to a nondisabled peer. For this criterion, accuracy, fluency, and quality of performance are measured. This criterion is used most often in integrated settings for social skills and for vocational tasks where competitive performance is expected.

What we traditionally consider as academics are as much a part of the curriculum for students with moderate disabilities as they are for the general education student. However, academics also must meet the test of being functional. They must be identified as skills necessary to perform functional activities within each of the curriculum domains as illustrated by the following examples (see box below).

An important consideration in writing objectives for students with severe disabilities, especially multiple disabilities, is the concept of **partial participation** (Baumgart et al., 1982). Although it acknowledges that for some students the ability to perform an entire task or chain of skills may not be cognitively or physically possible, most students can participate in a functional task by completing some of the steps in a chain independently, and/or by assisting someone else to perform it for them. This concept is important in broadening our view of instructional potential for this population of students. It refutes the once held hypotheses that long lists of prerequisite skills are needed before a student can be taught to do a task and that if a student cannot do a task with complete independence, then it should not be included in the program (Baumgart et al., 1982).

Simply because a student cannot learn to prepare a snack independently, read a science textbook, play a video game or soccer, or use a computer or bunsen burner, it does not mean the student cannot participate in some part of the activity and learn something cognitively or socially from the experience. It is true that participation may be partial and require using a method of engagement that is different from others. Participation may be demonstrated

Domestic—write name, address, and phone number; set an alarm clock for work; read contents and directions on food packages; identify poison labels.

Community—identify bus; identify coins for vending machines, movies, bus ride, or paying a cashier in a store; read numbers on price labels; read size labels on clothing; read menus, signs on buildings and in the community, directions for washer and dryer; counting money for purchases and transportation.

Leisure—tell time for a TV show or movie; address greeting cards, write notes to others to convey thoughts, wishes, or needs; money skills to pay for movie, bowling.

Vocational—tell time for start and end of break; operate microwave and vending machine; read work schedules.

simply by touching, holding, or looking when using adapted materials and devices or receiving assistance from a peer or adult. Suppose, for example, that a group of third grade students are engaged in a science lesson on how plants grow. Each student may have a particular assignment for the activity. With a severe disability, it may be difficult for a student to perform all of the activities the other students are doing, but it may be possible to participate by completing some of them. For example, the student may be unable to retrieve items from a shelf when planting seeds, but could spoon dirt into a pot and push a seed into the soil. The student may be able to make such actions alone or with the assistance of the teacher, the teacher's assistant, or another student. Regardless, this form of participation by the student can represent an important aspect of the educational experience while at the same time contributing to the group activity in a meaningful way (Westling & Fox, 1995).

Partial participation in chronologically age-appropriate environments and activities are educationally more advantageous than exclusion from such environments and activities. Students with severe disabilities, regardless of their degree of dependence or level of functioning, should be allowed to participate at least partially in a wide range of school and nonschool environments and activities. The type and degree of partial participation should be increased through direct and systematic instruction. Partial participation should result in a student being perceived by others as a more valuable, contributing, and productive member of the community. Partial participation can be reflected in IEP objectives as seen in **Figure 12.6** with Dario's dressing objective and his partial participation in the changing of his

Figure 12.6 Examples of IEP Objectives for Students with Moderate to Severe Intellectual Disabilities

Dario

- During his scheduled trips to the bathroom, given a verbal prompt from the teacher, Dario will partially participate in changing his adult undergarments by unzipping his pants and releasing the velcro tabs, when he is assisted to a standing position, 100% of occasions for three consecutive weeks.

   When told what number the big hand should be at on a clock, Dario will indicate when it is time to go to the cafeteria for lunch and time to go to his key-boarding class, within a 5 minute error limit, for 4 consecutive weeks.

   When in the break room at his job training site at a local department store, Dario will match the correct coins with those on a picture prompt card in order to get a soft drink from the vending machine independently 4 out of 5 days per week for 1 school quarter.

Shandra

- Given natural opportunities for putting on and taking off garments requiring buttoning (e.g., putting on and taking off her sweater for school arrival and departure, community-based instructional activities, her art shirt, and recess), Shandra will independently button at least two buttons in the appropriate holes within 4 minutes on 90% of opportunities, for 2 weeks.

   Given a four-step sequence of material gathering for morning and afternoon snack, Shandra will independently follow a sequence of picture prompts with only two errors in placement for 1 month.

   When not provided immediate assistance with opening her milk carton at lunch and snack, Shandra will verbally say "need help" to seek assistance from an adult, with less than three occurrences of body rocking, for 4 consecutive weeks.

Ross

- Given the amount of $10 entered into his calculator and a shopping list of six items, Ross will find each item, read the price label, and deduct it from the total on his calculator with 100% accuracy over six trips to the grocery store.

   When at the Red Cross Center to perform his two job assignments (assembling mailing materials and blood donation kits), in the presence of a table clock, Ross will indicate when the 30 minutes allotted to each has expired, within a 5 minute error limit, for 1 school quarter.

   During language expansion activities that focus on a specific topic, Ross will engage in turn-taking in conversations by limiting his verbalization to one sentence each time it is his turn, with 80% compliance, in each session.

Figure 12.7   Changing Curriculum Focus Across School Years

Preschool/Primary	Elementary/Middle	Secondary
Goal: Personal Competence	**Goal:** Local Competence	**Goal:** Transition Competence
Domain Foci:	**Domain Foci:**	**Domain Foci:**
Domestic—Personal Care	**Domestic**—Personal Care	**Domestic**—Residential Care Personal Care
Leisure—Play skills, social skills	**Leisure**—Individual and group	**Leisure**—Individual and group in community
Community—Familiarity with environmental features in the community, social skills	**Community**—With functional academics, community social skills, safety skills	**Community**—With functional academics, community social skills, safety skills
	Vocational—Pre-community based vocational instruction	**Vocational**—Resume development

Develop, Refine, and Generalize
Communication System
Mobility System

undergarments. Additional examples of IEP objectives for Dario, Shandra, and Ross are shown in Figure 12.6. These objectives demonstrate active participation by the student and give examples of objectives in various domains with activities in various settings.

As illustrated in **Figure 12.7**, as students get older, the curriculum focus changes to include skills needed for adult participation across each of the domains. During the preschool and primary years, the goal for students is development of personal competence. Objectives focus on the development of personal care skills, play skills, early social skills with peers, and trips into the community to familiarize the student with basic elements such as street crossing, crowds, elevators, and appropriate public social skills. During the elementary and middle school years, the goal for students is the development of competence in functioning in the local community. Objectives focus on the continuing development of personal care skills, skills required for individual and group leisure activities and play, instruction in the community in which functional academic skills are identified, and activities of prevocational instruction such as following a schedule or remaining on task. During the high school years, the goal for students is the development of competence for the transition from school to adult life. Objectives focus on personal care skills that are needed for the maturing adolescent, skills in residential care, leisure skills needed to participate in community settings, continued instruction of academics to include, reading, arithmetic, and money skills that are required for functioning in the community, and on-site job training in a variety of settings to identify vocational strengths and weakness, likes and dislikes, needed adaptations, and level of supervision required.

Over the past decade there has been a shift in the focus on instruction and assessment for students with intellectual disabilities. This shift was preceded by legislation requiring access to the general education curriculum for all students, including students with disabilities, and participation in state assessments by all students, including students with most significant cognitive disabilities (IDEA, 1997; NCLB, 2002). NCLB provides regulations for students with significant cognitive disabilities (i.e., 1% of the total school population) to be assessed through an alternate assessment based on alternate achievement standards that are aligned with the general education standards. Although this allows for some flexibility, this shift has required teachers of students with moderate to severe intellectual disabilities to incorporate curriculum choices within the framework of a state's general education curriculum and its content standards. General education content standards do not substitute for a functional curriculum's concept, content, and objectives. Doing so would go against the knowledge derived from decades of research and would be contrary to the requirement for use of research-based educational programming (Ayres, Lowrey, Douglas, & Sievers, 2011). Rather there should be alignment of the functional curriculum needs of these students with the broad concepts represented by certain content standards. For example, functional cognitive and functional academic objectives can be aligned within the various traditional academic content areas in the general education curriculum. At the younger grades one-to-one correspondence and basic arithmetic functions of addition and subtraction may be easily aligned. In the upper grades, a functional objective such as direction following can be aligned with science content standards in the performance of an experiment or social studies content standards in understanding maps. The functional concept of sorting by variables—such as used and unused, broken and unbroken, full and not full—can be aligned within academic and vocational standards. Even essential hygiene objectives can be aligned with biology in the study of identification and function of body parts, or ecology and earth science in discussion of the functions of water and how it cleanses the earth and its contents.

At younger ages there should be a considerable number of content standards, the modification of which will make them appropriate for these students. Indeed, in most instances alignment reinforces the need for skills such as literacy which has always been a part of a functional curriculum, and can be aligned throughout a student's educational career. However, as current discussions include selection of grade level equivalent standards, teachers of students with moderate to severe intellectual disabilities may have increasing difficulty aligning content as students get older. Their functional curriculum needs become more divergent from the content standards in grades 8 or 10 or 12 in the general education curriculum. In an attempt to assist teachers with aligning instruction to general education standards, the majority of states have provided extended standards (Cameto et al., 2009). Extended standards reduce the complexity of the general education standard and/or address prerequisite skills that relate to the standard and may be more appropriate for students with moderate to severe intellectual disabilities. Whereas the general education curriculum content advances to algebra, the needs of these students advances to broader applications of functional objectives for maintenance and generalization. Is alignment worth the time spent on an objective that diverts from functional reading in order to access *Romeo and Juliet* as a modification of that content standard? The process of alignment should be a conversation that brings into focus two educational perspectives that can strengthen the purpose and goals of both (Ayers, Lowrey, Douglas, & Sievers, 2011; Courtade-Little & Browder, 2005). Such a conversation can encourage IEP committees to think in terms of students' functional needs alongside the content prescribed for nondisabled peers thereby providing common ground in which students have opportunities to be educated and interact together.

Literacy

Reading instruction is an example of how functional curriculum and alignment with general education content standards can be complimentary. As noted earlier, the ongoing necessity of literacy skills to be part of a student's IEP allows alignment throughout a student's educational career. The field has recently noted the importance of a comprehensive approach to literacy instruction for students with moderate to severe intellectual disabilities (Allor, Mathes, Kyle, Jones, & Champlin, 2010; Browder, Ahlgrim-Delzell, Courtade, Gibbs, & Flowers, 2008; Fredrick, Davis, Alberto, & Waugh, 2013). In order to provide a comprehensive approach to literacy a more inclusive definition of literacy beyond solely reading text must be considered. Alberto, Fredrick, Hughes, McIntosh, and Cihak (2007) define literacy as "the ability to obtain information—from the environment, through a variety of modes—

with which to make decisions and choices, alter the environment, and gain pleasure" (p. 234). This definition of literacy expands beyond simple text to include pictures and logos.

Pictures commonly are used to relay messages in classrooms and community settings. In classrooms, pictures are used in storybooks (e.g., wordless books), to label common objects (e.g., activity boxes), relay basic concepts (e.g., the water cycle), and establish classroom routines (e.g., picture schedules). In community settings pictures are used to convey services, activities, and products available (e.g., logos). For students with moderate to severe intellectual disabilities, the ability to interact with pictures may be especially important in order to gain information and express a thought or need. Pictures are often used as a mode of communication for these students (e.g., Picture Exchange Communication System, PECS). Alberto et al. (2007) established a seven-step sequence for teaching picture reading to students with moderate to severe intellectual disabilities that begins with identifying individual pictures of classmates and advances to two- and three-step sequences. In this picture reading sequence, students identify information (e.g., who, what) in a picture and then are required to do something with the information obtained (e.g., imitate an action from the picture; locate an item in the picture). Logo reading is well established in the literature for students with moderate to severe intellectual disabilities (Alberto, Fredrick, Hughes, McIntosh, & Cihak, 2007). Logos are a combination of a graphic design, color, and/or written word(s). For some students, literacy instruction may focus on identifying common community logos and services or products associated with the logo.

The most common instructional practice and the majority of reading research conducted with students with moderate intellectual disabilities focuses on sight-word instruction. With sight-word instruction students learn through repeated practice to recognize/read words based on the configuration of the letters. A sight-word approach is used because of students' articulation difficulties and the complexity of letter-sound correspondence in the English language. There are two typical methods for selecting sight words: a basal reading approach and/or a functional approach. In a basal reading approach, the words selected for instruction are based on the words needed to provide students with access to storybooks. Examples of commercial basal reading programs for students with moderate to severe intellectual disabilities include the Edmark Reading Program (1972) and the PCI Reading Program (2009). In a functional reading approach, the words selected for instruction are functional words that will facilitate access to, and independence in, current and future environments. Students are taught words and phrases in the formats they appear in natural settings. The words and phrases provide information (e.g., signs and product labels), directions (e.g., pull, stop, exit), safety warnings (e.g., do not enter, caution), and those that affect job performance.

Although sight-word instruction can teach individual words, it does not provide word analysis skills that would allow a student to read untaught words they encounter (Browder & Lalli, 1991; Browder & Xin, 1998; Conners, 1992). For this reason it is important to consider additional approaches to reading instruction. Phonics instruction is successful with nondisabled students, students with mild intellectual disabilities, and increasing evidence indicates it holds promise for some students with moderate intellectual disabilities (Allor et al., 2010; Bradford, Shippen, Alberto, Houchins, & Flores, 2005; Browder et al., 2008; Fredrick et al., 2013). Phonics instruction consists of basic identification of letter-sound correspondences and then blending of letter-sound correspondences to identify unknown words.

Some students with moderate intellectual disabilities will achieve reading at the second grade level through phonics (Bradford et al., 2005). However, the primary purpose of phonics with this population is not to be able to read books, but rather to have a tool with which to decode untaught words and phrases in various environments, and thereby increase their independence. The overall programming of reading instruction for students with moderate intellectual disabilities should provide a comprehensive approach that includes exposure or access to a combination of pictures, sight words, and phonics instruction. Due to the complexity of the written English language and the various sound combinations of letters-sounds, a complete phonics approach to learning to read all words may not be practical. Not all functional words in the environment conform to common phonics rules for decoding. If a phonics approach is not successful, the student's literacy instruction will focus on pictures and/or sight words.

Two common strategies to teach literacy skills to students with moderate intellectual disabilities are time delay (Browder, Ahlgrim-Delzell, Spooner, Mims, & Baker, 2009) and simultaneous prompting (Waugh, Alberto, & Fredrick, 2011). When teaching time delay, the student is asked the word and given 3 to 4 seconds to respond. If the student incorrectly identifies the word or does not respond, the teacher provides assistance (a prompt) for correct identification. When teaching with simultaneous prompting, the student is presented with a word, asked to read it, and immediately told what the word is so the response will be correct and then they respond.

Mathematics

In order to promote independence, a mathematics curriculum should focus on the skills critical for students to possess in order to acquire, maintain, and generalize the skills necessary for them to participate as independently as possible in their community. This functional approach to mathematics provides the context in which skills will be used and the real materials, variables, and outcomes (a naturally successful experience or a naturally correcting experience). The scope of mathematics curriculum content for these students includes three areas: basic concepts, basic manipulation and computation, and functional uses (Browder, Spooner, Ahlgrim-Delzell, Harris, & Wakeman, 2008; Falvey, 1989; Ford et al., 1989; Snell & Brown, 2011).

The content includes: (1) *basic concepts*: rote counting, rational counting, sorting and matching (e.g., by color, size, amount, and function, such as things you eat versus things you wear), sequencing, one-to-one correspondence (e.g., setting places for snack by putting one plate and one glass at each place, passing out one book per student); (2) *basic manipulation and computation*: object manipulation (e.g., putting objects in your lunch box or bookbag, moving the pieces on a game board), recognizing parts and a whole, addition (and counting on from a specific number), subtraction, math literacy (e.g., reading graphemes and identification of corresponding number of objects, and terms such as more, less, add); (3) *functional uses of mathematics*: money recognition and management, time recognition and management (e.g., daily activity schedules, reading a clock, understanding appointment times, duration of an activity), environment-specific required skills derived from ecological assessment (e.g., counting four across when stocking shelves).

Teaching mathematics skills within a functional framework requires the application of systematic instructional strategies in the classroom and in settings where the need to use the skill naturally occurs, such as in community businesses. This is also known as *in vivo instruction*. This provides experience with actual variables the student will encounter, such as real materials, real distractions, and real criteria for performance. Instruction should be designed around an activity that allows the student to experience and understand the place of mathematics in a larger context (e.g., the function of addition and money skills within the larger activity of shopping).

Systematic instruction involves consistent use of instructional strategies that make use of prompting and corrective feedback, and both guided and independent practice, to teach students specific skills. These prompting systems are discussed in this chapter. Systematic instruction may include adaptations and assistive devices. *In vivo* instruction allows the teacher to evaluate the need for, design, and assess adaptations. Adaptations are considered for use when a student cannot learn to perform a skill in the same manner as a typical student. For mathematics these include use of coin-matching cards that have pictures of the coins needed for a particular activity, use of a calculator (Westling & Fox, 2004), a number line (Sandknop, Schuster, Wolery, & Cross, 1992), or use of strategies such as the "and-one-dollar-more" strategy for money handling (Test, Howell, Burkhart, & Beroth, 1993), or use of touchpoints for basic calculations (Cihak & Foust, 2008), commercialized by Touch Math.

With the passage of the No Child Left Behind Act of 2001, educators of students with moderate to severe intellectual disabilities may be asked to align their mathematics objectives with general education curriculum standards. Because decades of research that address best educational practices for students within this population have consistently yielded evidence in favor of a functional curriculum concept, content, and objectives, the adaptation of general education standards should be aligned within a functional curriculum framework that focuses on individual student needs. Functional cognitive and functional academic objectives can be aligned within the various traditional academic content areas in the general education curriculum. For example, in the early grades, one-to-one correspondence and basic mathematical functions of addition and subtraction may be aligned with general education objectives. For students in secondary grades who need basic arithmetic instruction, teachers may be required to restate basic addition or subtraction principles in the terms used by general education in the secondary grades. For example, it may require the teacher to view the basic math questions with which these students must deal (if you have two and need five, how many more do you need?) as if they were a basic algebraic equation ($x + 2 = 5$) in order to meet a requirement for alignment (Jimenez, Browder, & Courtade, 2008). Although this may seem forced, it helps to bring the language of special and general education into alignment. The process of alignment should be a conversation that brings into focus two educational perspectives which can strengthen the purpose and goals of both (Courtade-Little & Browder, 2005).

Instructional Strategies

As noted previously, the learning characteristics of students with moderate to severe intellectual disabilities influence the design of instructional strategies. Given each student's particular array of characteristics, each student will have unique learning requirements. Learning requirements will be affected by the student's particular combination of cognitive level, type and level of physical disability, and type and level of sensory disability. These will determine the extent to which tasks must be broken down into simpler parts, the need for assistance in performance, and the need for various types of technology. Despite the variety of characteristics across students, certain criteria for instruction must be maintained. Instruction must be systematic and consistent in its application. Such instruction would provide a very narrow opportunity for student error so as not to slow down the learning process. Instruction must be concrete in terms of both the skills being taught and the materials selected. Instruction must be distributed across time, with significant opportunities for ongoing practice. Most importantly, the student must be an active participant in the instructional process rather than a passive receiver of instruction. In order to meet these criteria various strategies are employed.

Activity-Based Instruction

Activity-based instruction is a strategy in which individual skills are taught in the context of an activity rather than in isolation. Within and across activities, students learn specific communication, motor, social, and academic skills in the context of the broader activity rather than in isolated half-hour time blocks at their desks. This strategy provides students with repeated learning opportunities in functional activities scheduled across the day and week. For students with moderate disabilities such as Ross, rather than teaching coin recognition with ditto sheets or matching piles of coins at his desk, he would be taught to recognize actual coins while paying for his lunch in the cafeteria, buying a snack from a vending machine, or purchasing pencils and paper in a store. In addition to learning to read by using flash cards in a classroom group lesson, he would learn to read product labels and price tags in stores and words on signs around the school building and neighborhood. For students with severe disabilities such as Shandra, rather than putting colored cubes in piles, she would be taught to sort by color when separating clothes for washing, glass for recycling, and/or colored napkins for table setting. Rather than rote recitation of numbers during circle time, she would learn to count by counting out various task materials for classmates in her special and general education class settings. An adolescent such as Dario, who is engaged in vocational training in a discount store unpacking shoes in the stock room, would have a variety of activities in which to learn and/or practice skills. When unpacking shoes, he would have an opportunity to work on sorting skills by separating the shoes from their packaging and sorting by size, counting when setting up the shoe display, and communication when he asks for assistance from coworkers using his communication device. When getting ready for work, he would practice self-help skills when dressing in his work uniform and using the restroom. During break, he would receive experience using money to purchase a soda from the vending machine, practice in reading words and logos when he makes his selection, and reinforcement of appropriate social skills when he uses his communication device to converse with his coworkers. Throughout his time at the store, Dario would have multiple opportunities to learn and practice his mobility skills as he navigates his wheelchair around the various subenvironments in the store.

Task Analysis

Many tasks performed are chains of skills rather than individual, discrete skills. For example, eating, dressing, washing, leisure tasks of playing board games, ball games, video games, vocational tasks of assembly, unwrapping, and storing shoes are all tasks that combine several behaviors. Chains make use of individual skills in various combinations or series in order to achieve new behaviors. Chains may result in a complex behavior such as brushing your teeth, or a series of activities such as taking a bus to a store and returning home.

Chained tasks are taught by breaking down the chain into small steps for the student to master. The process of identifying these steps is known as **task analysis**. This allows parts of a task to be taught individually while still in the context of the whole task. The component steps of the chain are arranged in sequence from first to last. The number of steps into which a chain is divided is determined by the student's ability level. One student may learn to wash dishes through a sequence of 10 steps, whereas another may need 20 steps. There should be just enough steps in the task analysis to allow efficient and systematic teaching that results in student performance over time. If a student has particular difficulty with a step, it can be further analyzed into smaller components for instruction. For example, if the step is to remove the top of the toothpaste tube, that step can be further broken down into: (a) hold tube with left hand, (b) place right hand on cap, (c) twist cap with right hand, (d) pull cap straight up, and (e) place cap on sink-top.

Steps in a chain can be taught as individual units, in sequence, from the first step in the chain to the last (**forward chaining**), or from the last step in the chain to the first (**backward chaining**). However, the preferred procedure is known as **total task programming** (Wilcox & Bellamy, 1982). In total task programming, the student is given the opportunity to perform all the steps in the chain in ordinal sequence and, as needed, is provided assistance by the teacher to complete steps that are difficult. This procedure has at least three advantages. First, it allows the student to perform the entire chain at each opportunity, thereby seeing the purpose or end product of performing the chained behavior. This procedure also provides repeated motor practice in completing the entire chain, and lastly, it allows for instructional assistance as needed.

Presented in **Figure 12.8** is a task analysis appropriate for teaching Ross to buy a snack from a vending machine. He can use this skill across environments such as his school, community, and vocational settings.

Even when a task has been analyzed into its component steps, some students may still be unable to perform the entire task. This is especially true for students with the most severe intellectual disabilities or those with complicating physical disabilities. An application of the Principle of Partial Participation differentiates competence within a chain as opposed to competence performing the entire chain (Logan, Alberto, Kana, & Waylor-Bowen, 1994). For some students, the ability to perform some of the steps is an appropriate performance criterion. For example, a student may be able to complete all the steps in putting on pants except zipping and fastening the belt. This partial completion of the activity may be the student's highest level of participation for the activity. For a student with multiple impairments, this may be considered a valid criterion level of participation because it reduces dependence on someone else.

Activity based instruction teaches this student to recognize the money he needs to use in the vending machine.

Behavioral Prompting Strategies

In order to provide instruction that is direct, systematic, and consistent, a behavioral approach is used with this population of students. The precision of a behavioral instructional approach makes clear to the student the behavior to be performed and reduces the possible range of error. The behavioral instructional approach is summarized in the sequence of A-B-C (antecedent-behavior-consequence). For the behavior or skill to be taught, the focus is on the selection of an appropriate antecedent condition, such as materials, opportunity, cues, or environment, and a detailed definition of the expected behavior or desired outcome. This is

---

Figure 12.8   Task Analysis for Buying a Snack from a Vending Machine

1. Locate the vending machine
2. Scan through items and choose one to purchase
3. Find the price
4. Using the "one-dollar-more method," calculate how many dollars are needed for the snack
5. Take out money from wallet
6. Find the desired snack and locate its item number
7. Deposit money into the vending machine
8. Enter the item number
9. Retrieve snack from compartment
10. Wait for change to be dispensed
11. Take change from tray

followed by the consequence in the environment and/or an administration of a reinforcer or correction by the teacher. The relationships among these components can be seen in **Figure 12.9**.

During initial instruction, a verbal direction may not be sufficient to occasion student performance of a new behavior or skill. This is to be expected when asking students to perform responses that are not part of their behavioral repertoire. Skinner (1968) referred to this as the "problem of the first instance." This first instance must occur so that a response can be reinforced that will increase the probability of continued performance, or so an incorrect response can be corrected, or an approximation of the response can be shaped. Performance of a new behavior can be effected by teacher assistance known as **prompting**. A prompt may be placed in relation to different components of the instructional equation. Various antecedent prompts can augment the antecedent event(s), and various response prompts can be paired with the instructional cue to assist response performance.

Antecedent prompts are alterations of, or additions to, the instructional material that focuses student attention on the natural cue(s) for making correct responses. Antecedent prompts include:

- Highlighting natural cues such as color coding the label of a sweater so the student can determine front from back, or writing initial word sounds in capital or red letters to bring them to the student's attention (relevant feature prompts).
- Teaching names of eating utensils in an array of utensils and dishes during snack and lunch rather than a random array of objects at their desks (natural context prompts).
- Teaching new words paired with pictures (associative prompts).
- Providing a model for performance before the student is asked to perform (antecedent modeling).
- Spatially arranging materials so initially correct choices are closer to the student (proximity prompts).

Response prompts are types of assistance needed for behavior performance. They require the teacher to assist the student in performing the response. These are used when a natural cue for a behavior, or an instructional cue, such as the bell ringing at the end of the school

Figure 12.9 A-B-C Analysis of Behavior

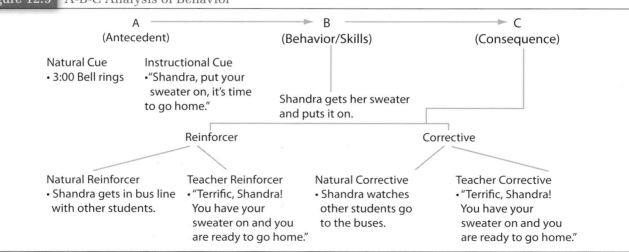

day, telling the student to put on her sweater, are not sufficient for the student to perform the behavior. Response prompts include:

- A verbal prompt that restates the instructional cue or provides the student added information or encouragement.
- A gesture prompt where the teacher points to or touches the material.
- A concurrent model in which the teacher demonstrates performance simultaneously with the student.
- Partial physical assistance where the teacher provides physical assistance for initiation of the behavior.
- Full physical assistance where the teacher guides the student through the entire behavior.

These types of prompts can be used individually (e.g., instructional strategies such as time delay or simultaneous prompting). They can also be used in combination, sequencing from the most amount of assistance (hand-over-hand assistance) to the least amount of assistance (verbal assistance), or from the least to the most amount of assistance. **Figure 12.10** illustrates how these response prompts may be used with Shandra.

Prompts are not used to make the student indefinitely dependent on the teacher or some third person. Relief from such dependence is accomplished in one of two ways: prompt fading and using self-operated prompts. Prompt fading is the procedure by which antecedent prompts such as color coding of relevant features are faded slowly until they disappear after the student has acquired the skill. For example, the color code on the sweater label or the print size of the initial word sound is reduced to normal. In response prompting, the fading of the teacher assistance is built into the procedure and the amount of assistance provided is reduced until the student responds to only the natural or instructional cues. The second procedure for reduced prompt dependence is the use of self-operated prompts. There are three types of self-operated prompts: pictures as prompts (Wacker & Berg, 1983), audio prompts (Alberto, Sharpton, Briggs, & Stright, 1986), and videos as prompts (Banda, Dogoe, & Matuszny, 2011). These prompts are used most often when teaching chained behavior. For each step in a chain, one of three options may be used in which a picture is taken, an oral direction is recorded, or video is taken. The student is given a booklet, DVD player (e.g., including an iPod), or a tape recording of step directions. For example, when teaching Dario to assemble the blood donation kits at the Red Cross using video prompting, the teacher would video tape Dario doing each step in the assembly. The number of prompts is

---

Figure 12.10   Examples of Response Prompts

Natural Cue	• The lunch bell rings. Teacher says "It's lunch time."
Instructional Cue	• "Shandra, get your lunch bag."
Verbal Prompt	• "Shandra, go to your cubby and get your lunch bag."
Gesture Prompt	• Teacher goes to student's cubby, points and says, "Shandra, get your lunch bag."
Model	• Teacher demonstrates taking out lunch bag and says, "Shandra, get your lunch bag."
Partial Physical Prompt	• Teacher assists student in getting up from her chair and says, "Shandra, get your lunch bag."
Full Physical Prompt	• Teacher takes student's hand and guides her through the entire task and says, "Shandra, get your lunch bag."

faded as the student acquires independent task performance. However, for chains that are very complex or very long, some students may always need the prompt. This is an acceptable alternative to relying upon another person for prompting if the student is able to operate the prompts independently.

Alternative Performance Strategies

When planning instruction for students with moderate to severe intellectual disability, it is important to understand the difference between the form of a behavior and the function of a behavior (White, 1980). There are a variety of ways to perform a task in order to achieve a desired outcome. If, for cognitive or physical reasons, the student cannot perform a task in the same manner as a nondisabled peer, the teacher designs an alternative performance strategy that will achieve the same functional outcome. An alternative performance strategy is a different way of engaging in a behavior (form) to achieve the same result (function). Designing an alternative form is especially important for critical activities (Brown et al., 1979). Critical activities are those that if the student cannot perform them, it will be essential for someone else to do them. This limits the student's independence. These activities typically include self-help, communication, and mobility. Alternative performance strategies are essential for reduction of dependency by these students. Examples of the use of an alternative performance strategy include:

- Using matching cards for selecting the coins for bus fare
- Using a picture language board to communicate
- Shopping from a picture list rather than a word list
- Using a pressure switch to turn on appliances

A hierarchical sequence of alternative performance strategies for purchasing items is presented in **Figure 12.11**.

The usual academic sequence approach focuses on the normal form of a behavior such as telling time, rather than on the function of the behavior which is time management. The normal form of behavior, in many cases, requires prerequisite skills quite different from those of a functional alternative. For example, being able to "tell time" on a standard watch or wall clock requires that the student be able to count by fives to 55, to count by ones from any multiple of 5 (30, 31, 32, 33, 34), and so on. In contrast, a time management strategy requires that the student be able to match-to-sample a clock and a picture of a clockface and comprehend the symbol (word, rebus, photograph) designating the target activity. A curriculum based on a usual academic sequence would clearly include instruction on the prerequi-

Figure 12.11   Hierarchical Sequence of Alternative Performance Strategies

Task: Ordering at a candy counter, movie theater ticket booth, fast food counter, etc.
1. Student verbally orders item from memory.
2. Student verbally orders using picture card as a prompt.
3. Student points to item desired.
4. Student points to a photo of desired item in a picture booklet.
5. Student activates an electronic communication board by touching the corresponding symbol and the board "says" the word.
6. Student activates digital recorder to place order.
7. Teacher or peer gives order card to the salesperson and the student touches the card (partial participation).

Figure 12.12   Correlation between Student Learning Characteristics and Curriculum/Instructional Strategies

Learning Characteristic	Curriculum/Instructional Strategy
1. Developmental delay	• Functional objectives • Age-appropriate materials and settings • Alternative performance strategies • Partial participation
2. Learn fewer skills and takes longer to learn skills	• Functional objectives based on ecological analysis • Community-based instruction • Antecedent and response prompting
3. Deficit in generalization	• Natural, integrated contexts • Activity-based instruction
4. Deficit in memory	• Functional objectives • Ongoing distributed practice • Natural contexts
5. Deficit in attention	• Antecedent prompting
6. Deficit in incidental learning	• Direct, systematic instruction
7. Deficit in information synthesis and anticipation	• Activity-based instruction • Task analysis
8. Deficit in language	• Alternative performance strategies • Natural contexts and settings
9. Deficit in social skills	• Integrated settings • Direct, systematic instruction
10. Challenging behaviors	• Alternative performance strategies • Task analysis • Prompting strategies • Partial participation

sites for standard time-telling and not those required for the functional alternative (Wilcox & Bellamy, 1982).

Students with moderate to severe intellectual disabilities exhibit learning characteristics that directly influence curriculum selection and instructional strategies. These learning characteristics are summarized in **Figure 12.12**. A curriculum that focuses on specific instructional skills and strategies is necessary to enable an outcome of graduates who live, work, and participate in integrated neighborhoods with a considerable degree of independence.

Instructional Settings

In recent years, educators serving students with moderate to severe intellectual disabilities began to examine the settings in which educational services are delivered to their students. Traditionally, instruction took place in self-contained classrooms on general education campuses where special educators were able to implement systematic instructional procedures to address specific student objectives. Although students were able to master many of the skills outlined on their IEPs in these classrooms, students had little opportunity to practice those skills in a variety of settings and few chances to interact socially with their nondisabled peers. Thus, educators now ask *What are the most appropriate settings for students to learn and practice new skills?* and *Where will they have a maximum opportunity to do so with their peers?* Because students with moderate to severe intellectual disabilities typically require a number of concrete experiences to master educational objectives, educators consider instructional settings beyond the self-contained special education classroom. They examine environments that not only provide students an opportunity to learn and practice new skills, but also offer the social benefit of interacting with their nondisabled peers.

General Education Settings

The legislative force behind integrated educational opportunities is the mandate for the provision of a free appropriate education in the least restrictive environment (LRE). In the

The lunchroom may be an inclusive setting.

1980s, educators defined LRE as mainstreaming. Mainstreaming referred to the placement of students with disabilities in general education programs whenever possible (Grenot-Scheyer & Falvey, 1986; MacMillan, 1982). However, mainstreamed placements often were determined by a student's ability to acquire the skills and subject matter being taught in these classroom settings. Thus, students with moderate to severe intellectual disabilities who lacked the cognitive skills to acquire classroom subject matter generally were not considered for mainstreamed placements. Instead, for these students, mainstreaming often was limited to attendance at school assemblies; participation in some art, music, and physical education classes; and taking part in the regular lunch periods.

Today, the term **inclusion** is used to refer to the provision of educational services to students with disabilities in integrated settings. Instead of making the student ready for the classroom, inclusion promotes making the classroom ready for the student. Inclusive settings may include:

- regular day-care or preschool settings
- school campus settings such as the library and lunchroom
- general education classroom settings such as exploratory classes (e.g., culinary arts, visual art, chorus) and appropriately selected academic classes
- community settings such as shopping malls, recreational centers, and vocational training sites.

Access to these settings provides students with moderate to severe intellectual disabilities numerous opportunities to learn and generalize skills across settings, and to interact with their peers. With inclusion, instead of being concerned with the student's cognitive readiness to acquire general curriculum subject matter, educators are interested in co-mingling a student's IEP objectives within the instructional format and with the supports and instructional methods necessary to accommodate the learning needs of all students.

Inclusion Defined

Inclusion may be defined as educating all children and youth in one system of education. Characteristics of an inclusive educational system include the following principles (York-Barr, Kronberg, & Doyle, 1996):

- Students with disabilities are members of the same school community as neighbors and siblings.

- A natural proportion of students with disabilities occurs at any school site.

- A zero-rejection philosophy exists so that typically no student would be excluded on the basis of type or extent of disability.

- Students with disabilities are placed in age- and grade-appropriate school and general education classrooms.

- The focus of the instructional design and curriculum are individualized to promote independent or partial participation in current and future environments.

- Supports are provided in the context of general school and community environments which include special education and related services.

Inclusion was conceptualized with the intent of providing students with disabilities equal access to educational settings with maximum opportunities to be educated alongside and develop social relationships with their peers. However, inclusion does not mean students with disabilities spend all of their instructional time in general education classrooms, never receive one-to-one or small group instruction, or only participate in parallel instruction that is unrelated to their nondisabled classmates. Nor is the goal of inclusion for all students to learn the core curriculum or content in a given class period (York-Barr, Kronberg, & Doyle, 1996). Instead, inclusion focuses on ensuring that students with disabilities are equal members of a class, school, and community where their specific instructional needs are met in appropriate, least restrictive, and integrated settings.

Continuum of Services

When considering options for where curriculum content and IEP objectives should be taught, IEP committee members must bear in mind the mandate that "to the maximum extent appropriate, children with disabilities are educated with children who are not disabled" (Least Restrictive Environment 34 CFR 300.550 (b)(2)). Therefore, initial priority is given to instruction in general education settings. IDEA also guarantees that instruction in a general education class be considered with the addition of supplementary aids and services, modifications, and personnel supports as needed to ensure access to learning. It is following consideration of general education class placement that alternative options in special education and community settings are reviewed. It is unlikely for students with moderate to severe intellectual disabilities that all of a student's instruction will occur in any one setting. It is typical across a day or week that the student will receive instruction in various general education, special education, and community settings. Various general education classes may be determined appropriate for a student to acquire and then generalize communication and social skills among nondisabled peers. It may also be determined that a special education setting is most appropriate for instruction of certain self-care objectives. It is often the case that instruction coordinated across settings is planned. An IEP committee may decide to address money skills in a general education math class, and generalize the skills during community-based instruction in a neighborhood retail store.

In order for the IEP committee and the school system to meet the mandate of education in the least restrictive environment (LRE) a variety of modifications and personnel supports must be available for use in a general education class.

The variety of modifications and personnel supports that may be used to support a student's placement in a general education class include:

1. **Material Modifications.** Materials may be modified in many ways to facilitate student learning and participation. Using real objects and/or manipulatives will adjust the cognitive demand through making the materials more functional and concrete. Teachers may also accommodate motor or sensory requirements by changing the size, highlighting specific parts, and incorporating assistive technology. Worksheets and tests can be adapted to include more spacing, fewer items, and bold or highlighted directions.

2. **Activity Modifications.** Activities are modified to allow for access and student participation. Activity modifications may include allowing a student, who is nonverbal, to respond by using a switch to activate a computer or an augmentative and alternative communication device. Partial participation is allowing students to participate in an activity to their maximum level of independence rather than denying access to the activity because the student could not complete the entire activity (Baumgart et al., 1983). For example, identifying, gathering, and sorting all the necessary materials for cooking while another student actually cooks. A teacher may also reduce the number of required responses, provide additional time, or identify different outcomes. An example of requiring a different outcome would be having a student complete a picture, collage, or typed report instead of a written report. The student could use a tee to hit a ball or use a bowling ramp to participate in physical education or extracurricular activities.

3. **Instructional Modifications.** A teacher may modify the instructional setting by using large and small groups. Also, the teacher could implement peer tutors and individualized instruction. Additionally, shortening the length of a lesson or decreasing the rate at which the instruction is delivered may assist in the facilitation of learning. For example, the teacher may use vocabulary that matches the student's understanding during instruction. The teacher may also use visual aids across lessons and provide copies of overheads, class notes, and recordings of lectures to assist with note taking.

4. **Environmental Modifications.** The environment may be modified to accommodate a student's physical, sensory, academic, and behavioral needs. Teachers may implement daily schedules for students working on self-management skills, proximity seating for students who uses wheel chairs, or lamps instead of overhead lighting to reduce the glare for a student with visual impairments.

5. **Personnel Supports.** Support may also be provided through the presence of another adult outside or within the general education classroom. Support outside the classroom is typically conducted on a consultative model. A special educator or related service personnel, such as a speech-language pathologist, adaptive physical education teacher, or physical therapist, may consult with the general education teacher regarding how to address specific student IEP objectives, how to implement modifications, and how to individualize teaching strategies that promote academic, social, and behavioral outcomes.

Personnel supports within the general education classroom may consist of collaboration, co-teaching, and supportive instruction models. The collaboration model is defined as a special education teacher providing direct services in the general education classroom for at least 50% of the course segment. Co-teaching is defined as a special education teacher and general education teacher sharing the teaching responsibilities of the general education classroom for 100% of the course segment. Supportive instruction is the assistance of a paraprofessional in the general education classroom either to provide direct service to one student or a group of students. Although the primary role of additional personnel is to facilitate learning and access to the general education environment for students with disabilities, their role is not limited to only assisting students with disabilities. The additional adult may work with all students during some activities and work one-to-one with a student during other activities. The goal of personnel supports is to systematically fade direct services to natural classroom conditions in which the student functions independently in the LRE.

Figure 12.13   Expanded Continuum of Instructional Placement Options

1. General education classroom with no modifications or personnel supports
2. General education classroom with modifications
3. General education classroom with special education consultation
4. General education classroom with supportive instruction from paraprofessional
5. General education classroom with supportive instruction from a special educator
6. Integrated community-based instructional and vocational settings
7. Special education classroom

Figure 12.13 illustrates such a continuum that emphasizes the use of modifications and supports. This continuum ranges from general education placement without modifications and supports, to placement within a separate special education class.

Addressing the IEP Goals and Objectives in an Inclusive Setting

When considering an age appropriate general education class, the IEP committee must determine what classes and segments are available to students at their grade level. For example, a schedule for a typical first grade student may include calendar time, center time, reading, writing, math, recess, music, art, and physical education. Whereas, a sixth grade student schedule may include language arts, literature, social studies, math, health, and physical education. An effective method for determining appropriate classes for implementing IEP objectives is the use of a scheduling matrix. Matrices provide a graphic view of opportunities to learn IEP objectives across a daily schedule matrix or within a class schedule matrix.

To complete a daily schedule matrix, a student's IEP objectives are listed vertically down the left column and a typical class schedule is listed horizontally across the top of the matrix. Committee members then discuss and indicate the classes in which objectives could be implemented. For example, as presented in **Figure 12.14a**, Ross's IEP indicates that he needs to work on conversational turn taking, assembling specific items in a given amount of time, reading labels, and using a calculator. When looking across the matrix at a typical sixth grade schedule of classes, Ross's IEP committee indicates with check marks the range of options in which Ross may receive instruction in general education classes. Selecting specific classes is based on student preferences, school building schedule, scheduling of community activities, and prior experiences and training of teachers. Sixth grade science will provide Ross multiple opportunities to address each of his IEP objectives.

Committee members also examine specific opportunities to address IEP objectives within a class. To complete a class schedule matrix, a student's IEP objectives are listed vertically down the left column. The within class schedule of activities is listed across the

Figure 12.14a   Daily Schedule Matrix of Ross' IEP Objectives Across a Typical School Day

IEP Objectives	Reading	English	Math	Science	Social Studies	Art	Phys. Ed.
Conversational turn taking	✓	✓⁻		✓	✓	✓	✓
Assemble item			✓	✓		✓	
Read labels	✓	✓	✓	✓	✓	✓	✓
Use a calculator			✓	✓			

Adapted from Falvey, M. (1995). *Inclusive and heterogeneous schooling* (p. 101). Baltimore, MD: Paul H. Brookes.

Figure 12.14b   Class Schedule Matrix of Ross' IEP Objectives within a General Education Classroom

| IEP Objectives | Roll Call and Lesson Preview | Science Class | | Work Review of Lesson and Clean-up |
		Material Distribution	Group (Lab)	
Conversational turn taking	✓	✓	✓	✓
Assemble item	✓	✓	✓	✓
Read labels	✓	✓	✓	
Use a calculator			✓	✓

Adapted from Falvey, M. (1995). *Inclusive and heterogeneous schooling* (p. 101). Baltimore, MD: Paul H. Brookes.

top of the matrix. Committee members then discuss and indicate activities in which each objective can be instructed. For example, as seen in **Figure 12.14b**, Ross's IEP objectives can be included in any and/or each of the science class activities.

Once an IEP committee determines which settings are the most appropriate for addressing a student's IEP goals and objectives, a daily schedule can be developed. For Shandra, Ross, and Dario, the following IEP objectives were developed to be addressed in their general education classroom placements (see box below).

The team of individuals involved in developing a student's daily schedule, as well as designing instructional adaptations, usually includes the classroom teacher(s), the special education teacher, related service professionals, and the student. This team generally meets on a regular basis to develop specific instructional plans for the student while at the same time completing the general classroom lesson plans. An instructional plan developed for the student with a disability might indicate the following: the specific IEP and non-IEP objectives addressed on that particular day for a student, the time(s) of day in which a student is included, the specific class, instructional support personnel, and the activity for the class period(s). In addition, this plan would indicate instructional adaptations and materials necessary to assure relevant learning opportunities are available. As illustrated in **Figure 12.15**, the instructional plan also provides the classroom teacher an opportunity to indicate whether planned activities occurred and whether alternative activities or remediations need to be implemented in future class periods.

Shandra: "When given the opportunity to choose between team games in which to participate during her physical education class in the gym, Shandra will indicate which sport she would like to play and physically move to that location of the gym 100% of the time, with no more than one verbal prompt for 6 consecutive weeks."

Ross: "During physical science class, Ross will participate in lab activities by reading and gathering the materials presented on a written list, sharing his materials with his lab partner, and assisting in putting materials away independently, 2 days per week for 5 weeks."

Dario: "During computer class, Dario will use a switch to turn his computer on and off, use his communication device to indicate which computer program he needs to use, and will type his name and social security number using an adapted keyboard with no more than two physical prompts, twice per week for 6 weeks."

Figure 12.15   Example Instruction Plan for Shandra in Two General Education Classroom Placements

STUDENT: Shandra   DAY OF WEEK: Wednesday
TIME: 9:00–9:55

DATE: August 16
TIME: 1:05–2:00

Class: Physical Education
Support: Mr. Jones until 9:30

Class: Social Studies
Support: Ms. Archer

- Class Activity: Warm-up exercises, activities introduction, choosing activities, participate in chosen activity. Choices include: soccer skills, floor hockey drills, tether ball, four-square.
- IEP Obj.: 1. Choose an activity. During activity selection, the P.E. teacher will ask Shandra to select an activity in which to participate. Any prompts or reminders of which activities are available will be reviewed at this time.
  2. Participate in activity. Shandra does not require physical assistance in participation in activities. However, she may require teacher and peer guidance in rule-following.
- Non-IEP Obj: 3. Share materials and equipment with her peers and teammates. Shandra may need verbal reminders for sharing.
  4. Keep her shoe laces tied. Shandra is still learning to tie her shoes and may require assistance in "making loops." She also may require reminders to ask for assistance (if needed) when she needs help with her shoe laces.
- Activities completed as planned?
  1. Yes
  2. Yes
  3. Yes
  4. No
- Alternative Activities/Remediation: Although Shandra's shoe lace did come untied during the class period, she did not have an opportunity to ask for assistance nor retie her own shoe laces because a peer completed the task for her. We may need to remind Shandra's class peers of the importance for Shandra to learn to ask for help as well as tie her own shoes.

- Class Activity: Map reading, learning to read the map legend, learning to read map directions (north, south, east, west).
- IEP Obj.: 1. Locating places within the school building. Activity: Using a map of the school, Shandra and one peer will use the school map to physically locate the library, cafeteria, gym, math class, computer room, and front office. In addition, Shandra and her peer will review these places on the map in the classroom.
  2. Concepts. Activity: while her peers are reading their maps, the teacher will ask questions to the class and to Shandra as to the activities conducted in various community businesses and what you might find there. For example, "at the library we check out books."
- Non-IEP Obj.: 3. Keep her personal items put away during activity time. Shandra may require verbal reminders and physical assistance in putting away her items.
- Activities completed as planned?
  1. Yes
  2. Yes
  3. No
- Alternative Activities/Remediation: Shandra has continued to have difficulty following the verbal reminders of her teachers and peers for keeping her personal items stored during activity time. Therefore, a picture prompt system was developed and attached to the top of Shandra's desk to act as a reminder to put away items. Data on training and Shandra's ability to follow this prompting system will be taken by Ms. Archer for the first 2 weeks of its implementation.

Instructional Adaptations

The planning team that develops a student's daily class schedule also may be responsible for determining the curricular adaptations needed in order for a student to learn. Thus, team members must determine what to teach in specific curricular areas as well as how to teach activities and to evaluate student progress. If it is decided the student with a disability will be able to actively participate in a lesson without modifications while achieving the same learning outcomes as nondisabled peers, then no adaptations would be developed. For example, during recess for the second grade, Shandra is able to socialize with her peers and utilize the playground equipment independently. Therefore, no adaptations were developed for Shandra during recess. However, if adaptations are needed, then the committee may develop modifications for the teaching style, instructional format, materials, environment, or support structure. For example, in his art class, Ross was unable to complete his projects during the allotted class time without ongoing teacher attention and assistance. Therefore, the instructional format was changed, and students were assigned to work in small groups to complete a single group project. This adaptation provided Ross with immediate support in completing his projects as well as a means of addressing his social interaction skills. In Dario's computer class, two adaptations were developed to assist him in utilizing the computer. First, Dario could not reach the switch on the floor to turn his computer on and off. Therefore, a tabletop switch was created for Dario's use. Second, Dario had difficulty isolating the correct keys to push on the keyboard to type his personal information. His special education teacher and occupational therapist developed a keyboard overlay highlighting specific letters for him to use when typing his personal information.

Community-Based Instruction

Community-based instruction (CBI) is an instructional model that provides students with disabilities an opportunity to learn and practice functional skills across a variety of community settings. In this model, educators present curriculum content in natural settings while addressing student deficits in generalization. It is a replication of the systematic, individualized instruction of the classroom where IEP objectives are targeted, instructional strategies are applied, and evaluation procedures are employed. The instruction that takes place in the community occurs on a regular, weekly basis. In order for CBI to be efficient, it makes use of small group instruction with no more than three to four students per adult in an instructional group.

Objectives and activities selected for instruction in the community are coordinated with classroom instruction. Skills often are taught in both settings simultaneously which provides multiple opportunities for practicing and generalizing functional skills. Those community settings selected as instructional sites influence the selection of instructional content. For example, at a shopping mall, students are required to locate various stores on the mall directory, purchase their lunches in the food court, and locate and use the restrooms. Thus, instructional content might include map reading, reading vocabulary words, math skills for using money, and self-care skills.

Various criteria are used in the selection of appropriate community sites for teaching selected student objectives. These include the opportunities available to teach targeted objectives; the opportunities available for generalizing learned skills; the age-appropriateness of the site; how often the student, nondisabled peers, or family may visit the site; the current and future appropriateness of the site for the student; and how safe the CBI setting is for the student. Once selected, the community sites are used continually throughout the school year to provide the student multiple opportunities to learn and practice new skills.

Scheduling the number of sites to be visited during a CBI session generally is based on the ages and grade levels of participating students. Initially, with young students, CBI sessions are short, with instruction taking place in no more than one community site at a time. However, as students get older or the academic year progresses, CBI often is extended to incorporate sites and activities for each of the domains of the curriculum. Chains of sites are selected and scheduled in as normal a sequence as possible for the student to experience a normal progression of a day in the community. **Figure 12.16** presents a full day expansion of CBI sessions for an elementary, middle, and high school student.

Community-based instruction contains three components:

CBI preview in the classroom

community on-site instruction

post-CBI follow-up activities in the classroom

Figure 12.16 Expanded CBI Session Sequences for Elementary, Middle, and High School Students

Elementary	Middle School	High School

1. Pre-CBI Session
  a. Where are we going
  b. What will we do
  c. How we behave
  d. What to do if (20 mins.)
2. Go to school bus
  a. Enter
  b. Find seat
  c. Buckle up
  d. Exit (10 mins.)
3. Locate Target store
  a. Enter
  b. Find paints & paper
  c. Find cashier & pay
  d. Exit (20 mins.)
4. Locate grocery store
  a. Enter
  b. Find popcorn
  c. Find cashier & pay
    (30 mins.)
5. Locate McDonalds
  a. Get in counter line
  b. Order
  c. Pay
  d. Find seat
  e. Eat
  f. Clear trash
  g. Use bathroom
  h. Exit (50 mins.)
6. Stop at pet shop or park
  (30 mins.)
7. Find bus and return (10 mins.)
8. Classroom follow-up with paints
  & popcorn (40 mins.)
	1. Pre-CBI Session
	  a. Where and what
	  b. Behavior
	  c. Academics (20 mins.)
	2. Go to school bus (10 mins.)
	3. Local drug store
	  a. Enter
	  b. Locate 3-item list
	  c. Find cashier & pay
	  d. Exit (30 mins.)
	4. Locate card shop
	  a. Enter
	  b. Locate card
	  c. Find cashier & pay
	  d. Exit (20 mins.)
	5. Go to school bus (10 mins.)
	6. Locate volunteer office
	  and complete day's task
	  (40 mins.)
	7. Go to school bus (10 mins.)
	8. McDonalds sequence
	  (50 mins.)
	9. Go to school bus (10 mins.)
	10. Back at school
	  a. Complete activity with card
	  b. Rake school grounds
	    (40 mins.)
		1. Pre-CBI Session (20 mins.)
		2. Walk to corner and cross street
		  a. Locate bus stop
		  b. Identify bus
		  c. Enter
		  d. Deposit money
		  e. Find seat
		  f. Identify stop
		  g. Exit bus (20 mins.)
		3. Walk to CBI site
		  a. Entrance routine
		  b. Go to work area
		  c. Perform job task(s)
		  d. Break room
		  e. Exit routine (90 mins.)
		4. Health club
		  a. Change shirt
		  b. Use 3 machines
		  c. Exit (30 mins.)
		5. Lunch sequence in cafeteria style
		  restaurant (60 mins.)
		6. Arrive at local group home for
		  residential care training
		  a. Complete one room
		  b. Exit (45 mins.)
		7. Walk to Target store
		  a. Enter
		  b. Complete purchasing routine
		  c. Exit (30 mins.)
		8. Bus sequence (20 mins.)
		9. Classroom simulation
		  (40 mins.)

CBI Preview in the Classroom

Prior to each CBI session, participating students receive a preview of the upcoming instructional session. Preview activities would include:

- a review of where they will be going, what activities will take place there, and the people they will encounter.
- a review of the general and location-specific vocabulary, reading/logos, and arithmetic skills required.
- behavioral expectations.
- a safety review such as *What would you do if . . . you need to go to the bathroom, don't see me, get lost, drop something, are spoken to by a stranger?*

On-site Instruction

Once in the community, teachers would implement the identified instructional objectives for each student. In addition, the teacher would employ the same systematic instructional strategies used in the classroom such as appropriate cues, prompts, consequences, task analyses, and alternative performance strategies. Because the instructional objectives may differ for each student, teachers may vary the levels of instruction or learning requirements. At a typical community site, such as a department store, the teacher would know which students are at the observation, acquisition, or generalization stages when purchasing clothing items in the following shopping activities.

1. Enter the store (mobility)
2. Take out shopping list (written or picture) (reading, motor)
3. Find the first item (reading or matching)
4. Check size labels (reading)
5. Check price tags (numbers)
6. Deduct cost from total on a calculator (arithmetic)
7. Repeat steps 3 to 6 for second and third items
8. Locate check-out register (mobility, reading)
9. Locate end of line and wait (social)
10. Hand items to cashier (communication)
11. Pay using appropriate strategy (money skills)
12. Take package and leave the store (mobility)

Post-CBI

Following each CBI session, there should be a review of the activities that took place in the community. In the classroom, students might review where they went, the activities they completed, the people they encountered (language expansion and memory activity), the functional academics used, and the behaviors they employed in certain situations (while eating, when speaking to the cashier). In addition, students may participate in carryover activities that provide closure to the instructional session. These activities might include cooking popcorn purchased at the grocery store, making a collage with art supplies purchased at a craft store, or totaling the prices of their purchases using a calculator.

Community-based instruction brings distinct advantages to the educational program. Given the proper selection of sites, it is functional by definition. Since students are taught skills in natural settings using materials that are naturally available in those settings, it is noninferential. In CBI settings, the teacher has an opportunity to use real (natural) criteria for evaluating student performance, and students have an opportunity to experience the natural sequences of events, distractions, and cues and consequences for correct and incorrect completion of activities. In addition, CBI provides multiple opportunities for the generalization of communication, mobility, and social skills with distributed practice across the various community sites.

Preparing for Post-School Options

The purpose of education for any student is preparation to be an active and contributing member of society by providing an opportunity to learn the skills necessary to live, work, and recreate in integrated community settings. For students without disabilities, this education typically consists of academic instruction in preparation for entering higher education

or the military, vocational instruction in preparation for entering specific jobs or further voca-
tional/technical training, and programming that
prepares students for obtaining a job, maintaining a home, managing finances, and caring for
children. For many of these students, services
provided by the high school guidance counselor are sufficient for obtaining these post-
school outcomes. However, for students with
moderate to severe intellectual disabilities, it is
essential that systematic planning and specific
instruction take place early in the student's
school years to achieve desired post-school
outcomes. Transition services is the term used
to describe the systematic planning and instruction which takes place to achieve a student's
desired post-school outcomes. According to
IDEA, transition services are "a coordinated

Community experiences are just one part of the transition
services provided to achieve a student's desired post-school
outcome.

set of activities for a student . . . which promotes movement from school to post-school
activities" (Public Law 105-17, Section 1401 [30][A] of IDEA). These services include
"instruction, related services, community experiences, the development of employment and
other post-school adult living objectives, and when appropriate, acquisition of daily living
skills and functional vocational evaluation" (Section 1401 [30][C] of IDEA). Because these
services require long-term planning and systematic instruction to achieve post-school goals,
transition must be addressed in a student's IEP no later than age 14. With the 1997 Reauthorization of IDEA, IEP team members must begin planning for a student's transition
beginning at age 14. At this time, it is the team's responsibility to develop a statement of the
student's transition needs and focus on the course of study that will facilitate transition. This
law further requires team members to develop "a statement of needed transition services . . .
including, when appropriate, a statement of the interagency responsibilities or any needed
linkages no later than age 16 for a student" (Section 1414 [vii][I] of IDEA). In addition,
coordination among elementary, middle, secondary, and adult programs must take place to
ensure that instructional programming results in each student's smooth transition to post-
school activities (Alberto, Elliott, Taber, Houser, & Andrews, 1993).

    For students with moderate to severe intellectual disabilities, an educational model that
leads to desired post-school outcomes is one that addresses instructional content and settings
throughout a student's school career as well as the individuals and agencies who may be
involved in the delivery of services. A continuum of programming that begins in the elementary grades and follows a student through the secondary level, provides a system for establishing linkages with adult agencies and an instructional foundation for the planning and
delivery of educational and post-school services. As illustrated in **Figure 12.17**, students
with moderate to severe intellectual disabilities receive instructional services by educators
in both school and community-based settings during the elementary and middle school
grades.

    The curriculum content may include instruction in domestic and self-help skills such as
making a bed and grooming, community skills such as learning to cross a street or shop in
a grocery store, recreation and leisure skills such as learning to play age-appropriate games
and team sports, and prevocational skills such as following a schedule and remaining on
task. As these students enter the secondary program, instructional settings are expanded to
include **community-based vocational instruction** (CBVI) sites. CBVI is an instructional

Figure 12.17   Continuum of Educational Programming for Transition

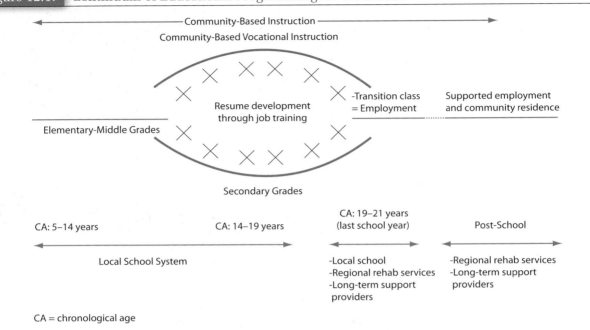

From Alberto, P., Elliott, N., Taber, T., Houser, E., & Andrews, P. (1993). Vocational content for students with moderate and severe disabilities in elementary and middle grades. *Focus on Exceptional Children, 25*(9), 1–10.

model in which students with moderate to severe disabilities experience vocational training in a variety of community businesses. These range from retail, food services, and office or clerical experiences to building maintenance, hotel guest services, and jobs in light industry. During a given school year, a student would have an opportunity to experience training in two or three vocational training settings. As preparation for future employment, students receive instruction on a variety of work-related skills and behaviors while remaining under the direct supervision of school personnel. However, they also receive training from community business employees as they begin to develop a repertoire of specific vocational skills required to obtain and maintain employment. During the final school year, students receive services from not only the local school system but also from adult agencies identified in each student's Individual Transition Plan (ITP). Once the student exits the school program, it is these agencies that continue to provide ongoing support throughout the individual's adult life.

Individual Transition Plan (ITP)

For students with moderate to severe intellectual disabilities, the development of a comprehensive ITP is critical in planning for an individual's future. It provides a means of determining needed areas of instruction and support for working and living in an integrated community. It also provides an organized format for accessing those agencies whose support will be required for a young adult exiting a school program. Because students with moderate to severe intellectual disabilities require extensive educational training prior to graduation and coordination with numerous post-school services from adult agencies, the development of a comprehensive ITP will take several years. Generally, the more services and supports a student requires as an adult, the earlier transition planning should occur. Thus, transition planning may need to begin well before a student's 14th birthday.

The ITP is a part of the IEP. For students with mild disabilities, transition recommendations may be incorporated in the standard IEP format. However, for students with moderate to severe disabilities requiring extensive transition planning, a separate set of pages addressing transition issues may be attached to the IEP. Regardless of where ITP recommendations are made in the IEP, they provide a foundation for developing IEP goals and objectives. For example, 18-year-old Dario and his family would like for him to be employed in a part-time job that provides medical and dental benefits. As part of Dario's high school program, he participated in some community-based vocational instruction (CBVI) but has yet to experience a job that

During a given school year, a student would have an opportunity to train in two or three vocational settings.

he really enjoys. In his last IEP meeting, through his brother, Dario indicated that he would like to participate in training at a local movie theater. For the next school year, Dario's teacher indicated on the ITP that Dario will continue to participate in the school's CBVI program and will receive vocational training in at least three vocational sites, one being a movie theater. Thus, an IEP goal might be that Dario will participate in CBVI training at a restaurant, a pharmacy, and a movie theater over the next year. A specific objective under this goal might be as follows:

> Upon entering his vocational training site, Dario will greet his coworkers, clock in, and collect tickets for the 1:00 movie with only verbal assistance from a coworker, 100% of the time for 3 consecutive weeks.

As illustrated in **Figure 12.18**, the ITP is comprised of two major components. The first is student information, which includes the student's name and birth date as well as present skills, needs, and experiences.

This section expands the descriptive information contained in the "present levels of performance" portion of the IEP to include a concise description of the student's current skills and instructional needs in the vocational, community, domestic, and leisure domains. After completing this section, members of the IEP/ITP committee should have a clear understanding of how the student currently functions in various integrated settings and what skills remain as a needed focus for future instruction.

The second portion of the ITP identifies the specific adult outcome areas for a student and the committee recommendations for achieving those outcomes. In addition, individual and agency responsibilities are assigned and a time line is established for completing those responsibilities. For example, Dario would like to live outside the family home once he graduates from school, and his family is interested in receiving information about group homes. As noted in Figure 12.18, a recommendation was made regarding a group home placement following Dario's graduation. Responsibilities were assigned to each of the participating individuals and agencies who will be involved in the transition process, and a time line was established for completing assigned responsibilities. Each of the recommendations and responsibilities are then reviewed and updated in future IEP/ITP meetings.

Figure 12.18   Sample Portion of an ITP for Dario

Student Name: Dario Williams   Birthdate: 06/14 Date: 05/13

Summary of Student's Present Skills, Needs and Experiences: Dario is in a self-contained class for students with moderate to severe intellectual disabilities at a regular high school. He also is included in computer and home economics classes. Dario uses a wheelchair and an AAC device for communication. Dario independently feeds himself and partially participates in changing his undergarments. Dario can assemble 3-part items using picture cues, wash dishes in an adapted sink, wipe tables, spray and wipe to clean, and can manipulate a variety of switches to activate items. Dario can fold paper and stuff envelopes. He accesses the community through the school CBI program and his parents taking him to grocery stores, restaurants, movies, spectator sporting events, and vocational training. Dario needs to learn to fold clothes and linens with more accuracy. Dario wants to learn to operate a drink dispenser. He also has expressed a desire to work in a movie theater. Dario needs more leisure skills and opportunities for participation in community recreational activities.

A. Transition Issues for Education Planning	Recommendations	Responsibilities						
		Parent/Guardian		School		Adult Service Providers		
		Action	Time Line	Action	Time Line	Action	Time Line	
2. Post-school Community Living Arrangements: Options and Training Needs • Group homes • Apartments • Remain at home	• It is recommended that Dario be placed on a waiting list for a group home opening.	• Contact group home closest to his present neighborhood and take care of paperwork to have Dario placed on waiting list. • Continue working on home-living and self-help skills to produce more independence.	• From present until graduation	• IEP objectives need to concentrate on shaving and washing hair for self-help. IEP goals will be written for learning to operate a washing machine and dryer and simple cooking preparation for home living to help in group home environment.	• Present–June	• Provide parents with all information concerning group homes and let parents and Dario tour group home sites.	• Immediately	

Adult Outcome Options

In order to successfully plan for the comprehensive transition needs of students with moderate to severe intellectual disabilities, transition team members must address a variety of adult outcome areas for a student. These areas include:

- Employment preparation and placement,
- Post-school community living arrangements,
- Independent living skills,
- Community and leisure options,
- Transportation training needs,
- Social behavior training,
- Medical needs,
- Transportation access,
- Financial and other benefits,
- Advocacy and legal trust,
- Communication needs.

Options in each of these areas can vary from learning to use the city bus under the transportation training needs area to applying for social security benefits under the financial and other benefits section of the ITP. Although considerable planning is required for each of these areas, two areas that entail significant planning, training, and supports are the areas of employment and community living.

Employment preparation models typically available to high school students are the cooperative preparation and work-study models. Both of these training models prepare students for post-school vocational/technical training and competitive employment. Students receiving vocational training in either of these models typically require little to no support once they exit the secondary school program. However, individuals with moderate to severe intellectual disabilities who require long-term support from an adult agency following graduation to maintain employment may receive training in the supported employment model. As illustrated in **Figure 12.19**, the adult outcome for this model differs from the cooperative preparation and work study models in that the goal for individuals with moderate to severe disabilities is supported rather than competitive employment.

According to the Rehabilitation Act Amendments of 1986 (PL 99-506), supported employment is "paid employment in integrated settings" for individuals with the most severe disabilities. Individuals employed under this model receive ongoing support from an adult agency job coach for the length of their employment. Support may include assistance in locating and securing employment, on-the-job training and retraining, transportation training, and advocacy support. Students who participate in this training model receive vocational experiences across a wide range of community-based businesses in order to develop employment-related skills.

Community living is the second area for which significant transition planning and preparation is required. As illustrated in **Figure 12.20**, post-school adult options in the community living area may be divided into four levels.

Students without disabilities and the majority of students with mild disabilities will live independently and be fully integrated into the community. These individuals will receive no assistance from agencies or organizations that specialize in disabilities. Student preparation for this level of independent living may include instruction in academics related to daily

Figure 12.19   Comparison of Community-Based Vocational Instruction and Work Study Programs

Item	CBVI	Work Study
Purpose	• Job sampling for resume development and ongoing assessment	• Proficiency in a specific vocational field
Target Student Population	• Students who will be eligible for supported employment	• Students who will be eligible for competitive employment
Curriculum	• Part of IEP; clusters are identified by goals and objectives	• Part of IEP; job usually relates to vocational courses in which the student is enrolled
School Credit	• Yes	• Yes
Job Development	• Special education teacher or Job Developer for CBVI	• Special education teacher or Rehabilitation Services Counselor in cooperation with Vocational coordinator for Work Study
Transportation	• Supervised and/or provided by the school system	• Student provides own
Wages	• Non-paid	• Paid; minimum wage or more
Status	• Trainee	• Employee
Supervision	• Constant by designated school personnel	• Two visits per week by special education teacher
Evaluation	• Data collected daily; e.g., work adjustment, task analysis, level of supervision, production rate, and anecdotal notes	• Daily in the beginning tapering to monthly
Benefit to Employer	• Student does not provide benefit to employer; primary benefit is to the student	• Student does provide benefit to employer as a paid employee completing assigned tasks
Time at Site	• Average 6 hours per week (2 hrs/3 days), for no more than 215 hours per site	• Daily, for two or three segments for school term
Sites per Year	• Two to four	• One

living, household maintenance, self-advocacy skills, community access, and a range of leisure activities.

It is the goal of education that students with moderate to severe intellectual disabilities be able to live in the community in supported living arrangements away from the family home. These options include semi-independent living, life sharing, and group homes. Support for individuals living in the community at this level would be provided by agencies, programs, or persons that typically assist individuals with disabilities. Student preparation for this level of community living may include instruction in functional academics related to daily living, money management, household safety, leisure activities, cooking and shopping, household maintenance and cleaning, self-advocacy, and community access skills.

Some families choose for their sons or daughters to continue to reside in the family home. The level of dependence on family members may vary significantly from complete dependence to participating and contributing to the daily household management. Instruction related to community living for individuals choosing this option may include functional academics related to daily living, household management and maintenance skills, self-advocacy, leisure activities, and community access training.

Figure 12.20   Continuum of Community Living Options

	Level One	Level Two	Level Three	Level Four
Support Services	• Independent, only natural supports from the community and family.	• Living away from the family home with support provided by an agency that typically works with individuals with disabilities.	• Continued residence in the family home with total support from the family.	• Facility based; total support for the individual, 24 hour supervision.
Responsibilities	• Choice for all aspects of life, responsible for entire household and personal management.	• Instruction and support is provided for all areas of household responsibility such as money management, cooking, cleaning, maintenance, shopping, etc. Support is faded only when and if the individual becomes independent with these skills.	• Usually very little, some simple chores and financially to household budget.	• Usually no responsibilities.
Related Curriculum Content	• Self-advocacy, self-determination; budgeting, functional academics, community skills and experiences; awareness of post-school support services, public benefits and programs.	• Self-advocacy and self-determination; community living skills and experiences; instruction in cooking, cleaning, shopping, etc.; transportation training and use of leisure time.	• Self-determination; daily living skills of personal hygiene, feeding; simple household chores such as snack preparation, dish-washing, laundry, etc.; leisure skill and activities.	• Self-determination; activities of daily living such as feeding, dressing, and bathing; leisure activities.
Examples	• Own home, apartment with a friend or spouse, live in a dormitory.	• Semi-independent living, life sharing, group homes.	• Family home with no outside agency involvement.	• Personal care homes, nursing homes, institutions.
Amount of Community Integration	• Totally integrated	• Partially integrated	• Dependent on family and amount of time they spend in the community.	• Little or no integration.

Viewed as most restrictive are community living options consisting of residing in community facilities, personal care homes, nursing homes, and public institutions that provide a great deal of structure and supervision. Individuals participating in this level are those who require constant medical care or, because of behavioral or psychiatric reasons, require intense supervision. Instructional content for these students may include: communication training, self-help skills (grooming, feeding, dressing), a range of leisure activities, self-advocacy skills, and skills leading to greater independence such as motor skills and mobility training.

Because transition planning begins early in a student's school career (no later than age 14), instructional programming may be established and implemented with specific adult outcomes in mind. In addition, educators, families, and adult service providers are able to assess future vocational, community, domestic, and leisure demands establish early linkages with agencies that will assist a student in community participation and provide a specific focus for a student's support, education, and on-going training. It is the responsibility of educators to serve as part of a team to assure a student has the opportunity to learn skills leading to increased independence based on real adult outcomes. It also is their responsibility to work on a team to establish a working relationship with service agencies which will assist in supporting an individual in an integrated community.

Figures 12.21 to **12.23** present descriptions of Shandra, Ross, and Dario 15 years from now. These descriptions provide an account of how each individual obtains access to the community, where they are living and working, and the types of recreational and leisure activities in which they may participate as adults.

Figure 12.21   Description of Shandra at 22 Years of Age

Shandra

- At 22 years of age, Shandra continues to live at home. Over the last few years in public school, Shandra and her family expressed some interest in a group home. However, they prefer that Shandra continue to live in the family home for a while. After making several inquiries about group homes, Shandra's parents placed her name on a waiting list. It is anticipated that an opening will be available in the next few years.

  While living at home, Shandra's responsibilities increased around the house. She is responsible for helping with household chores such as setting the table, dusting furniture once a week, vacuuming the rugs, and cleaning the bathrooms. She was taught to make simple meals such as sandwiches and has learned to warm food in a microwave oven. She continues to rely on reminders to take a shower; however, she recently began using a picture schedule to complete her grooming routine which has been successful so far. Financially, Shandra contributes money for her share of groceries, new clothing, and gasoline for the car.

  After graduation, Shandra began working for a major food company. She is a supported employee who works in a small group with two other adults with severe disabilities. She also has a job coach who provides daily support on the job. She works 20 hours per week packaging and pricing snack items and folding the boxes for packing. She currently earns minimum wage, and after 1 year on the job she will be eligible for limited medical benefits.

  During her time away from work, Shandra enjoys shopping in the mall with her older sister. On Wednesday and Sunday evenings, Shandra sings with her church chorus during services and attends chorus practice every Thursday night. One day each week Shandra volunteers with her next door neighbor at the local Red Cross Center. There she distributes cookies and juice to blood donors.

  Shandra's family is hesitant about allowing her to use public transportation at this time. Therefore, they provide most of the transportation for Shandra around the community. She can, however, ride a bicycle in the neighborhood and walk to neighbors' homes.

| Figure 12.22 | Description of Ross at 27 Years of Age |

Ross

- At 27, Ross shares an apartment with a friend who also has intellectual disability. Ross and his roommate receive support services from a local non-profit housing agency for persons with disabilities. This support allows Ross to live semi-independently in the community. The support services he receives include writing checks for bills and assistance with balancing his checkbook, developing and maintaining a budget, and morning telephone calls to ensure he is out of bed and getting ready for work. A support person from the agency also takes Ross and his roommate to the grocery store to do their weekly shopping. Ross is responsible for sharing half of the household chores and paying half of the bills.

  For the past 3 years, Ross has worked as a stock clerk at a large retail pet store. Some of his duties include pricing items, replacing stock on the shelves, cleaning the stock room, and assembling and building store displays. Ross works 40 hours per week, receives full medical and dental benefits, and earns an hourly wage of $10.50. He receives limited supported employment services. His job coach, who initially visited him daily, now visits him on the job once a week. Most of the support Ross receives on the job comes from his coworkers.

  During his time away from work, Ross has a variety of interests and activities. Ross and his roommate participate in the Parks and Recreation softball league during the spring and summer months. He also enjoys collecting and renting videos. He has an extensive Star Trek video collection and is a member of the Star Trek fan club.

  Occasionally on Saturdays, you can find Ross at the local library where he enjoys reading the latest magazines. Ross also enjoys camping and hiking with his friends and family. He is currently planning an upcoming weekend camping trip which will involve primitive camping and a great deal of hiking.

  Because Ross lives within 2 miles of his work, he usually rides his bicycle to work. On days when it rains or snows, Ross calls a coworker to pick him up. His coworkers established a phone system for Ross on days when he needs a ride. They provided him a list of coworkers' names and phone numbers to call when he needs assistance or a ride to work. All other transportation around the community is provided by family members, friends, and support staff. No public transportation is available in the area where Ross lives.

| Figure 12.23 | Description of Dario at 33 Years of Age |

Dario

- At 33, Dario lives in a group home with four other adults with disabilities and a full-time support person. At home Dario is responsible for maintaining his room, sharing in the household chores, and assisting with the grocery shopping twice each month. His household chores include washing the dishes, laundry, dusting, and keeping the kitchen counters clean. Dario also participates in some meal preparation such as making salads and operating the microwave oven.

  Dario is employed part-time at a local movie theater for the past 7 years. He works 30 hours per week as a ticket taker. Some of his other work responsibilities include keeping the front counters clean, stocking candy in the cases, and sweeping the front lobby with an adapted broom and dust pan. Because Dario's job responsibilities rarely change, his job coach provides only periodic visits to the job site. However, the job coach does maintain weekly phone contact with the movie theater manager. Dario has received several raises over the years and he currently earns an hourly salary of $12.50. After his first 6 months of employment, Dario was able to receive medical and dental benefits from the company's HMO.

  During his leisure time, Dario enjoys attending basketball games at the local college, Parks and Recreation Department, and going into the city to watch the hometown professional basketball team. Every Sunday he attends religious services at his church. In addition, Dario is a member of a Unified Bowling team which bowls every Friday night. His favorite part of being a member of this bowling team is going out to eat with other team members after they are finished bowling. Twice each month Dario attends social events for adults sponsored by the local intellectual disability service center. He has made several friends at these events and often calls them on the phone between social activities.

  Transportation for Dario is provided by several individuals. The full-time support person at his group home provides transportation to the grocery store, shopping mall, and doctor's office. Dario rides to work with a coworker or he uses specially equipped buses provided by the public department of transportation. He also uses the public bus to go to church on Sundays.

Summary

Students with moderate to severe intellectual disabilities are a heterogeneous population. However, certain learning characteristics result from their significant cognitive deficits and overall developmental delay. In particular, these students exhibit deficits in the number of skills they learn, in generalization of learned skills, and in the synthesis of learned skills. These characteristics have a direct relationship to the selection of a curriculum model and a set of instructional strategies. These characteristics, and post-school goals of supported work and community living have led to a functional curriculum model with objectives selected based on the students' ability to function in current and future environments. Instruction, based on behavioral teaching strategies, is conducted in community settings that are viewed as an extension of the classroom. Additionally, to the greatest extent possible, learning environments also should include opportunities in a variety of general education settings. This relationship among characteristics, post-school goals, and curriculum is necessary to ensure an outcome of graduates who live, work, and participate in integrated neighborhoods with a considerable degree of independence.

Classroom Application Activities

1. Jamie's IEP committee decided that, as another step toward independence, in the cafeteria she should be required to bring her tray from the lunch line to her table. Jamie has a severe intellectual disability and has a physical disability that requires her to use a four-legged walker. What adaptations and/or alternative performance strategies might be tried to enable Jamie to do this task?

2. As noted in this chapter, students with moderate to severe intellectual disabilities may engage in challenging behaviors. One reason for these behaviors is that students become bored in class. What are potential reasons for this boredom, and what might teachers do to prevent boredom?

3. Conduct an ecological assessment to determine the tasks required to order an ice cream cone in an ice cream shop. Then, for one of the identified tasks, perform a task analysis to determine the steps that make up the task, and the skills required for performance.

4. Carol can print most of the letters of the alphabet. Her teacher wants to begin to shape her ability to print on a line. How might the teacher use antecedent prompts to teach Carol to print on a line, and to begin at the left side of the page?

5. What training would you provide a general education student who will take a turn being the peer tutor/buddy for a student with moderate intellectual disability?

6. If you were the house leader of a group home for six adolescent and young adults with moderate intellectual disability, what leisure skills would you program for evenings in the group home and for participation in the community?

7. Ross is a middle school student with moderate intellectual disability described in this chapter (see Figure 12.2). Ross currently attends exploratory and science class with his nondisabled peers and is an active participant in the after school chorus. What modifications and/or supports might be employed to enable Ross to participate in the class unit on weather in the general education science class he attends?

8. Following Ross's science class, he attends after school chorus. What skills are required for changing classes in a middle school? What supports may be put in place to assist Ross to go from his science class to chorus?

Internet Resources

American Association on Intellectual and Developmental Disabilities
www.aaidd.org

National Transition Research Institute
www.ed.uiuc.edu/coe/sped/tri/institute.html

Office of Disability Employment Policy
www.dol.gov/odep

The Association for Persons with Severe Handicaps (TASH)
www.tash.org

Council for Exceptional Children Division on Developmental Disabilities
www.dddcec.org

What Works Clearinghouse
ies.ed.gov/ncee/wwc

References

Alberto, P., Elliott, N., Taber, T., Houser, E., & Andrews, P. (1993). Vocational content for students with moderate and severe disabilities in elementary and middle grades. *Focus on Exceptional Children, 25*(9), 1–10.

Alberto, P.A., & Fredrick, L.D. (2000). Teaching picture reading as an enabling skill. *TEACHING Exceptional Children, 33*, 60–64.

Alberto, P.A., Fredrick, L.D., Hughes, M., McIntosh, L., & Cihak, D. (2007). Components of visual literacy: Teaching logos. *Focus on Autism and Other Developmental Disabilities, 22*, 234–243.

Alberto, P., Sharpton, W., Briggs, A., & Stright, M. (1986). Facilitating task acquisition through the use of a self-operated auditory prompting system. *Journal of the Association for Persons with Severe Handicaps, 11*(2), 85–91.

Alberto, P., & Troutman, A. (2003). *Applied behavior analysis for teachers* (6th ed.). Columbus, OH: Merrill Prentice-Hall.

Allor, J.H., Mathes, P.G., Kyle, R.J., Jones, F.G., & Champlin, T.M. (2010). Teaching students with moderate intellectual disabilities to read: An experimental examination of a comprehensive reading intervention. *Education and Training in Autism and Developmental Disabilities, 45*, 3–22.

American Association on Mental Retardation (AAMR). (2002). *Mental retardation: Definition, classification, and systems of supports* (10th ed.). Washington, DC: American Association on Mental Retardation.

Ayres, K., Lowrey, K.A., Douglas, K.H., & Sievers, C. (2011). I can identify Saturn but I can't brush my teeth: What happens when the curricular focus for students with severe disabilities shifts. *Education and Training in Autism and Developmental Disabilities, 46*, 11–21.

Banda, D.R., Dogoe, M.S., & Matuszny, R.M. (2011). Review of video prompting studies with persons with developmental disabilities. *Education and Training in Autism and Developmental Disabilities, 46*, 514–527.

Barudin, S., & Hourcade, J. (1990). Relative effectiveness of three methods of reading instruction in developing specific recall and transfer skills in learners with moderate and severe mental retardation. *Education and Training in Mental Retardation, 25*, 286–291.

Baumgart, D., Brown, L., Pumpian, I., Nisbet, J., Ford, A., Sweet, M., Messina, R., & Schroeder, J. (1982). Principle of partial participation and individualized adaptations in educational programs for severely handicapped students. *Journal of the Association for Persons with Severe Handicaps, 7*, 17–27.

Bradford, S., Shippen, M., Alberto, P., Houchins, D., & Flores, M. (2005). Using systematic instruction to teach decoding skills to middle school students with moderate intellectual disabilities. *Education and Training in Developmental Disabilities.*

Browder, D. (Ed.). (1991). *Assessment of individuals with severe disabilities* (2nd ed.). Baltimore: Paul H. Brookes.

Browder, D., & Lalli, J. (1991). Review of research on sight word instruction. *Research in Developmental Disabilities, 12*, 203–228.

Browder, D., & Minarovic, T. (2000). Utilizing sight words in self-instruction training for employees with moderate mental retardation in competitive jobs. *Education and Training in Mental Retardation and Developmental Disabilities, 35*, 78–89.

Browder, D., Spooner, F., Ahlgrim-Delzell, L., Harris, A., & Wakeman, S. (2008). A meta-analysis on teaching mathematics to students with significant cognitive disabilities. *Exceptional Children, 74*, 407–432.

Browder, D., & Xin, Y. P. (1998). A meta-analysis and review of sight word research and its implications for teaching functional reading to individuals with moderate and severe disabilities. *The Journal of Special Education, 32*, 130–153.

Browder, D.M., Ahlgrim-Delzell, L., Courtade, G., Gibbs, S.L., & Flowers, C. (2008). Evaluation of the effectiveness of an early literacy program for students with significant developmental disabilities. *Exceptional Children, 75*, 33–52.

Browder, D.M., Ahlgrim-Delzell, L., Spooner, F., Mims, P.J., & Baker, J.N. (2009). Using time delay to teach literacy to students with severe developmental disabilities. *Exceptional Children, 75,* 343–364.

Brown, L., Long, E., Udvari-Solner, A., Schwarz, P., VanDeventer, P., Ahlgren, C., Johnson, F., Gruenewald, L., & Jorgensen, J. (1989). Should students with severe intellectual disabilities be based in regular or in special education classrooms in home schools? *Journal of the Association for Persons with Severe Handicaps, 14*(1), 8–12.

Brown, L., McClean, M.B., Baumgart, D., Vincent, L., Falvey, M., & Schroeder, J. (1979). Using the characteristics of current and subsequent least restrictive environments in the development of curricular content for severely handicapped students. *AAESPH Review, 4*(4), 407–424.

Cameto, R., Knokey, A.M., Nagle, K., Sanford, C., Blackorby, J., Sinclair, B., & Riley, D. (2009). *State Profiles on Alternate Assessment Based on Alternate Achievement Standards: A Report from the National Study on Alternate Assessments* (NNCSER 2009-3013). Menlo Park, CA: SRI International.

Carr, E., & Durand, V.M. (1985). Reducing behavior problems through functional communication training. *Journal of Applied Behavior Analysis, 18,* 111–126.

Cihak, D., & Foust, J. (2008). Comparing number lines and touch points to teach addition facts to students with autism. *Focus on Autism and Other Developmental Disabilities, 23,* 131–137.

Conners, F. (1992). Reading instruction for students with moderate mental retardation: Review and analysis of research. *American Journal on Mental Retardation, 96,* 577–598.

Courtade-Little, G., & Browder, D. (2005). *Aligning IEPs to academic standards for students with moderate and severe disabilities.* Verona, WI: Attainment Co.

Edmark Reading Program. (1972). Belleveue, WA: Edmark Corp.

Ellis, N. (1970). Memory processes in retardates and normals. In N. Ellis (Ed.), *International review of research in mental retardation, Vol. 9.* New York: Academic Press.

Farlow, L., & Snell, M. (1994). *Making the most of student performance data.* Washington, DC: American Association on Mental Retardation.

Falvey, M. (1989). *Community-based curriculum: Instructional strategies for students with severe handicaps.* Baltimore, MD: Paul H. Brookes.

Falvey, M. (1995). *Inclusive and heterogeneous schooling.* Baltimore, MD: Paul H. Brookes

Ford, A., Schnorr, R., Meyer, L., Davern, L., Black, J., & Dempsey, P. (1989). *The Syracuse community-referenced curriculum guide for students with moderate and severe disabilities.* Baltimore, MD: Paul H. Brookes.

Fredrick, L.D., Davis, D., Alberto, P.A., & Waugh, R.E. (2013). From initial phonics to functional phonics: Teaching word-analysis skills to students with moderate intellectual disabilities. *Education and Training in Autism and Developmental Disabilities.*

Gast, D., Ault, M., Wolery, M., Doyle, P., & Belanger, S. (1988). Comparison of constant time delay and the system of least prompts in teaching sight words to students with moderate retardation. *Education and Training in Mental Retardation, 23,* 117–128.

Gast, D., Wolery, M., Morris, L., Doyle, P., & Meyer, S. (1990). Teaching sight word reading in a group instructional arrangement using constant time delay. *Exceptionality, 1,* 81–96.

Gaylord-Ross, R., & Peck, C. (1984). Integration efforts for students with severe mental retardation. In D. Bricker & J. Fuller (Eds.), *Severe mental retardation: From theory to practice,* (pp. 185–207). Reston, VA: Division on Mental Retardation of the Council for Exceptional Children.

Grenot-Scheyer, M., & Falvey, M. (1986). Integration issues and strategies. In M. Falvey (Ed.), *Community-based curriculum: Instructional strategies for students with severe handicaps* (pp. 217–233) Baltimore, MD: Paul H. Brookes.

Haring, N. (Ed.). (1988). *Generalization for students with severe handicaps: Strategies and solutions.* Seattle, WA: University of Washington Press.

Hodapp, R., & Zigler, E. (1997). New issues in the developmental approach to mental retardation. In W. MacLean, Jr. (Ed.), *Ellis' handbook of mental deficiency, psychological theory, and research* (3rd ed., pp. 115–136). Mahwah, NJ: Lawrence Erlbaum Associates.

Hoogeveen, F., Smeets, P., & Lancioni, G. (1989). Teaching moderately mentally retarded children basic reading skills. *Research in Developmental Disabilities, 10,* 1–18.

Individuals with Disabilities Education Act of 1997. 120, U.S.C. Section 1400et seq, Law Revision Council, U.S. House of Representatives.

Iwata, B., Dorsey, M., Slifer, K., Bauman, K., & Richman, G. (1982). Toward a functional analysis of self-injury. *Analysis and Intervention in Developmental Disabilities, 2,* 3–20.

Jimenez, B., Browder, D., & Courtade, G. (2008). Teaching an algebraic equation to high school students with moderate developmental disabilities. *Education and Training in Developmental Disabilities, 43,* 266–274.

Kasari, C., Freeman, S., & Hughes, M. (2001). Emotion recognition by children with Down Syndrome. *American Journal on Mental Retardation, 106,* 59–72.

Kennedy, C., Horner, R., & Newton, J. (1989). Social contacts of adults with severe disabilities living in the community. *Journal of the Association for Persons with Severe Handicaps, 14,* 190–196.

Logan, K., Alberto, P., Kana, T., & Waylor-Bowen, T. (1994). Curriculum development and instructional design for students with profound disabilities (pp. 333–383). In L. Sternberg (Ed.), *Individuals with profound disabilities*. Austin, TX: PRO-ED.

MacMillan, D. (1982). *Mental retardation in school and society* (2nd ed.). Boston: Little, Brown and Co.

Mar, H., & Sall, N. (1999). Profiles of the expressive communication skills of children and adolescents with severe cognitive disabilities. *Education and Training in Mental Retardation and Developmental Disabilities, 34*, 77–89.

McLaughlin, S. (1998). *Introduction to language development*. San Diego, CA: Singular.

McLean, L., Brady, N., & McLean, J. (1996). Reported communication abilities of individuals with severe mental retardation. *American Journal on Mental Retardation, 100*, 580–591.

McLean, L., Brady, N., McLean, J., & Behrens, G. (1999). Communication forms and functions of children and adults with severe mental retardation in community and institutional settings. *Journal of Speech, Language, and Hearing Research, 42*, 231–240.

Nietupski, J., & Hamre-Nietupski, S. (1987). An ecological approach to curriculum development. In L. Goetz, D. Guess, & K. Stremel-Campbell (Eds.), *Innovative program design for individuals with dual sensory impairments*. Baltimore, MD: Paul H. Brookes.

No Child Left Behind Act of 2001. 2002, Pub. L. No 107-110, 115 Stat. 1425.

PCI Reading Program. (2009). San Antonio, TX: PCI Education.

Pruess, J., Vadasy, P., & Fewell, R. (1987). Language development in children with Down Syndrome: An overview of recent research. *Education and Training in Mental Retardation, 22*, 44–55.

Sandknop, P., Schuster, J., Wolery, M., & Cross, D. (1992). The use of an adaptive device to teach students with moderate mental retardation to select lower priced grocery items. *Education and Training in Mental Retardation, 27*, 219–229.

Siperstein, G., & Bak, J. (1989). Social relationships of adolescents with moderate mental retardation. *Mental Retardation, 27*, 5–10.

Skinner, B. F. (1968). *The technology of teaching*. New York: Appleton-Century-Crofts.

Snell, M., & Brown, F. (2011). *Instruction of students with severe disabilities*. Columbus, OH: Pearson-Prentice Hall-Merrill.

Sullivan, C., Vitello, S., & Foster, W. (1988). Adaptive behavior of adults with mental retardation: An intensive case study. *Education and Training in Mental Retardation, 23*(1), 76–81.

Taylor, R., Richards, S., & Brady, M. (2005). *Mental Retardation: Historical perspectives, current practices, and future directions*. Boston: Pearson/Allyn and Bacon.

Test, D., Howell, A., Burkhart, K., & Beroth, T. (1993). The one-more-than technique as a strategy for counting money for individuals with moderate mental retardation. *Education and Training in Mental Retardation, 28*, 232–241.

Test, D., Spooner, F., Keul, P., & Grossi, T. (1990). Teaching adolescents with severe disabilities to use the public telephone. *Behavior Modification, 14*(2), 157–171.

Wacker, D., & Berg, W. (1983). Effects of picture prompts on the acquisition of complex vocational tasks by mentally retarded adolescents. *Journal of Applied Behavior Analysis, 16*, 417–433.

Walsh, B., & Lamberts, F. (1979). Errorless discrimination and picture fading as techniques for teaching sight words to TMR students. *American Journal on Mental Deficiency, 83*, 473–479.

Waugh, R.E., Alberto, P.A., & Fredrick, L.D. (2011). Simultaneous prompting: An instructional strategy for skill acquisition. *Education and Training in Autism and Developmental Disabilities, 46*, 528–543.

Westling, D., & Fox, L. (1995). *Teaching students with severe disabilities*. Columbus, OH: Charles Merrill.

Westling, D., & Fox, L. (2004). Teaching students with severe disabilities. Columbus, OH: Prentice Hall-Merrill.

White, O. (1980). Adaptive performance objectives: Form versus function. In W. Sailor, B. Wilcox, & L. Brown (Eds.), *Methods of instruction for severely handicapped students*. Baltimore, MD: Paul H. Brookes.

Wilcox, B., & Bellamy, G.T. (1982). *Design of high school programs for severely handicapped students*. Baltimore, MD: Paul H. Brookes.

York-Barr, J., Kronberg, R., & Doyle, M. (1996). Module 1: A shared agenda for general and special educators. In J. York-Bar (Ed.), *Creating inclusive school communities: A staff development series for general and special educators*. Baltimore, MD: Paul H. Brookes.

Zeaman, D., & House, B. (1979). A review of attention theory. In N. Ellis (Ed.), *Handbook of mental deficiency: Psychological theory and research* (2nd ed.). Hillsdale, NJ: Erlbaum.

Zigler, E. (1969). Developmental vs. differential theory of mental retardation and the problem of motivation. *American Journal of Mental Deficiency, 73*(4), 536–556.

CHAPTER THIRTEEN

Gifted and Talented: The Overlooked Exceptionality

John E. Kesner and Teresa Pawlik

CHAPTER OBJECTIVES

- to provide an overview of the history of gifted education;
- to describe the characteristics of students who are talented or gifted;
- to review the ways in which students are assessed and identified as talented or gifted;
- to describe the service delivery models used by schools for students who are talented and gifted; and
- to present instructional strategies classroom teachers can use to address the needs of these students.

KEY TERMS

creativity · divergent thinking · cluster grouping · enrichment · acceleration · curriculum compacting

The distribution of talents and abilities in our society varies widely. If we accept that some individuals have abilities below the norm, we are forced to recognize that some individuals will be blessed with talents and abilities far above the norm. Recognition of those gifted individuals is difficult because in our efforts to attain an egalitarian society, we confuse equality of individuals with equality of opportunity. Some have even suggested dropping the label gifted. The argument is that all students should receive the quality of instruction usually received by gifted children (Sternberg, Jarvin, & Grigorenko, 2011). Striving for an egalitarian society does not mean that all are equal in ability, but rather that all should be afforded the same opportunities to develop to their full potential.

Students who are talented and gifted have been viewed by some as being handicapped, because their abilities lie outside the norm and their needs are not met in regular education curricula (Coleman & Cross, 2001). If the myriad of problems facing humankind are to be solved, the talents and abilities of these students are our brightest hope. Too often, however, they are met with suspicion, ridicule, and even scorn. In our efforts to help those with abilities below the norm, gifted students are often forgotten or relegated to programs on the margin of the educational spectrum. The No Child Left Behind (NCLB) legislation, which has become the national educational obsession, is a prime example. NCLB has the laudable goals of bringing all students to proficiency, yet does little to assist those students above the median (Colangelo, Assouline, & Gross, 2004). Although considered by many as special education, programs for students who are gifted and talented are not subject to the same state and federal regulations that govern other special education services.

We believe that students who are talented and gifted have special needs that are not fully met by the general education curriculum in most schools. It is important that schools identify and nurture these students to ensure they have the opportunity to develop to their fullest potential. Due to limited resources in many schools, this often becomes the responsibility of the classroom teacher. This chapter reviews the history of gifted education and examines the ways in which giftedness is defined and identified. In addition, we provide suggestions for teachers to assist them in enriching the curriculum and meeting the needs of their students who are talented or gifted.

History of Gifted Education

Historically, concern for individuals who are gifted is as old and varied as humankind. The Greeks and the Romans believed that exceptionally competent individuals should be identified and educated to become future leaders of the state. The Ottoman Empire sent scouts to locate gifted students and bring them to Istanbul to be educated. Thomas Jefferson believed that gifted students should be identified and educated at state expense (Coleman & Cross, 2001).

Sir Francis Galton is credited with the first scientific investigation of giftedness. Galton's 1869 treatise, *Hereditary Genius,* provided a systematic exposition using statistical methods to identify giftedness. Galton concluded from his studies that intelligence is an inherited trait. Today, although most psychologists agree heredity is a major contributor to intelligence, disagreement continues as to the relative role of nature (genetics) and nurture (environment) in its development. Current pioneering research suggests the experiences of childhood aid in forming the brain's circuits for language, mathematics, music, and emotion. Sir Francis Galton's conclusions had an effect on educational and social policies from the mid-nineteenth to the mid-twentieth centuries. However, his belief that eugenics or selective breeding could improve the general level of intellectual development is open to challenge in a democratic society.

French psychologist Alfred Binet raised interest in measuring intelligence when he constructed the first developmental scale for children in the early 1900s. He developed the scale by observing children of various ages and their ability to perform specific tasks. Children then could be identified as developmentally advanced or delayed by comparing their performance on these tasks to what was expected given their chronological age. Lewis Terman further refined Binet's scale and adapted it for use in the United States. This test, renamed the *Stanford-Binet Intelligence Scale,* became the most often used test of individual intelligence for many years. Terman began using the term intelligence quotient (IQ) and his test allowed the examiner to calculate a person's aptitude for performing cognitive tasks (IQ score). Other names for IQ include mental ability or cognitive ability. Today's edition of the *Stanford-Binet,* the fifth edition (SB5), is used widely; however, Spruill (1987) advises that the ceiling may be much too low for very bright persons.

In 1939 another mental ability instrument was developed by David Wechsler. The *Wechsler Intelligence Scale for Children* (WISC-IV) is currently (2003) in its fourth edition and is used throughout the world. Later developments in the Wechsler series include the *Wechsler Adult Intelligence Scales* (WAIS) and the *Wechsler Preschool and Primary Scales of Intelligence* (WPPSI).

Terman (1925) conducted a longitudinal study of more than 1,500 children with Stanford-Binet IQ scores of 140 and above. The Terman study followed these subjects into adulthood, examining their physical characteristics, personality attributes, and educational and career achievements. Terman found bright children become bright adults. These individuals enjoyed better health and adjusted better to the problems of life than did others. Also, they were more productive than their average colleagues. Terman's research stimulated interest in the systematic study of giftedness.

In the United States, interest in educating students who are talented and gifted has waxed and waned. In 1957, the launching of the Soviet Union's Sputnik satellite triggered concern that the United States was no longer the world leader in science and technology. Public and private funds were allocated to establish programs to develop the talents of students who were gifted in this country. In 1958 the National Defense Education Act (Public Law 85-864) was passed to support the development of math, science, and foreign language talent. In addition, the Association for the Gifted, an affiliate of the Council for Exceptional Children, was created (Clark, 2007). In 1965 provisions for the development of model gifted programs and funding for state personnel in gifted education were contained in the Elementary and Secondary Education Act (Public Law 89-10). Federal recognition of the need for educating gifted and talented students was established in the Elementary and Secondary Education Act of 1970 (Public Law 91-230, Section 306).

Interest was heightened following the publication of *Education of the Gifted and Talented* by Sidney Marland (Marland, 1972). This congressionally mandated a national survey of gifted programs and needs. The Marland Report noted that only a small number of students who were talented or gifted were receiving special services. The report emphasized three main areas of concern relative to gifted programming:

1. The need to develop curricula emphasizing high level thinking processes and concepts.
2. The need to develop appropriate teaching strategies to accommodate the learner who is gifted.
3. The need to develop educational delivery systems and administrative procedures adequate to provide differential educational services for specific groups of students who are gifted.

As a result of the Marland Report (Marland, 1972), the U.S. Office of Gifted and Talented was created, with a budget of $2.5 million. The first federal definition of giftedness was adopted, and funds for training, technical assistance, and continuing education continued to increase until they peaked at $6.2 million in 1980 (Jenkins-Friedman & Nielsen, 1990).

In the 1980s, during the Reagan administration, gifted education funding was cut and the Office of Talented and Gifted eliminated. Fortunately, the 100th Congress re-established the Office and provided funding for teacher training and technical assistance to school districts (Jenkins-Friedman & Nielsen, 1990). Passage of Public Law 100-297, the Jacob K. Javits Gifted and Talented Students Education Act of 1988, and its reauthorization in 1994 reflected the national concern that the talents and gifts of students were not being recognized and developed.

Currently there is no federal requirement to provide gifted programs in the schools, as gifted education is only mentioned once in the Individuals with Disabilities Education Improvement Act of 2004. Consequently, little federal or state money is targeted for students with gifts and talents. The only federally funded program for gifted education is the Javits Gifted and Talented Grants program. This program, however, has had continual budget cuts since a high of $11,250,000 in 2002 to the present $7,596,070 for 2007 (U.S. Department of Education, 2008). In recent years, funding for gifted education has not been a high priority compared to funding for other special education programs. The Obama administration's fiscal year 2013 budget provides no funds for gifted education. The budget for the Jacob K. Javits Gifted and Talented Students Education Act was zeroed out in the budget sent to Congress. Thus, the only federally funded program for gifted education faces elimination (Council for Exceptional Children, 2012).

The No Child Left Behind Act (Public Law 107-110; Elementary and Secondary Education Amendments of 2001) has created quite a stir in the educational community. This "comprehensive" law is designed to ensure that all students achieve at a higher level, especially those at-risk for academic failure. It is generally agreed that NCLB ignores the needs of gifted and talented students (Gallagher, 2004; Kaplan, 2004). Its "high stakes testing" requirements ensure that curricula will be replaced with instruction designed to enable students to do well on these tests. Testing will be done at a basic conceptual level, thus not providing the necessary intellectual challenge for gifted and talented students (Gallagher, 2004; Mendoza, 2006).

With the trend toward inclusive classrooms and the popularity of the teaching strategy of cooperative learning, students who are gifted often remain in the general education classroom and may be encouraged to assist their less able peers. These methods may be highly effective teaching strategies for many students, but they do little to challenge students who are gifted and ensure they have the opportunity to reach their maximum potential (Colangelo & Davis, 1997). The controversy remains as to whether separate programs are necessary for these students. Siegle (2008) has asserted that if, as a group, those in gifted education were to focus on the present educational needs of gifted children, rather than on their potential for future performance, more people might be accepting and supportive of services for gifted and talented children.

Definition

Defining giftedness and talent is not a simple task, yet it has a significant impact on both the identification of students and the types of services and special programs provided. A close examination of attempts to define giftedness reveals tremendous variety (Gagne, 2004; Cramond, 2004). This variety is most likely the result of influences such as the values of the person making the definition, the social climate of the time, and the impact of new knowledge of human intelligence (Coleman & Cross, 2001). Prior to systematic attempts, defining giftedness relied on ex post facto definitions (Lucito, 1963). That is, a person was considered gifted after making some outstanding and novel contribution to society. Initial systematic attempts at defining giftedness focused on measuring intelligence. For example, students having an IQ score of above 130 or those who ranked in the upper 5% on academic achievement tests would be labeled gifted and often placed in special classes or provided an advanced curriculum. Despite their widespread popularity in defining giftedness, intelligence tests are only modestly correlated to school performance. Students with high IQs often do not do well in school, leading some to propose that definitions of giftedness that stress academic achievement might better serve gifted students (Gallagher & Gallagher, 1994). However, such definitions excluded students who exhibited outstanding talent in other areas such as music, art, dance, athletics, and leadership. In the 1950s, Guilford (1950, 1959) proposed that intelligence was not a single ability or capacity that could be measured by an IQ score. Rather he viewed intelligence as a diverse range of intellectual and creative abilities. Other researchers (Cattell, 1971; Renzulli, 1978; Torrance, 1965; Sternberg, 1981, 1982, 1988; Gardner, & Hatch, 1989) championed the concept of giftedness as a multidimensional construct that requires the use of multidimensional assessments. As a result, the definitions of these terms began to be more inclusive of creativity and performance talents.

Although there is no universally accepted definition for this group of students, the definition included in the Jacob K. Javits Gifted and Talented Students Education Act of 1988 (Public Law 100-297) often is used by states and school systems:

> The term "gifted and talented students" means children and youth who give evidence of high performance capability in areas such as intellectual, creative, artistic, or leadership capacity, or in specific academic fields, and who require services or activities not ordinarily provided by the school in order to fully develop such capabilities (Section 4103).

Another widely accepted definition created by a group of experts commissioned by the U.S. Department of Education's Office of Educational Research and Improvement (1993) states:

> Children and youth with outstanding talent perform or show the potential for performing at remarkably high levels of accomplishment when compared with others of their age, experience, or environment.
>
> These children and youth exhibit high performance capability in intellectual, creative and/or artistic areas, possess an unusual leadership capacity, or excel in specific academic fields. They require services or activities not ordinarily provided by the schools. Outstanding talents are present in children and youth from all cultural groups, across all economic strata, and in all areas of human endeavor (p. 26).

Unlike early definitions, this includes students with talents in the arts and leadership as well as those who are intellectually gifted. In addition, they also emphasize performance rather than just the potential for high achievement.

The research of Renzulli and his colleagues (Renzulli, 1978; Renzulli, Reis, & Smith, 1981; Renzulli & Smith, 1980) has influenced the thinking of professionals about the definition of giftedness. They suggest that giftedness is an interaction of three traits and that all three must be present to be truly gifted. These traits or behaviors are:

1. Above-average intellectual ability, as indicated by the student achieving in the upper 15 to 20% of the class.
2. A high level of task-commitment, as demonstrated by clear evidence of persistence and achievement.
3. A high level of creativity, as evidenced in original ways of thinking which lead to new solutions or new definitions of problems.

The label of giftedness (or any other educational label) is not static. A child does not reach the threshold of giftedness, stop, and remain static for the rest of her life. Rather gifted students (along with all other students) can improve their skills and knowledge throughout their lifetimes (Sternberg et al., 2011).

Other researchers (Gardner, 1983; Gardner & Hatch, 1989; Ramos-Ford & Gardner, 1997) view giftedness based on a theory of multiple intelligences. This theory proposes that there are at least eight areas in which intelligence manifests itself:

- Logical-mathematical,
- Linguistic,
- Musical,
- Spatial,
- Bodily-kinesthetic,
- Naturalist,
- Interpersonal, and
- Intrapersonal.

Individuals might exhibit special gifts or talents in any one or more of these areas. These multiple intelligences are described in **Table 13.1**.

TABLE 13.1

Gardner's Multiple Intelligences*

Intelligence	Processing Operations	End-State Performance Possibilities
Logical-mathematical	Sensitivity to, and capacity to detect, logical or numerical patterns; ability to handle long chains of logical reasoning	Mathematician
Linguistic	Sensitivity to the sounds, rhythms, and meaning of words and the functions of language	Poet, journalist
Musical	Ability to produce and appreciate pitch, rhythm (or melody), and aesthetic quality of the forms of musical expressiveness	Instrumentalist, composer
Spatial	Ability to perceive the visual-spatial world accurately, to perform transformations on those perceptions, and to re-create aspects of visual experience in the absence of relevant stimuli	Sculptor, navigator
Bodily-kinesthetic	Ability to use the body skillfully for expressive as well as goal-directed purposes; ability to handle objects skillfully	Dancer, athlete
Naturalist	Ability to recognize and classify all varieties of animals, minerals, and plants	Biologist
Interpersonal	Ability to detect and respond appropriately to the moods, temperaments, motivations, and intentions of others	Therapist, salesperson
Intrapersonal	Ability to discriminate complex inner feelings and to use them to guide one's own behavior; knowledge of one's own strengths, weaknesses, desires, and intelligences	Person with detailed, accurate self-knowledge

*Gardner also has proposed a possible spiritual intelligence (gift for religion, mysticism, or the transcendent), existential intelligence (concern with "ultimate" issues, such as the significance of life and death), and moral intelligence (capacity to recognize and reason about moral issues). However, these potential intelligences are less well defined and more controversial than the eight intelligences listed above.

From Berk, L. (2003). *Child Development* (6th ed.). Boston, MA: Allyn & Bacon.

Characteristics

Misperceptions and stereotypes of individuals who are talented and gifted can lead to a misunderstanding of these students. As late as the late 1800s, some experts viewed giftedness as being linked to emotional imbalance and were concerned that it might lead to society's decline (Henson, 1976). Early research in giftedness (MacKinnon, 1962; Terman, 1925) sought to identify the characteristics of gifted individuals. This initial research used a restricted population of subjects that included few girls or individuals from diverse ethnic or racial groups. The result was a stereotypical profile of gifted individuals that did not control for gender, socioeconomic, or cultural variables. It is important to remember that the talented and gifted are a heterogeneous group with differences and similarities as great as any other group of students. They exhibit a wide range of specific aptitudes, abilities, and interests that makes it difficult for researchers to reduce giftedness to a recognizable set of characteristics (Neumeister, Adams, Pierce, & Dixon, 2007).

Clark (2007) synthesized the work of previous researchers to develop a list of the differentiating characteristics of the gifted as shown in **Table 13.2**. It is unlikely that gifted

---

TABLE 13.2

Common Characteristics of Highly and Exceptionally Gifted Individuals

- An extraordinary speed in processing information
- A rapid comprehension of the whole idea or concept
- An unusual ability to perceive essential elements and underlying structures and patterns in relationships and ideas
- A need for precision in thinking and expression, resulting in need to correct errors and argue extensively
- An ability to relate to a broad range of ideas and synthesize commonalities among them
- A high degree of ability to think abstractly that develops early
- Appreciation of complexity; finding myriad alternative meanings in even the most simple issues or problems
- An ability to learn in an integrative, intuitively nonlinear manner
- An extraordinary degree of intellectual curiosity
- An unusual capacity for memory
- A long concentration span
- A fascination with ideas and words
- An extensive vocabulary
- An ability to perceive many sides of an issue
- Argumentativeness
- Advanced visual and motor skills
- An ability from an early age to think in metaphors and symbols and a preference for doing so
- An ability to visualize models and systems
- An ability to learn in great intuitive leaps
- Highly idiosyncratic interpretations of events
- An awareness of detail
- An unusual intensity and depth of feeling
- A high degree of emotional sensitivity
- Highly developed morals and ethics and early concern for moral and existential issues
- Unusual and early insight into social and moral issues
- An ability to empathetically understand and relate to ideas and other people
- An extraordinarily high energy level
- A need for the world to be logical and fair
- A conviction of correctness and personal ideas and beliefs

From Clark, B. (2007). *Growing up gifted* (7th ed.) Englewood Cliffs, NJ: Prentice Hall.

students will manifest all of these characteristics, but they will most likely exhibit more of these characteristics when compared to their peers. It is important that teachers are familiar with these characteristics because teacher nomination for gifted programs plays a significant role in the identification process in most schools today. However, teachers must remember that these characteristics can be observed in students who do not necessarily have the best grades or highest academic performance. Some students who are talented or gifted may not be performing at their highest potential. Teachers need to be alert to the possible display of gifted characteristics in any of their students.

It is an interesting paradox that some of the behaviors exhibited by students who are gifted can be misinterpreted as behavior problems as shown in **Table 13.3**. Because these students learn new skills more easily and rapidly than their peers, they may irritate teachers by shouting out answers, showing impatience to move on to the next task, or engaging in off-task behaviors when they are bored with the regular curriculum. So too, peers may become annoyed when gifted students dominate class discussions, consistently score the highest on exams, or receive special attention from the teacher.

Identification

As with the lack of clarity on a definition, identification of students who are talented and gifted is equally vague. Many claim that an ideal identification system does not exist (Feldhusen, Hoover, & Sayler, 1990; Belanger & Gagne, 2006), and given the political incorrectness of labeling one student superior to another in any area suggests that one is not likely to be devised. Identification must be based on a value-free universally accepted definition of giftedness.

Historically, identification procedures have relied heavily on measures of intellectual ability. IQ scores were regularly used to identify students for gifted programs. However, many students, for a variety of reasons, do not perform well on IQ and other standardized tests of mental ability, thus these gifted students were excluded from these programs. More recently, a number of states have moved to a multi-modal method for assessing giftedness. In Georgia, for example, students are assessed on mental ability, achievement, creativity,

---

TABLE 13.3

Possible Behaviors of Students Who Are Gifted

Positive	*Not-So-Positive*
1. Persistent, goal-directed behavior	1. Stubbornness
2. Power of concentration	2. Resistance to interruption
3. Large vocabulary; highly verbal	3. Escape into verbalism
4. Ability to see relationships	4. Difficulty in accepting the illogical
5. Willingness to examine the unusual	5. Possible gullibility
6. Power of critical thinking; skepticism	6. Critical of others
7. High expectations for self	7. Critical of self
8. High energy, alertness, eagerness	8. Frustration with lack of progress or inactivity
9. Independence in work and study	9. Possible difficulty working in groups
10. Self-reliance; need for freedom	10. Possible rebellion against constraints
11. Likes new ways of doing things	11. Dislike of routine and drill
12. Diversity of interests and abilities	12. Need to build basic competencies in major interests
13. Sensitivity, intuitiveness, empathy	13. Need for success and recognition; sensitive to criticism, vulnerable to peer group rejection

and motivation in determining eligibility for gifted services. However, many state assessments still mostly rely on standardized tests.

As previously discussed, not all gifted students are identified and served in gifted programs. Certain minorities and students from low socioeconomic backgrounds are overrepresented in remedial programs and underrepresented in programs for the gifted. African American and Hispanic students are far more likely to be participating in remedial programs than in programs for the gifted (Grantham, Ford, Henfield, Scott, Harmon, Porcher, & Price, 2011). Currently there are two theories that attempt to explain the causes of underrepresentation of certain minority groups in gifted programs. The *Distribution Theory* suggests that giftedness may indeed not be distributed equally among racial and ethnic groups due to a lack of resources most often found in those communities. The *Discrimination Theory* focuses on identification procedures which may be biased against certain racial and ethnic groups. It is likely that both theories offer insight into the problem of underrepresentation (Stein, Hetzel, & Beck, 2012). However, this is not true of all minority groups. Asian and Pacific Americans are commonly perceived as being overrepresented in programs for the gifted (Kitano & Dijiosia, 2002). Educators are encouraged to consider the following abilities as described in the Marland Report (1972) when assessing students who are potentially gifted.

General Intellectual Ability

Usually measured by individually or group administered mental abilities tests, this generally gives teachers an indication of how well the student will adapt to the academic environment. Often, high performance in this area requires special learning provisions for the student.

Specific Academic Aptitude

Regularly measured by outstanding performance on standardized achievement tests, this relates to high aptitude in a specific subject area that allows the student to exceed beyond peers and requires a special program in that particular content field.

Creative/Productive Thinking

Tests of creative/productive thinking are helpful in finding this population of original thinkers. Opportunities allowing students with this ability to demonstrate **divergent thinking** and manipulate information to arrive at new and unique solutions to problems are important needs.

Leadership Ability

Performance in social settings both in and out of the classroom, positions of responsibility held in clubs and organizations, sociograms, and personality inventories are some of the tools used as possible indicators of leadership ability.

Visual and Performing Arts

Expert opinion, performance, portfolio assessment, and, if available, valid and reliable standardized instruments can be useful in locating students with ability in the arts. Special opportunities in school should be provided for these youngsters to excel.

It is important to remember that students who are gifted and talented are found at all grade levels in the schools. Some aspects of giftedness may emerge early in a child's development (e.g., an exceptionally large vocabulary or self-taught reading ability at a young age) and be identified by parents. Other aspects may not appear until the student matures (e.g., exceptional academic performance, athletic skills, or artistic abilities) and may be noted first by classroom teachers, counselors, or even peers. To appropriately determine an individual's giftedness at any age, a multidimensional assessment should be performed. Such an assessment might include teacher nominations, developmental inventories, mental ability tests, achievement tests, creativity tests, newly developed information-processing tests, student interview and observation, motivation assessment, and student portfolios (Benbow & Minor, 1990; Sowell, Bergwall, Zeigler, & Cartwright, 1990). These expanded criteria will be helpful in locating a broader range of students who are gifted including those who often do not score highly enough on tests of mental abilities and/or standard achievement tests to be included in typical gifted programs. Several of these assessment strategies are discussed in the following section.

Sternberg et al. (2011) suggest a "pentagonal" theory for the identification of gifted individuals. These five include: (1) excellence, (2) rarity, (3) productivity, (4) demonstrability, and (5) value. The *excellence* criteria states that an individual is "superior in some dimension or set of dimensions relative to peers" (Sternberg et al. 2011, p. 2). However, excellence is not enough—the aforementioned excellence must be relatively rare for the individual's peer group, thus meeting the *rarity* criteria. In order to meet the *productivity* criteria, the dimension in which the individual is rated as excellent must at least have the potential for productivity utilizing the superior dimension(s). The *demonstrability* criteria state that the dimension or dimensions in which the individual excels must be measureable in some way. Finally, in order to meet the *value* criteria, the dimension in which one excels must be valued in some way by the individual's society (Sternberg et al., 2011).

Teacher Nomination

The accuracy of teachers as identifiers of students who are potentially gifted has been questioned, particularly with younger children and students from diverse ethnic, cultural, or linguistic populations (Baldwin, 1991; Hallahan, Kauffman, & Pullen, 2009; Kitano, 1989). Although teacher referral is the most common method of identifying gifted children, a study by Pegnato and Birch (1959) of an entire junior high school population indicated teachers missed 55% of the eligible students when asked to nominate the gifted students in their classes. This study has been criticized for its research methodology and results from a newer analysis have indicated that teachers are no less effective in identifying gifted children when compared to other sources (Bianco, Harris, Garrison-Wade, & Leech, 2011). Teachers tend to identify the stereotypical student who is gifted (see **Figure 13.1**). This means that students who are bright, cooperative, task-oriented, and well adjusted

The accuracy of teacher identification of gifted students has been questioned, particularly with younger children and students from diverse ethnic, cultural, or linguistic populations.

to school will be nominated for gifted programs. Students who are bright, but disruptive, bored with routine tasks, nonconforming, underachievers, or who exhibit unusual skills and abilities are often overlooked. **Figure 13.2** provides a description of a student who is gifted, but not identified.

Teachers may receive no specific criteria to use when asked to nominate students for gifted programs, but their observations tend to improve when they are made familiar with

Figure 13.1   Description of a Stereotypical Student Who Is Gifted

David's parents did not realize that their first child was exceptional until he started school. He was clearly inquisitive and eager to learn. He wanted to be read to and often woke his mother early in the morning to read his favorite Richard Scarry book. He would follow his father as he went about his chores and attempted to help. At age 4 he tried to "wire" his house by using ropes and cords to connect outlets and appliances. His parents were supportive of this activity and allowed the "wires" to remain until David found a new interest. As a result of his investigations, he was able to write a book explaining electricity for his kindergarten class.

David was reading when he entered kindergarten, but it was not just his ability to read but also his keen memory and wealth of knowledge which alerted his teacher to his special abilities. David's mathematical ability was well above his age peers. He could not only add and subtract, but could multiply and divide as well. With his parents' permission, David's kindergarten teacher referred David for the gifted program.

David scored a school ability index of 150/99th percentile. On the instrument that was used, David did not answer a single question incorrectly. It was not necessary to do further testing, and David was found to be eligible for the gifted program.

David was accelerated in mathematics in the third grade by receiving instruction with fourth graders. In his last year of elementary school, David received individual mathematics instruction from an administrator with a doctorate in mathematics education.

David, though profoundly gifted in mathematics, achieved beyond his age expectations in all areas of school. Although a quiet and serious young man, David was well liked by his peers and was always selected for team or group work. His work habits were recognized by his peers, and he was voted the most outstanding gifted student.

In middle school, David continued to develop his mathematics ability. He took all gifted math classes and worked with a teacher after school as part of a math team. David also continued to excel in other academic areas, but his mathematical abilities were truly outstanding. He earned a perfect score on the American Junior High School Mathematics Examination, won numerous prizes with Mathcounts and Mathematics League, and participated in mathematics competitions on the state and national level.

In high school, David continued his outstanding achievement. He was ranked first in his class and was valedictorian of an extremely large class. While in high school David earned enough advanced placement credits that will enable him to earn both a bachelor's and a master's degree in 4 years.

David has stated that his curiosity drove him to investigate and learn independently. He felt that he was self-motivated and learned for the joy of learning. He said that he was inspired by teachers who were enthusiastic about learning and the material they were teaching.

Figure 13.2   Description of a Student Who Is Gifted but Not Identified

Joe's parents are very concerned about him. He has always been a difficult child, having intense feelings and views about things. He seems to be on a roller coaster in terms of his emotions, and gets upset when others don't agree with his point of view. He expects that everyone sees the world as he does. Other times he seems to have blinders on, only focusing on what he is doing and oblivious to others and the world around him. He is frequently argumentative with peers and other adults, claiming that they don't know anything. He is disorganized and has trouble making friends.

Not surprisingly, Joe is having difficulty at school. He has been diagnosed with Attention Deficit Hyperactivity Disorder (ADHD) and is on Ritalin. Joe's teachers believe that although he is extremely bright, he is not working up to his potential. They claim that he often fails to try new things because he is afraid he won't do well. Surprisingly, he usually scores in the 90th percentile or higher on standardized achievement tests, but his schoolwork is often sloppy and his grades are poor.

His teachers echo his parents' concerns that he has trouble making and keeping friends. They worry that his challenging authority will escalate as he gets older, causing him further, more serious problems. They all agree that Joe is "different" from his classmates. He sees the world differently and has trouble fitting in with the group. He seems to relish being a nonconformist which further alienates him from his peers. The school counselor thinks that Joe is depressed and overly anxious and worries that he is becoming a loner. Her attempts to counsel Joe have been met with resistance and resentment. Joe says that he is picked on because he is different. Without the proper intervention, the outlook for Joe is bleak.

Figure 13.3   Sample Statements from the *Scales for Rating the Behavioral Characteristics of Superior Students*

	Seldom or Never	Occasionally	Considerably	Almost Always
• Carries responsibility well; can be counted on to do what he has promised and usually does it well.	❑	❑	❑	❑
• Adapts readily to new situations; is flexible in thought and action and does not seem disturbed when the normal routine is changed.	❑	❑	❑	❑
• Arrives at unique, unconventional solutions to artistic problems as opposed to traditional, conventional ones.	❑	❑	❑	❑
• Shows a sustained interest in music—seeks out opportunities to hear and create music.	❑	❑	❑	❑
• Modifies and adjusts expression of ideas for maximum reception.	❑	❑	❑	❑
• Is good at games of strategy where it is necessary to anticipate several moves ahead.	❑	❑	❑	❑

Renzulli, Smith, White, Callahan, & Hartman, 1976.

the behavior characteristics of students who are gifted. Scales such as the *Scales for Rating the Behavioral Characteristics of Superior Students* (Renzulli, Smith, White, Callahan, & Hartman, 1976) can improve teacher judgment. This scale, as shown in **Figure 13.3**, allows the teacher to rate a student's performance in areas of learning, motivation, and creativity.

Frasier (1994) also has developed rating scales including the *Frasier Talent Assessment Profile* (FTAP), a comprehensive assessment system to facilitate the use of information from multiple sources, to help classroom teachers assess and summarize student performance. The information gained from such scales as these is useful for both identification and educational planning. In addition, Kitano (1989) offers suggestions for teachers to improve their accuracy in identifying gifted students. These are presented in **Table 13.4**.

TABLE 13.4

Suggestions for Teachers to Identify Students Who Are Gifted

- Consider all students as potential candidates for giftedness. For example, a hyperactive, disruptive, or unkempt youngster may also be gifted.
- Recognize that "negative traits" . . . do not disqualify a student from consideration as gifted. Although gifted and average students may display negative behaviors, gifted students will also demonstrate their strengths when provided opportunities to do so.
- Look for and analyze the strengths exhibited by all students, including those who do not display stereotypical achieving, cooperating, and conforming behaviors. For example, the individual who touches expensive equipment after being admonished not to touch may be exhibiting extreme curiosity rather than defiance.
- Provide opportunities for and encourage students to express their abilities. For example, the teacher can informally assess reading and writing skills by inviting students to read to them at the book center and encouraging volunteer efforts to write.
- Use parents as informants. Parents serve as effective identifiers of gifted individuals and they can provide accurate observations about what their children can and cannot do (p. 60).

From Kitano, M. K. (1989). The K–3 teacher's role in recognizing and supporting young gifted children. *Young Children, 44*(3), 57–63.

Intelligence Tests

Individual IQ tests are considered the single most reliable indicator of intellectual giftedness. The *Stanford-Binet Intelligence Scale IV* and the *Wechsler Intelligence Scale for Children–Fourth Edition* (WISC–IV) are the most widely used individual tests. Scores derived from these two instruments are useful in pinpointing strengths and weaknesses of students, but these tests may only be administered by a licensed psychologist. Consequently, many school systems rely on results from group tests such as the *Otis-Lennon School Ability Test* and the *Cognitive Abilities Test* for referral and placement in gifted programs. These tests may be administered by classroom teachers or administrators.

There are many reasons that IQ scores derived from these measures should not be the sole selection criterion for gifted programs. These scores are predictors of school related abilities not measures of innate ability. Their accuracy is questionable in measuring the abilities of students who have disabilities or come from diverse ethnic, cultural, or linguistic groups. IQ tests are a predictor of school performance and may be biased in favor of individuals from middle- and upper-class socioeconomic groups. Lyman (1997) states that no intelligence test gets at all cognitive functions. Because of this, critics point out that IQ tests are unable to assess adequately many of the higher mental processes that characterize the thinking and learning of individuals who are gifted. Because they were not developed to do so, IQ tests do not assess such abilities as creativity, leadership, and specific talents. As Kaufman (1992) stresses, the appropriate use of IQ tests to screen or identify students who are gifted, or potentially gifted, demands that they be used in conjunction with other tests and selection criteria.

Achievement Tests

Critics of the typical identification process for students who are potentially gifted also warn teachers about the limitations of academic achievement tests. Although these tests may identify students who are bright, have received outstanding instruction, and are adept at taking standardized tests, some students who are potentially gifted may be missed because they have received inadequate instruction, are bored by routine tests, have extreme test anxiety, or purposely score poorly because they don't want to stand out from their peers. In addition, it is important to realize that achievement tests are not designed to measure the true achievement of students who are academically gifted. These tests have a restricted range of test items that prevents some students from demonstrating their achievement at higher levels beyond the limits of the test range. Like IQ tests, academic achievement tests cannot assess such abilities as creativity, leadership, or artistic talents.

Creativity Tests

As the definition of giftedness has expanded, there have been increased attempts to measure the wider range of abilities and capacities included in the newer definition, particularly in the area of creativity. As Davis and Rimm (1998) note, this is a formidable task. The nature of creativity and the many ways in which it can be expressed have made it difficult to develop tests to determine its presence and magnitude. Callahan (1991) recommends that multiple measures of creativity be used to demonstrate a student's exceptionality. These measures could include analysis of a student's creative products or performances as well as direct observation of the student's behavior. Tests designed to assess creative or divergent thinking include the *Torrance Tests of Creative Thinking* (Torrance, 1966) and *Thinking Creatively in Action and Movement* (TCAM) (Torrance, 1981). Clasen, Middleton, and Connell (1994) have developed tests of problem solving and drawing to identify students who exhibit creativity in these areas. Although creativity tests may offer insight into a student's thinking and reasoning style or artistic ability, they are more subjective than most other tests to assess the intellectual ability of students who are potentially gifted.

Neglected Gifted

Given the traditionally narrow definition placed on giftedness, there are many neglected students who are talented and gifted who are not included in gifted education programs. The U.S. Department of Education (1993) described several groups of neglected gifted: under-achievers, students with disabilities, students from certain minority and ethnic groups, and girls. More recently a new category of neglected gifted students has emerged—the "tough bright" child (Peterson, 1997; McClusky, Baker, & McClusky, 2005). In addition, there is evidence that a lack of diversity among gifted program participants is a continuing national concern. For example, Pfeiffer (2003) solicited views from a national panel of experts in the field of gifted education to get their perspective on recent and emerging concerns and trends in gifted education. Among the most frequent categories mentioned was the need to develop new identification procedures to decrease the underrepresentation of gifted minority students in programs. Specifically, the concern was with the disproportionate number of potentially gifted students of color, economic disadvantage, or both and students who are female, linguistically different, handicapped, or from rural communities who were not being adequately identified and served. Second language learners face difficulties related to their identification for gifted programs. Often their lack of proficiency in English becomes the focus of intervention rather than recognizing their potential giftedness. Of course, this problem is exacerbated by the use of identifying tools that are in English (Stein, Hetzel, & Beck, 2012).

Underachievers

The gifted underachiever presents a paradox. High ability students not performing to their abilities represent an enormous loss of potential, as well as immense potential for change (Davis & Rimm, 1998). Van Tassel-Baska (1998) reports that as many as 63% of gifted students are underachievers. Gifted underachievers can be defined as those students who have a significant discrepancy between their intelligence or standardized tested abilities (scoring in the gifted range on these tests) and their performance in class (average or even failing grades). There is no single cause for the underachievement of some students who are gifted. The many possible factors related to this problem include poor study skills or habits, a lack of motivation for academic achievement, low self-esteem, the absence of a supportive or nurturing environment at home or school, and a boring or nonchallenging curriculum. According to Reis (2005), there appears to be a relationship between inappropriate or too easy content in elementary school and underachievement in middle and high school.

Just as there is no single cause for underachievement, there is no single solution to this problem. It is a generally accepted fact, however, that these students will need special services to develop to their fullest potential (Emerick, 1992). The strategies found to be effective for some students include counseling, acceleration (subject or grade skipping), using non-competitive learning strategies (mastery learning, cooperative learning, contracts), mentoring, school-sponsored community service or work-study programs, and the integration of personal interests into school work (Covington, 1984; Feldhusen, 1989; Rimm & Lovance, 1992). Reis (2005) further asserts that positive peer relationships can play a major role in keeping underachievement from occurring in friends. Finally, adolescents who are involved in clubs and other extracurricular activities tend to be effective learners in school and develop regular patterns of work and practice that seem to be beneficial in developing self-regulation strategies.

Students with Disabilities

Students with disabilities often are overlooked as potential candidates for gifted programs for several reasons (Lovett & Lewandowski, 2006). The nature of the disability may mask the true talents or abilities of the student. Individuals with severe physical impairments or visual or hearing impairments may not have the exceptional communication skills parents and teachers generally associate with giftedness. Identification of the gifted students with these disabilities is equally problematic. The usual identification procedures and protocols may be wholly inappropriate for students with physical or visual or hearing impairments (Willard-Holt, 1994). **Figure 13.4** is a description of a gifted student with a visual impairment.

Figure 13.4 Donna, A Creatively Gifted Child with a Visual Impairment

Donna was a first grade student when I first noticed her in my talent development class. I was immediately intrigued by her thought processes but was not able to transfer this intrigue to her teacher. I taught her in talent development for first and second grade and part of third grade. In first grade I realized Donna's creative potential early on. She had a very developed ability in fluency and flexibility in creative problem-solving as evidenced by her work samples in my class. Her teacher was startled by Donna's work samples because she had not demonstrated that ability in her classwork.

Donna was also a bit of a behavior problem in her class. She was not a particularly instigating type of child, but she did have a tendency to strike out inappropriately when challenged. She was respectful with teachers and adults, but she was aggressive with her classmates. She was a tiny little thing but never afraid to strike back if thwarted, no matter how big the other child was. She also had trouble finishing classwork.

In second grade, I again taught Donna in the talent development class and saw her shrink before my eyes. She was not happy, and her teacher was unimpressed with her work. The teacher was a middle-aged woman who had been a substitute teacher and paraprofessional for several years before getting her certification and moving to her own classroom. Her first year as a teacher coincided with Donna's second grade year. In addition, the class was what is commonly called "a revolving door" class. That is, the class was the smallest at the grade level so any time a new second grade student enrolled from a shelter or from other areas, the student was placed in Donna's class. The shelter students had many other issues, and two of them met eligibility for self-contained behavioral disorders by the end of the year. In the meantime, the entire class, including the teacher, was tense all the time. As mentioned before, Donna never shrank from a physical challenge even though the child causing the problem might be several heads taller than she was. She was not a whiner or a crier, but she did dive right into a confrontation. Donna was moved a lot during the school year because she was always in the thick of any controversy involving the problem children. In order to separate her from a situation, the teacher would often send her to the library to finish her work and calm down. Fortunately, the librarian took a shine to her, and a special relationship developed between the two of them.

When I first saw Donna, I noted that the entire left side of her face appeared atrophied. Further review of her permanent record revealed that she was blind in her left eye. There was, however, no doctor's report in the record and no mention of her blindness. I talked to Donna's mother when I first realized the problem, and she advised me that Donna was born blind in her left eye as a result of the optic nerve being detached from the retina. At age 2, Donna had unsuccessful surgery to correct the problem. During the surgery, the doctor did insert a "shelf" under her blind eye to give her a more normal look.

When I understood the vision problem, I also realized that Donna's sensory disability would have to be considered in eligibility decisions concerning gifted program placement. Although she is creative, that does not necessarily mean she has a gifted IQ. There is a relationship between creativity and IQ, but not when an IQ is over 120. Her achievement tests were not qualifying, but this could be due to her not having any accommodation for her vision problem when she was taking the tests.

Donna's behavior problems may also be a function of her vision problems. She may not possess the ability to "read" other children's eyes and looks since she has limited peripheral vision. Finally, she may not be as intuitive as other children who have full use of both eyes and communicate with eye movement and looks (Malcomson, 1988).

(continued on next page)

| Figure 13.4 | Donna, A Creatively Gifted Child with a Visual Impairment *(continued)* |

Donna's third grade teacher was perfect for her learning style. She is a traditional type of disciplinarian with a "no-nonsense" attitude. She does not appear to be a particularly nurturing type of teacher, but she is devoted to her students' achievement. The class moves smoothly with little disruption and fewer distractions. It is a good environment for Donna. The teacher put her toward the front of the room with her "good-eye side" facing the board. We often talked about Donna, and she told me that she thought she might be gifted. She had an advanced vocabulary for certain subjects, particularly in science. She also confirmed my analysis that Donna was creative with a dry sense of humor that often went over the heads of the other students.

Because Donna has always done relatively well in school and scored well (not in the gifted range) on her achievement tests, she has never been referred for assistance from a vision therapist. It seems a shame that this avenue of support has never been attempted because it might help us to draw out Donna's talent. When the time came for recommendations for gifted testing, however, her teacher also asked about vision support for Donna. Her idea was that Donna's vision could be supported in terms of special environmental aids such as lighting and optical aids (Corn & Riser, 1989).

Although Donna's achievement testing did not qualify her for gifted program placement, her mental ability testing did. Her score was 128/96% on the composite of the *Otis Lennon*. She took the test alone with only a proctor and was given extra time to complete it. It was interesting to note that the proctor said that Donna put her hand over her blind eye toward the end of her testing period as though she were getting tired. She also scored above 90% in motivation and creativity.

Having multiple criteria for gifted program placement was beneficial for Donna. She has met eligibility for the gifted program and is doing well in her regular class as well as in the gifted program. It took a long time and perseverance for school personnel to draw out her giftedness, but the result was well worth it. This little girl's giftedness has been affirmed.

Donna is now receiving support from a vision therapist with special optical aids. Her textbooks have large print, and her testing also has large print. Her latest achievement scores in reading and math are both over 90%.

Teachers may be so focused on the student's disability (attention deficit/hyperactivity disorder, learning disability, etc.) and its effect on the student's classroom performance that they overlook the individual's abilities or special talents. In some cases, the disability may not be readily apparent. Many gifted students suffer from learning disabilities. Baum (1990) describes three types of learning disabilities that may affect gifted students:

"1. identified gifted students who have subtle learning disabilities,
2. unidentified students whose gifts and disabilities may be masked by average achievement, and
3. identified learning disabled students who are also gifted."

For some students with disabilities, restrictions in their home or school environment may have resulted in limited opportunities to demonstrate their talents. Johnson, Karnes, and Carr (1997) note that gifted programs must pay special attention to include and meet the needs of students with disabilities. Betts and Neihart (2004) refer to the disabled gifted student as a Type V or double-labeled student. The vast majority of gifted programs do not identify these children, nor do they offer differentiated programming that addresses and integrates their special needs. Fortunately, research on the effective identification of these children has been promising, and suggestions do exist for ways to provide programming.

Students from Minority Cultures

Individuals who are gifted and talented exist in every culture and linguistic group. The U.S. Department of Education reports that in 2010 approximately 48% of public school children were non-white (Chen, Sable, & Noel, 2010). Given these statistics, it is logical to assume that more non-white students would be involved in gifted programs. The situation in our schools today is that students from certain minority groups (African American, Latino, and Native American) are not identified as gifted in numbers reflecting their proportion in the general population (Kitano & Dijiosia, 2002). Analyzing data from 2006 (the most recent data available), Ford states that 48% more African American students should be identified as gifted. Similarly, Hispanic students should comprise 38% more of the gifted student population than they currently do (Ford, 2010). Numerous reasons for this disproportional representation have been cited. Many students from minority groups live in poverty and come from families with low socioeconomic status (SES) which limit the student's opportunities for enrichment and learning in the home environment.

Educators and policy makers have long been concerned about the lack of diversity in gifted programs (Ford, Grantham, & Whiting, 2008; Borland & Wright, 1994; Ford & Harris, 1990; Van Tassel-Baska, Patton, & Prillaman, 1989). This lack of diversity also extends to students who are socioeconomically deprived, and/or are limited in English proficiency. Minority children, especially African American children, are disproportionately found in low SES environments (Halle, Kurtz-Costes, & Mahoney, 1997), and low SES environments are often associated with poor academic performance (Hill, 2001). Gifted minority children typically underachieve (Ford & Thomas, 1997), and thus their true cognitive abilities may not be identified. Finally, minority children tend to do poorly on intelligence tests that emphasize verbal abilities (Ford, 1998), tests which are often described as culturally biased (Scott & Delgado, 2005). Stein, Hetzel, and Beck (2012) point out that poor and/or limited English proficient gifted students may "fall through the cracks" because the focus is on these issues and not on their potential giftedness.

Ambrose (2002) stated that an awareness of the suppressive effects of socioeconomic deprivation on talent development puts the responsibility on all who influence public policy to ensure that all children, especially those who are deprived, have access to adequate primary goods such as educational opportunities and adequate health care. He further advised that educators of the gifted must recognize that deprivation does indeed stunt aspiration development which, in turn, undermines talent development. Consequently, they must work harder to find potential within children by alternative methods of identification for these children's motivation to achieve is often undermined by oppressive outside forces.

Some agree with Ford (1998) that traditional standardized tests used to identify gifted students are unfair and biased to students from minority cultures requiring a familiarity with the dominant culture. Research has indicated that there is validity to this argument; however, not all minority groups seem to be adversely effected by this bias. Recent research suggests that Asian and Pacific Americans may in fact be overrepresented in gifted programs (Kitano & Dijiosia, 2002). It is unlikely that students from this minority group are more familiar with the dominant culture, thus this argument needs further research.

Schools in some districts have attempted to maximize the likelihood that students from diverse cultures will be appropriately identified by using a variety of selection criteria for gifted programs. These include flexible cut-off scores on standardized tests and the use of checklists for parents and teachers to rate students' behaviors and skills in areas other than academic performance. In addition, it is important for all teachers to have an awareness and understanding of the cultural differences of their students and how these may affect students' performance and behavior in the classroom (see Chapter 1). When designing gifted programs for students from minority cultures, Feldhusen (1989) has recommended increased parental involvement, the use of experiential learning strategies, and the inclusion of mentors and role models. A description of a creative young African American child is in **Figure 13.5**.

Figure 13.5   Ricky, A Creatively Gifted African American First Grader

Ricky was a quiet African American child in my talent development class in first grade. He was handsome, well dressed, and well behaved, but his teacher and his mother were concerned about his school work. His teacher told me that he was having problems learning to read. He had little realization of the connection of sounds to letters and often mixed up his first name with his last name. They began with the same two letters.

Ricky's mother was a single parent and told us that she did not have a lot of time to read to him after school. She asked his teacher for extra help from the remedial program for Ricky's reading.

The first inclination I had that Ricky was creative was when I gave the class an assignment in flexibility in creative problem-solving. The students were given a paper with 16 items of "junk," called spare parts, on it. The task was to use as many of the "spare parts" as possible to build a kind of boat for a kangaroo to use to cross a pond. Ricky worked diligently on his drawing. He did not use his crayons or markers but preferred using just his pencil. The result was a picture of a boat using all 16 spare parts. He was the only student in any of the first grade classes to use all the spare parts. When I questioned him about the uses of the different parts, he gave me detailed explanations of how they worked together. There was one detail that I could not figure out. One of the spare parts was a doghouse that Ricky used as the basis for his boat. When I looked at the door of the doghouse, I noticed something poking out of it. I asked him what it was because it was not on the spare parts paper. He smiled at me and said that it was the tail of the kangaroo because the kangaroo was inside the doghouse with its tail sticking out.

There were several other examples of Ricky's creativity during the first weeks of school; however, Ricky did not stay very long. In the middle of the first semester, he moved and we were not able to complete the process to identify Ricky for gifted program placement. He had been receiving remedial help with his reading, which was improving. The problem we have in a large urban school system is that many students are transient and do not stay long enough for their gifts to be affirmed. It was sad for me to watch this happen to Ricky. Unfortunately, we were not able to track his move from our school so we were never able to inform the personnel at his new school about his potential. Gifted program assessment takes a long time. For those children who may be difficult to assess correctly, there is just not enough time to do so.

Women

Although males and females do not differ in intellectual ability, significant differences exist in their achievement and their identification for gifted programs. Girls generally score higher than boys on achievement tests until puberty, when boys begin to excel, especially in math and science (Kerr, 1997). Differences in enrollment in gifted programs by gender may be due to a variety of factors. The gender role socialization that girls receive can impact on the way they behave and perform in school (Bianco et al., 2011). Some behaviors associated with giftedness (competitiveness, risk-taking, independence) typically are not encouraged in girls. Traditional cultural and societal expectations regarding educational performance and occupational choices continue to influence girls' behavior. Many families and cultures place a higher value on academic achievement in boys than in girls. Females frequently disguise their abilities and limit their achievement to what are perceived as socially acceptable levels (Parke, 1989). Some girls deliberately sabotage their own grades (leaving answers blank on exams, not turning in assignments) to avoid being identified as smarter or different from their peers. Terwilliger and Titus (1995) found that when nominated for accelerated programs, girls who are gifted do not accept enrollment as often as boys. Widespread discrimination against females from teachers, texts, and tests (American Association of University Women, 1992) also may affect their enrollment in gifted programs. Teachers pay less attention to girls than boys (Sadker & Sadker, 1985) and underestimate their female students' mathematical abilities (Kimball, 1989). Some tests remain biased against girls and textbooks used in schools often stereotype or ignore women (American Association of University Women, 1992).

Tremendous strides have been taken in recent years; however, the expectations of society continue to have a negative effect on many women who are gifted (Pendarvis, 1993). In addition, women's perception of their academic ability factors into how they view their success or failure. Whereas gifted boys tend to attribute academic success to their ability and failure to lack of effort (Hebert, 2001, 2002), gifted girls often attribute their success to luck and effort and their failures to lack of ability (Reis, 1987, 1998; Rimm, 1999). Further, Siegle, and Reis (1994) found that adolescent gifted girls believed that they had higher ability than boys in language arts and reading only, while adolescent gifted boys believed that they had higher ability in math, science, and social studies. It is important that gifted girls and boys develop a strong belief in their abilities in elementary and middle school because, by the adolescent years, their perceptions of their own ability begin to influence their achievement independent of any objective measures of ability (Meece, Blumenfeld, & Hoyle, 1988).

A phenomenon called stereotype threat (Spencer, Steele, & Quinn, 1999; Steele, 1997) has been found to adversely affect some groups, including gifted women, on standardized achievement tests. This phenomenon has been seen to raise anxiety and doubt about performance by certain groups. Although the SAT achievement gap has lessened in the last decade (ETS, 2006; Halpern, 1989; Rosser, 1989), current differences in standardized tests suggest that, overall, high school aged males continue to score higher in verbal and quantitative areas. For 2006, the achievement in SAT math for males was 34 points higher than for females and 3 points higher in SAT verbal. This SAT test gap also exists even when females earn the same grades as their male counterparts. The results may have a detrimental effect on gifted girls with fewer opportunities for selective colleges and programs for the gifted particularly in high school. Further, there may be a negative impact on girls' desire to enter graduate school and select careers (Reis, 1998). Finally, adolescents across the board tend to estimate their math and verbal abilities close to their SAT scores with the result that girls tend to underestimate their own abilities and lower their expectations resulting in underachievement in college and later in life.

Although the identification and development of giftedness in females has improved in the last few years, there are many factors that still impact the fulfillment of female potential. Walker, Reis, and Leonard (1992) noted that when women who are gifted were questioned about the problem of underachieving women, the issues raised were a lack of role models for such females, the denial of giftedness, the lack of organized mentoring, and lower expectations for women.

Program Delivery Models

Because students spend over 15,000 hours of life in school, it is crucial that educational programming be appropriately stimulating and challenging for all students including students who are gifted. As Tomlinson (2004) notes, "Fair will mean that all of us must live by the class rules, all of us must work hard, all of us must respect one another and encourage one another. It does not mean that we will all do the same things all the time" (p. 71). In an age of standards-based reform, school systems are becoming more aware of the need to develop content-based approaches to curriculum for gifted learners (VanTassel-Baska, 2005). No longer can gifted programs survive if they are not fundamentally connected to the business of schools—that is, preparing all students for proficiency in key areas of learning. There are a variety of administrative arrangements for service delivery of gifted programs. These administrative arrangements are used to varying degrees throughout the country with each school system generally responsible for selecting the arrangement it implements. These arrangements can include special schools, resource classrooms, special classes, cluster

grouping, collaboration, mentorships, joint enrollment options, and inclusion within the general education classroom. These models deliver either direct or indirect services.

Direct Services

Special Schools

Typical schools may be unable to offer the number of advanced courses and the diverse curriculum needed to challenge students identified as gifted. Establishing special schools for these students allows for the development of a wide range of advanced courses and a unique educational experience. Such schools also offer students a supportive climate for unlimited interaction with others of similar ability. Some school systems have developed special schools, often called magnet schools, to provide unique learning opportunities in specific fields for students with superior ability in those areas (e.g., language arts, music, math, science). The New York School of Performing Arts (commonly known as the Fame school) is an example of this type institution.

There is a growing trend to develop special residential high schools for students who are gifted and talented (Kolloff, 1997). These schools offer students an educational experience designed for them, taught by expert faculty, with peers who have similar interests and comparable abilities. The programs often incorporate mentorships, internships, and opportunities for independent study. Some residential schools are located on university campuses which allow the students access to university classes, laboratory facilities, and cultural events.

Resource Model

The resource model generally is a "pull-out" program where students are grouped with other students who are gifted and talented for part of their school day. Resource models can also include options for weekend programs, summer programs, workshops, and special programs sponsored by national or state agencies such as Odyssey of the Mind or Future Problem Solving. In most school systems this is the model used at the elementary level. The lack of a standard curriculum for the elementary model means that there may be a vast difference in the nature of specific gifted programs. For example, some resource rooms are highly academic in nature and may require teachers to cover standards for language arts, math, science, or social studies. Other programs may be more ancillary in nature in that teachers use interest inventories to drive the nature of their classes.

It should also be noted that many states have class size limitations for these resource classrooms. For example, in Georgia the elementary gifted resource room is limited to 17 students. For middle and high schools, class size is limited to 21 students.

Special Classes

When students who are gifted are taken out of the general education classroom and placed together in a special class for part or all of the school day in the school setting, a school-within-a-school concept has been created. These special classes are designed primarily to provide a variety of educational opportunities above and beyond those of the typical school curriculum. Activities may extend from academic acceleration to cultural enrichment. Honors courses, electives, mentoring programs, and the study of topics generally not available to the rest of the student body are examples of special class strategies. Offering special classes before or after school, on weekends, or during summers are other alternatives used by schools. High schools often offer special advanced placement classes that have strict content area and requirements and can assist the student in receiving college credit through examination. The class size limitations also apply to these classes.

Cluster Grouping

In a **cluster grouping** model, identified gifted students are placed as a group into an otherwise heterogeneous general education classroom. The general education teacher must have the gifted endorsement and must document curriculum modifications made for the gifted students such as separate lesson plans and individual student contracts. Here again, there is generally a class size limit.

Indirect Services

Collaborative Teaching

In this model, a teacher with a gifted education teaching endorsement, the classroom teacher, and the gifted student (when appropriate) collaborate in the development of challenging assignments that substitute for or extend core curriculum objectives. Direct instruction may be provided by the classroom teacher, but there must be collaborative planning between this teacher and the gifted specialist. In addition, teacher-partners document curriculum modifications through separate lesson plans, student contracts, and collaborative planning time logs.

Mentorship/Internship

In a mentorship or internship model, identified gifted students work with mentors to explore professions of interest. The teacher with gifted endorsement supervises these experiences by collaborating with the student and mentor in documenting student contracts for work to be done, learning objectives, assessment strategies, and data logs.

In a mentorship or internship model, identified gifted students work with mentors to explore professions of interest.

Joint Enrollment/Postsecondary Options

In this option, students who have completed the secondary curriculum in a specific content area in a school can opt to attend a college or university near the school on a part-time basis. There should be a demonstrated need for an advanced curriculum not offered otherwise and the experience should be monitored by the gifted specialist in the secondary school.

Inclusion

Presently, the most frequently offered educational experience for students who are gifted involves attending a special resource class for a period of time that may range from 45 minutes to 5 or more hours each week. When these students are in the general education classroom, it is the responsibility of the classroom teacher to make adaptations in the curriculum.

The classroom teacher should make no assumptions about the knowledge base of a student who is identified as academically gifted. Classroom adaptations can be made for those who excel in a particular area, but regular instruction may meet the needs of those who need instruction in some basic skills. Students may have academic gifts and talents in only one area of the curriculum. They can be extremely gifted in one area and average in another. Teachers should familiarize themselves with test results to determine the strengths and weaknesses of those students in their classroom. With this model, the gifted education specialist can be of invaluable assistance in helping the classroom teacher modify the curriculum for the gifted student.

Including gifted students in the general education classroom imposes some administrative challenges. Effective inclusion requires flexible scheduling, and the collaboration of other school personnel requires coordination of schedules. Without proper administrative support, these challenges can make including gifted students in the classroom impossible, even though it may be the most financially efficient way to deliver programming for students who are talented and gifted (Coleman & Cross, 2001).

Within these varied models the approach taken for delivery of the services can be offered as enrichment or acceleration or a combination of the two. The term **enrichment** refers to richer, more varied educational experiences and can apply to both service delivery and curriculum (Schiever & Maker, 1997). **Acceleration** involves increasing the pace of teaching and learning and also can apply to service delivery (grade skipping) as well as curriculum (completing 2 years of the math curriculum in a single year) (Schiever & Maker, 1997).

Enrichment and Acceleration in the General Education Classroom

Schools that rely on resource room instruction for a portion of the school day must ensure that the general education classroom teacher and the teacher of the gifted collaborate to develop and implement a plan to supplement resource room instruction with enrichment or acceleration of content in the general classroom. The resource room delivery model allows these students to be academically challenged and remain with their same-age peers while participating in other school activities. Enrichment and acceleration are methods by which general education can be modified to meet the needs of students with gifts and talents.

Enrichment

Typically, enrichment is viewed as a supplement to the school's general education curriculum, adding depth and breadth to the normally studied content. The classroom teacher dispenses lessons and materials distinctive to students who are gifted as they remain in the classroom for most or all of the school day. Independent study projects, investigations of a unit in more depth and breadth than other students in the class, Internet contacts with authorities in fields of interest to the student, special high-level materials and activities supplementing the class content being studied, and pursuit of special topics under the guidance of the classroom teacher, a mentor, or the teacher of the gifted are some ways enrichment may be accomplished.

Program coordination among elementary, middle, and secondary schools is important to the expansion and long-range planning of content offered in an enrichment program. Doing this helps eliminate the add-on nature of many enrichment programs that offer fragmented or non-intellectually challenging subject matter to students as they move through the school experience. Offerings of enrichment should be above and beyond the general school curriculum, yet supplemental to it. Enrichment content should include the application of acquired knowledge to actual situations, breaking down a problem or situation into its component parts and analyzing each for its relevance to a solution, combining information in new and unique ways, and evaluating the value a process or product possesses when compared to established criteria. Renzulli and Reis (1997) offer a schoolwide enrichment model that incorporates a triad of activities and strategies. The first component is the use of general exploratory activities to expose students to disciplines, topics, persons, places, and other content typically not included in the general education curriculum. The second part of the triad involves the development of specific skills in creative thinking, problem solving, and communication related to various disciplines, topics, persons, places, and other content typically not included in the general education curriculum. The third component is the self-selected investigation of real-life problems by individuals and small groups with the possible development of an original product. This enrichment triad is a widely used approach for instruction of students who are gifted because it provides opportunities to stimulate and encourage their natural curiosity, interests, and abilities. **Figure 13.6** gives an example of a Schoolwide Enrichment Program.

Figure 13.6	An Example of a Schoolwide Enrichment Program (SEM)

For the Schoolwide Enrichment Program (SEM), the first component is always exploratory in nature with topics often chosen from interest inventories not typically included in the general curriculum. These activities are generally called Type I activities, and they are open to all students, not just the gifted ones. An example of a Type I activity in science might be an assembly with a dermatologist discussing various skin disorders and their causes.

The Type II activity, which would evolve from the Type I session with the dermatologist, might be a research project on skin types, pigmentation, and skin disorders. The students involved in this project would do research and interview different scientists who might be studying skin disorders and people with skin disorders. There would be primary as well as secondary research.

The Type III activity would be an independent project done by the gifted student and supervised by the gifted education specialist. This activity draws on the information gathered from the Type II activity and includes a publication or a presentation about some aspect of dermatology. This activity always requires a live audience and is geared toward this presentation. One good example is a book on warts written by a gifted student and aimed at sharing with children who are in a dermatologist's office to have their warts removed—a sort of *Berenstain Bears Have Their Warts Removed* kind of book.

Acceleration

With acceleration, students who are gifted move through the general education curriculum at a faster rate than their grade-level peers. Academic achievement is a major factor in a program emphasizing acceleration. Strategies for acceleration include:

- Early admission to school at the primary, secondary, or college level;
- Skipping grades;
- Telescoping or compacting the curriculum typically covered in two or more grades into 1 year; and
- Taking high school courses for credit in middle school, or college courses for credit in high school.

Advanced placement courses often are used at the high school level as well as credit by exam allowing the student to test out of courses, units, or grades and in some cases to graduate early. Acceleration for some students may involve the entire curriculum, but for others acceleration may be appropriate in only one or two subjects. Many school systems allow cross-grade placement (i.e., a fourth grade student is enrolled in grade-level social studies and language arts and in sixth grade math and science) or joint enrollment between high school and college. In addition, a school might set up a mentorship for selected students. The mentor may be a person in the community or school who has the time to offer expertise in certain areas on a consistent basis.

Enrichment and Acceleration Opportunities for Gifted and Talented Students Outside the General Education Classroom

In the continuing debate over how best to serve the educational needs of students, current popular thinking suggests that inclusion in the general education classroom is best for most, if not all, students. However, research generally suggests that homogeneous grouping of gifted and talented students is more advantageous. Recent reviews of the research on grouping clearly suggest that homogeneous grouping of gifted and talented students has a significant positive effect on academic achievement (Shields, 2002). Homogeneous grouping can vary from situations where students spend a few hours each week in a gifted classroom, to placement in full-time gifted classrooms, to attendance at a special school for the gifted and talented.

Controversies Associated with Enrichment and Acceleration

There is long-standing controversy surrounding the issue of acceleration and enrichment. Some parents and teachers may express concern about acceleration and resist its implementation due to possible negative effects on students' social-emotional development. VanTassel-Baska (1994) found no such negative effects and noted higher achievement rates in students who were accelerated than those who were not. Kulik (1992) also reported that students from accelerated classes outperform their non-accelerated peers on achievement tests.

Some educators claim that true enrichment does not exist and that many enrichment activities are often pointless and unrelated to each other (Stanley & Benbow, 1986). Stanley (1978) suggested that enrichment without acceleration is potentially dangerous to the gifted student. Others argue that acceleration is simply allowing students to progress at their own natural rate through curriculum without predetermined institution-imposed parameters as to when and at what rate students should learn certain academic material. This debate notwithstanding, acceleration and enrichment can often be complementary pieces in a gifted education program. Allowing students to progress at their own rate and receive enrichment will lead to greater knowledge and skills as well as develop creativity and other cognitive skills. Regardless of the model or approach chosen, Coleman and Cross (2001) suggest that program planners base their program on several premises. These premises should form the foundation for all program planning:

1.   The child's strengths are to be encouraged and developed.
2.   The learning environment should provide opportunities for expanding one's knowledge, and building more effective cognitive, affective, and creative capabilities.
3.   Arrangements must be made to accommodate individual differences, such as interests, abilities, learning rates, and learning styles.
4.   Contact with other gifted children promotes social-emotional development.
5.   A program should be responsive to the community it serves and involve families of children.
6.   The curricula should promote these premises.
7.   Evaluation is an indispensable part of effective program planning.

Davis and Rimm (1998) propose that any program serving the needs of gifted students must contain four core components. Based in part on Treffinger's model, they suggest that program planners should attend to these four components:

1.   Program philosophy and goals. Key questions:
     a.   What is our attitude toward gifted children?
     b.   Why are we doing this?
     c.   What do we wish to accomplish?
2.   Definition and identification. Key questions:
     a.   What do we mean by "gifted and talented"?
     b.   Which categories of gifts and talents will this program serve?
     c.   How will we select them?

3. Instruction-grouping, acceleration, and enrichment. Key questions:
    a. What are students' needs?
    b. How can we best meet those needs?
    c. How can we implement our instructional plans?
4. Evaluation and modification. Key questions:
    a. Was the program successful?
    b. How do we know?
    c. What did we do right?
    d. What did we do wrong?
    e. What changes shall we make?

It is important that while planning instructional activities teachers include activities for those who finish their work early. These should be meaningful activities that would benefit all students not just those who have been identified gifted. Kennedy (1995) proposes the suggestions listed in **Table 13.5** to promote the well-being of gifted students in the general education classroom. These suggestions are important for every classroom teacher to understand and implement as they teach gifted students.

Recent reforms in education have stressed the inclusion of all students in the general education classroom and have resulted in a reduction of the number of special classes found in schools. The limited number of special classes and resource room programs for students who are gifted concerns some educators and parents for several reasons. They believe that classroom teachers must focus on the typical students in their classes and are unable to

---

TABLE 13.5

Promoting the Well-Being of Gifted Children in Regular Classrooms

1. Resist policies requiring more work of those who finish assignments quickly and easily. Instead, explore ways to assign different work, which may be more complex, more abstract, and both deeper and wider. Find curriculum compacting strategies that work, and use them regularly.
2. Seek out supplemental materials and ideas that extend, not merely reinforce, the curriculum. Develop interdisciplinary units and learning centers that call for higher level thinking. Don't dwell on comprehension-level questions and tasks for those who have no problems with comprehension. Encourage activities that call for analysis, synthesis, and critical thinking, and push beyond superficial responses.
3. De-emphasize grades and other extrinsic rewards. Encourage learning for its own sake, and help perfectionists establish realistic goals and priorities. Try to assure that the self-esteem of talented learners does not rest solely on their products and achievements.
4. Encourage intellectual and academic risk-taking. The flawless completion of a simple worksheet by an academically talented student calls for little or no reward, but struggling with a complex, open-ended issue should earn praise. Provide frequent opportunities to stretch mental muscles.
5. Help all children develop social skills to relate well to one another. For gifted children this may require special efforts to see things from other viewpoints. Training in how to "read" others and how to send accurate verbal and nonverbal messages may also be helpful. Tolerate neither elitist attitudes nor anti-gifted discrimination.
6. Take time to listen to responses that may at first appear to be off-target. Gifted children often are divergent thinkers who get more out of a story or remark and have creative approaches to problems. Hear them out, and help them elaborate on their ideas.
7. Provide opportunities for independent investigations in areas of interest. Gifted children are often intensely, even passionately, curious about certain topics. Facilitate their in-depth explorations by teaching research skills as needed, directing them to good resources, and providing support as they plan and complete appropriate products.
8. Be aware of the special needs of gifted girls. Encourage them to establish realistically high-level educational and career goals, and give them additional encouragement to succeed in math and science.

provide the enrichment and acceleration needed by students who are gifted. Westberg, Archabault, Dobyns, and Slavin (1993) observed third and fourth grade general education classrooms in which students identified as gifted were placed and found the majority of these students were not receiving instruction or curriculum appropriate to their abilities. Grouping students who are gifted allows for increased opportunities for interaction and accelerated learning which can have positive effects on both their achievement and their attitudes (Barnett & Durden, 1993; Sowell, 1993).

Instructional Strategies

While avoiding the controversy of whether the identification of students who are talented and gifted is elitist, it is important to recognize that gifted students are "differently abled" (Morelock, 1996, p. 11) and thus require different instructional strategies. Students who exhibit exceptional intellectual abilities must be allowed to develop and demonstrate those abilities in the classroom. If they are not provided with appropriate opportunities, they could become underachievers or behavior problems. Core content areas are important for instructional focus for these students and the general education curriculum should not be abandoned. A classroom teacher can differentiate the curriculum by taking into account the characteristics, educational needs and interests of the student, and then adapt the standard curriculum appropriately. Techniques that will help teachers differentiate instructional strategies and make curriculum adaptations for students with gifts and talents include curriculum compacting, flexible grouping, tiered assignments, questioning techniques, independent study centers or projects, and interest centers.

Curriculum compacting, a strategy which allows students to identify content that they already know, is an effective method for differentiating instruction for students who are gifted. Curriculum compacting allows students to move at a more rapid pace and "buy" time for individual projects of interest. Winebrenner (1992) suggests the following guidelines for teaching students who are gifted in the general education classroom:

- First, find out what they already know.
- Give them "credit" for the concepts they have mastered.
- Don't have them repeat grade level work if they show they know it.
- Provide alternate challenging activities for them to do instead of drill and practice or already mastered work. Provide opportunities for them to work with complex and abstract ideas.
- Discover what their interests are, and build their projects around their interests.
- Allow them flexibility in the way they use the time they "buy back" by mastering a concept early.
- Allow them to learn at a faster pace than their age peers.
- Use discovery-learning techniques often.
- Trust students to learn in nontraditional ways.
- Help them find students just like themselves. Try not to judge their social skills solely on the way they interact with their age peers.
- Give them lots of experience with setting their own goals and evaluating their own work.
- Offer choice, choices, and more choices! (p. 138).

The main idea in curriculum compacting is not to repeat skills already mastered. A good method is to give a pretest to see where the students are in skill mastery. If they have mastered the skill at the 90th percentile or above, they should be allowed to skip that skill and move on. There might be several groups working on different things at the same time, but careful management techniques will help to avoid confusion.

In flexible grouping, students are grouped for instruction within the classroom by demonstrated strengths. Thus an identified gifted student might be in a high level group for math but in an average group for reading. However, as the students demonstrate their strengths it is important to include opportunities to move in and out of groups so that students receive appropriate instruction. In some classes where flexible grouping is used, students will be moving into different groups several times

In flexible grouping, students are grouped for instruction within the classroom by demonstrated strengths.

each day, depending on the assignment. As long as students do not feel stuck in any one particular group, this is fine. Flexible grouping dovetails easily with curriculum compacting because you are always assessing for mastery and affirming the students' levels.

Tiered assignment strategy includes large group instruction with differing activities depending on the ability of the students. Thus, a class may be studying the Civil Rights movement in a social studies class; however, they may be assigned different projects appropriate for their instructional level. If there are book assignments on a topic for instance, different students might be assigned different books to read and discuss. Other important considerations include that the assignments should never make the gifted students feel as though they are being punished for being smart by the amount of work expected of them nor should the assignments for the gifted students look like too much fun to the students in the other groups. Much thought needs to go into the development of activities in order to avoid these pitfalls. An example of a tiered assignment in reading for third grade may be that the students are reading different books on the same topic. The gifted group might be reading *Charlie and the Chocolate Factory* whereas another group may be reading *Chocolate Fever*, and yet another group is reading *Chocolate Touch*. *Charlie and the Chocolate Factory* would be for the more advanced readers—the other two books are for the average and below-average readers. The theme is the same, but the levels are different. When assignments are given out for each of these books, there should be the same number of assignments per group, and each group should have some choices within the assignments.

Questioning techniques is another appropriate strategy for differentiating instruction in the classroom. When asking questions about material in the content area, the classroom teacher takes care to ask more probing questions, designed to encourage the development of higher order thinking skills. It is important to make sure students have understood the material taught, but it is equally important to ask them questions that require them to analyze, synthesize, and evaluate what they have learned. To ask a student to predict what happened after Goldilocks woke up and ran away or to compare and contrast different versions of the Cinderella story are the kinds of questions that may stimulate thoughtful responses in students who have never had to think like that before. Finally, open-ended questions such as the one for the Goldilocks story encourage students to be risk-takers and realize that there are sometimes no "right" answers to problems. The Junior Great Book series has many questions that stimulate open-ended thinking, analysis, and evaluation. Inquiry techniques in this series are excellent methods of getting away from simple recall of events.

Independent study projects can be used to stimulate gifted students because they allow a degree of ownership in choosing and designing the project. Gifted students, in particular, can be encouraged through this strategy to take risks and explore topics in more depth than they would be able to in the classroom setting. Also, at the end of the project, students should present their projects affording them the opportunity to develop poise and self-confidence. Independent projects should include a contract which the teacher and the students develop. This way the students know exactly what is expected of them. If, for example, the class is studying the Civil War and the students are interested in civil rights laws that were enacted, the gifted students demonstrate that they know the material by a mastery test and then choose several laws that were enacted as a part of post-Civil War events.

A final strategy in differentiating instruction for gifted learners within the general education classroom is through the use of interest centers. In the beginning of the school year, students are asked to fill out an interest inventory, not unlike the "Interest-a-lyzer" developed by Dr. Joseph Renzulli. Using this inventory as a guide, the teacher would set up interest centers in the classroom for student use. Thus, all the students, including the gifted students, have the opportunity to explore subject matter beyond the scope of the general education classroom curriculum. The result of the interest centers is much like that of the independent project strategy in that students have ownership of their projects, but with the bonus result that they may also discover a new area of interest and become passionate about it. The interest center may also serve as a stimulus for Type I and II activities in place of a schoolwide program. Thus, within the regular classroom, students are able to explore subject matter which may not be part of the regular curriculum.

Although the above techniques are considered to be appropriate differentiation strategies for modifying the curricular experiences for gifted students, the following points should be considered as any and/or all of the techniques are employed:

- Differentiation can occur with respect to one, two, or all of the following:
  — content (the subject matter or body of knowledge to be acquired)
  — process (mastery of skills, development of concepts, thinking)
  — product (the way in which the learning is demonstrated).
- Differentiation may also occur in the way the curriculum is presented (e.g., separate setting, itinerant teacher, integrated classroom).
- One approach to differentiating curriculum is to extend or study in depth an existing curriculum area. Another approach is to shift to curriculum that arises out of the student's own interests and concerns. Both concepts are important, and both emphasize the processes of learning, thinking, applying, and creating.
- Working together to develop this curriculum, student and teacher share the responsibility for the following levels of a chosen area of study:
  — planning (independent study contract)
  — implementation (student independent study log)
  — evaluation (student self-evaluation)
- The teacher's role in this partnership involves:
  — serving as a mentor or facilitator of learning and thinking rather than as a dispenser of information
  — creating a learning environment that is both secure and stimulating
  — helping the student receive a good balance of learning experiences
  — keeping the focus on the quality of the learning experience.

- Discussions, brainstorming sessions, and related follow-up activities can promote the development of higher level thinking skills. Higher level thinking involves analyzing, synthesizing, and evaluating information as opposed to simple knowledge gathering.
- Skills work in the basic subject areas should be an integral part of the gifted student's differentiated curriculum:
  - Basic skills can be taught by using materials that are at the student's instructional level and adapting them so there is less repetition and more opportunity for creative application and critical thinking
  - Independent study provides an ideal vehicle for incorporating basic skills work with the development of higher level thinking skills.
- Independent study enables the gifted student to become involved in selecting, structuring, executing, and judging his or her work in partnership with the teacher. Sharing the results of this study with others can be beneficial to the gifted students and to others in the class.[1]

Particularly in the early grades, teachers may need to assist students to become independent learners by defining a continuum of skills from the totally dependent to the totally independent learner and the variety of study, research, and communication skills used at each step. It is possible to move them toward becoming totally independent learners.

Task commitment, according to Renzulli (1978), is one of three components constituting giftedness. In many schools, students are identified as gifted because of above average intelligence, but little or nothing is done regarding the area of task commitment. Often students who are gifted have a wide variety of interests and find it difficult to stay focused on one. By being a guide and helping students acquire and maintain task commitment, teachers will be providing them a great service.

Students who are gifted need opportunities to go beyond what is already known to generate new ideas, judge long-held assumptions, and solve complex problems. For these students curriculum and its adaptations should be developed in accord with individualized aims and objectives to parallel their mental abilities and talents, and in accord with the role these students can be expected to play in society. The curriculum for gifted and talented should differ from that for other students in degree of challenge, depth, rigor, sophistication, and required excellence.

Traditionally, curriculum for students who are gifted has been differentiated in three ways: content, process, and product (Howley, Howley, & Pendarvis, 1986; Kaplan, 1974). Differentiated content may include courses the student ordinarily would not encounter until a later date and time. For example, the student may be taking an advanced mathematics class a year or two sooner than same age peers. Differentiated process may include expanding the breadth and depth of the content being studied. For instance, when studying The Great Depression, students may compare and contrast it to The Depression of 1893 and examine them at a higher and more abstract level than just knowledge and understanding. Differentiated product would be using the most acceptable and creative form to report the results of a student's study. For example, if a video would be the best method to convey the results of a student's study of videography, then that should be the product form used. **Table 13.6** presents a guide for adaptations in the curriculum.

As noted previously in this chapter, creativity is considered a key component of giftedness. Creative individuals are curious and adventurous. They are able to speculate and gener-

---

[1]From the Council for Exceptional Children (1981). *Gifted and talented multi-media kit, meeting the needs of gifted and talented students.* Reston, VA: Author.

TABLE 13.6

Curriculum Adaptations

Subject Matter Accommodations

- **Facts** should be learned but not as the sole focus of study. Emphasis should be more on abstract, divergent thinking processes.
- **Interconnectedness** of concepts should be encouraged as much as possible.
- **Diversity** of material and topics should be provided especially for in depth, individual study.
- **Orderliness and Parsimony** are paramount to synthesizing key concepts in a functional format.
- **Histories** of diverse groups who have overcome obstacles and solved problems creatively can be explored.
- **Analysis of Methods** includes understanding the methods of inquiry and disciplines as means of increasing the depth understanding.

Cognitive Accommodations

- **Advanced Cognitive Processing** uses application, synthesis, and evaluation as vital tools in the process of learning.
- **Thinking Out Loud** requires students to explain their rationale for what they think without fear of rejection.
- **Open-Mindedness** includes withholding judgment and encouraging healthy debate, divergent thinking, and "out there" ideas.
- **Cooperative Learning** allow students to work as a team to solve problems and create an atmosphere of respect and acceptance.
- **Discovery** produces those "aha" moments which build interest, curiosity, confidence, and self-motivated learning.
- **Self-Selection** allows students more autonomy in the learning process, activities, and topics.
- **Self-Regulation and Diversity** through pretesting provides a challenge and helps maintain interest.

Product Accommodations

- **Visibility** includes taking the product of the students' work on the road, that is demonstrating their work to larger appropriate audiences.
- **Metamorphosis** includes altering existing information through the incorporation of divergent subject matter rather than simply summarizing it.
- **Authentic Issues** includes current life situations in the world (inter-personal, inter-societal, scientific, and artistic) and provides students with ownership of solutions.
- **Assessment** allows students the opportunity to have their products used and critically evaluated in real life situations.

ate many different ideas or solutions to problems and questions. Their responses are unusual, unique, or clever and evidence both imagination and knowledge. Hammer (1961) defines creativity as "the unique innovation, the unique configuration, whether it be artistic, philosophical, or scientific. It must be new, fresh and original, and it must be worthwhile, important or highly valued. If it is creativity in the arts as opposed to creativity in the sciences, it must have richness of communicated emotion" (p. 18). Creativity is natural in many students who are gifted, however, the classroom climate, instructional strategies, activities, and curricular approaches must support and enhance that creativity (Daniels, 1997). Gallagher (1985) emphasizes that a person engages in different activities or different ways of treating products during the stages of the creative process. These stages and characteristics are presented in **Table 13.7**.

Gallagher (1985) discusses the problem of our educational programs concentrating on the encouragement of students in the stages of preparation and verification and not in the stages of incubation and illumination. For example, compositions may be evaluated for neatness and organization and not for divergent thinking. How often do teachers encourage

TABLE 13.7

The Stages of the Creative Process

Stage of Creative Process	Expected Form	Predominant Thinking Operation	Personality Factor or Aptitude
• Preparation	• Well organized and well stated	• Cognitive	• Studiousness and sustained attention
• Incubation	• Often confused and sloppy	• Memory	• Intellectual freedom and risk taking
• Illumination	• Incoherent	• Divergent thinking	• Tolerance of failure and ambiguity
• Verification	• Neat, well organized, clearly following a logical sequence	• Convergent thinking	• Intellectual

the efforts of students whose ideas are in the incubation period, by accepting confusing and sloppy work?

Give students opportunities to develop their creative abilities. Allow them to be original, divergent thinkers. Brainstorming and creative problem solving techniques foster fluency, flexibility, elaboration, and originality—the four creative cognitive processes. Programs such as Odyssey of the Mind and Future Problem Solving encourage this behavior. Recognize that students have individual styles for generating creative ideas. Creativity might best occur while walking rather than while sitting, when working in short segments rather than in a long session, with background noise or music rather than in silence, and in cooperation with another rather than alone. Remember that creativity comes in a variety of forms, not only in the arts, but also in an unusual way to display a model aircraft collection, or a working heart made from sandwich bags and drinking straws. Be accepting of the possibility that a student who is creatively gifted may choose to discard what appears to be a perfectly acceptable, wonderfully creative idea. Some of the most important things you can provide these students are an environment conducive to creativity free from too much structure, the necessary resources and materials to work creatively, and support and encouragement to continue even when students initially fail.

Students demonstrate various types of creative behaviors at different ages. The type and level of their creativity depend on their experience, their physical development, and also their cognitive development (Amabile, 1989). Very young children may show their creativity through singing inventive songs, drawing, building while experimenting with different materials, and experimenting with sounds and instruments. As young children mature, their creativity may be seen through dancing, painting or combining colors in new ways, playing with sounds and meanings of words, and inventing and playing imaginary characters as they play.

Amabile (1989) further asserted that problem solving involves the creativity process in all four steps, beginning with problem finding. Once the problem has been defined, resources and data are gathered which will help solve the problem. The next stage of problem solving is the generation of many ideas and possibilities, no matter how wild and seemingly impractical. Since judgment of ideas is withheld in this stage, creative talent is allowed free rein. Finally, the validation stage of problem solving proceeds with testing the various possibilities and ideas produced. Young children can be encouraged and observed demonstrating their engagement in the creative process especially when they are in a flexible classroom that encourages independence, acceptance, and creativity.

One of the dangers in recognizing creativity in young children, according to Cramond (2001), is that many of the behaviors that identify creativity in these children also can be used to identify learning and/or behavior problems. The child who is different may be misdiagnosed as having Attention Deficit Hyperactivity Disorder (ADHD). Both highly creative children as well as ADHD children tend to daydream, be impulsive, take risks, and have poor social skills and generally difficult personalities. Both groups also demonstrate high energy levels and higher levels of sensation seeking behavior.

The early childhood teacher who is in tune with this conundrum in the overlapping of creative behavior and ADHD behavior will do the highly creative child (or any child for that matter) a great service simply by being careful not to place an ADHD label on the child too quickly. Also, the most important thing that the teacher can do for this child is simply to recognize and encourage creativity. Offering a safe haven for the highly creative child to express new ideas and to take risks without fear of rejection or ridicule is vital to this child's self-esteem and builds confidence. The creative child learns to accept his different feelings as valuable in an adult's eyes.

Researchers (Getzels & Jackson, 1962; Torrance, 1984) have indicated that many teachers consider students who are high on intelligence but low on creativity to be more ambitious, more studious, and more hard working than the highly creative student. They tell us teachers best like students who work industriously on teacher designated tasks, obey authority and rules readily and without conflict, and retain knowledge well. So, attempt to be accepting of your students who are creatively gifted and supportive of their ability. **Table 13.8** offers suggestions for encouraging creativity.

Although many students who are gifted are natural leaders and will assume many leadership roles, they must understand there also will be occasions when they must be part of a team effort. Classroom teachers can foster leadership skills by providing opportunities for students to serve as both leaders and followers in the classroom and to participate as members of teams. Allowing students the opportunity to be followers teaches them that a good leader must, at times, be willing to follow. Encourage your students who are gifted to participate in a variety of school organizations and activities (band, athletic teams, drama club, etc.) so they can encounter the diverse talents of others. Participating in an organization gives students the opportunity to encounter a variety of leadership role models. Provide your students with information about leaders in the fields in which they have an interest and discuss the characteristics and attributes these individuals possessed to become leaders.

Technology, the Internet, and Gifted Education

The recent advances in technology have offered opportunities for enhanced educational experiences for all students. These technological advances have significant implications for the education of gifted and talented students, particularly disadvantaged students. The proliferation of computer software for students and teachers has made learning and facilitating learning easier and more interesting. The use of email and distance learning can offer those disadvantaged students learning opportunities that were previously inaccessible. However, there remains a "digital divide" that separates students who have access to technology and the internet from those who do not. Typically these divisions occur along economic, racial, and geographic lines (Roach, 2002).

For gifted and talented students the internet offers opportunities that were previously unavailable. At the touch of a button, vast amounts of information are available to the gifted learner. No longer are teachers bound by the physical resources on hand (maps, textbooks, encyclopedias, trade books, etc.), they can tailor an individualized education plan for the gifted student in their classroom. Online and distance learning allows gifted students the

TABLE 13.8

Suggestions for Encouraging Creativity

- To stimulate students' powers of close examination, inquisitiveness, and alertness, ask them to look out the school bus window on a field trip and record only things that are living, or things of a certain color, or shape, etc. You may ask them to mentally record their observations while traveling and later make a written list. On the return trip, they can check to see what they overlooked or missed.

- To stimulate fluency, ask students to propose as many uses as possible for everyday items such as a cereal box, a pliers, a nail clipper, a shopping bag, etc. You can ask them to list as many things as they can that are shiny, sharp, slimy, or dry; round, square, or rectangular; black, white, yellow, or blue; etc.

- To stimulate inventiveness and imagination, ask students what they think would happen if:
  - animals wore clothes
  - we were born with wheels on our feet
  - we all lived in the trees
  - there were no electrical appliances
  - everyone became some kind of animal/flower/bird/fish/insect
  - we were transported to Ancient Egypt/Merry Old England/Prehistoric times.

- Try brainstorming by proposing a question affecting the entire school, such as where to go on a field trip. Have your students generate as many ideas as possible for answering the question or solving the problem, no matter how bizarre, and record them on paper or a computer. When the list is complete, select the best responses and elaborate on them.

- Do "pass it on" stories. Begin an extemporaneous story that each student must continue as the previous student stops. For instance, you may begin a story by saying, "One day, a boy and girl were strolling through a deep woods when they saw a . . ." and at this point pass the story on to the next participant. This procedure continues for as long as you choose. Sometimes it's fun to tape record the stories for later listening.

- Try play-making by acting out fictitious scenes, such as playing basketball against Michael Jordan, interviewing Columbus on his return to Spain, or pretending to have a conversation between Rosa Parks and Harriet Beecher Stowe.

- Expose your creatively gifted students to other creative individuals. This might include reading comic strips such as "Calvin and Hobbs" or "The Far Side" together; viewing videotapes about Edison, Van Gogh, Martin Luther King Jr., etc.; visiting museums and art institutes to encounter firsthand the works of creative masters in various fields; reading biographies and autobiographies of highly creative individuals; and viewing and discussing films and videotapes produced by highly creative people such as Disney, Spielberg, Lee, and Lucas. Use the work of such creative individuals to intrigue and encourage exploration, not as a model to be emulated.

opportunity for acceleration and enrichment as they move through curriculum at their own pace and pursue topics in depth.

Suggestions for Classroom Teachers

In the section that follows, suggestions for classroom activities are presented by subject area.

Art

1. Write a numeral, a letter of the alphabet, or a squiggly line and use it as a part of a larger drawing. Try to disguise your choice of letter, numeral, or squiggly line so it will be difficult for others to find it without a search.

2. Given several objects such as string, a paper clip, an empty paper towel roll, rubber band, glue, coat hangers, construction paper, scissors, etc., construct a mobile.

3. Given four letters of the alphabet and/or numerals, randomly invent a variety of monogram designs for your school, your name, your state, etc.

4. Design your own recreational vehicle and describe the function of each major feature.

5. Design the ideal bedroom you would like to have and describe the function of each major feature of the room.

6. Design a clothing outfit you would like to own. Be original with color, material, style, etc.

7. Design a school you think would be more fun to attend. Describe the function of each major feature and how it would improve your learning.

8. Using items such as construction paper, paper clips, paper towel rolls, rubber bands, tape, glue, post-it notes, etc., make something no one else will think of doing.

9. Brainstorm many different uses for a shoe string.

10. Design a new cage for a gerbil.

Language Arts

1. Orally describe in class what you would do with a ***pumglitz*** if given one. What would it look like; smell like; do? What can be done with it? Write a two person play with a partner about the day you were given a ***pumglitz*** and the adventures you had with it. Perform the play in class with your partner.

2. You are an "object." Tell your life story in a short story format, illustrations optional, using all the features a good short story should possess. An alternate project would be to create an illustrated story book using the same theme. Possible objects may include: a mirror, a foreign coin, a well travelled penny, one of Michael Jordan's shoes, etc.

3. Name three occupations that would well fit someone with the following names:

    Hy Pancake

    Sally Forth

    Noel Belle

    Ben Fender

    Create a children's story about one of your choices.

4. If you could create a new television show, about what would it be? Who would be the main characters? What actors would you cast to play these roles? What would be the title of the show? Write a 5 minute script for the introductory show.

5. What could you do if you were 12 feet tall you now can't do? Write a short story about your imaginary experiences.

6. To what uses other than wearing to play football can a football helmet be put?

7. Create an idea for a web site that has not been done but you think would be a success.

8. Women's dress hats are no longer fashionable. Develop a strategy to return them to popularity. What will be the main medium you will use in your effort (e.g., television, newspapers, magazines, point-of-purchase display, motion pictures, etc.)? In what ways will you use this medium?

9. Write four new cheers for your school's athletic team. Will they be humorous, musical, rhyming, tough, friendly, congratulatory, encouraging, etc.? Will they follow a particular presentation style such as rap, hip-hop, etc.?

10. Brainstorm designs to make a computer table more useful, practical, and/or portable. Select 10 improvements you like best and add as many of these as possible to a drawing or a model of your improved computer table. Style, practicality, aesthetics, and utility should be important considerations in your plan.

11. What are seven new ideas for the use of post-it notes. Try to think of uses other than those of anyone else. If possible, demonstrate in class the new use for this product.

12. What major lead news story might be hidden in:

    a circus parade

    a howling dog

    a jack-o-lantern

    a man's stocking

13. Invent a snack food you think would be well-liked but is different from anything with which you are familiar on today's market. What research and marketing steps must you follow before your new product is mass produced?

14. Write five equally effective headlines for the lead story in today's sports section of the newspaper. Try to make your headline four words or fewer yet descriptive of the sporting event that occurred. Try to make it provocative so readers will choose to complete the article. Without reading the newspaper article, write one of your own describing the sporting event. Read the newspaper article and compare and contrast your work with the newspaper's. Did you cover all pertinent information? Did you use a writing style conducive to newspaper articles, etc.?

15. Design, name, and develop a magazine ad for a cartoon character who represents a sport's shoe company. Decide on the major advertising approach you will use (e.g., propaganda, celebrity endorsement, prestige, etc.). Learn the characteristics of a good magazine advertisement and incorporate as many as possible into your ad. If you have access to a computer program and/or camcorder allowing animation do an animated commercial in lieu of a magazine advertisement.

16. What would be a suitable name for a home for retired NASCAR drivers? Write a newspaper article about the home's dedication ceremony and residents by succinctly answering the questions who, what, when, where, why, how, and how many.

17. Create a single word to describe each of the following:
    - hometown fans who throw back onto the field an opposing team's home run ball.
    - a curved foot long hot dog containing bacon, three cheeses, special sauce, onion rings, french fries, tomato, lettuce, pickle, mustard, jalapeno peppers, and catsup served on a croissant roll.

18. What is the title of your favorite book, magazine, movie, or television show? Propose five other titles you think would be equally or more effective.

19. Make a list of things that go up and down.

20. Make a list of things that are round.

Science

1. Create an invention that demonstrates the principle of the simple pulley using a soda straw, a cup, two yards' length of string, a stapler, a piece of cardboard 3 feet long, 2 feet wide and a minimum of one-fourth inch thick, two empty soda pop bottles, transparent tape, a scissors, four empty spools, a small saw, and two 3-foot dowels. You may alter the materials as desired and do not need to use all of the listed items in your final invention. Some of the items may serve only as tools. Explain and demonstrate your invention to the class.

2. Classify the following gibberish words into as many categories as possible:

hmda	kmor	ftam	ecto	wyrr
belk	cvst	arf	turr	reg
xel	jul	sdo	ghak	botts

3. Create original similes using content you studied in science (biology, zoology, chemistry, physics, etc.):

flexible as . . .   twinkling like . . .   odorous as . . .   clear as . . .

strong as . . .   screaming like . . .   blue as . . .   elusive as . . .

bright as . . .   treacherous as . . .   mild as . . .   elegant as . . .

   Explain your choices to the class.

4. Create a unique name for a store selling together the following: pharmaceuticals, playground equipment, electric appliances, exotic animals, and Harley-Davidson motorcycles. Design a layout for the store and indicate where the various merchandise would be located and how they would be displayed. What considerations must be made to ensure the merchandise does not interfere one with the other?

5. List seven things we encounter regularly that operate on the principle of the simple incline.

6. Make a thorough drawing or a scale model of an invention for:

   tying a bow tie

   a practical total home car wash

   an inflatable playhouse

   a retractable stair lift for the kitchen

   Detail is important as are the scientific principles needed to be considered to successfully complete a life-size prototype of this invention.

7. Brainstorm ways to reduce the ozone pollution in your town. What things will you need to know when you complete generating possible solutions to the problem before you can decide which solutions are best? What may be helpful to know before you begin your brainstorming session?

8. Describe five ways in which a simple telescope, microscope, Bunsen burner, barometer, tachometer, etc., may be improved to make it more effective and useful.

9. Of what new and useful functions can you think for a Segway®? Draw or make a model of your favorite idea and demonstrate it to your class. To your knowledge, are there things not yet invented necessary to the actual completion of your idea? Can you name the genius from the Renaissance era who created a model of the helicopter, but could not successfully complete a manned aircraft because other discoveries had not yet been made making this possible?

   Can the new functions for your Segway® help in:

   environmental research

   medical assistance

   oceanographic research

   space exploration

   wildlife conservation?

   If so, how? If not, what will be the vehicle's primary use? What will you need to know prior to starting this exercise?

10. List five items to which Vitamin E may be added to increase their marketability. What information will you need to gain about the items and Vitamin E before you can make cogent recommendations for their combining? Prepare a defense for your favorite choice to present to your class.

11. Using your ideas as a guide, decorate a van or truck for your store.

12. Invent a new cereal for children. Consider taste, uniqueness, and health.

13. Create a chain reaction to: (a) wash a dog, (b) crack an acorn, (c) wake a person up in the morning.

14. Develop an underground city, a city in the ocean, or a city on the moon.

Social Studies

1. If you were an individual with truly super powers, how would you use them? Generate a list of super powers you would like to possess. From this list, choose three powers you would most want. Generate a list of things you could do with these combined powers. Choose the one you best like and create a comic book about your exploits. Will it benefit humankind? Will it benefit the environment? Will it benefit wildlife? Will it benefit you? Or, will your super powers be used in other ways?

2. Many fairy tales have universal similarity. Although some of the details may differ, the basic plot is the same. Locate as many cultures as possible having a Cinderella story. Try to find translations of the original tale from each country. Compare and contrast those tales with the version told in the Walt Disney movie/video. What assumptions can be drawn about the various cultures based upon their version of Cinderella? Compare and contrast your assumptions about the various cultures. Do you think your assumptions accurately describe the culture as a whole? Why or why not?

3. Premiums given with the purchase of a product are intended to enhance that product's sale. Yet, to the seller, the premium cannot be of great cost compared to the original product's cost.

     For instance, a fast food chain may offer a pressed plastic model, of very little cost to them, as their prize with the sale of their childrens' meal. Oftentimes, these premiums have tie-ins to movies or TV shows the sellers hope will be popular with their primary user. Extensive demographic information is collected and analyzed when premium choices are made. Develop a survey instrument asking anonymous, nonthreatening information about your school mates. Tabulate this information and develop a profile of demographic information about the student body in your school. Next, develop a questionnaire asking a representative group of your classmates to list the premiums most motivating in their hypothetical purchase of:

     a man's cologne

     a hair dryer

     a woman's high school graduation ring

     a dune buggy

     a Recreational Van

     Establish the criteria a response from your pilot group must meet to be reasonable to include in a list to be presented to the total school body. Tabulate your lists and develop a questionnaire containing the most reasonable responses asking the total school to prioritize the three premiums they would most like for the purchase of each of the products.

4. How might our country and/or world be different if:

     Columbus had landed on the west coast of America

     Elvis Presley had been an opera singer

     George Washington had been born in England

     Adolf Hitler had been accidentally killed as a youth

     Abraham Lincoln had not been assassinated

     JFK's brother, Joseph Kennedy, had not been killed in World War II

5. Pretend you are an archeologist in the year 3000 A.D. having just completed an excavation of a room in your house without having any prior knowledge of what the things in it actually were or how they were used. Develop an imaginary log of what you, as a future archeologist, may think the things in the room of your choice were and how they were used. Be creative. The wilder the better!

6. What is the name of your town? How did it get that name? Was it originally called what it is today? If you were asked to rename your town, what would you call it? Why?

7. Compare and contrast the nonviolent protest movement of Gandhi and Martin Luther King, Jr.

Mathematics

1. Measure the length of one of your paces and record it using the metric and/or U.S. measurement system. Pace-off a selected area such as a parking lot, a hallway, a gymnasium, etc. Translate the number of your paces into linear measure. Next, measure the same area with an accurate measuring device. Is there a difference? If so, what is it? How could using pacing instead of accurate measurement affect some of your school sporting events?

2. Given an answer to a problem, brainstorm the number of ways in which that answer may be arrived.

3. Amount of shelf space in a supermarket is important to product manufacturers. Contact a manufacturer and ask about the mathematics involved in designing packages for optimum usage of shelf space. Ask about things such as volume, weight, size, product type, package shape, etc.

4. Discover how mathematics is used in the following occupations:

   animator

   veterinarian

   chiropractor

   film and/or video tape editor

   NASCAR mechanic and/or pit crew boss

5. Design a geodesic house using geometric principles.

Summary

Students who are talented and gifted can be found in every school and their identification is the first step in ensuring that they have the opportunity to develop to their fullest potential. Because the classroom teacher plays an important role in that process, this chapter has provided a description of the characteristics of students who are gifted and a review of the ways in which they are assessed and identified. Although differentiated services for these students are not mandated by federal law, their unique abilities require special attention in the schools. Unfortunately, programming for these students typically receives less funding and focus than programming for other students who have special needs. As a result of the limited funding and the trend toward inclusive classrooms, the primary responsibility for the education of students who are gifted may be delegated to the classroom teacher. Although some school districts do provide resource room or special class placements for these students, many of them will continue to remain in the general education classroom for at least part of their educational experience. The instructional strategies presented in this chapter assist classroom teachers as they nurture and encourage the development of these students' unique abilities.

Classroom Application Activities

1. Generate a list of individuals you consider to be gifted. Would these individuals qualify for placement in a gifted program using the definitions in this chapter? In your state or school district?

2. Discuss inclusion. Should students who are gifted be served only by an inclusion model? What would be the advantages of this service delivery model? The disadvantages?

3. Gina does not have an IQ score above 130. She is an extremely motivated and creative young lady. If she has above grade level achievement, could she qualify for gifted placement in some states? What about in your state or district?

4. Gifted education has been controversial over the years. Why? What is the controversy?

5. Discuss the difference between the two types of IQ tests described in this chapter. Why would a district or school system choose to use one over the other?

6. Discuss the neglected gifted. Why do you suppose that these groups are underrepresented?

7. Administrative models for gifted programs vary from state to state. Should there be a national norm for service and/or identification procedures for gifted education? Why or why not?

Internet Resources

Center for Talent Development
www.ctd.northwestern.edu/index.html

Council for Exceptional Children
http://www.cec.sped.org

Educational Resources Information Center (ERIC)
http://www.ericec.org

Gifted and Talented Resources List
http://www.isd77.k12.mn.us/resources/g&tresources.txt

Center for Talented Youth
http://www.jhu.edu/~gifted

Free Spirit Publishing, Serving kids' emotional needs
www.freespirit.com

Great Potential Press, Guiding the Gifted Learner
www.greatpotentialpress.com

Interact: Learn through Experience
www.teachinteract.com

National Research center on the Gifted and Talented
http://www.gifted.uconn.edu/nrcgt.html

National Association For Gifted Children
http://www.nagc.org

Pieces of Learning, Specializing in Differentiated Instruction
www.piecesoflearning.com

Providing Curriculum Alternatives to Motivate Gifted Students
http://www.kidsource.com/education/motivate.gifted.html

Prufrock Press
http://www.prufrock.com

Blending Gifted Education and School Reform
http://www.kidsource.com/kidsource/content/Blending_Gifted_Ed.html

Supporting the Emotional Needs of the Gifted
www.sengifted.org

Ten Tips for Parents of Gifted Children
http://www.hoagiesgifted.org/ten_tips.htm

World Council for Gifted and Talented Children
http://www.worldgifted.org

References

Amabile, T.M. (1989). *Growing up creative: Nurturing a lifetime of creativity.* New York: Crown Publishers, Inc.

Ambrose, D. (2002). Socioeconomic stratification and its influence on talent development: Some interdisciplinary perspectives. *Gifted Child Quarterly, 46*(3), 170–180.

American Association of University Women (1992). *How schools short-change girls.* Washington, DC: AAUW Educational Foundation.

Baldwin, A.Y. (1991). Ethnic and cultural issues. In N. Colangelo & G.A. Davis (Eds.), *Handbook of gifted education* (pp. 416–427). Boston: Allyn & Bacon.

Barnett, L., & Durden, W. (1993). Education patterns of academically talented youth. *Gifted Child Quarterly, 37,* 161–168.

Baum, S. (1990). *Gifted but learning disabled: A puzzling paradox.* Reston, VA: Council for Exceptional Children (ERIC Digest E479).

Belanger, J., & Gagne, F. (2006). Estimating the size of the gifted/talented population from multiple identification criteria. *Journal for the Education of the Gifted, 30*(2), 131–163.

Benbow, C.P., & Minor, L.L. (1990). Cognitive profiles of verbally and mathematically precocious students: Implications for identifications of the gifted. *Gifted Child Quarterly, 34*(1), 21–26.

Berk, L. (2003). *Child development* (6th ed.). Boston: Allyn & Bacon.

Betts, G., & Neihart, M. (2004, Fall). Profiles of the gifted and talented. *Gifted Child Quarterly.*

Bianco, M., Harris, B., Garrison-Wade, D., & Leech, N. (2011). Gifted girls: Gender bias in gifted referrals. *Roeper Review, 33,* 170–181.

Borland, J.H., & Wright, L. (1994). Identifying young, potentially gifted, economically disadvantaged students. *Gifted Child Quarterly, 38,* 164–171.

Callahan, C.M. (1991). The assessment of creativity. In N. Colangelo & G.A. Davis (Eds.), *Handbook of gifted education* (pp. 219–235). Boston: Allyn & Bacon.

Cattell, R.B. (1971). *Abilities: Their structure, growth, and action.* Boston: Houghton Mifflin.

Chen, C., Sable, J., & Noel, A.M. (2011). *Documentation to the Common Core of Data State Nonfiscal Survey of Public Elementary/Secondary Education: School Year 2009–10* (NCES 2011-350rev). U.S. Department of Education. Washington, DC: National Center for Education Statistics. From http://nces.ed.gov/pubsearch/pubsinfo.asp?pubid=2011350rev.

Clark, B. (2007). *Growing Up Gifted* (7th ed.). Englewood Cliffs, NJ: Prentice-Hall.

Clasen, D.R., Middleton, J.A., & Connell, T.J. (1994). Assessing artistic and problem-solving performance in minority and nonminority students using a nontraditional multidimensional approach. *Gifted Child Quarterly, 38,* 27–32.

Colangelo, N., Assouline, S.G., & Gross, M. (2004). *A nation deceived: How schools hold back America's brightest students.* Connie Belin & Jacqueline N. Blank International Center for Gifted Education and Talent Development, Iowa City, Iowa.

Colangelo, N., & Davis, G.A. (1997). Introduction and overview. In N. Colangelo & G.A. Davis (Eds.), *Handbook of gifted education* (2nd ed., pp. 3–9). Boston: Allyn & Bacon.

Coleman, L.J., & Cross, T.L. (2001). *Being Gifted in School: An introduction to development, guidance, and teaching.* Waco, TX: Prufrock Press.

Corn, A.L., & Ryser, B. (1989). Access to print for students with low vision. *Journal of Visual Impairment & Blindness, 83,* 340–349.

Council for Exceptional Children (1981). *Gifted and talented multi-media kit, Meeting the needs of gifted and talented students.* Reston, VA: Author.

Council for Exceptional Children. (2012). *The President's FY 2013 Budget: What does it mean for Special and Gifted Education?* Policy Insider, http://www.policyinsider.org/2012/02/the-presidents-fy-2013-budget-what-does-it-mean-for-special-and-gifted-education.html#more.

Covington, M.V. (1984). The self-worth theory of academic motivation: Findings and applications. *Elementary School Journal, 85,* 5–20.

Cramond, B. (2001). Fostering creative thinking. In F. Karnes & S. Bean (Eds.). *Methods and materials for teaching the gifted* (pp. 399–406). Waco, TX: Prufrock Press.

Cramond, B. (2004). Can we, should we, need we agree on a definition of giftedness? *Roeper Review, 27*(1), 15–16.

Daniels, S. (1997). Creativity in the classroom: Characteristics, climate, and curriculum. In N. Colangelo & G.A. Davis (Eds.), *Handbook of gifted education* (2nd ed., pp. 292–307). Boston: Allyn & Bacon.

Davis, G.A., & Rimm, S.B. (1998). *Education of the gifted and talented* (4th ed.). Boston: Allyn & Bacon.

Educational Testing Service (2006). *2006 college-bound seniors: A profile of SAT program test takers.* Princeton, NJ: Author.

Emerick, L.J. (1992). Academic underachievement among the gifted: Students' perceptions of factors that reverse the pattern. *Gifted Child Quarterly, 36,* 140–146.

Feldhusen, J.F. (March, 1989). Synthesis of research on gifted youth. *Educational Leadership,* 6–11.

Feldhusen, J.F., Hoover, S.M., & Sayler, M.F. (1990). *Identifying and educating gifted students at the secondary level.* New York: Trillium Press.

Ford, D.Y. (1998). The under-representation of minority students in gifted education: Problems and promises in recruitment and retention. *The Journal of Special Education, 32,* 4–14.

Ford, D.Y. (2010). Underrepresentation of culturally different students in gifted education: Reflections about current problems and recommendations for the future. *Gifted Child Today, 33*(3), 31–35.

Ford, D.Y., Grantham, T.C., & Whiting, G.W. (2008). Culturally and linguistically diverse students in gifted education: Recruitment and retention issues. *Exceptional Children, 74*(3), 289–306.

Ford, D.Y., & Harris, J.J. (1990). On discovering the hidden treasures of gifted and talented African-American children. *Roeper Review, 13,* 27–32.

Ford, D.Y., & Thomas, A. (1997). *Underachievement among gifted minority students: Problems and promises.* (Report No. EDO-EC 95-7). Washington, DC: Office of Educational Research and Improvement. (ERIC Document Reproduction Service No. ED409660.)

Frasier, M.M. (1994). *Frasier Talent Assessment Profile—Revised*. Athens, GA: The University of Georgia.

Gagne, F. (2004). An imperative, but alas, improbable consensus! *Roeper Review, 27*(1), 12–14.

Gallagher, J.J. (1985). *Teaching the gifted child* (3rd ed.). Boston: Allyn & Bacon.

Gallagher, J.J. (2004). No Child Left Behind and gifted education. *Roeper Review, 26*, 121–12.

Gallagher, J.J., & Gallagher, S.A. (1994). *Teaching the gifted* (4th ed.). Boston: Allyn & Bacon.

Galton, F. (1869). *Hereditary genius*. London: Macmillan.

Gardner, H. (1983). *Frames of mind: The theory of multiple intelligences*. New York: Basic Books.

Gardner, H., & Hatch, T. (1989). Multiple intelligences go to school: Educational implications of the theory of multiple intelligences. *Educational Researcher, 18*(8), 6.

Getzels, J.W., & Jackson, P.W. (1962). *Creativity and intelligence*. New York: Wiley.

Grantham, T.C., Ford, D.Y., Henfield, M.S., Scott, M.T., Harmon, D.A., Porcher, S., & Price, C. (2011). *Gifted and advanced black students in school*. Waco, TX: Prufrock Press.

Guilford, J.P. (1950). Creativity. *American Psychologist, 5*, 444–454.

Guilford, J.P. (1959). Three faces of intellect. *American Psychologist, 14*, 469–479.

Hallahan, D.P., Kauffman, J.M., & Pullen, P.C. (2009). *Exceptional learners*. Needham Heights, MA: Allyn & Bacon.

Halle, T.G., Kurtz-Costes, B., & Mahoney, J.L. (1997). Family influences on school achievement in low income African American children. *Journal of Educational Psychology, 89*, 527–537.

Halpern, D. (1989). The disappearance of cognitive gender differences: What you see depends on where you look. *American Psychologist, 44*, 1156–1158.

Hammer, E.F. (1961). Creativity. New York: Random House.

Hebert, T.P. (2001). *"If I had a new notebook, I know things would change"*, Bright achieving young men in urban classrooms. *Gifted Child Quarterly, 45*, 174–194.

Hebert, T.P. (2002). Gifted males. In M. Neihart, S.M. Reis, N.M. Robinson, & S.M. Moon (Eds.), *The social and emotional development of gifted children: What do we know?* (pp. 137–144). Waco, TX: Prufrock Press.

Henson II, F.O. (1976). *Mainstreaming the gifted*. Austin, TX: Learning Concepts.

Hill, N.E. (2001). Parenting and academic socialization as they relate to school readiness: The roles of ethnicity and family income. *Journal of Educational Psychology, 93*, 686–697.

Howley, A., Howley, C.B., & Pendarvis, E.D. (1986). *Teaching gifted children*. Boston: Little Brown.

Jenkins-Friedman, R., & Nielsen, M.E. (1990). Gifted and talented students. In E. L. Meyen (Ed.), *Exceptional children in today's schools* (2nd ed., pp. 451–493). Denver, CO: Love.

Johnson, L.J., Karnes, M.B., & Carr, V.W. (1997). Providing services to children with gifts and disabilities: A critical need. In N. Colangelo & G.A. Davis (Eds.), *Handbook of gifted education* (2nd ed., pp. 516–527). Boston: Allyn & Bacon.

Kaplan, S. (1974). *Providing programs for the gifted and talented: A handbook*. Ventura, CA: Office of the Ventura County Superintendent of Schools.

Kaplan, S.N. (2004). Where we stand determines the answer to the question: Can the No Child Left Behind legislation be beneficial to gifted students? *Roeper Review, 26*, 124–125.

Kaufman, A.S. (1992). Evaluation of WISC-R and WIPSI-R for gifted children. *Roeper Review, 15*, 154–158.

Kennedy, D.M. (1995). Plain talk about creating a gifted-friendly classroom. *Roeper Review, 17*(4), 232–234.

Kerr, B. (1997). Developing talents in girls and young women. In N. Colangelo & G.A. Davis (Eds.), *Handbook of gifted education* (2nd ed., pp. 483–497). Boston: Allyn & Bacon.

Kimball, M. (1989). A new perspective on women's math achievement. *Psychological Bulletin, 105*, 198–214.

Kitano, M.K. (1989). The K-3 teacher's role in recognizing and supporting young gifted children. *Young Children, 44*(3), 57–63.

Kitano, M.K., & Dijiosia, M. (2002). Are Asian and Pacific Americans over represented in programs for the gifted? *Roeper Review, 24*(2), 76–80.

Kolloff, P.B. (1997). Special residential high schools. In N. Colangelo & G.A. Davis (Eds.), *Handbook of gifted education* (2nd ed., pp. 198–206). Boston: Allyn & Bacon.

Kulik, J.A. (1992). *An analysis of the research on ability grouping: Historical and contemporary perspectives*. Research-Based Decision Making Series. Storrs, CT: National Research Center on the Gifted and Talented, University of Connecticut.

Lovett, B.J., & Lewandowski, L.J. (2006). Gifted students with leaning disabilities: Who are they? *Journal of Learning Disabilities, 39*(6), 515–527.

Lucito, L. (1963). Gifted children. In L. Dunn (Ed.), *Exceptional children in the schools* (pp. 179–238). New York: Holt, Rinehart and Winston.

Lyman, H. (1997). *Test scores and what they mean* (6th ed.). Boston: Allyn and Bacon.

MacKinnon, D.W. (1962). The nature and nurture of creative talent. *American Psychologist, 17*(7), 484–495.

Malcomson, B. (1988). Opening your eyes. *Gifted Children Today*, May/June, 2–6.

Marland, S. (1972). *Education of the gifted and talented.* Report to the Subcommittee on Education, Committee on Labor and Public Welfare, U.S. Senate. Washington, DC: GPO.

McClusky, K.W., Baker, P.A., & McClusky, A.L. (2005). Creative problem solving with marginalized populations: Reclaiming lost prizes through in the trenches interventions. *Gifted Child Quarterly, 49,* 330–341.

Meece, J.L., Blumenfeld, P.C., & Hoyle, R.H. (1988). Students' goal orientations and cognitive engagements in classroom activities. *Journal of Educational Psychology, 80,* 514–523.

Mendoza, C. (2006). Inside today's classrooms: Teacher voices on No Child Left Behind and the education of gifted children. *Roeper Review, 29*(1), 28–31.

Morelock, M. (1996). The nature of giftedness and talent: Imposing order on chaos. *Roeper Review, 19*(1), 4–12.

Neumeister, K.L., Adams, C.M., Pierce, R.L., & Dixon, F.A. (2007). Fourth-grade teachers' perceptions of giftedness: Implications for identifying and serving diverse gifted students. *Journal for the Education of the Gifted, 30*(4), 479–499.

Parke, B.N. (1989). *Gifted students in regular classrooms.* Boston: Allyn & Bacon.

Pegnato, C.C., & Birch, J.W. (1959). Locating gifted children in junior high school. *Exceptional Children, 25,* 300–304.

Pendarvis, E.D. (1993). Students with unique gifts and talents. In A.E. Blackhurst & W.H. Berdine (Eds.), *An introduction to special education* (3rd ed., pp. 563–599). New York: Harper Collins.

Peterson, J.S. (1997). Bright, tough, and resilient—and not in a gifted program. *Journal of Secondary Gifted Education, 8*(3), 121–136.

Pfeiffer, S.I. (2003). Challenges and opportunities for students who are gifted: What the experts say. *Gifted Child Quarterly, 47*(2), 161–169.

Ramos-Ford, V., & Gardner, H. (1997). Giftedness from a multiple intelligence perspective. In N. Colangelo & G.A. Davis (Eds.), *Handbook of gifted education* (2nd ed., pp. 54–66). Boston: Allyn & Bacon.

Reis, S. (2005, March). *Why Gifted and Talented Students Underachieve in School.* Presented at the Georgia Association for Gifted Children Conference.

Reis, S.M. (1987). We can't change what we don't recognize: Understanding the special needs of gifted females. *Gifted Child Quarterly, 31*(2), 83–88.

Reis, S.R. (1998). *Work left undone: Compromises and challenges of talented females.* Mansfield Center, CT: Creative Learning Press.

Renzulli, J.S. (1978). What makes giftedness? Reexamining a definition. *Phi Delta Kappan, 60*(3), 180–184, 261.

Renzulli, J.S., & Reis, S.M. (1997). The schoolwide enrichment model: New directions for developing high-end learning. In N. Colangelo & G.A. Davis (Eds.), *Handbook of gifted education* (2nd ed., pp. 136–154). Boston: Allyn & Bacon.

Renzulli, J., Reis, S., & Smith, L. (1981). *The revolving door identification model.* Mansfield Center, CT: Creative Learning Press.

Renzulli, J., & Smith, L. (1980). An alternative approach to identifying and programming for gifted and talented students. *Gifted/Creative/Talented, 15,* 4–11.

Renzulli, J.S., Smith, L.H., White, A.J., Callahan, C.M., & Hartman, R.K. (1976). *Scales for rating the behavior characteristics of superior students.* Mansfield Center, CT: Creative Learning Press.

Rimm, S. (1999). *See Jane run.* New York: Random House.

Rimm, S.B., & Lovance, K.J. (1992). The use of subject and grade skipping for the prevention and reversal of underachievement. *Gifted Child Quarterly, 36,* 100–105.

Roach, R. (2002). Report touts federal role in solving digital divide. *Black Issues in Higher Education, 19*(12), 23–27.

Robinson, A., Bradley, R.H., & Stanley, T.D. (1990). Opportunity to achieve: Identifying mathematically gifted Black students. *Contemporary Educational Psychology, 15*(1), 1–2.

Rosser, P. (1989). *Sex bias in college admission tests: Why women lose out.* Cambridge, MA: National Center for Fair and Open Testing.

Sadker, M., & Sadker, D. (1985). Sexism in the schoolroom in the '80s. *Psychology Today, 19,* 54–57.

Schiever, S.W., & Maker, C.J. (1997). Enrichment and acceleration: An overview and new directions. In N. Colangelo & G.A. Davis (Eds.), *Handbook of gifted education* (2nd ed., pp. 113–125). Boston: Allyn & Bacon.

Scott, M., & Delgado, C. (2005). Identifying cognitively gifted minority students in preschool. *Gifted Child Quarterly, 49*(3), 199–210.

Shields, C.M. (2002). A comparison study of student attitudes and perceptions in homogeneous and heterogeneous classrooms. *Roeper Review, 24*(3), 115–119.

Siegel, D. (2008, June). Why we should have gifted education programs. *Parenting for High Potential,* 3.

Siegle, D., & Reis, S.M. (1994). Gender differences in teacher and student perceptions of students' abilities and effort. *Journal of Secondary Gifted Education, 6*(2), 86–92.

Sowell, E. (1993). Programs for mathematically gifted students: A review of empirical research. *Gifted Child Quarterly, 37,* 124–132.

Sowell, E.J., Bergwall, L.K., Zeigler, A.J., & Cartwright, R.M. (1990). Identification and description of mathematically gifted students: A review of empirical research. *Gifted Child Quarterly, 34*(4), 147–154.

Spencer, S.J., Steele, C.M., & Quinn, D.M. (1999). Stereotype threat and women's math performance. *Journal of Experimental Social Psychology, 35,* 4–28.

Spruill, J. (1987). Stanford-Binet Intelligence Scale (4th ed.). In D. Keyser & R. Sweetland (Eds.), *Test critiques: Volume VI,* (pp. 544–559). Kansas City, MO: Test Corporation of America.

Stanley, J.C. (1978). Identifying and nurturing the intellectually gifted. In R. E. Clasen & B Robinson (Eds.), *Simple gifts.* Madison, WI: University of Wisconsin Extension.

Stanley, J.C., & Benbow, C.P. (1986). Youths who reason exceptionally well mathematically. In R.J. Sternberg & J.E. Davidson (Eds.), *Conceptions of giftedness* (pp. 361–387). New York: Cambridge University Press.

Steele, C.M. (1997). A threat in the air: How stereotypes shape the intellectual identities and performance of women and African-Americans. *American Psychologist, 52,* 613–629.

Stein, J.C., Hetzel, J., & Beck, R. (2012). Twice exceptional: The plight of the gifted English language learner. *Delta Kappa Gamma Bulletin, 78*(2), 36–41.

Sternberg, R.J. (1981). A componential theory of intellectual giftedness. *Gifted Child Quarterly, 25,* 86–93.

Sternberg, R.J. (1982). Lies we live by: Misapplication of tests in identifying the gifted. *Gifted Child Quarterly, 26,* 157–161.

Sternberg, R.J. (1988). A triarchic theory of intellectual giftedness. In R.J. Sternberg & J.E. Davidson (Eds.), *Conceptions of Giftedness* (pp. 223–243). New York: Cambridge University Press.

Sternberg, R.J., Jarvin, L., & Grigorenko, E.L. (2011). *Explorations in giftedness,* Cambridge: Cambridge University Press.

Terman, L.M. (1925). *Genetic studies of genius.* Vol. 1. Mental and physical traits of a thousand gifted children. Stanford, CA: Stanford University Press.

Terwilliger, J.S., & Titus, J.C. (1995). Gender differences in attitudes and attitude changes among mathematically talented youth. *Gifted Child Quarterly, 39,* 29–35.

Tomlinson, C.A. (2004). *How to Differentiate Instruction in Mixed-Ability Classrooms.* Upper Saddle River, NJ: Prentice-Hall.

Torrance, E.P. (1965). *Rewarding creative behavior.* Englewood Cliffs, NJ: Prentice-Hall.

Torrance, E.P. (1966). *Torrance tests of creative thinking.* Princeton, NJ: Personnel.

Torrance, E.P. (1981). *Thinking creatively in action and movement.* Bensonville, IL: Scholastic Testing Services.

Torrance, E.P. (1984). *Mentor relationships.* Buffalo, NY: Bearly Limited.

U.S. Department of Education (1991). *National educational longitudinal study 88. Final report: Gifted and talented education programs for eighth grade public school students.* Washington, DC: Author.

U.S. Department of Education. Office of Communications and Outreach. (2008). *Guide to U.S. Department of Education programs,* Washington, DC: Author.

U.S. Department of Education's Office of Educational Research and Improvement. (1993). *National Excellence: A case for developing America's talent.* Washington DC: U.S. Government Printing Office.

VanTassel-Baska, J. (1994). *Comprehensive curriculum for gifted learners* (2nd ed.). Boston: Allyn & Bacon.

VanTassel-Baska, J. (1998). Appropriate curriculum for the talented learner. In J. Van Tassel-Baska (Ed.), *Excellence in educating gifted and talented learners* (3rd ed., pp. 339–361). Denver, CO: Love.

VanTassel-Baska, J. (2005). Politics and children with high potential. *Parenting for High Potential,* September, 3.

VanTassel-Baska, J., Patton, J., & Prillaman (1989). Disadvantaged gifted learners at risk for educational attention. *Focus on Exceptional Children, 22*(3), 1–15.

Walker, B.A., Reis, S.M., & Leonard, J.S. (1992). A developmental investigation of the lives of gifted women. *Gifted Child Quarterly, 36,* 201–206.

Westberg, K., Archambault, F., Dobyns, S., & Slavin, T. (1993). The classroom practices observation study. *Journal for the Education of the Gifted, 16,* 120–146.

Willard-Holt, C. (1994). Strategies for individualizing instruction in regular classrooms. *Roeper Review, 17*(1), 43–45.

Winebrenner, S. (1992). *Teaching gifted kids in the regular classroom.* Minneapolis, MN: Free Spirit Publishing Inc.

What Is Your Classroom Management Profile?

Answer these 12 questions and learn more about your classroom management profile. The steps are simple:

- Read each statement carefully.
- Write your response, from the scale below, on a sheet of paper.
- Respond to each statement based upon either actual or imagined classroom experience.
- Then, follow the scoring instructions below. It couldn't be easier!

1 = Strongly Disagree   2 = Disagree   3 = Neutral   4 = Agree   5 = Strongly Agree

1. If a student is disruptive during class, I assign him/her to detention, without further discussion.
2. I don't want to impose any rules on my students.
3. The classroom must be quiet in order for students to learn.
4. I am concerned about both what my students learn and how they learn.
5. If a student turns in a late homework assignment, it is not my problem.
6. I don't want to reprimand a student because it might hurt his/her feelings.
7. Class preparation isn't worth the effort.
8. I always try to explain the reasons behind my rules and decisions.
9. I will not accept excuses from a student who is tardy.
10. The emotional well-being of my students is more important than classroom control.
11. My students understand that they can interrupt my lecture if they have a relevant question.
12. If a student requests a hall pass, I always honor the request.

To score your quiz,

Add your responses to statements 1, 3, and 9. This is your score for the *authoritarian style*.
Statements 4, 8 and 11 refer to the *authoritative style*.
Statements 6, 10, and 12 refer to the *laissez-faire style*.
Statements 2, 5, and 7 refer to the *indifferent style*.

The result is your classroom management profile. Your score for each management style can range from 3 to 15. A high score indicates a strong preference for that particular style. After you have scored your quiz, and determined your profile, read the descriptions of each management style. You may see a little bit of yourself in each one.

As you gain teaching experience, you may find that your preferred style(s) will change. Over time, your profile may become more diverse or more focused. Also, it may be suitable to rely upon a specific style when addressing a particular situation or subject. Perhaps the successful teacher is one who can evaluate a situation and then apply the appropriate style. Finally, remember that the intent of this exercise is to inform you and arouse your curiosity regarding classroom management styles.

Authoritarian

The authoritarian teacher places firm limits and controls on the students. Students will often have assigned seats for the entire term. The desks are usually in straight rows and there are no deviations. Students must be in their seats at the beginning of class and they frequently remain there throughout the period. This teacher rarely gives hall passes or recognizes excused absences.

Often, it is quiet. Students know they should not interrupt the teacher. Since verbal exchange and discussion are discouraged, the authoritarian's students do not have the opportunity to learn and/or practice communication skills.

This teacher prefers vigorous discipline and expects swift obedience. Failure to obey the teacher usually results in detention or a trip to the principal's office. In this classroom, students need to follow directions and not ask why.

At the extreme, the authoritarian teacher gives no indication that he/she cares for the students. Mr. Doe is a good example of an authoritarian teacher. His students receive praise and encouragement infrequently, if at all. Also, he makes no effort to organize activities such as field trips. He feels that these special events only distract the students from learning. After all, Mr. Doe believes that students need only listen to his lecture to gain the necessary knowledge.

Students in this class are likely to be reluctant to initiate activity, since they may feel powerless. Mr. Doe tells the students what to do and when to do it. He makes all classroom decisions. Therefore, his style does little to increase achievement motivation or encourage the setting of personal goals.

One middle school pupil reacts to this teaching style:

I don't really care for this teacher. He is really strict and doesn't seem to want to give his students a fair chance. He seems unfair, although that's just his way of getting his point across.

Authoritative

The authoritative teacher places limits and controls on the students but simultaneously encourages independence. This teacher often explains the reasons behind the rules and decisions. If a student is disruptive, the teacher offers a polite, but firm, reprimand. This teacher sometimes metes out discipline, but only after careful consideration of the circumstances.

The authoritative teacher is also open to considerable verbal interaction, including critical debates. The students know that they can interrupt the teacher if they have a relevant question or comment. This environment offers the students the opportunity to learn and practice communication skills.

Ms. Smith exemplifies the authoritative teaching style. She exhibits a warm and nurturing attitude toward the students and expresses genuine interest and affection. Her classroom abounds with praise and encouragement. She often writes comments on homework and offers positive remarks to students. This authoritative teacher encourages self-reliant and socially competent behavior and fosters higher achievement motivation. Often, she will guide the students through a project, rather than lead them.

A student reacts to this style:

I like this teacher. She is fair and understands that students can't be perfect. She is the kind of teacher you can talk to without being put down or feeling embarrassed.

Laissez-faire

The laissez-faire teacher places few demands or controls on the students. "Do your own thing" describes this classroom. This teacher accepts the students' impulses and actions and is less likely to monitor their behavior.

Mr. Jones uses a laissez-faire style. He strives to not hurt the students' feelings and has difficulty saying no to a student or enforcing rules. If a student disrupts the class, Mr Jones may assume that he is not giving that student enough attention. When a student interrupts a lecture, Mr. Jones accepts the interruption with the belief that the student must surely have something valuable to add. When he does offer discipline, it is likely to be inconsistent.

Mr. Jones is very involved with his students and cares for them very much. He is more concerned with the students' emotional well-being than he is with classroom control. He sometimes bases classroom decisions on his students' feelings rather than on their academic concerns.

Mr. Jones wants to be the students' friend. He may even encourage contact outside the classroom. He has a difficult time establishing boundaries between his professional life and his personal life.

However, this overindulgent style is associated with students' lack of social competence and self-control. It is difficult for students to learn socially acceptable behavior when the teacher is so permissive. With few demands placed upon them, these students frequently have lower motivation to achieve.

Regardless, students often like this teacher. A middle school student says:

This is a pretty popular teacher. You don't have to be serious throughout the class. But sometimes things get out of control and we learn nothing at all.

Indifferent

The indifferent teacher is not very involved in the classroom. This teacher places few demands, if any, on the students and appears generally uninterested. The indifferent teacher just doesn't want to impose on the students. As such, he/she often feels that class preparation is not worth the effort. Things like field trips and special projects are out of the question. This teacher simply won't take the necessary preparation time. Sometimes, he/she will use the same materials, year after year.

Also, classroom discipline is lacking. This teacher may lack the skills, confidence, or courage to discipline students.

The students sense and reflect the teacher's indifferent attitude. Accordingly, very little learning occurs. Everyone is just "going through the motions" and killing time. In this aloof environment, the students have very few opportunities to observe or practice communication skills. With few demands placed on them and very little discipline, students have low achievement motivation and lack self-control.

The classroom management styles are adaptations of the parenting styles discussed in *Adolescence,* by John W. Santrock. They were adapted by Kris Bosworth, Kevin McCracken, Paul Haakenson, Marsha Ritter Jones, Anne Grey, Laura Versaci, Julie James, and Ronen Hammer.

Ms. Johnson is a good example of an indifferent teacher. She uses the same lesson plans every year, never bothering to update them. For her, each day is the same. She lectures for the first 20 minutes of class. Sometimes she will show a film or a slideshow. When she does, it becomes a substitute for her lecture, not a supplement. If there is any time left (and there always is) she allows students to study quietly and to talk softly. As long as they don't bother her, she doesn't mind what they do. As far as she is concerned, the students are responsible for their own education.

According to one student:
This teacher can't control the class and we never learn anything in there. There is hardly ever homework and people rarely bring their books.

Source: Used with permission from *Teacher Talk: A Publication for Secondary Education Teachers, 1*(2). Available under the "Resources" link at www. indiana.edu/~cafs/

GLOSSARY

A

ABC MODEL A behavioral model encompassing antecedents, behaviors, and consequences with a focus on observable actions. Chapter 9

ABERRANT BEHAVIOR Behavior that differs from typical behavior in the same situation. It would be aberrant for a 12-year-old student to hit a peer if he lost a game. Chapter 10

ACADEMIC LEARNING TIME Time during which students are making a high rate of correct responses. Chapter 7

ACCELERATION Instructional strategy for students who are gifted that emphasizes advanced subject matter content to be learned and mastered at a faster than usual rate. Included in this are practices such as credit by examination, grade-skipping, advanced placement, joint enrollment, and telescoping grade levels. Chapter 13

ACCOMMODATIONS Any changes made to the instruction or materials that do not change the curriculum expectations. Chapter 1

ADAPTIVE BEHAVIOR The degree to which individuals meet standards of personal independence. Chapter 6

ADHD Abbreviation for "Attention Deficit Hyperactivity Disorder," in which a person has a hard time sustaining attention and completing tasks. Individuals are easily distracted and frequently interrupt others. Students with ADHD may appear as if they are not listening and will fail to follow directions. These attention deficits are accompanied by impulsivity and frequent motor movements, including fidgeting, tapping, and shaking legs. Adolescents may describe that they feel "restless." Chapter 8

ADVANCE ORGANIZER Used to assist students in learning content area material. Assists students in identifying their prior knowledge about a topic and provide information about the goals of the lesson, the activities that will take place during the lesson, and the teacher's expectations of the students. Chapter 7

ALLOCATED LEARNING TIME The amount of time an instructor assigns for instructional tasks. Chapter 7

ALTERNATIVE PERFORMANCE STRATEGY A manner of performing a behavior (form), other than that usually done by a nondisabled person, which achieves the same result (function). Chapter 12

ANTECEDENT An event preceding a behavior and serving as a cue or inhibition of a response. Chapter 12

AMERICAN SIGN LANGUAGE (ASL) A manual communication system used by the deaf community in the United States. Chapter 11

ARTICULATION DISORDER A type of speech-sound disorder in which a child has difficulty moving the structures of the mouth precisely to make a speech sound. Chapter 11

ASSISTIVE TECHNOLOGY DEVICES Items or equipment designed to increase, maintain, or improve the functional capabilities of individuals with disabilities. Chapter 11

AUTHORITARIAN TEACHING STYLE Teachers who use an authoritarian style tend to create unrealistically high expectations, demand strict conformity, and impose harsh sanctions on students who violate the rules. These teachers tend to emphasize the punitive consequences for rule violations rather than the positive consequences for rule adherence. People who adopt an authoritarian style behave similarly to oppressive dictators. Unfortunately, this style is associated with high student dropout rates. Chapter 9

AUTHORITATIVE TEACHING STYLE The teaching style that has been found to be most effective for promoting achievement. Authoritative teachers have realistic expectations for students and establish clear expectations for academic and social behavior. Rules are enforced consistently, and authoritative teachers use reasoning and positive approaches to discipline. Chapter 9

AUTISM SPECTRUM DISORDERS Current term being used to refer to the diverse population of individuals with autism and autism-related disorders (i.e., Asperger's, Rett's, Childhood Disintegrative disorder, and pervasive developmental disorders). This term reflects that each individual with autism is uniquely affected and can be impaired on a continuum from mild to severe. Chapter 10

B

BASIC PSYCHOLOGICAL PROCESSES Functions that the brain performs in order to interpret, apply, and store stimuli and information. This term includes short- or long-term memory; auditory, visual, and haptic discrimination; sequencing; attention; organization; psychomotor skills and visual motor integration; conceptualization and reasoning; and social perception. Chapter 6

BEHAVIOR DISORDERS OR EMOTIONAL DISTURBANCES Behaviors that are chronically and significantly different from those others; mannerisms or behaviors that are considered unacceptable. Chapter 1

BEHAVIOR INTERVENTION PLAN A plan mandated in the IDEA 1997 Amendments for any special education student exhibiting behavioral difficulties. The behavior intervention plan is to be based upon the results of a functional behavioral assessment and should have a positive orientation. The behavior intervention plan must also address contingencies and supports for the student and teachers in addressing behavioral difficulties. Chapter 9

BEHAVIOR PAIRS Effective teachers identify the opposite of the misbehavior and use reinforcement to increase students' demonstration of the alternative. For example, the behavior pair of calling out in class is to raise the hand and wait to be called on. Reinforcement is used to increase students' abilities to raise their hands and wait to be called on before speaking. Chapter 9

BIPOLAR DISORDER A mood disorder that affects the brain as well as the nervous system and causes extreme mood swings from severe depression involving suicidal thoughts or actions to mania or elation. Chapter 8

BLIND A term to describe individuals who are totally without vision or who have only light perception and use other senses (i.e., hearing and touch) as primary channels for receiving information. Chapter 11

BRAILLE A system of raised dots that represents letters or whole words that allows individuals who have severe visual impairments or who are blind to read. Chapter 11

C

CENTRAL HEARING LOSS A type of hearing loss caused by damage to the auditory cortex of the brain. Chapter 11

CLOCS-RAM A mnemonic for the eight keys to providing effective instruction (clarity, level, opportunities, consequences, sequence, relevance, application, monitoring). Chapter 9

CLUSTER GROUPING Gathering groups of students with similar abilities together in the regular classroom for learning opportunities suited to their aptitudes. Chapter 13

COCHLEAR IMPLANT A device that delivers electrical stimulation to the auditory nerve through an implanted electrode. It is an amplification option for individuals with severe to profound hearing loss. Chapter 11

COGNITIVE DISABILITIES Disabilities that affect the student's ability to acquire and/or express knowledge; may be demonstrated by difficulties with attention, perception, memory, and the generalization of knowledge and skills. Chapter 1

COLLABORATION Working jointly with others in an endeavor. Chapter 4

COLLABORATIVE LEARNING An instructional strategy in which students work in teams on a project, problem, or task such as studying for a test or creating a presentation. Chapter 7

COMMUNICATION DISORDER An impairment in the ability to receive, send, process, and comprehend concepts or verbal, nonverbal, and graphic symbol systems. Chapter 1

COMMUNITY-BASED INSTRUCTION (CBI) An instructional model that uses community settings as an extension of the classroom. Community-based instruction provides the opportunity for the student to learn and/or practice skills directly in the settings in which performance is required. Chapter 12

COMMUNITY-BASED VOCATIONAL INSTRUCTION (CBVI) A subset of community-based instruction that focuses on job training skills identified in actual community businesses. Chapter 12

COMMUNITY-REFERENCED CURRICULUM Curriculum content based on activities and tasks required in actual community settings. This content is derived from an ecological assessment. Chapter 12

CONCEPT MAP A graphical representation designed to indicate the relationships that exist in a framework of concepts or ideas. Chapter 7

CONDUCT DISORDERS A diagnosis in the DSM-IV, conduct disorders describe antisocial patterns of rule-violating behavior, often directed with the intent to harm others or property. Some authorities describe conduct disorders as failing to have an emotional basis and describe those who have conduct disorders as making a conscious choice to engage in the behaviors, thereby differentiating conduct disorders from emotional disturbances. Chapter 8

CONDUCTIVE HEARING LOSS A type of hearing loss caused by damage to the outer or middle ear. It usually is treatable by medication or surgery. Chapter 11

CONGENITAL A condition or disorder that is existing at birth. Chapter 11

CONSEQUENCE An event following a behavior and strengthening or weakening the chance of the behavior occurring again in the future. Chapter 9

CONTINGENCY A planned or structured relationship between antecedents and consequences. Chapter 12

COOPERATIVE LEARNING Heterogeneous groups of students work together to achieve a common goal. Groups are rewarded based on the progress of the entire group. Chapter 7

CREATIVITY The process of sensing gaps or missing elements; forming ideas or hypotheses; testing these hypotheses; and communicating the results, possibly modifying and retesting the hypotheses. Chapter 13

CULTURALLY AND LINGUISTICALLY DIVERSE STUDENT A student whose primary home culture, race, ethnicity, or language is not that of the mainstream group in a specific society. For example, in the United States, culturally and linguistically diverse students include students from African American, Hispanic/Latino, and Native American racial/ethnic backgrounds, as well as students whose primary home language or dialect is not mainstream American English. Chapter 5

CULTURALLY DIVERSE STUDENT See culturally and linguistically diverse student. Chapter 5

CULTURALLY RELEVANT PEDAGOGY An effective instructional practice and theoretical model that promotes student achievement, supports students' cultural identity, and helps students to develop the critical perspectives needed to challenge inequities in schools and society (Ladson-Billings, 1995). Chapter 5

CULTURE A broad and comprehensive concept that encompasses multiple characteristics, practices, and all the ways of being that one learns throughout the life span as a member of a particular social group, including language use, dress, behavioral norms, values, beliefs, and worldviews. Chapter 5

CURRICULUM The set of instructional knowledge, skills, and activities that comprise a school's program of study. Typically, the curriculum is a reflection of the texts and materials used. Chapter 3

CURRICULUM COMPACTING An instructional strategy for students who are gifted that allows for faster acceptable mastery of the necessary and required content components in a subject area to provide time to work with that content in a more enriching way. Chapter 13

D

DE NOVO MUTATIONS A genetic mutation that neither parent possessed nor transmitted. De novo mutations appear to be responsible for the neurological differences in autism spectrum disorders. Chapter 10

DEAF/deaf Individuals who have a hearing loss and use sign language as their primary mode of communication. Chapter 11

DECONTAMINATION Removing distracting and/or dangerous objects from classrooms so that students are more likely to focus on the instruction and assignments. Chapter 9

DEPENDENT GROUP CONTINGENCY The ability to access reinforcement based on the behavior of a particular student or small group of students. For example, everyone in the class can have 5 minutes of free time if Jerrord stays in his seat all period. Chapter 9

DEPRESSION A pervasive feeling that everything is hopeless and the person experiencing the depression is inadequate or worthless. The feeling is accompanied by a loss of interest in previously enjoyed activities and a low level of energy. Often, depression in children manifests as anger while depression in older adolescents is more similar to that seen in adults (e.g., sadness, lethargy, withdrawal). Chapter 8

DEVELOPMENTAL DELAY Progression at a slower rate than that of typically developing children in areas such as communication, cognition, motor, or social development. Chapter 12

DIFFERENTIAL REINFORCEMENT Providing reinforcement for the desired behavior but withholding reinforcement if the inappropriate behavior occurs. For example, students are called on when they raise their hands but ignored if they speak out of turn. Chapter 9

DIRECT INSTRUCTION A systematic form of instruction that includes explicit step-by-step teaching procedures that account for student mastery, immediate student feedback, student practice, and gradual fading of teaching direction. Chapter 7

DISCREPANCY ANALYSIS The format of direct observation of students performing functional skills to identify current performance capabilities and skills that require instruction. Chapter 12

DIVERGENT THINKING Independent or liberal thinking. It includes producing original work, being open-minded and intellectually curious, and considering many approaches or possible solutions to a problem. Chapter 13

DYSREGULATED Something that is no longer regulated, but is out of balance. Some people become dysregulated when they get upset and will do and say things they regret later. Chapter 10

E

ECHOLALIA The repetition of others' oral speech; often mimicking of the intonation and pitch. Chapter 10

ECOLOGICAL ASSESSMENT Observation of individuals in community settings to identify tasks performed in particular settings. The results of this assessment contribute to the content of a functional curriculum. Chapter 12

EDUCATION The process of learning and developing as a result of schooling and other experiences. Chapter 1

ELIGIBILITY TEAM Those who determine a student's eligibility for special education services, including a school psychologist, special educator, general educator, and parents. Other professionals may be included. Chapter 3

EMOTIONAL/BEHAVIORAL DISORDERS Preferred name for the federal category of emotional disturbances. Chapter 8

EMPATHY Empathy is the act of understanding others from their point of view. It requires active listening, attention to nonverbal communication, and suspension of judgment. It is a helping skill that conveys that a teacher is trying to understand a student's feeling state and cares about the student (You feel ___ when ____). Chapter 4

EMOTIONAL SELF-REGULATION The ability to keep emotions under control and in balance is emotional self-regulation. Some people take deep breaths and count to 10 when they get upset to maintain their emotional self-regulation. Chapter 10

ENGAGED LEARNING TIME The portion of the scheduled time during which students are actually working. Same as time-on-task. Chapter 7

ENRICHMENT PROGRAMS A supplement to the regular curriculum offerings for students who are gifted to expand depth and breadth of understanding. Offerings include independent study programs and electives. Chapter 13

ETHNICITY Referring to the term ethnic group, used to classify a group whose members have a shared national origin, genealogy, or ancestry. Chapter 5

ETIOLOGY The cause of a disability or condition, usually related to biologic or environmental factors. Chapter 11

EXPLICIT INSTRUCTION Model of teaching that includes three main components: (a) demonstration and modeling, (b) guided practice, and (c) independent practice. Chapter 7

EXPRESSIVE LANGUAGE Refers to the production of language and messages sent to others. Chapter 11

EXTERNALIZING DISORDERS When an emotional/behavioral disorder is directed outward at others, it is called externalizing (e.g., aggression, bullying, harassment, cruelty to animals, vandalism). Chapter 8

F

FAMILY CENTERED APPROACH The view that families are competent decision makers who must be equal team members in the decision making process for a child with special needs. Chapter 4

FLUENCY DISORDER An interruption in the flow of oral language. It is a type of communication disorder. Chapter 11

FM (FREQUENCY MODULATED) SYSTEM An assistive listening device often used in classrooms for students who have a hearing loss. Chapter 11

FREE, APPROPRIATE, PUBLIC EDUCATION (FAPE) Mandated with the passage in 1975 of Public Law 94-142, the Education for All Handicapped Children Act; states are required to provide a free, appropriate, public education to all students with disabilities. Chapter 1

FUNCTIONAL BEHAVIOR ASSESSMENT An assessment to determine the function of a special education student's disruptive behavior through an analysis of the antecedents and consequences surrounding the behavior. Specific functions of behavior could include escape (i.e., getting out of an assignment) or attention (either peer or adult). A functional behavior assessment is the initial step in the development of a behavior intervention plan as specified by IDEA 97. Chapter 9

FUNCTIONAL CURRICULUM A curriculum model for students with moderate and severe disabilities. Content is selected based on identified skills needed for functioning in current and future integrated community, residential, and vocational environments. Chapter 12

FUNCTIONAL SKILL A skill required for living an independent and productive adult life (e.g., reading signs, managing money). Chapter 6

FUNCTIONAL VISION EXAM An exam performed by a teacher certified in visual impairments to determine how well a student is using vision and what modifications and adaptations are needed. Chapter 11

G

GROUP ALERTING Teachers use strategies to capture the attention of all students in order to present, clarify, or expand on information about academic content or social expectations. Chapter 9

GUIDED PRACTICE Students work directly under the teacher's supervision on tasks that are new and difficult. Teacher may assist students in producing correct responses through additional models, prompts, or cues. Chapter 7

H

HARD OF HEARING A term to describe individuals who have some amount of hearing loss, but still rely on hearing and listening to communicate and learn. Chapter 11

HEALTH IMPAIRMENTS Chronic or acute health problems that limit an individual's strength, vitality, or alertness. Chapter 11

HEARING IMPAIRMENTS A generic term used to described any type or amount of hearing loss. Chapter 11

HYPERACTIVITY Excessive motor movement given the child's age and gender. Chapter 8

I

IEP TEAM Those who develop and monitor the Individualized Education Program. It includes at least a special educator, general educator, and parent or guardian. Other specialists and the student may be included. Chapter 3

IMPLICIT INSTRUCTION An instructional approach that emphasizes the use of inquiry, hypothesis-testing, and problem solving by the student. Chapter 7

IMPULSIVITY Lack of self-control and inhibition that results in acting before thinking and poor choice making. Chapter 8

INATTENTION Inability to focus on relevant information or sustain a focus that would be expected for a student of a particular age. Chapter 8

INCIDENCE Related to disabilities, incidence is the number of new cases in a given time period. The ability to calculate incidence requires multiple years of prevalence data that are collected in the same manner using the same definition of a phenomenon. Chapter 10

INCLUSION The process of educating students with disabilities in the general education setting. Chapter 1

INDEPENDENT GROUP CONTINGENCY The ability to access reinforcement is based on each individual's behavior and each group member who reaches the criterion gets the same consequence. For example, each person who brings in two cans of food for the food drive will get a certificate. Chapter 9

INDEPENDENT PRACTICE Practice that students complete without direct teacher supervision. Students should not independently practice new skills until they are performing them accurately under guided practice conditions. Chapter 7

INDIVIDUALIZED EDUCATION PROGRAM (IEP) The formal plan that teachers and parents develop to meet the educational needs of a student who is eligible for special education services. The IEP includes a description and management plan for the special services provided by the general and special educators. Chapter 3

INDIVIDUALIZED FAMILY SERVICE PLAN (IFSP) The formal plan that describes the child's and family's needs and the services to be provided for children with disabilities from birth through age three. Chapter 3

INDIVIDUALIZED TRANSITION PROGRAM (ITP) The plan developed by teachers, parents, and often the student that specifies what special activities will occur to prepare the student for work, leisure, and independent living after leaving school. It is required for students with disabilities age 14 and above. Chapter 3

INELIGIBLE The student evaluated for special education services did not meet the criteria for any of the disability categories. Chapter 3

INSISTENCE Culturally responsive management suggests that teachers should "insist" on students behaving appropriately. When students make behavioral mistakes, teachers insist that the students try again in order to practice correct behavior. Chapter 9

INTERDEPENDENT GROUP CONTINGENCY Everyone in the group must meet the criterion in order for anyone in the group to access the reinforcement. For example, if everyone scores 80% or better on the quiz, the group will get a night off from homework. Chapter 9

INTERIM ALTERNATIVE EDUCATION SETTING (IAES) An educational placement designated by the IEP team for a special education student after involvement in a weapons or illicit substance violation at school. The IAES can be determined from a number of options including alternative school placement or after-school program placement and have a duration of 45 calendar days. Chapter 9

INTERNALIZING DISORDERS When an emotional/behavioral disorder is directed inward at one's self instead of outward at others, it is called internalizing (e.g., depression, self-mutilation, anorexia, bulimia, drug/alcohol abuse). Chapter 8

L

LANGUAGE A dynamic communication system used by a cultural group, which includes verbal, nonverbal, spoken, and written components. Chapter 5

LANGUAGE DISORDERS Difficulty with the comprehension or use of spoken or written language. The term includes disorders of morphology, syntax, semantics, and pragmatics. Chapter 11

LEARNING STYLE The perceptual strength a person uses when learning. It can include visual, auditory, and kinesthetic modes of learning. Chapter 5

LEAST RESTRICTIVE ENVIRONMENT (LRE) The policy mandated by IDEA that students with disabilities be educated in the general school environment with their nondisabled peers to the greatest extent possible and appropriate. Chapter 1

LEGAL BLINDNESS Central visual acuity of 20/200 or less in the better eye with best correction, or widest diameter of visual field subtending an angle of no greater than 20 degrees. Chapter 11

LINGUISTICALLY DIVERSE STUDENT See culturally and linguistically diverse student. Chapter 5

LOGICAL CONSEQUENCES Logical consequences are consequences known to both teacher and student that are related directly to a misbehavior. The student can then choose to cooperate or experience the agreed upon logical consequence. The student chooses, and the teacher is removed from the role of punisher. Chapter 9

LOW VISION This term refers to individuals who have significant visual impairments with best correction, but still have usable vision. Chapter 11

LOW VISION DEVICES Devices that magnify items, including print. Chapter 11

LOW VISION EXAM An exam performed by an optometrist to determine if an individual would benefit from the use of low vision devices (e.g., magnifiers, telescopes, etc.). Chapter 11

MAINSTREAMED A delivery model in which special education students received their special education in a separate class for the majority of the school day and participated in the same learning and social activities as their peers for the remainder of the day. Chapter 1

MEAN The average score obtained when all of the scores are added together and divided by the number of people that took the test. Chapter 6

METACOGNITION Awareness and self-regulation of one's own cognitive processes. Chapter 5

MODELING Showing the students exactly what to do. Same as demonstration. Chapter 7

MODIFICATIONS Significant changes made to instruction or mterials that result in the student no longer meeting the standards of the general education curriculum. Chapter 1

MOMENTUM Term used by Kounin to describe the effective instructional practice of teachers who keep lessons moving at a brisk pace, make efficient transitions between activities, and bring lessons to clear conclusions. Chapter 9

MORPHOLOGY The rules for the structure of words. Chapter 11

MOTIVATION An individual's interest in participating with a task to completion; motivation has been described as one of the major deficits in ADHD. Chapter 8

NEUROTYPICAL A person who has a typical neurological system. In contrast, individuals with autism spectrum disorders do not have typical neurological systems. Chapter 10

NO CHILD LEFT BEHIND (NCLB) 2001 Federal legislation that requires schools to provide effective instruction for all children, including students with disabilities; all states are also required to demonstrate the effectiveness of this instruction by assessing and measuring the progress of all students, including those with disabilities, in major content areas such as reading and math each academic year. Chapter 1

NONVERBAL BEHAVIOR Nonverbal behavior includes body movement, eye contact (or lack of it), tone of voice, etc. that is critical to attend to in effective interpersonal communication. Chapter 4

NORMALIZATION The belief that individuals with disabilities should be integrated into the mainstream of society and should live, learn, and work in environments as similar to the norm as possible. Chapter 1

O

OBSERVATIONAL LEARNING The acquisition of skills or behaviors being taught to other students, which were not being directly taught to a student. This ability is essential for students to benefit from group instruction. Chapter 12

OPPORTUNITIES TO RESPOND (OTR) Any strategy used to facilitate active engagement, such as asking questions, choral responding, assigning written work, having students quiz each other, etc. Chapter 9

OPPOSITIONAL DEFIANT DISORDER (ODD) A DSM-IV diagnosis with criteria including a recurrent pattern of negativistic, defiant, disobedient, and hostile behavior toward authority figures that persists for at least 6 months. Chapter 8

ORTHOPEDIC IMPAIRMENTS Disorders that are the result of diseases or conditions that interfere with the normal functioning of muscles or bones. Chapter 11

OVERLAPPING Term used by Kounin to describe effective teachers' abilities to juggle a variety of activities at the same time. Chapter 9

P

PARTIAL PARTICIPATION The curriculum and instruction philosophy that states that for students with severe disabilities it is desirable and appropriate for the development of curriculum objectives that target participation within a task in lieu of the ability to independently perform a task. Chapter 12

PEER TUTORING A student who is competent in an area serves as a teacher/monitor of another student who needs additional practice. Chapter 7

PERINATAL The period of time during labor and delivery. Chapter 11

PERMANENT RECORDS The accumulation of school information about a student, including attendance records, achievement test scores, grades, and comments from teachers. Chapter 3

PERMISSIVE TEACHING STYLE Also known as the "laissez-faire" style. Teachers who use a permissive style are those who do not want to do anything to make the students dislike them. Everything is negotiable, and few rules are enforced. These are teachers who want to be "friends" with their students, and they think that by letting their students do whatever they want, the students will like them. Unfortunately, this style is detrimental to students' learning and achievement and results in the lowest levels of engagement when compared to authoritarian and authoritative teaching styles. Chapter 9

PERSEVERATION Repeating the same actions, thoughts, or behaviors, without functional purpose (e.g., turning on/off the light switch over and over, talking about rabbits in every conversation, refusing to step on the cracks in sidewalks). Commonly associated with autism and obsessive compulsive disorders. Chapter 10

PERVASIVE DEVELOPMENTAL DISORDER (PDD) The umbrella term used in the DSM-IV which includes subcategories of autism spectrum disorders (i.e., Autism, Asperger's, Rett's, Childhood Disintegrative disorder, Pervasive developmental disorders-Not otherwise specified). Chapter 10

PHONOLOGICAL DISORDER A type of speech sound disorder in which a child consistently uses patterns of errors that affect a group of sounds or particular parts of words. Chapter 11

PHONOLOGY The sound system of a language and the rules for combining sounds. Chapter 11

PHYSICAL DISABILITIES Disabilities that result from diseases or disorders that affect normal physical development or functioning. Chapter 1

PHYSICAL IMPAIRMENTS Another term for orthopedic impairments. Chapter 11

POSITIVE BEHAVIORAL INTERVENTIONS AND SUPPORTS (PBIS) A three-tiered (universal, targeted, intensive) proactive model that emphasizes the importance of teaching all students to behave appropriately and recognizing compliance prior to intervening with students who have chronic behavior challenges. Chapter 9

POSTLINGUAL Occurring after the acquisition of spoken language. Chapter 11

POSTNATAL The period of time following birth. Chapter 11

PRAGMATICS The study of the rules that govern the use of language for social interaction. Chapter 11

PRECISION REQUESTS An empirically based method for increasing student cooperation with teacher requests. Teachers give a concise, specific request and wait 5 seconds. If the student responds appropriately, the teacher praises the student. If the student does not respond appropriately, the teacher repeats the request and states the probable consequences for complying. If the student responds appropriately, the teacher praises the student. If the student does not respond appropriately, a behavior reduction strategy is used. Chapter 9

PRECORRECTION Giving students a clear description of expected behavior before the student engages in an inappropriate behavior. Chapter 9

PRELINGUAL Occurring before the acquisition of spoken language. Chapter 11

PREMACK PRINCIPLE The use of preferred activities to increase performance of nonpreferred activities. Also called "Grandma's Law" with the example being "First eat your vegetables, then you can have dessert." Chapter 9

PRENATAL The period of time between conception and birth. Chapter 11

PREVALENCE An indication of how many people have a specific condition in a given population at a particular time. Prevalence can vary widely based on differences in the definitions used for the condition and the methods used to collect data. Chapter 10

PROJECT-BASED LEARNING A learner-centered instructional strategy in which students working in collaboration are engaged in learning knowledge and skills through an inquiry approach over an extended period of time. Learning is demonstrated through the tasks completed and projects produced. Chapter 13

PROMPTING Assistance provided by a teacher to enable a student to perform a skill or behavior. Chapter 12

PROXIMITY CONTROL The visual and physical monitoring of a classroom by a teacher to reduce disruptive behavior. Chapter 9

PUNISHMENT Any consequence that follows a behavior that prevents the behavior from being demonstrated again in the future. Chapter 9

R

RACE A term used to classify human beings into distinct groups according to phenotypes or physical traits (e.g., skin color, eye shape). Chapter 5

READING COMPREHENSION The ability to gain meaning from text. Requires fluent decoding, knowledge of semantics and syntax, and activation of prior knowledge about the topic of the text. Chapter 7

READING DECODING The ability to accurately identify unknown words when reading. Chapter 7

READING FLUENCY The ability to decode words accurately at an efficient word per minute rate. Chapter 7

RECEPTIVE LANGUAGE Refers to the comprehension of language and the communication and messages sent by others. Chapter 11

REINFORCEMENT Any consequence that follows a behavior and results in the behavior being demonstrated again in the future. Chapter 9

RELATED SERVICES Services to assist special education students in categories such as transportation, both to and from school as well as within the school; or developmental, corrective, and other supportive services. Chapter 1

RESPONSE COST Making a behavior "cost" something as a way of reducing the likelihood that the behavior will occur. If a driver is caught speeding, the behavior (speeding) will result in a monetary fine. Students who continue to call out after they have been taught to raise their hands and wait to be called on may lose minutes of free time for each occurrence. Chapter 9

RESPONSE TO INTERVENTION (RTI) A prereferral strategy that is applicable to all students but is particularly useful for students with special needs. Chapter 1

S

SCHIZOPHRENIA Individuals must have two or more of the following symptoms during a 1-month period to be diagnosed with schizophrenia: delusions, hallucinations, disorganized speech, grossly disorganized or catatonic behavior, flat affect, deficiency of speech, lack of resolve, bizarre behavior, and poor attention. Chapter 8

SELF-INJURIOUS BEHAVIORS Behaviors that seem to be directed at causing injuries to a person's own body (e.g., biting, hitting, or scratching oneself). Chapter 10

SELF-STIMULATING Behaviors that are repetitious actions that serve no apparent purpose (e.g., rocking, flapping hands in front of eyes). Chapter 10

SEMANTICS Knowledge of word meaning, vocabulary. Chapter 11

SENSORY DISABILITIES Disabilities that occur whenever any sensory system (vision, hearing, taste, touch, etc.) is impaired. Chapter 1

SENSORY (SENSORINEURAL) HEARING LOSS A type of hearing loss caused by damage to the inner ear. It usually is a permanent hearing loss for which individuals will be fit with hearing aids. Chapter 11

SIGNAL CONTROL The use of teacher cue either audibly, visually, or kinesthetically to prompt students to perform or cease actions (i.e., rapping the desk three times to indicate the class should stop talking). Chapter 9

SIGNIFICANTLY SUBAVERAGE INTELLECTUAL FUNCTIONING Refers to intellectual ability at least two standard deviations below the mean as measured by a standardized IQ test. Chapter 6

SOCIAL CLASS See socioeconomic status. Chapter 5

SOCIOECONOMIC STATUS A relative measure of an individual's or family's social and/or economic position in a society that usually takes into account income, occupation, education, and other indicators of wealth.

The terms "socioeconomic status" and "social class" are often used interchangeably. Chapter 5

SPECIAL EDUCATION The instruction and services designed to meet the unique learning needs of students with disabilities. Chapter 1

SPEECH DISORDERS Difficulty with the production of oral language. The term includes disorders of articulation, voice, and fluency. Chapter 11

SPEECH SOUND DISORDER A type of speech disorder that includes problems with articulation or with phonological rules. Chapter 11

STANDARD DEVIATION A unit of measure that indicates how much an individual score differs from the mean. Chapter 6

STANDARD INTERVENTION PROTOCOL Predetermined, research-based interventions that schools make available to address areas of weakness identified by universal screenings. Chapter 3

STORY MAP A strategy for teaching reading comprehension in which students identify the structural components of a story (e.g., plot, setting, characters, etc.) and place them on a story diagram. Chapter 7

STUDENT ACCOUNTABILITY Using strategies that increase levels of engagement and hold students accountable for their own learning. Teachers often ask questions, request demonstrations, solicit explanations, give exams, etc. in order to allow students to demonstrate their mastery of material. Chapter 9

STUDENT-DIRECTED APPROACH Students take responsibility of monitoring and recording their own progress. Also called self-management strategies. Chapter 7

STUDENT SUPPORT TEAM A team of professionals from the school that meets during Tier 3 of the RTI process to develop research-based interventions for students struggling with academic or behavioral issues. Chapter 3

SYNTAX Knowledge of grammar; structure of sentences. Chapter 11

T

TASK ANALYSIS The process of breaking down a complex task into its component steps. This allows for analysis of student competence in performance of each step and for structuring instruction. Chapter 12

TIME-ON-TASK The portion of the scheduled time during which students are actually working. Same as engaged time. Chapter 7

TIME-OUT Short for "time-out from reinforcement" and is the contingent removal of reinforcement when students misbehave. Attention and/or materials may be removed for inclusion timeout. Students move away from the group or activity for exclusion timeout. Chapter 9

TOKEN ECONOMY Teachers give tokens (e.g., check marks, stars, marbles, poker chips) to recognize desirable academic and social behavior. Students accumulate the tokens and then trade them in for preferred items (e.g., snacks, CDs, homework passes) and activities (e.g., lunch with the janitor, 5 minutes to visit with peers). Based on a real-life model in which adults work to earn money that they can use to buy things they want and need. Chapter 9

TORCH An acronym for the maternal infections of Toxoplasmosis, Other, Rubella, Cytomegalovirus, and Herpes. Chapter 11

TOTAL COMMUNICATION (TC) A communication system used by individuals with a hearing loss that incorporates both auditory/oral communication and manual communication. Chapter 11

TOTAL COMMUNICATION APPROACH The use of multiple modalities simultaneously with speech to facilitate communication development in children with autism. Total communication typically consists of speech plus augmentative and alternative communication (e.g., speech accompanied by sign language, Picture Exchange Communication System [PECS], devices with Dynavox, Big Mac). Chapter 10

U

UNIVERSAL SCREENING The assessment conducted with large groups of students to identify academic areas of weakness. Chapter 3

V

VENN DIAGRAMS Graphical representations that are used to display compare-contrast relationships between ideas. Chapter 7

VISUAL ACUITY A term that describes how clear or sharp a visual image appears. Chapter 11

VOICE DISORDER Any abnormality in the pitch, loudness, resonance, or quality of the voice. It is a type of communication disorder. Chapter 11

W

WARM DEMANDER Teachers who are effective with students who are culturally and linguistically diverse tend to communicate their warmth and caring while continuing to demand that the students succeed. Chapter 9

WITHITNESS Term used by Kounin to describe the effective instructional practice of teachers who are aware of what is going on at all times in all parts of their classrooms. Chapter 9

Z

ZONE OF PROXIMAL DEVELOPMENT (ZPD) The difference between the levels at which a student can perform independently and the levels at which support from an adult or a more competent peer are required. Chapter 7

INDEX

M